Haynes
THE BOOK ®

Vauxhall/Opel Corsa
Service and Repair Manual

A. K. Legg LAE MIMI and Peter T. Gill

Models covered

(4079 - 384)

Hatchback, Corsavan & Combo Van models, including special/limited editions

Petrol engines: 1.0 litre (973cc) 3-cyl, 1.2 litre (1199cc) and 1.4 litre (1389cc) 4-cyl
Diesel engines: 1.7 litre (1686cc) turbo

Does NOT cover 1.8 litre (1796cc) petrol engines
Does NOT cover 'facelifted' range introduced October 2003

© Haynes Publishing 2004

ABCDE
FGHIJ
KLM

A book in the **Haynes Service and Repair Manual Series**

ISBN 1 84425 079 2

British Library Cataloguing in Publication Data
A catalogue record for this book is available from the British Library.

Printed in the USA

Haynes Publishing
Sparkford, Yeovil, Somerset BA22 7JJ, England

Haynes North America, Inc
861 Lawrence Drive, Newbury Park, California 91320, USA

Editions Haynes
4, Rue de l'Abreuvoir
92415 COURBEVOIE CEDEX, France

Haynes Publishing Nordiska AB
Box 1504, 751 45 UPPSALA, Sverige

Contents

LIVING WITH YOUR VAUXHALL CORSA

Roadside Repairs

Weekly Checks

MAINTENANCE

Routine maintenance and servicing

Contents

Many people see the words 'advanced driving' and believe that it won't interest them or that it is a style of driving beyond their own abilities. Nothing could be further from the truth. Advanced driving is straightforward safe, sensible driving - the sort of driving we should all do every time we get behind the wheel.

An average of 10 people are killed every day on UK roads and 870 more are injured, some seriously. Lives are ruined daily, usually because somebody did something stupid. Something like 95% of all accidents are due to human error, mostly driver failure. Sometimes we make genuine mistakes - everyone does. Sometimes we have lapses of concentration. Sometimes we deliberately take risks.

For many people, the process of 'learning to drive' doesn't go much further than learning how to pass the driving test because of a common belief that good drivers are made by 'experience'.

Learning to drive by 'experience' teaches three driving skills:

☐ Quick reactions. (Whoops, that was close!)
☐ Good handling skills. (Horn, swerve, brake, horn).
☐ Reliance on vehicle technology. (Great stuff this ABS, stop in no distance even in the wet...)

Drivers whose skills are 'experience based' generally have a lot of near misses and the odd accident. The results can be seen every day in our courts and our hospital casualty departments.

Advanced drivers have learnt to control the risks by controlling the position and speed of their vehicle. They avoid accidents and near misses, even if the drivers around them make mistakes.

The key skills of advanced driving are **concentration,** effective all-round **observation, anticipation** and **planning.** When **good vehicle handling** is added to

these skills, all driving situations can be approached and negotiated in a safe, methodical way, leaving nothing to chance.

Concentration means applying your mind to safe driving, completely excluding anything that's not relevant. Driving is usually the most dangerous activity that most of us undertake in our daily routines. It deserves our full attention.

Observation means not just looking, but seeing and seeking out the information found in the driving environment.

Anticipation means asking yourself what is happening, what you can reasonably expect to happen and what could happen unexpectedly. (One of the commonest words used in compiling accident reports is 'suddenly'.)

Planning is the link between seeing something and taking the appropriate action. For many drivers, planning is the missing link.

If you want to become a safer and more skilful driver and you want to enjoy your driving more, contact the Institute of Advanced Motorists at www.iam.org.uk, phone 0208 996 9600, or write to IAM House, 510 Chiswick High Road, London W4 5RG for an information pack.

Working on your car can be dangerous. This page shows just some of the potential risks and hazards, with the aim of creating a safety-conscious attitude.

General hazards

Scalding

• Don't remove the radiator or expansion tank cap while the engine is hot.
• Engine oil, automatic transmission fluid or power steering fluid may also be dangerously hot if the engine has recently been running.

Burning

• Beware of burns from the exhaust system and from any part of the engine. Brake discs and drums can also be extremely hot immediately after use.

Crushing

• When working under or near a raised vehicle, always supplement the jack with axle stands, or use drive-on ramps. *Never venture under a car which is only supported by a jack.*
• Take care if loosening or tightening high-torque nuts when the vehicle is on stands. Initial loosening and final tightening should be done with the wheels on the ground.

Fire

• Fuel is highly flammable; fuel vapour is explosive.
• Don't let fuel spill onto a hot engine.
• Do not smoke or allow naked lights (including pilot lights) anywhere near a vehicle being worked on. Also beware of creating sparks (electrically or by use of tools).
• Fuel vapour is heavier than air, so don't work on the fuel system with the vehicle over an inspection pit.
• Another cause of fire is an electrical overload or short-circuit. Take care when repairing or modifying the vehicle wiring.
• Keep a fire extinguisher handy, of a type suitable for use on fuel and electrical fires.

Electric shock

• Ignition HT voltage can be dangerous, especially to people with heart problems or a pacemaker. Don't work on or near the ignition system with the engine running or the ignition switched on.

• Mains voltage is also dangerous. Make sure that any mains-operated equipment is correctly earthed. Mains power points should be protected by a residual current device (RCD) circuit breaker.

Fume or gas intoxication

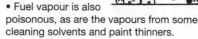

• Exhaust fumes are poisonous; they often contain carbon monoxide, which is rapidly fatal if inhaled. Never run the engine in a confined space such as a garage with the doors shut.
• Fuel vapour is also poisonous, as are the vapours from some cleaning solvents and paint thinners.

Poisonous or irritant substances

• Avoid skin contact with battery acid and with any fuel, fluid or lubricant, especially antifreeze, brake hydraulic fluid and Diesel fuel. Don't syphon them by mouth. If such a substance is swallowed or gets into the eyes, seek medical advice.
• Prolonged contact with used engine oil can cause skin cancer. Wear gloves or use a barrier cream if necessary. Change out of oil-soaked clothes and do not keep oily rags in your pocket.
• Air conditioning refrigerant forms a poisonous gas if exposed to a naked flame (including a cigarette). It can also cause skin burns on contact.

Asbestos

• Asbestos dust can cause cancer if inhaled or swallowed. Asbestos may be found in gaskets and in brake and clutch linings. When dealing with such components it is safest to assume that they contain asbestos.

Special hazards

Hydrofluoric acid

• This extremely corrosive acid is formed when certain types of synthetic rubber, found in some O-rings, oil seals, fuel hoses etc, are exposed to temperatures above 400ºC. The rubber changes into a charred or sticky substance containing the acid. *Once formed, the acid remains dangerous for years. If it gets onto the skin, it may be necessary to amputate the limb concerned.*
• When dealing with a vehicle which has suffered a fire, or with components salvaged from such a vehicle, wear protective gloves and discard them after use.

The battery

• Batteries contain sulphuric acid, which attacks clothing, eyes and skin. Take care when topping-up or carrying the battery.
• The hydrogen gas given off by the battery is highly explosive. Never cause a spark or allow a naked light nearby. Be careful when connecting and disconnecting battery chargers or jump leads.

Air bags

• Air bags can cause injury if they go off accidentally. Take care when removing the steering wheel and/or facia. Special storage instructions may apply.

Diesel injection equipment

• Diesel injection pumps supply fuel at very high pressure. Take care when working on the fuel injectors and fuel pipes.

⚠️ *Warning: Never expose the hands, face or any other part of the body to injector spray; the fuel can penetrate the skin with potentially fatal results.*

Remember...

DO

• Do use eye protection when using power tools, and when working under the vehicle.

• Do wear gloves or use barrier cream to protect your hands when necessary.

• Do get someone to check periodically that all is well when working alone on the vehicle.

• Do keep loose clothing and long hair well out of the way of moving mechanical parts.

• Do remove rings, wristwatch etc, before working on the vehicle – especially the electrical system.

• Do ensure that any lifting or jacking equipment has a safe working load rating adequate for the job.

DON'T

• Don't attempt to lift a heavy component which may be beyond your capability – get assistance.

• Don't rush to finish a job, or take unverified short cuts.

• Don't use ill-fitting tools which may slip and cause injury.

• Don't leave tools or parts lying around where someone can trip over them. Mop up oil and fuel spills at once.

• Don't allow children or pets to play in or near a vehicle being worked on.

The original Corsa models were first introduced to the European market in Spring 1993 and are covered in manual SRM 1985. The Corsa then had a facelift from April 1997 onward models which was covered in manual SRM 3921. This manual covers versions from October 2000, which were the subject of another model facelift, together with mechanical revisions.

A variety of engines are available in the Corsa range, of 1.0, 1.2, and 1.4 litre petrol engines and two versions of the 1.7 litre diesel engines. All engines are of the four-cylinder double overhead camshaft (DOHC) configuration, in-line type, with the exception of the 1.0 litre engine which is a three-cylinder unit. The engines all have fuel injection, and are fitted with a range of emission control systems. The 1.6 and 1.8 litre petrol engines are not covered in this manual.

The Corsa is available in 3- and 5-door Hatchback, Corsavan (3-door Van based on Hatchback), and Combo Van body styles, with a wide range of fittings and interior trim depending on the model specification.

Fully-independent front suspension is fitted; the rear suspension is semi-independent, with a torsion beam and trailing arms.

The manual gearbox is of the five-speed all synchromesh type, and a four-speed electronically-controlled transmission is available as an option on certain models. An 'Easytronic' manual/automatic transmission is also available.

A wide range of standard and optional equipment is available within the Corsa range to suit most tastes, including central locking, electric windows, electric sunroof, anti-lock braking system, electronic alarm system and supplemental restraint systems.

For the home mechanic, the Corsa is a relatively straightforward vehicle to maintain, and most of the items requiring frequent attention are easily accessible.

Your Vauxhall Corsa Manual

The aim of this manual is to help you get the best value from your vehicle. It can do so in several ways. It can help you decide what work must be done (even should you choose to get it done by a garage), provide information on routine maintenance and servicing, and give a logical course of action and diagnosis when random faults occur. However, it is hoped that you will use the manual by tackling the work yourself. On simpler jobs it may even be quicker than booking the car into a garage and going there twice, to leave and collect it. Perhaps most important, a lot of money can be saved by avoiding the costs a garage must charge to cover its labour and overheads.

The manual has drawings and descriptions to show the function of the various components so that their layout can be understood. Tasks are described and photographed in a clear step-by-step sequence.

References to the 'left' and 'right' of the vehicle are in the sense of a person in the driver's seat facing forward.

Acknowledgements

Certain illustrations are the copyright of Vauxhall Motors Limited, and are used with their permission. Thanks are due to Draper Tools Limited, who provided some of the workshop tools, and to all those people at Sparkford who helped in the production of this Manual.

We take great pride in the accuracy of information given in this manual, but vehicle manufacturers make alterations and design changes during the production run of a particular vehicle of which they do not inform us. No liability can be accepted by the authors or publishers for loss, damage or injury caused by errors in, or omissions from, the information given.

The following pages are intended to help in dealing with common roadside emergencies and breakdowns. You will find more detailed fault finding information at the back of the manual, and repair information in the main chapters.

If your car won't start and the starter motor doesn't turn

- ☐ If it's a model with automatic transmission, make sure the selector is in the P or N position.
- ☐ Open the bonnet and make sure that the battery terminals are clean and tight.
- ☐ Switch on the headlights and try to start the engine. If the headlights go very dim when you're trying to start, the battery is probably flat. Try jump starting (see next page) using another car.

If your car won't start even though the starter motor turns as normal

- ☐ Is there fuel in the tank?
- ☐ Is there moisture on electrical components under the bonnet? Switch off the ignition, then wipe off any obvious dampness with a dry cloth. Spray a water-repellent aerosol product (WD-40 or equivalent) on ignition and fuel system electrical connectors like those shown in the photos. Pay special attention to the ignition coil, wiring connector and HT leads, as applicable.

1 On petrol engines, check that the wiring to the ignition DIS module is connected firmly.

2 Check that the air mass meter wiring is connected securely.

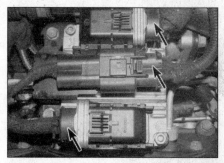

3 On diesel engines, check that the wiring to the engine ECU is connected securely.

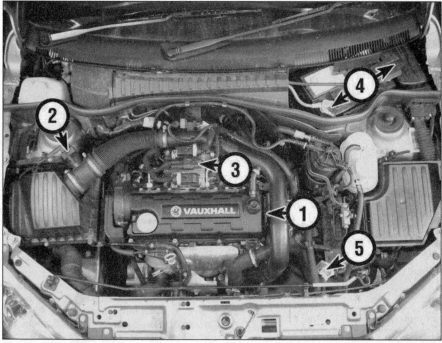

Check that electrical connections are secure (with the ignition switched off) and spray with water dispersant if you suspect a problem due to damp.

4 Check the security and condition of the battery connections.

5 Check all multi-plugs and wiring connectors for security.

Jump starting

When jump-starting a car using a booster battery, observe the following precautions:

✔ Before connecting the booster battery, make sure that the ignition is switched off.

✔ Ensure that all electrical equipment (lights, heater, wipers, etc) is switched off.

✔ Take note of any special precautions printed on the battery case.

✔ Make sure that the booster battery is the same voltage as the discharged one in the vehicle.

✔ If the battery is being jump-started from the battery in another vehicle, the two vehicles MUST NOT TOUCH each other.

✔ Make sure that the transmission is in neutral (or PARK, in the case of automatic transmission).

 HAYNES HiNT *Jump starting will get you out of trouble, but you must correct whatever made the battery go flat in the first place. There are three possibilities:*

1 *The battery has been drained by repeated attempts to start, or by leaving the lights on.*

2 *The charging system is not working properly (alternator drivebelt slack or broken, alternator wiring fault or alternator itself faulty).*

3 *The battery itself is at fault (electrolyte low, or battery worn out).*

1 Connect one end of the red jump lead to the positive (+) terminal of the flat battery

2 Connect the other end of the red lead to the positive (+) terminal of the booster battery.

3 Connect one end of the black jump lead to the negative (-) terminal of the booster battery

4 Connect the other end of the black jump lead to a bolt or bracket on the engine block, well away from the battery, on the vehicle to be started.

5 Make sure that the jump leads will not come into contact with the fan, drivebelts or other moving parts of the engine.

6 Start the engine using the booster battery and run it at idle speed. Switch on the lights, rear window demister and heater blower motor, then disconnect the jump leads in the reverse order of connection. Turn off the lights etc.

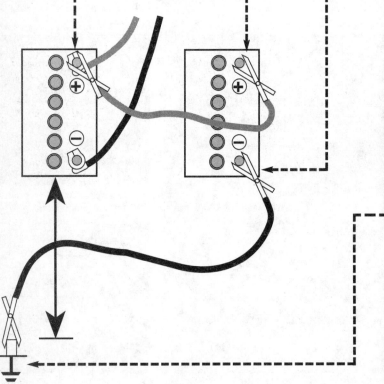

Wheel changing

 Warning: Do not change a wheel in a situation where you risk being hit by another vehicle. On busy roads, try to stop in a lay-by or a gateway. Be wary of passing traffic while changing the wheel - it is easy to become distracted by the job in hand.

Preparation

- When a puncture occurs, stop as soon as it is safe to do so.
- Park on firm level ground, if possible, and well out of the way of other traffic.
- Use hazard warning lights if necessary.
- If you have one, use a warning triangle to alert other drivers of your presence.
- Apply the handbrake and engage first or reverse gear.
- Chock the wheel diagonally opposite the one being removed – a couple of large stones will do for this.
- If the ground is soft, use a flat piece of wood to spread the load under the foot of the jack.

Changing the wheel

1 Lift the floor covering and unscrew the spare wheel clamp nut. Note on Combo models, the spare wheel is stored in a cradle beneath the floor; the cradle is lowered by unscrewing the bolt in the rear floor, using the wheelbrace. Lift out the spare wheel.

2 Remove the tools from the toolbag stored beneath the spare wheel. Use the special clip to pull off the wheel trim.

3 Slacken each wheel bolt by half a turn.

4 Make sure the jack is located on firm ground, and engage the jack head correctly with the sill. Raise the jack until the wheel is clear of the ground.

5 Unscrew the wheel bolts and remove the wheel. Fit the spare wheel and screw in the bolts. Lightly tighten the bolts with the wheelbrace then lower the car to the ground.

6 Securely tighten the wheel bolts in a diagonal sequence then refit the wheel trim. Stow the punctured wheel and tools back in the luggage compartment or cradle (as applicable).

Finally...

- Check the tyre pressure on the wheel just fitted. If it is low, or if you don't have a pressure gauge with you, drive slowly to the next garage and inflate the tyre to the correct pressure.
- The wheel bolts should be slackened and retightened to the specified torque at the earliest possible opportunity.
- Have the damaged tyre or wheel repaired as soon as possible, or another puncture will leave you stranded.

Identifying leaks

Puddles on the garage floor or drive, or obvious wetness under the bonnet or underneath the car, suggest a leak that needs investigating. It can sometimes be difficult to decide where the leak is coming from, especially if the engine bay is very dirty already. Leaking oil or fluid can also be blown rearwards by the passage of air under the car, giving a false impression of where the problem lies.

 Warning: Most automotive oils and fluids are poisonous. Wash them off skin, and change out of contaminated clothing, without delay.

 HAYNES HiNT *The smell of a fluid leaking from the car may provide a clue to what's leaking. Some fluids are distinctively coloured. It may help to clean the car carefully and to park it over some clean paper overnight as an aid to locating the source of the leak.*
Remember that some leaks may only occur while the engine is running.

Sump oil

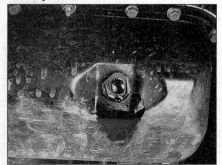

Engine oil may leak from the drain plug...

Oil from filter

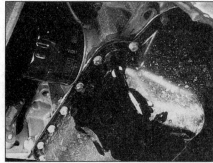

...or from the base of the oil filter.

Gearbox oil

Gearbox oil can leak from the seals at the inboard ends of the driveshafts.

Antifreeze

Leaking antifreeze often leaves a crystalline deposit like this.

Brake fluid

A leak occurring at a wheel is almost certainly brake fluid.

Power steering fluid

Power steering fluid may leak from the pipe connectors on the steering rack.

Towing

When all else fails, you may find yourself having to get a tow home – or of course you may be helping somebody else. Long-distance recovery should only be done by a garage or breakdown service. For shorter distances, DIY towing using another car is easy enough, but observe the following points:

☐ Use a proper tow-rope – they are not expensive. The vehicle being towed must display an ON TOW sign in its rear window.
☐ Always turn the ignition key to the 'on' position when the vehicle is being towed, so that the steering lock is released, and that the direction indicator and brake lights work.

☐ The towing eye is supplied in the vehicle toolkit which is stored in the luggage compartment with the spare wheel (see *Wheel Changing*). To fit the eye, unclip the access cover from the relevant bumper and screw the eye firmly into position. Note that the eye has an **anticlockwise** thread. The wheelbrace can be used to tighten the eye.
☐ Before being towed, release the handbrake and select neutral on the transmission.
Caution: On models with automatic transmission, do not tow the car at speeds in excess of 50 mph (80 kph) or for a distance greater than 60 miles (100 km). If towing speeds/distances are to exceed

these limits, then the car must be towed with its front wheels off the ground.
☐ Note that greater-than-usual pedal pressure will be required to operate the brakes, since the vacuum servo unit is only operational with the engine running.
☐ The driver of the car being towed must keep the tow-rope taut at all times to avoid snatching.
☐ Make sure that both drivers know the route before setting off.
☐ Only drive at moderate speeds and keep the distance towed to a minimum. Drive smoothly and allow plenty of time for slowing down at junctions.

Introduction

There are some very simple checks which need only take a few minutes to carry out, but which could save you a lot of inconvenience and expense.

These *Weekly checks* require no great skill or special tools, and the small amount of time they take to perform could prove to be very well spent, for example;

☐ Keeping an eye on tyre condition and pressures, will not only help to stop them wearing out prematurely, but could also save your life.

☐ Many breakdowns are caused by electrical problems. Battery-related faults are particularly common, and a quick check on a regular basis will often prevent the majority of these.

☐ If your car develops a brake fluid leak, the first time you might know about it is when your brakes don't work properly. Checking the level regularly will give advance warning of this kind of problem.

☐ If the oil or coolant levels run low, the cost of repairing any engine damage will be far greater than fixing the leak, for example.

Underbonnet check points

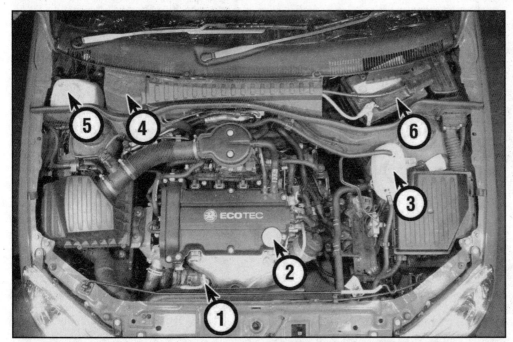

◀ 1.2 litre petrol engine

1 *Engine oil level dipstick*

2 *Engine oil filler cap*

3 *Coolant expansion tank cap*

4 *Brake (and clutch) fluid reservoir*

5 *Screen washer fluid reservoir*

6 *Battery*

◀ 1.7 litre diesel engine

1 *Engine oil level dipstick*

2 *Engine oil filler cap*

3 *Coolant expansion tank cap*

4 *Brake (and clutch) fluid reservoir*

5 *Screen washer fluid reservoir*

6 *Battery*

Engine oil level

Before you start

✔ Make sure that your car is on level ground.
✔ Check the oil level before the car is driven, or at least 5 minutes after the engine has been switched off.

 **HAYNES HINT** *If the oil is checked immediately after driving the vehicle, some of the oil will remain in the upper engine components, resulting in an inaccurate reading on the dipstick.*

The correct oil

Modern engines place great demands on their oil. It is very important that the correct oil for your car is used (See *'Lubricants and fluids'*).

Car Care

● If you have to add oil frequently, you should check whether you have any oil leaks. Place some clean paper under the car overnight, and check for stains in the morning. If there are no leaks, the engine may be burning oil, or the oil may only be leaking when the engine is running.
● Always maintain the level between the upper and lower dipstick marks (see photo 3). If the level is too low severe engine damage may occur. Oil seal failure may result if the engine is overfilled by adding too much oil.

1 The dipstick is brightly coloured for easy identification (see *Underbonnet check points* on page 0•11 for exact location). Withdraw the dipstick.

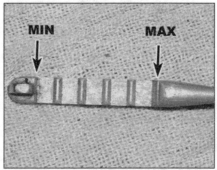

3 Note the level on the end of the dipstick, which should be between the upper (MAX) mark and lower (MIN) mark.

2 Using a clean rag or paper towel remove all oil from the dipstick. Insert the clean dipstick into the tube as far as it will go, then withdraw it again.

4 Oil is added through the filler cap. Unscrew the cap and top-up the level. A funnel may help to reduce spillage. Add the oil slowly, checking the level on the dipstick frequently. Avoid overfilling (see *Car Care*).

Coolant level

⚠ **Warning:**
DO NOT attempt to remove the expansion tank pressure cap when the engine is hot, as there is a very great risk of scalding. Do not leave open containers of coolant about, as it is poisonous.

Car Care

● Adding coolant should not be necessary on a regular basis. If frequent topping-up is required, it is likely there is a leak. Check the radiator, all hoses and joint faces for signs of staining or wetness, and rectify as necessary.

● It is important that antifreeze is used in the cooling system all year round, not just during the winter months. Don't top-up with water alone, as the antifreeze will become too diluted.

1 The coolant level varies with the temperature of the engine. When the engine is cold, the coolant level should be near the COLD (or KALT) mark.

2 If topping-up is necessary, **wait until the engine is cold**. Slowly unscrew the cap to release any pressure present in the cooling system and remove it.

3 Add a mixture of water and antifreeze to the expansion tank until the coolant level is up to the COLD/KALT mark.

Brake and clutch fluid level

Warning:
● Brake fluid can harm your eyes and damage painted surfaces, so use extreme caution when handling and pouring it.
● Do not use fluid that has been standing open for some time, as it absorbs moisture from the air, which can cause a dangerous loss of braking effectiveness.

 HAYNES HiNT The fluid level in the reservoir will drop slightly as the brake pads wear down, but the fluid level must never be allowed to drop below the MIN mark.

Before you start
✔ Make sure that your car is on level ground.

Safety First!
● If the reservoir requires repeated topping-up this is an indication of a fluid leak somewhere in the system, which should be investigated immediately.

● If a leak is suspected, the car should not be driven until the braking system has been checked. Never take any risks where brakes are concerned.

1 The MIN and MAX marks are indicated on the reservoir. The fluid level must be kept between the marks at all times.

2 If topping-up is necessary, first lift the plastic cover then wipe clean the area around the filler cap to prevent dirt entering the hydraulic system. Unscrew the reservoir cap.

3 Carefully add fluid, taking care not to spill it onto the surrounding components. Use only the specified fluid; mixing different types can cause damage to the system. Then securely refit the cap and wipe off any spilt fluid.

Washer fluid level

● Screenwash additives not only keep the windscreen clean during foul weather, they also prevent the washer system freezing in cold weather - which is when you are likely to need it most. Don't top up using plain water as the screenwash will become too diluted, and will freeze during cold weather.

On no account use coolant antifreeze in the washer system - this could discolour or damage paintwork.

1 The screenwasher fluid reservoir is located at the rear right-hand corner of the engine compartment.

2 When topping-up the reservoir, a screen-wash additive should be added in the quantities recommended on the bottle.

Tyre condition and pressure

It is very important that tyres are in good condition, and at the correct pressure - having a tyre failure at any speed is highly dangerous. Tyre wear is influenced by driving style - harsh braking and acceleration, or fast cornering, will all produce more rapid tyre wear. As a general rule, the front tyres wear out faster than the rears. Interchanging the tyres from front to rear ("rotating" the tyres) may result in more even wear. However, if this is completely effective, you may have the expense of replacing all four tyres at once!

Remove any nails or stones embedded in the tread before they penetrate the tyre to cause deflation. If removal of a nail does reveal that the tyre has been punctured, refit the nail so that its point of penetration is marked. Then immediately change the wheel, and have the tyre repaired by a tyre dealer.

Regularly check the tyres for damage in the form of cuts or bulges, especially in the sidewalls. Periodically remove the wheels, and clean any dirt or mud from the inside and outside surfaces. Examine the wheel rims for signs of rusting, corrosion or other damage. Light alloy wheels are easily damaged by "kerbing" whilst parking; steel wheels may also become dented or buckled. A new wheel is very often the only way to overcome severe damage.

New tyres should be balanced when they are fitted, but it may become necessary to re-balance them as they wear, or if the balance weights fitted to the wheel rim should fall off. Unbalanced tyres will wear more quickly, as will the steering and suspension components. Wheel imbalance is normally signified by vibration, particularly at a certain speed (typically around 50 mph). If this vibration is felt only through the steering, then it is likely that just the front wheels need balancing. If, however, the vibration is felt through the whole car, the rear wheels could be out of balance. Wheel balancing should be carried out by a tyre dealer or garage.

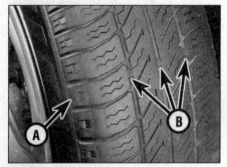

1 *Tread Depth - visual check*
The original tyres have tread wear safety bands (B), which will appear when the tread depth reaches approximately 1.6 mm. The band positions are indicated by a triangular mark on the tyre sidewall (A).

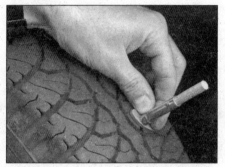

2 *Tread Depth - manual check*
Alternatively, tread wear can be monitored with a simple, inexpensive device known as a tread depth indicator gauge.

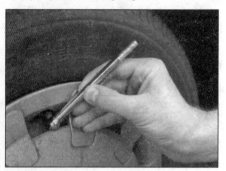

3 *Tyre Pressure Check*
Check the tyre pressures regularly with the tyres cold. Do not adjust the tyre pressures immediately after the vehicle has been used, or an inaccurate setting will result.

Tyre tread wear patterns

Shoulder Wear

Underinflation (wear on both sides)
Under-inflation will cause overheating of the tyre, because the tyre will flex too much, and the tread will not sit correctly on the road surface. This will cause a loss of grip and excessive wear, not to mention the danger of sudden tyre failure due to heat build-up.
Check and adjust pressures
Incorrect wheel camber (wear on one side)
Repair or renew suspension parts
Hard cornering
Reduce speed!

Centre Wear

Overinflation
Over-inflation will cause rapid wear of the centre part of the tyre tread, coupled with reduced grip, harsher ride, and the danger of shock damage occurring in the tyre casing.
Check and adjust pressures

If you sometimes have to inflate your car's tyres to the higher pressures specified for maximum load or sustained high speed, don't forget to reduce the pressures to normal afterwards.

Uneven Wear

Front tyres may wear unevenly as a result of wheel misalignment. Most tyre dealers and garages can check and adjust the wheel alignment (or "tracking") for a modest charge.
Incorrect camber or castor
Repair or renew suspension parts
Malfunctioning suspension
Repair or renew suspension parts
Unbalanced wheel
Balance tyres
Incorrect toe setting
Adjust front wheel alignment
Note: *The feathered edge of the tread which typifies toe wear is best checked by feel.*

Wiper blades

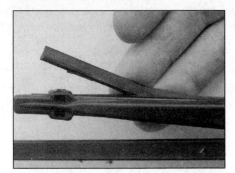

1 Check the condition of the wiper blades; if they are cracked or show any signs of deterioration, or if the glass swept area is smeared, renew them. Wiper blades should be renewed annually.

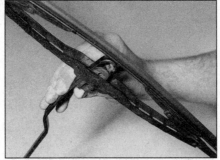

2 To remove a windscreen wiper blade, pull the arm fully away from the screen until it locks. Swivel the blade through 90º, press the locking tab with your fingers and slide the blade out of the arm's hooked end.

3 Don't forget to check the tailgate wiper blade as well. To remove the blade, depress the retaining tab and slide the blade out of the hooked end of the arm.

Battery

Caution: Before carrying out any work on the vehicle battery, read the precautions given in 'Safety first!' at the start of this manual.

✔ Make sure that the battery tray is in good condition, and that the clamp is tight. Corrosion on the tray, retaining clamp and the battery itself can be removed with a solution of water and baking soda. Thoroughly rinse all cleaned areas with water. Any metal parts damaged by corrosion should be covered with a zinc-based primer, then painted.

✔ Periodically (approximately every three months), check the charge condition of the battery, as described in Chapter 5A.

✔ If the battery is flat, and you need to jump start your vehicle, see *Roadside Repairs*.

1 The battery is located at the rear left-hand side of the engine compartment. The exterior of the battery should be inspected periodically for damage such as a cracked case or cover.

2 Check the tightness of the battery cable clamps to ensure good electrical connections. You should not be able to move them. Also check each cable for cracks and frayed conductors.

Battery corrosion can be kept to a minimum by applying a layer of petroleum jelly to the clamps and terminals after they are reconnected.

3 If corrosion (white, fluffy deposits) is evident, remove the cables from the battery terminals, clean them with a small wire brush, then refit them. Automotive stores sell a tool for cleaning the battery post . . .

4 . . . as well as the battery cable clamps

Electrical systems

✔ Check all external lights and the horn. Refer to the appropriate Sections of Chapter 12 for details if any of the circuits are found to be inoperative.

✔ Visually check all accessible wiring connectors, harnesses and retaining clips for security, and for signs of chafing or damage.

 If you need to check your brake lights and indicators unaided, back up to a wall or garage door and operate the lights. The reflected light should show if they are working properly.

1 If a single indicator light, brake stop-light or headlight has failed, it is likely that a bulb has blown and will need to be renewed. Refer to Chapter 12 for details. If both stop-lights have failed, it is possible that the switch has failed (see Chapter 9).

2 If more than one indicator light or tail light has failed it is likely that either a fuse has blown or that there is a fault in the circuit (see Chapter 12). The main fuses are located in the fusebox situated at the left-hand front corner of the engine compartment.

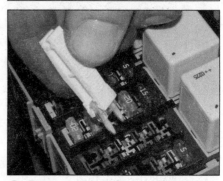

3 To renew a blown fuse, remove it, where applicable, using the plastic tool provided. Fit a new fuse of the same rating, available from car accessory shops. It is important that you find the reason that the fuse blew (see *Electrical fault finding* in Chapter 12).

Lubricants and fluids

Engine

Petrol	Multigrade engine oil, viscosity SAE 5W/30, 5W/40, 5W/50, 10W/30, 10W/40 or 10W/50 to ACEA A3, ACEA A3/B3 or ACEA A3/B3/B4
Diesel	Multigrade engine oil, viscosity SAE 5W/30, 5W/40, 5W/50, 10W/30, 10W/40 or 10W/50 to ACEA B3, ACEA A3/B3 or ACEA A3/B3/B4
Manual gearbox	Vauxhall/Opel gear oil No 09 120 541
Easytronic transmission	Vauxhall/Opel gear oil No 09 120 541
Automatic transmission	Vauxhall/Opel A/T fluid 09 117 946
Cooling system	Vauxhall/Opel antifreeze 19 40 650/09 194 431
Brake fluid reservoir	Hydraulic fluid to DOT 4

Choosing your engine oil

Engines need oil, not only to lubricate moving parts and minimise wear, but also to maximise power output and to improve fuel economy.

HOW ENGINE OIL WORKS

• *Beating friction*

Without oil, the moving surfaces inside your engine will rub together, heat up and melt, quickly causing the engine to seize. Engine oil creates a film which separates these moving parts, preventing wear and heat build-up.

• *Cooling hot-spots*

Temperatures inside the engine can exceed 1000° C. The engine oil circulates and acts as a coolant, transferring heat from the hot-spots to the sump.

• *Cleaning the engine internally*

Good quality engine oils clean the inside of your engine, collecting and dispersing combustion deposits and controlling them until they are trapped by the oil filter or flushed out at oil change.

OIL CARE - FOLLOW THE CODE

To handle and dispose of used engine oil safely, always:

OIL CARE
0800 66 33 66
www.oilbankline.org.uk

- *Avoid skin contact with used engine oil. Repeated or prolonged contact can be harmful.*
- *Dispose of used oil and empty packs in a responsible manner in an authorised disposal site. Call 0800 663366 to find the one nearest to you. Never tip oil down drains or onto the ground.*

Tyre pressures (cold)

Note: *Pressures are quoted for standard tyre fitments (see Chapter 10); consult a dealer or tyre specialist for alternative or revised recommendations.*

Corsa and Corsavan	Front	Rear
Normal load (up to 3 passengers)		
1.0 litre petrol except ECO models:		
155/80 R 13	2.2 bars (32 psi)	1.8 bars (26 psi)
175/65 R 14	2.2 bars (32 psi)	1.8 bars (26 psi)
1.0 litre petrol ECO models:		
175/65 R 14 (for minimum fuel consumption)	2.7 bars (39 psi)	2.5 bars (36 psi)
175/65 R 14 (for improving driving comfort)	2.4 bars (35 psi)	2.4 bars (35 psi)
1.2 litre petrol models:		
155/80 R 13	2.2 bars (32 psi)	1.8 bars (26 psi)
175/65 R 14	2.2 bars (32 psi)	1.8 bars (26 psi)
185/55 R 15	2.2 bars (32 psi)	1.8 bars (26 psi)
1.4 litre petrol models:		
175/65 R 14	2.3 bars (33 psi)	2.1 bars (30 psi)
185/55 R 15	2.3 bars (33 psi)	2.1 bars (30 psi)
1.7 litre diesel models:		
175/65 R 14	2.3 bars (33 psi)	2.1 bars (30 psi)
185/55 R 15	2.3 bars (33 psi)	2.1 bars (30 psi)
Fully laden		
All models except 1.0 litre ECO models	2.4 bars (35 psi)	2.8 bars (41 psi)
1.0 litre petrol ECO models	2.7 bars (39 psi)	3.0 bars (44 psi)

Combo Van	Front	Rear
Normal load (2 persons and 100kg luggage)		
175/65 R 14	2.4 bars (35 psi)	2.4 bars (35 psi)
175/65 R 14	2.4 bars (35 psi)	2.4 bars (35 psi)
185/60 R 15	2.4 bars (35 psi)	2.4 bars (35 psi)
Fully laden		
All models	2.4 bars (35 psi)	3.5 bars (51 psi)

Chapter 1 Part A:
Routine maintenance and servicing – petrol models

Contents

Degrees of difficulty

Easy, suitable for novice with little experience	**Fairly easy,** suitable for beginner with some experience	**Fairly difficult,** suitable for competent DIY mechanic	**Difficult,** suitable for experienced DIY mechanic	**Very difficult,** suitable for expert DIY or professional

Lubricants and fluids .... Refer to *Weekly checks* on page 0•17

Capacities

Engine oil
Oil change, including filter:
    1.0 litre engines .... 3.0 litres
    1.2 litre engines .... 3.5 litres
    1.4 litre engines .... 3.5 litres
Difference between MAX and MIN dipstick marks .... 1.0 litre

Cooling system
1.0 litre engines .... 4.9 litres
1.2 litre engines .... 5.0 litres
1.4 litre engines:
    Manual transmission .... 6.1 litres
    Automatic transmission .... 6.5 litres

Fuel tank
All models .... 44.0 litres

Manual gearbox .... 1.6 litres

Easytronic transmission .... 1.6 litres

Automatic transmission
Drain and refill .... Approximately 4.0 litres

Washer fluid reservoir
Without headlight washers .... 2.2 litres
With headlight washers .... 3.5 litres

Cooling system
Antifreeze mixture:
    50% antifreeze .... Protection down to -37°C
    55% antifreeze .... Protection down to -45°C

Ignition system

	Type	Electrode gap
Spark plugs:		
All engines	Bosch FLR 8 LD+U	1.0 mm

Suspension and steering
Tyre pressures .... Refer to end of *Weekly checks* on page 0•18

Torque wrench settings

	Nm	lbf ft
Oil filter housing cap to filter housing:		
1.0 and 1.2 litre engines	10	7
Oil filter:		
1.4 litre engines	15	11
Reversing light switch	20	15
Right-hand engine mounting-to-body bolts	40	30
Right-hand engine mounting-to-engine bracket bolts:		
Stage 1	60	44
Stage 2	Angle-tighten by a further 30°	
Stage 3	Angle-tighten by a further 15°	
Roadwheel bolts	110	81
Spark plugs	25	18
Sump drain plug	10	7

The maintenance intervals in this manual are provided with the assumption that you, not the dealer, will be carrying out the work. These are the minimum maintenance intervals based on the schedule recommended by the manufacturer for vehicles driven daily. If you wish to keep your vehicle in peak condition at all times, you may wish to perform some of these procedures more often. We encourage frequent maintenance, because it enhances the efficiency, performance and resale value of your vehicle.

If the vehicle is driven in dusty areas, used to tow a trailer, or driven frequently at slow speeds (idling in traffic) or on short journeys, more frequent maintenance intervals are recommended.

When the vehicle is new, it should be serviced by a factory-authorised dealer service department, in order to preserve the factory warranty.

Every 250 miles (400 km) or weekly

☐ Refer to *Weekly checks*

Every 10 000 miles (15 000 km) or 6 months – whichever comes first

☐ Renew the engine oil and filter (Section 3)

Note: *Vauxhall recommend that the engine oil and filter are changed every 20 000 miles (30 000 km) or 12 months. However, oil and filter changes are good for the engine and we recommend that the oil and filter are renewed more frequently, especially if the vehicle is used on a lot of short journeys.*

Every 20 000 miles (30 000 km) or 12 months – whichever comes first

☐ Check all underbonnet and underbody components, pipes and hoses for leaks (Section 4)
☐ Check the auxiliary drivebelt and tensioner (Section 5)
☐ Check the operation of the horn, all lights, and the wipers and washers (Section 6)
☐ Check the tightness of the roadwheel bolts (Section 7)
☐ Check the condition of the brake pads (renew if necessary), the calipers and discs (Section 8)
☐ Check the operation of the handbrake and adjust if necessary (Section 9)
☐ Check the headlight beam alignment (Section 10)
☐ Check the condition of all brake fluid pipes and hoses (Section 11)
☐ Check the Easytronic clutch hydraulic fluid level (Section 12)
☐ Check the bodywork and underbody for damage and corrosion, and check the condition of the underbody corrosion protection (Section 13)
☐ Check the condition of the exhaust system components (Section 14)
☐ Lubricate all door, bonnet and tailgate hinges and locks (Section 15)
☐ Check the condition of the front suspension and steering components, particularly the rubber gaiters and seals (Section 16)
☐ Check the condition of the rear suspension components (Section 17)
☐ Check the condition of the driveshaft joint gaiters, and the driveshaft joints (Section 18)
☐ Carry out a road test (Section 19)
☐ Reset the service interval indicator (Section 20)

Every 20 000 miles (30 000 km) or 2 years – whichever comes first

☐ Renew the pollen filter (Section 21)

Every 40 000 miles (60 000 km) or 2 years – whichever comes first

☐ Renew the battery for the remote control (Section 22)
☐ Renew the brake and clutch fluid (Section 23)
☐ Renew the coolant (Section 24)

Every 40 000 miles (60 000 km) or 4 years – whichever comes first

☐ Renew the air cleaner filter element (Section 25)
☐ Renew the spark plugs (Section 26)
☐ Renew the timing belt (1.4 litre engines) (Section 27)*
☐ Renew the fuel filter (Section 28)
☐ Renew the automatic transmission fluid (Section 29)
☐ Check the condition of the rear brake shoes (renew if necessary), drums and wheel cylinders (Section 30)

* Note: *For 2003 models, the normal interval for timing belt renewal is increased to 60 000 miles (90 000 km) or 6 years, however, it is strongly recommended that the interval used is 40 000 miles (60 000 km) on vehicles which are subjected to intensive use, ie, mainly short journeys or a lot of stop-start driving. The actual belt renewal interval is therefore very much up to the individual owner, but bear in mind that severe engine damage will result if the belt breaks.*

Underbonnet view of a 1.2 litre model

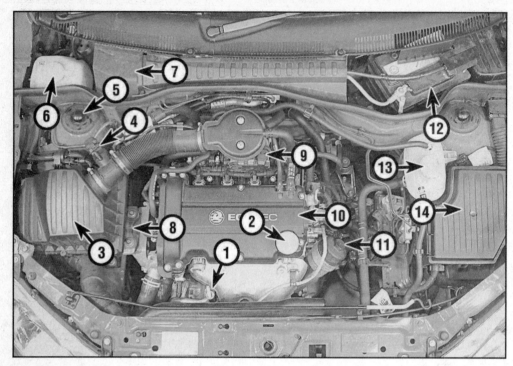

1 Engine oil level dipstick
2 Engine oil filler cap
3 Air cleaner assembly
4 Air mass meter
5 Front suspension strut
   upper mounting
6 Windscreen/headlamp
   washer fluid reservoir
7 Brake (and clutch) fluid
   reservoir
8 Engine mounting
9 Air box and throttle body
10 Distributorless ignition
   system (DIS) module
11 Oil filter
12 Battery
13 Coolant expansion tank
14 Engine compartment fuse
   and relay box

Front underbody view of a 1.2 litre model

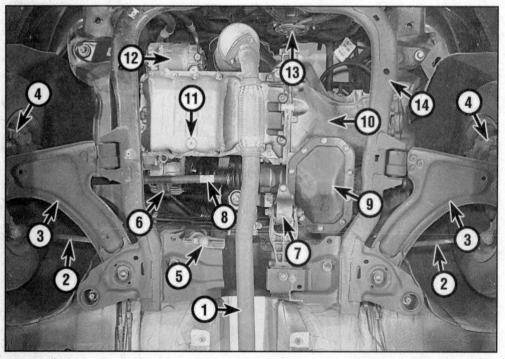

1 Exhaust front pipe
2 Steering track rods
3 Front suspension lower
   arms
4 Front brake calipers
5 Steering gear
6 Alternator
7 Engine mounting rear
   torque link
8 Right-hand driveshaft
9 Final drive cover plate
10 Manual transmission
11 Engine oil drain plug
12 Air conditioning
   compressor
13 Electric cooling fan
14 Front suspension
   subframe

Rear underbody view of a 1.2 litre model

1   *Handbrake cable*
2   *Rear suspension coil springs*
3   *Exhaust tailpipe and silencer*
4   *Exhaust heat shield*
5   *Rear anti-roll bar*
6   *Rear suspension trailing arms and rear axle*
7   *Fuel filter*
8   *Fuel tank*

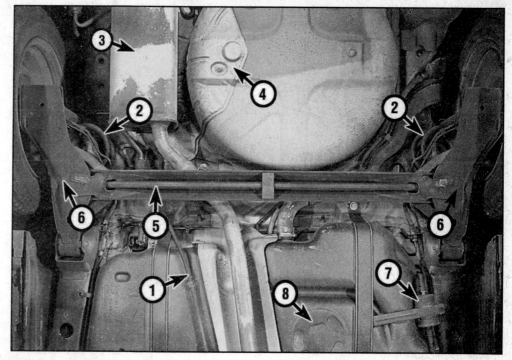

Maintenance procedures

1   General information

1 This Chapter is designed to help the home mechanic maintain his/her vehicle for safety, economy, long life and peak performance.
2 The Chapter contains a master maintenance schedule, followed by sections dealing specifically with each task on the schedule. Visual checks, adjustments, component renewal and other helpful items are included. Refer to the accompanying illustrations of the engine compartment and the underside of the vehicle for the locations of the various components.
3 Servicing of your vehicle in accordance with the mileage/time maintenance schedule and the following sections will provide a planned maintenance programme, which should result in a long and reliable service life. This is a comprehensive plan, so maintaining some items but not others at the specified service intervals will not produce the same results.
4 As you service your vehicle, you will discover that many of the procedures can – and should – be grouped together, because of the particular procedure being performed, or because of the close proximity of two otherwise-unrelated components to one another. For example, if the vehicle is raised for any reason, the exhaust can be inspected at the same time as the suspension and steering components.

5 The first step in this maintenance programme is to prepare yourself before the actual work begins. Read through all the sections relevant to the work to be carried out, then make a list and gather together all the parts and tools required. If a problem is encountered, seek advice from a parts specialist, or a dealer service department.

2   Regular maintenance

1 If, from the time the vehicle is new, the routine maintenance schedule is followed closely, and frequent checks are made of fluid levels and high-wear items, as suggested throughout this manual, the engine will be kept in relatively good running condition, and the need for additional work will be minimised.
2 It is possible that there will be times when the engine is running poorly due to the lack of regular maintenance. This is even more likely if a used vehicle, which has not received regular and frequent maintenance checks, is purchased. In such cases, additional work may need to be carried out, outside of the regular maintenance intervals.
3 If engine wear is suspected, a compression test (Chapter 2A or 2B) will provide valuable information regarding the overall performance of the main internal components. Such a test can be used as a basis to decide on the extent of the work to be carried out. If for

example a compression test indicates serious internal engine wear, conventional maintenance as described in this Chapter will not greatly improve the performance of the engine, and may prove a waste of time and money, unless extensive overhaul work (Chapter 2D) is carried out first.
4 The following series of operations are those most often required to improve the performance of a generally poor-running engine:

Primary operations
a) *Clean, inspect and test the battery ('Weekly checks').*
b) *Check all the engine-related fluids ('Weekly checks').*
c) *Check the condition and tension of the auxiliary drivebelt (Section 5).*
d) *Renew the spark plugs (Section 26).*
e) *Renew the fuel filter (Section 28).*
f) *Check the condition of the air cleaner filter element, and renew if necessary (Section 25).*
g) *Check the condition of all hoses, and check for fluid leaks (Section 4).*
5 If the above operations do not prove fully effective, carry out the following secondary operations:

Secondary operations
All items listed under *Primary operations*, plus the following:
a) *Check the ignition system (Chapter 5B).*
b) *Check the charging system (Chapter 5A).*
c) *Check the fuel system (Chapter 4A or 4B).*

3.3 Removing the oil filler cap

HAYNES HiNT

As the drain plug threads release, move it sharply away so the stream of oil issuing from the sump runs into the container, not up your sleeve.

3.8 The oil filter is located at the front left-hand side on 1.0 and 1.2 litre engines

Every 10 000 miles (15 000 km) or 6 months

3 Engine oil and filter renewal

HAYNES HiNT *Frequent oil and filter changes are the most important preventative maintenance procedures which can be undertaken by the DIY owner. As engine oil ages, it becomes diluted and contaminated, which leads to premature engine wear.*

1 Before starting this procedure, gather together all the necessary tools and materials. Also make sure that you have plenty of clean rags and newspapers handy, to mop up any spills. Ideally, the engine oil should be warm, as it will drain more easily, and more built-up sludge will be removed with it. Take care not to touch the exhaust or any other hot parts of the engine when working under the vehicle. To avoid any possibility of scalding, and to protect yourself from possible skin irritants and other harmful contaminants in used engine oils, it is advisable to wear gloves when carrying out this work.

2 Access to the underside of the vehicle will be greatly improved if it can be raised on a lift, driven onto ramps, or jacked up and supported on axle stands (see *Jacking and vehicle support*). Whichever method is

chosen, make sure that the vehicle remains level, or if it is at an angle, that the drain plug is at the lowest point. The drain plug is located at the rear of the sump.

3 Remove the oil filler cap from the camshaft cover (twist it through a quarter-turn anti-clockwise and withdraw it) **(see illustration)**.

4 Using a spanner, or preferably a suitable socket and bar, slacken the drain plug about half a turn. Position the draining container under the drain plug, then remove the plug completely. If possible, try to keep the plug pressed into the sump while unscrewing it by hand the last couple of turns.

5 Allow some time for the oil to drain, noting that it may be necessary to reposition the container as the oil flow slows to a trickle.

6 After all the oil has drained, wipe the drain plug and the sealing washer with a clean rag. Examine the condition of the sealing washer, and renew it if it shows signs of scoring or other damage which may prevent an oil-tight seal. Clean the area around the drain plug opening, and refit the plug complete with the washer. Tighten the plug securely, preferably to the specified torque, using a torque wrench.

7 Two different types of oil filter will be encountered on engines covered by this manual. On 1.0 and 1.2 litre engines, the oil filter is of the element type, which is removed from the oil filter housing and then a new element is fitted to the housing. On the 1.4 engine, the filter is of the metal container type, which is unscrewed and removed as a unit from the

engine, and then a new container is screwed into position. Proceed as described under the following sub-Sections, according to engine type.

1.0 and 1.2 litre engines

8 The oil filter housing is located at the front left-hand side of the engine **(see illustration)**.

9 Move the container into position under the oil filter housing. Note, on some models it may be necessary to undo the retaining bolts and remove the engine undertray.

10 Unscrew the oil filter housing cap and withdraw the cap together with the filter from the oil filter housing.

11 Withdraw the filter from the oil filter housing cap.

12 Use clean rags to remove all remaining oil, dirt and sludge from the oil filter housing.

13 Remove the sealing O-ring from the oil filter housing cap.

14 Fit a new sealing O-ring to the oil filter housing cap then clip the new oil filter element to the cap **(see illustrations)**.

15 Fit the cap and filter element assembly to the oil filter housing and screw the cap into position. Finally, tighten the cap to the specified torque **(see illustrations)**.

1.4 litre engines

16 The oil filter is located at the front left-hand side of the engine. Note that access is most easily obtained from underneath the front of the vehicle.

3.14a Fit a new sealing O-ring to the oil filter housing cap . . .

3.14b . . . then clip the new oil filter element to the cap

3.15a Fit the cap and filter element assembly to the oil filter housing . . .

17 Move the container into position under the oil filter.

18 Using an oil filter removal tool if necessary, slacken the filter initially, then unscrew it by hand the rest of the way **(see illustration)**. Empty the oil in the old filter into the container. To ensure that the old filter is completely empty before disposal, puncture the filter dome in at least two places and allow any remaining oil to drain through the punctures and into the container.

19 Use a clean rag to remove all oil, dirt and sludge from the filter sealing area on the engine. Check the old filter to make sure that the rubber sealing ring has not stuck to the engine. If it has, carefully remove it.

20 Apply a light coating of clean engine oil to the sealing ring on the new filter, then screw the filter into position on the engine. Tighten the filter firmly by hand only – **do not** use any tools.

21 Remove the old oil and all tools from under the vehicle then, if applicable, lower the vehicle to the ground.

All engines

22 Fill the engine through the filler hole in the camshaft cover, using the correct grade and type of oil (refer to *Weekly checks* for details

3.15b ... screw the assembly into place and tighten the cap to the specified torque

3.18 Using an oil filter removal tool to slacken the filter

of topping-up). Pour in half the specified quantity of oil first, then wait a few minutes for the oil to drain into the sump. Continue to add oil, a small quantity at a time, until the level is up to the lower mark on the dipstick. Adding a further 1.0 litre will bring the level up to the upper mark on the dipstick.

23 Start the engine and run it for a few minutes, while checking for leaks around the oil filter and the sump drain plug. Note that there may be a delay of a few seconds before the oil pressure warning light goes out when the engine is first started, as the oil circulates through the new oil filter and the engine oil

galleries before the pressure builds-up.

24 Stop the engine, and wait a few minutes for the oil to settle in the sump once more. With the new oil circulated and the filter now completely full, recheck the level on the dipstick, and add more oil as necessary.

25 Dispose of the used engine oil and filter safely, with reference to *General repair procedures* in the Reference Chapter of this manual. Do not discard the old filter with domestic household waste. The facility for waste oil disposal provided by many local council refuse tips generally has a filter receptacle alongside.

Every 20 000 miles (30 000 km) or 12 months

4 Hose and fluid leak check

1 Visually inspect the engine joint faces, gaskets and seals for any signs of water or oil leaks. Pay particular attention to the areas around the camshaft cover, cylinder head, oil filter and sump joint faces. Similarly, check the transmission and (where applicable) the air conditioning compressor for oil leakage. Bear in mind that, over a period of time, some very slight seepage from these areas is to be expected; what you are really looking for is any indication of a serious leak. Should a leak be found, renew the offending gasket or oil seal by referring to the appropriate Chapters in this manual.

2 Also check the security and condition of all the engine-related pipes and hoses. Ensure that all cable ties or securing clips are in place, and in good condition. Clips which are broken or missing can lead to chafing of the hoses pipes or wiring, which could cause more serious problems in the future.

3 Carefully check the radiator hoses and heater hoses along their entire length. Renew any hose which is cracked, swollen or deteriorated. Cracks will show up better if the hose is squeezed. Pay close attention to the hose clips that secure the hoses to the cooling system components. Hose clips can pinch and puncture hoses, resulting in cooling

system leaks. If wire-type hose clips are used, it may be a good idea to replace them with screw-type clips.

4 Inspect all the cooling system components (hoses, joint faces, etc) for leaks. Where any problems of this nature are found on system components, renew the component or gasket with reference to Chapter 3 **(see Haynes Hint)**.

5 Where applicable, inspect the automatic transmission fluid cooler hoses for leaks or deterioration.

6 With the vehicle raised, inspect the petrol tank and filler neck for punctures, cracks and other damage. The connection between the filler neck and tank is especially critical. Sometimes, a rubber filler neck or connecting hose will leak due to loose retaining clamps or deteriorated rubber.

7 Carefully check all rubber hoses and metal fuel lines leading away from the petrol tank. Check for loose connections, deteriorated hoses, crimped lines and other damage. Pay particular attention to the vent pipes and hoses, which often loop up around the filler neck and can become blocked or crimped. Follow the lines to the front of the vehicle, carefully inspecting them all the way. Renew damaged sections as necessary. Similarly, whilst the vehicle is raised, take the opportunity to inspect all underbody brake fluid pipes and hoses.

8 From within the engine compartment, check the security of all fuel hose attachments and pipe unions, and inspect the fuel hoses

and vacuum hoses for kinks, chafing and deterioration.

9 Where applicable, check the condition of the automatic transmission fluid pipes.

5 Auxiliary drivebelt check

Checking

1 The ribbed type auxiliary drivebelt drives the alternator, coolant pump and the air conditioning compressor where applicable. An automatic drivebelt tensioner is fitted, and there is no requirement to check the drivebelt tension.

A leak in the cooling system will usually show up as white- or rust-coloured deposits on the area adjoining the leak.

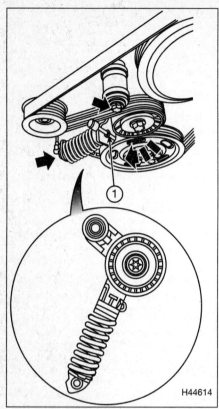

5.7a Auxiliary drivebelt tensioner on 1.0 and 1.2 litre petrol engines without air conditioning

1 *Locking bolt*
Arrows indicate tensioner mounting bolts and direction to release tension

2 The belt should be inspected along its entire length, and if it is found to be worn, frayed or cracked, it should be renewed as a precaution against breakage in service.

Removal

Note: *The manufacturers recommend that the tensioner roller is checked and if necessary renewed at the same time as the drivebelt.*

3 Apply the handbrake, then jack up the front of the vehicle and support it on axle stands (see *Jacking and vehicle support*). Remove the right-hand front roadwheel and the wheel arch liner cover for access to the right-hand side of the engine.
4 With reference to the appropriate part of Chapter 4, remove the air cleaner housing.
5 If the drivebelt is to be re-used, mark it to indicate its normal running direction.
6 On 1.0 and 1.2 litre petrol engines, support the engine and remove the right-hand engine mounting with reference to Chapter 2A. **Note:** *On 1.0 and 2.0 litre petrol engines the engine mounting locates within the auxiliary drivebelt.*
7 Note the routing of the drivebelt, then, using a Torx key or spanner (as applicable) on the pulley centre bolt, turn the tensioner clockwise (1.0 and 1.2 litre petrol engines) or anti-clockwise (1.4 litre petrol engine) against

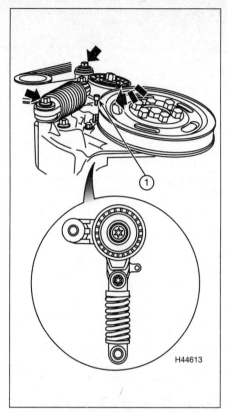

5.7b Auxiliary drivebelt tensioner on 1.0 and 1.2 litre petrol engines with air conditioning

1 *Locking bolt*
Arrows indicate tensioner mounting bolts and direction to release tension

the spring tension. Hold the tensioner in this position by inserting a suitable locking bolt through the special hole provided. Note the

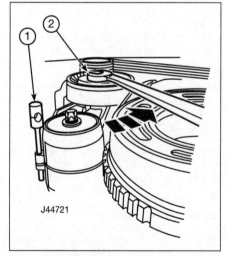

5.7c Auxiliary drivebelt tensioner on the 1.4 litre petrol engine

1 *Locking bolt*
2 *Turn the tensioner as indicated to release the tension*

different tensioners fitted to 1.0 and 1.2 litre petrol engines (**see illustrations**).
8 Slip the auxiliary drivebelt off of the pulleys.

Refitting

9 Locate the auxiliary drivebelt onto the pulleys in the correct routing. If the drivebelt is being re-used, make sure it is fitted the correct way around.
10 Turn back the tensioner and remove the locking bolt, then release it, making sure that the drivebelt ribs locate correctly on each of the pulley grooves.
11 Refit the air cleaner housing, then refit the wheel arch liner and roadwheel, and lower the vehicle to the ground.

6 Electrical system check

1 Check the operation of all the electrical equipment, ie, lights, direction indicators, horn, etc. Refer to the appropriate sections of Chapter 12 for details if any of the circuits are found to be inoperative.
2 Note that the stop-light switch is described in Chapter 9.
3 Check all accessible wiring connectors, harnesses and retaining clips for security, and for signs of chafing or damage. Rectify any faults found.

7 Roadwheel bolt tightness check

1 Where applicable, remove the wheel trims from the wheels.
2 Using a torque wrench on each wheel bolt in turn, ensure that the bolts are tightened to the specified torque.
3 Where applicable, refit the wheel trims on completion, making sure they are fitted correctly.

8 Brake pad and disc check

1 With the vehicle on level ground, chock the rear wheels, apply the handbrake, then jack up the front of the vehicle and support securely on axle stands; remove the roadwheels (see *Jacking and vehicle support*).
2 Check the thickness of the friction material on each brake pad.

> **HAYNES HiNT** *For a quick check, the thickness can be measured through the aperture in the caliper body.*

3 If any pad is worn to the specified minimum thickness or less, all four pads must be renewed (see Chapter 9).

4 The view through the caliper inspection hole gives a rough indication of the state of the brake pads. For a comprehensive check, the brake pads should be removed and cleaned. This will allow the operation of the caliper to be checked, and the condition of the brake disc itself to be fully examined on both sides. Chapter 9 contains a detailed description of how the brake disc should be checked for wear and/or damage.

5 On completion, refit the roadwheels and lower the vehicle to the ground.

9 Handbrake operation and adjustment check

1 With the vehicle on a slight slope, apply the handbrake lever by 4 or 5 notches, and check that it holds the vehicle stationary, then release the lever and check that there is no resistance to movement of the vehicle.

2 If necessary, adjust the handbrake lever as described in Chapter 9.

10 Headlight beam alignment check

1 Accurate adjustment of the headlight beam is only possible using optical beam-setting equipment, and this work should therefore be carried out by a Vauxhall dealer or service station with the necessary facilities.

2 Basic adjustments can be carried out in an emergency, and further details are given in Chapter 12.

11 Brake fluid pipe and hose check

1 The brake hydraulic system includes a number of metal pipes, which run from the master cylinder to the front and rear brake assemblies, and the hydraulic modulator on models with an anti-lock braking system (ABS). Flexible hoses are fitted between the pipes and the front and rear brake assemblies, to allow for steering and suspension movement.

2 When checking the system, first look for signs of leakage at the pipe or hose unions, then examine the flexible hoses for signs of cracking, chafing or deterioration of the rubber. Bend the hoses sharply between the fingers (but do not actually bend them double, or the casing may be damaged) and check that this does not reveal previously-hidden cracks, cuts or splits. Check that the pipes and hoses are securely fastened in their clips.

3 Carefully working along the length of the metal pipes, look for dents, kinks, damage of any sort, or corrosion. Light corrosion can be polished off, but if the depth of pitting is significant, the pipe must be renewed.

12 Clutch hydraulic fluid level check (Easytronic models)

1 The clutch hydraulic fluid level markings are on the side of the fluid reservoir located on the front of the transmission. The use of a mirror will be helpful.

2 Check that the level of the fluid is at or near the MAX marking on the side of the reservoir (see illustration).

3 If topping-up is required, unscrew the filler cap and pour in fresh fluid until the level is at the MAX marking. Retighten the cap on completion.

13 Bodywork and underbody condition check

Note: *This work should be carried out by a Vauxhall dealer in order to validate the vehicle warranty. The work includes a thorough inspection of the vehicle paintwork and underbody for damage and corrosion.*

Bodywork damage/ corrosion check

1 Once the car has been washed, and all tar spots and other surface blemishes have been cleaned off, carefully check all paintwork, looking closely for chips or scratches. Pay particular attention to vulnerable areas such as the front panels (bonnet and spoiler), and around the wheel arches. Any damage to the paintwork must be rectified as soon as possible, to comply with the terms of the manufacturer's anti-corrosion warranties; check with a Vauxhall dealer for details.

2 If a chip or light scratch is found which is recent and still free from rust, it can be touched-up using the appropriate touch-up stick which can be obtained from Vauxhall dealers. Any more serious damage, or rusted stone chips, can be repaired as described in Chapter 11, but if damage or corrosion is so severe that a panel must be renewed, seek professional advice as soon as possible.

3 Always check that the door and ventilation opening drain holes and pipes are completely clear, so that water can drain out.

Corrosion protection check

4 The wax-based underbody protective coating should be inspected annually, preferably just prior to Winter, when the underbody should be washed down as thoroughly as possible without disturbing the protective coating. Any damage to the coating should be repaired using a suitable wax-based sealer. If any of the body panels are disturbed for repair or renewal, do not forget to re-apply the coating. Wax should be injected into door cavities, sills and box sections, to maintain the level of protection provided by the vehicle manufacturer – seek the advice of a Vauxhall dealer.

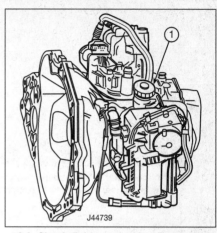

12.2 Clutch fluid reservoir on Easytronic models

14 Exhaust system check

1 With the engine cold (at least an hour after the vehicle has been driven), check the complete exhaust system from the engine to the end of the tailpipe. The exhaust system is most easily checked with the vehicle raised on a hoist, or suitably-supported on axle stands, so that the exhaust components are readily visible and accessible (see *Jacking and vehicle support*).

2 Check the exhaust pipes and connections for evidence of leaks, severe corrosion and damage. Make sure that all brackets and mountings are in good condition, and that all relevant nuts and bolts are tight. Leakage at any of the joints or in other parts of the system will usually show up as a black sooty stain in the vicinity of the leak.

3 Rattles and other noises can often be traced to the exhaust system, especially the brackets and mountings (see illustration). Try to move the pipes and silencers. If the components are able to come into contact with the body or suspension parts, secure the system with new mountings. Otherwise separate the joints (if possible) and twist the pipes as necessary to provide additional clearance.

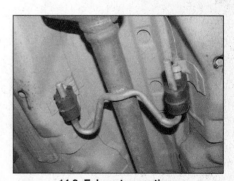

14.3 Exhaust mountings

16.4 Check for wear in the hub bearings by grasping the wheel and trying to rock it

15 Hinge and lock lubrication

1 Work around the vehicle and lubricate the hinges of the bonnet, doors and tailgate with a light machine oil.
2 Lightly lubricate the bonnet release mechanism and exposed section of inner cable with a smear of grease.
3 Check the security and operation of all hinges, latches and locks, adjusting them where required (see Chapter 11). Check the operation of the central locking system.
4 Check the condition and operation of the tailgate struts, renewing them both if either is leaking or no longer able to support the tailgate securely when raised.

16 Front suspension and steering check

1 Apply the handbrake, then raise the front of the vehicle and securely support it on axle stands (see *Jacking and vehicle support*).
2 Inspect the balljoint dust covers and the steering gear gaiters for splits, chafing or deterioration.
3 Any wear of these components will cause loss of lubricant, and may allow water to enter the components, resulting in rapid deterioration of the balljoints or steering gear.
4 Grasp each roadwheel at the 12 o'clock

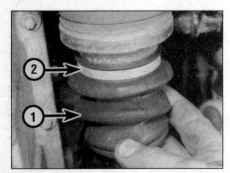

18.1 Check the condition of the driveshaft gaiters (1) and retaining clips (2)

and 6 o'clock positions, and try to rock it **(see illustration)**. Very slight free play may be felt, but if the movement is appreciable, further investigation is necessary to determine the source. Continue rocking the wheel while an assistant depresses the footbrake. If the movement is now eliminated or significantly reduced, it is likely that the hub bearings are at fault. If the free play is still evident with the footbrake depressed, then there is wear in the suspension joints or mountings.
5 Now grasp each wheel at the 9 o'clock and 3 o'clock positions, and try to rock it as before. Any movement felt now may again be caused by wear in the hub bearings or the steering track rod end balljoints. If the track rod end balljoint is worn, the visual movement will be obvious.
6 Using a large screwdriver or flat bar, check for wear in the suspension mounting bushes by levering between the relevant suspension component and its attachment point. Some movement is to be expected, as the mountings are made of rubber, but excessive wear should be obvious. Also check the condition of any visible rubber bushes, looking for splits, cracks or contamination of the rubber.
7 Check for any signs of fluid leakage around the suspension strut/shock absorber bodies, or from the rubber gaiters around the piston rods. Should any fluid be noticed, the suspension strut/shock absorber is defective internally, and should be renewed. **Note:** *Suspension struts/shock absorbers should always be renewed in pairs on the same axle.*
8 With the vehicle standing on its wheels, have an assistant turn the steering wheel back-and-forth about an eighth of a turn each way. There should be very little, if any, lost movement between the steering wheel and roadwheels. If this is not the case, closely observe the joints and mountings previously described, but in addition check the steering column rubber coupling for wear, and also check the steering gear itself.
9 The efficiency of each suspension strut/shock absorber may be checked by bouncing the vehicle at each corner. Generally speaking, the body will return to its normal position and stop after being depressed. If it rises and returns on a rebound, the suspension strut/shock absorber is probably suspect. Also examine the suspension strut/shock absorber upper and lower mountings for any signs of wear.

17 Rear suspension check

1 Chock the front wheels, then jack up the rear of the vehicle and support securely on axle stands (see *Jacking and vehicle support*).
2 Inspect the rear suspension components for any signs of obvious wear or damage. Pay particular attention to the rubber

mounting bushes, and renew if necessary (see Chap-ter 10).
3 Grasp each roadwheel at the 12 o'clock and 6 o'clock positions **(see illustration 16.4)**, and try to rock it. Any excess movement indicates incorrect adjustment or wear in the wheel bearings. Wear may also be accompanied by a rumbling sound when the wheel is spun, or a noticeable roughness if the wheel is turned slowly. The wheel bearing can be renewed as described in Chapter 10.
4 Check the rear shock absorbers in a similar manner to that described previously for the front shock absorbers.

18 Driveshaft check

1 With the vehicle raised and securely supported on stands, turn the steering onto full-lock, then slowly rotate each front roadwheel. Inspect the condition of the outer constant velocity (CV) joint rubber gaiters **(see illustration)**, while squeezing the gaiters to open out the folds. Check for signs of cracking, splits or deterioration of the rubber, which may allow the grease to escape and lead to water and grit entering the joint. Also check the security and condition of the retaining clips. Repeat these checks on the inner CV joints. If any damage or deterioration is found, the gaiters should be renewed as described in Chapter 8.
2 At the same time, check the general condition of the CV joints themselves by first holding the driveshaft and attempting to rotate the wheel. Repeat this check by holding the inner joint and attempting to rotate the driveshaft. Any appreciable movement indicates wear in the joints, wear in the driveshaft splines, or a loose front hub nut.

19 Road test

Instruments and electrical equipment

1 Check the operation of all instruments and electrical equipment.
2 Make sure that all instruments read correctly, and switch on all electrical equipment in turn, to check that it functions properly.

Steering and suspension

3 Check for any abnormalities in the steering, suspension, handling or road 'feel'.
4 Drive the vehicle, and check that there are no unusual vibrations or noises.
5 Check that the steering feels positive, with no excessive 'sloppiness', or roughness, and check for any suspension noises when cornering and driving over bumps.

Drivetrain

6 Check the performance of the engine, clutch (where applicable), gearbox/transmission and driveshafts.

7 Listen for any unusual noises from the engine, clutch and gearbox/transmission.

8 Make sure that the engine runs smoothly when idling, and that there is no hesitation when accelerating.

9 Check that, where applicable, the clutch action is smooth and progressive, that the drive is taken up smoothly, and that the pedal travel is not excessive. Also listen for any noises when the clutch pedal is depressed.

10 On manual gearbox models, check that all gears can be engaged smoothly without noise, and that the gear lever action is smooth and not abnormally vague or 'notchy'.

11 On automatic transmission models, make sure that all gearchanges occur smoothly, without snatching, and without an increase in engine speed between changes. Check that all the gear positions can be selected with the vehicle at rest. If any problems are found, they

should be referred to a Vauxhall dealer.

12 Listen for a metallic clicking sound from the front of the vehicle, as the vehicle is driven slowly in a circle with the steering on full-lock. Carry out this check in both directions. If a clicking noise is heard, this indicates wear in a driveshaft joint, in which case renew the joint if necessary (see Chapter 8).

Braking system

13 Make sure that the vehicle does not pull to one side when braking, and that the wheels do not lock when braking hard.

14 Check that there is no vibration through the steering when braking.

15 Check that the handbrake operates correctly without excessive movement of the lever, and that it holds the vehicle stationary on a slope.

16 Test the operation of the brake servo unit as follows. With the engine off, depress the footbrake four or five times to exhaust the vacuum. Hold the brake pedal depressed, then start the engine. As the engine starts, there should be a noticeable 'give' in the

brake pedal as vacuum builds-up. Allow the engine to run for at least two minutes, and then switch it off. If the brake pedal is depressed now, it should be possible to detect a hiss from the servo as the pedal is depressed. After about four or five applications, no further hissing should be heard, and the pedal should feel considerably harder.

20 Service interval indicator reset

1 With the ignition switched off, depress and hold the reset button located on the instrument panel.

2 Switch on the ignition and press and hold the reset button for two more seconds at least. The InSP indicator should flash for two seconds, after which the text '___' should appear before releasing the reset button. When the button is released, the odometer or clock will appear again.

Every 20 000 miles (30 000 km) or 2 years

21 Pollen filter renewal

1 Peel the bonnet seal off the engine compartment bulkhead, and remove it from the vehicle.

2 Lift the brake fluid reservoir cover, and remove the battery wiring harness cover from the water deflector.

3 Release the battery wiring harness from the water deflector and move to one side. It may be necessary to unclip the wiring harness from the bracket on the right-hand inner panel.

4 Lift the water deflector shield, then release

the two retaining clips and lift the pollen filter out from its housing, noting which way round it is fitted.

5 Wipe clean the filter housing and install the new filter, making sure it is the correct way up. Ensure that the filter is correctly seated, and secure it in position with the retaining clips.

6 Refitting is the reverse of the removal procedure.

Every 40 000 miles (60 000 km) or 2 years

22 Remote control battery renewal

Note: *The following procedure must be*

performed within 3 minutes, otherwise the remote control unit will have to be reprogrammed.

1 Using a screwdriver, prise the key section from the remote control unit. Then prise the battery cover from the remote

control unit **(see illustrations)**.

2 Note how the battery is fitted, then carefully remove it from the contacts.

3 Fit the new battery and refit the cover making sure that it clips fully onto the base. Refit the key section.

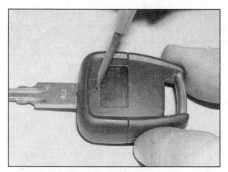

22.1a Prise the key section away . . .

22.1b . . . from the remote control . . .

22.1c . . . and open the battery cover

23 Brake and clutch fluid renewal

Note: *It is not possible for the home mechanic to bleed the clutch hydraulic system on Easytronic models.*

> **Warning: Brake hydraulic fluid can harm your eyes and damage painted surfaces, so use extreme caution when handling and pouring it. Do not use fluid that has been standing open for some time, as it absorbs moisture from the air. Excess moisture can cause a dangerous loss of braking effectiveness.**

1 The procedure is similar to that for the bleeding of the hydraulic system as described in Chapters 9 (brake) and 6 (clutch).

2 Working as described in Chapter 9, open the first bleed screw in the sequence, and pump the brake pedal gently until nearly all the old fluid has been emptied from the master cylinder reservoir. Top-up to the MAX level with new fluid, and continue pumping until only the new fluid remains in the reservoir, and new fluid can be seen emerging from the bleed screw. Tighten the screw, and top the reservoir level up to the MAX level line.

Old hydraulic fluid is invariably much darker in colour than the new, making it easy to distinguish the two.

3 Work through all the remaining bleed screws in the sequence until new fluid can be seen at all of them. Be careful to keep the master cylinder reservoir topped-up to above the MIN level at all times, or air may enter the system and greatly increase the length of the task.

4 When the operation is complete, check that all bleed screws are securely tightened, and that their dust caps are refitted. Wash off all traces of spilt fluid, and recheck the master cylinder reservoir fluid level.

5 Check the operation of the brakes before taking the car on the road.

6 Similarly, bleed the clutch hydraulic system with reference to Chapter 6.

24 Coolant renewal

Note: *Vauxhall do not specify renewal intervals for the antifreeze mixture, as the mixture used to fill the system when the vehicle is new is designed to last the lifetime of the vehicle. However, it is strongly recommended that the coolant is renewed at the intervals specified in the 'Maintenance schedule', as a precaution against possible engine corrosion problems. This is particularly advisable if the coolant has been renewed using an antifreeze other than that specified*

by Vauxhall. With many antifreeze types, the corrosion inhibitors become progressively less effective with age. It is up to the individual owner whether or not to follow this advice.

Cooling system draining

> **Warning: Wait until the engine is cold before starting this procedure. Do not allow antifreeze to come in contact with your skin, or with the painted surfaces of the vehicle. Rinse off spills immediately with plenty of water. Never leave antifreeze lying around in an open container, or in a puddle on the driveway or garage floor. Children and pets are attracted by its sweet smell, but antifreeze is fatal if ingested.**

1 To drain the cooling system, first cover the expansion tank cap with a wad of rag, and slowly turn the cap anti-clockwise to relieve the pressure in the cooling system (a hissing sound will normally be heard). Wait until any pressure remaining in the system is released, then continue to turn the cap until it can be removed.

2 Where necessary, remove the splash guard from under the radiator and engine.

3 The coolant drain plug is located at the bottom of the radiator right-hand end tank. Position a container beneath the radiator then unscrew the drain plug and allow the coolant to drain.

4 As no cylinder block drain plug is fitted, it is not possible to drain all of the coolant. Due consideration must be made for this when refilling the system, in order to maintain the correct concentration of antifreeze.

5 If the coolant has been drained for a reason other than renewal, then provided it is clean and less than two years old, it can be re-used.

Cooling system flushing

6 If coolant renewal has been neglected, or if the antifreeze mixture has become diluted, then in time the cooling system may gradually lose efficiency, as the coolant passages become restricted due to rust, scale deposits, and other sediment. The cooling system efficiency can be restored by flushing the system clean.

7 The radiator should be flushed independently of the engine, to avoid unnecessary contamination.

8 To flush the radiator, disconnect the top hose at the radiator, then insert a garden hose into the radiator top inlet. Direct a flow of clean water through the radiator, and continue flushing until clean water emerges from the radiator bottom outlet (the bottom radiator hose should have been disconnected to drain the system). If after a reasonable period, the water still does not run clear, the radiator can be flushed with a good proprietary cleaning agent. It is important that the cleaning agent manufacturer's instructions are followed carefully. If the contamination is particularly bad, insert the hose in the radiator bottom

outlet, and flush the radiator in the reverse direction ('reverse-flushing').

9 To flush the engine block, the thermostat must be removed, because it will be shut, and would otherwise prevent the flow of water around the engine. The thermostat can be removed as described in Chapter 3. Take care not to introduce dirt or debris into the system if this approach is used.

10 With the radiator top and bottom hoses disconnected from the radiator, insert a hose into the top hose. Direct a clean flow of water through the engine, and continue flushing until clean water emerges from the radiator bottom hose.

11 On completion of flushing, refit the thermostat with reference to Chapter 3, and reconnect the hoses.

Cooling system filling

12 Before attempting to fill the cooling system, make sure that all hoses and clips are in good condition, and that the clips are tight. Note that an antifreeze mixture must be used all year round, to prevent corrosion of the alloy engine components.

13 On 1.4 litre engines, unscrew the bleed screw which is situated in the thermostat housing cover.

14 Remove the expansion tank cap, and fill the system by slowly pouring the coolant into the expansion tank to prevent airlocks from forming.

15 If the coolant is being renewed, begin by pouring in a couple of litres of water, followed by the correct quantity of antifreeze, then top-up with more water.

16 When coolant free of air bubbles emerges from the orifice, refit the bleed screw and tighten it securely (1.4 litre engines).

17 Top-up the coolant level to the KALT (or COLD) mark on the expansion tank, then refit the expansion tank cap.

18 Start the engine and run it until it reaches normal operating temperature, then stop the engine and allow it to cool.

19 Check for leaks, particularly around disturbed components. Check the coolant level in the expansion tank, and top-up if necessary. Note that the system must be cold before an accurate level is indicated in the expansion tank. If the expansion tank cap is removed while the engine is still warm, cover the cap with a thick cloth, and unscrew the cap slowly to gradually relieve the system pressure (a hissing sound will normally be heard). Wait until any pressure remaining in the system is released, then continue to turn the cap until it can be removed.

Antifreeze mixture

20 Always use an ethylene-glycol based antifreeze which is suitable for use in mixed-metal cooling systems. The quantity of antifreeze and levels of protection are indicated in the Specifications.

21 Before adding antifreeze, the cooling system should be completely drained,

preferably flushed, and all hoses and clips checked for condition and security.

22 After filling with antifreeze, a label should be attached to the radiator or expansion tank, stating the type and concentration of antifreeze used, and the date installed. Any subsequent topping-up should be made with the same type and concentration of antifreeze.

23 Do not use engine antifreeze in the windscreen/tailgate washer system, as it will cause damage to the vehicle paintwork. A screenwash should be added to the washer system in the quantities recommended on the bottle.

Every 40 000 miles (60 000 km) or 4 years

25 Air cleaner filter element renewal

1 Disconnect the wiring plug from the air mass meter **(see illustration)**.
2 Unclip the purge valve from the side of the air cleaner cover **(see illustration)**.
3 Undo the screws, lift off the air cleaner cover **(see illustration)**.

25.1 Disconnect the wiring plug from the air mass meter . . .

4 Lift out the air cleaner element **(see illustration)**.
5 Wipe out the casing and the cover.
6 Fit the new filter, noting that the rubber locating flange should be uppermost, and secure the cover with the screws.
7 Reconnect the air mass meter to the cover and tighten the clip, then reconnect the wiring.

26 Spark plug check and renewal

1 The correct functioning of the spark plugs is vital for the correct running and efficiency of the engine. It is essential that the plugs fitted are appropriate for the engine, the suitable type being specified at the beginning of this Chapter.
2 If the correct type of plug is used and the engine is in good condition, the spark plugs should not need attention between scheduled renewal intervals, except for adjustment of their gaps. Spark plug cleaning is rarely

necessary, and should not be attempted unless specialised equipment is available, as damage can easily be caused to the firing ends.
3 To gain access to the spark plugs, remove the engine top cover followed by the DIS module as described in Chapter 5B.
4 Unscrew the plugs using a spark plug spanner, a suitable box spanner, or a deep socket and extension bar **(see illustrations)**. Keep the socket in alignment with the spark plugs, otherwise if it is forcibly moved to either side, the porcelain top of the spark plug may be broken off. As each plug is removed, examine it as follows.
5 Examination of the spark plugs will give a good indication of the condition of the engine. If the insulator nose of the spark plug is clean and white, with no deposits, this is indicative of a weak mixture or too hot a plug (a hot plug transfers heat away from the electrode slowly, while a cold plug transfers heat away quickly).
6 If the tip and insulator nose are covered with hard black-looking deposits, then this is indicative that the idle mixture is too rich. Should the plug be black and oily, then it is

25.2 . . . unclip the purge valve . . .

25.3a . . . then undo the screws . . .

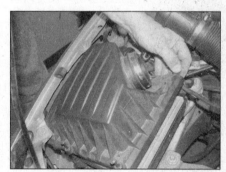

25.3b . . . remove the cover . . .

25.4 . . . and lift out the air cleaner element

26.4a Unscrew the spark plugs . . .

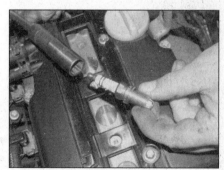

26.4b . . . and remove them

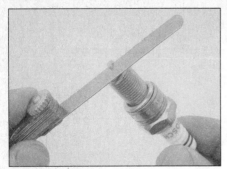

26.9a Measuring a spark plug electrode gap using a feeler blade

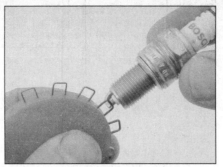

26.9b Measuring a spark plug electrode gap using a wire gauge

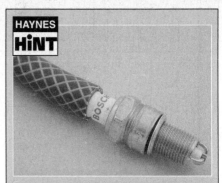

It's often difficult to insert spark plugs into their holes without cross-threading them. To avoid this possibility, fit a short piece of rubber hose over the end of the spark plug. The flexible hose acts as a universal joint, to help align the plug with the plug hole. Should the plug begin to cross-thread, the hose will slip on the spark plug, preventing thread damage.

likely that the engine is fairly worn, as well as the mixture being too rich.

7 If the insulator nose is covered with light-tan to greyish-brown deposits, then the mixture is correct and it is likely that the engine is in good condition.

8 The spark plug gap is of considerable importance as, if it is too large or too small, the size of the spark and its efficiency will be seriously impaired. For the best results, the spark plug gap should be set in accordance with the Specifications at the beginning of this Chapter.

9 To set the spark plug gap, measure the gap between the electrodes with a feeler blade, and then bend open, or close, the outer plug electrode until the correct gap is achieved **(see illustrations)**. The centre electrode should never be bent, as this may crack the insulation and cause plug failure, if nothing worse.

10 Special spark plug electrode gap adjusting tools are available from most motor accessory shops.

11 Before fitting the new spark plugs, check that the threaded connector sleeves on the top of the plug are tight, and that the plug exterior surfaces and threads are clean.

12 Screw in the spark plugs by hand where possible, then tighten them to the specified torque. Take extra care to enter the plug threads correctly, as the cylinder head is of light alloy construction **(see Haynes Hint)**.

13 Refit the DIS module as described in Chapter 5B, then refit the engine top cover.

27 Timing belt renewal (1.4 litre engines)

Renew the timing belt and tensioner with reference to Chapter 2B.

28 Fuel filter renewal

1 The fuel filter is located under the rear of the vehicle **(see illustration)**.

2 Depressurise the fuel system as described in Chapter 4A or 4B.

3 Chock the front wheels, then jack up the rear of the vehicle, and support securely on axle stands (see *Jacking and vehicle support*). On ECO models, unbolt the air guide plates and stone protectors from the underbody.

4 Undo the clamp screw and release the filter. Note the orientation of the fuel flow direction arrow.

5 Position a suitable container below the fuel filter, to catch spilt fuel.

6 Disconnect the quick-release fittings and remove the fuel hoses from the fuel filter, noting their locations to ensure correct refitting. A Vauxhall special tool is available to disconnect the hose connectors, but provided care is taken, the connections can be released using a pair of long-nosed pliers, or a similar tool, to depress the retaining tangs. Be prepared for fuel spillage, and take adequate precautions. Vauxhall recommend that the connecting clips of the quick-release connectors are renewed whenever removed.

7 Fitting the new filter is a reversal of removal, bearing in mind the following points.

a) Ensure that the filter is fitted with the flow direction arrow on the filter body pointing in the direction of fuel flow **(see illustration)**.

b) Ensure that the hoses are reconnected to their correct locations, as noted before removal.

c) Before lowering the vehicle to the ground (and refitting the air guide plates on ECO models), run the engine and check for leaks. If leakage is evident, stop the

engine immediately and rectify the problem without delay.

29 Automatic transmission fluid renewal

Draining

1 This operation is much quicker and more efficient if the vehicle is first taken on a journey of sufficient length to warm the engine/transmission up to normal operating temperature.

2 Apply the handbrake, then jack up the front of the vehicle and support it on axle stands (see *Jacking and vehicle support*).

3 Place a suitable container under the drain plug located at the lower right-hand side of the transmission housing.

4 Wipe clean the area around the drain plug, then unscrew the plug and allow the fluid to drain into the container.

5 After all the fluid has drained, wipe the drain plug and the sealing washer with a clean rag. Examine the condition of the sealing washer,

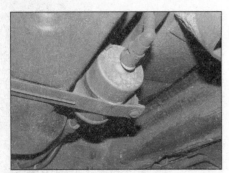

28.1 Fuel filter location

28.7 Ensure that the flow direction arrow points in the direction of the fuel flow

and renew it if it shows signs of scoring or other damage which may prevent a perfect seal. Clean the area around the drain plug opening, and refit the plug complete with the washer. Tighten the plug securely and lower the car to the ground.

Refilling

6 Refill the transmission through the dipstick tube with the correct quantity and type of fluid, then check the level as follows.

7 Lower the vehicle to the ground. Note that the vehicle must be parked on level ground for an accurate level check.

8 If the transmission fluid is cold (ie, if the engine is cold), the level check must be completed with the engine idling, within one minute of the engine being started.

9 With the engine idling, fully depress the brake pedal, and move the gear selector lever smoothly through all positions, finishing in position P.

10 With the engine still idling, withdraw the transmission fluid level dipstick (located at the left-hand side of the engine compartment, next to the engine oil level dipstick). Pull up the lever on the top of the dipstick to release it from the tube. Wipe the dipstick clean with a lint-free rag, re-insert it and withdraw it again.

11 If the transmission fluid was cold at the beginning of the procedure, the fluid level should be on the MIN mark on the side of the dipstick marked +20°C. Note that 0.4 litres of fluid is required to raise the level from the MIN to the MAX mark **(see illustration)**.

12 If the transmission fluid was at operating temperature at the beginning of the procedure (ie, if the vehicle had been driven for at least 12 miles/20 km), the fluid level should be between the MIN and MAX marks on the side of the dipstick marked +80°C. Note that 0.2 litres of fluid is required to raise the level from the MIN to the MAX mark.

13 If topping-up is necessary, stop the engine, and top-up with the specified type of fluid through the transmission dipstick tube.

14 Recheck the level, and refit the dipstick on completion.

30 Rear brake shoe, drum and wheel cylinder check

1 Chock the front wheels, then jack up the rear of the vehicle, and support it securely on axle stands (see *Jacking and vehicle support*).

2 For a quick check, the thickness of friction material remaining on one of the brake shoes can be observed through the hole in the brake backplate which is exposed by prising out the sealing grommet. If a rod of the same

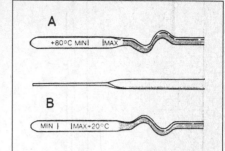

29.11 Automatic transmission fluid level dipstick markings

A Markings for fluid at operating temperature
B Markings for cold fluid

diameter as the specified minimum friction material thickness is placed against the shoe friction material, the amount of wear can be assessed. An electric torch or inspection light will probably be required. If the friction material on any shoe is worn down to the specified minimum thickness or less, all four shoes must be renewed as a set.

3 For a comprehensive check, the brake drum should be removed and cleaned. This will allow the wheel cylinders to be checked, and the condition of the brake drum itself to be fully examined (see Chapter 9).

Chapter 1 Part B:
Routine maintenance and servicing – diesel models

Contents

Degrees of difficulty

Easy, suitable for novice with little experience

Fairly easy, suitable for beginner with some experience

Fairly difficult, suitable for competent DIY mechanic

Difficult, suitable for experienced DIY mechanic

Very difficult, suitable for expert DIY or professional

Lubricants and fluids .... Refer to Weekly checks on page 0•17

Capacities

Engine oil
Oil change, including filter .... 4.5 litres
Difference between MAX and MIN dipstick marks .... 1.0 litre

Cooling system
All engines .... 7.1 litres

Fuel tank
Hatch and Corsavan models .... 44.0 litres
Combo models .... 52.0 litres

Manual gearbox .... 1.6 litres

Washer fluid reservoir
Without headlight washers .... 2.2 litres
With headlight washers .... 3.5 litres

Cooling system

Antifreeze mixture:
   50% antifreeze .... Protection down to -37°C
   55% antifreeze .... Protection down to -45°C

Suspension and steering

Tyre pressures .... Refer to end of *Weekly checks* on page 0•18

Torque wrench settings

	Nm	lbf ft
Balance weight to driveshaft	10	7
Fuel filter housing cover centre bolt	8	6
Oil filter housing cover	25	18
Reversing light switch	20	15
Roadwheel bolts	110	81
Sump drain plug	78	58

1 The maintenance intervals in this manual are provided with the assumption that you, not the dealer, will be carrying out the work. These are the minimum maintenance intervals recommended by us for vehicles driven daily. If you wish to keep your vehicle in peak condition at all times, you may wish to perform some of these procedures more often. We encourage frequent maintenance, because it enhances the efficiency, performance and resale value of your vehicle.
2 If the vehicle is driven in dusty areas, used to tow a trailer, or driven frequently at slow speeds (idling in traffic) or on short journeys, more frequent maintenance intervals are recommended.
3 When the vehicle is new, it should be serviced by a factory-authorised dealer service department, in order to preserve the factory warranty.

Every 250 miles (400 km) or weekly

☐ Refer to *Weekly checks*

Every 10 000 miles (15 000 km) or 6 months – whichever comes first

☐ Renew the engine oil and filter (Section 3)

Note: *Vauxhall recommend that the engine oil and filter are changed every 20 000 miles (30 000 km) or 12 months. However, oil and filter changes are good for the engine and we recommend that the oil and filter are renewed more frequently, especially if the vehicle is used on a lot of short journeys.*

Every 20 000 miles (30 000 km) or 12 months – whichever comes first

☐ Check all underbonnet and underbody components, pipes and hoses for leaks (Section 4)
☐ Check the auxiliary drivebelt and tensioner (Section 5)
☐ Check the operation of the horn, all lights, and the wipers and washers (Section 6)
☐ Check the tightness of the roadwheel bolts (Section 7)
☐ Check the condition of the brake pads (renew if necessary), the calipers and discs (Section 8)
☐ Check the operation of the handbrake and adjust if necessary (Section 9)
☐ Check the headlight beam alignment (Section 10)
☐ Check the condition of all brake fluid pipes and hoses (Section 11)
☐ Check the bodywork and underbody for damage and corrosion, and check the condition of the underbody corrosion protection (Section 12)
☐ Check the condition of the exhaust system components (Section 13)
☐ Drain water from the fuel filter (Section 14)
☐ Lubricate all door, bonnet and tailgate hinges and locks (Section 15)
☐ Check the condition of the front suspension and steering components, particularly the rubber gaiters and seals (Section 16)
☐ Check the condition of the rear suspension components (Section 17)
☐ Check the condition of the driveshaft joint gaiters, and the driveshaft joints (Section 18)
☐ Carry out a road test (Section 19)
☐ Reset the service interval indicator (Section 20)

Every 20 000 miles (30 000 km) or 2 years – whichever comes first

☐ Renew the fuel filter (Section 21)
☐ Renew the pollen filter (Section 22)

Every 40 000 miles (60 000 km) or 2 years – whichever comes first

☐ Renew the battery for the remote control (Section 23)
☐ Renew the brake (and clutch) fluid (Section 24)
☐ Renew the coolant (Section 25)

Every 40 000 miles (60 000 km) or 4 years – whichever comes first

☐ Renew the air cleaner filter element (Section 26)
☐ Check the condition of the rear brake shoes (renew if necessary), the drums and wheel cylinders (Section 27)

Every 60 000 miles (100 000 km) or 6 years – whichever comes first

☐ Renew the timing belt and tensioner (Section 28), and the auxiliary drivebelt (Section 5)

Note: *The normal interval for timing belt renewal, as recommended by Vauxhall, is 100 000 miles (150 000 km) or 10 years, however, it is strongly recommended that the interval is reduced to 60 000 miles (100 000 km) or 6 years on vehicles which are subjected to intensive use, ie, mainly short journeys or a lot of stop-start driving. The actual belt renewal interval is therefore very much up to the individual owner, but bear in mind that severe engine damage will result if the belt breaks.*

Every 100 000 miles (150 000 km) or 10 years – whichever comes first

☐ Check and adjust the valve clearances (Section 29)

Underbonnet view of a 1.7 litre Y17DTL model

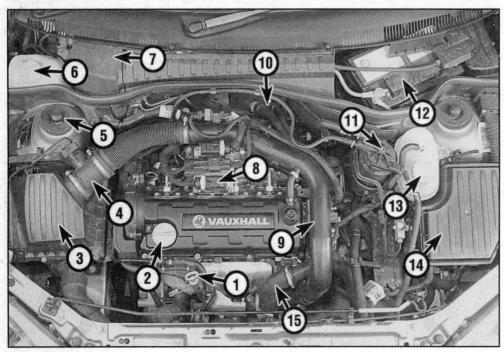

1 Engine oil level dipstick
2 Engine oil filler cap
3 Air cleaner assembly
4 Hot film mass airflow meter
5 Front suspension strut upper mountings
6 Washer fluid reservoir
7 Brake fluid reservoir
8 Engine electronic control unit (ECU)
9 Air inlet duct
10 Coolant hoses on heater matrix
11 Fuel filter
12 Battery
13 Coolant expansion tank
14 Engine compartment fuse and relay box
15 Turbocharger

Front underbody view of a 1.7 litre Y17DTL model

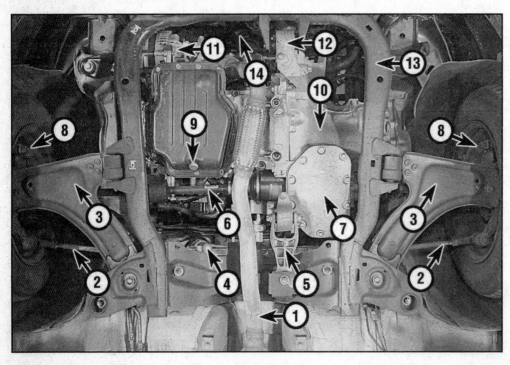

1 Exhaust front pipe
2 Steering track rods
3 Front suspension lower arms
4 Steering gear
5 Engine mounting rear torque link
6 Right-hand driveshaft
7 Final drive cover plate
8 Front brake calipers
9 Engine oil drain plug
10 Manual transmission
11 Air conditioning compressor
12 Engine mounting front torque link
13 Front suspension subframe
14 Electric cooling fan

Rear underbody view of a 1.7 litre Y17DTL model

1   *Handbrake cable*
2   *Rear suspension coil springs*
3   *Exhaust tailpipe and silencer*
4   *Exhaust heatshield*
5   *Rear anti-roll bar*
6   *Rear brake proportioning valve*
7   *Rear suspension trailing arms and rear axle*

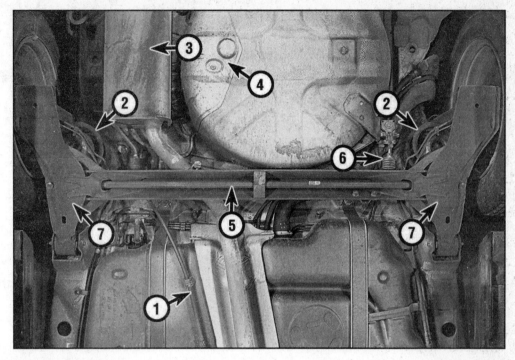

Maintenance procedures

1   General information

1 This Chapter is designed to help the home mechanic maintain his/her vehicle for safety, economy, long life and peak performance.

2 The Chapter contains a master maintenance schedule, followed by sections dealing specifically with each task on the schedule. Visual checks, adjustments, component renewal and other helpful items are included. Refer to the accompanying illustrations of the engine compartment and the underside of the vehicle for the locations of the various components.

3 Servicing of your vehicle in accordance with the mileage/time maintenance schedule and the following sections will provide a planned maintenance programme, which should result in a long and reliable service life. This is a comprehensive plan, so maintaining some items but not others at the specified service intervals will not produce the same results.

4 As you service your vehicle, you will discover that many of the procedures can – and should – be grouped together, because of the particular procedure being performed, or because of the close proximity of two otherwise-unrelated components to one another. For example, if the vehicle is raised for any reason, the exhaust can be inspected at the same time as the suspension and steering components.

5 The first step in this maintenance programme is to prepare yourself before the actual work begins. Read through all the sections relevant to the work to be carried out, then make a list and gather together all the parts and tools required. If a problem is encountered, seek advice from a parts specialist, or a dealer service department.

2   Regular maintenance

1 If, from the time the vehicle is new, the routine maintenance schedule is followed closely, and frequent checks are made of fluid levels and high-wear items, as suggested throughout this manual, the engine will be kept in relatively good running condition, and the need for additional work will be minimised.

2 It is possible that there will be times when the engine is running poorly due to the lack of regular maintenance. This is even more likely if a used vehicle, which has not received regular and frequent maintenance checks, is purchased. In such cases, additional work may need to be carried out, outside of the regular maintenance intervals.

3 If engine wear is suspected, a compression test (refer to Chapter 2C) will provide valuable information regarding the overall performance of the main internal components. Such a test can be used as a basis to decide on the

extent of the work to be carried out. If, for example, a compression test indicates serious internal engine wear, conventional maintenance as described in this Chapter will not greatly improve the performance of the engine, and may prove a waste of time and money, unless extensive overhaul work (Chapter 2D) is carried out first.

4 The following series of operations are those most often required to improve the performance of a generally poor-running engine:

Primary operations

a) *Clean, inspect and test the battery ('Weekly checks').*
b) *Check all the engine-related fluids ('Weekly checks').*
c) *Check the condition and tension of the auxiliary drivebelt (Section 5).*
d) *Check the condition of the air filter, and renew if necessary (Section 26).*
e) *Renew the fuel filter (Section 21).*
f) *Check the condition of all hoses, and check for fluid leaks (Section 4).*

5 If the above operations do not prove fully effective, carry out the following secondary operations:

Secondary operations

All items listed under *Primary operations*, plus the following:

a) *Check the charging system (Chapter 5A).*
b) *Check the preheating system (Chapter 5C).*
c) *Check the fuel system (Chapter 4C)*

3.3 Removing the oil filler cap

3.4 Sump drain plug

As the drain plug threads release, move it sharply away so the stream of oil issuing from the sump runs into the container, not up your sleeve.

Every 10 000 miles (15 000 km) or 6 months

3 Engine oil and filter renewal

HAYNES HiNT
Frequent oil and filter changes are the most important preventative maintenance procedures which can be undertaken by the DIY owner. As engine oil ages, it becomes diluted and contaminated, which leads to premature engine wear.

1 Before starting this procedure, gather together all the necessary tools and materials. Also make sure that you have plenty of clean rags and newspapers handy, to mop up any spills. Ideally, the engine oil should be warm, as it will drain more easily, and more built-up sludge will be removed with it. Take care not to touch the exhaust or any other hot parts of the engine when working under the vehicle. To avoid any possibility of scalding, and to protect yourself from possible skin irritants and other harmful contaminants in used engine oils, it is advisable to wear gloves when carrying out this work.

2 Firmly apply the handbrake then jack up the front of the vehicle and support it on axle stands (see *Jacking and vehicle support*). Remove the undertray from under the engine compartment.

3 Remove the oil filler cap **(see illustration)**.

4 Using a spanner, or preferably a suitable socket and bar, slacken the drain plug about half a turn **(see illustration)**.

5 Position the draining container under the drain plug, then remove the plug completely. If possible, try to keep the plug pressed into the sump while unscrewing it by hand the last couple of turns **(see Haynes Hint)**.

6 Allow some time for the oil to drain, noting that it may be necessary to reposition the container as the oil flow slows to a trickle.

7 Make sure there is a container below the position of the oil filter, which is located on the rear, left-hand side of the cylinder block **(see illustration)**.

8 Using a large socket, unscrew the cover and remove it from the top of the oil filter housing **(see illustrations)**. Lift out the old filter element.

9 Fit the new filter element to the housing or cover **(see illustration)**.

10 Renew the sealing rings then refit the oil filter cover and tighten it to the specified torque **(see illustration)**.

11 After all the oil has drained, wipe the drain plug and the sealing washer with a clean rag. Examine the condition of the sealing washer, and renew it if it shows signs of scoring or other damage which may prevent an oil-tight seal. Clean the area around the drain plug opening, and refit the plug complete with the washer and tighten it to the specified torque.

12 Remove the old oil and all tools from under the vehicle then lower the vehicle to the ground.

13 Fill the engine through the filler hole, using

3.7 The oil filter is located on the rear of the cylinder block

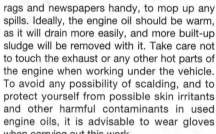

3.8a Unscrew the cover . . .

3.8b . . . and remove the filter element

3.9 Fitting the element to the cover

3.10 Sealing rings on the cover and pin

the correct grade and type of oil (refer to *Weekly Checks* for details of topping-up). Pour in half the specified quantity of oil first, then wait a few minutes for the oil to drain into the sump. Continue to add oil, a small quantity at a time, until the level is up to the lower mark on the dipstick. Adding approximately a further 1.0 litre will bring the level up to the upper mark on the dipstick.

14 Start the engine and run it for a few minutes, while checking for leaks around the oil filter seal and the sump drain plug. Note that there may be a delay of a few seconds before the low oil pressure warning light goes out when the engine is first started, as the oil circulates through the new oil filter and the engine oil galleries before the pressure buildsup.

15 Stop the engine, and wait a few minutes for the oil to settle in the sump once more. With the new oil circulated and the filter now completely full, recheck the level on the dipstick, and add more oil as necessary.

16 Dispose of the used engine oil safely with reference to *General repair procedures*.

Every 20 000 miles (30 000 km) or 12 months

4 Hose and fluid leak check

1 Visually inspect the engine joint faces, gaskets and seals for any signs of water or oil leaks. Pay particular attention to the areas around the camshaft cover, cylinder head, oil filter and sump joint faces. Similarly, check the transmission and (where applicable) the air conditioning compressor for oil leakage. Bear in mind that, over a period of time, some very slight seepage from these areas is to be expected; what you are really looking for is any indication of a serious leak. Should a leak be found, renew the offending gasket or oil seal by referring to the appropriate Chapters in this manual.

2 Also check the security and condition of all the engine-related pipes and hoses. Ensure that all cable ties or securing clips are in place, and in good condition. Clips which are broken or missing can lead to chafing of the hoses pipes or wiring, which could cause more serious problems in the future.

3 Carefully check the radiator hoses and heater hoses along their entire length. Renew any hose which is cracked, swollen or deteriorated. Cracks will show up better if the hose is squeezed. Pay close attention to the hose clips that secure the hoses to the cooling system components. Hose clips can pinch and puncture hoses, resulting in cooling system leaks. If wire-type hose clips are used, it may be a good idea to replace them with screw-type clips (see Haynes Hint).

4 Inspect all the cooling system components (hoses, joint faces, etc) for leaks. Where any

problems of this nature are found on system components, renew the component or gasket with reference to Chapter 3.

5 With the vehicle raised, inspect the petrol tank and filler neck for punctures, cracks and other damage. The connection between the filler neck and tank is especially critical. Sometimes, a rubber filler neck or connecting hose will leak due to loose retaining clamps or deteriorated rubber.

6 Carefully check all rubber hoses and metal fuel lines leading away from the petrol tank. Check for loose connections, deteriorated hoses, crimped lines and other damage. Pay particular attention to the vent pipes and hoses, which often loop up around the filler neck and can become blocked or crimped. Follow the lines to the front of the vehicle, carefully inspecting them all the way. Renew damaged sections as necessary. Similarly, whilst the vehicle is raised, take the opportunity to inspect all underbody brake fluid pipes and hoses.

7 From within the engine compartment, check the security of all fuel hose attachments and pipe unions, and inspect the fuel hoses and vacuum hoses for kinks, chafing and deterioration.

5 Auxiliary drivebelt check and renewal

Checking

1 Drivebelts are prone to failure after a long period of time and should therefore be inspected regularly.

2 With the engine stopped, inspect the full length of the drivebelt for cracks and separation of the belt plies. It will be necessary to turn the engine (using a spanner or socket and bar on the crankshaft pulley bolt) in order to move the belt from the pulleys so that the belt can be inspected thoroughly. Twist the belt between the pulleys so that both sides can be viewed. Also check for fraying, and glazing which gives the belt a shiny appearance. Check the pulleys for nicks, cracks, distortion and corrosion.

3 If the belt shows signs of wear or damage, it must be renewed.

Renewal

Note: *The manufacturers recommend that the tensioner roller is checked and if necessary renewed at the same time as the drivebelt.*

4 Apply the handbrake, then jack up the front of the vehicle and support it on axle stands (see *Jacking and vehicle support*). Remove the right-hand front roadwheel and the wheel arch liner cover for access to the right-hand side of the engine. Also remove the undertray from under the engine compartment.

5 With reference to Chapter 4C, remove the air cleaner housing.

6 If the drivebelt is to be re-used, mark it to indicate its normal running direction. Note the run of the drivebelt around the pulleys **(see illustration)**.

7 Using a Torx key or spanner (as applicable) on the pulley centre bolt, turn the tensioner clockwise against the spring tension. Hold the tensioner in this position by inserting a suitable locking bolt through the special hole provided **(see illustration)**.

A leak in the cooling system will usually show up as white- or rust-coloured deposits on the area adjoining the leak.

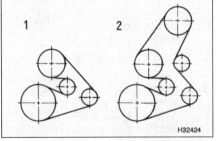

5.6 Auxiliary drivebelt configuration

1 *Models without air conditioning*
2 *Models with air conditioning*

5.7 Turn the tensioner clockwise and insert the locking bolt

5.8 Removing the auxiliary drivebelt

8 Slip the drivebelt from the pulleys **(see illustration).**

9 Locate the new drivebelt on the pulleys in the correct routing. If the drivebelt is being re-used, make sure it is fitted the correct way around.

10 Turn back the tensioner and remove the locking bolt, then release it, making sure that the drivebelt ribs locate correctly on each of the pulley grooves.

11 Refit the air cleaner housing and undertray, then refit the wheel arch liner and roadwheel, and lower the vehicle to the ground.

6 Electrical system check
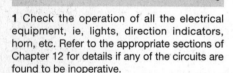

1 Check the operation of all the electrical equipment, ie, lights, direction indicators, horn, etc. Refer to the appropriate sections of Chapter 12 for details if any of the circuits are found to be inoperative.

2 Note that the stop-light switch is described in Chapter 9.

3 Check all accessible wiring connectors, harnesses and retaining clips for security, and for signs of chafing or damage. Rectify any faults found.

7 Roadwheel bolt tightness check

1 Where applicable, remove the wheel trims from the wheels.

2 Using a torque wrench on each wheel bolt in turn, ensure that the bolts are tightened to the specified torque.

3 Where applicable, refit the wheel trims on completion, making sure they are fitted correctly.

8 Brake pad and disc check

1 With the vehicle on level ground, chock the rear wheels, apply the handbrake, then jack up the front of the vehicle and support securely on axle stands; remove the roadwheels (see *Jacking and vehicle support*).

2 Check the thickness of the friction material on each brake pad.

 For a quick check, the thickness can be measured through the aperture in the caliper body.

3 If any pad is worn to the specified minimum thickness or less, all four pads must be renewed (see Chapter 9).

4 The view through the caliper inspection hole gives a rough indication of the state of the brake pads. For a comprehensive check, the brake pads should be removed and cleaned. This will allow the operation of the caliper to be checked, and the condition of the brake disc itself to be fully examined on both sides. Chapter 9 contains a detailed description of how the brake disc should be checked for wear and/or damage.

5 On completion, refit the roadwheels and lower the vehicle to the ground.

9 Handbrake operation and adjustment check

1 With the vehicle on a slight slope, apply the handbrake lever by 4 or 5 notches, and check that it holds the vehicle stationary, then release the lever and check that there is no resistance to movement of the vehicle.

2 If necessary, adjust the handbrake lever as described in Chapter 9.

10 Headlight beam alignment check

1 Accurate adjustment of the headlight beam is only possible using optical beam-setting equipment, and this work should therefore be carried out by a Vauxhall dealer or service station with the necessary facilities.

2 Basic adjustments can be carried out in an emergency, and further details are given in Chapter 12.

11 Brake fluid pipe and hose check

1 The brake hydraulic system includes a number of metal pipes, which run from the master cylinder to the front and rear brake assemblies, and the hydraulic modulator on models with an anti-lock braking system (ABS). Flexible hoses are fitted between the pipes and the front and rear brake assemblies, to allow for steering and suspension movement.

2 When checking the system, first look for signs of leakage at the pipe or hose unions, then examine the flexible hoses for signs of cracking, chafing or deterioration of the rubber. Bend the hoses sharply between the fingers (but do not actually bend them double, or the casing may be damaged) and check that this does not reveal previously-hidden cracks, cuts or splits. Check that the pipes and hoses are securely fastened in their clips.

3 Carefully working along the length of the metal pipes, look for dents, kinks, damage of any sort, or corrosion. Light corrosion can be polished off, but if the depth of pitting is significant, the pipe must be renewed.

12 Bodywork and underbody condition check

Note: *This work should be carried out by a Vauxhall dealer in order to validate the vehicle warranty. The work includes a thorough inspection of the vehicle paintwork and underbody for damage and corrosion.*

Bodywork damage/ corrosion check

1 Once the car has been washed, and all tar spots and other surface blemishes have been cleaned off, carefully check all paintwork, looking closely for chips or scratches. Pay particular attention to vulnerable areas such as the front panels (bonnet and spoiler), and around the wheel arches. Any damage to the paintwork must be rectified as soon as possible, to comply with the terms of the manufacturer's anti-corrosion warranties; check with a Vauxhall dealer for details.

2 If a chip or light scratch is found which is recent and still free from rust, it can be touched-up using the appropriate touch-up stick which can be obtained from Vauxhall dealers. Any more serious damage, or rusted stone chips, can be repaired as described in Chapter 11, but if damage or corrosion is so severe that a panel must be renewed, seek professional advice as soon as possible.

3 Always check that the door and ventilation opening drain holes and pipes are completely clear, so that water can drain out.

Corrosion protection check

4 The wax-based underbody protective coating should be inspected annually, preferably just prior to Winter, when the underbody should be washed down as thoroughly as possible without disturbing the protective coating. Any damage to the coating should be repaired using a suitable wax-based sealer. If any of the body panels are disturbed for repair or renewal, do not forget to re-apply the coating. Wax should be injected into door cavities, sills and box sections, to maintain the level of protection provided by the vehicle manufacturer – seek the advice of a Vauxhall dealer.

3 Rattles and other noises can often be traced to the exhaust system, especially the brackets and mountings **(see illustration)**. Try to move the pipes and silencers. If the components are able to come into contact with the body or suspension parts, secure the system with new mountings. Otherwise separate the joints (if possible) and twist the pipes as necessary to provide additional clearance.

quick-release fuel lines can be disconnected from the filter with reference to Chapter 4C. A Vauxhall special tool is available to disconnect the hose connectors, but provided care is taken, the connections can be released using a pair of long-nosed pliers, or a similar tool, to depress the retaining tangs **(see illustrations)**. Vauxhall recommend that the connecting clips of the quick-release connectors are renewed whenever removed.

3 In addition to taking the precautions noted above to catch any fuel spillages, connect a tube to the drain screw on the base of the fuel filter. Place the other end of the tube in a clean jar or can.

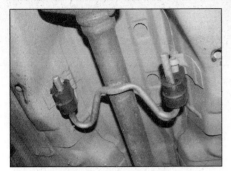

13.3 Exhaust mountings

14 Fuel filter water draining

Caution: Before starting any work on the fuel filter, wipe clean the filter assembly and the area around it; it is essential that no dirt or other foreign matter is allowed into the system. Obtain a suitable container into which the filter can be drained and place rags or similar material under the filter assembly to catch any spillages. Do not allow diesel fuel to contaminate components such as the starter motor, the coolant hoses and engine mountings, and any wiring.

1 The fuel filter is located on the left-hand side of the bulkhead at the rear of the engine compartment, next to the coolant expansion tank. First, disconnect the wiring from the fuel filter cover **(see illustration)**.

2 Using a screwdriver inserted from the right-hand side, depress the retaining clip and lift the filter from the crash box. If necessary, the

4 Loosen the drain screw approximately one complete turn and allow the filter to drain until clean fuel, free of dirt or water, emerges from the tube (approximately 100 cc is usually sufficient) **(see illustration)**.

5 Remove the drain tube, then tighten the drain screw securely.

6 Insert the filter in the crash box making sure that the retaining clip engages. Where applicable, reconnect the fuel lines.

7 Reconnect the wiring.

8 On completion, dispose of the drained fuel safely. Check all disturbed components to ensure that there are no leaks (of air or fuel) when the engine is restarted.

9 Start the engine and bleed the fuel system as described in Chapter 4C.

15 Hinge and lock lubrication

1 Work around the vehicle and lubricate the hinges of the bonnet, doors and tailgate with a light machine oil.

2 Lightly lubricate the bonnet release mechanism and exposed section of inner cable with a smear of grease.

3 Check the security and operation of all hinges, latches and locks, adjusting them where required (see Chapter 11). Check the operation of the central locking system.

4 Check the condition and operation of the tailgate struts, renewing them both if either is leaking or no longer able to support the tailgate securely when raised.

13 Exhaust system check

1 With the engine cold (at least an hour after the vehicle has been driven), check the complete exhaust system from the engine to the end of the tailpipe. The exhaust system is most easily checked with the vehicle raised on a hoist, or suitably-supported on axle stands, so that the exhaust components are readily visible and accessible (see *Jacking and vehicle support*).

2 Check the exhaust pipes and connections for evidence of leaks, severe corrosion and damage. Make sure that all brackets and mountings are in good condition, and that all relevant nuts and bolts are tight. Leakage at any of the joints or in other parts of the system will usually show up as a black sooty stain in the vicinity of the leak.

14.1 Disconnecting the wiring from the fuel filter

14.2a Depress the retaining clip . . .

14.2b . . . and lift the fuel filter from the crash box

14.2c Using the special plastic tool to disconnect the quick-release fuel lines from the fuel filter

14.4 Drain screw on the fuel filter

16 Front suspension and steering check

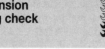

1 Apply the handbrake, then raise the front of the vehicle and securely support it on axle stands (see *Jacking and vehicle support*).
2 Inspect the balljoint dust covers and the steering gear gaiters for splits, chafing or deterioration.
3 Any wear of these components will cause loss of lubricant, and may allow water to enter the components, resulting in rapid deterioration of the balljoints or steering gear.
4 Grasp each roadwheel at the 12 o'clock and 6 o'clock positions, and try to rock it **(see illustration)**. Very slight free play may be felt, but if the movement is appreciable, further investigation is necessary to determine the source. Continue rocking the wheel while an assistant depresses the footbrake. If the movement is now eliminated or significantly reduced, it is likely that the hub bearings are at fault. If the free play is still evident with the footbrake depressed, then there is wear in the suspension joints or mountings.
5 Now grasp each wheel at the 9 o'clock and 3 o'clock positions, and try to rock it as before. Any movement felt now may again be caused by wear in the hub bearings or the steering track rod end balljoints. If the track rod end balljoint is worn, the visual movement will be obvious.
6 Using a large screwdriver or flat bar, check for wear in the suspension mounting bushes by levering between the relevant suspension component and its attachment point. Some movement is to be expected, as the mountings are made of rubber, but excessive wear should be obvious. Also check the condition of any visible rubber bushes, looking for splits, cracks or contamination of the rubber.
7 Check for any signs of fluid leakage around the suspension strut/shock absorber bodies, or from the rubber gaiters around the piston rods. Should any fluid be noticed, the suspension strut/shock absorber is defective internally, and should be renewed. **Note:** *Suspension struts/shock absorbers should always be renewed in pairs on the same axle.*
8 With the vehicle standing on its wheels, have an assistant turn the steering wheel back-and-forth about an eighth of a turn each way. There should be very little, if any, lost movement between the steering wheel and roadwheels. If this is not the case, closely observe the joints and mountings previously described, but in addition check the steering column rubber coupling for wear, and also check the steering gear itself.
9 The efficiency of each suspension strut/shock absorber may be checked by bouncing the vehicle at each corner. Generally speaking, the body will return to its normal position and stop after being depressed. If it rises and returns on a rebound, the suspension strut/shock

16.4 Check for wear in the hub bearings by grasping the wheel and trying to rock it

absorber is probably suspect. Also examine the suspension strut/shock absorber upper and lower mountings for any signs of wear.

17 Rear suspension check

1 Chock the front wheels, then jack up the rear of the vehicle and support securely on axle stands (see *Jacking and vehicle support*).
2 Inspect the rear suspension components for any signs of obvious wear or damage. Pay particular attention to the rubber mounting bushes, and renew if necessary (see Chapter 10).
3 Grasp each roadwheel at the 12 o'clock and 6 o'clock positions **(see illustration 16.4)**, and try to rock it. Any excess movement indicates incorrect adjustment or wear in the wheel bearings. Wear may also be accompanied by a rumbling sound when the wheel is spun, or a noticeable roughness if the wheel is turned slowly. The wheel bearing can be renewed as described in Chapter 10.
4 Check the rear shock absorbers in a similar manner to that described previously for the front shock absorbers.

18 Driveshaft check

1 With the vehicle raised and securely supported on stands, turn the steering onto

18.1 Check the condition of the driveshaft gaiters (1) and retaining clips (2)

full-lock, then slowly rotate each front roadwheel. Inspect the condition of the outer constant velocity (CV) joint rubber gaiters **(see illustration)**, while squeezing the gaiters to open out the folds. Check for signs of cracking, splits or deterioration of the rubber, which may allow the grease to escape and lead to water and grit entering the joint. Also check the security and condition of the retaining clips. Repeat these checks on the inner CV joints. If any damage or deterioration is found, the gaiters should be renewed as described in Chapter 8.
2 At the same time, check the general condition of the CV joints themselves by first holding the driveshaft and attempting to rotate the wheel. Repeat this check by holding the inner joint and attempting to rotate the driveshaft. Any appreciable movement indicates wear in the joints, wear in the driveshaft splines, or a loose front hub nut.

19 Road test

Instruments and electrical equipment

1 Check the operation of all instruments and electrical equipment.
2 Make sure that all instruments read correctly, and switch on all electrical equipment in turn, to check that it functions properly.

Steering and suspension

3 Check for any abnormalities in the steering, suspension, handling or road 'feel'.
4 Drive the vehicle, and check that there are no unusual vibrations or noises.
5 Check that the steering feels positive, with no excessive 'sloppiness', or roughness, and check for any suspension noises when cornering and driving over bumps.

Drivetrain

6 Check the performance of the engine, clutch (where applicable), gearbox and driveshafts.
7 Listen for any unusual noises from the engine, clutch and gearbox.
8 Make sure that the engine runs smoothly when idling, and that there is no hesitation when accelerating.
9 Check that the clutch action is smooth and progressive, that the drive is taken up smoothly, and that the pedal travel is not excessive. Also listen for any noises when the clutch pedal is depressed.
10 Check that all gears can be engaged smoothly without noise, and that the gear lever action is smooth and not abnormally vague or 'notchy'.
11 Listen for a metallic clicking sound from the front of the vehicle, as the vehicle is driven slowly in a circle with the steering on full-lock.

Carry out this check in both directions. If a clicking noise is heard, this indicates wear in a driveshaft joint, in which case renew the joint if necessary (see Chapter 8).

Braking system

12 Make sure that the vehicle does not pull to one side when braking, and that the wheels do not lock when braking hard.
13 Check that there is no vibration through the steering when braking.
14 Check that the handbrake operates correctly without excessive movement of the lever, and that it holds the vehicle stationary on a slope.

15 Test the operation of the brake servo unit as follows. With the engine off, depress the footbrake four or five times to exhaust the vacuum. Hold the brake pedal depressed, then start the engine. As the engine starts, there should be a noticeable 'give' in the brake pedal as vacuum builds-up. Allow the engine to run for at least two minutes, and then switch it off. If the brake pedal is depressed now, it should be possible to detect a hiss from the servo as the pedal is depressed. After about four or five applications, no further hissing should be heard, and the pedal should feel considerably harder.

20 Service interval indicator reset

1 With the ignition switched off, depress and hold the reset button located on the instrument panel.
2 Switch on the ignition and press and hold the reset button for two more seconds at least. The InSP indicator should flash for two seconds, after which the text '____' should appear before releasing the reset button. When the button is released, the odometer or clock will appear again.

Every 20 000 miles (30 000 km) or 2 years

21 Fuel filter renewal

1 Completely drain the fuel filter with reference to Section 14.
2 With the filter body upright in a suitable container, undo the centre screw, and remove the lid from the filter body **(see illustration)**. Note the position of the cover in relation to the body to ensure correct refitting.
3 Remove the upper seal, filter element, spring and lower seal **(see illustrations)**. Discard the seals as a new ones must be fitted.
4 Empty the fuel from the filter body and dispose of it safely.
5 Wipe clean the filter body and lid.
6 Fit the lower seal and spring inside the housing.

7 Insert the new filter element, then if possible fill the filter body with fresh fuel in order to assist the self-purging process. Ideally the fuel level should be just below the rim of the body.
8 Refit the cover to the housing together with a new upper seal, then refit the centre bolt and tighten it to the specified torque. **Do not** overtighten the cover screw.
9 Refit the fuel filter with reference to Section 14.
10 Start the engine and bleed the fuel system as described in Chapter 4C.

22 Pollen filter renewal

1 Peel the bonnet seal off the engine compartment bulkhead, and remove it from the vehicle.
2 Lift the brake fluid reservoir cover, and remove the battery wiring harness cover from the water deflector.
3 Release the battery wiring harness from the water deflector and move to one side. It may be necessary to unclip the wiring harness from the bracket on the right-hand inner panel.
4 Lift the water deflector shield, then release the two retaining clips and lift the pollen filter out from its housing, noting which way round it is fitted.
5 Wipe clean the filter housing and install the new filter, making sure it is the correct way up. Ensure that the filter is correctly seated, and secure it in position with the retaining clips.
6 Refitting is the reverse of the removal procedure.

21.2 Remove the cover . . .

21.3a . . . upper seal . . .

21.3b . . . and filter element

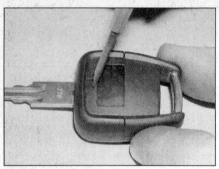

23.1a Prise the key section away . . .

23.1b . . . from the remote control . . .

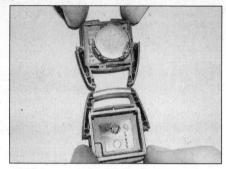

23.1c . . . and open the battery cover

Every 40 000 miles (60 000 km) or 2 years

23 Remote control battery renewal

Note: *The following procedure must be performed within 3 minutes, otherwise the remote control unit will have to be reprogrammed.*

1 Using a screwdriver, prise the key section from the remote control unit. Then prise the battery cover from the remote control unit **(see illustrations).**

2 Note how the battery is fitted, then carefully remove it from the contacts.

3 Fit the new battery and refit the cover making sure that it clips fully onto the base. Refit the key section.

24 Brake and clutch fluid renewal

⚠ **Warning: Brake hydraulic fluid can harm your eyes and damage painted surfaces, so use extreme caution when handling and pouring it. Do not use fluid that has been standing open for some time, as it absorbs moisture from the air. Excess moisture can cause a dangerous loss of braking effectiveness.**

1 The procedure is similar to that for the bleeding of the hydraulic system as described in Chapters 9 (brake) and 6 (clutch).

2 Working as described in Chapter 9, open the first bleed screw in the sequence, and pump the brake pedal gently until nearly all the old fluid has been emptied from the master cylinder reservoir. Top-up to the MAX level with new fluid, and continue pumping until only the new fluid remains in the reservoir, and new fluid can be seen emerging from the bleed screw. Tighten the screw, and top the reservoir level up to the MAX level line.

HAYNES HiNT *Old hydraulic fluid is invariably much darker in colour than new fluid, making it easy to distinguish the two.*

3 Work through all the remaining bleed screws in the sequence until new fluid can be seen at all of them. Be careful to keep the master cylinder reservoir topped-up to above the MIN level at all times, or air may enter the system and greatly increase the length of the task.

4 When the operation is complete, check that all bleed screws are securely tightened, and that their dust caps are refitted. Wash off all traces of spilt fluid, and recheck the master cylinder reservoir fluid level.

5 Check the operation of the brakes before taking the car on the road.

6 Similarly, bleed the clutch hydraulic system with reference to Chapter 6.

25 Coolant renewal

Note: *Vauxhall do not specify renewal intervals for the antifreeze mixture, as the mixture used to fill the system when the vehicle is new is designed to last the lifetime of the vehicle. However, it is strongly recommended that the coolant is renewed at the intervals specified in the 'Maintenance schedule', as a precaution against possible engine corrosion problems. This is particularly advisable if the coolant has been renewed using an antifreeze other than that specified by Vauxhall. With many antifreeze types, the corrosion inhibitors become progressively less effective with age. It is up to the individual owner whether or not to follow this advice.*

Cooling system draining

⚠ **Warning: Wait until the engine is cold before starting this procedure. Do not allow antifreeze to come in contact with your skin, or with the painted surfaces of the vehicle. Rinse off spills immediately with plenty of water. Never leave antifreeze lying around in an open container, or in a puddle on the driveway or garage floor. Children and pets are attracted by its sweet smell, but antifreeze is fatal if ingested.**

1 To drain the cooling system, first cover the expansion tank cap with a wad of rag, and slowly turn the cap anti-clockwise to relieve the pressure in the cooling system (a hissing sound will normally be heard). Wait until any pressure remaining in the system is released, then continue to turn the cap until it can be removed.

2 Where necessary, remove the splash guard from under the radiator and engine.

3 The coolant drain plug is located at the bottom of the radiator right-hand end tank. Position a container beneath the radiator then unscrew the drain plug and allow the coolant to drain.

4 As no cylinder block drain plug is fitted, it is not possible to drain all of the coolant. Due consideration must be made for this when refilling the system, in order to maintain the correct concentration of antifreeze.

5 If the coolant has been drained for a reason other than renewal, then provided it is clean and less than two years old, it can be re-used.

Cooling system flushing

6 If coolant renewal has been neglected, or if the antifreeze mixture has become diluted, then in time, the cooling system may gradually lose efficiency, as the coolant passages become restricted due to rust, scale deposits, and other sediment. The cooling system efficiency can be restored by flushing the system clean.

7 The radiator should be flushed independently of the engine, to avoid unnecessary contamination.

8 To flush the radiator, disconnect the top hose at the radiator, then insert a garden hose into the radiator top inlet. Direct a flow of clean water through the radiator, and continue flushing until clean water emerges from the radiator bottom outlet (the bottom radiator hose should have been disconnected to drain the system). If after a reasonable period the water still does not run clear, the radiator can be flushed with a good proprietary cleaning agent. It is important that the cleaning agent manufacturer's instructions are followed carefully. If the contamination is particularly bad, insert the hose in the radiator bottom

outlet, and flush the radiator in the reverse direction ('reverse-flushing').

9 To flush the engine block, the thermostat must be removed, because it will be shut, and would otherwise prevent the flow of water around the engine. The thermostat can be removed as described in Chapter 3. Take care not to introduce dirt or debris into the system if this approach is used.

10 With the radiator top and bottom hoses disconnected from the radiator, insert a hose into the top hose. Direct a clean flow of water through the engine, and continue flushing until clean water emerges from the radiator bottom hose.

11 On completion of flushing, refit the thermostat with reference to Chapter 3, and reconnect the hoses.

Cooling system filling

12 Before attempting to fill the cooling system, make sure that all hoses and clips are in good condition, and that the clips are tight. Note that an antifreeze mixture must be used all year round, to prevent corrosion of the alloy engine components.

13 Remove the expansion tank cap, and fill the system by slowly pouring the coolant into the expansion tank to prevent airlocks from forming.

14 If the coolant is being renewed, begin by pouring in a couple of litres of water, followed by the correct quantity of antifreeze, then top-up with more water.

15 Top-up the coolant level to the KALT (or COLD) mark on the expansion tank, then refit the expansion tank cap.

16 Start the engine and run it until it reaches normal operating temperature, then stop the engine and allow it to cool.

17 Check for leaks, particularly around disturbed components. Check the coolant level in the expansion tank, and top-up if necessary. Note that the system must be cold before an accurate level is indicated in the expansion tank. If the expansion tank cap is removed while the engine is still warm, cover the cap with a thick cloth, and unscrew the cap slowly to gradually relieve the system pressure (a hissing sound will normally be heard). Wait until any pressure remaining in the system is released, then

continue to turn the cap until it can be removed.

Antifreeze mixture

18 Always use an ethylene-glycol based antifreeze which is suitable for use in mixed-metal cooling systems. The quantity of antifreeze and levels of protection are indicated in the Specifications.

19 Before adding antifreeze, the cooling system should be completely drained, preferably flushed, and all hoses and clips checked for condition and security.

20 After filling with antifreeze, a label should be attached to the radiator or expansion tank, stating the type and concentration of antifreeze used, and the date installed. Any subsequent topping-up should be made with the same type and concentration of antifreeze.

21 Do not use engine antifreeze in the windscreen/tailgate washer system, as it will cause damage to the vehicle paintwork. A screenwash should be added to the washer system in the quantities recommended on the bottle.

Every 40 000 miles (60 000 km) or 4 years

26 Air cleaner filter element renewal

1 The air cleaner is located in the front right-hand corner of the engine compartment.

2 Loosen the clip and disconnect the hot film mass airflow meter from the air cleaner cover **(see illustration)**.

3 Undo the screws and lift the cover from the air cleaner **(see illustrations)**.

4 Lift out the element **(see illustration)**.

5 Wipe out the casing and the cover.

6 Fit the new filter, noting that the rubber locating flange should be uppermost, and secure the cover with the screws.

7 Reconnect the hot film mass airflow meter to the cover and tighten the clip.

26.2 Disconnect the hot film mass airflow meter . . .

26.3a . . . then undo the screws . . .

26.3b . . . lift off the cover . . .

26.4 . . . and lift out the element

27 Rear brake shoe, drum and wheel cylinder check

1 Chock the front wheels, then jack up the rear of the vehicle, and support it securely on axle stands (see *Jacking and vehicle support*).

2 For a quick check, the thickness of friction material remaining on one of the brake shoes can be observed through the hole in the brake backplate which is exposed by prising out the sealing grommet. If a rod of the same diameter as the specified minimum friction material thickness is placed against the shoe friction material, the amount of wear can be assessed. An electric torch or inspection light will probably be required. If the friction material on any shoe is worn down to the specified minimum thickness or less, all four shoes must be renewed as a set.

3 For a comprehensive check, the brake drum should be removed and cleaned. This will allow the wheel cylinders to be checked, and the condition of the brake drum itself to be fully examined (see Chapter 9).

Every 60 000 miles (100 000 km) or 6 years

**28 Timing belt and tensioner
renewal**

Renew the timing belt and tensioner with
reference to Chapter 2C.

Every 100 000 miles (150 000 km) or 10 years

**29 Valve clearance
check and adjustment**

Refer to Chapter 2C.

Chapter 2 Part A:
1.0 and 1.2 litre petrol engine in-car repair procedures

Contents

Degrees of difficulty

| Easy, suitable for novice with little experience | | Fairly easy, suitable for beginner with some experience | | Fairly difficult, suitable for competent DIY mechanic | | Difficult, suitable for experienced DIY mechanic | | Very difficult, suitable for expert DIY or professional | |

Specifications

General

Engine type:
1.0 litre engine	Three-cylinder, in-line, water-cooled. Double overhead camshafts, chain-driven, acting on rocker arms and hydraulic valve lifters
1.2 litre engine	Four-cylinder, in-line, water-cooled. Double overhead camshafts, chain-driven, acting on rocker arms and hydraulic valve lifters

Manufacturer's engine codes*:
1.0 litre engine	Z10XE and Z10XE-ECO
1.2 litre engine	Z12XE
Bore	72.50 mm

Stroke:
1.0 litre engine	78.60 mm
1.2 litre engine	72.60 mm

Capacity:
1.0 litre engine	973 cc
1.2 litre engine	1199 cc

Firing order:
1.0 litre engine	1-2-3 (No 1 cylinder at timing chain end of engine)
1.2 litre engine	1-3-4-2 (No 1 cylinder at timing chain end of engine)
Direction of crankshaft rotation	Clockwise (viewed from timing chain end of engine)
Compression ratio	10.1:1

*For details of engine code location, see 'Vehicle identification' in the Reference Chapter.

Lubrication system

Minimum oil pressure at 80°C	1.5 bars at idle speed
Oil pump type	Gear-type, driven directly from crankshaft
Gear-to-housing clearance (endfloat)	0.035 to 0.070 mm

Flywheel

Maximum permissible lateral run-out of starter ring gear	0.500 mm
Refinishing limit (maximum depth of material which may be removed from clutch friction surface)	0.300 mm

Torque wrench settings

	Nm	lbf ft
Air conditioning compressor to cylinder block	20	15
Auxiliary drivebelt tensioner to cylinder block:		
M8 bolt	20	15
M10 bolt	55	41
Big-end bearing cap bolts*:		
M6 bolts:		
Stage 1	10	7
Stage 2	Angle-tighten a further 60°	
Stage 3	Angle-tighten a further 15°	
M6.5 bolts (marked RIBE from engine number 19P13554):		
Stage 1	13	10
Stage 2	Angle-tighten a further 60°	
Stage 3	Angle-tighten a further 15°	
Camshaft bearing cap bolts	8	6
Camshaft sprocket bolt*:		
Stage 1	50	37
Stage 2	Angle-tighten a further 60°	
Catalytic converter support bracket bolts	20	15
Catalytic converter-to-exhaust manifold nuts	35	26
Coolant pump pulley bolts	20	15
Crankshaft pulley hub-to-crankshaft bolt*:		
Stage 1	150	111
Stage 2	Angle-tighten a further 45°	
Cylinder block baseplate to cylinder block*:		
M6 bolts:		
Stage 1	10	7
Stage 2	Angle-tighten a further 60°	
M8 bolts:		
Stage 1	25	18
Stage 2	Angle-tighten a further 60°	
Cylinder block closure bolt (for TDC setting tool)	60	44
Cylinder head bolts*:		
Stage 1	25	18
Stage 2	Angle-tighten a further 60°	
Stage 3	Angle-tighten a further 60°	
Stage 4	Angle-tighten a further 60°	
Engine mountings:		
Left-hand:		
Mounting bracket-to-engine bolts	25	18
Mounting-to-body bolts	80	59
Rear mounting/torque reaction link	80	59
Right-hand:		
Mounting-to-engine bracket bolts:		
Stage 1	60	44
Stage 2	Angle-tighten a further 30°	
Stage 3	Angle-tighten a further 15°	
Mounting-to-body bolts	40	30
Engine-to-transmission bolts	60	44
Exhaust manifold securing nuts*	22	16
Flywheel/driveplate bolts*:		
Stage 1	35	26
Stage 2	Angle-tighten a further 30°	
Front suspension subframe*:		
Stage 1	90	66
Stage 2	Angle-tighten a further 45°	
Stage 3	Angle-tighten a further 15°	
Fuel feed and return hose unions	15	11
Inlet manifold support bracket to cylinder block	20	15
Oil filter housing cap to filter housing	15	11
Oil filter housing to cylinder block	20	15
Sump to transmission:		
M10 bolts	40	30
M8 bolts	20	15
Timing chain tension rail pivot bolt	20	15
Timing chain tensioner closure bolt (for locking pin access)	50	37

Torque wrench settings (continued)

	Nm	lbf ft
Timing cover bolts:		
M10	35	26
M6	8	6
Timing cover oil fill channel closure plug	50	37
Torque converter to driveplate*	50	37

*Use new fasteners.

---

1 General information

How to use this Chapter

This Part of Chapter 2 describes the repair procedures which can reasonably be carried out on the engine while it remains in the vehicle. If the engine has been removed from the vehicle and is being dismantled as described in Chapter 2D, any preliminary dismantling procedures can be ignored.

Note that, while it may be possible physically to overhaul items such as the piston/connecting rod assemblies while the engine is in the vehicle, such tasks are not usually carried out as separate operations, and usually require the execution of several additional procedures (not to mention the cleaning of components and of oil ways); for this reason, all such tasks are classed as major overhaul procedures, and are described in Chapter 2D.

Chapter 2D describes the removal of the engine/transmission unit from the vehicle, and the full overhaul procedures which can then be carried out.

Engine description

The engine is of three-cylinder (1.0 litre) or four-cylinder (1.2 litre) in-line type, with double overhead camshafts (DOHC). The engine is mounted transversely at the front of the vehicle. Apart from the obvious difference in the number of cylinders, the two engines are virtually identical in all other respects.

The crankshaft runs in four (1.0 litre) or five (1.2 litre) shell-type main bearings with crankshaft endfloat being controlled by thrust-washers which are an integral part of No 3 main bearing shells (1.0 litre engines), or No 4 main bearing shells (1.2 litre engines).

The connecting rods are attached to the crankshaft by horizontally-split shell-type big-end bearings. The pistons are attached to the connecting rods by gudgeon pins, which are an interference fit in the connecting rod small-end bores. The aluminium-alloy pistons are fitted with three piston rings – two compression rings and an oil control ring.

The camshafts are driven from the crankshaft by a hydraulically tensioned timing chain. Each cylinder has four valves (two inlet and two exhaust), operated via rocker arms which are supported at their pivot ends by hydraulic self-adjusting valve lifters (tappets). One camshaft operates the inlet valves, and the other operates the exhaust valves.

The inlet and exhaust valves are each closed by a single valve spring, and operate in guides pressed into the cylinder head.

A rotor-type oil pump is located in the timing cover attached to the cylinder block, and is driven directly from the crankshaft.

The coolant pump is located externally on the timing cover, and is driven by the auxiliary drivebelt.

Operations with engine in place

The following operations can be carried out without having to remove the engine from the vehicle.

a) Removal and refitting of the cylinder head.
b) Removal and refitting of the timing cover.
c) Removal and refitting of the timing chain, tensioner and sprockets.
d) Removal and refitting of the camshafts.
e) Removal and refitting of the sump.
f) Removal and refitting of the big-end bearings, connecting rods, and pistons*.
g) Removal and refitting of the oil pump.
h) Renewal of the crankshaft oil seals.
i) Renewal of the engine mountings.
j) Removal and refitting of the flywheel/driveplate.

*Although the operation marked with an asterisk can be carried out with the engine in the vehicle (after removal of the sump), it is preferable for the engine to be removed, in the interests of cleanliness and improved access. For this reason, the procedure is described in Chapter 2D.

2 Compression test – description and interpretation

Note: *A suitable compression gauge will be required to carry out this test.*

1 When engine performance is down, or if misfiring occurs which cannot be attributed to the ignition or fuel systems, a compression test can provide diagnostic clues as to the engine's condition. If the test is performed regularly, it can give warning of trouble before any other symptoms become apparent.

2 The engine must be fully warmed-up to normal operating temperature, and the battery must be fully charged. The aid of an assistant will also be required.

3 Remove the DIS module from the top of the camshaft cover as described in Chapter 5B. Ensure that the ignition is switched off then disconnect the two wiring plugs from the engine management electronic control unit located on the left-hand side of the inlet manifold.

4 Remove all of the spark plugs from the engine (see Chapter 1A).

5 Fit a compression tester to the No 1 spark plug hole (No 1 cylinder is nearest the timing chain end of the engine) – the type of tester which screws into the plug thread is to be preferred.

6 Have an assistant hold the accelerator pedal fully depressed, at the same time cranking the engine over for approximately four seconds on the starter motor. After one or two revolutions, the compression pressure reading on the gauge should build-up to a maximum figure and then stabilise. Record the highest reading obtained.

7 Repeat the test on the remaining cylinders, recording the pressure in each.

8 All cylinders should produce very similar pressures. Note that the compression should build-up quickly in a healthy engine; low compression on the first stroke, followed by gradually-increasing pressure on successive strokes, indicates worn piston rings. A low compression reading on the first stroke, which does not build-up during successive strokes, indicates leaking valves or a blown head gasket (a cracked head could also be the cause). Deposits on the undersides of the valve heads can also cause low compression.

9 If the pressure in any cylinder is significantly lower than that in the remaining cylinders, carry out the following test to isolate the cause. Introduce a teaspoonful of clean engine oil into the relevant cylinder through its spark plug hole, and repeat the test.

10 If the addition of oil temporarily improves the compression pressure, this indicates that bore or piston wear is responsible for the pressure loss. No improvement suggests that leaking or burnt valves, or a blown head gasket may be to blame.

11 A low reading from two adjacent cylinders is almost certainly due to the head gasket having blown between them; the presence of coolant in the engine oil will confirm this.

12 If one cylinder is about 20 percent lower than the others, and the engine has a slightly rough idle, a worn camshaft lobe could be the cause.

13 If the compression reading is unusually high, the combustion chambers are probably coated with carbon deposits. If this is the case, the cylinder head should be removed and decarbonised (see Chapter 2D).

14 On completion of the test, refit the spark plugs, reconnect the electronic control unit wiring plugs (ensure that the ignition is switched off), and refit the DIS module.

3.2a Disconnect the wiring connectors at the air mass meter . . .

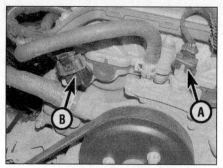

3.2b . . . coolant temperature sensor (A) and camshaft position sensor (B) . . .

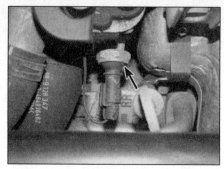

3.2c . . . and at the oil pressure switch

3 Camshaft cover –
removal and refitting

Note: *A new camshaft cover rubber seal will be required for refitting, and a suitable silicone sealant will be required to seal the timing cover-to-cylinder head upper joint.*

Removal

1 Disconnect the battery negative terminal (refer to *Disconnecting the battery* in the Reference Chapter).
2 Disconnect the wiring connectors at the air mass meter, coolant temperature sensor, camshaft position sensor and oil pressure switch **(see illustrations)**.
3 Lift the wiring harness trough from the camshaft cover and move it to one side **(see illustration)**.

4 Disconnect the two breather hoses at the rear of the camshaft cover **(see illustration)**.
5 Remove the DIS module from the centre of the camshaft cover as described in Chapter 5B.
6 Progressively slacken the camshaft cover retaining bolts until they are all fully unscrewed. Note that the bolts are captive and will remain in place in the cover as it is removed.
7 Lift the camshaft cover up and off the cylinder head **(see illustration)**.

Refitting

8 Remove the old seal from the camshaft cover, then examine the inside of the cover for a build-up of oil sludge or any other contamination, and if necessary clean the cover with paraffin, or a water-soluble solvent. Dry the cover thoroughly before refitting.
9 Check the condition of the rubber seals on the camshaft cover retaining bolts. If the seals

are in any way damaged or deformed, carefully tap the bolts out of the camshaft cover using a soft-faced mallet and fit new seals to the bolts **(see illustrations)**.
10 Fit a new rubber seal to the cover ensuring that it is correctly located in the camshaft cover groove **(see illustration)**.
11 Inspect the joint between the timing cover and cylinder head, and cut off any projecting timing cover gasket using a sharp knife **(see illustration)**.
12 Thoroughly clean the mating faces of the camshaft cover and cylinder head.
13 Apply a 2 mm diameter bead of silicone sealant to the joint between the timing cover and cylinder head on each side **(see illustration)**.
14 Locate the camshaft cover on the cylinder head and screw in the retaining bolts. Progressively and evenly tighten the retaining bolts securely.

3.3 Lift the wiring harness trough from the camshaft cover and move it to one side

3.4 Breather hoses on the rear of the camshaft cover

3.7 Lift the camshaft cover up and off the cylinder head

3.9a If necessary, tap the bolts out of the camshaft cover . . .

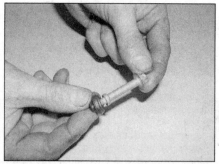

3.9b . . . and fit new seals to the bolts

3.10 Fit a new rubber seal to the camshaft cover ensuring that it is correctly located in the cover groove

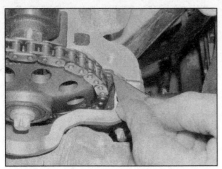

3.11 Cut off any projecting timing cover gasket using a sharp knife

15 Refit the DIS module from the centre of the camshaft cover as described in Chapter 5B.

16 Reconnect the two breather hoses to the right-hand rear of the camshaft cover.

17 Locate the wiring harness trough in the camshaft cover slots then reconnect the air mass meter, coolant temperature sensor, camshaft position sensor and oil pressure switch wiring connectors.

18 Reconnect the battery negative terminal on completion.

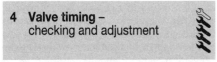

4 Valve timing – checking and adjustment

Note: *Certain special tools will be required for this operation. Read through the entire procedure to familiarise yourself with the work involved, then either obtain the manufacturer's*

4.6 Turn the crankshaft until the TDC notch (A) on the pulley is located just before the cast lug (B) on the timing cover

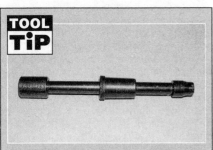

Tool Tip 1: A commercially-available clutch aligning tool can be used as a TDC positioning tool.

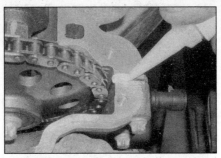

3.13 Apply a bead of silicone sealant to the joint between the timing cover and cylinder head on each side

special tools, or use the alternatives described. New gaskets and sealing rings will also be required for all disturbed components.

Checking

1 Disconnect the battery negative terminal (refer to *Disconnecting the battery* in the Reference Chapter).

2 Remove the air cleaner assembly as described in Chapter 4A.

3 Remove the camshaft cover as described in Section 3.

4 Firmly apply the handbrake, then jack up the front of the car and support it securely on axle stands (see *Jacking and vehicle support*). Remove the right-hand front roadwheel and the wheel arch liner for access to the crankshaft pulley.

5 On models with air conditioning, release the tension on the auxiliary drivebelt and lock the tensioner in the released position as described

4.7 With No 1 piston on the compression stroke, the camshaft lobes for No 1 cylinder should be pointing outwards

4.10a The end of the tool must engage with the slot in the crankshaft web (arrowed) – shown with engine partially dismantled

in the auxiliary drivebelt renewal procedure in Chapter 1A. Note that it is not necessary to completely remove the drivebelt, as this would entail removal of the right-hand engine mounting bracket. With the drivebelt tension released, slip the belt off the compressor pulley. Unbolt the compressor from the cylinder block, release the refrigerant lines from their brackets and support the compressor clear of the engine. **Do not** disconnect the refrigerant lines from the compressor.

6 Using a socket or spanner on the crankshaft pulley hub bolt, turn the crankshaft in the normal direction of rotation (clockwise as viewed from the right-hand side of the car) until the TDC notch on the crankshaft pulley is located just before the cast lug on the timing cover **(see illustration)**.

7 Check that No 1 piston is on the compression stroke by observing No 1 cylinder camshaft lobes. All four lobes should be pointing outwards (away from the engine) **(see illustration)**. If they are not, No 1 piston is on the exhaust stroke and the crankshaft should be turned through a further full turn, stopping once again just before the TDC notch aligns with the lug on the timing cover.

8 Undo the closure bolt from the crankshaft TDC position setting hole. The plug is located on the front facing side of the cylinder block baseplate, adjacent to the timing cover joint. Note that a new closure bolt sealing ring will be required for refitting.

9 If the Vauxhall TDC positioning pin KM-952 is available, insert the tool into the TDC position setting hole. Slowly turn the crankshaft in the normal direction of rotation until the tool engages with the TDC slot in the crankshaft, and moves fully in, up to its stop.

10 In the absence of the Vauxhall tool, a typical commercially-available clutch aligning tool of the type having interchangeable cones and collars of various diameters can be used as an alternative **(see Tool Tip 1)**. Assemble the tool so that the end collar (the part that normally engages with the crankshaft spigot bearing) is of 12 mm diameter, and the sliding cone (the part that normally engages with the clutch disc hub) is of 17.5 mm diameter. Insert the tool into the TDC position setting hole, and slowly turn the crankshaft in the normal direction of rotation until the end collar engages with the TDC slot in

4.10b Clutch aligning tool in position in the TDC setting hole

4.12 Camshaft setting tool (arrowed) made from steel strip and inserted into the camshaft slots

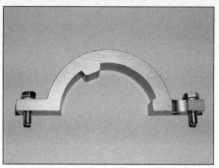

4.15a Vauxhall/Opel camshaft sensor phase disc positioning tool (KM-954)

4.15b Home-made cardboard alternative camshaft sensor phase disc positioning tool in place

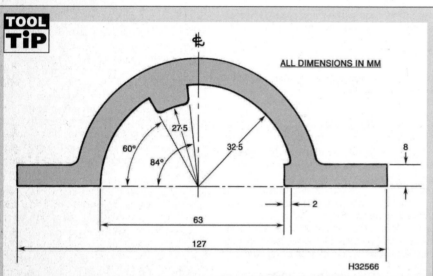

TOOL TiP

ALL DIMENSIONS IN MM

27·5
60°
84°
32·5
8
2
63
127

H32566

Tool Tip 2: A home-made camshaft sensor phase disc positioning tool can be fabricated using the dimensions shown.

the crankshaft web. Push the cone fully into the setting hole as far as it will go, and the crankshaft should now be locked in the TDC position **(see illustrations)**.

11 If the Vauxhall camshaft setting tool KM-953 is available, insert the tool into the slots in the left-hand end of the camshafts. Ensure that the tool is inserted fully, up to its stop, to lock both camshafts.

12 In the absence of the Vauxhall tool, a camshaft setting tool can be made out of 5 mm

thick flat steel strip, approximately 20 mm wide and long enough to engage both camshaft slots. Insert the setting tool into the camshaft slots to lock the camshafts in the TDC position **(see illustration)**. Note that a ready-made equivalent is available from tool stockists.

13 If it is not possible to insert the camshaft setting tool, then the valve timing must be adjusted as described in paragraphs 17 to 35 below.

14 If all is satisfactory so far, the position of the camshaft position sensor phase disc on the inlet camshaft should be checked. This check entails the use of Vauxhall camshaft sensor phase disc positioning tool KM-954. If this tool is not available, an alternative can be fabricated as follows.

15 The Vauxhall positioning tool (KM-954) is a relatively substantial die-casting, the purpose of which is to check the position of the phase disc, and also to hold the phase disc in the correct position on the camshaft sprocket if adjustment is required. During the workshop procedures undertaken for the preparation of this manual, we discovered that a tool made from stiff cardboard (such that used for the cover of a Haynes manual) worked just as well as the factory tool **(see illustrations and Tool Tip 2)**.

16 Using the Vauxhall positioning tool, or the home-made alternative, check to see if the tool will engage with the phase disc on the camshaft, and also seat squarely on the timing cover surface. If it does, proceed to paragraph 31. If adjustment is required, proceed as follows.

Adjustment

Note: *New camshaft sprocket retaining bolts will be required for this operation.*

17 Remove the camshaft sensor phase disc positioning tool, and the tool used to lock the camshafts in position.

18 Unscrew the timing chain tensioner closure plug from the timing cover, located just below the heater hose union on the coolant pump. Note that a new closure bolt sealing ring will be required for refitting **(see illustration)**.

19 Using a suitable spanner engaged with the flats provided on the inlet camshaft, apply tension in a clockwise direction (as viewed from the right-hand side of the car) to the camshaft, to take up any slack in the timing chain **(see illustration)**. This will push the timing chain tensioner plunger fully into its bore.

20 Hold the camshaft in this position and retain the tensioner plunger in the released position by inserting a 2 mm diameter roll pin, approximately 30 mm long, through the

4.18 Unscrew the timing chain tensioner closure plug from the timing cover

4.19 Use a spanner on the flats of the inlet camshaft to take up any slack in the timing chain

closure plug aperture and into the hole on the tensioner body **(see illustrations)**.

21 Slacken and remove the sprocket retaining bolts for both camshafts, using a spanner to counterhold each camshaft as the bolts are slackened.

22 Fit the new bolts to both camshaft sprockets and tighten them finger tight only at this stage. Check that the phase disc on the inlet camshaft can still be turned.

23 Again, using the spanner on the camshaft flats, turn the camshafts slightly, as necessary, until the camshaft setting tool can be reinserted into the slots in the ends of the camshafts.

24 Remove the roll pin used to hold the timing chain tensioner plunger in the retracted position.

25 Turn the camshaft sensor phase disc slightly, as necessary, and locate the Vauxhall positioning tool (KM-954), or the home-made alternative over the disc and in contact with the timing cover. If the Vauxhall tool is being used, bolt it into position on the timing cover.

26 Tighten the camshaft sprocket retaining bolts to 10 Nm (7 lbf ft). The inlet camshaft sprocket bolts should be tightened first. Note that this is just an initial torque loading to hold the sprockets and the phase disc in position when the setting tools are removed.

27 Remove the crankshaft, camshaft and phase disc setting tools, then tighten the camshaft sprocket retaining bolts to the specified torque in the stages given in the Specifications. The inlet camshaft sprocket bolts should be tightened first. Counterhold the camshafts using the spanner on the camshaft flats as the sprocket bolts are tightened.

28 Turn the crankshaft through two complete revolutions, stopping just before the TDC notch on the crankshaft pulley aligns with the cast lug on the timing cover **(see illustration 4.6)**. Check that all four lobes for No 1 cylinder are pointing outwards (away from the engine).

29 Slowly turn the crankshaft further until the TDC position setting tool can once again be inserted to lock the crankshaft.

30 It should now be possible to re-insert the camshaft setting tool into the slots in the camshafts, and to fit the camshaft sensor phase disc setting tool over the disc. If this is not possible repeat the entire adjustment procedure.

31 If all is satisfactory, remove all the setting/aligning tools and refit the timing chain tensioner and cylinder block closure bolts using new sealing rings. Tighten both closure bolts to the specified torque.

32 On models with air conditioning, refit the compressor to the cylinder block and tighten the mounting bolts to the specified torque. Refit the refrigerant lines to their relevant clips or brackets, then refit the auxiliary drivebelt as described in Chapter 1A.

33 Refit the wheel arch liner and the roadwheel. Tighten the roadwheel bolts to the

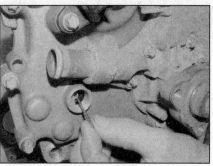

4.20a Insert a 2 mm diameter roll pin, approximately 30 mm long, through the closure plug aperture . . .

specified torque, then lower the vehicle to the ground.

34 Refit the camshaft cover as described in Section 3.

35 Refit the air cleaner assembly as described in Chapter 4A, then reconnect the battery negative terminal.

5 Crankshaft pulley – removal and refitting

Removal

1 Firmly apply the handbrake, then jack up the front of the car and support it securely on axle stands (see *Jacking and vehicle support*). Remove the right-hand roadwheel and the wheel arch liner. Where necessary remove the engine undertray.

2 Release the tension on the auxiliary drivebelt and lock the tensioner in the released position as described in the auxiliary drivebelt renewal procedure in Chapter 1A. Note that it is not necessary to completely remove the drivebelt, as this would entail removal of the right-hand engine mounting bracket.

3 With the drivebelt tension released, slip the belt off the crankshaft pulley.

4 Using quick-drying paint, or similar, make an alignment mark between the crankshaft pulley and the pulley hub. It should only be possible to refit the pulley in one position, but it is advisable to make an alignment mark anyway.

5 Unscrew the six crankshaft pulley retaining bolts and remove the pulley from the hub **(see illustration)**. If necessary, prevent the crankshaft from turning as the pulley bolts are slackened using a spanner or socket on the pulley hub bolt.

Refitting

6 Align the marks made on removal and locate the pulley on the hub.

7 Refit the six retaining bolts and progressively tighten them securely.

8 Refit the auxiliary drivebelt over the crankshaft pulley and ensure that it is correctly seated in the other pulleys.

4.20b . . . and into the hole on the tensioner body (arrowed)

9 Unlock the auxiliary drivebelt tensioner as described in Chapter 1A to retension the drivebelt.

10 Refit the wheel arch liner and the roadwheel and tighten the wheel bolts to the specified torque.

11 Lower the car to the ground.

6 Timing cover and chain – removal and refitting

Note: *The special tools described in Section 4 will also be required for this operation. Read through the entire procedure and also the procedures contained in Section 4 to familiarise yourself with the work involved, then either obtain the manufacturer's special tools, or use the alternatives described. New gaskets and sealing rings will also be required for all disturbed components, together with new camshaft sprocket retaining bolts. A tube of silicone sealant will be needed to seal the joint between the cylinder block and cylinder head.*

Removal

1 Disconnect the battery negative terminal (refer to *Disconnecting the battery* in the Reference Chapter).

2 Apply the handbrake, then jack up the front of the vehicle and support it on axle stands (see *Jacking and vehicle support*). Remove the right-hand roadwheel. On ECO models, remove the engine undertray sections.

5.5 Undo the six bolts and remove the crankshaft pulley from the pulley hub

6.9 Radiator lower hose on the water pump

3 Drain the cooling system as described in Chapter 1A. Tighten the drain plug after draining the system.

4 Remove the air cleaner assembly as described in Chapter 4A.

5 At the right-hand end of the engine, loosen the clip and disconnect the throttle body preheater hose from the thermostat housing.

6 Loosen the clip and disconnect the heater feed hose from the water pump.

7 Disconnect the wiring from the oil pressure switch, coolant temperature sensor and camshaft position sensor, then unclip the wiring conduit and move it to one side.

8 Loosen the clips and disconnect the radiator upper hose from the radiator and thermostat housing.

9 Loosen the clip and disconnect the radiator lower hose from the water pump **(see illustration)**.

10 Remove the ignition module cover by moving it to the right, then disconnect the wiring from the left-hand end of the ignition module. Unscrew the two mounting bolts and remove the module, taking care not to distort it. Vauxhall technicians use two special holders to remove the module, although two suitable threaded rods screwed into the holes can be used instead.

11 Disconnect the crankcase ventilation hose from the camshaft cover.

12 Progressively slacken the camshaft cover retaining bolts until they are all fully unscrewed. Note that the bolts are captive and will remain in place in the cover as it is removed. Lift the camshaft cover up and off the cylinder head.

13 Remove the auxiliary drivebelt cover from under the right-hand wheel arch.

14 Position a container beneath the engine sump, then unscrew the drain plug and drain the engine oil. Clean, refit and tighten the drain plug on completion.

15 Refer to Chapter 4A, Section 10, and disconnect the wiring from the oxygen sensor on the catalytic converter, then unbolt the exhaust front pipe from the exhaust manifold, taking care to support the flexible section. **Note:** *Angular movement in excess of 10° can cause permanent damage to the flexible section.*

16 Release the mounting rubbers and support the front of the exhaust pipe to one side.

6.17 The coolant pump pulley retaining bolts

17 Slacken, but do not remove, the three coolant pump pulley retaining bolts **(see illustration)**.

18 On models without air conditioning, turn the auxiliary drivebelt tensioner pulley bolt clockwise then insert a suitable pin through the spring centre shaft to lock the spring in its compressed state. Note the routing of the drivebelt, then remove it from the pulleys – mark the drivebelt for fitted direction. **Note:** *The drivebelt cannot be removed completely until the right-hand engine mounting has been removed.* Unscrew the auxiliary drivebelt tensioner lower mounting bolt and the tensioner roller upper pivot bolt. Remove the tensioner from the timing cover.

19 On models with air conditioning, turn the auxiliary drivebelt tensioner pulley bolt clockwise to tension the spring, then insert a suitable pin through the hole in the tensioner body and into the hole in the timing cover to lock the spring. Note the routing of the drivebelt, then remove it from the pulleys – mark the drivebelt for fitted direction. **Note:** *The drivebelt cannot be removed completely until the right-hand engine mounting has been removed.* Turn the tensioner pulley bolt clockwise again and remove the locking pin, then gradually release the tensioner until it is fully released. Unbolt the tensioner from the timing cover. Store the tensioner upright in its normally fitted position after removal. **Note:** *If the tensioner is not stored upright, it must be bled before refitting. To do this, mount it in a vice and slowly operate it through 5 complete strokes.*

20 Remove the alternator as described in Chapter 5A.

6.31 Slacken the crankshaft pulley hub retaining bolt (arrowed)

21 Remove the sump as described in Section 11.

22 The engine must now be supported while the right-hand engine mounting is removed. To do this, use a hoist attached to the top of the engine, or make up a wooden frame to locate on the crankcase and use a trolley jack.

23 Remove the right-hand engine mounting bracket with reference to Section 15, then remove the auxiliary drivebelt.

24 Fully unscrew the bolts and remove the coolant pump pulley from its drive flange.

25 On models with air conditioning, unbolt the compressor from the cylinder block, release the refrigerant lines from their brackets and support the compressor clear of the engine. **Do not** disconnect the refrigerant lines from the compressor.

26 Undo the three bolts securing the thermostat housing cover to the coolant pump. Remove the sealing ring from the housing cover noting that a new one will be required for refitting.

27 Using a socket or spanner on the crankshaft pulley hub bolt, turn the crankshaft in the normal direction of rotation (clockwise as viewed from the right-hand side of the car) until the TDC notch on the crankshaft pulley is located just before the cast lug on the timing cover **(see illustration 4.6)**.

28 Check that No 1 piston is on the compression stroke by observing No 1 cylinder camshaft lobes. All four lobes should be pointing outwards (away from the engine). If they are not, No 1 piston is on the exhaust stroke and the crankshaft should be turned through a further full turn, stopping once again just before the TDC notch aligns with the lug on the timing cover.

29 Using quick-drying paint, or similar, make an alignment mark between the crankshaft pulley and the pulley hub. It should only be possible to refit the pulley in one position, but it is advisable to make an alignment mark anyway.

30 Unscrew the six crankshaft pulley retaining bolts and remove the pulley from the hub. If necessary, prevent the crankshaft from turning as the pulley bolts are slackened, using a spanner or socket on the pulley hub bolt.

31 Using a suitable socket, initially slacken (but do not remove) the crankshaft pulley hub retaining bolt **(see illustration)**. The crankshaft can be prevented from turning as the bolt is slackened, using Vauxhall special tool KM-956 or a similar tool which will engage with the flats on each side of the pulley hub. Alternatively, remove the starter motor, and lock the flywheel ring gear teeth using a suitable hooked tool bolted to the bellhousing.

32 Undo the closure bolt from the crankshaft TDC position setting hole. The plug is located on the front facing side of the cylinder block baseplate, adjacent to the timing cover joint. Note that a new closure bolt sealing ring will be required for refitting.

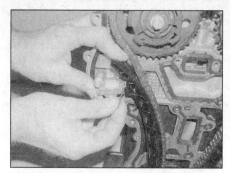

6.42 Push back the timing chain tensioner plunger and secure it in the released position with a 2 mm diameter roll pin

6.43 Undo the two bolts (arrowed) and remove the timing chain sliding rail from the cylinder head

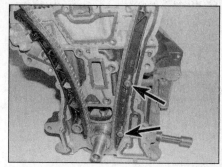

6.44 Undo the two bolts (arrowed) and remove the timing chain guide rail from the cylinder block

33 Temporarily place the crankshaft pulley back on the hub and check that the TDC notch is still positioned just before the lug on the timing cover.

34 Slowly turn the crankshaft in the normal direction of rotation until the TDC positioning pin (or suitable alternative) described in Section 4, engages with the TDC slot in the crankshaft.

35 Remove the crankshaft pulley, if still in place, and check that the punch mark on the pulley hub is in the 11 o'clock position.

36 Insert the camshaft setting tool described in Section 4 into the slots in the ends of the camshafts.

37 Unscrew the coolant pump retaining bolts, noting the locations of the three short bolts. The short bolts secure the pump to the timing cover, and the long bolts secure the pump and the timing cover to the cylinder block and cylinder head.

38 Withdraw the coolant pump from the timing cover, noting that it may be necessary to tap the pump lightly with a soft-faced mallet to free it from the locating dowels.

39 Recover the pump sealing ring noting that a new one must be used for refitting.

40 Unscrew the previously slackened crankshaft pulley hub retaining bolt and remove the hub from the crankshaft. Note that a new bolt will be required for refitting.

41 Undo the timing cover retaining bolts and remove the timing cover from the engine. The cover will be initially tight as it is located on dowels and secured by sealant. If necessary, gently tap it off using a soft-faced mallet.

42 Fully push back the timing chain tensioner plunger and secure it in the released position by inserting a 2 mm diameter roll pin, approximately 30 mm long, in the hole on the tensioner body **(see illustration)**.

43 Undo the two bolts and remove the timing chain sliding rail from the top of the cylinder head **(see illustration)**.

44 Undo the two bolts and remove the timing chain (front) guide rail from the cylinder block **(see illustration)**.

45 Undo the lower pivot bolt and remove the timing chain (rear) tension rail from the cylinder block **(see illustration)**.

46 Lift the timing chain off the sprockets and

remove the chain, then remove the drive sprocket from the crankshaft **(see illustrations)**.

47 Remove the composite gasket from the cylinder block baseplate, cylinder block, and cylinder head, using a plastic spatula if necessary to release the sealant **(see illustration)**. Note that if the cylinder head has ever been previously removed, the gasket will be a two-piece type, with a split at the cylinder head-to cylinder block joint. A new gasket will be required for refitting.

48 Thoroughly clean the timing cover and remove all traces of gasket and sealant from all the mating surfaces. Similarly clean the cylinder block baseplate, cylinder block and cylinder head mating surfaces. Ensure that all traces of old sealant are removed, particularly from the area of the cylinder head-to-cylinder block joint.

49 Inspect the timing chain, sprockets,

6.45 Undo the lower pivot bolt and remove the timing chain tension rail from the cylinder block

6.46b . . . then remove the drive sprocket from the crankshaft

sliding rail, guide rail and tension rail for any sign of wear or deformation, and renew any suspect components as necessary. Renew the crankshaft timing chain end oil seal in the timing cover as a matter of course using the procedures described in Section 13.

50 It is advisable to check the condition of the timing chain tensioner at this stage, as described in Section 7.

51 Obtain all new gaskets and components as necessary ready for refitting.

Refitting

52 Commence refitting by inserting a new coolant pump seal into the groove in the timing cover.

53 Check that the locating dowels are in place, and that the mating surfaces are clean and dry, then locate the pump in position on the timing cover.

6.46a Lift the timing chain off the sprockets and remove the chain . . .

6.47 Remove the timing cover composite gasket from the cylinder block baseplate, cylinder block, and cylinder head

6.55 Apply a 2 mm diameter bead of silicone sealant to the joint between the cylinder block and cylinder head on each side

6.57 Slide the timing chain drive sprocket onto the crankshaft with the markings facing outwards

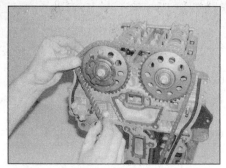

6.58 Keeping the timing chain tight on the exhaust camshaft side, locate the chain over the sprockets

54 Refit the three coolant pump short retaining bolts, ensuring that the bolts are fitted to their correct locations (refer to Chapter 3 if necessary). Tighten the bolts to the specified torque.

55 Apply a 2 mm diameter bead of silicone sealant to the joint between the cylinder block and cylinder head on each side **(see illustration)**. The bead should be long enough to fill the joint in the area covered by the timing cover gasket. Similarly, apply silicone sealant to the joint between the cylinder block and baseplate.

56 Ensure that the locating dowels are in position, then locate the new timing cover gasket in place on the cylinder head, cylinder block and baseplate.

57 Slide the timing chain drive sprocket onto the crankshaft with the markings facing outwards **(see illustration)**.

58 Engage the timing chain with the drive sprocket then, keeping it tight on the exhaust camshaft side, feed the chain up and over the camshaft sprockets **(see illustration)**.

59 Place the timing chain tension rail in position, refit the lower pivot bolt and tighten the bolt to the specified torque.

60 Attach the timing chain guide rail to the cylinder block and secure with the two bolts tightened securely.

61 Refit the timing chain sliding rail to the cylinder head and secure with the two bolts tightened securely.

62 Remove the roll pin used to secure the timing chain tensioner plunger in the released position.

63 Locate the timing cover in position and refit all the retaining bolts, finger tight only at this stage. Now tighten all the bolts to the specified torque, starting with the bolts

around the coolant pump first, followed by the bolts around the periphery of the cover.

64 Refit the sump as described in Section 11.

65 Remove the position setting tools used to lock the crankshaft and camshafts in the TDC position.

66 Lubricate the crankshaft pulley hub with engine oil, then refit the hub to the crankshaft, ensuring that the punch mark on the hub is in the 11 o'clock position **(see illustration)**.

67 Screw in the new pulley hub retaining bolt and tighten it to the specified torque, in the stages given in the Specifications **(see illustrations)**. Prevent crankshaft rotation as the bolt is tightened, using the method employed for removal.

68 Refit the crankshaft pulley to the pulley hub, with the marks made on removal aligned, and tighten the six bolts securely.

69 Turn the crankshaft through two complete revolutions, stopping just before the TDC notch on the crankshaft pulley aligns with the cast lug on the timing cover. Check that all four lobes for No 1 cylinder are pointing outwards (away from the engine).

70 Slowly turn the crankshaft further until the TDC position setting tool can once again be inserted to lock the crankshaft.

71 It should now be possible to re-insert the camshaft setting tool into the slots in the camshafts. If the setting tool cannot be inserted, carry out the valve timing adjustment procedures contained in Section 4.

72 If all is satisfactory, remove all the setting/aligning tools and refit the closure bolt to the cylinder block using a new sealing ring. Tighten the closure bolt to the specified torque.

73 Refit the coolant pump pulley and tighten the three bolts to the specified torque. To prevent the pulley turning as the bolts are tightened, hold the pulley using a screwdriver engaged with one of the bolts and the pump centre spindle. Alternatively, wait until the auxiliary drivebelt has been refitted and tighten the bolts then.

74 Ensure that the mating surfaces are clean, then fit a new sealing ring to the thermostat housing cover. Refit the cover to the coolant pump and tighten the bolts securely.

75 On models with air conditioning, refit the

6.66 Lubricate the crankshaft pulley hub, then refit the hub to the crankshaft

6.67a Screw in the new pulley hub retaining bolt . . .

6.67b . . . tighten it to the specified torque . . .

6.67c . . . then through the specified angle in the stages given in the Specifications

compressor to the cylinder block and tighten the mounting bolts to the specified torque. Refit the refrigerant lines to their relevant clips or brackets.

76 Refit the alternator as described in Chapter 5A.

77 Refit the auxiliary drivebelt tensioner and tighten the mounting bolts to the specified torque.

78 Rotate the tensioner pulley bolt clockwise as for removal, refit the auxiliary drivebelt as previously noted and release the tensioner.

79 Refit the right-hand engine mounting bracket with reference to Section 15.

80 Refit the exhaust front pipe and oxygen sensor with reference to Chapter 4A.

81 Refill the engine with fresh oil with reference to Chapter 1A.

82 Refit the auxiliary drivebelt cover.

83 Refit the camshaft cover and reconnect the crankcase ventilation hose as described in Section 3.

84 Refit the ignition module and cover.

85 Reconnect the radiator top and bottom hoses and heater hose to their respective connections.

86 Reconnect the wiring to the oil pressure switch, coolant temperature sensor and camshaft position sensor, then clip the wiring conduit in position.

87 Reconnect the throttle body preheater hose and tighten the clip.

88 Refit the air cleaner assembly as described in Chapter 4A.

89 Refill the cooling system as described in Chapter 1A, then reconnect the battery negative terminal.

90 Refit the engine undertray as necessary, then refit the roadwheel and lower the vehicle to the ground.

---

7 Timing chain tensioner – removal, inspection and refitting

Removal

1 Remove the timing cover as described in Section 6.

2 Undo the two tensioner retaining bolts and remove the tensioner from the cylinder head **(see illustration)**.

3 Extract the roll pin used to retain the tensioner plunger in the retracted position and withdraw the tensioner plunger and spring **(see illustrations)**.

Inspection

4 Examine the components for any sign of wear, deformation or damage and, if evident, renew the complete tensioner assembly.

Refitting

5 Lubricate the tensioner spring and plunger, then insert the spring, followed by the plunger into the tensioner body.

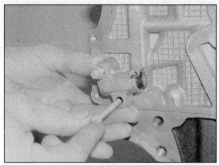

7.2 Undo the two retaining bolts and remove the timing chain tensioner from the cylinder head

6 Fully compress the tensioner plunger and reinsert the retaining roll pin **(see illustration)**.

7 Refit the tensioner assembly to the cylinder head and tighten the retaining bolts securely.

---

8 Camshaft sprockets – removal and refitting

Note: *The special tools described in Section 4 will also be required for this operation. Read through the entire procedure and also the procedures contained in Section 4 to familiarise yourself with the work involved, then either obtain the manufacturer's special tools, or use the alternatives described. New gaskets and sealing rings will also be required for all disturbed components, together with new camshaft sprocket retaining bolts.*

Removal

1 Disconnect the battery negative terminal (refer to *Disconnecting the battery* in the Reference Chapter).

2 Remove the air cleaner assembly as described in Chapter 4A.

3 Disconnect the wiring from the oil pressure switch, coolant temperature sensor and camshaft position sensor, then unclip the wiring conduit and move it to one side.

4 Remove the ignition module cover by moving it to the right, then disconnect the wiring from the left-hand end of the ignition module. Unscrew the two mounting bolts and remove the module, taking care not to distort

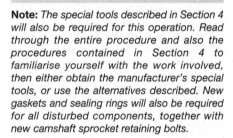

7.3b . . . and withdraw the tensioner plunger and spring

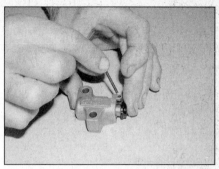

7.3a Extract the roll pin used to retain the tensioner plunger in the retracted position . . .

it. Vauxhall technicians use two special holders to remove the module, although two suitable threaded rods screwed into the holes can be used instead.

5 Disconnect the crankcase ventilation hose from the camshaft cover.

6 Progressively slacken the camshaft cover retaining bolts until they are all fully unscrewed. Note that the bolts are captive and will remain in place in the cover as it is removed. Lift the camshaft cover up and off the cylinder head.

7 Firmly apply the handbrake, then jack up the front of the car and support it securely on axle stands (see *Jacking and vehicle support*). Remove the right-hand front roadwheel and the wheel arch liner for access to the crankshaft pulley.

8 On models with air conditioning, release the tension on the auxiliary drivebelt and lock the tensioner in the released position as described in the auxiliary drivebelt renewal procedure in Chapter 1A. Note that it is not necessary to completely remove the drivebelt, as this entails removal of the right-hand engine mounting bracket. With the drivebelt tension released, slip the belt off the compressor pulley. Unbolt the compressor from the cylinder block, release the refrigerant lines from their brackets and support the compressor clear of the engine. **Do not** disconnect the refrigerant lines from the compressor.

9 Using a socket or spanner on the crankshaft pulley hub bolt, turn the crankshaft in the normal direction of rotation (clockwise

7.6 Timing chain tensioner plunger fully retracted and locked with the roll pin

as viewed from the right-hand side of the car) until the TDC notch on the crankshaft pulley is located just before the cast lug on the timing cover **(see illustration 4.6)**.

10 Check that No 1 piston is on the compression stroke by observing No 1 cylinder camshaft lobes. All four lobes should be pointing outwards (away from the engine). If they are not, No 1 piston is on the exhaust stroke and the crankshaft should be turned through a further full turn, stopping once again just before the TDC notch aligns with the lug on the timing cover.

11 Unscrew the timing chain tensioner closure bolt from the front of the timing cover, below the heater hose union on the coolant pump. Note that a new closure bolt sealing ring will be required for refitting.

12 Obtain a suitable roll pin or similar of 2 mm diameter and approximately 30 mm long to use as a timing chain tensioner locking tool.

13 Using a suitable spanner engaged with the flats provided on the inlet camshaft, apply tension in a clockwise direction (as viewed from the right-hand side of the car) to the camshaft, to take up any slack in the timing chain. This will push the timing chain tensioner plunger fully into its bore.

14 Hold the camshaft in this position and retain the tensioner plunger in the released position by inserting the roll pin through the closure plug aperture and into the hole on the tensioner plunger body.

15 Undo the two bolts and remove the timing chain sliding rail from the top of the cylinder head.

16 Slacken the sprocket retaining bolts for both camshafts, using the spanner to counterhold each camshaft as the bolts are slackened **(see illustration)**. Remove the bolt for the sprocket(s) being removed together with the camshaft position sensor phase disc, if removing the inlet camshaft. Withdraw the relevant sprocket(s) from the camshaft(s), disengage the timing chain and remove the sprocket(s) from the engine.

Refitting

17 Engage the sprocket(s) with the timing chain and locate the sprocket(s) on the camshaft(s). Fit the new retaining bolt(s) together with the phase disc, if working on the inlet camshaft. Note that new retaining bolts must be fitted to **both** sprockets, even if only one sprocket was removed. Tighten the bolts finger tight only at this stage and check that the phase disc on the inlet camshaft can still be turned.

18 Refit the timing chain sliding rail to the top of the cylinder head and secure with the two bolts tightened securely.

19 Using the spanner on the camshaft flats, turn the camshafts slightly, as necessary, until the camshaft setting tool described in Section 4 can be inserted into the slots in the ends of the camshafts.

20 Turn the camshaft sensor phase disc as necessary until the phase disc positioning tool (or suitable alternative) described in Section 4

8.16 Slacken the camshaft sprocket retaining bolts using a spanner to counterhold each camshaft as the bolts are slackened

can be located over the phase disc. If the Vauxhall tool is being used, bolt it to the top of the timing cover. If the alternative tool described is being used, ensure that its base is in contact with the timing cover.

21 Remove the roll pin used to hold the timing chain tensioner plunger in the retracted position.

22 Undo the closure bolt from the crankshaft TDC position setting hole. The plug is located on the front facing side of the cylinder block baseplate, adjacent to the timing cover joint. Note that a new closure bolt sealing ring will be required for refitting.

23 Slowly turn the crankshaft in the normal direction of rotation until the TDC positioning pin (or suitable alternative), described in Section 4, engages with the TDC slot in the crankshaft.

24 Tighten the camshaft sprocket retaining bolts to 10 Nm (7 lbf ft). Note that this is just an initial torque loading to hold the sprockets and the phase disc in position when the setting tools are removed.

25 Remove the crankshaft, camshaft and phase disc setting tools, then tighten the camshaft sprocket retaining bolts to the specified torque in the stages given in the Specifications. Counterhold the camshafts using the spanner on the camshaft flats as the sprocket bolts are tightened.

26 Turn the crankshaft through two complete revolutions, stopping just before the TDC notch on the crankshaft pulley aligns with the cast lug on the timing cover. Check that all

9.2 Camshaft bearing cap identification numbers (arrowed)

four lobes for No 1 cylinder are pointing outwards (away from the engine).

27 Slowly turn the crankshaft further until the TDC position setting tool can once again be inserted to lock the crankshaft.

28 It should now be possible to re-insert the camshaft setting tool into the slots in the camshafts, and to fit the camshaft sensor phase disc setting tool over the disc. If this is not possible carry out the valve timing adjustment procedure contained in Section 4.

29 If all is satisfactory, remove all the setting/aligning tools and refit the timing chain tensioner and cylinder block closure bolts using new sealing rings. Tighten both closure bolts to the specified torque.

30 On models with air conditioning, refit the compressor to the cylinder block and tighten the mounting bolts to the specified torque. Refit the refrigerant lines to their relevant clips or brackets, then refit the auxiliary drivebelt as described in Chapter 1A.

31 Refit the wheel arch liner and the roadwheel. Tighten the roadwheel bolts to the specified torque, then lower the vehicle to the ground.

32 Refit the camshaft cover as described in Section 3.

33 Refit the ignition module and cover, and reconnect the wiring.

34 Reconnect the wiring to the oil pressure switch, coolant temperature sensor and camshaft position sensor, then clip the wiring conduit into position.

35 Refit the air cleaner assembly as described in Chapter 4A, then reconnect the battery negative terminal.

9 Camshafts, hydraulic tappets and rocker arms – removal and refitting

Removal

1 Remove the camshaft sprocket(s) as described in Section 8.

2 Observe the identification numbers and markings on the camshaft bearing caps **(see illustration)**. On the project car used during the compilation of this manual, the bearing caps with odd numbers were fitted to the exhaust camshaft, and the caps with the even numbers were fitted to the inlet camshaft. However, this may not be the case on other engines. Also, as it is possible to fit the caps either way round, it will be necessary to mark the caps with quick-drying paint, or identify them in some way, so that they can be refitted in exactly the same position. On the project car, all the numbers could be read the correct way up, when viewed from the exhaust camshaft side of the engine. Again, this may not always be the case.

3 With the bearing caps correctly identified, and working in a spiral pattern from the outside to the inside, initially slacken the bearing cap bolts, one at a time, by half a turn.

When all the bolts have been initially slackened, repeat the procedure, slackening the bolts by a further half a turn. Continue until all the bolts have been fully slackened. The camshaft will rise up under the action of the valve springs as the bolts are slackened. Ensure that the camshaft rises uniformly and does not jam in its bearings.

4 When all the bolts have been slackened, remove the bolts and lift off the bearing caps, keeping them in order according to the identification method decided on **(see illustration)**.

5 Note the installed position of the camshafts before removal – the cam lobes for No 1 cylinder should be pointing outwards (ie, away from the centre). Carefully lift the camshafts from their locations in the cylinder head. If both camshafts are removed, identify them as exhaust and inlet **(see illustration)**.

6 Obtain sixteen small, clean plastic containers, and number them inlet 1 to 8 and exhaust 1 to 8; alternatively, divide a larger container into sixteen compartments and number each compartment accordingly. Withdraw each rocker arm and hydraulic tappet in turn, and place them in their respective container **(see illustrations)**. Do not interchange the rocker arms and tappets, or the rate of wear will be much increased.

Inspection

7 Examine the camshaft bearing surfaces and cam lobes for signs of wear ridges and scoring. Renew the camshaft if any of these conditions are apparent. Examine the condition of the bearing surfaces, both on the camshaft journals and in the cylinder head/bearing caps. If the head bearing surfaces are worn excessively, the cylinder head will need to be renewed.

8 Examine the rocker arm and hydraulic tappet bearing surfaces for wear ridges and scoring. Renew any rocker arm or tappet on which these conditions are apparent.

9 If either camshaft is being renewed, it will be necessary to renew all the rocker arms and tappets for that particular camshaft also.

Refitting

10 Before refitting, thoroughly clean all the components and the cylinder head and bearing cap journals.

11 Liberally oil the cylinder head hydraulic tappet bores and the tappets. Carefully refit the tappets to the cylinder head, ensuring that each tappet is refitted to its original bore.

12 Lay each rocker arm in position over its respective tappet.

13 Liberally oil the camshaft bearings in the cylinder head and the camshaft lobes, then place the camshafts in the cylinder head. Turn the camshafts so that the cam lobes for No 1 cylinder are pointing outwards as noted during removal.

14 Refit all the bearing caps to their respective locations ensuring they are fitted the correct way round as noted during removal.

9.4 Lift off the camshaft bearing caps, keeping them in order – shown with cylinder head removed

15 Working in a spiral pattern from the inside to the outside, initially tighten the bearing cap bolts, one at a time, by half a turn. When all the bolts have been initially tightened, repeat the procedure, tightening the bolts by a further half a turn. Continue until all the bearing caps are in contact with the cylinder head and the bolts are lightly tightened.

16 Again, working in a spiral pattern from inside to outside, tighten all the bolts to the specified torque.

17 Refit the camshaft sprockets as described in Section 8.

10 Cylinder head – removal and refitting

Note 1: The engine must be cold when removing the cylinder head. A new cylinder head gasket, timing cover gasket, cylinder head bolts, camshaft sprocket bolts together with seals and sealing rings will be required for refitting. A suitable sealant will also be needed to seal the timing cover-to-cylinder block joint.

Note 2: The special tools described in Section 4 will also be required for this operation. Read through the entire procedure and also the procedures contained in Section 4 to familiarise yourself with the work involved, then either obtain the manufacturer's special tools, or use the alternatives described.

Removal

1 Apply the handbrake, then jack up the front

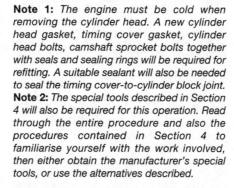

9.6a Withdraw each rocker arm . . .

9.5 Lift the camshafts from their locations in the cylinder head. Shown with cylinder head removed

of the vehicle and support it on axle stands (see *Jacking and vehicle support*). Remove the right-hand roadwheel. On ECO models, remove the engine undertray sections.

2 Disconnect the battery negative terminal (refer to *Disconnecting the battery* in the Reference Chapter), then remove the battery and battery tray as described in Chapter 5A.

3 Drain the cooling system as described in Chapter 1A.

4 On 1.2 litre models, remove the front bumper as described in Chapter 11.

5 Remove the air cleaner assembly as described in Chapter 4A. Also remove the air inlet duct from the front of the engine compartment by unscrewing the single bolt.

6 Remove the throttle body as described in Chapter 4A, Section 10.

7 Disconnect the heater feed hose from the coolant pump and position it to one side.

8 Disconnect the brake servo vacuum line from the inlet manifold. Where applicable, also disconnect the evaporative system hose from the manifold.

9 Undo the two bolts and release the wiring harness support bracket from the rear of the inlet manifold.

10 From under the car, undo the bolt securing the support bracket to the base of the inlet manifold. Slacken the bolt securing the bracket to the cylinder block and twist the bracket to one side **(see illustration)**.

11 On 1.0 litre engines, detach the additional lower wiring harness bracket from the inlet manifold.

12 Disconnect the heater return hose from

9.6b . . . and hydraulic tappet in turn, and place them in their respective containers – shown with cylinder head removed

10.10 Undo the bolt (arrowed) securing the support bracket to the base of the inlet manifold

the EGR coolant flange, and unclip the wiring harness.

13 Depressurise the fuel system as described in Chapter 4A, then disconnect the fuel feed and return hoses from the fuel rail, noting their locations to aid refitting. Be prepared for fuel spillage, and take adequate precautions. Clamp or plug the open ends of the hoses, to minimise further fuel loss.

14 Disconnect the wiring from the following components:
a) Oil pressure switch.
b) Coolant temperature sensor.
c) Camshaft position sensor.
d) Fuel injectors.
e) Throttle valve adjuster.
f) Engine electronic control unit (LH end of engine).
g) Wiring combination plug (LH end of engine).
h) EGR valve.

15 Release the DIS ignition module cover from the centre of the camshaft cover and remove it toward the transmission end of the engine. Disconnect the wiring plug from the left-hand end of the DIS module.

16 Disconnect the earth cables from the electronic control unit bracket.

17 Undo the two bolts, one at each end, securing the plastic fuel injector wiring trough to the top of the fuel rail. Note that these bolts also secure the fuel rail to the inlet manifold. With the injector wiring disconnected, lift the wiring trough up and off the injectors. Place the trough to one side.

18 Remove the auxiliary drivebelt cover from under the right-hand wheel arch.

19 Refer to Chapter 4A, Section 10, and disconnect the wiring from the oxygen sensor on the catalytic converter, then unbolt the exhaust front pipe/catalytic converter from the exhaust manifold, taking care to support the flexible section. **Note:** *Angular movement in excess of 10° can cause permanent damage to the flexible section.*

20 Release the mounting rubbers and support the front of the exhaust pipe to one side.

21 Slacken, but do not remove, the three coolant pump pulley retaining bolts.

22 Unscrew the nuts and disconnect the wiring from the starter motor. Also, release the cable ties.

23 Unbolt the two wiring harness brackets from the inlet manifold.

24 On models without air conditioning, turn the auxiliary drivebelt tensioner pulley bolt clockwise

then insert a suitable pin through the spring centre shaft to lock the spring in its compressed state. Note the routing of the drivebelt, then remove it from the pulleys – mark the drivebelt for fitted direction. **Note:** *The drivebelt cannot be removed completely until the right-hand engine mounting has been removed.* Unscrew the auxiliary drivebelt tensioner lower mounting bolt and the tensioner roller upper pivot bolt. Remove the tensioner from the timing cover.

25 On models with air conditioning, turn the auxiliary drivebelt tensioner pulley bolt clockwise to tension the spring, then insert a suitable pin through the hole in the tensioner body and into the hole in the timing cover to lock the spring. Note the routing of the drivebelt, then remove it from the pulleys – mark the drivebelt for fitted direction. **Note:** *The drivebelt cannot be removed completely until the right-hand engine mounting has been removed.* Turn the tensioner pulley bolt clockwise again and remove the locking pin, then gradually release the tensioner until it is fully released. Unbolt the tensioner from the timing cover. Store the tensioner upright in its normally fitted position after removal. **Note:** *If the tensioner is not stored upright, it must be bled before refitting. To do this, mount it in a vice and slowly operate it through 5 complete strokes.*

26 Undo the bolt securing the oil dipstick guide tube to the exhaust manifold and withdraw the dipstick and guide tube from the cylinder block baseplate. To do this, turn the guide tube forward. Suitably cover or plug the guide tube aperture in the cylinder block baseplate to prevent dirt ingress.

27 Disconnect the wiring from the oxygen sensor on the exhaust manifold at the left-hand front of the engine, then unscrew the sensor from the head. Refer to Chapter 4A, Section 10, if necessary.

28 Unbolt the left-hand engine lifting eye from the cylinder head, complete with attached wiring harness.

29 Unbolt the exhaust manifold heat shield **(see illustration)**, then unscrew the mounting nuts and withdraw the exhaust manifold from the cylinder head. On 1.2 litre models it will be necessary to first unbolt the air conditioning compressor and suspend it to one side **(see illustration)**. Recover the gasket.

30 Remove the oil filter from the filter housing as described in Chapter 1A **(see illustration)**. Remove as much of the oil remaining in the filter housing as possible using clean rags.

31 Undo the three bolts and remove the oil filter housing from the cylinder block **(see illustration)**. Place absorbent rags below the housing as it is removed to catch any remaining oil. Recover the filter housing seal noting that a new seal will be required for refitting.

32 Loosen the clips and disconnect the radiator upper hose from the radiator and thermostat housing.

33 The engine must now be supported while the right-hand engine mounting is removed. To do this, use a hoist attached to the top of the

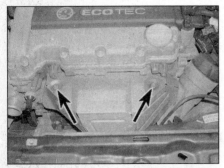

10.29a Undo the two bolts (arrowed) and remove the exhaust manifold heat shield

10.29b Air conditioning compressor – 1.2 litre engine

10.30 Oil filter cap and housing

10.31 Undo the three bolts and remove the oil filter housing from the cylinder block

engine, or make up a wooden frame to locate beneath the sump and use a trolley jack.

34 Remove the right-hand engine mounting bracket with reference to Section 15, then remove the auxiliary drivebelt.

35 Fully unscrew the bolts and remove the coolant pump pulley from its drive flange.

36 Undo the three bolts securing the thermostat housing cover to the coolant pump. Remove the sealing ring from the housing cover noting that a new one will be required for refitting.

37 Undo the bolts securing the coolant pump and timing cover to the cylinder head **(see illustration)**. Note that it is not necessary to remove all the coolant pump bolts as three are shorter than the rest, and only secure the pump to the timing cover.

38 Remove the camshaft cover as described in Section 3.

39 Using a socket or spanner on the crankshaft pulley hub bolt, turn the crankshaft in the normal direction of rotation (clockwise as viewed from the right-hand side of the car) until the TDC notch on the crankshaft pulley is located just before the cast lug on the timing cover (see Section 4).

40 Check that No 1 piston is on the compression stroke by observing No 1 cylinder camshaft lobes. All four lobes should be pointing outwards (away from the engine). If they are not, No 1 piston is on the exhaust stroke and the crankshaft should be turned through a further full turn, stopping once again just before the TDC notch aligns with the lug on the timing cover.

41 On models with air conditioning, unbolt the compressor from the cylinder block, release the refrigerant lines from their brackets and support the compressor clear of the engine. **Do not** disconnect the refrigerant lines from the compressor.

42 Undo the closure bolt from the crankshaft TDC position setting hole. The plug is located on the front facing side of the cylinder block

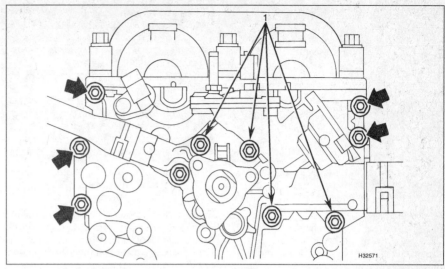

10.37 Undo the bolts (1) securing the coolant pump, and the bolts (arrowed) securing the timing cover to the cylinder head

baseplate, adjacent to the timing cover joint. Note that a new closure bolt sealing ring will be required for refitting.

43 Slowly turn the crankshaft in the normal direction of rotation until the TDC positioning pin (or suitable alternative), described in Section 4, engages with the TDC slot in the crankshaft.

44 Obtain a suitable roll pin, or similar, of 2 mm diameter and approximately 30 mm long, to use as a timing chain tensioner locking tool.

45 Using a suitable spanner engaged with the flats provided on the inlet camshaft, apply tension in a clockwise direction (as viewed from the right-hand side of the car) to the camshaft, to take up any slack in the timing chain. This will push the timing chain tensioner plunger fully into its bore.

46 Hold the camshaft in this position and retain the tensioner plunger in the released position by inserting the roll pin through the

closure plug aperture and into the hole on the tensioner body.

47 Undo the two bolts and remove the timing chain sliding rail from the top of the cylinder head.

48 Slacken the sprocket retaining bolts for both camshafts, using the spanner to counterhold each camshaft as the bolts are slackened. Remove both sprocket bolts together with the camshaft position sensor phase disc from the inlet camshaft. Ease the sprockets and chain off the camshafts and rest the sprockets on the top of the timing cover.

49 Undo the retaining bolt and remove the camshaft position sensor from the front of the timing cover.

50 Working in the specified sequence, progressively slacken the cylinder head retaining bolts half a turn at a time until all the bolts are loose **(see illustrations)**. Remove

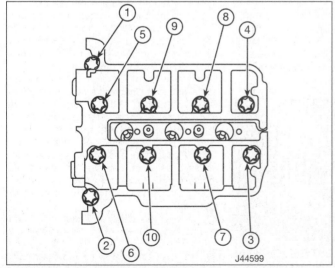

10.50a Cylinder head bolt slackening sequence – 1.0 litre engine

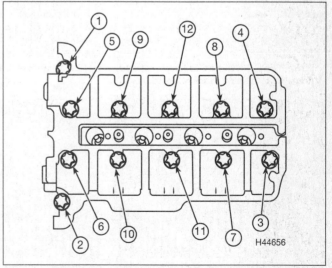

10.50b Cylinder head bolt slackening sequence – 1.2 litre engine

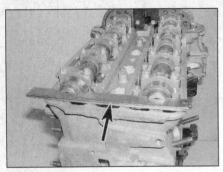

10.57 Before refitting the cylinder head, insert the camshaft setting tool (arrowed) into the slots in the ends of the camshafts

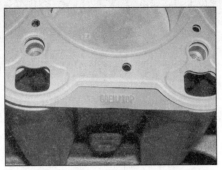

10.60 Position the cylinder head gasket on the block with the words OBEN/TOP uppermost

the bolts from their locations noting that new bolts will be required for refitting.

51 Slightly raise the cylinder head so it just clears the cylinder block face and move the head toward the transmission end of the engine. The head will be initially tight due to the sealant on the timing cover gasket and head gasket. Note that the locating dowel holes on the cylinder head are elongated to allow the head to move sideways slightly.

52 As soon as sufficient clearance exists, lift the cylinder head up and off the cylinder block. At the same time, release the timing chain guide rail from the peg on the cylinder head, and guide the chain tensioner clear of the tensioning rail. Check that the tensioner locking pin is not dislodged as the cylinder head is lifted up. Place the cylinder head on wooden blocks after removal to avoid damage to the valves. Recover the cylinder head gasket.

Preparation for refitting

53 The mating faces of the cylinder head and cylinder block must be perfectly clean before refitting the head. Scouring agents are available for this purpose, but acceptable results can be achieved by using a hard plastic or wood scraper to remove all traces of gasket and carbon. The same method can be used to clean the piston crowns. Take particular care to avoid scoring or gouging the cylinder head mating surfaces during the cleaning operations, as aluminium alloy is easily damaged. Make sure that the carbon is

not allowed to enter the oil and water passages – this is particularly important for the lubrication system, as carbon could block the oil supply to the engine's components. Using adhesive tape and paper, seal the water, oil and bolt holes in the cylinder block. To prevent carbon entering the gap between the pistons and bores, smear a little grease in the gap. After cleaning each piston, use a small brush to remove all traces of grease and carbon from the gap, then wipe away the remainder with a clean rag.

54 Check the mating surfaces of the cylinder block and the cylinder head for nicks, deep scratches and other damage. If slight, they may be removed carefully with a file, but if excessive, machining may be the only alternative to renewal. If warpage of the cylinder head gasket surface is suspected, use a straight-edge to check it for distortion. Refer to Part D of this Chapter if necessary.

55 Thoroughly clean the threads of the cylinder head bolt holes in the cylinder block. Ensure that the bolts run freely in their threads, and that all traces of oil and water are removed from each bolt hole.

56 Using a sharp knife, partially cut through the timing cover gasket flush with the top of the cylinder block. Release the gasket from the timing cover and bend it in half to break it off at the cut line. Remove the upper part of the gasket, and thoroughly clean the mating surface, paying particular attention to the cylinder block edge where it contacts the timing cover.

57 Before refitting the cylinder head, using the spanner on the camshaft flats, turn the camshafts slightly, as necessary, until the camshaft setting tool described in Section 4 can be inserted into the slots in the ends of the camshafts **(see illustration)**. With the tool in position, the camshaft lobes for No 1 cylinder should be pointing outward.

Refitting

58 Prior to locating the cylinder head gasket on the cylinder block, cut off the two protruding tabs at the timing cover end of the gasket, flush with the gasket edge.

59 Apply a 2 mm diameter bead of silicone sealant to the joint between the cylinder block and the timing cover on each side.

60 Check that the locating dowels are in position in the cylinder block, then lay the new gasket on the block face, with the words OBEN/TOP uppermost **(see illustration)**. Push the gasket hard up against the timing cover so that it engages with the sealant.

61 Position the new timing cover gasket upper part on the timing cover, so that its lower ends engage with the sealant. Temporarily insert the left- and right-hand upper timing cover mounting bolts to locate the gasket in the correct position.

62 Apply a further 2 mm diameter bead of silicone sealant to the joint between the cylinder block and the timing cover on each side.

63 Carefully lower the cylinder head into position on the gasket, guiding the chain tensioner past the tensioning rail and guiding the tensioner locking pin into the timing cover access hole. Check also that the timing chain guide rail engages with cylinder head peg.

64 Once the head is seated on its dowels, tap it towards the timing cover with a rubber mallet.

65 Refit the three lower timing cover retaining bolts (one at each side, and one below the coolant pump). Tighten the three bolts to the specified torque.

66 Remove the camshaft setting tool from the camshaft slots.

67 Fit the new cylinder head retaining bolts and screw in the bolts until they contact the cylinder head. Working in the reverse order to the loosening sequence shown earlier in this Section, tighten the cylinder head bolts to the Stage one torque setting given in the Specifications, using a torque wrench. Again working in the correct order, tighten all the bolts through the Stage two angle using an angle measuring gauge **(see illustrations)**. Repeat for Stage three and Stage four.

68 Slacken the three previously-fitted bolts securing the timing cover to the cylinder head.

69 Refit the bolts around the coolant pump and tighten them securely.

70 Refit the remaining timing cover retaining bolts and tighten them to the specified torque.

71 Using the spanner on the camshaft flats, turn the camshafts slightly, as necessary, until the camshaft setting tool can once again be inserted into the camshaft slots.

10.67a Tighten the cylinder head bolts to the Stage 1 torque setting using a torque wrench

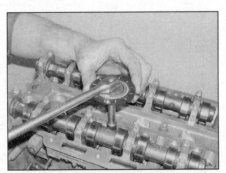

10.67b Tighten the cylinder head bolts through the Stage two, three and four angles using an angle tightening gauge

72 Engage the camshaft sprockets with their respective camshafts, and fit the new retaining bolts together with the phase disc on the inlet camshaft. Tighten the bolts finger tight only at this stage and check that the phase disc on the inlet camshaft can still be turned.

73 Refit the timing chain sliding rail to the top of the cylinder head and secure with the two bolts tightened securely.

74 Remove the roll pin used to hold the timing chain tensioner plunger in the retracted position.

75 Turn the camshaft sensor phase disc as necessary until the phase disc positioning tool (or suitable alternative), described in Section 4, can be located over the phase disc. If the Vauxhall tool is being used, bolt it to the top of the timing cover. If the alternative tool described is being used, ensure that its base is in contact with the timing cover.

76 Tighten the camshaft sprocket retaining bolts to 10 Nm (7 lbf ft). Note that this is just an initial torque loading to hold the sprockets and the phase disc in position when the setting tools are removed. Tighten the inlet camshaft sprocket bolt first, followed by the exhaust camshaft sprocket bolt.

77 Remove the crankshaft, camshaft and phase disc setting tools, then tighten the camshaft sprocket retaining bolts to the specified torque in the stages given in the Specifications. Counterhold the camshafts using the spanner on the camshaft flats as the sprocket bolts are tightened.

78 Turn the crankshaft through two complete revolutions, stopping just before the TDC notch on the crankshaft pulley aligns with the cast lug on the timing cover. Check that all four lobes for No 1 cylinder are pointing outwards (away from the engine).

79 Slowly turn the crankshaft further until the TDC position setting tool can once again be inserted to lock the crankshaft.

80 It should now be possible to re-insert the camshaft setting tool into the slots in the camshafts, and to fit the camshaft sensor phase disc setting tool over the disc. If this is not possible carry out the valve timing adjustment procedure contained in Section 4.

81 If all is satisfactory, remove all the setting/aligning tools and refit the timing chain tensioner and cylinder block closure bolts using new sealing rings. Tighten both closure bolts to the specified torque.

82 Refit the camshaft position sensor using a new sealing ring and tighten the retaining bolt securely.

83 On models with air conditioning, refit the compressor to the cylinder block and tighten the mounting bolts to the specified torque. Refit the refrigerant lines to their relevant clips or brackets.

84 Refit the camshaft cover as described in Section 3.

85 Ensure that the mating surfaces are clean, then fit a new sealing ring to the thermostat housing cover. Refit the cover to the coolant pump and tighten the bolts securely.

86 Refit the coolant pump pulley and tighten the three bolts to the specified torque. To prevent the pulley turning as the bolts are tightened, hold the pulley using a screwdriver engaged with one of the bolts and the pump centre spindle. Alternatively, wait until the auxiliary drivebelt has been refitted and tighten the bolts then.

87 Refit the right-hand engine mounting bracket together with the auxiliary drivebelt with reference to Section 15. Remove the hoist or trolley jack supporting the engine.

88 Reconnect the radiator top hose and tighten the clips.

89 Thoroughly clean the mating surfaces of the oil filter housing and cylinder block, and refit the housing using a new seal. Refit and tighten the retaining bolts to the specified torque.

90 Fit a new sealing O-ring to the oil filter housing cap, then clip the new oil filter element to the cap.

91 Fit the cap and filter element assembly to the oil filter housing and screw the cap into position. Finally, tighten the cap to the specified torque.

92 Refit the exhaust manifold, together with a new gasket, and tighten the mounting nuts to the specified torque. Refit the exhaust manifold heat shield.

93 Refit the left-hand engine lifting eye to the cylinder head and tighten the bolts securely. Attach the wiring harness.

94 Refer to Chapter 4A and refit the oxygen sensor to the exhaust manifold. Reconnect the wiring.

95 Renew the oil dipstick guide tube O-rings and lubricate the O-rings with petroleum jelly. Insert the guide tube into the cylinder block baseplate then secure the tube to the exhaust manifold with the retaining bolt.

96 Refit the auxiliary drivebelt tensioner and tighten the mounting bolts to the specified torque.

97 Rotate the tensioner pulley bolt clockwise as for removal, refit the auxiliary drivebelt as previously noted and release the tensioner.

98 Refit the wiring harness brackets to the inlet manifold.

99 Reconnect the wiring to the starter motor and tighten the nuts. Secure the cable with ties.

100 Reconnect the catalytic converter to the exhaust manifold using a new flange gasket. Tighten the converter-to-manifold nuts to the specified torque first, followed by the support bracket bolts. Refit the mounting rubbers, then refit the oxygen sensor with reference to Chapter 4A. Reconnect the wiring.

101 Refit the auxiliary drivebelt cover under the right-hand wheel arch.

102 Refit the injector wiring and trough to the top of the fuel rail.

103 Reconnect the earth cables to the electronic control unit bracket.

104 Refit the DIS ignition module with reference to Chapter 5B, and reconnect the wiring.

105 Reconnect the wiring to the following components:
a) Oil pressure switch.
b) Coolant temperature sensor.
c) Camshaft position sensor.
d) Fuel injectors.
e) Throttle valve adjuster.
f) Engine electronic control unit (LH end of engine).
g) Wiring combination plug (LH end of engine).
h) EGR valve.

106 Reconnect the fuel feed and return hoses to the fuel rail.

107 Disconnect the heater return hose to the EGR coolant flange, and secure the wiring harness.

108 On 1.0 litre engines, attach the lower wiring harness bracket to the inlet manifold.

109 Refit and tighten the bolt securing the support bracket to the base of the inlet manifold.

110 Refit the wiring harness support bracket to the rear of the inlet manifold.

111 Reconnect the brake servo vacuum line to the inlet manifold.

112 Reconnect the heater feed hose to the coolant pump and tighten the clip.

113 Refit the throttle body as described in Chapter 4A.

114 Refit the air cleaner assembly with reference to Chapter 4A. Also refit the air inlet duct to the front of the engine compartment.

115 Refit or reconnect the battery as applicable.

116 Refill the cooling system with reference to Chapter 1A.

117 Refit the roadwheel then lower the vehicle to the ground.

11 Sump and oil pick-up pipe – removal and refitting

Note: *A new sump gasket must be used on refitting. If the oil pick-up pipe is removed, a new O-ring should be used on refitting.*

Removal

1 Firmly apply the handbrake, then jack up the front of the car and support it securely on axle stands (see *Jacking and vehicle support*). Remove the right-hand roadwheel. On ECO models, remove the engine undertray sections.

2 Drain the engine oil, with reference to Chapter 1A, then refit and tighten the sump drain plug.

3 Refer to Chapter 4A, Section 10, and disconnect the wiring from the oxygen sensor on the catalytic converter, then unbolt the exhaust front pipe from the exhaust manifold, taking care to support the flexible section. **Note:** *Angular movement in excess of 10° can cause permanent damage to the flexible section.* Release the mounting rubbers and support the front of the exhaust pipe to one side to allow removal of the sump.

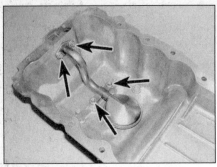

11.7a Undo the bolts (arrowed) . . .

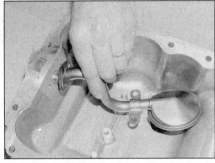

11.7b . . . remove the oil pick-up pipe . . .

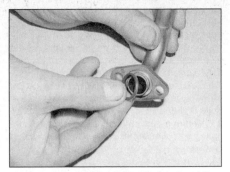

11.7c . . . and recover the O-ring from the flange

11.11a Apply a 2 mm diameter bead of silicone sealant to the joint between the timing cover and cylinder block on each side . . .

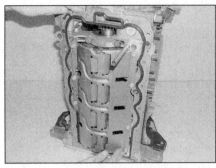

11.11b . . . then place a new gasket on the sump and locate the sump on the cylinder block baseplate – shown with engine removed

11.12 If the engine has been separated from the transmission, use a straight-edge to check the transmission mating face alignment when refitting the sump

4 Remove the auxiliary drivebelt cover from under the right-hand wheel arch.

5 Undo the bolts securing the sump to the cylinder block baseplate, timing cover and transmission bellhousing, then withdraw the sump. If necessary, tap the sump with a soft-faced mallet to free it from its location – do not lever between the sump and cylinder block baseplate mating faces. Recover the gasket.

6 To remove the oil baffle plate, undo the retaining bolts and remove the baffle plate from the cylinder block baseplate.

7 If desired, the oil pick-up pipe can be removed from the sump by unscrewing the two support bracket retaining bolts and the two bolts securing the flange to the end face of the sump. Lift out the pick-up pipe and recover the O-ring from the flange **(see illustrations)**. Note that a new O-ring will be required for refitting.

Refitting

8 Thoroughly clean the inside and outside of the sump ensuring that all traces of old gasket are removed from the mating face. Also clean the cylinder block baseplate mating face to remove all traces of old gasket.

9 If the oil pick-up pipe has been removed, fit a new O-ring to the flange, then refit the pipe to the sump. Refit the flange bolts and support bracket bolts, then tighten the flange bolts securely. Tighten the support bracket bolts securely.

10 If removed, refit the oil baffle plate and secure with the retaining bolts tightened securely.

11 Apply a 2 mm diameter bead of silicone sealant to the joint between the timing cover and cylinder block, on each side. Place a new gasket on the sump, then locate the sump on the cylinder block baseplate **(see illustrations)**. Refit the securing bolts and tighten them finger tight at this stage.

12 If the engine has been removed from the car and separated from the transmission, use a straight-edge to check that the transmission mating face is aligned with the cylinder block baseplate mating face **(see illustration)**.

13 Tighten the bolts securing the sump to the cylinder block baseplate and timing cover

12.2 Remove the securing screws and withdraw the oil pump cover from the rear of the timing cover

progressively and securely. Now tighten the bolts securing the sump to the transmission bellhousing to the specified torque.

14 Refit the auxiliary drivebelt cover under the right-hand wheel arch.

15 Reconnect the exhaust system front pipe/catalytic converter to the manifold as described in Chapter 4A. Also, reconnect the wiring to the oxygen sensor.

16 Refit the roadwheel, and where necessary the engine undertray sections, then lower the car to the ground and refill the engine with oil as described in Chapter 1A.

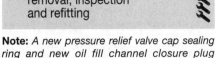

12 Oil pump –
removal, inspection and refitting

Note: *A new pressure relief valve cap sealing ring and new oil fill channel closure plug sealing ring will be required for refitting.*

Removal

1 Remove the timing cover and chain as described in Section 6.

2 Remove the securing screws and withdraw the oil pump cover from the rear of the timing cover **(see illustration)**.

3 Remove the inner and outer rotor from the timing cover and wipe them clean. Also clean the rotor location in the timing cover.

4 The oil pressure relief valve components can also be removed from the timing cover by unscrewing the cap. Withdraw the cap and sealing ring, the spring and plastic pin, and the plunger **(see illustrations)**.

Inspection

5 Locate the inner and outer rotor back in the timing cover, noting that the chamfer on the outer rotor outside diameter must face the timing cover.

6 Check the clearance between the end faces of the gears and the housing (endfloat) using a straight-edge and a feeler gauge **(see illustration)**.

7 If the clearance is outside the specified limits, renew the components as necessary.

8 Examine the pressure relief valve spring and plunger, and renew if any sign of damage or wear is evident.

9 Ensure that the rotor location in the interior of the timing cover is scrupulously clean before commencing reassembly.

Refitting

10 Thoroughly clean the pressure relief valve components, and lubricate them with clean engine oil before refitting. Insert the plunger, the spring and plastic pin, then refit the cap using a new sealing ring. Tighten the cap securely.

11 Ensure that the gears are clean, then lubricate them with clean engine oil, and refit them to the pump body. Ensure that the chamfer on the outer rotor outside diameter faces the timing cover.

12 Ensure that the mating faces of the rear cover and the pump housing are clean, then refit the rear cover. Refit and tighten the securing screws securely.

13 Fit a new crankshaft oil seal to the timing cover as described in Section 13.

14 Refit the timing chain and cover to the engine as described in Section 6.

15 After refitting the timing cover, unscrew the oil fill channel closure bolt from the lower front facing side of the timing cover. Using a pump type oil can filled with clean engine oil, insert the oil can spout into the oil channel, so that the spout pushes back the internal ball valve. Prime the pump by filling it with oil until the oil runs out of the fill channel. Refit the closure plug using a new sealing ring and tighten it to the specified torque.

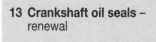

13 Crankshaft oil seals – renewal

Timing chain end oil seal

Note: *A new crankshaft pulley hub retaining bolt will be required for refitting.*

1 Disconnect the battery negative terminal (refer to *Disconnecting the battery* in the Reference Chapter).

2 Remove the air cleaner assembly as described in Chapter 4A.

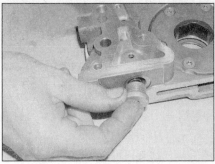

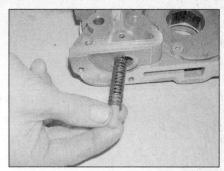

12.4a Unscrew the oil pressure relief valve cap and sealing ring . . .

12.4b . . . then withdraw the spring and plastic pin . . .

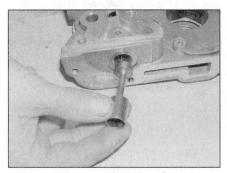

12.4c . . . and the plunger

12.6 Check the oil pump gear endfloat using a straight-edge and feeler gauge

3 Firmly apply the handbrake, then jack up the front of the car and support it securely on axle stands (see *Jacking and vehicle support*). Remove the right-hand front roadwheel and the wheel arch liner for access to the crankshaft pulley.

4 Release the tension on the auxiliary drivebelt and lock the tensioner in the released position as described in the auxiliary drivebelt renewal procedure in Chapter 1A. Note that it is not necessary to completely remove the drivebelt, as this would entail removal of the right-hand engine mounting bracket. With the drivebelt tension released, slip the belt off the crankshaft pulley.

5 Using a socket or spanner on the crankshaft pulley hub bolt, turn the crankshaft in the normal direction of rotation (clockwise as viewed from the right-hand side of the car) until the TDC notch on the crankshaft pulley is located just before the cast lug on the timing cover **(see illustration 4.6)**.

6 Using quick-drying paint, or similar, make an alignment mark between the crankshaft pulley and the pulley hub. It should only be possible to refit the pulley in one position, but it is advisable to make an alignment mark anyway.

7 Unscrew the six crankshaft pulley retaining bolts and remove the pulley from the hub. If necessary, prevent the crankshaft from turning as the pulley bolts are slackened, using a spanner or socket on the pulley hub bolt.

8 Using a suitable socket, slacken the crankshaft pulley hub retaining bolt. The crankshaft can be prevented from turning as

the bolt is slackened, using Vauxhall special tool KM-956 or a similar tool which will engage with the flats on each side of the pulley hub. Alternatively, remove the starter motor, and lock the flywheel ring gear teeth using a suitable hooked tool bolted to the bellhousing.

9 Unscrew the slackened crankshaft pulley hub retaining bolt and remove the hub from the crankshaft. Note that a new bolt will be required for refitting.

10 The seal can now be carefully prised out with a screwdriver or similar hooked tool **(see illustration)**.

11 Clean the oil seal seat with a wooden or plastic scraper.

12 Grease the lips of the new seal, and tap it into position until it is flush with the outer face of the timing cover, using a suitable socket or tube, or a wooden block **(see illustration)**.

13.10 Carefully prise out the crankshaft oil seal from the timing cover – shown with timing cover removed

13.12 Tap the new seal into position until it is flush with the outer face of the timing cover – shown with timing cover removed

13.23 Locate the seal over the crankshaft and into the recess – shown with engine removed

13.24 Tap the seal into position until it is flush – shown with engine removed

13 Refit the crankshaft pulley hub to the crankshaft, ensuring that the punch mark on the pulley hub is in the 11 o'clock position.

14 Screw in the new pulley hub retaining bolt and tighten it to the specified torque, in the stages given in the Specifications. Prevent crankshaft rotation as the bolt is tightened, using the method employed for removal.

15 Refit the crankshaft pulley to the pulley hub, with the marks made on removal aligned, and tighten the six bolts securely.

16 Refit the auxiliary drivebelt as described in Chapter 1A.

17 Refit the air cleaner assembly as described in Chapter 4A.

18 Refit the wheel arch liner and roadwheel, tightening the wheel bolts to the specified torque.

19 Lower the car to the ground, then reconnect the battery negative terminal.

Transmission end oil seal

20 Remove the flywheel/driveplate as described in Section 14.

21 Carefully prise out the old seal from its location using a screwdriver or similar hooked tool.

22 Clean the oil seal seat with a wooden or plastic scraper.

23 Grease the lips of the new seal, then carefully locate the seal over the crankshaft and into the recess in the cylinder block and baseplate **(see illustration)**.

24 Tap the seal into position using a suitable

socket or tube, or a wooden block, until it is flush with the outer faces of the cylinder block and baseplate **(see illustration)**.

25 Refit the flywheel/driveplate as described in Section 14.

14 Flywheel/driveplate – removal, inspection and refitting

Note: *New flywheel/driveplate securing bolts must be used on refitting.*

Removal

1 Remove the transmission as described in Chapter 7A, 7B or 7C, as applicable.

2 On manual gearbox or Easytronic transmission models, remove the clutch assembly as described in Chapter 6.

3 Although the flywheel/driveplate bolt holes are offset so that the flywheel/driveplate can only be fitted in one position, it will make refitting easier if alignment marks are made between the flywheel/driveplate and the end of the crankshaft.

4 Prevent the flywheel/driveplate from turning by jamming the ring gear teeth using a suitable tool **(see illustration)**.

5 Unscrew the securing bolts, and remove the flywheel/driveplate **(see illustration)**.

Caution: Take care, as the flywheel is heavy.

Inspection

6 If the teeth on the flywheel starter ring are badly worn, or if some are missing, then it will be necessary to remove the ring and fit a new one.

7 The old ring can be split with a cold chisel, after drilling a shallow hole between two gear teeth. Take great care not to damage the flywheel during this operation, and wear eye protection at all times. Once the ring has been split, it will spread apart, and can be lifted from the flywheel.

8 The new ring gear must be heated evenly to between 180 and 230ºC. Unless facilities for heating by oven or flame are available, leave the fitting to a Vauxhall dealer or engineering works. The new ring gear must not be overheated during this work, or the temper of the metal will be affected.

9 The ring should be tapped gently down onto its register, and left to cool naturally – the contraction of the metal on cooling will ensure that it is a secure and permanent fit.

Caution: Make sure that the ring is fitted the correct way round, so that the starter motor pinion teeth will engage the tooth 'lead-in' bevel machined on one side of the flywheel/driveplate teeth.

10 If the clutch friction disc contact surface of the flywheel is scored, or on close inspection shows signs of small hair cracks (caused by overheating), it may be possible to have the flywheel surface-ground, provided the overall thickness of the flywheel is not reduced too much. Consult a Vauxhall dealer or a specialist engine repairer and, if grinding is not possible, renew the flywheel complete.

Refitting

11 Offer the flywheel/driveplate to the end of the crankshaft, and align the previously-made marks on the flywheel and crankshaft.

12 Coat the threads of the new flywheel bolts with thread-locking compound (note that new bolts may be supplied ready-coated), then fit the bolts and tighten them to the specified torque, whilst preventing the flywheel from turning as during removal **(see illustrations)**.

14.4 If the engine is removed, lock the flywheel with a suitable tool

14.5 Unscrew the securing bolts, and remove the flywheel/driveplate – shown with engine removed

13 Where applicable refit the clutch as described in Chapter 6, then refit the transmission as described in Chapter 7A, 7B or 7C, as applicable.

15 Engine/transmission mountings – inspection and renewal

Inspection

1 To improve access, firmly apply the handbrake, then jack up the front of the vehicle and support it on axle stands (see *Jacking and vehicle support*).
2 Check the mounting blocks (rubbers) to see if they are cracked, hardened or separated from the metal at any point. Renew the mounting block if any such damage or deterioration is evident.
3 Check that all the mounting securing nuts and bolts are securely tightened, using a torque wrench to check if possible.
4 Using a large screwdriver, or a similar tool, check for wear in the mounting blocks by carefully levering against them to check for free play. Where this is not possible, enlist the aid of an assistant to move the engine/transmission unit back-and-forth, and from side-to-side, while you observe the mountings. While some free play is to be expected, even from new components, excessive wear should be obvious. If excessive free play is found, check first to see that the securing nuts and bolts are correctly tightened, then renew any worn components as described in the following paragraphs.

Renewal

Note: *Before slackening any of the engine mounting bolts/nuts, the relative positions of the mountings to their various brackets should be marked to ensure correct alignment upon refitting.*

Right-hand mounting

5 Apply the handbrake, then jack up the front of the vehicle and support it on axle stands (see *Jacking and vehicle support*). Remove the right-hand roadwheel and the wheel arch liner for access to the crankshaft pulley.

14.12a Tighten the flywheel bolts to the specified torque using a torque wrench . . .

6 Remove the air cleaner as described in Chapter 4A.
7 Attach a suitable hoist and lifting tackle to the engine lifting brackets on the cylinder head, and support the weight of the engine.
8 Unscrew the four mounting bolts and remove the right-hand mounting from the engine mounting bracket and body **(see illustration)**. If necessary, the engine mounting bracket may be unbolted from the cylinder block.
9 If necessary, refit the engine mounting bracket and tighten the bolts to the specified torque, then locate the new mounting block on the body and engine bracket, and tighten the bolts to the specified torque.
10 Remove the hoist, then refit the air cleaner.
11 Refit the wheel arch liner and right-hand roadwheel, then lower the vehicle to the ground.

Left-hand mounting

12 Attach a suitable hoist and lifting tackle to the engine lifting brackets on the cylinder head, and support the weight of the engine.
13 Using a Torx socket, unscrew the two bolts securing the engine mounting bracket to the body mounting bracket **(see illustration)**.
14 Unbolt the mounting brackets from the engine and body. On manual transmission models, slightly lower the engine, then unclip the clutch hydraulic line from the mounting bracket.
15 Locate the new mounting brackets in position, and, where necessary, clip the clutch

14.12b . . . then through the specified angle using an angle tightening gauge

hydraulic line onto the bracket.
16 Raise the engine and insert the bolts, then tighten them to the specified torque.
17 Disconnect the hoist and lifting tackle.

Rear mounting/torque link

18 Apply the handbrake, then jack up the front of the vehicle and support it on axle stands (see *Jacking and vehicle support*).
19 Attach a suitable hoist and lifting tackle to the engine lifting brackets on the cylinder head, and support the weight of the engine.
20 Refer to Chapter 4A, Section 10, and disconnect the wiring from the oxygen sensor on the catalytic converter, then unbolt the exhaust front pipe from the exhaust manifold, taking care to support the flexible section.
Note: *Angular movement in excess of 10° can cause permanent damage to the flexible section.*
21 Release the mounting rubbers and support the front of the exhaust pipe to one side.
22 Working under the vehicle, remove the nut and bolt securing the mounting to the transmission bracket.
23 Remove the bolts securing the mounting to the body, and withdraw the mounting/torque link.
24 Locate the new mounting/link in position. Insert the bolts and tighten to the specified torque.
25 Refit the exhaust front pipe with reference to Chapter 4A.
26 Remove the hoist and lower the vehicle to the ground.

15.8 Right-hand engine mounting

15.13 Left-hand engine mounting

Notes

Chapter 2 Part B:
1.4 litre petrol engine in-car repair procedures

Contents

Degrees of difficulty

Easy, suitable for novice with little experience		**Fairly easy,** suitable for beginner with some experience		**Fairly difficult,** suitable for competent DIY mechanic		**Difficult,** suitable for experienced DIY mechanic		**Very difficult,** suitable for expert DIY or professional	

Specifications

General

Engine type	Four-cylinder, in-line, water-cooled. Double overhead camshafts, belt-driven, acting on hydraulic valve lifters
Manufacturer's engine code*	Z14XE
Bore	77.60 mm
Stroke	73.40 mm
Capacity	1389 cc
Firing order	1-3-4-2 (No 1 cylinder at timing belt end)
Direction of crankshaft rotation	Clockwise (viewed from timing belt end of engine)
Compression ratio	10.5:1

*For details of engine code location, see 'Vehicle identification' in the Reference Chapter.

Camshaft

Endfloat	0.040 to 0.144 mm
Camshaft bearing journal diameter	27.939 to 27.960 mm
Maximum permissible radial run-out	0.040 mm

Lubrication system

Minimum oil pressure at 80ºC	1.5 bars at idle speed
Oil pump type	Gear-type, driven directly from crankshaft
Oil pump clearances:	
Inner-to-outer gear clearance (backlash)	0.10 to 0.20 mm
Gear-to-housing clearance (endfloat)	0.03 to 0.10 mm

Flywheel

Maximum permissible lateral run-out of starter ring gear	0.50 mm
Refinishing limit (maximum depth of material which may be removed from clutch friction surface)	0.30 mm

Torque wrench settings	Nm	lbf ft
Big-end bearing cap bolts*:		
Stage 1	25	18
Stage 2	Angle-tighten a further 30°	
Camshaft bearing cap bolts	8	6
Camshaft sprocket bolt*:		
Stage 1	50	37
Stage 2	Angle-tighten a further 60°	
Stage 3	Angle-tighten a further 15°	
Crankshaft pulley bolt*:		
Stage 1	95	70
Stage 2	Angle-tighten a further 30°	
Stage 3	Angle-tighten a further 15°	
Cylinder head bolts*:		
Stage 1	25	18
Stage 2	Angle-tighten a further 90°	
Stage 3	Angle-tighten a further 90°	
Stage 4	Angle-tighten a further 90°	
Stage 5	Angle-tighten a further 45°	
Driveplate bolts (automatic transmission models)*	60	44
Engine mountings:		
Left-hand:		
Mounting to body	25	18
Mounting adaptor block:		
Stage 1	80	59
Stage 2	Angle-tighten a further 45°	
Stage 3	Angle-tighten a further 15°	
Mounting to transmission:		
Stage 1	80	59
Stage 2	Angle-tighten a further 45°	
Stage 3	Angle-tighten a further 15°	
Rear:		
Torque link to subframe and transmission bracket	80	59
Torque link bracket to transmission:		
Stage 1	80	59
Stage 2	Angle-tighten a further 45°	
Stage 3	Angle-tighten a further 15°	
Right-hand:		
Mounting to body	40	30
Mounting to engine bracket:		
Stage 1	60	44
Stage 2	Angle-tighten a further 30°	
Stage 3	Angle-tighten a further 15°	
Engine-to-transmission bolts	60	44
Exhaust front pipe to manifold*	25	18
Exhaust manifold to cylinder head*	22	16
Flywheel bolts*:		
Stage 1	35	26
Stage 2	Angle-tighten a further 30°	
Stage 3	Angle-tighten a further 15°	
Front suspension subframe*:		
Stage 1	90	66
Stage 2	Angle-tighten a further 45°	
Stage 3	Angle-tighten a further 15°	
Inlet manifold support:		
To cylinder block	35	26
To manifold	20	15
Inlet manifold to cylinder head	20	15
Main bearing cap bolts*:		
Stage 1	50	37
Stage 2	Angle-tighten a further 45°	
Stage 3	Angle-tighten a further 15°	
Oil pressure relief valve plug to oil pump	50	37
Sump-to-cylinder block bolts	10	7
Sump-to-transmission bolts	40	30
Thermostat housing to cylinder head	20	15
Timing belt idler roller bolts	25	18
Timing belt tensioner bolt	20	15
Torque converter to driveplate*	50	37

*Use new bolts.

1 General information

How to use this Chapter

1 This Part of Chapter 2 describes the repair procedures which can reasonably be carried out on the engine while it remains in the vehicle. If the engine has been removed from the vehicle and is being dismantled as described in Chapter 2D, any preliminary dismantling procedures can be ignored.

2 Note that, while it may be *possible* physically to overhaul items such as the piston/connecting rod assemblies while the engine is in the vehicle, such tasks are not generally carried out as separate operations, and usually require the execution of several additional procedures (not to mention the cleaning of components and of oil ways); for this reason, all such tasks are classed as major overhaul procedures, and are described in Chapter 2D.

3 Chapter 2D describes the removal of the engine/transmission unit from the vehicle, and the full overhaul procedures which can then be carried out.

Engine description

4 The engine is of the in-line four-cylinder, double overhead camshaft (DOHC) type, mounted transversely at the front of the car, with the transmission attached to its left-hand end **(see illustration)**.

5 The crankshaft runs in five shell-type bearings, and the centre bearing incorporates thrust bearing shells to control crankshaft endfloat.

6 The connecting rods are attached to the crankshaft by horizontally-split shell-type big-end bearings. The pistons are attached to the connecting rods by gudgeon pins, which are an interference fit in the connecting rod small-end bores. The aluminium-alloy pistons are fitted with three piston rings – two compression rings and an oil control ring.

7 Both camshafts are driven from the crankshaft by a toothed composite-rubber timing belt. Each cylinder has four valves (two inlet and two exhaust), operated directly from the camshafts via hydraulic self-adjusting valve lifters (tappets). One camshaft operates the inlet valves, and the other operates the exhaust valves. The inlet and exhaust valves are each closed by a single valve spring, and operate in guides pressed into the cylinder head.

8 A gear-type oil pump is located in a housing attached to the front of the cylinder block, and is driven directly from the crankshaft.

9 The coolant pump is located at the front of the cylinder block, and is driven by the timing belt.

Operations with engine in place

10 The following operations can be carried out without having to remove the engine from the vehicle.

a) Removal and refitting of the cylinder head.
b) Removal and refitting of the timing belt and sprockets.
c) Removal and refitting of the camshafts.
d) Removal and refitting of the sump.
e) Removal and refitting of the big-end bearings, connecting rods, and pistons*.
f) Removal and refitting of the oil pump.
g) Renewal of the engine mountings.
h) Removal and refitting of the flywheel/ driveplate.

*Although the operation marked with an asterisk can be carried out with the engine in the vehicle (after removal of the sump), it is preferable for the engine to be removed, in the interests of cleanliness and improved access. For this reason, the procedure is described in Chapter 2D.

2 Compression test – description and interpretation

Note: *A suitable compression gauge will be required to carry out this test.*

1 When engine performance is down, or if misfiring occurs which cannot be attributed to the ignition or fuel systems, a compression test can provide diagnostic clues as to the engine's condition. If the test is performed regularly, it can give warning of trouble before any other symptoms become apparent.

2 The engine must be fully warmed-up to normal operating temperature, the battery must be fully charged, and all the spark plugs must be removed (see Chapter 1A). The aid of an assistant will also be required.

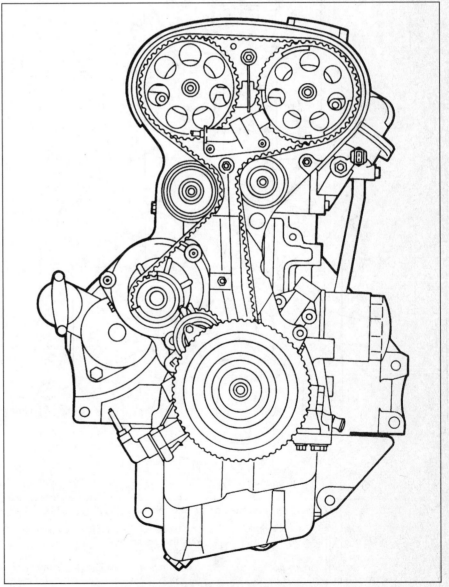

1.4 Front sectional view of engine

3 Disconnect the wiring plug from the DIS module, and remove the fuel pump relay (see Chapter 12 for details of relay locations).

4 Fit a compression tester to the No 1 spark plug hole (No 1 cylinder is nearest the timing belt end of the engine) – the type of tester which screws into the plug thread is to be preferred.

5 Have an assistant hold the accelerator pedal fully depressed, at the same time cranking the engine over for approximately four seconds on the starter motor. After one or two revolutions, the compression pressure reading on the gauge should build-up to a maximum figure and then stabilise. Record the highest reading obtained.

6 Repeat the test on the remaining cylinders, recording the pressure in each.

7 All cylinders should produce very similar pressures; a difference of more than 1 bar between any two cylinders indicates a fault. Note that the compression should build-up quickly in a healthy engine; low compression on the first stroke, followed by gradually-increasing pressure on successive strokes, indicates worn piston rings. A low compression reading on the first stroke, which does not build-up during successive strokes, indicates leaking valves or a blown head gasket (a cracked head could also be the cause). Deposits on the undersides of the valve heads can also cause low compression.

8 If the pressure in any cylinder is significantly lower than that in the remaining cylinders, carry out the following test to isolate the cause. Introduce a teaspoonful of clean engine oil into the relevant cylinder through its spark plug hole, and repeat the test.

9 If the addition of oil temporarily improves the compression pressure, this indicates that bore or piston wear is responsible for the pressure loss. No improvement suggests that leaking or burnt valves, or a blown head gasket may be to blame.

10 A low reading from two adjacent cylinders is almost certainly due to the head gasket having blown between them; the presence of coolant in the engine oil will confirm this.

11 If one cylinder is about 20 percent lower than the others, and the engine has a slightly rough idle, a worn camshaft lobe could be the cause.

12 If the compression reading is unusually high, the combustion chambers are probably coated with carbon deposits. If this is the case, the cylinder head should be removed and decarbonised (see Chapter 2D).

13 On completion of the test, refit the spark plugs, reconnect the DIS module wiring plug, and refit the fuel pump relay.

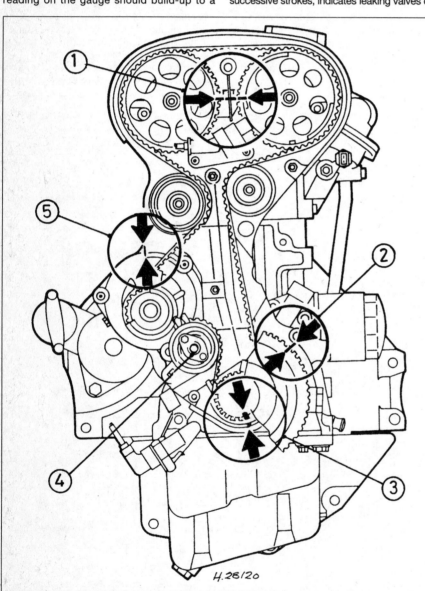

3.6a Timing mark positions with No 1 piston at TDC

1   *Camshaft sprocket timing marks aligned with top edge of cylinder head*

2   *TDC sensor wheel timing mark aligned with mark on timing belt cover*

3   *Crankshaft sprocket timing mark aligned with mark on timing belt cover*

4   *Timing belt tensioner bolt*

5   *Coolant pump mark aligned with mark on cylinder block (see Chapter 3 – not part of timing belt procedure)*

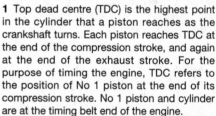

3   Top dead centre (TDC) for No 1 piston – locating

1 Top dead centre (TDC) is the highest point in the cylinder that a piston reaches as the crankshaft turns. Each piston reaches TDC at the end of the compression stroke, and again at the end of the exhaust stroke. For the purpose of timing the engine, TDC refers to the position of No 1 piston at the end of its compression stroke. No 1 piston and cylinder are at the timing belt end of the engine.

2 Disconnect the battery negative lead (refer to *Disconnecting the battery* at the end of this manual).

3 Remove the upper outer timing belt cover as described in Section 6.

4 Apply the handbrake, then jack up the front of the vehicle and support it on axle stands (see *Jacking and vehicle support*). Remove the right-hand front roadwheel, then remove the wheel arch inner cover for access to the crankshaft pulley.

5 Using a suitable spanner or socket on the crankshaft pulley bolt, rotate the crankshaft to bring No 1 piston to TDC. Note that turning the engine will be made much easier if the spark plugs are removed first (see Chapter 1A).

6 The timing marks must be aligned as follows **(see illustrations)**.

a) *The timing marks on the camshaft sprockets must be directly opposite each other, and aligned with the top edge of the cylinder head.*

3.6b Camshaft sprocket timing marks (A) aligned with top edge of cylinder head (B)

3.6c Crankshaft sprocket timing mark (A) aligned with mark (B) on timing belt cover

b) *The timing mark on the crankshaft speed/ position sensor wheel must be aligned with the pointer (raised line) on the timing belt cover. Note that if the crankshaft pulley and lower outer timing belt cover have been removed, the timing mark on the crankshaft sprocket can be used instead of the mark on the pulley. The mark on the crankshaft sprocket must align with the corresponding mark on the rear timing belt cover (there may be two marks on the sprocket, in which case ignore the mark with a cross stamped across it).*

4 Camshaft cover – removal and refitting

Removal

1 Disconnect the battery negative lead (refer to *Disconnecting the battery* at the end of this manual).
2 Unscrew the oil filler cap, then undo the bolts and remove the engine top cover. Refit the cap.
3 Remove the air cleaner assembly as described in Chapter 4B.
4 Remove the ignition module from the spark plugs with reference to Chapter 5B.
5 Disconnect the throttle valve module preheater hose from the thermostat housing.
6 Disconnect the two crankcase ventilation breather hoses from the camshaft cover.
7 Disconnect the oxygen sensor wiring and unclip it from the support.
8 Progressively loosen the camshaft cover securing bolts (preferably working from the ends of the cover towards the centre, in a spiral pattern), then withdraw the bolts.
9 Lift the camshaft cover from the cylinder head, and recover the gasket.

Refitting

10 Clean the mating surfaces of the camshaft cover and cylinder head.

11 Apply sealant to the two semi-circular cut-outs at the transmission end of the cylinder head, and to each side of the camshaft bearing caps at the timing belt end of the cylinder head **(see illustration)**.
12 Ensure that the gasket is located correctly on the camshaft cover (if necessary, smear it with light grease to hold it in place).
13 Fit the cover to the cylinder head, then refit the securing bolts. Progressively tighten the bolts securely, working from the centre to the ends of the cover, in a spiral pattern.
14 Reconnect the oxygen sensor wiring and clip it in the support.
15 Reconnect the crankcase ventilation breather hoses to the camshaft cover.
16 Reconnect the throttle valve module preheater hose to the thermostat housing.
17 Refit the ignition module to the spark plugs with reference to Chapter 5B.
18 Refit the air cleaner assembly as described in Chapter 4B.
19 Refit the engine top cover, then reconnect the battery negative lead.

5 Crankshaft pulley – removal and refitting

Note: A new crankshaft pulley bolt will be required for refitting.

Removal

1 Apply the handbrake, then jack up the front of the vehicle and support it on axle stands (see *Jacking and vehicle support*). Remove the right-hand front roadwheel, then remove the wheel arch inner cover for access to the crankshaft pulley.
2 Remove the auxiliary drivebelt as described in Chapter 1A.
3 To prevent the crankshaft from turning as the pulley bolt is unscrewed, select 4th gear and have an assistant apply the brakes hard (manual gearbox models only). Alternatively,

remove the starter motor, and lock the flywheel ring gear teeth using a suitable tool.
4 Unscrew the pulley bolt and recover the washer fitted behind it, then remove the pulley.

Refitting

5 On refitting, ensure that the notch in the pulley fits over the locating lug on the crankshaft sprocket.
6 Prevent the crankshaft from turning as during removal, then fit the new pulley securing bolt, ensuring that the washer is in place under the bolt head.
7 Tighten the bolt to the specified torque, in the stages given in the Specifications.
8 Refit and tension the auxiliary drivebelt, as described in Chapter 1A.

6 Timing belt covers – removal and refitting

Upper outer cover

Removal

1 Remove the air cleaner assembly as described in Chapter 4B.

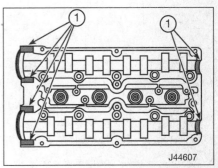

4.11 Apply sealant to the semi-circular cut-outs indicated (1)

6.2 Removing the upper outer timing belt cover

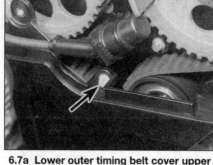

6.7a Lower outer timing belt cover upper securing bolt (arrowed) . . .

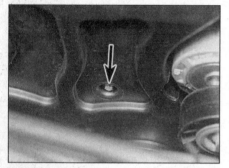

6.7b . . . and lower (arrowed) securing bolt

2 Unscrew the three securing bolts, and unclip the cover (see illustration).

Refitting

3 Refitting is a reversal of removal.

Lower outer cover

Removal

4 Apply the handbrake, then jack up the front of the vehicle and support it on axle stands (see *Jacking and vehicle support*). Remove the right-hand front roadwheel, then remove the wheel arch inner cover for access to the crankshaft pulley.

5 Remove the upper outer timing belt cover, as described previously in this Section.

6 Remove the crankshaft pulley, as described in Section 5.

7 Remove the two securing bolts, then release the four clips, and withdraw the lower outer cover (see illustrations).

7.13 Withdraw the camshaft position sensor

6.13 Rear timing belt cover securing bolts – arrowed (seen with timing belt and sprockets still fitted)

Refitting

8 Refitting is a reversal of removal, but fit the crankshaft pulley with reference to Section 5.

Rear cover

Removal

9 Remove the upper and lower outer covers as described previously in this Section.

10 Remove the timing belt, sprockets and inlet-side idler roller, as described in Sections 7 and 8.

11 Unscrew the securing bolt and remove the timing belt tensioner.

12 Unbolt the right-hand engine mounting bracket from the cylinder block.

13 Unscrew the two upper and two lower securing screws, and withdraw the rear cover from the engine (see illustration).

7.14 Timing belt tensioner securing bolt (1) and hexagon hole (2) in front plate

Refitting

14 Refitting is a reversal of removal, bearing in mind the following points:
  a) *Tighten the right-hand engine mounting bolts to the specified torque.*
  b) *Refit the timing belt sprockets as described in Section 8.*
  c) *Refit and tension the timing belt as described in Section 7.*
  d) *Refit the outer timing belt covers as described previously in this Section.*

---

7 Timing belt –
removal, refitting
and adjustment

Removal

1 Apply the handbrake, then jack up the front of the vehicle and support it on axle stands (see *Jacking and vehicle support*). Remove the right-hand front roadwheel, then remove the wheel arch inner cover for access to the crankshaft pulley.

2 Disconnect the battery negative lead (refer to *Disconnecting the battery* at the end of this manual).

3 Unscrew the oil filler cap, then undo the bolts and remove the engine top cover. Refit the cap.

4 Remove the air cleaner assembly and air duct as described in Chapter 4B.

5 Remove the auxiliary drivebelt as described in Chapter 1A. This involves locking the tensioner before removing the drivebelt.

6 With the auxiliary drivebelt removed, remove the locking pin then unscrew the bolt and remove the tensioner from the engine.

7 Turn the crankshaft to bring No 1 piston to top dead centre, as described in Section 3. If necessary, the spark plugs may be removed to enable the engine to be turned easier (refer to Chapter 1A).

8 Remove the crankshaft pulley with reference to Section 5. To enable the crankshaft to be turned, temporarily refit the crankshaft pulley retaining bolt.

9 Unscrew the bolt and unclip the lower timing belt cover.

10 Attach a suitable hoist and lifting tackle to the engine lifting brackets, and support the weight of the engine. Alternatively, support the engine with a trolley jack and block of wood positioned beneath the sump.

11 Unbolt and remove the right-hand engine mounting. There are two bolts on the engine and two bolts on the body panel.

12 Unscrew the bolts and unclip the upper timing belt cover.

13 Unscrew the two bolts securing the camshaft position sensor mounting bracket to the cylinder head, and move the sensor/bracket assembly to one side (see illustration). If necessary, disconnect the wiring.

14 Check that the timing marks are still aligned, then loosen the belt tensioner securing bolt sufficiently to completely relieve the tension in the belt. If necessary, turn the tensioner clockwise to relieve the tension, using a suitable hexagon bit or Allen key engaged with the hole provided in the tensioner front plate **(see illustration)**.

15 Slide the timing belt from the sprockets, and withdraw it from the engine **(see illustration)**. Take note of any arrows marked on the belt to indicate the direction of rotation (if necessary, mark the belt to aid correct refitting).

Refitting

16 Ensure that No 1 piston is still positioned at top dead centre, as described in Section 3.

17 If the coolant pump has been disturbed, check the position of the pump. The mark on the edge of the pump must be aligned with the corresponding mark on the cylinder block (see Chapter 3). If necessary, loosen the securing bolts, and turn the pump as required to align the marks, then tighten the bolts securely.

18 Refit the timing belt around the sprockets, starting at the crankshaft sprocket, and working in the order shown **(see illustration)**. **Note:** *When fitting the belt over the inlet camshaft sprocket, ensure that the belt does not jump a tooth on the sprocket, and make sure that the timing marks on both camshaft sprockets stay positioned directly opposite each other, and aligned with the top edge of the cylinder head. If the original timing belt is being refitted, make sure its direction of rotation is as noted before removal.*

Adjustment

Note: *The engine must be cold when checking and adjusting the timing belt tension.*

19 Check that the front section of the timing belt between the crankshaft pulley and exhaust camshaft sprocket is taut. This will ensure the slack is on the tensioner section of the belt.

20 With the tensioner securing bolt loosened, engage a suitable hexagon bit or Allen key with the hole provided in the tensioner front plate, and turn the tensioner anti-clockwise until the tension indicator pointer is positioned just before the left stop of the adjustment plate. Tighten the tensioner securing bolt in this position.

21 Using a suitable socket or spanner on the crankshaft pulley bolt, turn the crankshaft clockwise through two complete revolutions, until No 1 piston is again positioned at top dead centre. Check that the timing marks are correctly aligned as described in Section 3.

22 Engage the hexagon bit or Allen key with the hole in the tensioner adjustment plate, then slacken the tensioner securing bolt, and carefully turn the plate clockwise to slacken the belt. If a new timing belt has been fitted, the tension indicator pointer should be positioned on the NEW mark **(see illustration)**. If a 'run-in' belt has been fitted (one that has been used for more than a few hours), the tension indicator pointer should be

positioned on the USED mark. Tighten the tensioner securing bolt to the specified torque.

23 Turn the crankshaft clockwise through two complete revolutions, as described previously, and check that the tension indicator pointer is still positioned correctly – if not, repeat the procedure.

24 Where removed, refit the spark plugs with reference to Chapter 1A.

25 Refit the camshaft position sensor and mounting bracket. Clean the threads of the mounting bolts and apply locking fluid to them before inserting them and tightening them securely. Reconnect the wiring.

7.15 Sliding the timing belt from the sprockets

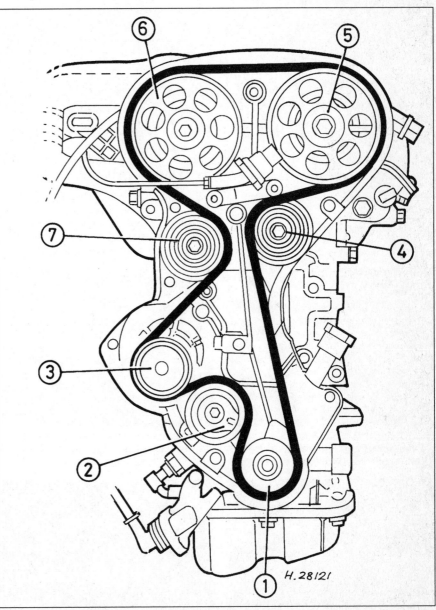

7.18 Fit the timing belt around the sprockets in the order shown

1 Crankshaft sprocket	*4 Exhaust-side idler roller*	*6 Inlet camshaft*
2 Timing belt tensioner	*5 Exhaust camshaft*	*sprocket*
3 Coolant pump sprocket	*sprocket*	*7 Inlet-side idler roller*

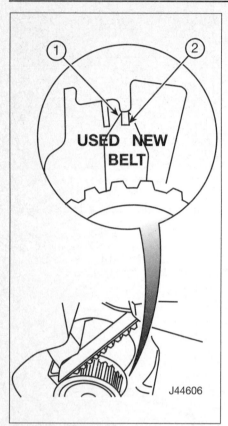

7.22 Align the pointer (1) with the relevant mark on the tensioner roller (2)

8.2a Using a Torx bit engaged with the rear timing belt cover bolt hole to counterhold the inlet camshaft sprocket

8.2b Counterholding the inlet camshaft using a spanner on the flats in front of No 1 cam lobe

8.3 Removing the inlet camshaft sprocket

8.11 Refit the crankshaft sprocket with the locating flange and pulley locating lug outermost

26 Refit the upper and lower timing belt covers.
27 Refit the right-hand engine mounting and tighten the bolts to the specified torque.
28 Remove the engine hoist or support jack.
29 Refit the crankshaft pulley with reference to Section 5.
30 Refit the auxiliary drivebelt tensioner and tighten the bolts, then refit the drivebelt with reference to Chapter 1A.
31 Refit the engine top cover, and reconnect the battery negative lead (refer to *Disconnecting the battery* at the end of this manual).
32 Refit the wheel arch inner cover, then refit the roadwheel and lower the vehicle to the ground.

8 Timing belt sprockets, tensioner and idler rollers – removal and refitting

Camshaft sprockets

Removal

1 Remove the timing belt as described in Section 7.
2 The camshaft sprocket bolt must be prevented from turning as the sprocket bolt is unscrewed, and this can be achieved in one of three ways as follows **(see illustrations)**.
   a) Pass a suitable Torx bit and extension bar through one of the holes in the camshaft sprocket, to engage with the rear timing belt cover bolt. Use the Torx bit and extension bar to counterhold the sprocket as the bolt is loosened.
   b) With the camshaft cover removed as described in Section 4, prevent the camshaft from turning by holding it with a suitable spanner on the flats provided in front of No 1 cam lobe.
   c) Make up a forked tool and use it to hold the sprocket stationary by means of the holes in the sprocket face.
3 Unscrew and remove the camshaft sprocket bolts, noting the washers under each bolt head **(see illustration)**.
4 Withdraw the sprockets from the end of the camshaft, keeping them identified for location. **Note:** *The exhaust camshaft sprocket is fitted with lugs which activate the camshaft position sensor.*

Refitting

5 Commence refitting by offering the camshaft sprockets to their respective camshafts. Each sprocket must be fitted so that the timing mark is visible on the outer face.
6 Refit the sprocket securing bolts, ensuring that the washers are in place, and tighten the bolts to the specified torque, preventing the camshaft from turning as during removal.
7 Where applicable, refit the camshaft cover as described in Section 4.
8 Refit and tension the timing belt as described in Section 7.

Crankshaft sprocket

Note: *A new crankshaft pulley retaining bolt will be required for refitting.*

Removal

9 Remove the timing belt as described in Section 7.
10 Remove the sprocket from the end of the crankshaft.

Refitting

11 Refit the crankshaft sprocket with the locating flange and locating lug for the crankshaft pulley outermost **(see illustration)**.
12 Refit and tension the timing belt as described in Section 7.

Tensioner

Removal

13 Remove the timing belt as described in Section 7.
14 Unscrew the central securing bolt, and withdraw the tensioner.

Refitting

15 Refit the tensioner, ensuring that the lug on the tensioner backplate engages with the corresponding hole in the oil pump.
16 Refit the tensioner securing bolt, but do not tighten the bolt fully until the timing belt has been tensioned.
17 Refit and tension the timing belt, as described in Section 7.

Idler rollers

Removal

18 Remove the timing belt as described in Section 7.

19 Unscrew the securing bolt, and remove the relevant idler roller.

Refitting

20 If both idler rollers have been removed, note that the larger-diameter roller fits on the inlet side of the engine (see illustration).
21 Refit the relevant idler roller, and tighten the securing bolt to the specified torque.
22 Refit the timing belt as described in Section 7.

9 Camshaft oil seals – renewal

1 Remove the relevant camshaft sprocket as described in Section 8.
2 Punch or drill a small hole in the centre of the now-exposed oil seal.
3 Screw in a self-tapping screw, and pull on the screw with pliers to extract the seal.
4 Clean the oil seal seat with a wooden or plastic scraper.
5 Wind a thin band of tape around the end of the camshaft, to protect the lips of the new oil seal as it is fitted.
6 Grease the lips of the new seal, then fit it to the housing. Ideally, the seal should be drawn into position using a suitable socket or tube and washer, and a suitable bolt (see illustration). Alternatively, the seal can be tapped into position. The seal should be fitted

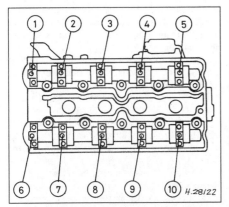

10.4a Camshaft bearing cap numbering sequence (No 1 at timing belt end)

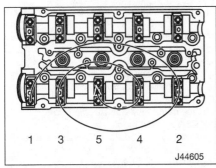

10.6 Camshaft bearing cap bolt loosening sequence

8.20 Timing belt idler rollers (arrowed)

with its outer face flush with the housing. Take care not to damage the seal lips during fitting.
7 Carefully remove the tape from the end of the camshaft.
8 Refit the camshaft sprocket as described in Section 8.

10 Camshafts and hydraulic tappets – removal, inspection and refitting

Note: New timing belt end oil seals, and a tube of suitable sealant will be required when refitting.

Removal

1 Remove the camshaft cover as described in Section 4.
2 Remove the camshaft sprockets as described in Section 8.

10.4b Camshaft bearing cap numbers (exhaust camshaft shown)

10.7a Removing a camshaft bearing cap

9.6 Fitting a new camshaft oil seal using a socket and bolt

3 Unbolt the timing belt rear cover from the cylinder head and block.
4 Check the camshaft bearing caps for identification marks, and if none are present, make corresponding marks on the bearing caps and the top surface of the cylinder head using a centre-punch (take care not to damage the cylinder head or bearing caps). Note the orientation of the bearing caps before removal, as they must be refitted in exactly the same positions from which they are removed. The inlet (rear) camshaft caps are usually numbered 1 to 5, and the exhaust (front) camshaft caps 6 to 10, with corresponding numbers cast into the cylinder head (see illustrations).
5 Before removing the camshaft, check the endfloat using a dial gauge or a feeler gauge. If the endfloat is outside the specified limits, the camshaft must be renewed.
6 Working on one camshaft at a time, progressively loosen the bearing cap bolts, a half or one turn at a time, in the inward spiral sequence shown (see illustration). This is necessary to progressively relieve the tension in the valve springs, and prevent undue stress on the camshaft.
7 With all of the bolts removed, withdraw the bearing caps from the cylinder head, then lift out the camshafts, keeping them identified for location (see illustrations).
8 Remove the hydraulic valve lifters (tappets) from their bores, using a rubber suction plunger tool – do not invert the cylinder head in order to remove the valve lifters. Keep the valve lifters upright at all times, with the oil groove at the bottom (see illustration). Immerse them, in

10.7b Lifting the exhaust camshaft from the cylinder head

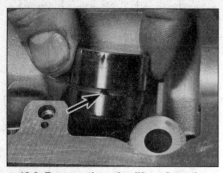

10.8 Remove the valve lifters from the cylinder head, and store with the oil groove (arrowed) at the bottom

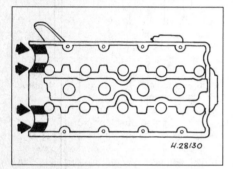

10.13 Coat the timing belt end bearing cap mating faces of the cylinder head (arrowed) with sealing compound

order of removal, in a container of clean engine oil until they are to be refitted.

Inspection

9 With the camshafts removed, examine the bearing surfaces in the cylinder head for signs of obvious wear or pitting. If evident, the cylinder head and all the bearing caps must be renewed as a matched set, as it is not possible to renew the bearings individually. The camshafts should show no marks or scoring on the journal or cam lobe surfaces. If evident, renew them.

10 It is advisable to renew the oil seals as a matter of course. Prise the old seals from the camshafts and discard them.

Refitting

11 Commence refitting by turning the

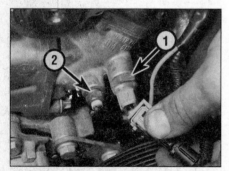

11.6 Disconnect the wiring from the coolant temperature sensor (1) and the temperature gauge sender (2)

10.12 Lubricate the contact faces of the valve lifters, camshaft lobes and bearings with molybdenum disulphide paste

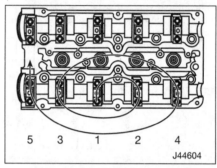

10.16 Camshaft bearing cap bolt tightening sequence (exhaust camshaft shown)

crankshaft anti-clockwise by 60°. This will position Nos 1 and 4 pistons a third of the way down the bore, and prevent any chance of the valves touching the piston crowns as the camshafts are being fitted. This could happen if any of the hydraulic valve lifters have excessive oil in them before the pressure of the valve springs forces it out.

12 Lubricate the cylinder head hydraulic tappet bores, tappets, camshaft lobes, and bearing surfaces (see illustration). Carefully refit the tappets to the cylinder head, ensuring that each tappet is refitted to its original bore.

13 Coat the timing belt end bearing cap mating faces on the cylinder head with sealant (see illustration).

14 Place the camshafts in their original positions on the cylinder head, temporarily refit the camshaft sprockets, and check that the timing marks are still aligned with No 1 piston at TDC, as described in Section 3. Remove the sprockets.

15 Loosely refit the bearing caps in their original positions as noted during removal, then insert the bolts and finger-tighten them.

16 Working on one camshaft at a time, progressively tighten the bearing cap bolts to the specified torque, one turn at a time, in the outward spiral sequence shown (see illustration).

17 Wipe away any excess sealant from the timing belt end bearing caps.

18 Lubricate the lips of the new camshaft oil seals with a little grease, and fit them as described in Section 9.

19 Refit the timing belt rear cover and tighten the bolts.

20 Refit the camshaft sprockets as described in Section 8.

21 Refit the camshaft cover as described in Section 4.

11 Cylinder head – removal and refitting

Note: *The engine must be cold when removing the cylinder head. A new cylinder head gasket and new cylinder head bolts must be used on refitting.*

Removal

1 Apply the handbrake, then jack up the front of the vehicle and support it on axle stands (see *Jacking and vehicle support*). Remove the right-hand front roadwheel, then remove the wheel arch inner cover for access to the crankshaft pulley.

2 Depressurise the fuel system as described in Chapter 4B.

3 Disconnect the battery negative lead (refer to *Disconnecting the battery* at the end of this manual).

4 Drain the cooling system as described in Chapter 1A.

5 Remove the camshaft cover as described in Section 4.

6 Disconnect the wiring from the coolant temperature sensor (and temperature gauge sender, if fitted) on the thermostat housing on the right-hand front of the cylinder head (see illustration).

7 Remove the camshaft sprockets, timing belt tensioner, and the timing belt idler rollers, as described in Section 8.

8 Remove the rear timing belt cover with reference to Section 6.

9 Refer to Chapter 4B and unbolt the exhaust front pipe from the exhaust manifold, taking care to support the flexible section. **Note:** *Angular movement in excess of 10° can cause permanent damage to the flexible section.* Release the mounting rubbers and support the front of the exhaust pipe to one side.

10 Unscrew the upper bolt securing the support bracket to the inlet manifold, and loosen only the bottom bolt.

11 Unscrew the bolt and remove the earth cable, then disconnect the engine management wiring loom from the following, noting its routing:

a) *Throttle body.*
b) *Knock sensor.*
c) *Inlet absolute pressure sensor.*
d) *EGR valve.*
e) *Engine control unit (throttle body).*
f) *Combination plug.*
g) *Crankshaft speed/position sensor (see illustration).*
h) *Oil pressure switch.*

12 Release the cable ties and place the wiring loom to one side.

11.11 Disconnect the wiring from the crankshaft speed/position sensor

11.14 Disconnecting the fuel return hose from the fuel pressure regulator

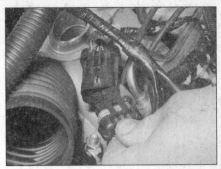

11.15 Disconnect the wiring connectors for the fuel injectors

11.18 Disconnect the coolant hose from the thermostat housing

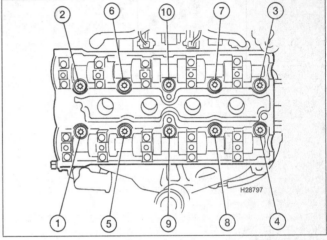

11.23a Cylinder head bolt loosening sequence

13 Unscrew the three securing bolts, and remove the upper alternator mounting bracket. Pivot the alternator rearwards away from the manifold as far as it will go.

14 Unscrew the union nut, and disconnect the return hose from the fuel pressure regulator **(see illustration)**. Be prepared for fuel spillage, and clamp or plug the hose to reduce fuel loss and to prevent dirt ingress. Similarly, disconnect the fuel supply hose from the fuel rail.

15 Disconnect the wiring from the injectors **(see illustration)**, then unscrew the bolts and remove the fuel rail.

16 Refer to Chapter 4B, Section 10, and remove the throttle body and the manifold absolute pressure sensor.

17 Remove the inlet manifold with reference to Chapter 4B.

18 Loosen the clips and remove the upper hose from the radiator and thermostat housing **(see illustration)**.

19 Loosen the clips and disconnect the two heater hoses from the left-hand end of the cylinder head.

20 Remove the engine vent flange from the engine control unit bracket.

21 Remove the exhaust manifold with reference to Chapter 4B. Recover the gasket.

22 Make a final check to ensure that all

relevant hoses, pipes and wires have been disconnected.

23 Working in a spiral pattern from the outside inwards, progressively loosen the cylinder head bolts. First loosen all the bolts by quarter of a turn, then loosen all the bolts by half a turn, then finally slacken all the bolts fully and withdraw them from the cylinder head. Recover the washers **(see illustrations)**.

24 Lift the cylinder head from the cylinder block **(see illustration)**. If necessary, tap the cylinder head gently with a soft-faced mallet to free it from the block, but **do not** lever at the mating faces. Note that the cylinder head is located on dowels.

11.23b Remove the cylinder head bolts and washers

25 Recover the cylinder head gasket, and discard it.

Refitting

26 Clean the cylinder head and block mating faces by careful scraping. Take care not to damage the cylinder head, which is made of light alloy, and is easily scored. Cover the coolant passages and other openings with masking tape or rag, to prevent dirt and carbon falling in. Mop out all the oil from the bolt holes; if oil is left in the holes, hydraulic pressure could crack the block when the bolts are refitted.

27 Turn the crankshaft so that all the pistons

11.24 Lifting the cylinder head from the cylinder block

11.28 Cylinder head gasket OBEN/TOP marking should be at timing belt end of engine

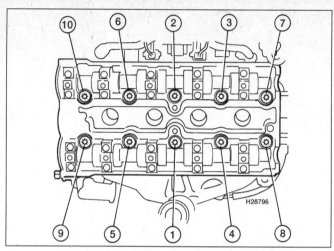
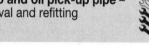

11.31a Cylinder head bolt tightening sequence

are positioned approximately half way down their bores. This will prevent the possibility of the valves contacting the pistons as the cylinder head is refitted.

28 Commence refitting by locating a new cylinder head gasket on the block, so that the word OBEN or TOP is uppermost at the timing belt end of the engine (see illustration).

29 With the mating faces scrupulously clean, locate the cylinder head on the block so that the positioning dowels engage in their holes.

30 Fit the **new** cylinder head bolts, ensuring that (where fitted) the washers are in place under their heads, and screw in the bolts *by hand* as far as possible.

31 Tighten the bolts in the sequence shown and in the five stages given in the Specifications – ie, tighten all bolts to the Stage 1 torque using a torque wrench, then tighten all bolts to Stage 2, and so on using an angle tightening gauge (see illustrations).

32 Refit the exhaust manifold together with a new gasket with reference to Chapter 4B.

33 Refit the engine vent flange to the engine control unit bracket.

34 Reconnect the two heater hoses to the left-hand end of the cylinder head and tighten the clips.

35 Refit the upper hose to the radiator and thermostat housing and tighten the clips.

11.31b Tightening a cylinder head bolt using an angle gauge

36 Refit the inlet manifold with reference to Chapter 4B.

37 Refer to Chapter 4B, and refit the throttle body and the manifold absolute pressure sensor.

38 Refit the fuel rail and tighten the mounting bolts, then reconnect the wiring to the injectors.

39 Reconnect the supply hose to the fuel rail, and the return hose to the fuel pressure regulator.

40 Refit the alternator upper mounting bracket and tighten the bolts.

41 Reconnect the wiring to the components listed in paragraph 11, then secure the wiring with cable ties.

42 Refit the inlet manifold support bracket and tighten the bolts.

43 Refer to Chapter 4B and refit the exhaust front pipe to the exhaust manifold. Refit the mounting rubbers.

44 Refit the rear timing belt cover with reference to Section 6.

45 Refit the camshaft sprockets, timing belt tensioner, and the timing belt idler rollers, with reference to Section 8.

46 Reconnect the wiring to the coolant temperature sensor (and temperature gauge sender, where fitted) on the thermostat housing on the right-hand front of the cylinder head.

47 Refit the camshaft cover with reference to Section 4.

48 Refit the wheel arch inner cover and front roadwheel, then lower the vehicle to the ground.

49 Reconnect the battery negative lead (refer to *Disconnecting the battery* at the end of this manual).

50 Check that all relevant hoses, pipes and wires, etc, have been reconnected. Check the security of the fuel hose connections.

51 Refill and bleed the cooling system with reference to Chapter 1A.

52 When the engine is started, check for signs of oil or coolant leakage.

12 Sump and oil pick-up pipe – removal and refitting

Removal

1 Apply the handbrake, then jack up the front of the vehicle and support it on axle stands (see *Jacking and vehicle support*). Remove the right-hand front roadwheel, then remove the wheel arch inner cover for access to the crankshaft pulley end of the engine.

2 Disconnect the battery negative lead (refer to *Disconnecting the battery* at the end of this manual).

3 Drain the engine oil as described in Chapter 1A, then clean the drain plug, renew the sealing ring, refit the plug and tighten it securely.

4 Disconnect the wiring from the oxygen sensor and release it from the support bracket.

5 Refer to Chapter 4B and unbolt the exhaust front pipe from the exhaust manifold, taking care to support the flexible section. **Note:** *Angular movement in excess of 10° can cause permanent damage to the flexible section.* Release the mounting rubbers and support the front of the exhaust pipe to one side.

6 Prise out the closure plug from the transmission end of the sump.

7 Unscrew and remove the bolts securing the sump to the transmission.

8 Unscrew and remove the bolts securing the sump to the oil pump housing.

9 Unscrew the securing bolts, and withdraw the sump. If necessary, tap the sump with a soft-faced mallet to free it from the cylinder block – **do not** lever between the sump and cylinder block mating faces.

10 If desired, the oil pick-up pipe can be removed by unscrewing the single bolt securing the support bracket to the cylinder block and the two bolts securing the pipe flange to the oil pump. Recover the O-ring.

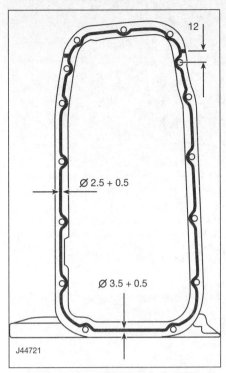

Ø 2.5 + 0.5

Ø 3.5 + 0.5

J44721

12.13 Apply an even bead of sealing compound to the sump mating face

Refitting

11 Clean all traces of the old gasket from the mating faces of the cylinder block and sump. Also clean the threads of the sump securing bolts.

12 If the oil pick-up pipe has been removed, refit it together with a new O-ring, and tighten the mounting bolts securely.

13 Apply an even bead of sealing compound to the sump mating face as shown **(see illustration)**. **Note:** *According to the sealant used, refitting must be completed within 10 minutes.*

14 Refit the sump to the cylinder block, insert the bolts, and tighten them progressively to the specified torque, noting that the transmission bolts are tightened to a higher torque than the remaining bolts.

15 Refit the closure plug.

16 Refer to Chapter 4B and refit the exhaust

13.7 Removing an oil pump rear cover securing screw

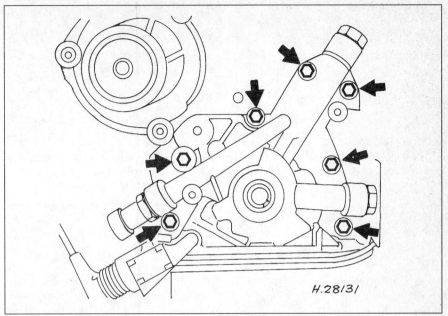

H.28/31

13.5 Oil pump securing bolts (arrowed)

front pipe to the exhaust manifold. Refit the mounting rubbers.

17 Reconnect the wiring to the oxygen sensor and clip it onto the support bracket.

18 Reconnect the battery negative lead (refer to *Disconnecting the battery* at the end of this manual).

19 Refit the wheel arch inner cover and roadwheel, then lower the vehicle to the ground.

20 Refill the engine with oil as described in Chapter 1A.

13 Oil pump –
removal, inspection and refitting

Note: *A new oil pump gasket and a new crankshaft oil seal must be used on refitting.*

Removal

1 Remove the rear timing belt cover as described in Section 6.

2 Remove the sump and oil pick-up pipe as described in Section 12.

3 Disconnect the wiring from the oil pressure switch mounted in the oil pump.

4 Where necessary, unbolt the crankshaft speed/position sensor bracket from the oil pump. Move the sensor/bracket assembly to one side, taking care not to damage the sensor.

5 Remove the securing bolts, and withdraw the oil pump from the cylinder block **(see illustration)**. Recover the gasket.

Inspection

Note: *A new pressure relief valve sealing ring should be used on reassembly, and sealing compound will be required to coat the pump housing mating face.*

6 With the oil pump removed, proceed as follows.

7 Remove the securing screws and withdraw the rear cover **(see illustration)**. The screws may be very tight, in which case it may be necessary to use an impact driver to remove them.

8 The oil pressure relief valve components can be removed from the pump by unscrewing the cap. Withdraw the cap, sealing ring, spring and plunger **(see illustration)**.

9 Prise the oil seal from the pump using a screwdriver.

10 Check the clearance between the inner and outer gear teeth (backlash) using a feeler gauge **(see illustration)**.

11 Check the clearance between the end faces of the gears and the housing (endfloat) using a straight-edge and a feeler gauge **(see illustration)**.

12 If any of the clearances are outside the specified limits, renew the components as necessary.

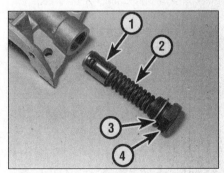

13.8 Oil pressure relief valve components

1 *Plunger*   3 *Sealing ring*
2 *Spring*   4 *Plug*

13.10 Check the clearance between the inner and outer gear teeth . . .

13.11 . . . and between the end faces of the gears and the housing

13.16 Gear outer face identification mark (arrowed)

13.18 Fitting a new crankshaft oil seal to the oil pump

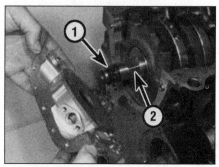

13.21 Refitting the oil pump (shown with engine removed from vehicle and inverted)

1 Tape wound around crankshaft
2 Flats on crankshaft engage with inner oil pump gear

22 Tighten the securing bolts securely, then carefully remove the tape from the crankshaft.
23 Where necessary, refit the crankshaft speed/position sensor and its securing bracket, and tighten the securing bolt.
24 Reconnect the wiring to the oil pressure switch.
25 Refit the oil pick-up pipe and sump, as described in Section 12.
26 Refit the rear timing belt cover as described in Section 6.

14 Crankshaft oil seals – renewal

Timing belt end oil seal

1 Remove the crankshaft sprocket as described in Section 8.
2 Punch or drill a small hole in the centre of the now-exposed oil seal.
3 Screw in a self-tapping screw, and pull on the screw with pliers to extract the seal **(see illustration)**. Several attempts may be necessary. Be careful not to damage the sealing face of the crankshaft.
4 Clean the oil seal seat with a wooden or plastic scraper.
5 Wind a thin band of tape around the end of the crankshaft, to protect the lips of the new oil seal as it is fitted.
6 Grease the lips of the new seal, and tap it into position until it is flush with the outer face of the oil pump body, using a suitable socket or tube **(see illustration)**. Take care not to damage the seal lips during fitting.
7 Carefully remove the tape from the end of the crankshaft.
8 Refit the crankshaft sprocket, as described in Section 8.

Flywheel end oil seal

9 Remove the flywheel/driveplate as described in Section 15.
10 Proceed as described in paragraphs 2 to 4 inclusive of this Section.
11 Grease the lips of the new seal, then tap the seal into position using a suitable tube, until flush with the outer faces of the cylinder block and main bearing cap.

13 Examine the pressure relief valve spring and plunger, and renew if any sign of damage or wear is evident.
14 Ensure that the interior of the pump body is scrupulously clean before commencing reassembly.
15 Discard the old pressure relief valve sealing ring, then thoroughly clean the pressure relief valve components, and lubricate them with clean engine oil before refitting. Use a new sealing ring.
16 Ensure that the gears are clean, then lubricate them with clean engine oil, and refit them to the pump body, noting that the outer gear is marked with a punch dot to indicate its outer face (ie, the face nearest the pump cover) **(see illustration)**.
17 Ensure that the mating faces of the rear cover and the pump housing are clean, then coat the pump housing mating face with

suitable sealing compound, and refit the rear cover. Refit and tighten the securing screws.
18 Fit a new crankshaft oil seal to the recess in the pump body, using a suitable socket or tube, so that the seal is flush with the outer face of the housing **(see illustration)**.

Refitting

19 Thoroughly clean the mating faces of the oil pump and cylinder block, then locate a new gasket on the block.
20 Wind a thin layer of tape around the end of the crankshaft, to prevent damage to the oil seal lips as the pump is refitted.
21 With the new oil seal fitted, grease the oil seal lips, then refit the pump, ensuring that the inner gear engages with the flats on the crankshaft **(see illustration)**.

14.3 Using a self-tapping screw and a pair of pliers to extract the crankshaft oil seal

14.6 Tapping a new crankshaft oil seal into position

HAYNES HiNT *Wind a length of tape around the end of the crankshaft to reduce the possibility of damage to the lips of the oil seal as the seal is fitted.*

12 Refit the flywheel/driveplate as described in Section 15.

15 Flywheel/driveplate – removal, inspection and refitting

Note: *New flywheel/driveplate securing bolts must be used on refitting.*

Removal

1 Remove the manual gearbox as described in Chapter 7A, or the automatic transmission as described in Chapter 7B, as applicable.
2 On manual gearbox models, remove the clutch as described in Chapter 6.
3 Although the flywheel/driveplate bolt holes are offset so that the flywheel/driveplate can only be fitted in one position, it will make refitting easier if alignment marks are made between the flywheel/driveplate and the end of the crankshaft.
4 Prevent the flywheel/driveplate from turning by locking the ring gear teeth using a suitable tool.
5 Unscrew the securing bolts, and remove the flywheel/driveplate **(see illustration)**.
Caution: Take care, as it is heavy.

Inspection

6 If the teeth on the starter ring are badly worn, or if some are missing, then it will be necessary to remove the ring and fit a new one.
7 The old ring can be split with a cold chisel, after drilling or making a cut with a hacksaw blade between two gear teeth. Take great care not to damage the flywheel during this operation, and wear eye protection at all times. Once the ring has been split, it will spread apart, and can be lifted from the flywheel.
8 The new ring gear must be heated evenly to between 180 and 230ºC. Unless facilities for heating by oven or flame are available, leave the fitting to a Vauxhall dealer or engineering works. The new ring gear must not be overheated during this work, or the temper of the metal will be affected.
9 The ring should be tapped gently down onto its register, and left to cool naturally – the contraction of the metal on cooling will ensure that it is a secure and permanent fit.
10 If the clutch friction disc contact surface of the flywheel is scored, or on close inspection, shows signs of small hair cracks (caused by overheating), it may be possible to have the flywheel surface-ground, provided the overall thickness of the flywheel is not reduced too much. Consult a Vauxhall dealer

or a specialist engine repairer, and if grinding is not possible, renew the flywheel complete.

Refitting

11 Offer the flywheel/driveplate to the end of the crankshaft, and align with the previously-made mark on the crankshaft.
12 Coat the threads of the new bolts with thread-locking compound (note that new bolts may be supplied ready-coated), then fit the bolts and tighten them as given in the Specifications, whilst preventing the flywheel/driveplate from turning as during removal **(see illustrations)**.
13 Where applicable, refit the clutch as described in Chapter 6.
14 Refit the manual gearbox, or automatic transmission as described in Chapter 7A or 7B, as applicable.

16 Engine/transmission mountings – inspection and renewal

Inspection

1 To improve access, firmly apply the handbrake, then jack up the front of the vehicle and support it on axle stands (see *Jacking and vehicle support*).
2 Check the mounting blocks (rubbers) to see if they are cracked, hardened or separated from the metal at any point. Renew the mounting block if any such damage or deterioration is evident.

15.5 Removing the flywheel

15.12b Tighten the flywheel securing bolts to the specified torque . . .

3 Check that all the mounting securing nuts and bolts are securely tightened, using a torque wrench to check if possible.
4 Using a large screwdriver, or a similar tool, check for wear in the mounting blocks by carefully levering against them to check for free play. Where this is not possible, enlist the aid of an assistant to move the engine/transmission unit back-and-forth, and from side-to-side, while you observe the mountings. While some free play is to be expected, even from new components, excessive wear should be obvious. If excessive free play is found, check first to see that the securing nuts and bolts are correctly tightened, then renew any worn components as described in the following paragraphs.

Renewal

Note: *Before slackening any of the engine mounting bolts/nuts, the relative positions of the mountings to their various brackets should be marked to ensure correct alignment upon refitting.*

Right-hand mounting

5 Apply the handbrake, then jack up the front of the vehicle and support it on axle stands (see *Jacking and vehicle support*). Remove the right-hand roadwheel and the wheel arch liner for access to the crankshaft pulley.
6 Remove the air cleaner as described in Chapter 4B.
7 Attach a suitable hoist and lifting tackle to the engine lifting brackets on the cylinder head, and support the weight of the engine.
8 Unscrew the four mounting bolts and

15.12a Tool for preventing the flywheel from turning, secured using an engine-to-gearbox bolt

15.12c . . . and then through the specified angle

remove the right-hand mounting from the engine mounting bracket and body. **Note:** *The lower mounting bracket can only be unbolted from the cylinder block after removal of the timing belt.*

9 Locate the new mounting block on the body and engine mounting bracket, and tighten the bolts to the specified torque.

10 Remove the hoist, then refit the air cleaner.

11 Refit the wheel arch liner and right-hand roadwheel, then lower the vehicle to the ground.

Left-hand mounting

12 Release the clips and position the coolant expansion tank to one side.

13 Attach a suitable hoist and lifting tackle to the engine lifting brackets on the cylinder head, and support the weight of the engine.

14 Using a Torx socket, unscrew the two bolts securing the engine mounting bracket to the body mounting bracket.

15 Unbolt the mounting brackets from the engine and body. On manual transmission models, slightly lower the engine, then unclip the clutch hydraulic line from the mounting bracket.

16 Unscrew the bolt and separate the adaptor block.

17 Fit the new adaptor block and tighten the bolt to the specified torque.

18 Locate the new mounting brackets in position and, where necessary, clip the clutch hydraulic line onto the bracket.

19 Raise the engine and insert the bolts, then tighten them to the specified torque.

20 Disconnect the hoist and lifting tackle.

21 Refit the coolant expansion tank and attach the clips.

Rear mounting/torque link

22 Apply the handbrake, then jack up the front of the vehicle and support it on axle stands (see *Jacking and vehicle support*).

23 Attach a suitable hoist and lifting tackle to the engine lifting brackets on the cylinder head, and support the weight of the engine.

24 Refer to Chapter 4B and unbolt the exhaust front pipe from the exhaust manifold, taking care to support the flexible section. **Note:** *Angular movement in excess of 10° can cause permanent damage to the flexible section.*

25 Release the mounting rubbers and support the front of the exhaust pipe to one side.

26 Working under the vehicle, remove the nut and bolt securing the mounting to the transmission bracket.

27 Remove the bolt securing the mounting to the subframe, and withdraw the mounting/torque link.

28 If necessary, unbolt the bracket from the transmission. **Note:** *The bracket bolts and link bolts are of different lengths.*

29 Refit the bracket to the transmission and tighten the bolts to the specified torque.

30 Locate the new mounting/link in position. Insert the bolts and tighten to the specified torque.

31 Refit the exhaust front pipe with reference to Chapter 4B.

32 Remove the hoist and lower the vehicle to the ground.

Chapter 2 Part C:
Diesel engine in-car repair procedures

Contents

Degrees of difficulty

Easy, suitable for novice with little experience	Fairly easy, suitable for beginner with some experience	Fairly difficult, suitable for competent DIY mechanic	Difficult, suitable for experienced DIY mechanic	Very difficult, suitable for expert DIY or professional

Specifications

Note: *Where specifications are given as N/A, no information was available at the time of writing.*
Refer to your Vauxhall dealer for the latest information available.

General

Engine type	Four-cylinder, in-line, water-cooled. Belt-driven double overhead camshaft, 16 valves
Manufacturer's engine code:	
With intercooler	Y17DT
Without intercooler	Y17DTL
Bore	79.0 mm
Stroke	86.0 mm
Capacity	1686 cc
Firing order	1-3-4-2 (No 1 cylinder at timing belt end)
Direction of crankshaft rotation	Clockwise (viewed from timing belt end of engine)
Compression ratio	18.4:1
Maximum power:	
Y17DT	55 kW at 4400 rpm
Y17DTL	48 kW at 4400 rpm
Maximum torque:	
Y17DT	165 Nm at 1800 to 3000 rpm
Y17DTL	130 Nm at 2000 to 3000 rpm

Compression pressures

Standard	26.0 to 30.0 bar
Maximum difference between any two cylinders	1.5 bar

Valve clearances

Engine cold:	
Inlet and exhaust	0.40 ± 0.05 mm

Camshaft

Endfloat	N/A
Maximum permissible radial run-out	0.05 mm

Camshaft lift:

Inlet valve	7.8 to 7.68 mm
Exhaust valve	7.95 to 7.77 mm

Bearing running clearance:

Standard	N/A
Service limit	N/A

Lubrication system

Oil pump type	Rotor-type, driven by timing belt
Minimum permissible oil pressure at idle speed, with engine at operating temperature (oil temperature of at least 80°C)	1.27 bar (18 psi)

Oil pump clearances:	Standard	Service limit
Outer rotor-to-body clearance	0.24 to 0.36 mm	0.40 mm
Inner-to-outer rotor clearance	0.13 to 0.15 mm	0.20 mm
Rotor endfloat	0.035 to 0.100 mm	0.150 mm

Torque wrench settings

	Nm	lbf ft
Alternator support bracket to block:		
M10 bolt	48	35
M14 bolt	68	50
Alternator to support bracket:		
M8 bolt	19	14
M10 bolt	46	34
Auxiliary belt guide roller to alternator support	38	28
Auxiliary belt tensioner to alternator support	50	37
Baffle plate-to-cylinder block bolts	19	14
Big-end bearing cap nuts*:		
Stage 1	24	18
Stage 2	Angle-tighten a further 100°	
Stage 3	Angle-tighten a further 15°	
Camshaft bearing cap nuts:		
M8 nuts	22	16
M10 nuts	43	32
Camshaft housing bolts	22	16
Camshaft sprocket bolt	64	47
Camshaft thrust plate	8	6
Coolant pipe to cylinder block	95	70
Coolant pump:		
Pulley retaining bolts	10	7
Pump retaining bolts	24	18
Crankshaft pulley/vibration damper to sprocket	20	15
Crankshaft sprocket bolt	196	145
Cylinder head bolts*:		
Stage 1	39	29
Stage 2	Angle-tighten a further 60°	
Stage 3	Angle-tighten a further 13°	
Stage 4	Angle-tighten a further 60°	
Stage 5	Angle-tighten a further 13°	
Engine control unit bracket to camshaft housing:		
Bolt	25	18
Nut	10	7
Engine mountings:		
Front torque link:		
Mounting-to-transmission bolts	60	44
Mounting to subframe	55	41
Left-hand:		
Mounting to body	25	18
Mounting adaptor block:		
Stage 1	80	59
Stage 2	Angle-tighten a further 45°	
Stage 3	Angle-tighten a further 15°	
Mounting to transmission:		
Stage 1	80	59
Stage 2	Angle-tighten a further 60°	
Stage 3	Angle-tighten a further 15°	

Torque wrench settings (continued)

	Nm	lbf ft
Engine mountings (continued):		
Rear torque link:		
Torque link to subframe and transmission bracket	80	59
Torque link bracket to transmission:		
Stage 1	80	59
Stage 2	Angle-tighten a further 45°	
Stage 3	Angle-tighten a further 15°	
Right-hand:		
Mounting to body	40	30
Mounting to engine bracket:		
Stage 1	60	44
Stage 2	Angle-tighten a further 30°	
Stage 3	Angle-tighten a further 15°	
Engine-to-transmission unit bolts:		
M10 bolts	40	30
M12 bolts	60	44
Engine transport shackles	20	15
Exhaust manifold	24	18
Front suspension subframe*:		
Stage 1	90	66
Stage 2	Angle-tighten a further 45°	
Stage 3	Angle-tighten a further 15°	
Flywheel bolts*:		
Stage 1	30	22
Stage 2	Angle-tighten a further 60°	
Stage 3	Angle-tighten a further 15°	
Injection pump sprocket nut	69	51
Injector pipe unions	23	17
Inlet manifold	25	18
Main bearing cap bolts	88	65
Oil drain plug	78	58
Oil filter housing cover	25	18
Oil filter housing to cylinder block	25	18
Oil pressure relief valve bolt	30	22
Oil pressure switch	21	15
Oil pump pick-up/strainer bolts	19	14
Oil pump sprocket to pump	44	32
Sump bolts:		
Sump pan-to-upper housing bolts	10	7
Upper housing-to-block bolts	10	7
Upper housing to transmission	40	30
Thermostat housing cover	24	18
Thermostat housing to cylinder head	24	18
Timing belt idler pulley bolt	80	59
Timing belt tensioner pulley to cylinder block	38	28

*Use new fasteners

1 General information

This Part of Chapter 2 describes those repair procedures that can reasonably be carried out on the 1.7 litre DOHC diesel engine while it remains in the car. If the engine has been removed from the car and is being dismantled as described in Part D, any preliminary dismantling procedures can be ignored.

Note that, while it may be possible physically to overhaul items such as the piston/connecting rod assemblies while the engine is in the car, such tasks are not normally carried out as separate operations.

Usually, several additional procedures (not to mention the cleaning of components and of oil ways) have to be carried out. For this reason, all such tasks are classed as major overhaul procedures, and are described in Part D of this Chapter.

Part D describes the removal of the engine/transmission unit from the vehicle, and the full overhaul procedures that can then be carried out.

Engine description

The 1.7 litre (1686 cc) direct injection diesel engine is of sixteen-valve, in-line four-cylinder, double overhead camshaft (DOHC) type, mounted transversely at the front of the car with the transmission attached to its left-hand end.

The crankshaft runs in five main bearings.

Thrustwashers are fitted to No 2 main bearing shell (upper half) to control crankshaft endfloat.

The connecting rods rotate on horizontally-split bearing shells at their big-ends. The pistons are attached to the connecting rods by gudgeon pins, which are a sliding fit in the connecting rod small-end eyes and retained by circlips. The aluminium-alloy pistons are fitted with three piston rings – two compression rings and an oil control ring.

The cylinder block is made of cast iron and the cylinder bores are an integral part of the block. On this type of engine the cylinder bores are sometimes referred to as having dry liners.

The inlet and exhaust valves are each closed by coil springs, and operate in guides pressed into the cylinder head.

The inlet camshaft is driven by the crankshaft by a timing belt and rotates directly in the camshaft housing. The exhaust camshaft is driven by the inlet camshaft via a spur gear. The camshafts operate the valves via followers, which are situated directly below the camshafts. Valve clearances are adjusted using shims which are fitted between the camshafts and followers.

Lubrication is by means of an oil pump, which is driven by the timing belt. It draws oil through a strainer located in the sump, and then forces it through an externally-mounted filter into galleries in the cylinder block/crankcase. From there, the oil is distributed to the crankshaft (main bearings) and camshaft. The big-end bearings are supplied with oil via internal drillings in the crankshaft, while the camshaft bearings also receive a pressurised supply. The camshaft lobes and valves are lubricated by splash, as are all other engine components. An oil cooler is fitted to keep the oil temperature stable under arduous operating conditions.

Operations with engine in place

The following work can be carried out with the engine in the car:
a) Compression pressure testing.
b) Camshaft cover – removal and refitting.
c) Timing belt cover – removal and refitting.
d) Timing belt – removal and refitting.
e) Timing belt tensioner and sprockets – removal and refitting.
f) Valve clearances – checking and adjustment.
g) Camshafts and followers – removal, inspection and refitting.
h) Cylinder head – removal and refitting.
i) Connecting rods and pistons – removal and refitting*.
j) Sump – removal and refitting.
k) Oil pump – removal, overhaul and refitting.
l) Oil cooler – removal and refitting.
m) Crankshaft oil seals – renewal.
n) Engine/transmission mountings – inspection and renewal.
o) Flywheel – removal, inspection and refitting.
p) Camshaft housing – removal and refitting.

3.5 Align the timing mark on the crankshaft pulley with the pointer on the oil pump cover to bring No 1 piston to TDC

* Although the operation marked with an asterisk can be carried out with the engine in the car after removal of the sump, it is better for the engine to be removed, in the interests of cleanliness and improved access. For this reason, the procedure is described in Chapter 2D.

2 Compression test – description and interpretation

Compression test

Note: *A compression tester specifically designed for diesel engines must be used for this test.*

1 When engine performance is down, or if misfiring occurs which cannot be attributed to the fuel system, a compression test can provide diagnostic clues as to the engine's condition. If the test is performed regularly, it can give warning of trouble before any other symptoms become apparent.

2 A compression tester specifically intended for diesel engines must be used, because of the higher pressures involved. The tester is connected to an adapter which screws into the glow plug or injector hole. On these models, an adapter suitable for use in the glow plug holes will be required, due to the design of the injectors. It is unlikely to be worthwhile buying such a tester for occasional use, but it may be possible to borrow or hire one – if not, have the test performed by a garage.

3 Unless specific instructions to the contrary are supplied with the tester, observe the following points:
a) The battery must be in a good state of charge, the air filter must be clean, and the engine should be at normal operating temperature.
b) All the glow plugs should be removed before starting the test (see Chapter 5C).
c) Release the retaining clip and disconnect the wiring connector from the fuel injection pump control unit (see Chapter 4C) to prevent the engine from running or fuel from being discharged.

4 There is no need to hold the accelerator pedal down during the test, because the diesel engine air inlet is not throttled.

5 Crank the engine on the starter motor; after one or two revolutions, the compression pressure should build-up to a maximum figure, and then stabilise. Record the highest reading obtained.

6 Repeat the test on the remaining cylinders, recording the pressure in each.

7 All cylinders should produce very similar pressures; any difference greater than that specified indicates the existence of a fault. Note that the compression should build-up quickly in a healthy engine; low compression on the first stroke, followed by gradually-increasing pressure on successive strokes, indicates worn piston rings. A low compression reading on the first stroke, which does not build-up during successive strokes, indicates leaking valves or a blown head gasket (a cracked head could also be the cause). **Note:** *The cause of poor compression is less easy to establish on a diesel engine than on a petrol one. The effect of introducing oil into the cylinders ('wet' testing) is not conclusive, because there is a risk that the oil will sit in the recess on the piston crown instead of passing to the rings.*

8 On completion of the test, reconnect the injection pump wiring connector then refit the glow plugs as described in Chapter 5C.

Leakdown test

9 A leakdown test measures the rate at which compressed air fed into the cylinder is lost. It is an alternative to a compression test, and in many ways it is better, since the escaping air provides easy identification of where pressure loss is occurring (piston rings, valves or head gasket).

10 The equipment needed for leakdown testing is unlikely to be available to the home mechanic. If poor compression is suspected, have the test performed by a dealership.

3 Top dead centre (TDC) for No 1 piston – locating

Note: *If the engine is to be locked in position with No 1 piston at TDC on its compression stroke then a M6 and M8 bolt will be required.*

1 In its travel up and down its cylinder bore, Top Dead Centre (TDC) is the highest point that each piston reaches as the crankshaft rotates. While each piston reaches TDC both at the top of the compression stroke and again at the top of the exhaust stroke, for the purpose of timing the engine, TDC refers to the No 1 piston position at the top of its compression stroke.

2 Number 1 piston (and cylinder) is at the right-hand (timing belt) end of the engine, and its TDC position is located as follows. Note that the crankshaft rotates clockwise when viewed from the right-hand side of the car.

3 Firmly apply the handbrake, then jack up the front of the car and support it securely on axle stands (see *Jacking and vehicle support*). Remove the right-hand front roadwheel and the inner wheel arch liner for access to the crankshaft pulley. Where necessary, remove the engine compartment undertray.

4 Remove the timing belt upper cover as described in Section 6.

5 Using a socket and extension bar on the crankshaft sprocket bolt, rotate the crankshaft until the notch on the crankshaft pulley rim is aligned with the pointer on the base of the oil pump cover **(see illustration)**. Once the mark

3.7a The camshaft sprocket can be locked using a 6 mm bolt . . .

3.7b . . . and the injection pump sprocket by an 8 mm bolt

is correctly aligned, No 1 and 4 pistons are at TDC.

6 To determine which piston is at TDC on its compression stroke, check the position of the timing holes in the camshaft and injection pump sprockets. When No 1 piston is at TDC on its compression stroke, both sprocket holes will be aligned with the threaded holes in the cylinder head/block, and both exhaust camshaft lobes for cylinder No 1 will be pointing upwards if viewed through the oil filler hole. If the timing holes are 180° out of alignment then No 4 cylinder is at TDC on its compression stroke; rotate the crankshaft through a further complete turn (360°) to bring No 1 cylinder to TDC on its compression stroke.

7 With No 1 piston at TDC on its compression stroke, if necessary, the camshaft and fuel injection pump sprockets can be locked in position. Secure the camshaft sprocket in position by screwing a M6 bolt into the hole in the cylinder head and lock the injection pump sprocket in position by screwing a M8 bolt into the cylinder block **(see illustrations)**.

4 Camshaft cover – removal and refitting

Removal

1 With reference to Chapter 4C, remove the air cleaner housing and air intake trunking complete with the hot film air mass meter.

2 On the Y17DT engine, unscrew the intercooler-to-turbocharger air inlet pipe mounting bolts, then release the crankcase ventilation hose from the camshaft cover. Move the air inlet pipe to one side.

3 Remove the engine control unit and bracket from the camshaft cover, as described in Chapter 4C, Section 8.

4 Unclip the wiring loom cable tie, undo the retaining screws/nut and remove the engine control unit bracket.

5 Undo the bolt, release the wiring loom retaining clip, and remove the engine transport shackle from the right-hand rear of

the cylinder head. Slacken the bolt securing the left-hand rear shackle.

6 Slacken the fuel injector pipe unions located at the fuel injection pump **(see illustration)**. Access to the unions on the pump is limited. We found it necessary to remove the oil cooler/filter housing retaining bolt, and prise the foam filling from between the injection pump and filter housing.

7 Undo the injector pipe unions at the injectors **(see illustration)**.

8 Remove the retaining bolts, and lift away the injector outer seals.

9 Unscrew the nuts and bolt and remove the oil dipstick tube bracket. Also, where necessary, unbolt the engine lifting eyes.

10 Note the locations of the 7 bolts and 3 studs securing the cover to the camshaft housing, then unscrew and remove them.

11 While an assistant carefully pushes the injection line to the rear, lift away the camshaft cover, complete with seal.

12 Examine the cover seal and O-rings for signs of damage or deterioration and renew if necessary **(see illustration)**.

4.6 Slacken the fuel injector pipe unions

4.7 Injector pipe unions at the injectors

4.12 Check the seal and O-ring on the underside of the cover

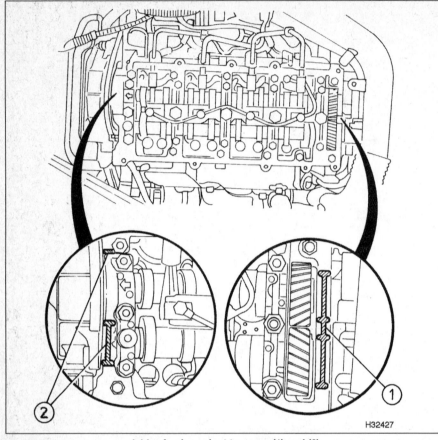

4.14a Apply sealant to areas (1) and (2)

4.14b Ensure the borehole is not covered in sealant

4.17 The injector seals are marked 'upper' and 'outside'

21 On the Y17DT engine, refit the turbocharger air inlet pipe and crankcase ventilation hose.

22 Refit the air cleaner housing, trunking and hot film air mass meter with reference to Chapter 4C.

Refitting

13 Ensure the cover and camshaft housing surfaces are clean and dry then fit the seal to the cover groove.

14 Apply sealant to the areas shown (see illustrations). Ensure that the oil borehole at the right-hand end of the exhaust camshaft is not covered in sealant or by the gasket.

15 While the assistant pushes the injection line to the rear, carefully lower the cover into position, ensuring the seal remains correctly seated. Insert the retaining bolts and studs in their correct locations, and tighten them securely.

16 Refit the oil dipstick tube bracket and tighten the nuts and bolt securely. Also refit the engine lifting eyes.

17 Refit the injector outer seals and tighten the bolts. The injector outer seals are marked 'upper' and 'outer'. Fit the seals and make sure that the centre of the seal is pushed over the injector taper (see illustration).

18 Refit the injector pipe unions and tighten them to the specified torque. Where necessary, refit the foam filling and tighten the oil cooler/filter housing retaining bolt.

19 Refit the engine transport shackles and the wiring loom retaining clip.

20 Refit the engine control unit and bracket with reference to Chapter 4C.

5 Crankshaft pulley – removal and refitting

Removal

1 Apply the handbrake, then jack up the front of the vehicle and support it on axle stands (see Jacking and vehicle support). Remove the right-hand front roadwheel and the inner wheel arch liner for access to the crankshaft pulley. Where necessary, remove the engine compartment undertray.

2 Remove the auxiliary drivebelt as described in Chapter 1B (see illustration). Prior to removal, mark the direction of rotation on the belt to ensure the belt is refitted the same way around.

3 Slacken and remove the small retaining bolts securing the pulley to the crankshaft sprocket and remove the pulley from the engine (see illustration). If necessary, prevent the crankshaft from turning by holding the sprocket retaining bolt with a socket.

Refitting

4 Refit the pulley to the crankshaft sprocket, aligning the pulley hole with the sprocket locating pin. Refit the pulley retaining bolts, tightening them to the specified torque.

5 Refit the auxiliary drivebelt as described in

5.2 Removing the auxiliary drivebelt

5.3 Removing the crankshaft pulley

5.5 Refitting the auxiliary drivebelt

6.4 Undo the bolts and remove the right-hand engine mounting lower bracket

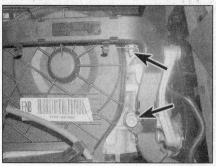

6.6 Undo the Torx bolt and release the wiring tray retaining clips (arrowed)

Chapter 1B using the mark made prior to removal to ensure the belt is fitted the correct way around **(see illustration)**.

6 Refit the engine undertray, wheel arch liner and roadwheel, then lower the car to the ground and tighten the wheel bolts to the specified torque.

6 Timing belt covers – removal and refitting

Removal

Upper cover

1 Disconnect the battery negative lead (see *Disconnecting the battery* at the end of this manual).
2 Remove the air cleaner assembly and ducting as described in Chapter 4C.

3 Support the weight of the engine using a trolley jack with a block of wood placed on its head.
4 Unbolt and remove the right-hand engine mounting and lower bracket with reference to Section 20 **(see illustration)**.
5 With reference to Chapter 5A if necessary, disconnect the wiring plug and connection from the alternator.
6 Unclip the brake servo and EGR vacuum lines then unscrew the bolt and remove the wiring harness trough from over the upper timing belt cover **(see illustration)**.
7 Unscrew the eight upper cover retaining bolts, noting they are of different lengths **(see illustrations)**. Remove the upper cover.

Lower cover

8 Apply the handbrake, then jack up the front of the vehicle and support it on axle stands (see *Jacking and vehicle support*). Remove

the right-hand front roadwheel and the inner wheel arch liner for access to the crankshaft pulley. Where necessary, remove the engine compartment undertray.
9 Remove the upper cover as described in paragraphs 1 to 7.
10 Loosen only the bolts securing the pulley to the coolant pump **(see illustration)**.
11 With reference to Chapter 1B, remove the auxiliary drivebelt. Prior to removal, mark the direction of rotation on the belt to ensure the belt is refitted the same way around.
12 Remove the crankshaft pulley with reference to Section 5.
13 Unscrew the bolts and remove the pulley from the coolant pump.
14 Undo the three retaining bolts, and remove the lower cover from the oil pump housing **(see illustrations)**.
15 Temporarily refit the bolt retaining the timing belt tensioner pulley bracket **(see illustration)**.

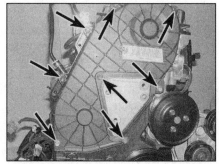

6.7a Unscrew the eight retaining bolts . . .

6.7b . . . and remove the upper timing belt cover

6.10 Bolts securing the pulley to the water pump

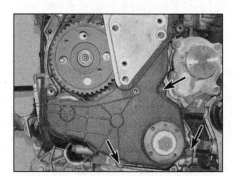

6.14a Lower cover retaining bolts

6.14b Removing the lower cover

6.15 Temporarily refit the timing belt tensioner lower retaining bolt (arrowed)

6.19 Rear timing belt cover bolts

7.2a Camshaft sprocket locked in the TDC position with a bolt

7.2b Injection pump sprocket locked in the TDC position with a bolt

Rear cover

16 Remove the timing belt as described in Section 7.

17 Remove the timing belt tension and guide rollers, camshaft sprocket and injection pump sprocket with reference to Section 8.

18 Detach the tensioner spring retainer.

19 Undo the four retaining bolts, and remove the rear timing belt cover (see illustration).

Refitting

20 Refitting is the reverse of removal, ensuring all retaining bolts are tightened securely.

7 Timing belt – removal and refitting

Note: *The timing belt must be removed and refitted with the engine cold.*

7.3 Removing the crankshaft pulley

7.5b Using an Allen key to release the tensioner on later models

Removal

1 Disconnect the battery negative lead (refer to *Disconnecting the battery* at the end of this manual).

2 Position No 1 cylinder at TDC on its compression stroke as described in Section 3. Lock the camshaft and injection pump sprockets in position by screwing the bolts into the threaded holes in the cylinder head/block (see illustrations).

3 Remove the crankshaft pulley as described in Section 5, then unbolt and remove the water pump pulley (see illustration).

4 Unbolt and remove the timing belt upper and lower covers with reference to Section 6.

5 Slacken the timing belt tensioner retaining bolt and, on early models, carefully unhook the tensioner spring from its locating pins. Note that on later models, the tensioner spring has been modified and is now attached

7.5a Unhooking the tensioner spring on early models

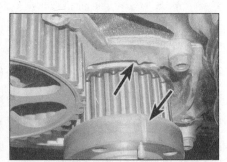

7.6 Removing the timing belt

to the bolt located above the tensioner – on these models, loosen the centre bolt then use an Allen key to turn the tensioner anti-clockwise to release the tension. Hold the tensioner in this position and tighten the bolt (see illustrations).

6 Slide the timing belt off its sprockets and remove it from the engine (see illustration). If the belt is to be re-used, use white paint or similar to mark the direction of rotation on the belt. **Do not** rotate the crankshaft until the timing belt has been refitted.

7 Check the timing belt carefully for any signs of uneven wear, splitting or oil contamination, and renew it if there is the slightest doubt about its condition. If the engine is undergoing an overhaul and is approaching the specified interval for belt renewal (see Chapter 1B) renew the belt as a matter of course, regardless of its apparent condition. If signs of oil contamination are found, trace the source of the oil leak and rectify it, then wash down the engine timing belt area and all related components to remove all traces of oil.

Refitting

8 On reassembly, thoroughly clean the timing belt sprockets and ensure the camshaft and injection pump sprockets are locked correctly in position. Temporarily refit the crankshaft pulley to the sprocket and check that the pulley cut-out is still aligned with the pointer on the oil pump cover; the mark on the crankshaft sprocket should also be aligned with the mark on the oil pump cover (see illustration).

7.8 Align the notch on the crankshaft sprocket with the pointer on the oil pump cover (arrowed)

9 Remove the pulley and fit the timing belt over the crankshaft, oil pump, injection pump and camshaft sprockets, ensuring that the belt rear run is taut (ie, all slack is on the tensioner pulley side of the belt). Do not twist the belt sharply while refitting it. Ensure that the belt teeth are correctly seated centrally in the sprockets, and that the timing marks remain in alignment. If a used belt is being refitted, ensure that the arrow mark made on removal points in the normal direction of rotation, as before (see illustration).

10 On early models, tension the belt by refitting the tensioner pulley spring, ensuring it is correctly located on its pins. On later models, loosen the tensioner centre bolt to allow it to tension the timing belt, then tighten the bolt to hold the tensioner in this position.

11 Check that the crankshaft sprocket timing mark is still correctly positioned then unscrew the locking bolts from the injection pump and camshaft sprockets.

12 Slacken the tensioner pulley retaining bolt then rotate the crankshaft pulley approximately 60° backwards (anti-clockwise) to automatically adjust the timing belt tension. Hold the crankshaft pulley stationary and securely tighten the tensioner pulley retaining bolt.

13 Rotate the crankshaft smoothly through two complete turns (720°) in the normal direction of rotation to settle the timing belt in position. Realign the crankshaft sprocket timing mark and check that the camshaft and injection pump sprocket locking bolts can be refitted.

14 Refit the timing belt covers, crankshaft pulley and water pump pulley as described in Sections 5 and 6.

15 Reconnect the battery negative lead (refer to *Disconnecting the battery* at the end of this manual).

8 Timing belt tensioner and sprockets – removal and refitting

Camshaft sprocket

Removal

1 Remove the timing belt as described in Section 7. Prior to attempting to unscrew the sprocket retaining bolt, turn the crankshaft 60° **backwards** (anti-clockwise) to prevent any accidental piston-to-valve contact.

2 With the locking bolt removed, hold the camshaft sprocket stationary using a tool engaged with the holes in the sprocket (see paragraph 8 of this Section).

3 Slacken and remove the retaining bolt, then remove the sprocket from the end of the camshaft, noting which way around it is fitted (see illustration). If the sprocket locating pin is a loose fit, remove it from the camshaft end and store it with the sprocket for safe-keeping.

7.9 Timing belt routing

Refitting

4 Ensure the locating pin is in position then refit the sprocket to the camshaft end, aligning its locating hole with the pin.

5 Refit the sprocket retaining bolt, and tighten it to the specified torque while holding the sprocket stationary with the special tool. Rotate the crankshaft 60° forwards (clockwise) until the groove in the crankshaft timing belt sprocket is at 12 o'clock and aligns with the cast-in mark on the oil pump cover.

6 Refit the timing belt as described in Section 7.

Injection pump sprocket

Removal

7 Remove the timing belt as described in Section 7.

8 With the sprocket locking bolt removed, hold the injection pump sprocket stationary

8.3 Remove the camshaft sprocket

8.10 Using a puller to remove the injection pump sprocket

using a tool engaged with the holes in the sprocket. The tool can be made using two lengths of steel strip (one long, the other short), and three nuts and bolts; one nut and bolt forms the pivot of a forked tool, with the remaining two nuts and bolts at the tips of the 'forks' to engage with the sprocket spokes (see illustration).

9 Slacken and remove the sprocket retaining nut.

10 Using a suitable puller, remove the sprocket from the injection pump shaft, noting which way around it is fitted. If the Woodruff key is a loose fit in the pump shaft, remove it and store it with the sprocket for safe-keeping (see illustration). Note: *The sprocket is a tapered-fit on the injection pump shaft.*

Refitting

11 Ensure the Woodruff key is correctly fitted to the pump shaft then refit the sprocket, aligning the sprocket groove with the key (see illustration).

12 Refit the retaining nut and tighten it to the specified torque whilst using the holding tool to prevent rotation.

13 If not already done, align the sprocket timing hole with the threaded hole in the cylinder block and screw in the locking bolt.

14 Refit the timing belt as described in Section 7.

Crankshaft sprocket

Removal

15 Remove the timing belt as described in Section 7.

8.8 Using a sprocket holding tool to prevent rotation as the injection pump sprocket nut is slackened

8.11 Align the keyway in the sprocket with the Woodruff key in the shaft

8.17 Slide the sprocket from the shaft

8.19 Fit the flanged spacer with the convex side away from the oil pump cover

8.21 Refit the sprocket retaining bolt and washer

16 Slacken the crankshaft sprocket retaining bolt. To prevent crankshaft rotation, have an assistant select 4th gear and apply the brakes firmly. If the engine is removed from the vehicle it will be necessary to lock the flywheel (see Section 18).

17 Unscrew the retaining bolt and washer and remove the crankshaft sprocket from the end of the crankshaft. If the sprocket is a tight fit, draw it off of the crankshaft using a suitable puller **(see illustration)**. If the Woodruff key is a loose fit in the crankshaft, remove it and store it with the sprocket for safe-keeping.

18 Slide the flanged spacer off of the crankshaft, noting which way around it is fitted.

Refitting

19 Refit the flanged spacer to the crankshaft with its convex surface facing away from the oil pump housing **(see illustration)**.

20 Ensure the Woodruff key is correctly fitted

then slide on the crankshaft sprocket aligning its groove with the key.

21 Refit the retaining bolt and washer then lock the crankshaft by the method used on removal, and tighten the sprocket retaining bolt to the specified torque setting **(see illustration)**.

22 Refit the timing belt as described in Section 7.

Oil pump sprocket

Removal

23 Remove the timing belt as described in Section 7.

24 Prevent the oil pump sprocket from rotating using a socket and extension bar fitted to one of the oil pump cover bolts then slacken and remove the sprocket retaining nut.

25 Remove the sprocket from the oil pump shaft, noting which way around it is fitted.

Refitting

26 Refit the sprocket, aligning it with the flat on the pump shaft, and fit the retaining nut. Tighten the sprocket retaining nut to the specified torque, using the socket and extension bar to prevent rotation **(see illustration)**.

27 Refit the timing belt as described in Section 7.

Tensioner assembly

Removal

28 Remove the timing belt as described in Section 7.

29 On early models, carefully unhook the tensioner spring, unscrew the retaining bolts and remove the tensioner assembly from the engine. On later models, unscrew the tensioner centre bolt, then unhook the spring from the stud, and remove the tensioner **(see illustrations)**.

Refitting

30 Fit the tensioner assembly to the engine, tightening its retaining bolts by hand only. Refit the tensioner spring on early models. Make sure that the spring is located correctly on the bolt on later models.

31 Refit the timing belt as described in Section 7.

Idler pulley

Removal

32 Remove the timing belt as described in Section 7.

33 Slacken and remove the retaining bolt and remove the idler pulley from the engine **(see illustration)**.

8.26 Use a socket and extension bar on one of the oil pump cover bolts to prevent the sprocket from turning

8.29a Timing belt tensioner spring on early models

8.29b Unhook the spring to remove the tensioner on later models

8.29c The later tensioner removed from the engine

8.33 Timing belt idler pulley retaining bolt

Refitting

34 Refit the idler pulley and tighten the retaining bolt to the specified torque.

35 Refit the timing belt as described in Section 7.

9 Camshaft oil seal – renewal

1 Remove the camshaft sprocket as described in Section 8.

2 Carefully punch or drill a small hole in the oil seal. Screw in a self-tapping screw, and pull on the screw with pliers to extract the seal **(see illustration)**.

3 Clean the seal housing, and polish off any burrs or raised edges which may have caused the seal to fail in the first place.

4 Lubricate the lips of the new seal with clean engine oil, and press it into position using a suitable tubular drift (such as a socket) which bears only on the hard outer edge of the seal. Take care not to damage the seal lips during fitting; note that the seal lips should face inwards **(see illustration)**.

5 Refit the camshaft sprocket as described in Section 8.

10 Valve clearances – checking and adjustment

Checking

1 The importance of having the valve clearances correctly adjusted cannot be overstressed, as they vitally affect the performance of the engine. The engine must be cold for the check to be accurate. The clearances are checked as follows.

2 Apply the handbrake, then jack up the front of the vehicle and support it on axle stands (see *Jacking and vehicle support*). Remove the right-hand front roadwheel and the inner wheel arch liner for access to the crankshaft pulley. Where necessary, remove the engine compartment undertray.

3 Remove the camshaft cover as described in Section 4, then remove the fuel injectors with reference to Chapter 4C.

4 Using a socket and extension on the crankshaft sprocket bolt, rotate the crankshaft in the normal direction of rotation (clockwise when viewed from the right-hand end of the engine) until the notch on the crankshaft pulley is correctly aligned with the pointer on the base of the oil pump cover.

5 Now rotate the crankshaft in the normal direction (clockwise) until the inlet camshaft lobes for No 1 cylinder (nearest the timing belt end of the engine) and the exhaust camshaft lobes for No 3 cylinder are pointing away from the followers. This indicates that these valves are completely closed, and the clearances can be checked.

9.2 Pull the screw to extract the seal

6 On a piece of paper, draw the outline of the engine with the cylinders numbered from the timing belt end. Show the position of each valve, together with the specified valve clearance. Note that the clearance for both the inlet and exhaust valves is the same.

7 With the cam lobes positioned as described in paragraph 5, using feeler blades, measure the clearance between the base of both No 1 cylinder inlet cam lobes and No 3 cylinder exhaust cam lobes and their followers. Record the clearances on the paper **(see illustration)**.

8 Rotate the crankshaft pulley through a half a turn (180°) to position No 3 cylinder inlet camshaft lobes and No 4 cylinder exhaust camshaft lobes pointing away from their followers. Measure the clearance between the base of the camshaft lobes and their followers and record the clearances on the paper.

9 Rotate the crankshaft pulley through a half a turn (180°) to position No 2 cylinder exhaust camshaft lobes and No 4 cylinder inlet camshaft lobes pointing away from their followers. Measure the clearance between the base of the camshaft lobes and their followers and record the clearances on the paper.

10 Rotate the crankshaft pulley through a half a turn (180°) to position No 1 cylinder exhaust camshaft lobes and No 2 cylinder inlet camshaft lobes pointing away from their followers. Measure the clearance between the base of the camshaft lobes and their followers and record the clearances on the paper.

11 If all the clearances are correct, refit the cylinder head cover (see Section 4), and

10.7 With the camshaft lobe pointing away from the follower measure the clearance

9.4 Press the oil seal into position using a tubular drift such as a socket

injectors (see Chapter 4C), then refit the roadwheel and lower the vehicle to the ground and tighten the wheel bolts to the specified torque. If any clearance measured is not correct, adjustment must be carried out as described in the following paragraphs.

Adjustment

12 Rotate the crankshaft clockwise until the inlet camshaft lobes for No 1 cylinder (nearest the timing belt end of the engine) and the exhaust camshaft lobes for No 3 cylinder are pointing away from the followers. With the crankshaft in this position, inlet valve No 1 and exhaust valve No 3 can be adjusted as follows.

13 Rotate the follower until the groove on its upper edge is facing towards the front of the engine (exhaust followers), or rear of the engine (inlet followers).

14 In the absence of the special Vauxhall tool (KM-6090), position a large flat-bladed screwdriver between the edge of the follower and the base of the camshaft. Use the screwdriver to carefully depress the follower until there is enough clearance to allow the shim to be slid out from between the follower and camshaft (a magnetic tool is particularly useful for this task) **(see illustration)**.

15 Clean the shim, and measure its thickness with a micrometer. The shims carry thickness markings, but wear may have reduced the original thickness, so be sure to double-check **(see illustration)**.

16 Add the measured clearance of the valve to the thickness of the original shim then subtract the specified valve clearance from

10.14 Carefully depress the follower and slide the shim out

10.15 The thickness of each shim should be stamped on one of its surfaces

this figure. This will give you the thickness of the shim required. For example:

Measured valve clearance	0.45 mm
Plus thickness of the original shim	2.70 mm
Equals	3.15 mm
Minus clearance required	0.40 mm
Thickness of shim required	2.75 mm

17 Obtain the correct thickness of shim required and lubricate it with clean engine oil. Carefully depress the follower and slide the shim into position, with the thickness number downwards, ensuring it is correctly located. Check that the valve clearance is within limits.

 HAYNES HiNT *It may be possible to correct the clearances by moving the shims around between the valves, but don't rotate the crankshaft with any shims missing. Keep a note of all the shim thicknesses to assist valve clearance adjustment when they need to be done again.*

18 Rotate the crankshaft through half a turn (180°) to position No 3 cylinder inlet camshaft lobes and No 4 cylinder exhaust camshaft lobes pointing away from their followers. Adjust No 3 inlet and No 4 exhaust valve clearances as described in paragraphs 13 to 17.
19 Rotate the crankshaft pulley through a half a turn (180°) to position No 2 cylinder exhaust camshaft lobes and No 4 cylinder inlet camshaft lobes pointing away from their followers. Adjust No 2 exhaust and No 4 inlet valve clearances as described in paragraphs 13 to 17.

11.6 Insert a screw through the fixed gear and into the backlash compensating gear (arrowed)

20 Rotate the crankshaft pulley through a half a turn (180°) to position No 1 cylinder exhaust camshaft lobes and No 2 cylinder inlet camshaft lobes pointing away from their followers. Adjust No 1 exhaust and No 2 inlet valve clearances as described in paragraphs 13 to 17.
21 Refit the camshaft cover (see Section 4) and the fuel injectors (Chapter 4C).
22 Refit the engine undertray, inner wheel arch liner and roadwheel, and lower the car to the ground.

11 Camshafts and followers – removal, inspection and refitting

Removal

1 Apply the handbrake, then jack up the front of the vehicle and support it on axle stands (see *Jacking and vehicle support*). Remove the right-hand front roadwheel and the inner wheel arch liner for access to the crankshaft pulley. Where necessary, remove the engine compartment undertray.
2 Remove the camshaft cover as described in Section 4.
3 Drain the cooling system as described in Chapter 1B. **Note:** *This is recommended by the manufacturers as a precaution against coolant entering the combustion chambers when the injectors are removed. The injector heat sleeves may become displaced, causing coolant to leak into the cylinders.*
4 Remove the fuel injectors with reference to Chapter 4C.
5 Remove the timing belt and camshaft sprocket as described in Sections 7 and 8.
6 The exhaust camshaft gear incorporates a backlash compensating gear. This must now be locked to the fixed exhaust camshaft gear by inserting a suitably-sized bolt/rod through the hole. This prevents the spring preload of the compensating gear being lost when either camshaft is removed. The Vauxhall tool (KM-955-2) is inserted from the compensating gear side, however, if preferred, a longer bolt may be inserted from the inner side of the camshaft gear after unscrewing the nuts and bolt, and removing

11.10 Lift out the cam followers and shims

the No 5 bearing cap from the left-hand (gearbox) end of the camshafts **(see illustration)**.
7 Working opposite to the tightening sequence given in paragraph 19, slacken the camshaft bearing cap retaining nuts by one turn at a time, to relieve the pressure of the valve springs on the bearing caps gradually and evenly. Once the valve spring pressure has been relieved, the nuts can be fully unscrewed and removed.
Caution: If the bearing cap nuts are carelessly slackened, the bearing caps may break. If any bearing cap breaks then the complete housing must be renewed, as the bearing caps are matched to the housing and are not available separately.
8 Remove the bearing caps, noting each caps correct fitted location. The bearing caps are numbered 1 to 5 and the arrow on each cap points towards the timing belt end of the engine.
9 Lift the camshafts out of the cylinder head, and recover the oil seal from the inlet camshaft.
10 Obtain sixteen small, clean plastic containers, and label them for identification. Alternatively, divide a larger container into compartments. Lift the followers and shims out from the top of the cylinder head and store each one in its respective fitted position. Make sure the followers and shims are not mixed up, to ensure the valve clearances remain correct on refitting **(see illustration)**.

Inspection

11 Examine the camshaft bearing surfaces and camshaft lobes for signs of wear ridges and scoring. Renew the camshaft if any of these conditions are apparent. Examine the condition of the bearing surfaces both on the camshaft journals and in the camshaft housing. If the housing bearing surfaces are worn excessively, the housing will need to be renewed.
12 Support the camshaft end journals on V-blocks, and measure the run-out at the centre journal using a dial gauge. If the run-out exceeds the specified limit, the camshaft should be renewed.
13 Examine the followers and their bores in the cylinder head for signs of wear or damage. If any follower is visibly worn it should be renewed.

Refitting

14 Where removed, lubricate the followers with clean engine oil and carefully insert each one into its original location in the cylinder head. Ensure each shim is correctly located in the top of its relevant follower **(see illustration)**.
15 Rotate the crankshaft approximately 60° backwards (anti-clockwise) as a precaution against accidental piston-to-valve contact. Lubricate the camshaft followers with clean engine oil then lay the camshafts in position. Check that the exhaust camshaft backlash compensating gear is still locked to the fixed

11.14 Ensure each shim is correctly located

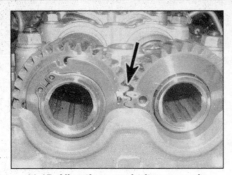

11.15 Align the camshaft gear marks (arrowed)

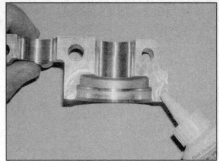

11.17 Apply a smear of sealant to the No 1 camshaft-bearing cap

gear. Ensure that the mark on the outer face exhaust camshaft gear lies between the two marks on the outer face of the inlet camshaft gear, and that the marks are approximately level with the upper edge of the camshaft housing **(see illustration)**. **Note:** *If the exhaust camshaft is being renewed, it will be necessary to obtain Vauxhall tool No KM 6092, and pretension the backlash compensating gear prior to installation.*

16 Ensure the mating surfaces of the bearing caps and camshaft housing are clean and dry and lubricate the camshaft journals and lobes with clean engine oil.

17 Apply a smear of suitable sealant (available from Vauxhall dealers) to the areas of the camshaft housing No 1 bearing cap mating surface **(see illustration)**.

18 Refit the camshaft bearing caps in their original locations on the cylinder head and tighten the nuts by hand only at this stage. The caps are numbered 1 to 5 (No 1 cap being at the timing belt end of the engine) and the arrow cast onto the top of each cap should point towards the timing belt end of the engine **(see illustration)**. Remove the locking bolt/rod from No 5 bearing cap (if the bolt/rod was fitted from the inside, refit

bearing caps 1 to 4 first, then remove the bolt/rod before refitting bearing cap 5.

19 Working in the specified sequence, tighten the nuts by one turn at a time to gradually impose the pressure of the valve springs evenly on the bearing caps **(see illustration)**. Repeat this sequence until all bearing caps are in contact with the cylinder head then go around in the specified sequence and tighten them to the specified torque.

Caution: If the bearing cap nuts are carelessly tightened, the bearing caps may break. If any bearing cap breaks then the complete housing must be renewed, as the bearing caps are matched to the housing and are not available separately.

20 Fit a new inlet camshaft oil seal as described in Section 9.

21 Refit the camshaft sprocket and timing belt as described in Sections 7 and 8.

22 Check the valve clearances as described in Section 10.

23 Refit the fuel injectors as described in Chapter 4C, and the camshaft cover as described in Section 4.

24 Refill the cooling system with reference to Chapter 1B.

11.18 The arrows on the camshaft bearing caps should point towards the timing belt end of the engine

12 Camshaft housing – removal, inspection and refitting

Removal

1 Remove the camshafts and followers as described in Section 11.

2 Remove the two bolts securing the rear timing belt cover to the camshaft housing **(see illustration)**.

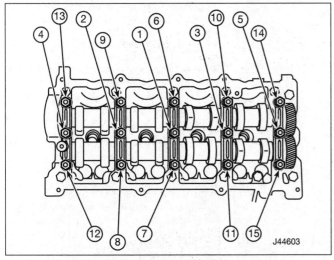

11.19 Camshaft bearing cap tightening sequence

12.2 Remove the two bolts securing the rear timing belt cover to the camshaft housing

12.3a Undo the charge air pipe bolts (arrowed)

12.3b Recover the EGR pipe gasket

3 Where applicable, remove the bolts securing the charge air pipe and bracket to the left-hand end of the camshaft housing and inlet manifold. Undo the retaining clips and release the pipe from the inlet trunking. Undo the bolts securing the EGR (exhaust gas recirculation) pipe to the exhaust manifold and the left-hand end of the camshaft housing. Undo the large union at the EGR valve, and remove the pipe **(see illustrations)**. It should now be possible to remove the left-hand rear transport eye from the camshaft housing.

4 Detach the hose from the leak-back pipe,

and disconnect the heater plug wiring connectors **(see illustration)**.

5 On models with air conditioning, release the refrigerant hoses from the retaining clip on the right-hand side inner wing. Without undoing the refrigerant pipes, disconnect the wiring plug, unbolt the air conditioning compressor from its support bracket (3 bolts), and position it clear of the engine. Use a cable tie or similar to tie the compressor to the bonnet slam panel out of the way. Undo the three bolts and remove the air conditioning support bracket **(see illustrations)**.

6 Slacken the camshaft housing-to-head retaining bolts 1/2 turn at a time, in the **reverse** sequence to that given in paragraph 12.

7 Undo the bolts completely and remove the camshaft housing. Remove and discard the gasket **(see illustration)**.

8 Unscrew the oil leak line banjo bolt and mounting bolt, and remove the line. Recover the sealing rings.

Inspection

9 Using a straight-edge, check the surface of the camshaft housing for distortion. It should be no more than that given for the cylinder head in Chapter 2D.

Refitting

10 Refit the oil leak line and tighten the banjo bolt and mounting bolt securely.

11 Ensure all mating surfaces are clean and free from any gasket or sealant residue.

12 With a new gasket in place, position the camshaft housing onto the cylinder head, and progressively tighten the housing bolts to the specified torque, in the sequence shown **(see illustration)**.

13 Where applicable, refit the air conditioning compressor and bracket, reconnect the wiring plug, and support the refrigerant hoses in the clips.

12.3c Undo the large EGR union nut

12.4 Disconnect the fuel leak-back pipe

12.5a Tie the compressor to the slam panel . . .

12.5b . . . and remove the compressor mounting bracket

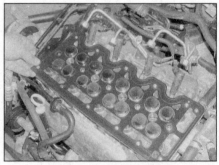

12.7 Remove the gasket

14 Reconnect the heater plug wiring connectors and the leak-back pipe hose.
15 Refit the transport eye, EGR valve and charge air pipe.
16 Refit and tighten the two bolts securing the rear timing belt cover.
17 Refit the camshafts and followers, and check the valve clearances, with reference to Sections 10 and 11.

13 Cylinder head – removal and refitting

Caution: Be careful not to allow dirt into the fuel injection pump or injector pipes during this procedure.
Note: *New cylinder head bolts will be required on refitting.*

Removal

1 Disconnect the battery negative lead (refer to *Disconnecting the battery* at the end of this manual).
2 Drain the cooling system as described in Chapter 1B.
3 Remove the camshaft housing and followers as described in Section 12 **(see illustration)**.
4 On models with air conditioning, release the refrigerant hoses from the retaining clip on the right-hand side inner wing. Without undoing the refrigerant pipes, disconnect the wiring plug, unbolt the air conditioning compressor from its support bracket (3 bolts), and position it clear of the engine. Use a cable tie or similar to tie the compressor to the bonnet slam panel out of the way. Undo the three bolts and remove the air conditioning support bracket.
5 Refer to Chapter 4C and unbolt the exhaust front pipe from the exhaust manifold/ turbocharger, taking care to support the flexible section. **Note:** *Angular movement in excess of 10° can cause permanent damage to the flexible section.* Release the mounting rubbers and support the front of the exhaust pipe to one side.
6 Unbolt and remove the oil dipstick tube and bracket. Also, release the vacuum hoses from the clips.
7 Release the clips and disconnect the

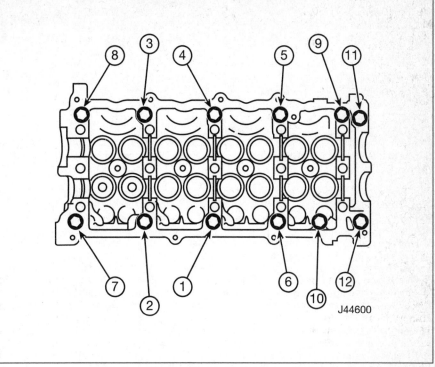

12.12 Camshaft housing bolts tightening sequence

turbocharger oil return hose from the turbocharger and drain tube.
8 Unscrew the nut while counterholding the threaded adapter, and remove the turbocharger oil feed line from the block.
9 Unscrew the turbocharger bracket mounting bolt.
10 Disconnect the vacuum hose from the turbocharger waste gate unit.
11 Release the clamp then disconnect the air intake pipe from the turbocharger.
12 Unbolt and remove the exhaust manifold heat shield.
13 Unscrew the bolts securing the EGR (exhaust gas recirculation) pipe to the exhaust manifold and remove the gasket.
14 Unscrew the bolt and remove the oil feed line banjo from the turbocharger. Recover the sealing rings.

15 Unscrew the nuts and bolts securing the exhaust manifold to the cylinder head, and recover the washers. Withdraw the manifold and recover the gasket.
16 Unscrew the nut and detach the brake servo vacuum line from the vacuum pump.
17 Slacken and remove the bolts securing the timing belt rear cover to the end of the cylinder head/camshaft housing.
18 Disconnect the wiring from the EGR solenoid valve and charge pressure sensor **(see illustrations)**.
19 Unscrew the nut and remove the starter/alternator wiring harness bracket from the EGR valve.
20 Disconnect the vacuum hose, unscrew the studs and bolts, and remove the EGR valve and gasket **(see illustration)**.
21 Place a container beneath the oil filter,

13.3 Store the followers the correct way up

13.18a Detach the EGR solenoid valve vacuum hose and wiring plug

13.18b Unplug the charge pressure sensor

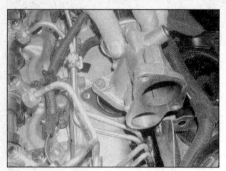

13.20 Remove the EGR valve

13.23 Disconnect the coolant pipe from the cylinder head

13.25a Coolant temperature sensor

then unscrew the filter cover and detach the return hose from the housing.

22 Remove the heater glow plugs with reference to Chapter 5C.

23 Loosen the clips and disconnect the coolant hoses from the thermostat housing. Also disconnect the hose from the left-hand rear of the cylinder head **(see illustration)**.

24 Unscrew the bolt and remove the wastegate unit vacuum hose bracket.

25 Disconnect the wiring from the coolant temperature sensor, unscrew the retaining bolts and pull the thermostat housing and wastegate vacuum pipe bracket away from the left-hand end of the cylinder head **(see illustrations)**.

26 Working in the **reverse** of the tightening sequence given in paragraph 43, progressively slacken the cylinder head bolts by half a turn at a time, until all bolts can be

unscrewed by hand. Remove the cylinder head bolts and recover the washers.

27 Lift the cylinder head away; seek assistance if possible, as it is a heavy assembly **(see illustration)**. Remove the gasket, noting the two locating dowels fitted to the top of the cylinder block. If they are a loose fit, remove the locating dowels and store them with the head for safe-keeping. Keep the head gasket for identification purposes (see paragraph 34).

28 If the cylinder head is to be dismantled for overhaul, then refer to Part D of this Chapter.

Preparation for refitting

29 The mating faces of the cylinder head and cylinder block/crankcase must be perfectly clean before refitting the head. Use a hard plastic or wood scraper to remove all traces of gasket and carbon; also clean the piston

crowns. Take particular care, as the surfaces are damaged easily. Also, make sure that the carbon is not allowed to enter the oil and water passages – this is particularly important for the lubrication system, as carbon could block the oil supply to any of the engine's components. Using adhesive tape and paper, seal the water, oil and bolt holes in the cylinder block/crankcase. To prevent carbon entering the gap between the pistons and bores, smear a little grease in the gap. After cleaning each piston, use a small brush to remove all traces of grease and carbon from the gap, then wipe away the remainder with a clean rag. Clean all the pistons in the same way.

30 Check the mating surfaces of the cylinder block/crankcase and the cylinder head for nicks, deep scratches and other damage. If slight, they may be removed carefully with a file, but if excessive, machining may be the only alternative to renewal.

31 Ensure that the cylinder head bolt holes in the crankcase are clean and free of oil. Syringe or soak up any oil left in the bolt holes. This is most important in order that the correct bolt tightening torque can be applied and to prevent the possibility of the block being cracked by hydraulic pressure when the bolts are tightened.

32 The cylinder head bolts must be discarded and renewed, regardless of their apparent condition.

33 If warpage of the cylinder head gasket surface is suspected, use a straight-edge to check it for distortion. Refer to Part D of this Chapter if necessary.

34 On this engine, the cylinder head-to-piston clearance is controlled by fitting different thickness head gaskets. The gasket thickness can be determined by looking at the left-hand front corner of the gasket and checking on the number of holes **(see illustration)**.

Holes in gasket	Gasket thickness
No holes	1.45 mm
One hole	1.50 mm
Two hole	1.55 mm

The correct thickness of gasket required is selected by measuring the piston protrusions as follows.

35 Ensure that the crankshaft is still correctly

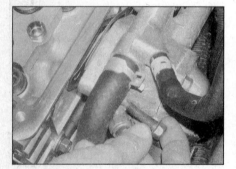

13.25b Remove the thermostat housing . . .

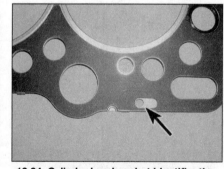

13.25c . . . and wastegate vacuum pipe bracket

13.27 Lift the cylinder head away

13.34 Cylinder head gasket identification hole (arrowed)

positioned in the TDC position. Mount a dial test indicator securely on the block so that its pointer can be easily pivoted between the piston crown and block mating surface. Zero the dial test indicator on the gasket surface of the cylinder block then carefully move the indicator over No 1 piston and measure the its protrusion at its highest point between the valve cut-outs, and then again at its highest point between the valve cut-outs at 90° to the first measurement (see illustration). Repeat this procedure with No 4 piston.

36 Rotate the crankshaft half a turn (180º) to bring No 2 and 3 pistons to TDC. Ensure the crankshaft is accurately positioned then measure the protrusions of No 2 and 3 pistons at the specified points. Once both pistons have been measured, rotate the crankshaft through a further one and a half turns (540º) to bring No 1 and 4 pistons back to TDC.

37 Select the correct thickness of head gasket required by determining the largest amount of piston protrusion, and using the following table.

Piston protrusion measurement	Gasket thickness required
0.630 to 0.696 mm	1.45 mm (no holes)
0.697 to 0.763 mm	1.50 mm (one hole)
0.764 to 0.830 mm	1.55 mm (two holes)

Refitting

38 Wipe clean the mating surfaces of the cylinder head and cylinder block/crankcase.

39 Check that the two locating dowels are in position then fit a new gasket to the cylinder block (see illustration).

40 If not already positioned at TDC, rotate the crankshaft so that No 1 piston is at its highest point in the cylinder. Now turn the crankshaft 60° backwards (anti-clockwise). This is to ensure that whilst the cylinder head and camshafts are being refitted, there is little chance of accidental piston-to-valve contact.

41 With the aid of an assistant, carefully refit the cylinder head assembly to the block, aligning it with the locating dowels.

42 Carefully enter each new cylinder head bolt into its relevant hole (do not drop them in). Screw all bolts in, by hand only, until finger-tight.

43 Working progressively in a spiral sequence from the centre outwards, tighten the cylinder head bolts to their Stage 1 torque setting, using a torque wrench and suitable socket (see illustration).

44 Once all bolts have been tightened to the Stage 1 torque, working again in the same sequence, go around and tighten all bolts through the specified Stage 2, 3, 4 and 5 angles. It is recommended that an angle-measuring gauge is used to ensure accuracy (see illustration). If a gauge is not available, use white paint to make alignment marks prior to tightening; the marks can then be used to check that the bolt has been rotated through the correct angle.

45 The remaining procedure is a reversal of

13.35 Measure the piston projection at the highest points between the valve cut-outs

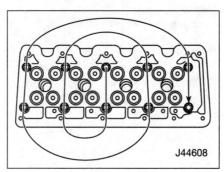

J44608

13.43 Tighten the bolts to the Stage 1 setting . . .

removal, but check the valve clearances as described in Section 10, and top up the coolant as described in Chapter 1B.

14 Sump –
removal and refitting

Removal

1 Disconnect the battery negative lead (refer to Disconnecting the battery at the end of this manual).

2 Apply the handbrake, then jack up the front of the vehicle and support it on axle stands (see Jacking and vehicle support). Remove the right-hand front roadwheel and the inner wheel arch liner for access to the right-hand side of the engine. Where necessary, undo the retaining screws and remove the engine undertray.

3 Drain the engine oil as described in Chapter 1B, then fit a new sealing washer and refit the drain plug, tightening it to the specified torque. It is also recommended that the oil filter is renewed at the same time.

4 Remove the front section of the exhaust system with reference to Chapter 4C.

5 Slacken and remove the bolts securing the sump lower pan to the upper housing then remove the sump pan from underneath the vehicle (see illustration).

6 Unscrew the bolts and remove the oil dipstick guide tube from the sump upper housing.

7 Progressively slacken and remove the nuts

13.39 Check the locating dowels are in place

13.44 . . . then to the Stage 2 setting

and bolts securing the upper housing to the base of the cylinder block/oil pump cover and transmission. Break the joint by striking the housing with the palm of the hand, or using a wide plastic spatula carefully inserted in the joint between the housing and cylinder block. Lower the housing away from the engine and withdraw it from underneath the vehicle.

8 While the sump is removed, take the opportunity to check the oil pump pick-up/strainer for signs of clogging or splitting. If necessary, unbolt the pick-up/strainer and remove it from the engine along with its sealing ring (see illustration). The strainer can then be cleaned easily in solvent or renewed.

Refitting

9 Remove all traces of dirt, oil and sealant from the mating surfaces of the sump upper housing and pan, the cylinder block and (where removed) the pick-up/strainer.

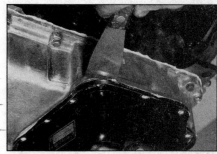

14.5 If the lower pan is stuck to the main casting, carefully ease it away using a wide-bladed scraper

14.8 Remove the oil pick-up pipe and strainer

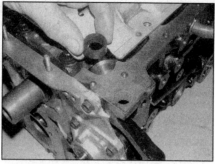

14.10 Fit a new oil pick-up pipe sealing ring

14.12 Position a new oil dipstick guide tube sealing ring

14.13 Refit the sump upper housing

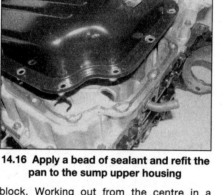

14.16 Apply a bead of sealant and refit the pan to the sump upper housing

then fill the engine with fresh oil, with reference to Chapter 1B.

19 Reconnect the battery negative lead (refer to *Disconnecting the battery* at the end of this manual).

15 Oil pump – removal, inspection and refitting

Note: *The oil pressure relief valve is screwed into the cylinder block and cannot be removed without disturbing the fuel injection pump (see paragraph 7).*

Removal

1 Remove the timing belt as described in Section 7.

2 Remove the oil pump and crankshaft timing belt sprockets as described in Section 8.

3 Remove the sump upper as housing described in Section 14.

4 Slacken and remove the retaining bolts then slide the oil pump cover off of the end of the crankshaft, taking great care not to lose the locating dowels. Remove the sealing ring, which is fitted around the oil pump housing section of the cover, and discard it.

5 Using a suitable marker pen, mark the surface of the pump outer rotor; the mark can then be used to ensure the rotor is refitted the correct way around.

6 Remove the oil pump inner and outer rotors from the cylinder block **(see illustrations)**.

7 If necessary, remove the fuel injection pump as described in Chapter 4C, and unscrew the oil pressure relief valve assembly from the rear of the cylinder block, where it is located on the right-hand side of the injection pump lower mounting bracket. Remove the sealing ring.

Inspection

8 Clean the components, and carefully examine the rotors, pump housing and cover for any signs of scoring or wear. Renew any component which shows signs of wear or damage. If the pump housing in the cylinder block is marked then seek the advice of a Vauxhall dealer on the best course of action.

10 Where necessary, fit a new sealing ring to the oil pump pick-up/strainer and fit the strainer to the base of the cylinder block **(see illustration)**. Refit the strainer retaining bolt and tighten it to the specified torque.

11 Ensure the upper housing and cylinder block mating surfaces are clean and dry, and apply a coat of suitable sealant (available from Vauxhall dealers) to the upper mating surface of the housing.

12 Position a new dipstick guide tube rubber seal on the main casting **(see illustration)**.

13 Offer up the upper housing and loosely refit all the retaining nuts and bolts **(see illustration)**. Note that the four long bolts correspond with the bolts holes at the rear of the housing. If the sump is being fitted with the engine removed from the vehicle and separated from the transmission, ensure that the rear face of the housing is flush with the transmission mounting face of the cylinder

block. Working out from the centre in a diagonal sequence, progressively tighten the upper housing retaining bolts to the specified torque setting.

14 Refit the bolts securing the upper housing to the transmission housing and tighten them to the specified torque.

15 Ensure that the oil dipstick guide tube is correctly positioned, refit the retaining bolts, and tighten securely.

16 Ensure the upper housing and sump pan mating surfaces are clean and dry and apply a coat of suitable sealant (available from Vauxhall dealers) to the upper mating surface of the pan. Refit the pan to the base of the upper housing and tighten its retaining bolts to the specified torque **(see illustration)**.

17 Refit the front section of the exhaust system with reference to Chapter 4C.

18 Where removed, refit the engine undertray, lower the vehicle to the ground

15.6a Remove the oil pump inner rotor . . .

15.6b . . . and outer rotor

15.9 Measure the inner rotor tip-to-outer rotor clearance

15.13 The seal fits flush with the housing

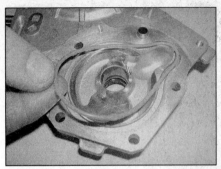

15.15 Fit a new seal to the oil pump cover

9 If the components appear serviceable, fit the rotors into the housing and measure the clearance between the outer rotor and pump housing, and the inner rotor tip-to-outer rotor clearance using feeler blades **(see illustration)**. Also measure the rotor endfloat, and check the flatness of the end cover. If the clearances exceed the specified tolerances, renew the worn components.

10 If the relief valve has been removed, check that the valve piston is free to move easily and return smoothly under spring pressure. If not renew the valve assembly.

Refitting

11 Where removed, fit a new sealing ring to the oil pressure relief valve then refit the valve assembly to the cylinder block and tighten it to the specified torque setting. Refit the fuel injection pump with reference to Chapter 4C.

12 Lubricate the pump rotors with clean engine oil and refit them to the pump housing, using the mark made prior to removal to ensure the outer rotor is fitted the correct way around.

13 Prior to refitting, carefully lever out the crankshaft and oil pump oil seals using a flat-bladed screwdriver. Fit the new oil seals, ensuring that each seals sealing lip is facing inwards, and press them squarely into the housing using a tubular drift which bears only on the hard outer edge of the seal. Press each seal into position so that it is flush with the housing then lubricate the oil seal lips with clean engine oil **(see illustration)**.

14 Ensure the mating surfaces of the oil pump and cylinder block are clean and dry and the locating dowels are in position. Remove all traces of sealant from the threads of the pump cover bolts.

15 Fit a new seal into the groove around the oil pump housing section of the cover, and apply a bead of suitable sealant (available from Vauxhall dealers) to the pump cover mating surface **(see illustration)**.

16 Carefully manoeuvre the oil pump cover into position, taking great care not to damage the oil seal lips on the crankshaft and inner rotor shaft. Locate the cover on the dowels making sure the pump sealing ring remains correctly positioned.

17 Apply a smear of sealant to the threads of each cover retaining bolt then refit all bolts and tighten them securely. Note that the longer bolt corresponds to the lower left-hand bolt hole in the cover.

18 Refit the timing belt sprockets and belt as described in Sections 7 and 8 then refit the sump as described in Section 14.

19 On completion refill the engine with clean oil as described in Chapter 1B.

16 Oil pump seal – renewal

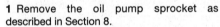

1 Remove the oil pump sprocket as described in Section 8.

2 Carefully punch or drill a small hole in the oil seal. Screw a self-tapping screw into the seal, and pull on the screw with pliers to extract the seal **(see illustration)**.

Caution: Great care must be taken to avoid damage to the oil pump.

3 Clean the seal housing, and polish off any burrs or raised edges which may have caused the seal to fail in the first place.

4 Lubricate the lips of the new seal with clean engine oil, and press it into position using a suitable tubular drift (such as a socket) which bears only on the hard outer edge of the seal. Take care not to damage the seal lips during fitting; note that the seal lips should face inwards.

5 Refit the oil pump sprocket as described in Section 8.

17 Oil cooler – removal and refitting

Removal

1 Apply the handbrake, then jack up the front of the vehicle and support it on axle stands (see *Jacking and vehicle support*). Where necessary, undo the retaining screws and remove the undertray to gain access to the oil cooler which is situated on the rear left-hand of the cylinder block.

2 Disconnect the battery negative lead (refer to *Disconnecting the battery* at the end of this manual).

3 Drain the cooling system as described in Chapter 1B. Alternatively, clamp the oil cooler coolant hoses directly above the cooler **(see illustration)**, and be prepared for some coolant loss as the hoses are disconnected. To improve access to the coolant hoses, remove the charge air pipe/hose.

4 With reference to Chapter 4C, remove the air cleaner housing and air intake trunking complete with the hot film air mass meter.

5 Disconnect the wiring from the engine control unit located over the inlet manifold, and release it from the support clip.

6 On the Y17DT engine, unscrew the intercooler-to-turbocharger air inlet pipe mounting bolts, then release the crankcase ventilation hose from the camshaft cover. Move the air inlet pipe to one side.

16.2 Pull the screw to extract the seal

17.3 Coolant hoses on the oil cooler

17.15 Fit a new sealing ring to the recess in the housing

7 Disconnect the engine management wiring and unbolt the support bracket.
8 Unscrew the nuts and remove the starter/alternator wiring harness bracket from the exhaust gas recirculation valve.
9 Remove the turbocharger centre air supply pipe, and recover the gasket.
10 Position a suitable container beneath the oil filter, then unscrew the filter cover. Undo the oil cooler return hose union, release the retaining clip and disconnect the return hose.
11 Release the clips and disconnect the coolant hoses from the oil cooler, and release the wiring loom retaining clip.
12 Remove the single bolt securing the oil filter housing to the cylinder block. Discard the sealing rings and obtain new ones.
13 Unscrew the mounting bolts and remove the oil cooler from the oil filter housing. Discard the sealing rings and obtain new ones.

Refitting

14 Refit the oil cooler to the oil filter housing, together with new sealing rings, and tighten the bolts securely.
15 Fit a new sealing ring to the recess in the rear of the oil filter housing, then locate the housing on the cylinder block. Insert the bolt and sealing washer, and tighten to the specified torque **(see illustration)**.
16 Reconnect the coolant hoses and tighten the clips. Clip the wiring in place.
17 Refit the oil filter return hose, and tighten the clips, then screw on the filter cover and tighten to the specified torque.
18 Refit the turbocharger centre air supply pipe, together with a new gasket.

18.2 Fabricate a locking tool to retain the flywheel

19 Remove the starter/alternator wiring harness bracket and tighten the nuts.
20 Refit the engine management wiring bracket and reconnect the wiring.
21 On the Y17DT engine, refit the air inlet pipe and tighten the bolts.
22 Reconnect the wiring to the engine control unit, and attach it to the support clip.
23 Refit the air cleaner housing and air intake trunking, complete with the hot film air mass meter, with reference to Chapter 4C.
24 Reconnect the battery negative lead (refer to *Disconnecting the battery* at the end of this manual).
25 Lower the vehicle to the ground. Top-up the engine oil level as described in *Weekly checks*.
26 Refill or top-up the cooling system as described in *Weekly checks* or Chapter 1B (as applicable). Start the engine, and check the oil cooler for signs of leakage.

18 Flywheel – removal, inspection and refitting

Note: *New flywheel retaining bolts will be required on refitting.*

Removal

1 Remove the transmission as described in Chapter 7A then remove the clutch assembly as described in Chapter 6.
2 Prevent the flywheel from turning by locking the ring gear teeth **(see illustration)**. Alternatively, bolt a strap between the flywheel and the cylinder block/crankcase. As an aid to refitting, make alignment marks between the flywheel and crankshaft using paint or a suitable marker pen. Note, however, that the flywheel will only fit in one position, as the bolts are slightly offset.
3 Slacken and remove the retaining bolts and plate, then remove the flywheel **(see illustration)**. Do not drop it, as it is very heavy.

Inspection

4 Examine the flywheel for wear or chipping of the ring gear teeth. Renewal of the ring gear is possible but is not a task for the home

18.3 Remove the flywheel bolts and recover the plate

mechanic; renewal requires the new ring gear to be heated (up to 180° to 230°C) to allow it to be fitted.
5 Examine the flywheel for scoring of the clutch face. If the clutch face is scored, the flywheel may be surface-ground, but renewal is preferable.
6 If there is any doubt about the condition of the flywheel, seek the advice of a Vauxhall dealer or engine reconditioning specialist. They will be able to advise if it is possible to recondition it or whether renewal is necessary.

Refitting

7 Clean the mating surfaces of the flywheel and crankshaft.
8 Apply a drop of locking compound to the threads of each of the new flywheel retaining bolts then refit the flywheel and retaining plate and install the new bolts. If the original is being refitted align the marks made prior to removal.
9 Lock the flywheel using the method employed on dismantling then, working in a diagonal sequence, evenly and progressively tighten the retaining bolts to the specified Stage 1 torque setting.
10 Once all bolts have been tightened to the Stage 1 torque, go around and tighten all bolts through the specified Stage 2 and Stage 3 angles. It is recommended that an angle-measuring gauge is used to ensure accuracy. If a gauge is not available, use white paint to make alignment marks prior to tightening. The marks can then be used to check that the bolt has been rotated through the correct angle.
11 Refit the clutch as described in Chapter 6 then remove the locking tool and refit the transmission as described in Chapter 7A.

19 Crankshaft oil seals – renewal

Timing belt end oil seal

1 Remove the crankshaft sprocket as described in Section 8.
2 Carefully punch or drill two small holes opposite each other in the oil seal. Screw a self-tapping screw into each and pull on the screws with pliers to extract the seal.
3 Clean the seal housing and polish off any burrs or raised edges which may have caused the seal to fail in the first place.
4 Lubricate the lips of the new seal with clean engine oil and ease it into position on the end of the shaft. Press the seal squarely into position until it is flush with the housing. If necessary, a suitable tubular drift which bears only on the hard outer edge of the seal can be used to tap the seal into position. Take great care not to damage the seal lips during fitting and ensure that the seal lips face inwards.
5 Wash off any traces of oil, then refit the crankshaft sprocket as described in Section 8.

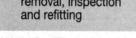

Flywheel end oil seal

6 Remove the flywheel as described in Section 18.

7 Renew the seal as described in paragraphs 2 to 4 **(see illustration)**.

8 Refit the flywheel as described in Section 18.

20 Engine/transmission mountings – inspection and renewal

Inspection

1 To improve access, firmly apply the handbrake, then jack up the front of the vehicle and support it on axle stands (see *Jacking and vehicle support*).

2 Check the mounting blocks (rubbers) to see if they are cracked, hardened or separated from the metal at any point. Renew the mounting block if any such damage or deterioration is evident.

3 Check that all the mounting securing nuts and bolts are securely tightened, using a torque wrench to check if possible.

4 Using a large screwdriver, or a similar tool, check for wear in the mounting blocks by carefully levering against them to check for free play. Where this is not possible, enlist the aid of an assistant to move the engine/gearbox unit back-and-forth, and from side-to-side, while you observe the mountings. While some free play is to be expected, even from new components, excessive wear should be obvious. If excessive free play is found, check first to see that the securing nuts and bolts are correctly tightened, then renew any worn components as described in the following paragraphs.

Renewal

Note: *Before slackening any of the engine mounting bolts/nuts, the relative positions of the mountings to their various brackets should be marked to ensure correct alignment upon refitting.*

Right-hand mounting

5 Apply the handbrake, then jack up the front of the vehicle and support it on axle stands (see *Jacking and vehicle support*). Remove

19.7 The seal fits flush with the housing

the right-hand roadwheel and the wheel arch liner for access to the crankshaft pulley.

6 Remove the air cleaner as described in Chapter 4C.

7 Attach a suitable hoist and lifting tackle to the engine lifting brackets on the cylinder head, and support the weight of the engine.

8 Mark the position of the mounting brackets and bolts, then unscrew the bolts and remove the right-hand mounting from the engine mounting bracket and body. If necessary, the lower mounting bracket may also be unbolted from the cylinder block **(see illustrations). Note:** *Take great care not to place any excess stress on the exhaust system when raising or lowering the engine. If necessary, disconnect the front pipe from the manifold (see Chapter 4C).*

9 If removed, refit the lower mounting bracket and tighten the bolts to the specified torque, then locate the new mounting block on the

body and engine mounting bracket, and tighten the bolts to the specified torque.

10 Remove the hoist, then refit the air cleaner.

11 Refit the wheel arch liner and right-hand roadwheel, then lower the vehicle to the ground.

Front mounting/torque link

12 Apply the handbrake, then jack up the front of the vehicle and support it on axle stands (see *Jacking and vehicle support*). Remove the right-hand roadwheel and the wheel arch liner for access to the crankshaft pulley.

13 Attach a suitable hoist and lifting tackle to the engine lifting brackets on the cylinder head, and support the weight of the engine.

14 Slacken and remove the nut and washer securing the mounting to the subframe bracket. Withdraw the bolt **(see illustration)**

15 Undo the bolts securing the mounting bracket to the transmission, then manoeuvre the mounting and bracket out of position. **Note:** *Take great care not to place any excess stress on the exhaust system when raising or lowering the engine. If necessary, disconnect the front pipe from the manifold (see Chapter 4C).*

16 Check all components for signs of wear or damage, and renew as necessary.

17 On reassembly, refit the mounting bracket (aligning the previously made marks) and tighten its bolts to the specified torque.

18 Locate the mounting in the subframe, ensuring it is fitted the correct way up, and manoeuvre the engine/transmission into position. Refit the mounting bolts and new nuts. Tighten them to the specified torque.

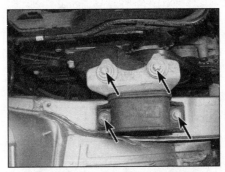

20.8a Right-hand engine mounting

20.8b Mark the position of the bolts before unscrewing them

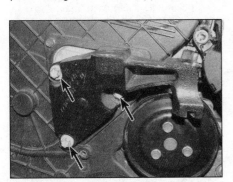

20.8c Bolts securing the lower mounting bracket to the cylinder block

20.8d Removing the lower mounting bracket

20.14 Front engine-to-subframe torque link

20.35 Rear engine-to-subframe torque link

19 Lower the vehicle to the ground.

Left-hand mounting

20 Release the clips and position the coolant expansion tank to one side.
21 Attach a suitable hoist and lifting tackle to the engine lifting brackets on the cylinder head, and support the weight of the engine.
22 Using a Torx socket, unscrew the two bolts securing the engine mounting bracket to the body mounting bracket.
23 Unbolt the mounting brackets from the engine and body. Slightly lower the engine, then unclip the clutch hydraulic line from the mounting bracket. **Note:** *Take great care not to place any excess stress on the exhaust system when raising or lowering the engine. If necessary, disconnect the front pipe from the manifold (see Chapter 4C).*
24 Unscrew the bolt and separate the adaptor block.
25 Fit the new adaptor block and tighten the bolt to the specified torque.
26 Locate the new mounting brackets in position and, where necessary, clip the clutch hydraulic line onto the bracket.
27 Raise the engine and insert the bolts, then tighten them to the specified torque.
28 Disconnect the hoist and lifting tackle.
29 Refit the coolant expansion tank and attach the clips.

Rear mounting/torque link

30 Apply the handbrake, then jack up the front of the vehicle and support it on axle stands (see *Jacking and vehicle support*).
31 Attach a suitable hoist and lifting tackle to the engine lifting brackets on the cylinder head, and support the weight of the engine.
32 Refer to Chapter 4C and unbolt the exhaust front pipe from the exhaust manifold, taking care to support the flexible section. **Note:** *Angular movement in excess of 10° can cause permanent damage to the flexible section.*
33 Release the mounting rubbers and support the front of the exhaust pipe to one side.
34 Working under the vehicle, remove the nut and bolt securing the mounting to the transmission bracket.
35 Remove the bolt securing the mounting to the subframe, and withdraw the mounting/torque link **(see illustration)**.
36 If necessary, unbolt the bracket from the transmission. **Note:** *The bracket bolts and link bolts are of different lengths.*
37 Refit the bracket to the transmission and tighten the bolts to the specified torque.
38 Locate the new mounting/link in position. Insert the bolts and tighten to the specified torque.
39 Refit the exhaust front pipe with reference to Chapter 4C.
40 Remove the hoist and lower the vehicle to the ground.

Chapter 2 Part D:
Engine removal and overhaul procedures

Contents

Degrees of difficulty

Easy, suitable for novice with little experience	**Fairly easy,** suitable for beginner with some experience	**Fairly difficult,** suitable for competent DIY mechanic 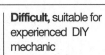	**Difficult,** suitable for experienced DIY mechanic	**Very difficult,** suitable for expert DIY or professional

Specifications

Note: *Where specifications are given as N/A, no information was available at the time of writing. Refer to your Vauxhall dealer for the latest information available.*

Engine identification

Engine type	Manufacturer's code
973 cc DOHC 12-valve petrol engine	Z10XE and Z10XE-ECO
1199 cc DOHC 16-valve petrol engine	Z12XE
1389 cc DOHC 16-valve petrol engine	Z14XE
1686 cc DOHC 16-valve diesel engine:	
Low-pressure turbo	Y17DTL
High-pressure turbo with intercooler	Y17DT

1.0 litre and 1.2 litre DOHC petrol engines

Cylinder block

Material	Cast iron
Maximum cylinder bore ovality	0.013 mm
Maximum cylinder bore taper	0.013 mm
Maximum permissible rebore oversize	0.500 mm

Cylinder bore diameters:
  Standard size:
    Identification mark 99 .... 72.485 to 72.495 mm
    Identification mark 00 .... 72.495 to 72.505 mm
    Identification mark 01 .... 72.505 to 72.515 mm
  0.500 mm oversize:
    Identification mark 9 + 0.5 .... 72.885 to 72.995 mm

Pistons

Piston-to-bore clearance:
  New .... 0.020 to 0.030 mm
  After rebore (oversize) .... 0.010 to 0.030 mm

Note: *Piston diameters: pistons carry identification marks corresponding to those listed previously for cylinder bore diameters. The appropriate piston diameter is 0.020 mm less than the corresponding bore diameter.*

Piston rings

Number of rings (per piston)	2 compression, 1 oil control

Ring end gap:
  Compression .... 0.200 to 0.400 mm
  Oil control (top and bottom sections) .... 0.400 to 1.400 mm
Ring gap offset (to gap of adjacent ring)* .... 180°

*For oil control ring sections, see text (Section 17).

Cylinder head

Material	Light alloy
Maximum permissible distortion of sealing face	0.025 mm
Overall height of cylinder head (sealing surface-to-sealing surface)	126.000 mm

Valve seat width:
  Inlet .... 1.000 to 1.400 mm
  Exhaust .... 1.400 to 1.800 mm
Valve seat angle .... 45°

Crankshaft and bearings

Number of main bearings:
  1.0 litre engines 4
  1.2 litre engines 5
Main bearing journal diameter:
  Standard size .... 50.004 to 50.017 mm (nominal). Undersize bearing shells are available
Big-end bearing journal diameter:
  Standard .... 42.971 to 42.987 mm (nominal). Undersize bearing shells are available
Crankshaft endfloat .... 0.100 to 0.200 mm
Connecting rod endfloat .... 0.013 to 0.049 mm

Valves and guides

Stem diameter:
  Inlet valve:
    Standard .... 4.955 to 4.970 mm. Oversize valves are available
  Exhaust valve:
    Standard .... 4.945 to 4.960 mm. Oversize valves are available
Valve head diameter:
  Inlet valve .... 27.900 to 28.100 mm.
  Exhaust valve .... 24.900 to 25.100 mm.
Maximum permissible valve stem play in guide:
  Inlet .... 0.018 to 0.052 mm.
  Exhaust .... 0.028 to 0.062 mm.
Valve seat angle (included) .... 90°40'
Valve clearances .... Automatic adjustment by hydraulic valve lifters
Valve guide bore:
  Standard .... 4.988 to 5.007 mm. Oversize valve guides are available
Valve guide length (inlet and exhaust) .... 38.750 to 39.250 mm
Valve guide fitted height above cylinder head (inlet and exhaust):
  Up to 2002 MY .... 11.700 to 12.000 mm
  From 2003 MY .... 12.700 to 13.000 mm

1.4 litre DOHC petrol engine

Cylinder block
Material . . . . Cast iron
Cylinder bore diameter . . . . 77.575 to 77.785 mm (nominal)

Pistons
Piston-to-bore clearance:
  New . . . . 0.020 mm
  After rebore (oversize) . . . . 0.010 to 0.030 mm
Note: *Piston diameters: pistons carry identification marks corresponding to those listed previously for cylinder bore diameters.*
The appropriate piston diameter is 0.020 mm less than the corresponding bore diameter.

Piston rings
Number of rings (per piston) . . . . 2 compression, 1 oil control
Ring end gap:
  Compression . . . . 0.300 to 0.500 mm
  Oil control (top and bottom sections) . . . . 0.400 to 1.400 mm
Compression ring gap offset (to gap of adjacent ring)* . . . . 180°
For oil control ring sections, see text (Section 17).

Cylinder head
Material . . . . Light alloy
Maximum permissible distortion of sealing face . . . . 0.025 mm
Overall height of cylinder head (sealing surface-to-sealing surface) . . . 134.900 to 135.100 mm
Valve seat width:
  Inlet . . . . 1.000 to 1.400 mm
  Exhaust . . . . 1.400 to 1.800 mm
Valve seat angle . . . . 45°

Crankshaft and bearings
Number of main bearings 5
Main bearing journal diameter:
  Standard (all engines) . . . . 54.980 to 54.997 mm (nominal). Undersize bearing shells are available
Big-end bearing journal diameter:
  Standard . . . . 42.971 to 42.987 mm (nominal). Undersize bearing shells are available
Crankshaft endfloat . . . . 0.100 to 0.202 mm
Connecting rod endfloat . . . . 0.070 to 0.142 mm

Valves and guides
Stem diameter:
  Inlet valve:
    Standard . . . . 5.955 to 5.970 mm (nominal)
  Exhaust valve:
    Standard . . . . 5.935 to 5.950 mm (nominal). Oversize valves are available
Valve head diameter:
  Inlet valve . . . . 30.900 to 31.100 mm
  Exhaust valve . . . . 27.400 to 27.600 mm
Maximum permissible valve stem play in guide:
  Inlet . . . . 0.030 to 0.057 mm
  Exhaust . . . . 0.050 to 0.077 mm
Valve seat angle (included) . . . . 90°40'
Valve clearances . . . . Automatic adjustment by hydraulic valve lifters
Valve guide bore:
  Standard . . . . 6.000 to 6.012 mm (nominal). Oversize valve guides are available
Valve guide length:
  Inlet . . . . 44.750 to 45.250 mm
  Exhaust . . . . 34.750 to 35.250 mm
Valve guide fitted height above cylinder head (inlet and exhaust) . . . . . 10.700 to 11.000 mm

1.7 litre DOHC diesel engine

Cylinder block
Material . . . . Cast iron
Cylinder bore diameters . . . . 79.00 to 79.03 mm (nominal)

Pistons
Piston-to-bore clearance . . . . 0.061 to 0.08 mm
Piston projection . . . . 0.63 to 0.83 mm

Piston rings
Number of rings (per piston) . . . . 2 compression, 1 oil control
Ring end gap:
    Top compression ring . . . . 0.25 to 0.35 mm
    Second compression ring . . . . 0.20 to 0.30 mm
    Oil control ring . . . . 0.20 to 0.40 mm

Cylinder head
Material . . . . Light alloy
Maximum gasket face distortion . . . . 0.1 mm
Cylinder head height . . . . 94.95 to 95.05 mm
Valve seat width . . . . 1.5 to 1.7 mm
Valve head depth below gasket face . . . . N/A
Valve seat angle . . . . 90°

Crankshaft and bearings
Endfloat . . . . 0.03 to 0.15 mm
Main bearing journal diameter . . . . 51.928 to 51.938 mm (nominal)
Big-end bearing journal (crankpin) diameter . . . . N/A

Valves and guides
Valve stem diameter:
    Inlet . . . . 6.00 mm
    Exhaust . . . . 6.00 mm
Valve guide bore diameter . . . . 7.000 to 7.015 mm
Valve guide length . . . . 41.75 to 42.25 mm

Stem-to-guide clearance:	Inlet	Exhaust
Standard	0.019 mm	0.0215 mm
Service limit	N/A	N/A
Valve length	98.45 mm	98.10 mm
Valve head diameter	27.5 mm	26.5 mm
Valve seat angle at valve head	89°	89°

Connecting rod
Big-end side clearance . . . . 0.25 to 0.58 mm
Maximum permissible weight difference between connecting rods . . . 4 grams

Torque wrench settings

1.0 litre and 1.2 litre DOHC petrol engine
Refer to Chapter 2A Specifications

1.4 litre DOHC petrol engine
Refer to Chapter 2B Specifications

1.7 litre DOHC diesel engine
Refer to Chapter 2C Specifications

1 General information

Included in this Part of Chapter 2 are details of removing the engine/transmission from the car and general overhaul procedures for the cylinder head, cylinder block/crankcase and all other engine internal components.

The information given ranges from advice concerning preparation for an overhaul and the purchase of replacement parts, to detailed step-by-step procedures covering removal, inspection, renovation and refitting of engine internal components.

After Section 6, all instructions are based on the assumption that the engine has been removed from the car. For information concerning in-car engine repair, as well as the removal and refitting of those external components necessary for full overhaul, refer to Part A, B or C of this Chapter (as applicable) and to Section 6. Ignore any preliminary dismantling operations described in Part A, B or C that are no longer relevant once the engine has been removed from the car.

Apart from torque wrench settings, which are given at the beginning of Part A, B or C (as applicable), all specifications relating to engine overhaul are at the beginning of this Part of Chapter 2.

2 Engine overhaul – general information

It is not always easy to determine when, or if, an engine should be completely overhauled, as a number of factors must be considered.

High mileage is not necessarily an indication that an overhaul is needed, while low mileage does not preclude the need for an overhaul. Frequency of servicing is probably the most important consideration. An engine which has had regular and frequent oil and filter changes, as well as other required maintenance, should give many thousands of miles of reliable service. Conversely, a neglected engine may require an overhaul very early in its life.

Excessive oil consumption is an indication that piston rings, valve seals and/or valve guides are in need of attention. Make sure that oil leaks are not responsible before deciding that the rings and/or guides are worn. Perform a compression test, as described in Part A or B (petrol engines) or C (diesel engine) of this Chapter, to determine the likely cause of the problem.

Check the oil pressure with a gauge fitted in place of the oil pressure switch, and compare it with that specified. If it is extremely low, the main and big-end bearings, and/or the oil pump, are probably worn out.

Loss of power, rough running, knocking or metallic engine noises, excessive valve gear noise, and high fuel consumption may also point to the need for an overhaul, especially if they are all present at the same time. If a complete service does not cure the situation, major mechanical work is the only solution.

An engine overhaul involves restoring all internal parts to the specification of a new engine. During an overhaul, the pistons and the piston rings are renewed. New main and big-end bearings are generally fitted; if necessary, the crankshaft may be renewed to restore the journals. The valves are also serviced as well, since they are usually in less-than-perfect condition at this point. While the engine is being overhauled, other components, such as the starter and alternator, can be overhauled as well. The end result should be an as-new engine that will give many trouble-free miles. **Note:** *Critical cooling system components such as the hoses, thermostat and coolant pump should be renewed when an engine is overhauled. The radiator should be checked carefully, to ensure that it is not clogged or leaking. Also, it is a good idea to renew the oil pump whenever the engine is overhauled.*

Before beginning the engine overhaul, read through the entire procedure, to familiarise yourself with the scope and requirements of the job. Overhauling an engine is not difficult if you follow carefully all of the instructions, have the necessary tools and equipment, and pay close attention to all specifications. It can, however, be time-consuming. Plan on the car being off the road for a minimum of two weeks, especially if parts must be taken to an engineering works for repair or reconditioning. Check on the availability of parts and make sure that any necessary special tools and equipment are obtained in advance. Most work can be done with typical hand tools, although a number of precision measuring tools are required for inspecting parts to determine if they must be renewed. Often the engineering works will handle the inspection of parts and offer advice concerning reconditioning and renewal. **Note:** *Always wait until the engine has been completely dismantled, and until all components (especially the cylinder block/crankcase and the crankshaft) have been inspected, before deciding what service and repair operations must be performed by an engineering works. The condition of these components will be the major factor to consider when determining whether to overhaul the original engine, or to buy a reconditioned unit. Do not, therefore, purchase parts or have overhaul work done on other components until they have been thoroughly inspected.* As a general rule, time is the primary cost of an overhaul, so it does not pay to fit worn or sub-standard parts.

As a final note, to ensure maximum life and minimum trouble from a reconditioned engine, everything must be assembled with care, in a spotlessly-clean environment.

3 Engine removal – methods and precautions

If you have decided that the engine must be removed for overhaul or major repair work, several preliminary steps should be taken.

Locating a suitable place to work is extremely important. Adequate work space, along with storage space for the car, will be needed. If a workshop or garage is not available, at the very least, a flat, level, clean work surface is required.

Cleaning the engine compartment and engine/transmission before beginning the removal procedure will help keep tools clean and organised.

An engine hoist or A-frame will also be necessary. Make sure the equipment is rated in excess of the combined weight of the engine and transmission. Safety is of primary importance, considering the potential hazards involved in lowering the engine/transmission out of the car.

If this is the first time you have removed an engine, an assistant should ideally be available. Advice and aid from someone more experienced would also be helpful. There are many instances when one person cannot simultaneously perform all of the operations required when lowering the engine out of the vehicle.

Plan the operation ahead of time. Before starting work, arrange for the hire of or obtain all of the tools and equipment you will need. Some of the equipment necessary to perform engine/transmission removal and installation safely and with relative ease (in addition to an engine hoist) is as follows: a heavy duty trolley jack, complete sets of spanners and sockets, wooden blocks, and plenty of rags and cleaning solvent for mopping-up spilled oil, coolant and fuel. If the hoist must be hired, make sure that you arrange for it in advance, and perform all of the operations possible without it beforehand. This will save you money and time.

Plan for the car to be out of use for quite a while. An engineering works will be required to perform some of the work which the do-it-yourselfer cannot accomplish without special equipment. These places often have a busy schedule, so it would be a good idea to consult them before removing the engine, in order to accurately estimate the amount of time required to rebuild or repair components that may need work.

During the engine removal procedure, it is advisable to make notes of the locations of all brackets, cable ties, earthing points, etc, as well as how the wiring harnesses, hoses and electrical connections are attached and routed around the engine and engine compartment.

Always be extremely careful when removing and refitting the engine/transmission. Serious injury can result from careless actions. Plan

4.15a Disconnect the wiring from the alternator . . .

ahead and take your time, and a job of this nature, although major, can be accomplished successfully.

On all Corsa models, the engine must be removed complete with the transmission as an assembly. There is insufficient clearance in the engine compartment to remove the engine leaving the transmission in the vehicle. The assembly is removed by raising the front of the vehicle, and lowering the assembly from the engine compartment.

4 Petrol engine and transmission unit – removal, separation and refitting

Note: *The engine can be removed from the car only as a complete unit with the transmission; the two are then separated for overhaul. The engine/transmission unit is lowered out of position, and withdrawn from under the vehicle. Bearing this in mind, ensure the vehicle is raised sufficiently so that there is enough clearance between the front of the vehicle and the floor to allow the engine/transmission unit to be slid out once it has been lowered out of position.*

Removal

1 Position the steering with the front roadwheels straight-ahead, and lock the steering by removing the ignition key.
2 Apply the handbrake, then jack up the front of the vehicle and support it on axle stands (see *Jacking and vehicle support*). Remove both front roadwheels, and the right-hand

4.15b . . . and from the starter motor solenoid (1.0 and 1.2 litre petrol)

inner wheel arch liner for access to the crankshaft pulley. Where necessary, remove the engine compartment undertray and the engine top cover. Note that the vehicle must be raised sufficiently high (approximately 650 mm) to enable the engine/transmission assembly to be withdrawn from under the front of the vehicle.
3 To improve access, remove the bonnet as described in Chapter 11.
4 Disconnect the battery negative lead (refer to *Disconnecting the battery* at the end of this manual).
5 If necessary, drain the engine oil as described in Chapter 1A.
6 Working in the driver's footwell, unscrew the nut and remove the bolt securing the column intermediate shaft to the steering gear pinion shaft. Separate the intermediate shaft from the pinion shaft by pulling the intermediate shaft upwards.
Caution: To prevent damage to the airbag clockspring, the steering lock must remain locked until the intermediate shaft is re-attached to the pinion shaft.
7 Remove the front bumper as described in Chapter 11.
8 Drain the cooling system as described in Chapter 1A, then refit and tighten the drain plug.
9 Remove the air cleaner assembly as described in Chapter 4A or 4B (as applicable).
10 Release the clip and disconnect the upper preheater hose from the throttle body.
11 On the bulkhead at the rear of the engine compartment, release the clips and disconnect the two hoses from the heater matrix.
12 Depressurise the fuel system with reference to Chapter 4A or 4B (as applicable), then disconnect the fuel line from the throttle body. Be prepared for fuel spillage, and take adequate precautions. Clamp or plug the open ends of the hoses, to minimise further fuel loss.
13 Disconnect the brake vacuum servo hose, and fuel evaporation purge hose.
14 Loosen the clips and remove the upper and lower radiator hoses.
15 Note the locations of the wiring to the various engine and transmission components, then disconnect them and move the wiring harness to one side **(see illustrations)**. At the same time, disconnect the battery positive lead and release the rubber seal from the engine compartment rear panel. Also disconnect the wiring harness combination plug located near the battery.
16 On standard manual transmission models (not Easytronic), place some cloth rags around the clutch hydraulic connection on the transmission, then disconnect the hose, plug it, and position to one side.
17 Tie the radiator to the engine compartment front crossmember in preparation for lowering the front subframe.
18 Remove the hub caps, then extract the split pins and unscrew the driveshaft outer

hub nuts while holding the hubs stationary. To do this, temporarily insert the wheel bolts and have an assistant depress the brake pedal while the nuts are loosened.
19 Remove the front brake discs with reference to Chapter 9.
20 Refer to Chapter 10 and disconnect the track rods from the hub carrier steering arms. Also detach the anti-roll bar links from the front suspension struts, and detach the front suspension lower arms from the hub carriers.
21 Disconnect the driveshafts from the hub carriers by carefully tapping them through the hubs while pulling out the carriers. Tie the struts and carriers to one side.
22 On models with air conditioning, remove the auxiliary drivebelt (Chapter 1A), then unbolt the compressor from the engine **without disconnecting the refrigerant lines** and support the compressor to one side.
23 Remove the exhaust system as described in Chapter 4A or 4B (as applicable).
24 Except on Easytronic models, refer to Chapter 7A or 7B and disconnect the gearchange/selector rod from the transmission.
25 On automatic transmission models, unscrew the union bolts and disconnect the fluid lines from the fluid cooler. Recover the copper sealing washers, and plug the openings to prevent entry of dust and dirt.
26 Support the front suspension subframe on trolley jacks, then mark the position of the subframe on the front underbody, and unscrew the four mounting bolts. Discard the bolts as new ones must be used for refitting. Unscrew and remove the bolt securing the engine rear torque link to the subframe. With the help of an assistant, carefully lower the subframe to the ground and withdraw from under the vehicle.

> **HAYNES HINT** *To ensure correct repositioning, we bolted two lengths of metal bar to the subframe, and marked their position on the underbody.*

27 Attach a suitable hoist and lifting tackle to the engine lifting brackets on the cylinder head, and support the weight of the engine/transmission.
28 Unscrew the two bolts securing the right-hand engine mounting to the engine lower mounting bracket. **Note:** *There is no need to remove the mounting, since the engine/transmission is lowered from the engine compartment.*
29 Unscrew the two bolts securing the left-hand engine mounting to the transmission.
30 Make a final check to ensure that all relevant pipes, hoses, wires, etc, have been disconnected, and that they are positioned clear of the engine and transmission.
31 With the help of an assistant, carefully lower the engine/transmission assembly to the ground. Make sure that the surrounding components in the engine compartment are

not damaged. Ideally, the assembly should be lowered onto a trolley jack or low platform with castors, so that it can easily be withdrawn from under the car.

32 Ensure that the assembly is adequately supported, then disconnect the engine hoist and lifting tackle, and withdraw the engine/transmission assembly from under the front of the vehicle.

33 Clean away any external dirt using paraffin or a water-soluble solvent and a stiff brush.

34 If necessary, remove the driveshafts from the transmission with reference to Chapter 8.

35 With reference to Chapter 7A, 7B or 7C, unbolt the transmission from the engine. Carefully withdraw the transmission from the engine. On manual transmission models, ensure that its weight is not allowed to hang on the input shaft while engaged with the clutch friction disc. On automatic transmission models, ensure that the torque converter is removed together with the transmission so that it remains engaged with the oil pump. Note that the transmission locates on dowels positioned in the rear of the cylinder block.

Refitting

36 With reference to Chapter 7A, 7B or 7C, refit the transmission to the engine and tighten the bolts to the specified torque.

37 If removed, refit the driveshafts to the transmission with reference to Chapter 8.

38 With the front of the vehicle raised and supported on axle stands, move the engine/transmission assembly under the vehicle, ensuring that the assembly is adequately supported.

39 Reconnect the hoist and lifting tackle to the engine lifting brackets, and carefully raise the engine/transmission assembly up into the engine compartment with the help of an assistant.

40 Reconnect the right- and left-hand engine/transmission mountings and tighten the bolts to the specified torque given in Chapters 2A, 2B or 2C.

41 Disconnect the hoist and lifting tackle from the engine lifting brackets.

42 With the aid of an assistant, raise the subframe onto the underbody, and at the same time, make sure that the radiator lower mounting pins engage with the rubbers in the subframe. Untie the radiator from the crossmember.

43 Check that the subframe is located in its previously-noted position and insert the mounting bolts. With the subframe held in position, tighten the (new) bolts to the specified torque and angles given in Chapters 2A, 2B or 2C.

44 Refit the bolt securing the engine rear torque link to the subframe, and tighten to the specified torque.

45 On automatic transmission models, reconnect the fluid lines to the fluid cooler together with new copper sealing washers,

and tighten the union bolts to the specified torque.

46 Except on Easytronic models, reconnect the gearchange/selector rod to the transmission with reference to Chapter 7A or 7B.

47 Refit the exhaust system with reference to Chapter 4A or 4B (as applicable).

48 On models with air conditioning, refit the compressor with reference to Chapter 3, then refit the auxiliary drivebelt with reference to Chapter 1A.

49 Reconnect the driveshafts to the hub carriers, then reconnect the lower arms, anti-roll bar links and track rods with reference to Chapter 10. At this stage the driveshaft/hub nuts can be tightened moderately, then fully tightened when the vehicle is lowered to the ground.

50 Refit the front brake discs with reference to Chapter 9.

51 On standard manual transmission models (not Easytronic), reconnect and bleed the clutch hydraulic connection at the transmission with reference to Chapter 6.

52 Reconnect the wiring to the various components as previously noted.

53 Reconnect the upper and lower radiator hoses and tighten the clips.

54 Reconnect the brake vacuum servo hose, and fuel evaporation purge hose.

55 Reconnect the fuel line to the throttle body.

56 Reconnect the heater matrix hoses and tighten the clips.

57 Reconnect the upper preheater hose to the throttle body and tighten the clips.

58 Refit the air cleaner assembly with reference to Chapter 4A or 4B (as applicable).

59 Refit the front bumper with reference to Chapter 11.

60 Reconnect the steering column inter-mediate shaft to the steering gear pinion shaft and tighten the bolt and nut with reference to Chapter 10.

61 Check and if necessary top-up the trans-mission oil level as described in Chapter 7A or 7C, as appropriate.

62 Make a final check to ensure that all relevant hoses, pipes and wires have been correctly reconnected.

63 Reconnect the battery negative lead (refer to *Disconnecting the battery* at the end of this manual).

64 Refit the right-hand inner wheel arch liner, front roadwheels, and engine compartment undertray (where fitted), then lower the vehicle to the ground.

65 Refill the engine with oil with reference to Chapter 1A.

66 Refill and bleed the cooling system with reference to Chapter 1A.

67 On automatic transmission models, check and top-up the fluid level with reference to Chapter 1A.

68 Fully tighten the driveshaft/hub nuts to the specified torque.

69 Refit the bonnet as described in Chapter 11.

5 Diesel engine and transmission unit – removal, separation and refitting

Note: *The engine can be removed from the car only as a complete unit with the transmission; the two are then separated for overhaul. The engine/transmission unit is lowered out of position, and withdrawn from under the vehicle. Bearing this in mind, ensure the vehicle is raised sufficiently so that there is enough clearance between the front of the vehicle and the floor to allow the engine/transmission unit to be slid out once it has been lowered out of position.*

Removal

1 Position the steering with the front roadwheels straight-ahead, and lock the steering by removing the ignition key.

2 Apply the handbrake, then jack up the front of the vehicle and support it on axle stands (see *Jacking and vehicle support*). Remove both front roadwheels, and the right-hand inner wheel arch liner for access to the crankshaft pulley. Where necessary, remove the engine compartment undertray and the engine top cover. Note that the vehicle must be raised sufficiently high (approximately 650 mm) to enable the engine/transmission assembly to be withdrawn from under the front of the vehicle.

3 To improve access, remove the bonnet as described in Chapter 11.

4 Disconnect the battery negative lead (refer to *Disconnecting the battery* at the end of this manual).

5 If necessary, drain the engine oil as described in Chapter 1B.

6 Working in the driver's footwell, unscrew the nut and remove the bolt securing the column intermediate shaft to the steering gear pinion shaft **(see illustration)**. Separate the intermediate shaft from the pinion shaft by pulling the intermediate shaft upwards.

Caution: To prevent damage to the airbag clockspring, the steering lock must remain locked until the intermediate shaft is re-attached to the pinion shaft.

7 Remove the front bumper as described in Chapter 11.

5.6 Removing the bolt securing the column intermediate shaft to the steering gear pinion shaft

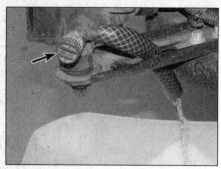

5.8 The drain plug is on the left-hand side of the radiator

5.10a Release the hoses from the clips . . .

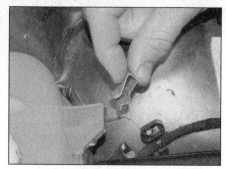

5.10b . . . and remove the coolant expansion tank mounting clips

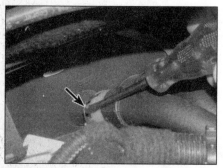

5.11a Pull out the locking spring clips . . .

5.11b . . . and disconnect the quick-release connections for the two heater matrix hoses

5.12a Disconnect the battery leads . . .

8 Drain the cooling system as described in Chapter 1B, then refit and tighten the drain plug **(see illustration)**.
9 Remove the air cleaner assembly as described in Chapter 4C.
10 Remove the clips and release the hoses,

then lift the coolant expansion tank from its mounting and position it to one side **(see illustrations)**.
11 On the bulkhead at the rear of the engine compartment, pull out the special locking spring clips and disconnect the quick-release

connections for two hoses from the heater matrix **(see illustrations)**. Also, where applicable, loosen the clips and disconnect the two hoses from the auxiliary heater.
12 Note the locations of the wiring to the relevant engine and transmission components, then disconnect them and move the wiring harness to one side. To do this, first disconnect the battery leads, release the rubber seal and plastic panel from the rear of the engine compartment, disconnect the wiring from the washer fluid reservoir warning switch, release the harness from the bulkhead and position it on the engine **(see illustrations)**. Where necessary, disconnect the wiring harness combination plug located near the battery. Depending on the reason for removing the engine/transmission, some wiring may remain connected.
13 Unclip the vacuum lines then unscrew the bolt and remove the wiring harness trough

5.12b . . . release the rubber seal . . .

5.12c . . . and plastic panel . . .

5.12d . . . disconnect the wiring from the washer fluid reservoir . . .

5.12e . . . and release the wiring harness from the bulkhead

5.13a Unclip the vacuum lines . . .

5.13b ... then unscrew the bolts ...

5.13c ... and remove the wiring harness trough

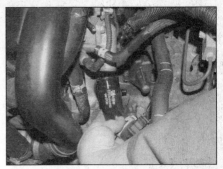

5.14a Disconnecting the radiator upper hose from the thermostat housing ...

5.14b ... and the lower hose from the water pump

5.16 Disconnecting the brake vacuum servo hose

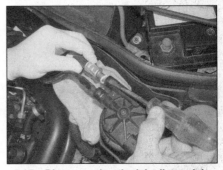

5.17a Disconnecting the inlet line quick-release connectors from the fuel filter

from over the upper timing belt cover (see illustrations).

14 Disconnect the wiring from the electric cooling fan, and position it to one side. Loosen the clips and remove the upper and lower radiator hoses (see illustration).

15 Place some cloth rags around the clutch hydraulic connection on the transmission, then pull out the clip to disconnect the hose, plug or cover it, and position to one side.

16 Disconnect the brake vacuum servo and EGR hoses from the vacuum pump (refer to Chapter 9 if necessary), or at the one-way valve located on the front of the engine (see illustration).

17 Disconnect the two fuel inlet lines from the fuel filter with reference to Chapter 1B and cover the ends (see illustrations). Also, disconnect the fuel return line from the injection pump.

18 Tie the radiator to the engine compart-

ment front crossmember in preparation for lowering the front subframe (see illustration).

19 Remove the hub caps (where fitted), then extract the split pins and unscrew the driveshaft outer hub nuts while holding the hubs stationary. To do this, temporarily insert

the wheel bolts and have an assistant depress the brake pedal while the nuts are loosened, or alternatively bolt a home-made retaining tool to the hub. Alternatively, the driveshafts can be removed from the transmission as described in Chapter 8 (see illustrations).

5.17b Cover the open ends of the fuel lines to prevent entry of dust and dirt

5.18 Use cable ties to tie the radiator to the front crossmember

5.19a Extract the split pin ...

5.19b ... then unscrew the hub nut

5.19c If preferred, lever the inner ends of the driveshafts from the transmission

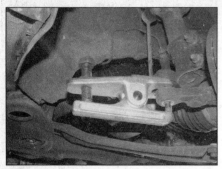

5.21a Using a separator tool to disconnect the track rod ends from the steering arms

5.21b Disconnecting the anti-roll bar links from the struts

5.21c Removing the lower balljoint retaining bolts

Use a long bar together with a block of wood and chain to lever down the lower arms.

20 If required, remove the front brake discs with reference to Chapter 9.

21 Refer to Chapter 10 and disconnect the track rods from the hub carrier steering arms. Also detach the anti-roll bar links from the front suspension struts, and detach the front suspension lower arms from the hub carriers. Pull down the lower arms and move the struts to one side **(see illustrations and Haynes Hint)**.

22 If the driveshafts are to remain in the transmission, disconnect them from the hub carriers by carefully tapping them through the hubs while pulling out the carriers. Tie the struts and carriers to one side.

23 On models with air conditioning, remove the auxiliary drivebelt (Chapter 1B), then unbolt the compressor from the engine **without disconnecting the refrigerant lines** and support the compressor to one side.

24 Remove the front section of the exhaust system with reference to Chapter 4C.

25 Refer to Chapter 7A and disconnect the gearchange rod from the transmission. Also, unbolt the gearchange rocking lever from the subframe. Alternatively, detach the gearchange from the top of the rocking lever **(see illustrations)**.

26 Support the front suspension subframe on trolley jacks, then mark the position of the subframe on the front underbody, and unscrew the four mounting bolts. Discard the bolts as new ones must be used for refitting. Unscrew and remove the bolt securing the engine rear torque link to the subframe, and also unbolt the front torque link from the subframe **(see illustrations and Haynes Hint opposite)**. With the help of an assistant, carefully lower the subframe to the ground and withdraw from under the vehicle.

27 Attach a suitable hoist and lifting tackle to the engine lifting brackets on the cylinder head, and support the weight of the engine/transmission.

28 Mark the position of the right-hand engine

5.25a Unscrew the clamp bolt . . .

5.25b . . . and disconnect the gearchange rod

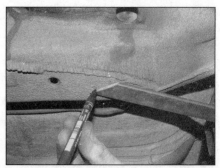

5.25c Disconnecting the gearchange linkage from the rocking lever

5.26a Front engine-to-subframe torque link

5.26b Rear engine-to-subframe torque link

5.26c Marking the position of the temporary position bars on the underbody

mounting, then unscrew the two bolts securing the upper mounting to the lower mounting bracket. **Note:** *There is no need to remove the mounting, since the engine/transmission is lowered from the engine compartment.*

29 Unscrew the two bolts securing the left-hand engine mounting to the transmission.

30 Make a final check to ensure that all relevant pipes, hoses, wires, etc, have been disconnected, and that they are positioned clear of the engine and transmission.

31 With the help of an assistant, carefully lower to the ground the engine/transmission assembly **(see illustration)**. Make sure that the surrounding components in the engine compartment are not damaged. Ideally, the assembly should be lowered onto a trolley jack or low platform with castors, so that it can easily be withdrawn from under the car.

32 Ensure that the assembly is adequately supported, then disconnect the engine hoist and lifting tackle, and withdraw the engine/transmission assembly from under the front of the vehicle.

Separation

33 With the engine/transmission assembly removed, support the assembly on suitable blocks of wood, on a workbench (or failing that, on a clean area of the workshop floor).

34 Clean away any external dirt using paraffin or a water-soluble solvent and a stiff brush.

35 If necessary, remove the driveshafts from the transmission with reference to Chapter 8. Be prepared for some loss of oil.

36 With reference to Chapter 5A, remove the starter motor.

37 With reference to Chapter 7A, unbolt the transmission from the engine. Carefully withdraw the transmission from the engine, ensuring that its weight is not allowed to hang on the input shaft while engaged with the clutch friction disc.

38 Note that the transmission locates on dowels positioned in the rear of the cylinder block. If they are loose, remove them and keep them in a safe place.

Refitting

39 Ensure the locating dowels are correctly positioned then carefully offer the transmission to the engine, until the locating dowels are engaged. Ensure that the weight of the transmission is not allowed to hang on the input shaft as it engages the clutch friction disc. With reference to Chapter 7A, complete the transmission refitting procedure and tighten the bolts to the specified torque.

40 Refit the starter motor with reference to Chapter 5A.

41 If removed, refit the driveshafts to the transmission with reference to Chapter 8. If necessary, renew the driveshaft oil seals with reference to Chapter 7A.

42 With the front of the vehicle raised and supported on axle stands, move the engine/transmission assembly under the vehicle,

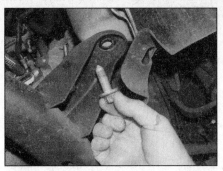

5.26d Removing the subframe mounting bolts

ensuring that the assembly is adequately supported.

43 Reconnect the hoist and lifting tackle to the engine lifting brackets, and carefully raise the engine/transmission assembly up into the engine compartment with the help of an assistant.

44 Reconnect the right- and left-hand engine/transmission mountings, making sure that the previously-made positional marks are complied with, and tighten the bolts to the specified torque given in Chapter 2C.

45 Disconnect the hoist and lifting tackle from the engine lifting brackets.

46 With the aid of an assistant, raise the subframe onto the underbody, making sure that it is located in its previously-noted position, then insert the mounting bolts. With the subframe held in position, tighten the (new) bolts to the specified torque and angles given in Chapter 2C. Ensure that the bulkhead packing on the steering gear is located correctly on the bulkhead **(see illustration)**.

47 Refit the front engine mounting bolt and tighten to the specified torque.

48 Refit the bolt securing the engine rear torque link to the subframe, and tighten to the specified torque.

49 Reconnect the gearchange rod to the transmission, and adjust with reference to Chapter 7A.

50 Refit the front section of the exhaust system with reference to Chapter 4C.

51 On models with air conditioning, refit the compressor with reference to Chapter 3, then refit the auxiliary drivebelt with reference to Chapter 1B.

5.31 Lowering the engine/transmission assembly from the engine compartment

To ensure correct repositioning, we bolted two lengths of metal bar to the subframe, and marked their position on the underbody.

52 Reconnect the driveshafts to the hub carriers, then reconnect the lower arms, anti-roll bar links and track rods with reference to Chapter 10. At this stage the driveshaft/hub nuts can be tightened moderately, then fully tightened when the vehicle is lowered to the ground.

53 Refit the front brake discs with reference to Chapter 9.

54 Reconnect the fuel return line to the injection pump, then reconnect the fuel inlet lines to the fuel filter.

55 Reconnect the brake vacuum servo hose.

56 Reconnect and bleed the clutch hydraulic connection at the transmission with reference to Chapter 6.

57 Reconnect the wiring to the electric cooling fan.

58 Refit the wiring harness trough over the upper timing belt cover, and clip the vacuum lines in place.

59 Reconnect the wiring to the various components as previously noted.

60 Reconnect the heater matrix hoses and tighten the clips.

61 Refit the coolant expansion tank and clip the hoses in place.

62 Refit the air cleaner assembly with reference to Chapter 4C.

63 Refit the front bumper with reference to Chapter 11.

64 Reconnect the steering column intermediate shaft to the steering gear pinion

5.46 Bulkhead packing on the steering gear

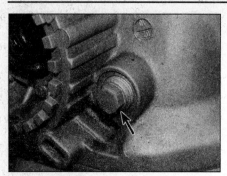

5.65 Gearbox oil level plug

shaft and tighten the bolt and nut with reference to Chapter 10.

65 Check and if necessary top-up the transmission oil level as described in Chapter 7A **(see illustration)**.

66 Make a final check to ensure that all relevant hoses, pipes and wires have been correctly reconnected.

67 Reconnect the battery negative lead (refer to *Disconnecting the battery* at the end of this manual).

68 Refit the right-hand inner wheel arch liner, front roadwheels, and engine compartment undertray (where fitted), then lower the vehicle to the ground.

69 Refill the engine with oil with reference to Chapter 1B.

70 Refill and bleed the cooling system with reference to Chapter 1B.

71 Fully tighten the driveshaft/hub nuts to the specified torque.

72 Refit the bonnet as described in Chapter 11.

6 Engine overhaul – dismantling sequence

1 It is much easier to dismantle and work on the engine if it is mounted on a portable engine stand. These stands can often be hired from a tool hire shop. Before the engine is mounted on a stand, the flywheel/driveplate should be removed, so that the stand bolts can be tightened into the end of the cylinder block/crankcase.

2 If a stand is not available, it is possible to dismantle the engine with it blocked up on a sturdy workbench, or on the floor. Be extra-careful not to tip or drop the engine when working without a stand.

3 If you are going to obtain a reconditioned engine, all the external components must be removed first, to be transferred to the replacement engine (just as they will if you are doing a complete engine overhaul yourself). These components include the following:
a) *Engine wiring harness and supports.*
b) *Alternator and air conditioning compressor mounting brackets (as applicable).*

c) *Coolant pump (where applicable) and inlet/outlet housings.*
d) *Dipstick tube.*
e) *Fuel system components.*
f) *All electrical switches and sensors.*
g) *Inlet and exhaust manifolds and, where fitted, the turbocharger.*
h) *Oil filter and oil cooler* **(see illustration)**.
i) *Flywheel/driveplate.*

Note: *When removing the external components from the engine, pay close attention to details that may be helpful or important during refitting. Note the fitted position of gaskets, seals, spacers, pins, washers, bolts, and other small items.*

4 If you are obtaining a 'short' engine (which consists of the engine cylinder block/crankcase, crankshaft, pistons and connecting rods all assembled), then the cylinder head, sump, oil pump, and timing belt/chains (as applicable) will have to be removed also.

5 If you are planning a complete overhaul, the engine can be dismantled, and the internal components removed, in the order given below.
a) *Inlet and exhaust manifolds (see Chapter 4A, 4B or 4C).*
b) *Timing belt, sprockets and tensioner (see Chapter 2B or 2C).*
c) *Coolant pump (see Chapter 3).*
d) *Cylinder head (see Chapter 2A, 2B or 2C).*
e) *Flywheel/driveplate (see Chapter 2A, 2B or 2C).*
f) *Sump (see Chapter 2A, 2B or 2C).*
g) *Oil pump (see Chapter 2A, 2B or 2C).*
h) *Timing chain and sprockets (see Chapter 2A).*
i) *Pistons/connecting rod assemblies (see Section 10).*
j) *Crankshaft (see Section 11).*

6 Before beginning the dismantling and overhaul procedures, make sure that you have all of the correct tools necessary. See *Tools and working facilities* for further information.

7 Cylinder head – dismantling

Note: *New and reconditioned cylinder heads are available from the manufacturer, and from*

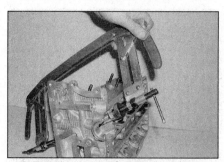

7.2 Fit a valve spring compressor tool, ensuring that the arms of the compressor are securely positioned

6.3 Oil filter and cooler housing on diesel engines

engine overhaul specialists. Due to the fact that some specialist tools are required for the dismantling and inspection procedures, and new components may not be readily available, it may be more practical and economical for the home mechanic to purchase a reconditioned head rather than to dismantle, inspect and recondition the original head. A valve spring compressor tool will be required for this operation.

1 With the cylinder head removed as described in Chapter 2A, 2B or 2C, clean away all external dirt, and remove the following components as applicable, if not already done:
a) *Manifolds (see Chapter 4A, 4B or 4C).*
b) *Spark plugs (petrol engines – see Chapter 1A).*
c) *Glow plugs (diesel engines – see Chapter 5C).*
d) *Camshafts and hydraulic tappets (petrol engines – see Chapter 2A or 2B).*
e) *Camshaft housing (diesel engine – see Chapter 2C).*
f) *Engine lifting brackets.*

2 To remove a valve, fit a valve spring compressor tool. Ensure that the arms of the compressor tool are securely positioned on the head of the valve and the spring cap **(see illustration)**. The valves are deeply-recessed on petrol engines, and a suitable extension piece may be required for the spring compressor.

3 Compress the valve spring to relieve the pressure of the spring cap acting on the collets.

> **HAYNES HINT** *If the spring cap sticks to the valve stem, support the compressor tool, and give the end a light tap with a soft-faced mallet to help free the spring cap.*

4 Extract the two split collets by hooking them out using a small screwdriver, then slowly release the compressor tool **(see illustration)**.

5 Remove the valve spring cap and the spring, then withdraw the valve through the combustion chamber. Remove the valve stem

7.4 Compress the valve spring and hook out the split collets using a small screwdriver

7.5a Remove the valve spring cap . . .

7.5b . . . spring and valve . . .

7.5c . . . then remove the valve stem oil seal . . .

7.5d . . . and spring seat

7.6 Place each valve assembly in a labelled polythene bag or similar container

oil seal (using long-nosed pliers if necessary), and the spring seat **(see illustrations)**.

6 Repeat the procedure for the remaining valves, keeping all components in strict order so that they can be refitted in their original positions, unless all the components are to be renewed. If the components are to be kept and used again, place each valve assembly in a labelled polythene bag or a similar small container **(see illustration)**. Note that as with cylinder numbering, the valves are normally numbered from the timing chain (or timing belt) end of the engine. Make sure that the valve components are identified as inlet and exhaust, as well as numbered.

8 Cylinder head and valve components – cleaning and inspection

1 Thorough cleaning of the cylinder head and valve components, followed by a detailed inspection, will enable a decision to be made on whether further work is necessary before reassembling the components.

Cleaning

2 Scrape away all traces of old gasket material and sealing compound from the cylinder head surfaces. Take care not to damage the cylinder head surfaces, as the head is made of light alloy.
3 Scrape away the carbon from the combustion chambers and ports, then wash the cylinder head thoroughly with paraffin or a suitable solvent.

4 Scrape off any heavy carbon deposits that may have formed on the valves, then use a power-operated wire brush to remove deposits from the valve heads and stems.

Inspection

Note: *Be sure to perform all the following inspection procedures before concluding that the services of a machine shop or engine overhaul specialist are required. Make a list of all items that require attention.*

Cylinder head

5 Inspect the head very carefully for cracks, evidence of coolant leakage, and other damage. If cracks are found, a new cylinder head should be obtained.
6 Use a straight-edge and feeler blade to check that the cylinder head surface is not distorted **(see illustration)**. If the specified distortion limit is exceeded on 1.0 and 1.2

8.6 Checking the cylinder head surface for distortion

petrol engines, the cylinder head must be renewed, as machining is not possible, however, on the 1.4 petrol and diesel engines, it may be possible to have the cylinder head resurfaced, provided that the overall height of the head is not reduced to less than the specified minimum.
7 Examine the valve seats in each of the combustion chambers. If the seats are severely pitted, cracked or burned, then they will need to be recut or renewed by an engine overhaul specialist. If only slight pitting is evident, this can be removed by grinding the valve heads and seats together with coarse, then fine, grinding paste, as described later in this Section.
8 If the valve guides are worn, indicated by a side-to-side motion of the valve, oversize valve guides are available, and valves with oversize stems can be fitted. This work is best carried out by an engine overhaul specialist. A dial gauge may be used to determine whether the amount of side play of a valve exceeds the specified maximum.
9 Check the tappet bores in the cylinder head for wear. If excessive wear is evident, the cylinder head must be renewed. Also check the tappet oil holes in the cylinder head for obstructions.

Valves

10 Examine the head of each valve for pitting, burning, cracks and general wear, and check the valve stem for scoring and wear ridges. Rotate the valve, and check for any obvious indication that it is bent. Look for pitting and excessive wear on the end of each

8.10 Measuring a valve stem diameter

valve stem. If the valve appears satisfactory at this stage, measure the valve stem diameter at several points using a micrometer **(see illustration)**. Any significant difference in the readings obtained indicates wear of the valve stem. Should any of these conditions be apparent, the valve(s) must be renewed. If the valves are in satisfactory condition, they should be ground (lapped) onto their respective seats to ensure a smooth gas-tight seal.

11 Valve grinding is carried out as follows. Place the cylinder head upside-down on a bench, with a block of wood at each end to give clearance for the valve stems.

A light spring placed under the valve head will greatly ease the grinding operation.

12 Smear a trace of coarse carborundum paste on the seat face in the cylinder head, and press a suction grinding tool onto the relevant valve head. With a semi-rotary action, grind the valve head to its seat, lifting the valve occasionally to redistribute the grinding paste. When a dull, matt, even surface is produced on the faces of both the valve seat and the valve, wipe off the paste and repeat the process with fine carborundum paste. When a smooth unbroken ring of light grey matt finish is produced on both the valve and seat faces, the grinding operation is complete. Carefully clean away every trace of grinding paste, taking great care to leave none in the ports or in the valve guides. Clean the valves and valve seats with a paraffin-soaked rag,

then with a clean rag, and finally, if an air line is available, blow the valves, valve guides and cylinder head ports clean.

Valve springs

13 Check that all the valve springs are intact. If any one is broken, all should be renewed.

14 If possible, check the free height of the springs against new ones, then stand each spring on a flat surface and check it for squareness. If a spring is found to be too short, or damaged in any way, renew all the springs as a set. Springs suffer from fatigue, and it is a good idea to renew them even if they look serviceable.

Rocker arm components (1.0 and 1.2 engines)

15 Check the rocker arm thrust faces (the areas that contact the tappets and valve stems) for pits, wear, score-marks or any indication that the surface-hardening has worn through. Check the rocker arm camshaft roller in the same manner. Renew any rocker arms which appear suspect.

Hydraulic tappets (petrol engines)

16 Inspect the tappets for obvious signs of wear on the contact faces, and check the oil holes for obstructions, particularly for oil sludge. If excessive wear is evident, or if any tappet has been noisy in operation, all the tappets must be renewed as a set.

9 Cylinder head – reassembly

Note: New valve stem oil seals should be used on reassembly. A valve spring compressor tool will be required for this operation.

1 With all the components cleaned, starting at one end of the cylinder head, fit the valve components as follows.

2 Insert the appropriate valve into its guide (if new valves are being fitted, insert each valve into the location to which it has been ground), ensuring that the valve stem is well-lubricated with clean engine oil **(see illustration)**. If the original components are being refitted, all components must be refitted in their original positions.

3 Fit the spring seat.

4 New valve stem oil seals may be supplied with a fitting sleeve, which fits over the collet groove in the valve stem, to prevent damage to the oil seal as it is slid down the valve stem. If no sleeve is supplied, wind a short length of tape round the top of the valve stem to cover the collet groove.

5 Lubricate the valve stem oil seal with clean engine oil, then push the oil seal down the valve stem using a suitable tube or socket, until the seal is fully engaged with the spring seat **(see illustration)**. Remove the fitting sleeve or the tape, as applicable, from the valve stem.

6 Fit the valve spring and the spring cap.

7 Fit the spring compressor tool, and compress the valve spring until the spring cap passes beyond the collet groove in the valve stem **(see illustration)**.

8 Refit the split collets to the groove in the valve stem, with the narrow ends nearest the spring.

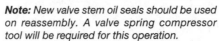
Apply a little grease to the split collets, then fit the split collets into the groove. The grease should hold the collets in the groove.

9 Slowly release the compressor tool, ensuring that the collets are not dislodged from the groove. When the compressor is fully released, give the top of the valve assembly a tap with a soft-faced mallet to settle the components.

10 Repeat the procedure for the remaining valves, ensuring that if the original components are being used, they are all refitted in their original positions.

11 Refit the components removed in Section 7, paragraph 1.

10 Piston/connecting rod assemblies – removal

Note: The mating faces of the connecting rods and the big-end bearing caps are 'rough' (not machined), which ensures perfect mating

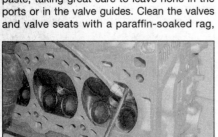

9.2 Insert the appropriate valve into its guide ensuring that the valve stem is well-lubricated

9.5 Push the oil seal into position using a suitable tube or socket

9.7 Compress the valve spring until the spring cap passes beyond the collet groove in the valve stem then refit the collets

10.3 Undo the bolts and remove the oil baffle plate from the cylinder block baseplate (1.0 and 1.2 litre petrol)

10.5 Unscrew the big-end cap bolts from the first connecting rod, and remove the cap

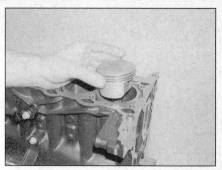

10.7 Push the piston/rod assembly up and out of the top of the cylinder bore

of each individual rod and bearing cap. When the components have been removed from the engine, extreme care should be taken not to damage the mating surfaces – eg, do not rest the bearing caps on the mating faces. Ensure that each bearing cap is kept together with its respective rod, to prevent any possibility of the components being refitted incorrectly. **Note:** New big-end cap bolts will be required for reassembly.

1.0 and 1.2 litre engines

1 Remove the cylinder head as described in Chapter 2A.
2 Remove the sump and oil pick-up pipe, as described in Chapter 2A.
3 Undo the retaining bolts and remove the oil baffle plate from the cylinder block baseplate **(see illustration)**.
4 If the connecting rods and big-end caps are not marked to indicate their positions in the cylinder block (ie, marked with cylinder numbers), suitably mark both the rod and cap with quick-drying paint or similar. Note which side of the engine the marks face and accurately record this also. There may not be any other way of identifying which way round the cap fits on the rod, when refitting.
5 Unscrew the big-end cap bolts from the first connecting rod, and remove the cap **(see illustration)**. If the bearing shells are to be re-used, tape the cap and the shell together.
6 Check the top of the cylinder bore for a wear ridge. If evident, carefully scrape it away with a ridge reamer tool, otherwise the piston

rings may jam against the ridge as the piston is pushed out of the block.
7 Place the wooden handle of a hammer against the bottom of the connecting rod, and push the piston/rod assembly up and out of the cylinder bore **(see illustration)**. Recover the bearing shell, and tape it to the connecting rod if it is to be re-used.
8 Remove the remaining assemblies in a similar way. Rotate the crankshaft as necessary to bring the big-end bolts to the most accessible position.

1.4 litre engine

9 Remove the cylinder head as described in Chapter 2B.
10 Remove the sump and oil pick-up pipe, as described in Chapter 2B.
11 If the connecting rods and big-end caps are not marked to indicate their positions in the cylinder block (ie, marked with cylinder numbers), centre-punch them at adjacent points either side of the cap/rod joint. Note to which side of the engine the marks face **(see illustration)**.
12 Unscrew the big-end cap bolts from the first connecting rod, and remove the cap. If the bearing shells are to be re-used, tape the cap and the shell together.
13 Check the top of the cylinder bore for a wear ridge. If evident, carefully scrape it away with a ridge reamer tool, otherwise the piston rings may jam against the ridge as the piston is pushed out of the block.

14 Place the wooden handle of a hammer against the bottom of the connecting rod, and push the piston/rod assembly up and out of the cylinder bore. Recover the bearing shell, and tape it to the connecting rod if it is to be re-used.
15 Remove the remaining three assemblies in a similar way. Rotate the crankshaft as necessary to bring the big-end bolts to the most accessible position.

1.7 litre engine

16 Referring to Chapter 2C, remove the cylinder head and sump and then unbolt the pick-up strainer from the base of the oil pump/cylinder block. Where fitted, unbolt and remove the baffle plate from the base of the cylinder block **(see illustration)**.
17 On all models, if there is a pronounced wear ridge at the top of any bore, it may be necessary to remove it with a scraper or ridge reamer, to avoid piston damage during removal. Such a ridge indicates excessive wear of the cylinder bore.
18 Prior to removal, using feeler blades, measuring the connecting rod big-end side clearance of each rod **(see illustration)**. If any rod exceeds the specified clearance, it must be renewed.
19 Using paint or similar, mark each connecting rod and its bearing cap with its respective cylinder number on the flat machined surface provided; if the engine has been dismantled before, note carefully any

10.11 Big-end cap centre-punched identification marks. Note that lug on bearing cap faces the flywheel end of engine

10.16 Where fitted, unbolt the baffle plate from the base of the cylinder block

10.18 Checking connecting rod big-end side clearance

10.19 Prior to removal make identification markings on the connecting rods and bearing caps (circled)

identifying marks made previously **(see illustration)**. Note that No 1 cylinder is at the timing belt end of the engine.

20 Turn the crankshaft to bring pistons 1 and 4 to BDC (bottom dead centre).

21 Unscrew the bolts from No 1 piston big-end bearing cap. Take off the cap and recover the bottom half bearing shell. If the bearing shells are to be re-used, tape the cap and the shell together.

22 Using a hammer handle, push the piston up through the bore, and remove it from the top of the cylinder block. Recover the bearing shell, and tape it to the connecting rod for safe-keeping.

23 Loosely refit the big-end cap to the connecting rod, and secure with the bolts – this will help to keep the components in their correct order.

24 Remove No 4 piston assembly in the same way.

25 Turn the crankshaft through 180° to bring pistons 2 and 3 to BDC (bottom dead centre), and remove them in the same way.

11 Crankshaft – removal

1 Remove the flywheel/driveplate as described in Chapter 2A, 2B or 2C.

2 Remove the pistons and connecting rods, as described in Section 10.

3 Invert the engine so that the crankshaft is uppermost.

4 Before removing the crankshaft, check the endfloat using a dial gauge in contact with the end of the crankshaft. Push the crankshaft fully one way, and then zero the gauge. Push the crankshaft fully the other way, and check the endfloat **(see illustration)**. The result should be compared with the specified limit, and will give an indication as to the size of the main bearing shell thrust journal width which will be required for reassembly.

5 If a dial gauge is not available, a feeler gauge can be used to measure crankshaft endfloat. Push the crankshaft fully towards one end of the crankcase, and insert a feeler gauge between the thrust flange of the main bearing shell and the machined surface of the crankshaft web **(see illustration)**. Before measuring, ensure that the crankshaft is fully forced towards one end of the crankcase, to give the widest possible gap at the measuring location. **Note:** *Measure at the bearing with the thrustwasher (see Section 18).*

1.0 and 1.2 litre engines

Note: *New cylinder block baseplate retaining bolts will be required for refitting.*

6 Working in a diagonal sequence, progressively slacken the outer (M6) bolts securing the cylinder block baseplate to the cylinder block.

7 When all the outer bolts have been slackened, repeat the procedure on the inner (M8) retaining bolts.

8 Remove all the bolts and lift the cylinder block baseplate off the cylinder block **(see illustration)**. If the baseplate is initially tight to remove, carefully tap it free using a soft-faced mallet.

9 As the baseplate is withdrawn check that the lower main bearing shells come away with the baseplate. If they remain on the crankshaft journals, lift them off and refit them to their respective locations in the baseplate.

10 Lift the crankshaft from the cylinder block and remove the crankshaft oil seal.

11 Extract the upper bearing shells, and identify them for position if they are to be re-used.

1.4 litre engine

Note: *New crankshaft main bearing bolts will be required for reassembly.*

12 Remove the oil pump as described in Chapter 2B.

13 The main bearing caps are normally numbered 1 to 4 from the timing belt end of the engine. The flywheel end cap is not marked. The numbers are read from the coolant pump side of the engine **(see illustration)**. If the bearing caps are not marked, centre-punch them to indicate their locations, and note to which side of the engine the marks face.

14 Unscrew and remove the main bearing cap bolts, and withdraw the bearing caps. If the bearing caps are stuck, tap them gently with a soft-faced mallet to free them. If the bearing shells are to be re-used, tape them to their respective caps.

15 Lift the crankshaft from the crankcase **(see illustration)**.

16 Extract the upper bearing shells, and identify them for position if they are to be re-used.

11.4 Using a dial gauge to check the crankshaft endfloat

11.5 Checking the crankshaft endfloat with a feeler gauge

11.8 Lift the cylinder block baseplate off the cylinder block

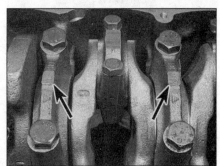

11.13 Main bearing cap identification marks (1.4 litre petrol)

11.15 Lifting the crankshaft from the crankcase

1.7 litre engine

Note: *New main bearing cap bolts will be required for reassembly.*

17 Working as described in Chapter 2C, remove the oil pump/cover and oil pick-up pipe.

18 Unbolt the crankshaft rear oil seal housing and remove it from the cylinder block. If the housing locating dowels are a loose fit, remove them and store them with the housing for safe-keeping.

19 Undo the retaining bolts, and remove the oil baffle plate from the cylinder block **(see illustration)**.

20 Remove the connecting rod bearing caps as described in Section 10.

21 Unscrew the main bearing cap bolts and remove the bearing caps. Note that the caps should are numbered 1 to 5, Number 1 cap being at the timing belt end, and the arrow on each cap should point towards the timing belt end of the engine.

22 Carefully remove the crankshaft, and recover the thrustwasher halves from the sides of Number 2 main bearing.

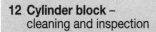

12 Cylinder block –
cleaning and inspection

Cleaning

1 For complete cleaning, remove all external components (senders, sensors, brackets, etc) from the cylinder block **(see illustration)**.

2 Scrape all traces of gasket and/or sealant from the cylinder block and cylinder block baseplate, taking particular care not to damage the cylinder head and sump mating faces.

3 Remove all oil gallery plugs, where fitted. The plugs are usually very tight – they may have to be drilled out and the holes retapped. Use new plugs when the engine is reassembled. On diesel engines, remove the piston oil spray nozzles from inside the cylinder block. The nozzles are a push-fit in the block and the use of a special Vauxhall tool is required for removal.

4 If the block and baseplate (1.0 and 1.2 petrol engines) are extremely dirty, they should be steam-cleaned.

12.1 Coolant elbow on the front of the cylinder block

11.19 Remove the oil baffle plate (1.7 litre diesel)

5 If the components have been steam-cleaned, clean all oil holes and oil galleries one more time on completion. Flush all internal passages with warm water until the water runs clear. Dry the block and, where necessary, the baseplate thoroughly and wipe all machined surfaces with a light oil. If you have access to compressed air, use it to speed-up the drying process, and to blow out all the oil holes and galleries.

⚠ *Warning: Wear eye protection when using compressed air.*

6 If the block and baseplate are relatively clean, an adequate cleaning job can be achieved with hot soapy water and a stiff brush. Take plenty of time, and do a thorough job. Regardless of the cleaning method used, be sure to clean all oil holes and galleries very thoroughly, dry everything completely, and coat all cast-iron machined surfaces with light oil.

7 The threaded holes in the cylinder block and baseplate must be clean, to ensure accurate torque readings when tightening fixings during reassembly. Run the correct-size tap (which can be determined from the size of the relevant bolt) into each of the holes to remove rust, corrosion, thread sealant or other contamination, and to restore damaged threads. If possible, use compressed air to clear the holes of debris produced by this operation. Do not forget to clean the threads of all bolts and nuts which are to be re-used, as well.

8 Where applicable, apply suitable sealant to the new oil gallery plugs, and insert them into

12.8 Oil spray nozzles (1.7 litre diesel)

the relevant holes in the cylinder block. Tighten the plugs securely. On diesel engines, press the oil spray nozzles into the block ensuring that each one is positioned exactly at a right-angle to the crankshaft axis **(see illustration)**.

9 If the engine is to be left dismantled for some time, cover the cylinder block with a large plastic bag to keep it clean and prevent corrosion. Where applicable, refit the baseplate and tighten the bolts finger-tight.

Inspection

10 Visually check the block for cracks, rust and corrosion. Look for stripped threads in the threaded holes (it may be possible to recut stripped threads using a suitable tap). If there has been any history of internal coolant leakage, it may be worthwhile asking an engine overhaul specialist to check the block using special equipment. If defects are found, have the block repaired if possible, otherwise a new block may be the only option.

11 Take the cylinder block to a Vauxhall dealer or engine overhaul specialist, who will have the equipment and experience to be able to accurately measure the bores, carry out a rebore and supply new pistons, etc, where necessary.

13 Piston/connecting rod
assemblies –
inspection

1 Before the inspection process can begin, the piston/connecting rod assemblies must be cleaned, and the original piston rings removed from the pistons.

2 Carefully expand the old rings over the top of the pistons. The use of two or three old feeler gauges will be helpful in preventing the rings dropping into empty grooves **(see illustration)**. Take care, however, as piston rings are sharp.

3 Scrape away all traces of carbon from the top of the piston. A hand-held wire brush, or a piece of fine emery cloth, can be used once the majority of the deposits have been scraped away.

4 Remove the carbon from the ring grooves

13.2 Using a feeler gauge to aid removal of a piston ring

14.8 Transfer the crankshaft speed/position sensor pulse pick-up ring to the new crankshaft

in the piston, using an old ring. Break the ring in half to do this (be careful not to cut your fingers – piston rings are sharp). Be very careful to remove only the carbon deposits – do not remove any metal, and do not nick or scratch the sides of the ring grooves.

5 Once the deposits have been removed, clean the piston/connecting rod assembly with paraffin or a suitable solvent, and dry thoroughly. Make sure that the oil return holes in the ring grooves are clear.

6 If the pistons and cylinder bores are not damaged or worn excessively, and if the cylinder block does not need to be rebored, the original pistons can be refitted. Normal piston wear shows up as even vertical wear on the piston thrust surfaces, and slight looseness of the top ring in its groove. New piston rings should always be used when the engine is reassembled.

7 Carefully inspect each piston for cracks around the skirt, at the gudgeon pin bosses, and at the piston ring lands (between the ring grooves).

8 Look for scoring and scuffing on the thrust faces of the piston skirt, holes in the piston crown, and burned areas at the edge of the crown. If the skirt is scored or scuffed, the engine may have been suffering from overheating, and/or abnormal combustion ('pinking') which caused excessively-high operating temperatures. The cooling and lubrication systems should be checked thoroughly. A hole in the piston crown, or burned areas at the edge of the piston crown indicates that abnormal combustion (pre-ignition, 'pinking', knocking or detonation) has

been occurring. If any of the above problems exist, the causes must be investigated and corrected, or the damage will occur again.

9 Corrosion of the piston, in the form of pitting, indicates that coolant has been leaking into the combustion chamber and/or the crankcase. Again, the cause must be corrected, or the problem may persist in the rebuilt engine.

10 Check the piston-to-bore clearance by measuring the cylinder bore (see Section 12) and the piston diameter. Measure the piston across the bottom of the skirt, at a 90° angle to the gudgeon pin. Subtract the piston diameter from the bore diameter to obtain the clearance. If this is greater than the figures given in the Specifications, the block will have to be rebored, and new oversize pistons and rings, together with new gudgeon pins and connecting rods will have to be fitted (see paragraph 12).

11 Check the fit of the gudgeon pin by twisting the piston and connecting rod in opposite directions. Any noticeable play indicates excessive wear, which must be corrected. If the pistons or connecting rods are to be renewed, have this work carried out by a Vauxhall dealer or a suitable engine overhaul specialist, who will have the necessary tooling.

12 It should be noted that if any of the components of a piston, gudgeon pin and connecting rod assembly are to be renewed, the manufacturers state that all the components of that assembly must be renewed as well (ie, if a new piston is required, a new gudgeon pin and connecting rod will be required also). A new piston must not be fitted to an old connecting rod and *vice versa*.

13 Check the alignment of the connecting rods visually, and if the rods are not straight, take them to an engine overhaul specialist for a more detailed check.

14 Crankshaft – inspection

1 Clean the crankshaft using paraffin or a suitable solvent, and dry it, preferably with compressed air if available. Be sure to clean

the oil holes with a pipe cleaner or similar probe, to ensure that they are not obstructed.

⚠️ *Warning: Wear eye protection when using compressed air.*

2 Check the main and big-end bearing journals for uneven wear, scoring, pitting and cracking.

3 Big-end bearing wear is accompanied by distinct metallic knocking when the engine is running (particularly noticeable when the engine is pulling from low revs), and some loss of oil pressure.

4 Main bearing wear is accompanied by severe engine vibration and rumble – getting progressively worse as engine revs increase – and again by loss of oil pressure.

5 Check the bearing journal for roughness by running a finger lightly over the bearing surface. Any roughness (which will be accompanied by obvious bearing wear) indicates that the crankshaft requires regrinding.

6 If the crankshaft has been reground, check for burrs around the crankshaft oil holes (the holes are usually chamfered, so burrs should not be a problem unless regrinding has been carried out carelessly). Remove any burrs with a fine file or scraper, and thoroughly clean the oil holes as described previously.

7 Take the crankshaft to a Vauxhall dealer or engine overhaul specialist, who will have the equipment and experience to accurately measure and inspect the crankshaft, and regrind the crankshaft as necessary.

8 If a new crankshaft is to be fitted on petrol engines, undo the screws securing the crankshaft speed/position sensor pulse pick-up ring to the crankshaft, and transfer the ring to the new crankshaft **(see illustration)**.

15 Main and big-end bearings – inspection

1 Even though the main and big-end bearing shells should be renewed during engine overhaul, the old bearing shells should be retained for close examination, as they may reveal valuable information about the condition of the engine. The bearing shells carry identification marks to denote their size in the form of a colour code, and/or a letter/number code marked on the back of the shell **(see illustrations)**. If the shells are to be renewed, without carrying out any crankshaft regrinding, the old shells should be taken along when obtaining new shells, to ensure that the correct shells are obtained.

2 Bearing failure occurs because of lack of lubrication, the presence of dirt or other foreign particles, overloading the engine, or corrosion **(see illustration)**. If a bearing fails, the cause must be found and eliminated before the engine is reassembled, to prevent the failure from happening again.

3 To examine the bearing shells, remove

15.1a Typical main bearing shell . . .

15.1b . . . and main thrust bearing shell identification marks

them from the cylinder block, the cylinder block baseplate, the connecting rods and the big-end bearing caps, and lay them out on a clean surface in the same order as they were fitted to the engine. This will enable any bearing problems to be matched with the corresponding crankshaft journal.

4 Dirt and other foreign particles can enter the engine in a variety of ways. Contamination may be left in the engine during assembly, or it may pass through filters or the crankcase ventilation system. Normal engine wear produces small particles of metal, which can eventually cause problems. If particles find their way into the lubrication system, it is likely that they will eventually be carried to the bearings. Whatever the source, these foreign particles often end up embedded in the soft bearing material, and are easily recognised. Large particles will not embed in the bearing, and will score or gouge the bearing and journal. To prevent possible contamination, clean all parts thoroughly, and keep everything spotlessly-clean during engine assembly. Once the engine has been installed in the vehicle, ensure that engine oil and filter changes are carried out at the recommended intervals.

5 Lack of lubrication (or lubrication breakdown) has a number of interrelated causes. Excessive heat (which thins the oil), overloading (which squeezes the oil from the bearing face), and oil leakage (from excessive bearing clearances, worn oil pump or high engine speeds) all contribute to lubrication breakdown. Blocked oil passages, which may be the result of misaligned oil holes in a bearing shell, will also starve a bearing of oil and destroy it. When lack of lubrication is the cause of bearing failure, the bearing material is wiped or extruded from the steel backing of the bearing. Temperatures may increase to the point where the steel backing turns blue from overheating.

6 Driving habits can have a definite effect on bearing life. Full-throttle, low-speed operation (labouring the engine) puts very high loads on bearings, which tends to squeeze out the oil film. These loads cause the bearings to flex, which produces fine cracks in the bearing face (fatigue failure). Eventually the bearing material will loosen in places, and tear away from the steel backing. Regular short journeys can lead to corrosion of bearings, because insufficient engine heat is produced to drive off the condensed water and corrosive gases which form inside the engine. These products collect in the engine oil, forming acid and sludge. As the oil is carried to the bearings, the acid attacks and corrodes the bearing material.

7 Incorrect bearing installation during engine assembly will also lead to bearing failure. Tight-fitting bearings leave insufficient bearing lubrication clearance, and will result in oil starvation. Dirt or foreign particles trapped behind a bearing shell results in high spots on the bearing which can lead to failure.

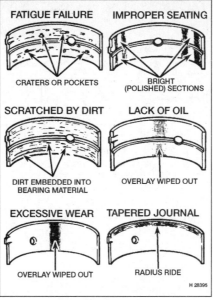

15.2 Typical bearing failures

16 Engine overhaul – reassembly sequence

1 Before reassembly begins, ensure that all necessary new parts have been obtained (particularly gaskets, and various bolts which must be renewed), and that all the tools required are available. Read through the entire procedure to familiarise yourself with the work involved, and to ensure that all items necessary for reassembly of the engine are to hand. In addition to all normal tools and materials, a thread-locking compound will be required. A tube of silicone sealant will be required to seal certain joint faces which are not fitted with gaskets.

2 In order to save time and avoid problems, engine reassembly can be carried out in the following order:

a) Piston rings (see Section 17).
b) Crankshaft (see Section 18).
c) Piston/connecting rod assemblies (see Section 19).

17.4 Measuring a piston ring end gap using a feeler gauge

d) Timing chain and sprockets (see Chapter 2A).
e) Oil pump (see Chapter 2A, 2B or 2C).
f) Sump (see Chapter 2A, 2B or 2C).
g) Flywheel/driveplate (see Chapter 2A, 2B or 2C).
h) Cylinder head (see Chapter 2A, 2B or 2C).
i) Coolant pump (see Chapter 3).
j) Timing belt, sprockets and tensioner (see Chapter 2B or 2C).
k) Inlet and exhaust manifolds (see Chapter 4A, 4B or 4C).

3 At this stage, all engine components should be absolutely clean and dry, with all faults repaired. The components should be laid out (or in individual containers) on a completely clean work surface.

17 Piston rings – refitting

1 Before refitting the new piston rings, the ring end gaps must be checked as follows.

2 Lay out the piston/connecting rod assemblies and the new piston ring sets, so that the ring sets will be matched with the same piston and cylinder during the end gap measurement and subsequent engine reassembly.

3 Insert the top ring into the first cylinder, and push it down the bore using the top of the piston. This will ensure that the ring remains square with the cylinder walls. On petrol engines, position the ring near the bottom of the cylinder bore, at the lower limit of ring travel. On diesel engines, push the ring down into the bore until it is positioned 15 to 20 mm down from the top edge of the bore, then withdraw the piston.

4 Measure the end gap using feeler gauges, and compare the measurements with the figures given in the Specifications **(see illustration)**.

5 If the gap is too small (unlikely if genuine Vauxhall parts are used), it must be enlarged or the ring ends may contact each other during engine operation, causing serious damage. Ideally, new piston rings providing the correct end gap should be fitted, but as a last resort, the end gap can be increased by filing the ring ends very carefully with a fine file. Mount the file in a vice equipped with soft jaws, slip the ring over the file with the ends contacting the file face, and slowly move the ring to remove material from the ends – take care, as piston rings are sharp, and are easily broken.

6 With new piston rings, it is unlikely that the end gap will be too large. If they are too large, check that you have the correct rings for your engine and for the particular cylinder bore size.

7 Repeat the checking procedure for each ring in the first cylinder, and then for the rings in the remaining cylinders. Remember to keep rings, pistons and cylinders matched up.

17.9 Fitting an oil control spreader ring

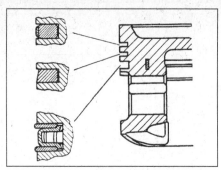

17.11 Sectional view showing correct orientation of piston rings

8 Once the ring end gaps have been checked and if necessary corrected, the rings can be fitted to the pistons.

9 The oil control ring (lowest one on the piston) is composed of three sections, and should be installed first. Fit the lower steel ring, then the spreader ring, followed by the upper steel ring **(see illustration)**.

10 With the oil control ring components installed, the second (middle) ring can be fitted. It is usually stamped with a mark (TOP) which must face up, towards the top of the piston. **Note:** *Always follow the instructions supplied with the new piston ring sets – different manufacturers may specify different procedures. Do not mix up the top and middle rings, as they have different cross-sections.* Using two or three old feeler blades, as for removal of the old rings, carefully slip the ring into place in the middle groove.

11 Fit the top ring in the same manner,

ensuring that, where applicable, the mark on the ring is facing up. If a stepped ring is being fitted, fit the ring with the smaller diameter of the step uppermost **(see illustration)**.

12 Repeat the procedure for the remaining pistons and rings.

18 Crankshaft – refitting

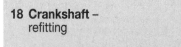

1 Refitting the crankshaft is the first step in the engine reassembly procedure. It is assumed at this point that the cylinder block, baseplate (where applicable) and crankshaft have been cleaned, inspected and repaired or reconditioned as necessary.

2 Position the cylinder block with the sump/baseplate mating face uppermost.

3 Clean the bearing shells and the bearing

recesses in both the cylinder block and the baseplate/caps. If new shells are being fitted, ensure that all traces of the protective grease are cleaned off using paraffin. Wipe the shells dry with a clean lint-free cloth.

4 Note that the crankshaft endfloat is controlled by thrustwashers located on No 3 bearing (1.0 and 1.4 petrol engines), No 4 bearing (1.2 petrol engine), or No 2 bearing (1.7 diesel engine). On all petrol engines, the thrustwashers are incorporated into the bearing shells, however, on diesel engines, they are separate.

5 If the original bearing shells are being re-used, they must be refitted to their original locations in the block and baseplate, or caps. On diesel engines use a little grease to hold the thrustwashers in position, and ensure that the oil way grooves on each thrustwasher face outwards **(see illustrations)**.

6 Fit the upper main bearing shells in place in the cylinder block.

1.0 and 1.2 litre engines

Note: *New cylinder block baseplate bolts must be used when refitting the crankshaft. A tube of silicone sealant will be required when fitting the baseplate to the cylinder block.*

7 Liberally lubricate each bearing shell in the cylinder block, and lower the crankshaft into position **(see illustration)**.

8 If necessary, seat the crankshaft using light taps from a soft-faced mallet on the crankshaft balance webs.

9 Fit the bearing shells in the baseplate.

10 Lubricate the crankshaft journals, and the bearing shells in the baseplate **(see illustration)**.

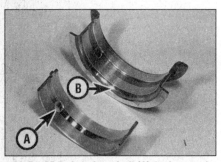

18.5a Main bearing shell (A) and central main bearing shell (B) with thrust flange (petrol)

18.5b Fitting a main bearing shell to the cylinder block

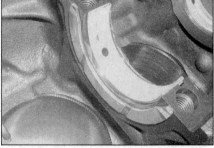

18.5c Fit the thrustwashers to the No 2 main bearing with the oil grooves facing outwards (diesel)

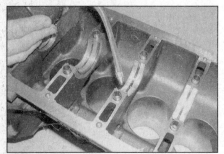

18.7 Liberally lubricate each bearing shell in the cylinder block then lower the crankshaft into position

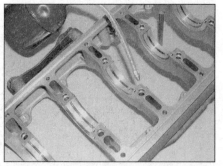

18.10 Lubricate the bearing shells in the baseplate

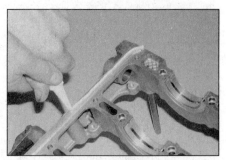

18.11 Apply a 2 mm diameter bead of silicone sealant to the outside of the groove in the baseplate

18.13a Fit the new baseplate inner bolts . . .

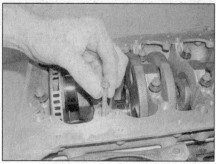

18.13b . . . and outer bolts

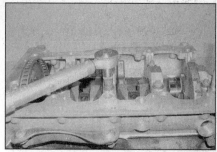

18.13c Tighten the inner bolts to the specified Stage 1 torque setting using a torque wrench . . .

18.13d . . . then through the specified Stage 2 angle using an angle tightening gauge

18.13e Similarly tighten the outer bolts to the specified torque . . .

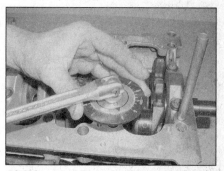

18.13f . . . and through the specified angle

11 Ensure that the cylinder block and baseplate mating surfaces are clean and dry, then apply a 2 mm diameter bead of silicone sealant to the outside of the groove (not in the groove itself) in the baseplate **(see illustration)**.

12 Locate the baseplate over the crankshaft and onto the cylinder block.

13 Fit the new baseplate retaining bolts, then working progressively and in a diagonal sequence, tighten the inner (M8) bolts to the specified torque, then through the specified angle, in the two stages given in the Specifications. Now similarly tighten the outer (M6) retaining bolts **(see illustrations)**.

1.4 litre engine

Note: *New main bearing cap bolts must be used when refitting the crankshaft. Suitable*

sealants will be required to coat the end main bearing caps.

14 Liberally lubricate each bearing shell in the cylinder block, and lower the crankshaft into position. Check that the oil seal is positioned correctly.

15 If necessary, seat the crankshaft using light taps from a soft-faced mallet on the crankshaft balance webs.

16 Fit the bearing shells into the bearing caps.

17 Lubricate the bearing shells in the bearing caps, and the crankshaft journals, then fit Nos 2, 3 and 4 bearing caps, and tighten the new bolts as far as possible by hand **(see illustration)**.

18 Fill the side grooves of the timing belt end (where applicable – not all engines have grooves in the timing belt end main bearing

cap) and flywheel end main bearing caps with RTV jointing compound (Vauxhall part No 15 03 295, or equivalent). Coat the lower surfaces of the bearing caps with sealing compound (Vauxhall part No 15 03 170, or equivalent). Fit the bearing caps, and tighten the new bolts as far as possible by hand **(see illustrations)**. Ensure that the timing belt end main bearing cap is exactly flush with the end face of the cylinder block.

19 Working from the centre main bearing cap outwards, tighten the bearing cap bolts to the specified torque in the three stages given in the Specifications; ie, tighten all bolts to Stage 1, then tighten all bolts to Stage 2, and so on **(see illustrations)**.

20 When all bolts have been fully tightened, inject further RTV jointing compound into the side grooves of the timing belt end (where

18.17 Fitting the centre main bearing cap (1.4 litre petrol)

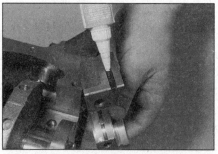

18.18a Fill the side grooves of the flywheel end main bearing cap with RTV jointing compound . . .

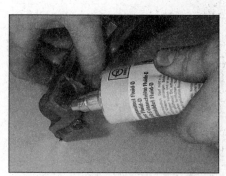

18.18b . . . and coat the lower surfaces with sealing compound (1.4 litre petrol)

18.19a Tighten the main bearing cap bolts to the specified torque . . .

18.19b . . . then through the specified angle

18.21 Lower the crankshaft into position (1.7 litre diesel)

18.24 Tighten the main bearing cap bolts to the specified torque (1.7 litre diesel)

18.26 Apply sealant to the oil seal housing mating surface (1.7 litre diesel)

19 Pistons/connecting rods – refitting

applicable) and flywheel end main bearing caps until it is certain that they are full.

1.7 litre engine

21 Lubricate the upper shells with clean engine oil then lower the crankshaft into position (see illustration).
22 If necessary, seat the crankshaft using light taps from a soft-faced mallet on the crankshaft balance webs.
23 Ensure the bearing shells are correctly located in the caps, then lubricate the shells and refit the caps to the cylinder block. Ensure the caps are fitted in their correct locations, with Number 1 cap at the timing belt end, and are fitted the correct way around so that the arrows all point towards the timing belt end of the engine. Prior to refitting No 1 cap, apply a smear of sealant to its mating surface.

19.2 Press the bearing shells into the connecting rods and caps in their correct positions

24 Apply a smear of clean engine oil to the threads and underneath the heads of the new main bearing cap bolts. Fit the bolts tightening them all by hand then working in a diagonal sequence from the centre outwards, evenly and progressively tighten them to the specified torque setting (see illustration).
25 Ensure that the mating surfaces of the crankshaft rear oil seal housing and cylinder block are clean and dry. Note the correct fitted depth of the oil seal then tap/lever the seal out of the housing.
26 Apply a smear of sealant to the oil seal housing mating surface, and make sure that the locating dowels are in position (see illustration). Slide the housing over the end of the crankshaft, and into position on the cylinder block. Put a drop of locking compound on the threads, then tighten the retaining bolts securely.
27 Refit the oil pump/cover together with new gaskets with reference to Chapter 2C.

All engines

28 Now rotate the crankshaft, and check that it turns freely, with no signs of binding or tight spots.
29 Check the crankshaft endfloat with reference to Section 11.
30 Fit a new crankshaft flywheel end oil seal as described in Chapter 2A, 2B or 2C.
31 Refit the pistons and connecting rods as described in Section 19.
32 Refit the flywheel/driveplate as described in Chapter 2A, 2B or 2C.

1 Clean the backs of the big-end bearing shells and the recesses in the connecting rods and big-end caps. If new shells are being fitted, ensure that all traces of the protective grease are cleaned off using paraffin. Wipe the shells, caps and connecting rods dry with a lint-free cloth.
2 Press the bearing shells into the connecting rods and caps in their correct positions (see illustration).
Note: *When finally refitting the piston/connecting rod assemblies, new big-end bearing cap bolts must be used. Ensure that the mating faces of the connecting rods and big-end bearing caps are clean before refitting (refer to Section 10).*
3 Lubricate No 1 piston and piston rings, and check that the ring gaps are correctly positioned. The gaps in the upper and lower steel rings of the oil control ring should be offset by 25 to 50 mm to the right and left of the spreader ring gap. The two upper compression ring gaps should be offset by 180° to each other.
4 Liberally lubricate the cylinder bore with clean engine oil.
5 Fit a ring compressor to No 1 piston, then insert the piston and connecting rod into the cylinder bore so that the base of the compressor stands on the block. With the crankshaft big-end bearing journal positioned at its lowest point, tap the piston carefully into the cylinder bore with the wooden handle of a hammer, and at the same time guide the connecting rod onto the bearing journal. Note that the arrow or notch (as applicable) on the piston crown must point towards the timing chain/belt end of the engine, and the lugs on the connecting rod (and big-end bearing cap where applicable) should point towards the flywheel end of the engine. On the 1.4 litre engine, the oil spray hole in the connecting rod should be on the coolant pump side of the engine (see illustrations).
6 Fit the bearing shells to the bearing caps.
7 Liberally lubricate the bearing journals and bearing shells, and fit the bearing cap in its

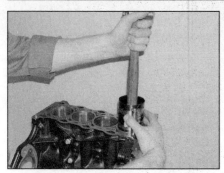

19.5a Tap the piston carefully into the cylinder bore with the wooden handle of a hammer . . .

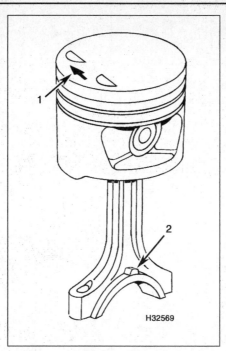

19.5b . . . ensuring that the arrow on the piston (1) points toward the timing chain and the lug (2) on the connecting rod is toward the flywheel

19.7a Tighten the big-end bearing cap bolts to the specified torque . . .

19.7b . . . then through the specified angle

original location. Tighten the new bearing cap bolts to the Stage 1 torque setting, then tighten all bolts through the specified angles **(see illustrations)**.

8 After refitting each piston/connecting rod assembly, rotate the crankshaft, and check that it turns freely, with no signs of binding or tight spots.

9 Refit the oil baffle plate and tighten the retaining bolts securely.

10 Refit the sump and oil pick-up pipe as described in Chapter 2A, 2B or 2C.

11 Refit the cylinder head as described in Chapter 2A, 2B or 2C.

20 Engine – initial start-up after overhaul

1 With the engine refitted in the vehicle, double-check the engine oil and coolant levels. Make a final check that everything has been reconnected, and that there are no tools or rags left in the engine compartment.

Petrol engine models

2 Remove the ignition module and spark plugs (see Chapters 5B and 1A), then remove the fuel pump relay from the fuse/relay box in the engine compartment. **Note:** *Do not disconnect the battery.* The fuel pump relay is located at the front of the fusebox, nearest to the engine compartment front left-hand corner.

3 Turn the engine on the starter several times in 4 second bursts; this will prime the oil lubrication circuit. Refit the fuel pump relay, spark plugs and ignition module.

4 Turn the ignition key to position II for 5

seconds in order to operate the fuel pump and prime the fuel system.

Diesel engine models

5 Remove the air cleaner assembly, fuel injection pump control unit and control unit mounting bracket (see Chapter 4C), then remove the glow plugs (see Chapter 5C). **Note:** *Do not disconnect the battery.*

6 Turn the engine on the starter several times in 4 second bursts in order to prime the oil lubrication circuit. The fuel injectors will not function at this stage as the pump control unit is disconnected.

7 Refit the glow plugs, the fuel injection pump control unit and the air cleaner with reference to Chapters 5C and 4C.

8 Prime the fuel system with reference to Chapter 4C. Although the system is self-priming, it will help if the ignition is switched on and off several times before attempting to start the engine in order to purge air from the system.

9 Turn the ignition key to position II and wait for the preheating warning light to go out.

All models

10 Start the engine, noting that this may take a little longer than usual.

11 While the engine is idling, check for fuel, water and oil leaks. Don't be alarmed if there are some odd smells and smoke from parts getting hot and burning off oil deposits.

12 Assuming all is well, keep the engine idling until hot water is felt circulating through the top hose, then switch off the engine.

13 After a few minutes, recheck the oil and coolant levels as described in *Weekly checks*, and top-up as necessary.

14 Note that there is no need to retighten the cylinder head bolts once the engine has first run after reassembly.

15 If new pistons, rings or crankshaft bearings have been fitted, the engine must be treated as new, and run-in for the first 600 miles (1000 km). *Do not* operate the engine at full-throttle, or allow it to labour at low engine speeds in any gear. It is recommended that the oil and filter be changed at the end of this period.

Chapter 3
Cooling, heating and ventilation systems

Contents

Degrees of difficulty

Easy, suitable for novice with little experience		Fairly easy, suitable for beginner with some experience		Fairly difficult, suitable for competent DIY mechanic		Difficult, suitable for experienced DIY mechanic		Very difficult, suitable for expert DIY or professional	

Specifications

Thermostat

Opening temperature .... 92°C

Air conditioning compressor

Lubricant capacity:
  Petrol engines .... 150 cc
  Diesel engines .... 120 cc
Lubricant type (synthetic PAG fluid) .... Vauxhall part number 90 509 933/19 49 870

Torque wrench settings

	Nm	lbf ft
Air conditioning:		
Petrol:		
Compressor lubricant drain bolt	18	13
Compressor-to-engine bolts (1.0 and 1.2 litre engines)	22	16
Compressor-to-bracket bolts (1.4 litre engines)	22	16
Compressor bracket to engine (1.4 litre engines)	20	15
Compressor clutch to shaft	11	8
Safety valve to compressor	8	6
Diesel:		
Compressor lubricant drain bolt	15	11
Compressor-to-bracket bolts	22	16
Compressor bracket to engine	43	32
Compressor clutch to shaft	18	13
Safety valve to compressor	10	7
Coolant pump blanking plug:		
1.0 and 1.2 litre engines	15	11
Coolant pump bolts:		
1.0 and 1.2 litre engines	8	6
1.4 litre engines	8	6
Diesel engines	24	18
Coolant pump cover bolts:		
1.0 and 1.2 litre engines	8	6
Coolant pump pulley bolts:		
1.0 and 1.2 litre engines	20	15
Diesel engines	10	7
Crankshaft pulley/vibration damper to sprocket:		
Diesel engines	20	15
Engine mounting-to-cylinder block retaining bolts:		
1.4 litre engines	50	37
Radiator lower mounting brackets to crossmember	15	11
Thermostat housing cover bolts		
Petrol engines	8	6
Diesel engines	23	17
Timing belt guide roller retaining bolts:		
1.4 litre engines	25	18
Timing belt tensioner roller retaining bolts:		
1.4 litre engines	20	15

1 General information and precautions

General information

The cooling system is of pressurised type, comprising a pump driven by the auxiliary drivebelt on all engine types except the 1.4 litre petrol engine, on which it is driven by the timing belt, an aluminium crossflow radiator, electric cooling fan, and a thermostat. The system functions as follows. Cold coolant from the radiator passes through the hose to the coolant pump, where it is pumped around the cylinder block and head passages. After cooling the cylinder bores, combustion surfaces and valve seats, the coolant reaches the underside of the thermostat, which is initially closed. The coolant passes through the heater, and is returned to the coolant pump.

When the engine is cold, the coolant circulates only through the cylinder block, cylinder head, expansion tank and heater. When the coolant reaches a predetermined temperature, the thermostat opens and the coolant passes through to the radiator. As the coolant circulates through the radiator, it is cooled by the inrush of air when the car is in forward motion. Airflow is supplemented by the action of the electric cooling fan when necessary. Once the coolant has passed through the radiator, and has cooled, the cycle is repeated.

The electric cooling fan, mounted on the rear of the radiator, is controlled by a thermostatic switch/sensor. At a predetermined coolant temperature, the fan is actuated.

An expansion tank is fitted to the left-hand side of the engine compartment to accommodate expansion of the coolant when it gets hot. The expansion tank is connected to the top of the radiator by a small bore rubber hose.

Precautions

⚠️ **Warning: Do not attempt to remove the expansion tank filler cap, or disturb any part of the cooling system, while the engine is hot; there is a high risk of scalding. If the expansion tank filler cap must be removed before the engine and radiator have fully cooled (even though this is not recommended) the pressure in the cooling system must first be relieved. Cover the cap with a thick layer of cloth, to avoid scalding, and slowly unscrew the filler cap until a hissing sound can be heard. When the hissing has stopped, indicating that the pressure has reduced, slowly unscrew the filler cap until it can be removed; if more hissing sounds are heard, wait until they have stopped before unscrewing the cap completely. At all times, keep well away from the filler cap opening.**

⚠️ **Warning: Do not allow antifreeze to come into contact with skin, or with the painted surfaces of the vehicle. Rinse off spills immediately, with plenty of water. Never leave antifreeze lying around in an open container, or in a puddle on the driveway or garage floor. Children and pets are attracted by its sweet smell, but antifreeze can be fatal if ingested.**

⚠️ **Warning: If the engine is hot, the electric cooling fan may start rotating even if the engine is not running; be careful to keep hands, hair and loose clothing well clear when working in the engine compartment.**

Warning: Refer to Section 11 for precautions to be observed when working on models equipped with air conditioning.

2 Cooling system hoses – disconnection and renewal

Note: *Refer to the warnings given in Section 1 of this Chapter before proceeding. Do not attempt to disconnect any hose while the system is still hot.*

1 If the checks described in Chapter 1A or 1B reveal a faulty hose, it must be renewed as follows.

2 First drain the cooling system (see Chapter 1A or 1B). If the coolant is not due for renewal, it may be re-used if it is collected in a clean container.

3 Before disconnecting a hose, first note its routing in the engine compartment, and whether it is secured by any additional retaining clips or cable ties. Use a pair of pliers to release the clamp-type clips, or a screwdriver to slacken the screw-type clips, then move the clips along the hose, clear of the relevant inlet/outlet union. Carefully work the hose free.

4 Note that the radiator inlet and outlet unions are fragile; do not use excessive force when attempting to remove the hoses. If a hose proves to be difficult to remove, try to release it by rotating the hose ends before attempting to free it.

HAYNES HiNT *If all else fails, cut the coolant hose with a sharp knife, then slit it so that it can be peeled off in two pieces. Although this may prove expensive if the hose is otherwise undamaged, it is preferable to buying a new radiator.*

5 When fitting a hose, first slide the clips onto the hose, then work the hose into position. If clamp-type clips were originally fitted, it is a good idea to use screw-type clips when refitting the hose. If the hose is stiff, use a little soapy water (washing-up liquid is ideal) as a lubricant, or soften the hose by soaking it in hot water.

6 Work the hose into position, checking that it is correctly routed and secured. Slide each clip along the hose until it passes over the flared end of the relevant inlet/outlet union, before tightening the clips securely.

7 Refill the cooling system with reference to Chapter 1A or 1B.

8 Check thoroughly for leaks as soon as possible after disturbing any part of the cooling system.

3 Radiator – removal, inspection and refitting

Removal

1 Disconnect the battery negative terminal (refer to *Disconnecting the battery* in the Reference Chapter).

2 Remove the front bumper as described in Chapter 11.

3 Drain the cooling system as described in Chapter 1A or 1B **(see illustration)**.

4 On diesel models with an intercooler, remove the intercooler as described in Chapter 4C.

5 Slacken the retaining clips, and disconnect the coolant top hose and the expansion tank hose from the top of the radiator **(see illustration)**.

6 Slacken the retaining clip, and disconnect the bottom hoses from the radiator **(see illustration)**.

7 Disconnect the cooling fan motor wiring connector(s), then unclip the wiring loom from the fan shroud **(see illustration)**.

8 Undo the retaining bolt(s), and remove the air cleaner assembly as described in the relevant part of Chapter 4.

9 Unclip any hoses from the fan shroud, then undo the two retaining bolts and release the fan assembly from the radiator. To remove, lift the fan assembly upwards taking care not to damage the radiator **(see illustrations)**.

10 Undo the retaining bolts, and release the radiator mounting brackets from the bottom of the radiator. Lower the radiator out through the bottom of the vehicle, disengaging it from its upper mountings **(see illustrations)**.

Inspection

11 If the radiator has been removed due to suspected blockage, reverse-flush it as

3.3 Fit a piece of hose pipe onto the end of the drain tap when draining the cooling system

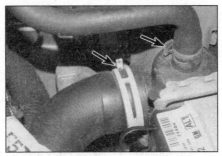

3.5 Release the retaining clips (arrowed) and disconnect the coolant hoses from the left-hand end of the radiator . . .

3.6 . . . and the coolant hose from the right-hand end of the radiator

3.7 Disconnect the wiring block connector from the cooling fan motor

3.9a Unclip the coolant hoses (arrowed) from the fan shroud . . .

3.9b . . . and undo the retaining bolts (right-hand side arrowed)

3.10a Remove the lower mounting brackets . . .

3.10b . . . and withdraw the radiator downwards from out of the radiator upper mounting bracket (arrowed)

3.15a Check the radiator upper mounting rubbers . . .

3.15b . . . and lower mounting rubbers for signs of damage, and renew if necessary

3.16a On refitting, ensure that the radiator pegs engage with lower mounting rubbers

3.16b Slight adjustment can be made on the left-hand upper mounting bracket (arrowed) if required

described in Chapter 1A or 1B. Clean dirt and debris from the radiator fins, using an air line (in which case, wear eye protection) or a soft brush.
Caution: Be careful, as the fins are easily damaged, and are sharp.
12 If necessary, a radiator specialist can perform a 'flow test' on the radiator, to establish whether an internal blockage exists.
13 A leaking radiator must be referred to a specialist for permanent repair. Do not attempt DIY repairs to a leaking radiator, as damage may result.
14 In an emergency, minor leaks from the radiator can be cured by using a suitable radiator sealant (in accordance with its manufacturer's instructions) with the radiator in situ.
15 Inspect the radiator mounting rubbers, and renew them if necessary **(see illustrations)**.

Refitting

16 Refitting is a reversal of removal, bearing in mind the following points:
  a) *Ensure that the lugs on the radiator are correctly engaged with the mounting rubbers in the mounting bracket* **(see illustrations)***.*
  b) *Ensure that all hoses are correctly reconnected, and their retaining clips securely tightened.*
  c) *Where applicable, reconnect the automatic transmission fluid cooler banjo unions using new copper washers.*
  d) *On completion, refill the cooling system as described in Chapter 1A or 1B.*
  e) *On models with automatic transmission, check and, if necessary, top-up the automatic transmission fluid as described in Chapter 1A.*

4 Thermostat – removal, testing and refitting

Removal

Petrol engines

1 Disconnect the battery negative terminal (refer to *Disconnecting the battery* in the Reference Chapter).
2 On 1.4 litre engines, remove the oil filler cap, undo the two retaining bolts and remove the engine cover, refit the oil filler cap.
3 Drain the cooling system (see Chapter 1A).
4 Slacken the retaining clip, and disconnect the coolant hose from the thermostat housing cover **(see illustration)**.
5 On 1.4 litre engines, slacken the retaining clip, and disconnect the small coolant hose from the thermostat housing cover.
6 Slacken and remove the three retaining bolts, and remove the thermostat housing cover **(see illustration)**.
7 Remove the thermostat. Note on some models, the thermostat is an integral part of the housing cover, and cannot be renewed separately.
8 Remove the sealing ring from the housing cover and discard it; a new one should be used on refitting.

Diesel engines

9 Disconnect the battery negative terminal (refer to *Disconnecting the battery* in the Reference Chapter).

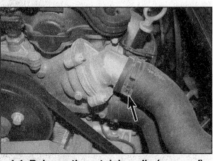

4.4 Release the retaining clip (arrowed) and disconnect the coolant hose from the thermostat housing cover

4.6 Remove the thermostat housing cover from the coolant pump – petrol engines

4.12 Undo the two bolts (arrowed) and remove the wiring harness bracket from the thermostat housing cover

10 Drain the cooling system (see Chapter 1B).
11 Slacken the retaining clip, and disconnect the coolant hose from the thermostat housing.
12 Undo the retaining bolt(s) and detach the wiring harness bracket from the thermostat housing **(see illustration)**.
13 Slacken and remove the two retaining bolts, and remove the thermostat housing from the engine **(see illustration 4.12)**.
14 Withdraw the thermostat from coolant housing unit.
15 Remove the gasket/sealing ring from the edge of the thermostat and discard it; a new one should be used on refitting.

Testing

16 A rough test of the thermostat's operation may be made by suspending it with a piece of string in a container full of water. Heat the water to bring it to the boil – the thermostat must open by the time the water boils. If not, renew it **(see illustration)**.
17 The opening temperature is marked on the thermostat. If a thermometer is available, the precise opening temperature of the thermostat may be determined, and compared with the value mark on the thermostat.
18 A thermostat which fails to close as the water cools must also be renewed.

Refitting

Petrol engines

19 Refitting is a reversal of removal, bearing in mind the following points:
a) Fit the new sealing ring to the thermostat housing cover **(see illustration)**.

4.16 Testing the thermostat opening temperature

b) Tighten the thermostat housing cover bolts to the specified torque setting.
c) On completion, refill the cooling system as described in Chapter 1A.
d) On 1.4 litre engines, refit the cover to the top of the engine.

Diesel engines

20 Refitting is a reversal of removal, bearing in mind the following points:
a) Fit the new gasket/sealing ring to the thermostat, and fit the thermostat to the cylinder head, ensuring that the thermostat is fitted the correct way round.
b) Tighten the thermostat housing bolts to the specified torque setting.
c) Refit the wiring loom bracket to the thermostat housing.
d) On completion, refill the cooling system as described in Chapter 1B.

---

5 Electric cooling fan –
testing, removal and refitting

⚠ **Warning: If the engine is hot, the cooling fan may start up at any time. Take extra precautions when working in the vicinity of the fan.**

Testing

1 The cooling fan is supplied with current via the ignition switch, relay(s) and a fuse (see Chapter 12). The circuit is activated by a control unit, which receives information from the temperature sensor.

4.19 Fitting a new sealing ring to the thermostat cover groove – 1.0 and 1.2 litre petrol engines

2 To test the electric fan, run the engine until normal operating temperature is reached, then allow it to idle. The fan should cut in within a few minutes (or before the temperature gauge indicates overheating). If it does not, check that the battery voltage is available at the feed wire to the fan motor, and at the relay (see Chapter 12). No voltage indicates a blown fuse, faulty relay, faulty ignition switch or a fault in the wiring circuit.
3 If the ignition switch, relay and wiring are in good working order, the fault must lie in the motor itself. The motor can be checked by disconnecting the motor wiring connector and connecting a fused, 12 volt supply directly to one of the motor terminals and an earth to the other terminal. If the motor fails to operate, it is proved faulty, and must be renewed complete.

Removal

4 Disconnect the battery negative terminal (refer to *Disconnecting the battery* in the Reference Chapter).
5 On some models with air conditioning, it may be necessary to remove the front bumper as described in Chapter 11.
6 Undo the retaining bolt(s), and remove the air cleaner assembly as described in the relevant part of Chapter 4.
7 Undo the retaining screw, and slide the air intake pipe to one side to release it from the radiator crossmember **(see illustrations)**. **Note:** *Where applicable, withdraw the dipstick from its tube.*
8 Disconnect the cooling fan motor wiring connector(s), then unclip the wiring loom from the fan shroud **(see illustration)**.

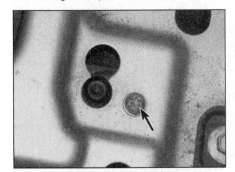

5.7a Undo the retaining screw (arrowed) . . . .

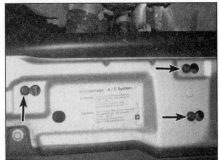

5.7b . . . then slide the locating pegs (arrowed) out from the crossmember

5.8 Disconnect the wiring block connector from the cooling fan motor

5.9 Unclip the coolant hoses (arrowed) from the fan shroud

5.10a Undo the retaining bolts (right-hand side arrowed) . . .

5.10b . . . and withdraw the fan assembly out from the radiator

5.11a Undo the retaining nut, withdraw the fan from the motor . . .

5.11b . . . and recover the washer

5.12 Undo the retaining bolts (arrowed) to remove the motor from the shroud

9 Unclip any hoses or wiring loom from the fan shroud (see illustration)

10 Unscrew the fan shroud retaining bolts, then tilt the assembly back slightly towards the engine, and withdraw it upwards away

from the radiator (see illustrations). Where necessary, push the coolant hoses aside to provide sufficient clearance for removal.

11 To remove the fan motor, first release the retaining nut and remove the fan from the

motor. Retrieve the washer from the motor spindle for refitting (see illustrations).

12 Turn the fan assembly over and unscrew the three retaining nuts, then remove the fan motor from the shroud (see illustration).

13 Undo the screw and detach the wiring plug and resistor from the shroud (see illustrations).

14 No spare parts are available for the motor, and if the unit is faulty, it must be renewed complete.

Refitting

15 Refitting is a reversal of removal, ensuring that the shroud is correctly located in the radiator clips (see illustrations).

16 On completion, start the engine and run it until it reaches normal operating temperature; continue to run the engine, and check that the cooling fan cuts in and functions correctly.

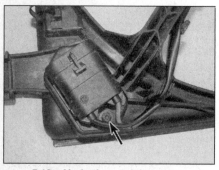

5.13a Undo the retaining screw (arrowed) . . .

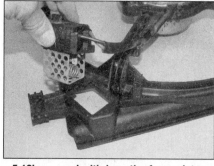

5.13b . . . and withdraw the fan resistor from the shroud

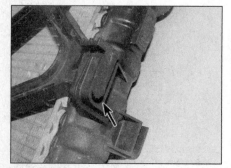

5.15a Ensure the fan is located correctly in the sides of the radiator (arrowed) . . .

5.15b . . . the top of the radiator (arrowed) . . .

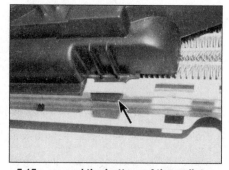

5.15c . . . and the bottom of the radiator (arrowed)

6 Coolant temperature sensor
– testing, removal and refitting

Testing

1 Testing of the coolant temperature sensor circuit is best entrusted to a Vauxhall dealer, who will have the necessary specialist diagnostic equipment.

Removal

2 On the diesel engines, the coolant sensor is located on the thermostat housing on the left-hand side of the cylinder head On the petrol engines, the coolant sensor is located on the thermostat housing on the right-hand front of the cylinder head **(see illustrations)**.

3 Remove the undertray from under the engine compartment, then position a suitable container beneath the sensor position to catch the spilled coolant.

4 With the engine cold, unscrew the cap from the coolant expansion tank to release the pressure, then refit and tighten it. This will reduce the loss of coolant when the sensor is removed. Have a suitable plug available to insert in the sensor hole.

5 Where applicable, remove the cover from the top of the engine.

6 Disconnect the wiring from the temperature sensor, then unscrew and remove it from the thermostat housing. Either insert the new sensor or fit a blanking plug to prevent the loss of coolant.

Refitting

7 Ensure the sender threads are clean, and apply a smear of suitable sealant to them.

8 Refit the sender, tightening it securely, and reconnect the wiring.

9 Top-up/refill the cooling system as described in Chapter 1A or 1B.

10 On completion, start the engine and check the operation of the temperature gauge. Also check for coolant leaks.

7 Coolant pump –
removal and refitting

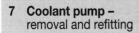

Removal

1.0 and 1.2 litre petrol engines

1 Disconnect the battery negative terminal (refer to *Disconnecting the battery* in the Reference Chapter).

2 Slacken the three coolant pump pulley retaining bolts **(see illustration)**.

3 Remove the auxiliary drivebelt as described in Chapter 1A.

4 Drain the cooling system as described in Chapter 1A.

5 Support the engine and remove the engine mounting as described in Chapter 2A.

6 Unscrew the previously-slackened coolant

**6.2a Coolant sensor (arrowed) –
diesel engines**

pump pulley bolts and withdraw the pulley from the pump.

7 Disconnect the coolant temperature sensor wiring plug(s).

8 Release the retaining clips and disconnect the hoses from the coolant pump and thermostat housing **(see illustrations)**.

9 Unscrew the coolant pump retaining bolts, noting the locations of the three short bolts **(see illustration)**. The short bolts secure the pump to the timing cover, and the long bolts secure the pump and the timing cover to the cylinder block and cylinder head.

10 Withdraw the coolant pump from the timing cover, noting that it may be necessary to tap the pump lightly with a soft-faced hammer to free it from the locating dowels. **Note:** *Coolant which is trapped in the cylinder block will leak out when the pump is removed.*

11 Recover the pump sealing ring/gasket, and discard it; a new one must be used on refitting.

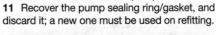

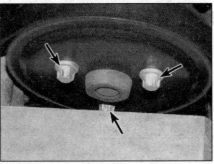

**7.2 Slacken the three coolant pump pulley
retaining bolts (arrowed)**

**7.8b . . . and release the retaining clips
(arrowed) and disconnect the coolant hoses
from rear of the coolant pump housing**

**6.2b Coolant sensor (arrowed) –
petrol engines**

12 Note that it is not possible to overhaul the pump. If it is faulty, the unit must be renewed complete.

13 If the pump is being renewed, remove the thermostat (referring to the procedures in Section 4) and temperature sensor(s) then transfer them to the new pump.

14 Similarly, unscrew the two bolts and withdraw the coolant pump top cover from the old pump and fit the cover to the new pump using a new seal. Tighten the cover bolts to the specified torque.

1.4 litre petrol engines

15 Disconnect the battery negative terminal (refer to *Disconnecting the battery* in the Reference Chapter).

16 Drain the cooling system with reference to Chapter 1A.

17 Remove the timing belt as described in Chapter 2B.

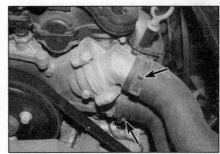

**7.8a Release the retaining clips (arrowed)
and disconnect the coolant hoses from the
front of the coolant pump housing . . .**

**7.9 Coolant pump short retaining bolt
locations (arrowed) – 1.0 and 1.2 litre petrol
engines (shown with timing cover removed)**

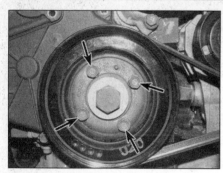

7.30 Undo the four retaining bolts (arrowed)

7.31 Withdraw the pulley from the coolant pump

7.32 Undo the five retaining bolts (arrowed) and remove the coolant pump – diesel engines

18 Undo the two timing belt guide roller centre bolts and remove them from the cylinder block.

19 Undo the three retaining bolts and remove the engine mounting bracket from the cylinder block.

20 Undo the timing belt tensioner roller centre bolt and remove it from the cylinder block.

21 Remove the timing belt drive gear from the end of the crankshaft, then undo the retaining bolts and remove the timing belt rear cover from the lower part of the cylinder block.

22 Unscrew and remove the three coolant pump securing bolts.

23 Withdraw the coolant pump from the cylinder block, noting that it may be necessary to tap the pump lightly with a soft-faced hammer to free it from the cylinder block. **Note:** *Coolant which is trapped in the cylinder block will leak out when the pump is removed.*

24 Recover the pump sealing ring, and discard it; a new one must be used on refitting.

25 Note that it is not possible to overhaul the pump. If it is faulty, the unit must be renewed complete.

Diesel engines

26 Disconnect the battery negative terminal (refer to *Disconnecting the battery* in the Reference Chapter).

27 Drain the cooling system with reference to Chapter 1B.

28 Remove the air filter assembly as described in Chapter 4C.

29 Slacken the retaining bolts on the coolant pump pulley, then remove the auxiliary drivebelt as described in Chapter 1B.

30 Undo the four retaining bolts and remove the crankshaft pulley/vibration damper from the end of the crankshaft **(see illustration)**.

31 Undo the retaining bolts and remove the coolant pump pulley from the coolant pump **(see illustration)**.

32 Unscrew and remove the five coolant pump retaining bolts **(see illustration)**.

33 Withdraw the coolant pump from the cylinder block, noting that it may be necessary to tap the pump lightly with a soft-faced hammer to free it from the cylinder block. **Note:** *Coolant which is trapped in the cylinder block will leak out when the pump is removed.*

34 Recover the pump gasket/sealing ring, and discard it; a new one must be used on refitting **(see illustration)**.

35 Note that it is not possible to overhaul the pump. If it is faulty, the unit must be renewed complete.

Refitting

1.0 and 1.2 litre petrol engines

36 Ensure that the pump and timing cover mating faces are clean and dry and locate a new seal in the timing cover groove **(see illustration)**.

37 Check that the locating dowels are in place and locate the pump in position on the timing cover.

38 Refit the pump retaining bolts, ensuring that the short bolts are fitted to their correct

locations **(see illustration 7.9)**. Tighten the bolts to the specified torque.

39 Refit the coolant pump pulley and tighten the three bolts to the specified torque. To prevent the pulley turning as the bolts are tightened, hold the pulley using a screwdriver engaged with one of the bolts and the pump centre spindle. Alternatively, wait until the auxiliary drivebelt has been refitted and tighten the bolts then.

40 Reconnect the coolant hoses and the coolant temperature sensor wiring plug.

41 Refit the auxiliary drivebelt and refill the cooling system as described in Chapter 1A or 1B.

42 If not already done, tighten the coolant pump pulley bolts to the specified torque. Refit the engine mounting with reference to Chapter 2A.

43 Refill the cooling system with reference to Chapter 1A.

44 Reconnect the battery negative terminal (refer to *Disconnecting the battery* in the Reference Chapter).

1.4 litre petrol engines

45 Ensure that the pump and cylinder block mating surfaces are clean and dry, and apply a smear of silicone grease to the pump mating surface in the cylinder block. Vauxhall recommend the use of their grease (Part No 90 167 353); in the absence of this, ensure a good-quality equivalent is used.

46 Fit a new sealing ring to the pump, and install the pump in the cylinder block.

47 Refit the pump retaining bolts, tightening them to the specified torque setting.

48 Refit the timing belt rear cover to the lower part of the cylinder block, then refit the timing belt drive gear to the end of the crankshaft.

49 Refit the timing belt tensioner roller centre bolt and refit it to the cylinder block.

50 Refit the engine mounting bracket to the cylinder block.

51 Refit the timing belt guide roller to the cylinder block.

52 Refit the timing belt as described in Chapter 2B.

53 Refill the cooling system with reference to Chapter 1A.

54 Reconnect the battery negative terminal

7.34 Coolant pump gasket – diesel engines

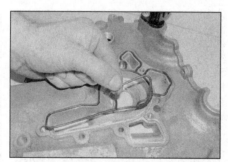

7.36 Locate a new rubber seal in the timing cover groove – 1.0 and 1.2 litre petrol engines (timing cover removed)

(refer to *Disconnecting the battery* in the Reference Chapter).

Diesel engines

55 Ensure that the pump and cylinder block mating surfaces are clean and dry.

56 Fit a new gasket/sealing ring to the pump, and install the pump in the cylinder block.

57 Refit the pump retaining bolts, tightening them to the specified torque setting.

58 Refit the crankshaft pulley/vibration damper to the end of the crankshaft tightening the retaining bolts to the specified torque setting.

59 Refit the coolant pump pulley to the coolant pump tightening it to the specified torque setting, if required wait until the auxiliary drivebelt has been refitted and tighten the bolts then.

60 Refit the auxiliary drivebelt as described in Chapter 1B.

61 Refit the air filter assembly as described in Chapter 4C.

62 Refill the cooling system with reference to Chapter 1B.

63 Reconnect the battery negative terminal (refer to *Disconnecting the battery* in the Reference Chapter).

8 Heater/ventilation system – general information

The heater/ventilation system consists of a four-speed blower motor which is inside the vehicle behind the facia to the left-hand side of the heater housing, face-level vents in the centre and at each end of the facia, and air ducts to the front footwells and windscreen.

The control unit is located in the facia to the right-hand side of the heater housing assembly. The controls operate flap valves to deflect and mix the air flowing through the various parts of the heater/ventilation system. The flap valves are contained in the air distribution housing, which acts as a central distribution unit, passing air to the various ducts and vents.

Cold air enters the system through the grille at the rear of the engine compartment. A pollen filter is fitted to the ventilation intake, to filter out dust, soot, pollen and spores from the air entering the vehicle.

The air (boosted by the blower fan if required) then flows through the various ducts, according to the settings of the controls. Stale air is expelled through ducts behind the doors. If warm air is required, the cold air is passed through the heater matrix, which is heated by the engine coolant.

A recirculation lever enables the outside air supply to be closed off, while the air inside the vehicle is recirculated. This can be useful to prevent unpleasant odours entering from outside the vehicle, but should only be used briefly, as the recirculated air inside the vehicle will soon deteriorate.

9.3a Undo the retaining screw . . .

9.3b . . . and withdraw the radio/cassette housing

9 Heater/ventilation system components – removal and refitting

Heater control panel

Removal

1 Disconnect the battery negative terminal (refer to *Disconnecting the battery* in the Reference Chapter).

2 Working inside the vehicle, remove the glove-box (see Chapter 11, Section 26), this will help to gain access to the rear of the control panel.

3 Remove the radio/cassette as described in Chapter 12, then undo the retaining screw and withdraw the radio/cassette housing, disconnecting the wiring connectors from the rear of the housing on removal **(see illustrations)**.

4 Carefully prise the trim from the heater control panel, starting at the top of the panel then working down each side, withdrawing the trim from the control panel, taking great care not to damage the panel **(see illustration)**.

5 From inside the radio aperture, unclip the direction control cable from the rear of the control panel **(see illustration)**.

6 From inside the radio aperture undo the two retaining screws from the top of the heater control panel **(see illustration)**.

7 Release the locating lugs and withdraw the heater control panel from the facia panel until access can be gained to release the temperature control cable from the rear of the control panel **(see illustrations)**.

8 Disconnect the wiring connectors from the control panel, noting the wiring's correct fitted location and routing.

9 If necessary, the control knobs can be

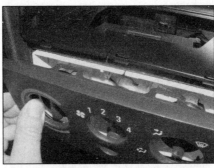

9.4 Carefully prise out the trim from the heater control panel

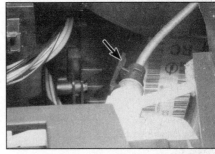

9.5 Unclip the direction control cable (arrowed) from the rear of the control panel

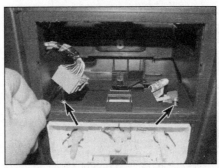

9.6 Undo the two retaining screws (arrowed) . . .

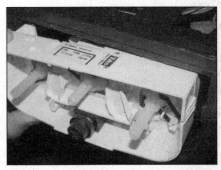

9.7a . . . then withdraw the control panel from the facia

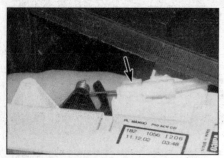

9.7b Unclip the remaining control cable (arrowed) from the rear of the control panel

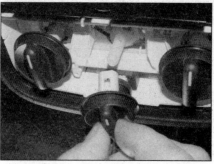

9.9 Pull the control knobs, to release them from the control panel

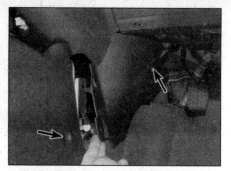

9.12a Undo the two retaining screws (arrowed) . . .

9.12b . . . and the two retaining screws (arrowed) from the lower trim panel

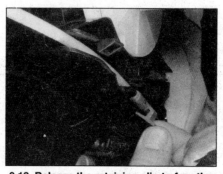

9.13 Release the retaining clip to free the outer cable

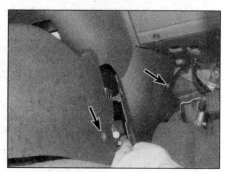

9.17a Undo the two retaining screws (arrowed) . . .

removed by carefully prising them from the control panel **(see illustration)**.

Refitting

10 Refitting is reversal of removal. Ensure that the wiring connectors and control cables are correctly routed and reconnected to the control panel, as noted before removal. Clip the outer cable(s) in position, and check the operation of each knob/lever before refitting the centre facia panel.

Temperature control cable

Removal

11 Remove the heater control panel from the facia, as described above in paragraphs 1 to 9.
12 Undo the two retaining screws and remove the trim from the side of the heater unit, then the two screws to remove the

driver's side lower trim panel **(see illustrations)**.
13 Release the retaining clip and disconnect the cable from the control valve lever on the lower part of the heater control drive unit **(see illustration)**.
14 Follow the run of the cable behind the facia, taking note of its routing, and if not already removed, disconnect the cable from the lever on the rear of the control panel. Note that the method of fastening is the same as that used at the control drive unit.

Refitting

15 Refitting is reversal of removal. Ensure that the wiring connectors and control cables are correctly routed and reconnected to the control panel, as noted before removal. Clip the outer cable(s) in position, and check the operation of each knob/lever before refitting the centre facia panel.

Heater control unit and cable

Removal

16 Remove the direction control cable from the rear of the control panel, as described above in paragraphs 1 to 5.
17 Undo the two retaining screws and remove the trim from the side of the heater unit, then the two screws to remove the driver's side lower trim panel **(see illustrations)**.
18 Release the retaining clip and disconnect the cable from the control valve lever on the lower part of the heater control drive unit **(see illustration)**.
19 Unclip the two operating levers from the air flap controls **(see illustration)**.
20 Undo the retaining bolt **(see illustration)** and withdraw the heater control drive unit from the heater housing, complete with direction control cable.

9.17b . . . and the two retaining screws from the lower trim panel and remove

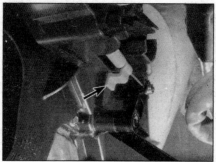

9.18 Release the retaining clip (arrowed) to free the outer cable

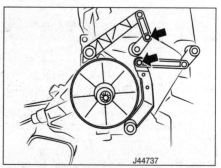

9.19 Carefully lever the two linkage rods (arrowed) from the air flap control unit

9.20 Undo the retaining bolt (arrowed)

9.21a Align the hole arrowed . . .

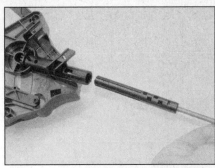

9.21b . . . then slide the cable from the housing

21 The cable can then be removed from the control drive unit, align the hole in the driveshaft, then pull the cable out of its housing **(see illustrations)**.

Refitting

22 Refitting is reversal of removal. Ensure that the wiring connectors and control cables are correctly routed and reconnected, as noted before removal **(see illustration)**. Clip the cables in position, and check the operation of each knob/lever before refitting the centre facia panel.

Heater matrix

Removal

23 With the engine cold, unscrew the expansion tank cap (referring to the warning note in Section 1) to release any pressure present in the cooling system, then securely refit the cap.

24 Clamp both heater hoses as close to the bulkhead as possible, to minimise coolant loss. Alternatively, drain the cooling system as described in Chapter 1A or 1B.

25 Working in the engine compartment, release the retaining clips, and disconnect both hoses from the heater matrix unions **(see illustrations)**.

26 Undo the two retaining screws and remove the trim from the side of the heater unit, then the two screws to remove the driver's side lower trim panel **(see illustrations 9.12a and 9.12b)**.

27 Release the retaining clip and remove the driver's side front footwell air duct **(see illustration)**.

28 Cover the carpet directly underneath the air distribution housing, to catch any coolant which may be spilt from the matrix as it is removed. Alternatively, release the carpet fasteners, and fold the carpet back from the

bulkhead so that any spilt coolant will go behind the carpet.

29 Undo the retaining screw and remove the bracket from the coolant pipes entering the air distribution housing, then undo the two retaining clips and disconnect the pipes from the heater matrix **(see illustration)**.

30 Slide the heater matrix out from the air distribution housing and remove the matrix from the vehicle. **Note:** *Keep the matrix unions uppermost as the matrix is removed, to prevent coolant spillage.* Mop up any spilt coolant immediately, and wipe the affected area with a damp cloth to prevent staining.

31 Where necessary, recover the sealing rings from the matrix unions and hoses, and renew them.

Refitting

32 Refitting is a reversal of the removal procedure, bearing in mind the following points:

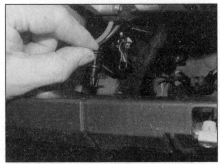

9.22 Align the peg (arrowed) on the housing with the slot in the cable

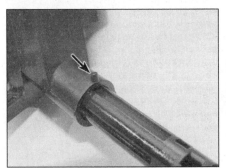

9.25a Release the retaining clips from the heater hoses . . .

9.25b . . . then disengage the hoses from the heater matrix pipes

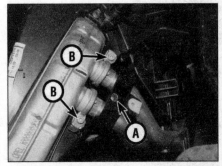

9.27a Withdraw the securing pin . . .

9.27b . . . and remove the heater air duct

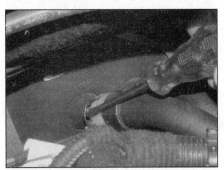

9.29 Undo the retaining screw (A), then the two retaining clips (B)

9.36 Remove the passenger side heater air duct

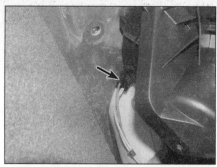

9.37 Disconnect the wiring connector (arrowed) from the blower motor

9.38a Undo the retaining screws (one arrowed) . . .

9.38b . . . then unclip the retaining clips (one arrowed) from around the motor housing . . .

9.38c and withdraw the motor from the housing

9.41 Disconnecting the wiring connector from the blower motor resistor . . .

a) Apply a smear silicone grease to the matrix sealing rings, to ease installation.
b) Ensure that the heater hose retaining clips are securely pressed back into position.
c) On completion, top-up/refill the cooling system as described in Chapter 1A or 1B.

Heater blower motor

Removal

33 Disconnect the battery negative terminal (refer to *Disconnecting the battery* in the Reference Chapter).
34 Working inside the vehicle, remove the glovebox as described in Chapter 11, Section 26.
35 Remove the lower trim panel from the facia above the passenger side footwell and the lower trim panel from the centre of the facia.
36 Release the retaining clip and remove the

passenger side front footwell air duct **(see illustration)**.
37 Disconnect the wiring connector from the fan motor, noting the correct routing of the wiring **(see illustration)**.
38 Working your way around the fan motor air distribution housing, undo the retaining screws, then unclip the motor from the housing **(see illustrations)**.

Refitting

39 Refitting is a reversal of the removal procedure, noting the following points:
a) Make sure that the motor wiring is correctly routed.
b) Make sure that the blower motor covers are correctly engaged with each other, and clipped securely in position.

Heater blower motor resistor

Removal

40 Remove the fan motor as described above in paragraphs 33 to 38.
41 From inside the vehicle, reach up behind the air distribution housing, and disconnect the wiring connector from the underside of the blower motor resistor, which is on the left-hand side of the air distribution housing **(see illustration)**.
42 Unclip the resistor from the air distribution housing **(see illustration)**.

Refitting

43 Refitting is the reverse of removal.

Air distribution housing

Note: *On models with air conditioning, it is not*

*possible to remove the air distribution housing without opening the refrigerant circuit (see Section 11). Therefore, this task **must** be carried out by qualified personnel.*

Removal

44 Remove the centre console and facia assembly as described in Chapter 11.
45 Unclip the wiring harness from the steering support crossmember, which is bolted across the front bulkhead behind the facia panel.
46 With the both front doors open, undo the retaining bolts (two each side), and withdraw the crossmember from the bulkhead **(see illustrations)**.
47 Drain the cooling system as described in Chapter 1A or 1B.
48 Working in the engine compartment, release the retaining clips, and disconnect both hoses from the heater matrix unions **(see illustrations 9.25a and 9.25b)**.

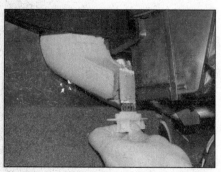

9.42 . . . and withdraw the blower motor resistor out of position

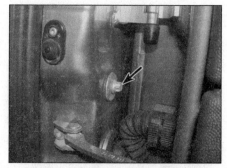

9.46a Undo the crossmember upper retaining bolt (right-hand side arrowed) . . .

49 Remove the windscreen wipers and water deflector as described in Chapter 12.

50 Remove the battery, then undo the four retaining bolts and withdraw the pollen filter housing from the bulkhead.

51 On models with air conditioning, the refrigerant line block connection will need to be disconnected from the expansion valve (*this task **must** be carried out by qualified personnel* – see **Note**).

52 Cover the carpet directly underneath the air distribution housing, to catch any coolant which may be spilt from the matrix as the housing assembly is removed.

53 Disconnect the wiring connector from the blower motor resistor on the left-hand side of the housing.

54 Working in the engine compartment, undo the two bolts where the heater hoses come out through the bulkhead and the one bolt which is located under the pollen filter housing **(see illustration)**

55 Working inside the vehicle withdraw the air distribution housing from the bulkhead.

Note: *Keep the matrix unions uppermost as the housing is removed, to prevent coolant spillage.* Mop up any spilt coolant immediately, and wipe the affected area with a damp cloth to prevent staining.

Refitting

56 Refitting is the reverse of removal. On completion, refill the cooling system as described in Chapter 1A or 1B. On models with air conditioning, have the system charged by the air conditioning engineer.

---

10 Heater/ventilation vents and ducts –
removal and refitting

Centre vents and housing

1 Unclip the hazard warning light switch cover from between the centre air vents **(see illustration)**.

2 Insert a small, flat-bladed screwdriver in through the gap, and carefully lever between the sides of the vent and the housing to release the vent from its locating pegs **(see illustration)**.

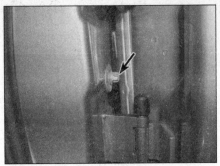

9.46b . . . and the lower retaining bolt (right-hand side arrowed)

3 Once the vent is free from both its locating pegs, it can be withdrawn from the facia.

4 Undo the four retaining screws and remove the air vent trim surround **(see illustration)**. Disconnect the wiring block connector from the housing.

5 On refitting, carefully manoeuvre the vent back into the facia, ensuring it is correctly engaged with the locating pegs.

Side vents

6 Remove the vents as described in paragraphs 2 to 3.

7 Refitting is a reversal of the removal procedure, ensuring that the housing is correctly located with the duct.

---

11 Air conditioning system –
general information
and precautions

General information

1 Air conditioning is available on certain models. It enables the temperature of incoming air to be lowered, and also dehumidifies the air, which makes for rapid demisting and increased comfort.

2 The cooling side of the system works in the same way as a domestic refrigerator. Refrigerant gas is drawn into a belt-driven compressor, and passes into a condenser mounted in front of the radiator, where it loses heat and becomes liquid. The liquid passes through an expansion valve to an evaporator,

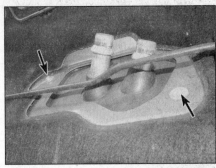

9.54 Undo the two retaining bolts arrowed

where it changes from liquid under high pressure to gas under low pressure. This change is accompanied by a drop in temperature, which cools the evaporator. The refrigerant returns to the compressor, and the cycle begins again.

3 Air blown through the evaporator passes to the air distribution unit, where it is mixed with hot air blown through the heater matrix, to achieve the desired temperature in the passenger compartment.

4 The heating side of the system works in the same way as on models without air conditioning (see Section 8).

5 The operation of the system is controlled electronically by the coolant temperature switches, which are screwed into the right-hand end of the radiator, and pressure switches which are screwed into the compressor high-pressure line. Any problems with the system should be referred to a Vauxhall dealer.

Precautions

6 It is necessary to observe special precautions whenever dealing with any part of the system, its associated components, and any items which necessitate disconnection of the system.

⚠️ *Warning: The refrigeration circuit contains a liquid refrigerant. This refrigerant is potentially dangerous, and should only be handled by qualified persons. If it is splashed onto the skin, it can cause frostbite. It is not itself*

10.1 Unclip the cover from the hazard switch

10.2 Carefully unclip the heater/ventilation ducts

10.4 Undo the four retaining screws and withdraw the vent housing from the facia

poisonous, but in the presence of a naked flame it forms a poisonous gas; inhalation of the vapour through a lighted cigarette could prove fatal. Uncontrolled discharging of the refrigerant is dangerous, and potentially damaging to the environment. It is therefore dangerous to disconnect any part of the system without specialised knowledge and equipment. If for any reason the system must be disconnected, entrust this task to your Vauxhall dealer or a refrigeration engineer.

7 Do not operate the air conditioning system if it is known to be short of refrigerant, as this may damage the compressor.

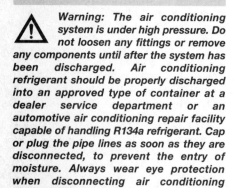

12 Air conditioning system components – removal and refitting

⚠️ *Warning: The air conditioning system is under high pressure. Do not loosen any fittings or remove any components until after the system has been discharged. Air conditioning refrigerant should be properly discharged into an approved type of container at a dealer service department or an automotive air conditioning repair facility capable of handling R134a refrigerant. Cap or plug the pipe lines as soon as they are disconnected, to prevent the entry of moisture. Always wear eye protection when disconnecting air conditioning system fittings.*

Note: *This Section refers to the components of the air conditioning system itself – refer to Sections 9 and 10 for details of components common to the heating/ventilation system.*

Condenser

1 Have the refrigerant discharged at a dealer service department or an automotive air conditioning repair facility.
2 Disconnect the battery negative (earth) lead (see *Disconnecting the battery* in the Reference Chapter).
3 Apply the handbrake, then raise the front of the vehicle and support on axle stands.
4 Remove the front bumper panel as described in Chapter 11.
5 Disconnect the refrigerant lines from the condenser. Immediately cap the open fittings, to prevent the entry of dirt and moisture.
6 Remove the two bolts from the top of the

radiator support bracket, then lift the condenser (complete with the receiver-dryer) to disengage it from the lower mounting brackets in the radiator.
7 Lower the condenser complete with receiver-dryer out from under the vehicle. Store it upright, to prevent fluid loss. Take care not to damage the condenser fins.
8 Refitting is the reverse of removal. Renew the O-rings and lubricate with refrigerant oil.
9 Have the system evacuated, charged and leak-tested by the specialist who discharged it.

Receiver-dryer

10 Have the refrigerant discharged at a dealer service department or an automotive air conditioning repair facility.
11 Disconnect the battery negative (earth) lead (see *Disconnecting the battery* in the Reference Chapter).
12 Apply the handbrake, then raise the front of the vehicle and support on axle stands.
13 Remove the front bumper panel as described in Chapter 11.
14 Undo the retaining bolts and detach the refrigerant lines from the receiver-dryer. Immediately cap the open fittings, to prevent the entry of dirt and moisture.
15 Release the receiver-dryer from the condenser, then remove the receiver-dryer downwards and withdraw it from the vehicle.
16 Refitting is the reverse of removal. Renew the O-rings and lubricate with refrigerant oil.
17 Have the system evacuated, charged and leak-tested by the specialist who discharged it.

Evaporator

18 The evaporator is mounted inside the heater housing with the heater matrix. Apart from the need to have the refrigerant discharged, and to disconnect the refrigerant lines, the procedure is as described in Section 9 of this Chapter.
19 Unbolt the heater unit assembly from the bulkhead to remove the evaporator. Refitting is the reverse of removal.
20 Have the system evacuated, charged and leak-tested by the specialist who discharged it.

Compressor

21 Have the refrigerant discharged at a dealer service department or an automotive air conditioning repair facility.
22 Disconnect the battery negative (earth)

lead (see *Disconnecting the battery* in the Reference Chapter).
23 Apply the handbrake, then raise the front of the vehicle and support on axle stands.
24 Remove the undershield and the slacken the auxiliary drivebelt as described in Chapter 1A or 1B.
25 Unscrew the clamping bolt to disconnect the refrigerant lines from the compressor. Plug the line connections to prevent entry of any dirt or moisture.
26 On 1.4 engine models undo the three retaining bolts and remove the exhaust front pipe from the catalytic converter.
27 Unbolt the compressor from the cylinder block/crankcase, unplug its electrical connector, then withdraw the compressor downwards from under the vehicle. On diesel models withdraw the compressor upwards and out through the top of the engine bay. **Note:** *Keep the compressor level during handling and storage. If the compressor has seized, or if you find metal particles in the refrigerant lines, the system must be flushed out by an air conditioning technician, and the accumulator/dehydrator must be renewed.*
28 Refit the compressor in the reverse order of removal; renew all seals disturbed.
29 If you are installing a new compressor, refer to the compressor manufacturer's instructions for adding refrigerant oil to the system.
30 Have the system evacuated, charged and leak-tested by the specialist that discharged it.
31 After installing a new compressor, always observe the following running-in procedure:
1) Open all instrument panel air outlet flaps.
2) Start vehicle engine and stabilise idle speed for approximately 5 seconds.
3) Switch fan to maximum speed.
4) Switch on the air conditioning and let it run for at least 2 minutes without interruption at engine speed under 1500 rpm.

Auxiliary fan

32 Remove the front bumper panel as described in Chapter 11.
33 Disconnect the wiring connector from the auxiliary fan.
34 Unclip the fan from the radiator by pressing the lugs inwards on the top mounting points, then lift the fan to release it from the radiator.
35 Withdraw the auxiliary fan downwards to remove from the vehicle.

Chapter 4 Part A:
Fuel and exhaust systems – 1.0 and 1.2 litre petrol engines

Contents

Degrees of difficulty

Easy, suitable for novice with little experience		Fairly easy, suitable for beginner with some experience		Fairly difficult, suitable for competent DIY mechanic		Difficult, suitable for experienced DIY mechanic		Very difficult, suitable for expert DIY or professional	

Specifications

General
System type .... Bosch Motronic ME 1.5.5 sequential multi-point fuel injection

Fuel pump
Type .... Electric, mounted in fuel tank

Fuel injection system data
System pressure .... 3.8 bars
Idle speed (not adjustable – for reference only):
   1.0 litre engines .... 790 to 990 rpm
   1.2 litre engines (manual and Easytronic) .... 750 to 970 rpm
Idle mixture CO content (not adjustable – for reference only) .... 0.4% maximum

Torque wrench settings

	Nm	lbf ft
Camshaft position sensor to timing cover	6	4
Coolant temperature sensor	18	13
Crankshaft speed/position sensor to cylinder block baseplate	8	6
Exhaust front pipe to manifold*	25	18
Exhaust manifold securing nuts*	22	16
Exhaust tailpipe-to-intermediate pipe clamp	50	37
Fuel tank	20	15
Knock sensor	20	15
Oxygen sensor (catalytic converter control)	40	30
Oxygen sensor (mixture regulation)	40	30

*Use new nuts

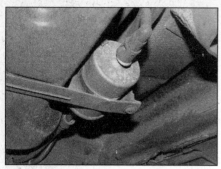

1.1 Fuel filter located next to the fuel tank

1 General information and precautions

General information

1 The fuel supply system consists of a fuel tank (which is mounted under the rear of the car, with an electric fuel pump immersed in it), a fuel filter, fuel feed and return lines. The fuel pump supplies fuel to the fuel rail, which acts as a reservoir for the fuel injectors which inject fuel into the inlet tracts. The fuel filter incorporated in the feed line from the pump to the fuel rail **(see illustration)** ensures that the fuel supplied to the injectors is clean. There is no return line from the engine compartment to the fuel tank, only a short line from the fuel filter (on the side of the tank) to the tank. The fuel pressure regulator is located on the fuel pump.

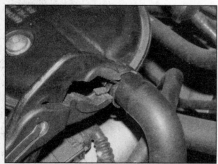

2.2 Disconnecting the breather hose

2.3b . . . and lift the airbox from the throttle body

2 The electronic control unit controls both the fuel injection system and the ignition system, integrating the two into a complete engine management system. Refer to Section 8 for further information on the operation of the fuel system and to Chapter 5B for details of the ignition side of the system.

3 The exhaust manifold incorporates an integral catalytic converter to reduce harmful exhaust gas emissions. The remaining exhaust system is in two sections. Further details can be found in Part D of this Chapter, along with details of the other emission control systems and components.

Precautions

Note: *Refer to Part D of this Chapter for general information and precautions relating to the catalytic converter.*

4 Before disconnecting any fuel lines, or working on any part of the fuel system, the system must be depressurised as described in Section 4.

5 Care must be taken when disconnecting the fuel lines. When disconnecting a fuel union or hose, loosen the union or clamp screw slowly, to avoid sudden uncontrolled fuel spillage. Take adequate fire precautions.

6 When working on fuel system components, scrupulous cleanliness must be observed, and care must be taken not to introduce any foreign matter into fuel lines or components.

7 After carrying out any work involving disconnection of fuel lines, it is advisable to check the connections for leaks; pressurise the system by switching the ignition on and off several times.

2.3a Undo the bolts . . .

2.4a Undo the screws . . .

8 Electronic control units are very sensitive components, and certain precautions must be taken to avoid damage to these units as follows.

 a) *When carrying out welding operations on the vehicle using electric welding equipment, the battery and alternator should be disconnected.*

 b) *Although the underbonnet-mounted control units will tolerate normal underbonnet conditions, they can be adversely affected by excess heat or moisture. If using welding equipment or pressure-washing equipment in the vicinity of an electronic control unit, take care not to direct heat, or jets of water or steam, at the unit. If this cannot be avoided, remove the control unit from the vehicle, and protect its wiring plug with a plastic bag.*

 c) *Before disconnecting any wiring, or removing components, always ensure that the ignition is switched off.*

 d) *Do not attempt to improvise fault diagnosis procedures using a test light or multi-meter, as irreparable damage could be caused to the control unit.*

 e) *After working on fuel injection/engine management system components, ensure that all wiring is correctly reconnected before reconnecting the battery or switching on the ignition.*

⚠ *Warning: Many of the procedures in this Chapter require the disconnection of fuel line connections, and the removal of components, which may result in some fuel spillage. Before carrying out any operation on the fuel system, refer to the precautions given in 'Safety first!' at the beginning of this manual, and follow them implicitly. Petrol is a highly-dangerous and volatile liquid, and the precautions necessary when handling it cannot be overstressed.*

2 Air cleaner assembly – removal and refitting

Removal

1 Disconnect the wiring plug from the air mass meter, located in the air inlet trunking.

2 Release the hose clamp and disconnect the breather hose from the side of the airbox **(see illustration)**. Also, unclip the purge valve.

3 Undo the bolts and lift off the airbox and inlet trunking from the throttle body **(see illustrations)**.

4 Undo the screws, lift off the air cleaner cover, and remove the trunking and airbox from the vehicle **(see illustrations)**.

5 Lift out the air cleaner element **(see illustration)**.

6 Disconnect the air inlet duct from the front of the air cleaner **(see illustration)**.

2.4b . . . lift off the air cleaner cover . . .

2.5 . . . then lift out the element

2.6 Removing the front inlet duct from the air cleaner

2.7a Remove the screw . . .

2.7b . . . and release the crossbar from the mounting pegs

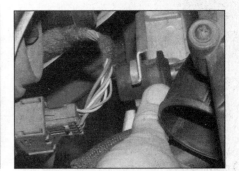

2.8 Pull the air cleaner from the front mounting rubber

7 Unscrew the crossbar mounting screw at the rear of the air cleaner, and release the crossbar rubber mountings from the mounting pegs. Note that the screw retains the purge valve-to-carbon canister line support **(see illustrations)**.
8 Pull the air cleaner body rearwards from the front mounting rubber **(see illustration)**, and withdraw from the engine compartment.

Refitting

9 Refitting is a reversal of removal.

 3 Accelerator pedal/ position sensor – removal and refitting

Removal

1 Disconnect the battery negative lead (refer

3.2 Disconnecting the wiring from the top of the accelerator pedal/position sensor

to *Disconnecting the battery* at the end of this manual).
2 Working in the driver's footwell under the facia, disconnect the wiring from the top of the accelerator pedal/position sensor **(see illustration)**. Where necessary, pull back the footwell carpet first.
3 Unscrew the three mounting nuts, and withdraw the sensor from the bulkhead.

Refitting

4 Refitting is a reversal of removal. After reconnecting the battery, have a Vauxhall dealer reprogram the volatile memories.

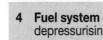 **4 Fuel system – depressurising**

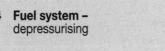 *Warning: The fuel system is pressurised all the time the ignition is switched on, and a high pressure will remain in the system even 20 minutes after switching off. It is therefore essential to depressurise the system before disconnecting fuel lines, or carrying out any work on the fuel system components. Failure to do this before carrying out work may result in a sudden release of pressure which may cause fuel spray – this constitutes a fire hazard, and a health risk. Note that, even when the system has been depressurised, fuel will still be present in the system fuel lines and components, and adequate precautions should still be taken when carrying out work.*

1 The fuel system referred to in this Section is defined as the tank-mounted fuel pump and pressure regulator, the fuel filter, the fuel injectors, the fuel rail, and the metal pipes and flexible hoses of the fuel lines between these components. All these contain fuel which will be under pressure while the engine is running, and/or while the ignition is switched on. High pressure will remain for at least 20 minutes after the ignition has been switched off, and must be relieved in a controlled fashion when any of these components are disturbed for servicing work.
2 Where necessary, remove the engine top cover.
3 Place a container beneath the fuel pressure testing point on the fuel rail and have a cloth rag ready to soak up any escaping fuel not being caught by the container.
4 Slowly loosen the cap and allow the fuel to escape. With the cap fully unscrewed, all fuel pressure will have escaped, and the cap can then be refitted and tightened.

 5 Fuel tank – removal and refitting

Note: *Refer to the precautions given in Section 1 before proceeding.*

Removal

1 Depressurise the fuel system (see Section 4).
2 Disconnect the battery negative lead (refer to *Disconnecting the battery* at the end of this manual).

6.5a Prise the plastic cover from the floor . . .

6.5b . . . to expose the fuel pump cover. Locking ring arrowed

6 Fuel gauge sender unit – removal and refitting

Note: Refer to the precautions given in Section 1 before proceeding.

Note: The fuel tank should be as empty as possible when carrying out this procedure.

Removal

1 Disconnect the battery negative lead (refer to *Disconnecting the battery* at the end of this manual).
2 Depressurise the fuel system as described in Section 4.
3 Syphon out any remaining fuel in the tank through the filler pipe into a clean metal container which can be sealed.
4 On Hatchback models, remove the rear seat as described in Chapter 11. On standard Van models, fold up the rear seat. On Combo Van models, unbolt the tank cover flap from the rear floor.
5 Fold up the acoustic insulation, then, using a screwdriver, carefully lever out the plastic cover to expose the fuel pump cover (see illustrations).
6 Disconnect the main wiring plug from the cover (see illustration).
7 Identify the position of the two fuel lines, then disconnect the quick-release fittings. Be prepared for some loss of fuel. A Vauxhall special tool is available to release the fuel line connectors, but provided care is taken, the connectors can be released using a pair of long-nosed pliers, or a similar tool, to depress the retaining tangs. Clamp or plug the open ends of the hoses, to prevent dirt ingress and further fuel spillage.
8 Release the fuel pump cover locking ring. A special tool (Vauxhall tool No KM-797) is available for this, but the ring can be removed by tapping anti-clockwise until the locking clips release.

⚠ **Warning: To prevent the possibility of any sparks which could ignite fuel vapour, use a plastic, wooden or brass tool to release the locking ring.**

9 Remove the locking ring, then carefully lift the cover from the top of the pump, noting the location of the wiring and hose connections.
10 Disconnect the sender unit wiring and the fuel pump wiring from the bottom of the cover.
11 On Van models, disconnect the earth wiring from the pressure regulator.
12 Release the clip and disconnect the fuel supply hose from the cover.
13 Disconnect the fuel return hose from the pressure regulator, and withdraw the cover.
14 Remove the cover sealing ring.
15 Using the hook provided, pull the sender unit from the clips on the side of the fuel pump housing (see illustrations).

3 Syphon out any remaining fuel in the tank through the filler pipe into a clean metal container which can be sealed.
4 Chock the front wheels then jack up the rear of the vehicle and support on axle stands (see *Jacking and vehicle support*). Remove both rear wheels.
5 Refer to Chapter 9 and disconnect the front ends of the rear (secondary) handbrake cables from the underbody clips after backing off the primary cable adjustment. Unclip the cables from the underbody and the right-hand side of the fuel tank, then tie them to one side, away from the fuel tank. Where necessary on ECO models, remove the underbody air guide plate.
6 Disconnect the rear of the exhaust system from its rubber mountings, and lower the system, then move it to one side sufficiently to enable removal of the fuel tank. Alternatively, remove the exhaust system completely to provide greater clearance (refer to Section 13).
7 Disconnect the wiring from the fuel pump and fuel gauge sensor at the connector on the underbody.
8 Disconnect the fuel feed line and the evaporative vent line at the quick-release connectors on the underbody (if necessary, detach the line retaining bracket from the underbody). Be prepared for some loss of fuel. A Vauxhall special tool is available to release the fuel line connectors, but provided care is taken, the connectors can be released using a pair of long-nosed pliers, or a similar tool, to depress the retaining tangs. Refer to *Fuel filter renewal* in Chapter 1A for further details.
9 Unscrew the lower filler hose mounting bolt, then unclip the ventilation and carbon canister purge hoses from the bottom of the fuel tank.
10 Loosen the clip and disconnect the fuel filler hose from the fuel tank.
11 Support the weight of the fuel tank on a jack with interposed block of wood.
12 Unbolt and remove the two securing straps from the fuel tank.
13 Lower the tank sufficiently to enable access to the fuel hoses on the tank, then disconnect them. Be prepared for some loss of fuel.
14 Continue to lower the tank until it can be removed from under the vehicle.

15 Plug or clamp the fuel and vent hoses to prevent entry of dust and dirt.
16 If necessary, remove the fuel lines and hoses, heat shield and wiring from the tank for transfer to the new tank. If a new tank is being fitted, it is recommended that the filter is renewed at the same time.
17 If the tank contains sediment or water, it may cleaned out with two or three rinses of clean fuel. Remove the fuel gauge sender unit and fuel pump as described in Sections 6 and 7 respectively. Shake the tank vigorously, and change the fuel as necessary to remove all contamination from the tank. *This procedure should be carried out in a well-ventilated area, and it is vital to take adequate fire precautions.*
18 Any repairs to the fuel tank should be carried out by a professional. Do not under any circumstances attempt any form of DIY repair to a fuel tank.

Refitting

19 Refitting is a reversal of removal, bearing in mind the following points:
  a) *Ensure that all hoses are securely reconnected to their correct locations.*
  b) *Check the handbrake cable adjustment, as described in Chapter 9.*
  c) *On completion, fill the fuel tank, then run the engine and check for leaks. If leakage is evident, stop the engine immediately and rectify the problem without delay.*

6.6 Disconnect the fuel gauge sender wiring plug

6.15a Using the hook . . .

6.15b . . . pull the sender unit from the fuel pump housing

Refitting

16 Refitting is a reversal of removal, bearing in mind the following points:
  a) *Ensure that the sender unit engages correctly with the clips on the fuel pump housing.*
  b) *Check the condition of the sealing ring on the underside of the fuel pump cover, and renew if necessary.*
  c) *Refit the fuel pump cover locking ring by tapping it clockwise until the locking clips 'click' into position.*

7 Fuel pump –
  testing, removal and refitting

Testing

1 If the pump is functioning, it should be possible to hear it 'buzzing' by listening under

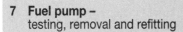

7.9 Disconnect the fuel pump wiring plug

7.13 Disconnect the wiring plugs from the underside of the cover

the rear of the vehicle when the ignition is switched on. Unless the engine is started, the fuel pump should switch off after approximately two seconds. If the noise produced is excessive, this may indicate a faulty pump.
2 If the pump appears to have failed completely, check the wiring to the pump, and check the appropriate fuse and relay.
3 To test the performance of the pump, special equipment is required, and it is recommended that any suspected faults are referred to a Vauxhall dealer.

Removal

Note: *Refer to the precautions given in Section 1 before proceeding. The fuel tank should be as empty as possible when carrying out this procedure.*
4 Disconnect the battery negative lead (refer to *Disconnecting the battery* at the end of this manual).

7.11 Releasing the fuel pump locking ring using a brass drift

7.18a Press the three retaining lugs (1 – one shown), and pull the housing from the tank using a hook on the eyelet (2)

5 Depressurise the fuel system as described in Section 4.
6 Syphon out any remaining fuel in the tank through the filler pipe into a clean metal container which can be sealed.
7 On Hatchback models, remove the rear seat (see Chapter 11). On standard Van models, fold up the rear seat. On Combo Van models, unbolt the tank cover flap from the rear floor.
8 Fold up the acoustic insulation then, using a screwdriver, carefully lever out the plastic cover to expose the fuel pump cover.
9 Disconnect the main wiring plug from the cover **(see illustration)**.
10 Identify the position of the two fuel lines, then disconnect the quick-release fittings. Be prepared for some loss of fuel. A Vauxhall special tool is available to release the fuel line connectors, but provided care is taken, the connectors can be released using a pair of long-nosed pliers, or a similar tool, to depress the retaining tangs. Clamp or plug the open ends of the hoses, to prevent dirt ingress and further fuel spillage.
11 Release the fuel pump cover locking ring. A special tool (Vauxhall tool No KM-797) is available for this, but the ring can be removed by tapping anti-clockwise until the locking clips release **(see illustration)**.

⚠ *Warning: To prevent the possibility of any sparks which could ignite fuel vapour, use a plastic, wooden or brass tool to release the locking ring.*

12 Remove the locking ring, then carefully lift the cover from the top of the pump, noting the location of the wiring and hose connections.
13 Disconnect the sender unit wiring and the fuel pump wiring from the bottom of the cover **(see illustration)**.
14 On Van models, disconnect the earth wiring from the pressure regulator.
15 Release the clip and disconnect the fuel supply hose from the cover.
16 Disconnect the fuel return hose from the pressure regulator, and withdraw the cover.
17 Remove the cover sealing ring.
18 Press the three pump housing retaining lugs to release them, and simultaneously pull the pump housing from the tank using a wire hook engaged with the eyelet provided **(see illustrations)**.

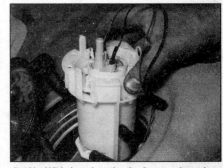

7.18b Withdrawing the fuel pump housing from the fuel tank

7.19 Removing the fuel filter from the base of the fuel pump

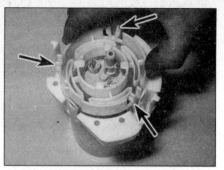

7.20a Compress the three locking tabs (arrowed) . . .

7.20b . . . and withdraw the pump from the housing

19 To remove the pump from the housing, first pull the filter from the base of the pump **(see illustration)** and disconnect the wires from the pump. Note the wire locations to ensure correct refitting.

20 Compress the three locking tabs, and pull the pump mounting plate and the pump from the housing **(see illustrations)**.

21 Disconnect the wiring and if necessary, remove the filter from the bottom of the fuel pump.

Refitting

22 Refitting is a reversal of removal, bearing in mind the following points:

a) *Before refitting the filter to the bottom of the pump, inspect the filter for contamination or blockage, and renew if necessary.*

b) *Ensure that the pump mounting plate engages correctly with the retaining clips on the housing.*

c) *Check the condition of the sealing ring on the underside of the fuel pump cover, and renew if necessary.*

d) *Refit the fuel pump cover locking ring by tapping it clockwise until the locking clips 'click' into position.*

---

8 Fuel injection system – general information

1 The system is under the overall control of the Motronic ME 1.5.5 engine management system, which also controls the ignition system (see Chapter 5B).

2 Fuel is supplied from the rear-mounted tank, via a fuel filter and a pressure regulator, to the fuel rail. Excess fuel is returned from the regulator to the tank. The fuel rail acts as a reservoir for the fuel injectors, which inject fuel into the cylinder inlet tracts, upstream of the inlet valves. The Motronic ME 1.5.5 system is a 'sequential' fuel injection system. This means that each of the three (1.0 litre engines), or four (1.2 litre engines) fuel injectors is triggered individually, just before the inlet valve on the relevant cylinder opens.

3 The duration of the electrical pulses to the fuel injectors determines the quantity of fuel

injected. The pulse duration is computed by the Motronic electronic control unit (ECU) on the basis of information received from the following sensors:

a) *Accelerator pedal position sensor – informs the ECU of accelerator pedal position, and the rate of throttle opening/closing.*

b) *Air mass meter – informs the ECU of the load on the engine (expressed in terms of the mass of air passing from the air cleaner to the throttle body).*

c) *Crankshaft speed/position sensor – informs the ECU of the crankshaft speed and position.*

d) *Camshaft position sensor – informs the ECU when No 1 cylinder is at top dead centre (TDC) on the firing stroke (expressed in terms of the position of the inlet camshaft).*

e) *Coolant temperature sensor – informs the ECU of engine temperature.*

f) *Exhaust gas oxygen sensors (two) – inform the ECU of the oxygen content of the exhaust gases (explained in greater detail in Chapter 4D).*

g) *Knock sensor – informs the ECU when engine 'knock' (pre-ignition) occurs (explained in greater detail in Chapter 5B).*

h) *Vehicle speed sensor (where fitted) – informs the ECU of the vehicle speed.*

4 The signals from the various sensors are processed by the ECU, and the optimum fuelling and ignition settings are selected for the prevailing engine operating conditions.

5 Idle speed is controlled by the idle speed control motor, which directly regulates the position of the throttle valve. The motor is controlled by the electronic control unit; there is no provision for direct adjustment of the idle speed.

6 Similarly, the fuel/air mixture is controlled within fine limits by the electronic control unit, via the fuel injectors. No manual adjustment of fuel/air mixture is possible.

7 A catalytic converter is incorporated in the exhaust manifold, to reduce harmful exhaust gas emissions. Details of this and other emissions control system equipment are given in Chapter 4D.

8 If certain sensors fail, and send abnormal signals to the ECU, the ECU has a back-up

programme. In this event, the abnormal signals are ignored, and a preprogrammed value is substituted for the sensor signal, allowing the engine to continue running, albeit at reduced efficiency. If the ECU enters its back-up mode, a warning light on the instrument panel will illuminate, and a fault code will be stored in the ECU memory. This fault code can be read using suitable specialist test equipment.

---

9 Fuel injection system components – testing

In order to safely test the fuel injection system components without the risk of damage to the components or electronic control unit, specialist test equipment is required.

The systems have a self-diagnosis function, and any faults are stored as codes in the electronic control unit memory. These fault codes can be read using suitable test equipment such as a fault code reader. If a fault code reader is available, it should be connected and operated according to the instructions supplied with the reader.

System sensors and actuators can be tested for continuity and resistance using a suitable multi-meter, but always ensure that the ignition is switched off, and that the relevant sensor or actuator is disconnected from the engine management system. Refer to the precautions given in Section 1 before attempting to carry out any fault diagnosis.

In the event of a suspected fault, and suitable test and diagnostic equipment is not available, the best course of action is to seek advice from a Vauxhall dealer, who will have access to the necessary equipment.

---

10 Fuel injection system components – removal and refitting

Throttle body

Removal

1 Disconnect the battery negative lead (refer to *Disconnecting the battery* in the Reference Chapter).

2 Remove the air cleaner cover, inlet trunking and airbox from the top of the throttle body, with reference to Section 2.

3 Disconnect the wiring from the throttle body module **(see illustration)**.

4 Partially drain the cooling system as described in Chapter 1A (drain sufficient coolant to empty the coolant expansion tank).

5 Release the retaining clips and disconnect the two coolant hoses from the rear of the throttle body.

6 Undo the four bolts and lift the throttle body off the inlet manifold **(see illustration)**. Recover the gasket.

7 It is not possible to obtain the idle speed control motor or throttle valve position sensor separately, so if either is faulty, the complete throttle body must be renewed.

Refitting

8 Refitting is a reversal of removal, but thoroughly clean the mating faces and use a new gasket. Tighten the bolts progressively and securely. Top-up the coolant level as described in *Weekly checks.* Finally, switch on the ignition for 30 seconds without starting the engine.

Air mass meter

Removal

9 Disconnect the wiring from the air mass meter at the right-hand rear corner of the engine compartment **(see illustration)**.

10 Release the retaining clips and remove the air mass meter from the air cleaner cover and inlet trunking **(see illustrations)**.

Refitting

11 Refitting is a reversal of removal, but ensure that the arrow on the air mass meter body points toward the throttle body when fitted.

Fuel injectors and fuel rail

Note: *Refer to the precautions given in Section 1 before proceeding. The seals at both ends of the fuel injectors must be renewed on refitting.*

Removal

12 Disconnect the battery negative lead (refer to *Disconnecting the battery* in the Reference Chapter).

13 Depressurise the fuel system as described in Section 4.

10.3 Disconnecting the wiring from the throttle body module

10.9 Air mass meter wiring

14 Remove the throttle body as described previously in this Section, however, it is not necessary to drain the cooling system, as the body can be placed to one side with the hoses still attached.

15 Loosen the clip and disconnect the engine breather hose from the camshaft cover.

16 Disconnect the wiring from the throttle body.

17 Disconnect the wiring from the injectors **(see illustration)**.

18 Disconnect the fuel feed hose quick-release connector at the fuel rail. Be prepared for some loss of fuel. A Vauxhall special tool is available to release the connector, but provided care is taken, it can be released using a pair of long-nosed pliers, or a similar tool, to depress the retaining tangs. Clamp or plug the open end of the hose, to prevent dirt ingress and further fuel spillage.

19 Unscrew the mounting bolts, then lift the

10.6 Throttle body retaining bolts

10.10a Release the clips . . .

fuel rail complete with the injectors off of the inlet manifold.

20 To remove an injector from the fuel rail, prise out the metal securing clip using a screwdriver or a pair of pliers, and pull the injector from the fuel rail. Remove and discard the injector sealing rings; new ones must be fitted on refitting.

21 Overhaul of the fuel injectors is not possible, as no spares are available. If faulty, an injector must be renewed.

Refitting

22 Before refitting, clean thoroughly the mating surfaces of the throttle body and inlet manifold.

23 Commence refitting by fitting new O-ring seals to both ends of the fuel injectors **(see illustration)**. Coat the seals with a thin layer of petroleum jelly before fitting.

10.10b . . . and remove the air mass meter

10.17 Wiring to the fuel injectors

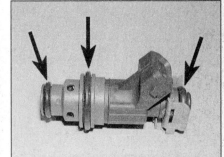

10.23 Fit new O-rings (arrowed) to the fuel injectors before refitting

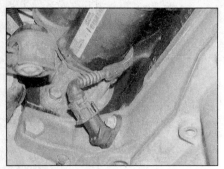

10.25 Crankshaft speed/position sensor location

10.33 Coolant temperature sensor located in the top of the coolant pump housing

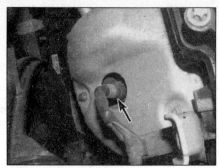

10.38 Exhaust gas oxygen sensor (mixture regulation)

24 Refitting is a reversal of removal, bearing in mind the following points:

a) *When refitting the injectors to the fuel rail, note that the groove in the metal securing clip must engage with the lug on the injector body.*

b) *Make sure that the quick-release connector audibly engages on the fuel rail.*

c) *Refit the throttle body as described previously in this Section.*

d) *Ensure that all wiring connectors are securely reconnected, and that the wiring is secured in the relevant clips and brackets.*

e) *Finally, it may be necessary to have a Vauxhall dealer program all volatile memories.*

Crankshaft speed/position sensor

Note: *A new O-ring seal must be used on refitting.*

25 The crankshaft speed/position sensor is located at the rear left-hand end of the cylinder block baseplate, below the starter motor **(see illustration)**.

26 Apply the handbrake, then jack up the front of the vehicle and support it on axle stands (see *Jacking and vehicle support*). On ECO models, remove the engine undertray.

27 Disconnect the sensor wiring connector, then undo the retaining bolt and withdraw the sensor from the cylinder block baseplate.

Refitting

28 Refitting is a reversal of removal, but

10.43 Exhaust gas oxygen sensor (catalytic converter control) located in the exhaust front pipe

ensure that the mating surfaces of the sensor and baseplate are clean and fit a new O-ring seal to the sensor before refitting. Tighten the bolt to the specified torque.

Camshaft position sensor

Removal

29 The camshaft position sensor is located on the timing cover, on the inlet camshaft side.

30 Disconnect the sensor wiring connector.

31 Undo the retaining bolt and withdraw the sensor from the timing cover.

Refitting

32 Refitting is a reversal of removal, but ensure that the mating surfaces of the sensor and timing cover are clean before fitting.

Coolant temperature sensor

33 The coolant temperature sensor is located in the top of the coolant pump housing **(see illustration)**.

34 Partially drain the cooling system as described in Chapter 1A.

35 Disconnect the sensor wiring plug.

36 Unscrew the sensor, and withdraw it from the coolant pump. Recover the sealing ring.

Refitting

37 Refitting is a reversal of removal, but use a new sealing ring, and tighten the sensor to the specified torque. On completion, top-up the cooling system as described in *Weekly checks*.

Oxygen sensor (mixture regulation)

Caution: The sensor will be very hot if the engine has been running within 10 or 15 minutes.

Removal

38 The mixture regulation oxygen sensor is located on the exhaust manifold/catalytic converter **(see illustration)**. First, trace the wiring back from the sensor to the connector next to the oil filter, and disconnect it. Release the wiring from the clip.

39 Unscrew the sensor from the exhaust manifold. Ideally, a special 'split' socket should be used, as this will locate over the sensor wiring.

Refitting

40 Clean the threads of the sensor then coat them with Vauxhall special grease for oxygen sensors. If a new sensor is being fitted, it will be supplied with the threads already coated with the special grease to prevent it seizing in the manifold.

41 Screw the sensor into the exhaust manifold/catalytic converter and tighten to the specified torque.

42 Reconnect the wiring and clip it in place.

Oxygen sensor (catalytic converter control)

Caution: The sensor will be very hot if the engine has been running within 10 or 15 minutes.

Removal

43 The catalytic converter control oxygen sensor is located in the exhaust front pipe, just behind the flexible section **(see illustration)**. First, apply the handbrake, then jack up the front of the vehicle and support it on axle stands (see *Jacking and vehicle support*).

44 Trace the wiring back from the sensor to the connector above the right-hand driveshaft, and disconnect it. Release the wiring from the clip.

45 Unscrew the sensor from the exhaust front pipe. Ideally, a special 'split' socket should be used, as this will locate over the sensor wiring.

Refitting

46 Clean the threads of the sensor then coat them with Vauxhall special grease for oxygen sensors. If a new sensor is being fitted, it will be supplied with the threads already coated with the special grease to prevent it seizing in the pipe.

47 Screw the sensor into the exhaust front pipe and tighten to the specified torque.

48 Reconnect the wiring and clip it in place.

Knock sensor

Removal

49 The knock sensor is located on the rear of the cylinder block, just above the starter motor.

50 Apply the handbrake, then jack up the

front of the vehicle and support it on axle stands (see *Jacking and vehicle support*). On ECO models, remove the engine undertray.

51 On the left-hand side of the engine, disconnect the wiring for the engine control unit by releasing it in the direction of the arrow.

52 Unscrew the bolt securing the earth wire to the cylinder head, then unbolt and remove the engine control unit.

53 Reach up behind the engine and disconnect the wiring from the knock sensor.

54 Note its position, then unscrew the bolt and remove the knock sensor from the block.

Refitting

55 Clean the contact surfaces of the sensor and block. Also clean the threads of the sensor mounting bolt.

56 Locate the sensor on the block and insert the mounting bolt. Position the sensor as previously noted, then tighten the bolt to the specified torque. Note that the torque setting is critical for the sensor to function correctly.

57 Reconnect the wiring, then refit the engine control unit together with its wiring and earth wire.

58 Reconnect the battery negative lead (refer to *Disconnecting the battery* in the Reference Chapter).

59 Refit the engine undertray where applicable, then lower the vehicle to the ground. Finally, it may be necessary to have a Vauxhall dealer program all volatile memories.

Electronic control unit (ECU)

Removal

60 The engine management electronic control unit is located on the rear, left-hand side of the engine.

61 Disconnect the battery negative lead (refer to *Disconnecting the battery* in the Reference Chapter).

62 Disconnect the wiring for the engine control unit by releasing it in the direction of the arrow marked on the connector **(see illustration)**.

63 Unscrew the bolt securing the earth wire to the cylinder head, then unbolt and remove the engine control unit.

Refitting

64 Refitting is a reversal of removal. Finally, it may be necessary to have a Vauxhall dealer program all volatile memories.

---

11 Inlet manifold –
removed and refitting

Removal

1 Apply the handbrake, then jack up the front of the vehicle and support it on axle stands (see *Jacking and vehicle support*). On ECO models, remove the engine undertray.

2 Disconnect the battery negative lead (refer

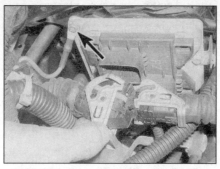

10.62 Disconnect the wiring connectors from the electronic control unit. Note the location of the earth lead (arrowed)

to *Disconnecting the battery* in the Reference Chapter).

3 Drain the coolant as described in Chapter 1A.

4 Remove the throttle body as described in Section 10.

5 Disconnect the fuel evaporation system hose from the inlet manifold.

6 Depressurise the fuel system as described in Section 4.

7 Disconnect the fuel supply line from the fuel rail and release it from the support clip. A quick-release connector is fitted and Vauxhall technicians use a special tool to release it, however, provided care is taken, the connector can be released using a pair of long-nosed pliers, or a similar tool, to depress the retaining tangs. Refer to *Fuel filter renewal* in Chapter 1A for further details.

8 Disconnect the crankcase ventilation hose from the camshaft cover, and the brake servo vacuum line from the inlet manifold.

9 Disconnect the wiring from the injectors and engine control unit (two locking levers), also unbolt the earth cable and unclip the wiring conduit. Place the wiring harness to one side.

10 Working beneath the vehicle, disconnect the wiring from the starter motor and release it from the supports on the inlet manifold.

11 Unbolt the EGR valve pipe from the EGR valve housing and position to one side. Discard the gasket; a new one must be used for refitting.

12 Unscrew the nuts and withdraw the inlet manifold from the cylinder head. Discard the seals; new ones must be used for refitting.

11.13 Fit new individual rubber seals to the grooves in the inlet manifold

Refitting

13 Thoroughly clean the mating face of the inlet manifold and cylinder head, then locate the new rubber seals in the grooves in the manifold mating face **(see illustration)**.

14 Locate the inlet manifold over the cylinder head studs and secure with the nuts tightened progressively and securely.

15 Refit the EGR valve pipe together with a new gasket, and tighten the bolts securely.

16 Reconnect the wiring to the starter, injectors and engine control unit, and tighten the earth cable bolt.

17 Reconnect the brake servo vacuum line and crankcase ventilation hose.

18 Reconnect the fuel supply line to the fuel rail, making sure that an audible click is heard as it engages.

19 Reconnect the fuel evaporation system hose to the inlet manifold.

20 Refit the throttle body with reference to Section 10.

21 Reconnect the battery negative lead (refer to *Disconnecting the battery* in the Reference Chapter).

22 Refill and bleed the cooling system with reference to Chapter 1A.

23 Refit the engine undertray where necessary, then lower the vehicle to the ground.

24 Finally, it may be necessary to have a Vauxhall dealer program all volatile memories.

---

12 Exhaust manifold/ catalytic converter –
removal and refitting

Note: *New manifold retaining nuts, a new manifold gasket, exhaust front pipe gasket and oil dipstick guide tube O-rings must be used on refitting.*

Removal

1 Apply the handbrake, then jack up the front of the vehicle and support it on axle stands (see *Jacking and vehicle support*).

2 Disconnect the battery negative lead (refer to *Disconnecting the battery* in the Reference Chapter).

3 Drain the coolant as described in Chapter 1A.

4 On air conditioning models, unbolt the compressor from the front of the engine with reference to Chapter 3, and support it to one side. **Do not** disconnect the refrigerant lines from the compressor.

5 Remove the throttle body as described in Section 10.

6 Refer to Section 10 and disconnect the wiring from the oxygen sensor (mixture regulation) on the catalytic converter, then unbolt the exhaust front pipe from the exhaust manifold/catalytic converter, taking care to support the flexible section **(see illustration)**. **Note:** *Angular movement in excess of 10° can cause permanent damage to the flexible section.* Recover the gasket.

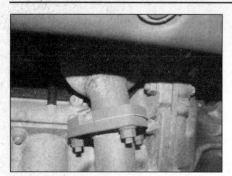

12.6 Exhaust front pipe-to-manifold/catalytic converter joint

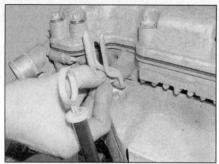

12.9 Remove the engine lifting bracket from the front of the cylinder head

12.11a Remove the exhaust manifold heat shield . . .

12.11b . . . then undo the exhaust manifold retaining nuts . . .

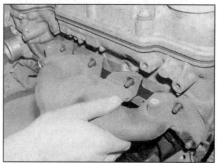

12.11c . . . and withdraw the manifold from the cylinder head studs

7 Release the mounting rubbers and support the front of the exhaust pipe to one side.
8 Remove the oxygen sensor (mixture regulation) from the exhaust manifold as described in Section 10.
9 Unbolt the engine lifting eye from the cylinder head **(see illustration)**.
10 Unbolt and remove the oil dipstick guide tube, and withdraw it from the baseplate. Remove and discard the O-ring seals.
11 Unbolt the heat shield (where fitted), then undo the retaining nuts and withdraw the exhaust manifold/catalytic converter downwards from the cylinder head studs **(see illustrations)**. Recover the gasket.

Refitting

12 Thoroughly clean the mating face of the exhaust manifold and cylinder head, then locate a new gasket over the studs.
13 Locate the exhaust manifold/catalytic converter over the cylinder head studs and secure with the (new) nuts tightened progressively to the specified torque.
14 Refit the heat shield and tighten the retaining bolts.
15 Fit the new O-ring seals to the oil dipstick guide tube, then insert the tube in the baseplate. Insert and tighten the retaining bolt.
16 Refit the left-hand lifting eye and tighten the bolt.
17 Refer to Section 10 and refit the oxygen sensor (mixture regulation) to the manifold/catalytic converter. Tighten to the specified torque.
18 Refit the exhaust front pipe to the manifold/catalytic converter together with a

new gasket, then tighten the (new) nuts to the specified torque.
19 Refit the throttle body with reference to Section 10.
20 On air conditioning models, refit the compressor to the front of the engine with reference to Chapter 3.
21 Lower the vehicle to the ground, then reconnect the battery negative lead (refer to *Disconnecting the battery* in the Reference Chapter).
22 Refill the cooling system with reference to Chapter 1A.
23 Finally, it may be necessary to have a Vauxhall dealer program all volatile memories.

13 Exhaust system – general information and component renewal

General information

1 The exhaust system is in two sections. The front section includes the oxygen sensor (catalytic converter control), silencer and intermediate pipe. The rear section consists of the tailpipe and silencer.
2 Periodically, the exhaust system should be checked for signs of leaks or damage. Also inspect the system rubber mountings, and renew if necessary.
3 Small holes or cracks can be repaired using proprietary exhaust repair products.
4 Before renewing an individual section of the exhaust system, it is wise to inspect the remaining section. If corrosion or damage is

evident, it may prove more economical to renew the entire system.

Component renewal

5 If either part of the system is to be renewed, it is important to ensure that the correct component is obtained.
6 To remove the rear tailpipe and silencer, chock the front wheels then jack up the rear of the vehicle and support on axle stands (see *Jacking and vehicle support*). Loosen the clamp securing the intermediate pipe to the tailpipe, then release the rubber mountings and slide the tailpipe from the intermediate pipe. If the tailpipe is rusted onto the intermediate pipe, tap around the joint with a hammer to free it. Twist the tailpipe in both directions while holding the intermediate pipe.
7 To remove the front section of the exhaust, jack up the front and rear of the vehicle and support it on axle stands (see *Jacking and vehicle support*). Remove the tailpipe and silencer as described in paragraph 6, then remove the oxygen sensor from the front pipe as described in Section 10. Unbolt the exhaust front pipe from the catalytic converter/exhaust manifold **(see illustration)**, taking care to support the flexible section. **Note:** *Angular movement in excess of 10° can cause permanent damage to the flexible section.* Recover the gasket. Release the rubber mountings and withdraw the exhaust from under the vehicle.
8 Refitting is a reversal of removal, but renew all gaskets and tighten the clamp and front pipe flange nuts to the specified torque.

13.7 Exhaust front pipe-to-catalytic converter/exhaust manifold joint (1.2 litre engine)

Chapter 4 Part B:
Fuel and exhaust systems – 1.4 litre petrol engine

Contents

Degrees of difficulty

Easy, suitable for novice with little experience		Fairly easy, suitable for beginner with some experience		Fairly difficult, suitable for competent DIY mechanic		Difficult, suitable for experienced DIY mechanic		Very difficult, suitable for expert DIY or professional	

Specifications

General

System type . . . . Multec S(F) sequential multi-point fuel injection

Fuel pump

Type . . . . Electric, mounted in fuel tank

Fuel injection system data

System pressure . . . . 3.8 ± 0.2 bars
Idle speed (not adjustable – for reference only) . . . . 710 to 930 rpm
Idle mixture CO content (not adjustable – for reference only) . . . . 0.3 % maximum

Torque wrench settings

	Nm	lbf ft
Accelerator pedal/position sensor	9	7
Coolant flange to inlet manifold	20	15
Coolant temperature sensor	20	15
Crankshaft speed/position sensor	8	6
EGR valve to lower inlet manifold	20	15
Engine control unit	8	6
Exhaust front pipe-to-manifold/catalytic converter nuts	25	18
Exhaust manifold/catalytic converter securing nuts*	22	16
Exhaust tailpipe-to-intermediate pipe clamp	50	37
Fuel tank	20	15
Inlet manifold lower section-to-cylinder head nuts*	20	15
Inlet manifold support:		
To inlet manifold	20	15
To cylinder block	35	26
Inlet manifold upper section to lower section	8	6
Knock sensor	20	15
Manifold absolute pressure sensor	8	6
Oxygen sensor (catalytic converter control)	30	22
Oxygen sensor (mixture regulation)	30	22

*Use new nuts

1 General information and precautions

General information

1 The fuel supply system consists of a fuel tank (which is mounted under the rear of the car, with an electric fuel pump immersed in it), a fuel filter, fuel feed and return lines. The fuel pump supplies fuel to the fuel rail, which acts as a reservoir for the fuel injectors which inject fuel into the inlet tracts. The fuel filter incorporated in the feed line from the pump to the fuel rail ensures that the fuel supplied to the injectors is clean. There is no return line from the engine compartment to the fuel tank, only a short line from the fuel filter (on the side of the tank) to the tank. The fuel pressure regulator is located on the fuel pump.

2 The electronic control unit controls both the fuel injection system and the ignition system, integrating the two into a complete engine management system. Refer to Section 8 for further information on the operation of the fuel system and to Chapter 5B for details of the ignition side of the system.

3 The exhaust manifold incorporates an integral catalytic converter to reduce harmful exhaust gas emissions. The remaining exhaust system is in two sections. Further details can be found in Part D of this Chapter, along with details of the other emission control systems and components.

Precautions

Note: *Refer to Part D of this Chapter for general information and precautions relating to the catalytic converter.*

4 Before disconnecting any fuel lines, or working on any part of the fuel system, the system must be depressurised as described in Section 4.

5 Care must be taken when disconnecting the fuel lines. When disconnecting a fuel union or hose, loosen the union or clamp screw slowly, to avoid sudden uncontrolled fuel spillage. Take adequate fire precautions.

6 When working on fuel system components, scrupulous cleanliness must be observed, and care must be taken not to introduce any foreign matter into fuel lines or components.

7 After carrying out any work involving disconnection of fuel lines, it is advisable to check the connections for leaks; pressurise the system by switching the ignition on and off several times.

8 Electronic control units are very sensitive components, and certain precautions must be taken to avoid damage to these units as follows.

a) *When carrying out welding operations on the vehicle using electric welding equipment, the battery and alternator should be disconnected.*

b) *Although the underbonnet-mounted control units will tolerate normal underbonnet conditions, they can be*

adversely affected by excess heat or moisture. If using welding equipment or pressure-washing equipment in the vicinity of an electronic control unit, take care not to direct heat, or jets of water or steam, at the unit. If this cannot be avoided, remove the control unit from the vehicle, and protect its wiring plug with a plastic bag.

c) *Before disconnecting any wiring, or removing components, always ensure that the ignition is switched off.*

d) *Do not attempt to improvise fault diagnosis procedures using a test light or multi-meter, as irreparable damage could be caused to the control unit.*

e) *After working on fuel injection/engine management system components, ensure that all wiring is correctly reconnected before reconnecting the battery or switching on the ignition.*

⚠️ **Warning: Many of the procedures in this Chapter require the disconnection of fuel line connections, and the removal of components, which may result in some fuel spillage. Before carrying out any operation on the fuel system, refer to the precautions given in 'Safety first!' at the beginning of this manual, and follow them implicitly. Petrol is a highly-dangerous and volatile liquid, and the precautions necessary when handling it cannot be overstressed.**

2 Air cleaner assembly – removal and refitting

Removal

1 Unscrew the oil filler cap, then unscrew the engine top cover securing bolts and lift off the cover. Screw the cap back into the camshaft cover.

2 Disconnect the wiring from the air temperature sensor and evaporative system purge valve. Unclip the valve from the side of the air cleaner cover.

3 Loosen the clip and disconnect the airbox crankcase ventilation hose from the camshaft cover.

4 Loosen the clip and remove the airbox from the throttle body. Loosen the clip and separate the airbox and duct from the air cleaner cover.

5 Disconnect the air inlet duct from the front of the air cleaner.

6 Unscrew the crossbar mounting bolt from the rear of the air cleaner, then pull the air cleaner body rearwards from the front mounting rubber, and withdraw from the engine compartment.

7 If necessary, release the securing clips and lift off the air cleaner cover. Lift out the air cleaner element.

Refitting

8 Refitting is a reversal of removal.

3 Accelerator pedal/ position sensor – removal and refitting

Removal

1 Disconnect the battery negative lead (refer to *Disconnecting the battery* at the end of this manual).

2 Working in the driver's footwell under the facia, disconnect the wiring from the top of the accelerator pedal/position sensor. Where necessary, pull back the footwell carpet first.

3 Unscrew the three mounting nuts, and withdraw the sensor from the bulkhead.

Refitting

4 Refitting is a reversal of removal. After reconnecting the battery, have a Vauxhall dealer reprogram the volatile memories.

4 Fuel system – depressurising

⚠️ **Warning: The fuel system is pressurised all the time the ignition is switched on, and a high pressure will remain in the system even 20 minutes after switching off. It is therefore essential to depressurise the system before disconnecting fuel lines, or carrying out any work on the fuel system components. Failure to do this before carrying out work may result in a sudden release of pressure which may cause fuel spray – this constitutes a fire hazard, and a health risk. Note that, even when the system has been depressurised, fuel will still be present in the system fuel lines and components, and adequate precautions should still be taken when carrying out work.**

1 The fuel system referred to in this Section is defined as the tank-mounted fuel pump and pressure regulator, the fuel filter, the fuel injectors, the fuel rail, and the metal pipes and flexible hoses of the fuel lines between these components. All these contain fuel which will be under pressure while the engine is running, and/or while the ignition is switched on. High pressure will remain for at least 20 minutes after the ignition has been switched off, and must be relieved in a controlled fashion when any of these components are disturbed for servicing work.

2 Where necessary, remove the engine top cover.

3 Place a container beneath the fuel pressure testing point on the fuel rail and have a cloth rag ready to soak up any escaping fuel not being caught by the container.

4 Slowly loosen the cap and allow the fuel to escape. With the cap fully unscrewed, all fuel pressure will have escaped, and the cap can then be refitted and tightened.

5 Fuel tank – removal and refitting

Note: *Refer to the precautions given in Section 1 before proceeding.*
Note: *The fuel tank should be as empty as possible when carrying out this procedure.*

Removal

1 Depressurise the fuel system as described in Section 4.
2 Disconnect the battery negative lead (refer to *Disconnecting the battery* at the end of this manual).
3 Syphon out any remaining fuel in the tank through the filler pipe into a clean metal container which can be sealed.
4 Chock the front wheels then jack up the rear of the vehicle and support on axle stands (see *Jacking and vehicle support*). Remove both rear wheels.
5 Refer to Chapter 9 and disconnect the front ends of the rear (secondary) handbrake cables from the underbody clips after backing off the primary cable adjustment. Unclip the cables from the underbody and the right-hand side of the fuel tank, then tie them to one side, away from the fuel tank.
6 Disconnect the rear of the exhaust system from its rubber mountings, and lower the system, then move it to one side sufficiently to enable removal of the fuel tank. Alternatively, remove the exhaust system completely to provide greater clearance (refer to Section 13).
7 Disconnect the wiring from the fuel pump and fuel gauge sensor, at the connector on the underbody.
8 Disconnect the fuel feed line and the evaporative vent line at the quick-release connectors on the underbody (if necessary, detach the line retaining bracket from the underbody). Be prepared for some loss of fuel. A Vauxhall special tool is available to release the fuel line connectors, but provided care is taken, the connectors can be released using a pair of long-nosed pliers, or a similar tool, to depress the retaining tangs. Refer to *Fuel filter renewal* in Chapter 1A for further details.
9 Loosen the clip and disconnect the fuel filler hose from the fuel tank.
10 Support the weight of the fuel tank on a jack with interposed block of wood.
11 Unbolt and remove the two securing straps from the fuel tank.
12 Lower the tank sufficiently to enable access to the fuel hoses on the tank, then disconnect them. Be prepared for some loss of fuel.
13 Continue to lower the tank until it can be removed from under the vehicle.
14 Plug or clamp the fuel and vent hoses to prevent entry of dust and dirt.
15 If necessary, remove the fuel lines and

6.5a Prise the plastic cover from the floor . . .

hoses, heat shield and wiring from the tank for transfer to the new tank. If a new tank is being fitted, it is recommended that the filter is renewed at the same time.

Refitting

16 If the tank contains sediment or water, it may cleaned out with two or three rinses of clean fuel. Remove the fuel gauge sender unit and fuel pump as described in Sections 6 and 7 respectively. Shake the tank vigorously, and change the fuel as often as is necessary to remove all contamination from the tank. *This procedure should be carried out in a well-ventilated area, and it is vital to take adequate fire precautions.*
17 Any repairs to the fuel tank should be carried out by a professional. Do not under any circumstances attempt any form of DIY repair to a fuel tank.
18 Refitting is a reversal of removal, bearing in mind the following points:
  a) Ensure that all hoses are securely reconnected to their correct locations.
  b) Check the handbrake cable adjustment, as described in Chapter 9.
  c) On completion, fill the fuel tank, then run the engine and check for leaks. If leakage is evident, stop the engine immediately and rectify the problem without delay.

6 Fuel gauge sender unit – removal and refitting

Note: *Refer to the precautions given in Section 1 before proceeding.*
Note: *The fuel tank should be as empty as possible when carrying out this procedure.*

Removal

1 Disconnect the battery negative lead (refer to *Disconnecting the battery* at the end of this manual).
2 Depressurise the fuel system as described in Section 4.
3 Syphon out any remaining fuel in the tank through the filler pipe into a clean metal container which can be sealed.
4 On Hatchback models, remove the rear seat as described in Chapter 11. On standard

6.5b . . . to expose the fuel pump cover. Locking ring arrowed

Van models, fold up the rear seat. On Combo Van models, unbolt the tank cover flap from the rear floor.
5 Fold up the acoustic insulation then, using a screwdriver, carefully lever out the plastic cover to expose the fuel pump cover (**see illustrations**).
6 Disconnect the main wiring plug from the cover (**see illustration**).
7 Identify the position of the two fuel lines, then disconnect the quick-release fittings. Be prepared for some loss of fuel. A Vauxhall special tool is available to release the fuel line connectors, but provided care is taken, the connectors can be released using a pair of long-nosed pliers, or a similar tool, to depress the retaining tangs. Clamp or plug the open ends of the hoses, to prevent dirt ingress and further fuel spillage.
8 Release the fuel pump cover locking ring. A special tool (Vauxhall tool No KM-797) is available for this, but the ring can be removed by tapping anti-clockwise until the locking clips release.

 Warning: To prevent the possibility of any sparks which could ignite fuel vapour, use a plastic, wooden or brass tool to release the locking ring.

9 Remove the locking ring, then carefully lift the cover from the top of the pump, noting the location of the wiring and hose connections.
10 Disconnect the sender unit wiring and the fuel pump wiring from the bottom of the cover.
11 On Van models, disconnect the earth wiring from the pressure regulator.

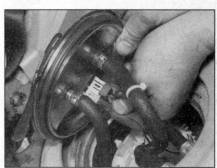

6.6 Disconnect the fuel gauge sender wiring plug

6.15a Using the hook . . .

6.15b . . . pull the sender unit from the fuel pump housing

12 Release the clip and disconnect the fuel supply hose from the cover.

13 Disconnect the fuel return hose from the pressure regulator, and withdraw the cover.

14 Remove the cover sealing ring.

15 Using the hook provided, pull the sender unit from the clips on the side of the fuel pump housing **(see illustrations)**.

Refitting

16 Refitting is a reversal of removal, bearing in mind the following points:

a) Ensure that the sender unit engages correctly with the clips on the fuel pump housing.

b) Check the condition of the sealing ring on the underside of the fuel pump cover, and renew if necessary.

c) Refit the fuel pump cover locking ring by tapping it clockwise until the locking clips 'click' into position.

7.9 Disconnect the fuel pump wiring plug – Hatchback models

7 Fuel pump – testing, removal and refitting

Testing

1 If the pump is functioning, it should be possible to hear it 'buzzing' by listening under the rear of the vehicle when the ignition is switched on. Unless the engine is started, the fuel pump should switch off after approximately two seconds. If the noise produced is excessive, this may indicate a faulty pump.

2 If the pump appears to have failed completely, check the wiring to the pump, and check the appropriate fuse and relay.

3 To test the performance of the pump, special equipment is required, and it is recommended that any suspected faults are referred to a Vauxhall dealer.

Removal

Note: Refer to the precautions given in Section 1 before proceeding.

4 Disconnect the battery negative lead (refer to Disconnecting the battery at the end of this manual).

5 Depressurise the fuel system as described in Section 4.

6 Syphon out any remaining fuel in the tank through the filler pipe into a clean metal container which can be sealed.

7 On Hatchback models, remove the rear seat as described in Chapter 11. On standard Van models, fold up the rear seat. On Combo

Van models, unbolt the tank cover flap from the rear floor.

8 Fold up the acoustic insulation, then, using a screwdriver, carefully lever out the plastic cover to expose the fuel pump cover.

9 Disconnect the main wiring plug from the cover **(see illustration)**.

10 Identify the position of the two fuel lines, then disconnect the quick-release fittings. Be prepared for some loss of fuel. A Vauxhall special tool is available to release the fuel line connectors, but provided care is taken, the connectors can be released using a pair of long-nosed pliers, or a similar tool, to depress the retaining tangs. Clamp or plug the open ends of the hoses, to prevent dirt ingress and further fuel spillage.

11 Release the fuel pump cover locking ring. A special tool (Vauxhall tool No KM-797) is available for this, but the ring can be removed by tapping anti-clockwise until the locking clips release **(see illustration)**.

Warning: To prevent the possibility of any sparks which could ignite fuel vapour, use a plastic, wooden or brass tool to release the locking ring.

12 Remove the locking ring, then carefully lift the cover from the top of the pump, noting the location of the wiring and hose connections.

13 Disconnect the sender unit wiring and the fuel pump wiring from the bottom of the cover **(see illustration)**.

14 On Van models, disconnect the earth wiring from the pressure regulator.

15 Release the clip and disconnect the fuel supply hose from the cover.

16 Disconnect the fuel return hose from the pressure regulator, and withdraw the cover.

17 Remove the cover sealing ring.

18 Press the three pump housing retaining lugs to release them, and simultaneously pull the pump housing from the tank using a wire hook engaged with the eyelet provided **(see illustrations)**.

19 To remove the pump from the housing, first pull the filter from the base of the pump **(see illustration)**, and disconnect the wires from the pump. Note the wire locations to ensure correct refitting.

20 Compress the three locking tabs, and pull the pump mounting plate and the pump from the housing **(see illustrations)**.

7.11 Releasing the fuel pump locking ring using a brass drift – Hatchback models

7.13 Disconnect the wiring plugs from the underside of the cover – Hatchback models

7.18a Press the three retaining lugs (1 – one shown), and pull the housing from the tank using a hook on the eyelet (2)

21 Disconnect the wiring and, if necessary, remove the filter from the bottom of the fuel pump.

Refitting

22 Refitting is a reversal of removal, bearing in mind the following points:
a) Before refitting the filter to the bottom of the pump, inspect the filter for contamination or blockage, and renew if necessary.
b) Ensure that the pump mounting plate engages correctly with the retaining clips on the housing.
c) Check the condition of the sealing ring on the underside of the fuel pump cover, and renew if necessary.
d) Refit the fuel pump cover locking ring by tapping it clockwise until the locking clips 'click' into position.

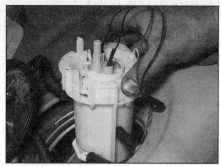

7.18b Withdrawing the fuel pump housing from the fuel tank – Hatchback models

7.19 Removing the fuel filter from the base of the fuel pump

---

8 Fuel injection system – general information

1 The multi-point injection system is under the overall control of the Multec S engine management system, which also controls the ignition system (see Chapter 5B).
2 Fuel is supplied from the rear-mounted tank, via a fuel filter and a pressure regulator, to the fuel rail. Excess fuel is returned from the regulator to the tank. The fuel rail acts as a reservoir for the four fuel injectors, which inject fuel into the cylinder inlet tracts, upstream of the inlet valves. The Multec S system is a 'sequential' fuel injection system. This means that each of the four fuel injectors is triggered individually, just before the inlet valve on the relevant cylinder opens.
3 The duration of the electrical pulses to the fuel injectors determines the quantity of fuel injected. The pulse duration is computed by the Multec S electronic control unit (ECU) on the basis of information received from the following sensors:
a) Accelerator pedal position sensor – informs the ECU of accelerator pedal position, and the rate of throttle opening/closing.
b) Manifold absolute pressure (MAP) sensor – informs the ECU of the load on the engine (expressed in terms of inlet manifold vacuum).
c) Intake air temperature sensor – informs the ECU of the temperature of the air passing through the air intake ducting.
d) Crankshaft speed/position sensor – informs the ECU of the crankshaft speed and position.
e) Camshaft position sensor – informs the ECU when No 1 cylinder is at top dead centre (TDC) on the firing stroke (expressed in terms of the position of the exhaust camshaft).
f) Coolant temperature sensor – informs the ECU of engine temperature.

g) Exhaust gas oxygen sensors (two) – inform the ECU of the oxygen content of the exhaust gases (explained in greater detail in Chapter 4D).
h) Knock sensor – informs the ECU when engine 'knock' (pre-ignition) occurs (explained in greater detail in Chapter 5B).
4 The signals from the various sensors are processed by the ECU, and the optimum fuelling and ignition settings are selected for the prevailing engine operating conditions.
5 Idle speed is controlled by the idle speed control motor, which regulates the quantity of air bypassing the throttle valve. The motor is controlled by the electronic control unit; there is no provision for direct adjustment of the idle speed.
6 Similarly, the fuel/air mixture is controlled within fine limits by the electronic control unit, via the fuel injectors. No manual adjustment of fuel/air mixture is possible.
7 A catalytic converter is incorporated in the exhaust manifold to reduce harmful exhaust gas emissions. Details of this and other emissions control system equipment are given in Chapter 4D.
8 If certain sensors fail, and send abnormal signals to the ECU, the ECU has a back-up programme. In this event, the abnormal signals are ignored, and a preprogrammed value is substituted for the sensor signal, allowing the engine to continue running, albeit at reduced efficiency. If the ECU enters its back-up mode, a warning light on the instrument panel will illuminate, and a fault

code will be stored in the ECU memory. This fault code can be read using suitable specialist test equipment.

---

9 Fuel injection system components – testing

In order to safely test the fuel injection system components without the risk of damage to the components or electronic control unit, specialist test equipment is required.

The systems have a self-diagnosis function, and any faults are stored as codes in the electronic control unit memory. These fault codes can be read using suitable test equipment such as a fault code reader. If a fault code reader is available, it should be connected and operated according to the instructions supplied with the reader.

System sensors and actuators can be tested for continuity and resistance using a suitable multi-meter, but always ensure that the ignition is switched off, and that the relevant sensor or actuator is disconnected from the engine management system. Refer to the precautions given in Section 1 before attempting to carry out any fault diagnosis.

In the event of a suspected fault, and suitable test and diagnostic equipment is not available, the best course of action is to seek advice from a Vauxhall dealer, who will have access to the necessary equipment.

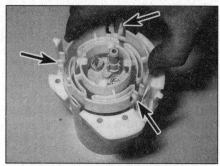

7.20a Compress the three locking tabs (arrowed) . . .

7.20b . . . and withdraw the pump from the housing

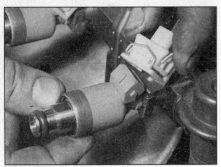

10.29a Disconnect the wiring plug . . .

10.29b . . . then remove the securing clip . . .

10.29c . . . and withdraw the injector

10 Fuel injection system components – removal and refitting

Throttle body

Removal

1 Disconnect the battery negative lead (refer to *Disconnecting the battery* in the Reference Chapter).
2 Remove the air cleaner cover, inlet trunking and airbox from the top of the throttle body, with reference to Section 2.
3 Disconnect the wiring from the throttle body module.
4 Partially drain the cooling system as described in Chapter 1A (drain sufficient coolant to empty the coolant expansion tank).
5 Release the retaining clips and disconnect the two coolant hoses from the rear of the throttle body.
6 Disconnect the crankcase ventilation hose and carbon canister vent hose from the throttle body.
7 Undo the four bolts and lift the throttle body off the upper section of the inlet manifold. Recover the gasket.
8 It is not possible to obtain the idle speed control motor or throttle valve position sensor separately, so if either is faulty, the complete throttle body must be renewed.

Refitting

9 Refitting is a reversal of removal, but thoroughly clean the mating faces and use a new gasket. Tighten the bolts progressively and securely. Top-up the coolant level as described in *Weekly checks*. Finally. switch on the ignition for 30 seconds without starting the engine.

Manifold absolute pressure (MAP) sensor

Removal

10 The sensor is located on the inlet manifold on the front of the cylinder head.
11 Disconnect the wiring from the sensor.
12 Unscrew the clamp nut, remove the clamp plate, and withdraw the sensor from the cylinder head.

Refitting

13 Refitting is a reversal of removal, but clean the contact faces of the sensor and manifold, and tighten the clamp nut to the specified torque.

Air temperature sensor

Removal

14 Disconnect the wiring from the air temperature sensor located on the rear of the air cleaner-to-throttle body duct.
15 Twist and pull the sensor from the duct, and recover the seal.

Refitting

16 Refitting is a reversal of removal, but renew the seal.

Fuel injectors and fuel rail

Note: *Refer to the precautions given in Section 1 before proceeding. The seals at both ends of the fuel injectors must be renewed on refitting.*

Removal

17 Disconnect the battery negative lead (refer to *Disconnecting the battery* in the Reference Chapter).
18 Depressurise the fuel system as described in Section 4.
19 Unscrew the oil filler cap, then unscrew the engine top cover securing bolts and lift off the cover. Screw the cap back into the camshaft cover.
20 Disconnect the wiring from the air temperature sensor on the rear of the air cleaner air duct, then loosen the clip and disconnect the crankcase ventilation hose from the camshaft cover.
21 Loosen the clip and remove the airbox and duct from the throttle body. Place the duct to one side.
22 Disconnect the wiring from the oil pressure switch on the front of the cylinder block.
23 Unscrew the union bolt and disconnect the fuel feed line from the fuel rail. Tape over or plug the rail aperture and the end of the line.
24 Disconnect the wiring from the following components:
a) *Engine management ECU.*

b) *Carbon canister purge valve located behind the air cleaner.*
c) *Coolant temperature sensor.*
d) *Camshaft position sensor.*
e) *Throttle body module.*
f) *Knock sensor.*
g) *Inlet manifold absolute pressure (MAP) sensor.*
25 Remove the catalytic converter control oxygen sensor as described later in this Section.
26 Remove the EGR valve as described in Chapter 4D, then release the wiring harness from the cable ties.
27 Release the heater hose for the throttle body from the bracket on the camshaft cover.
28 Unscrew the two mounting bolts and remove the fuel rail, together with the injectors and wiring conduit, from the lower section of the inlet manifold.
29 To remove an injector from the fuel rail and wiring conduit, first note the fitted position of the clips. Prise out the metal securing clip using a screwdriver or a pair of pliers, then release the wiring plug by carefully pulling the retaining spring clip downwards. Pull the injector from the fuel rail **(see illustrations)**. Remove and discard the injector sealing rings; new ones must be fitted on refitting.
30 Overhaul of the fuel injectors is not possible, as no spares are available. If faulty, an injector must be renewed.

Refitting

31 Commence refitting by fitting new O-ring seals to both ends of the fuel injectors. Coat the seals with a thin layer of petroleum jelly before fitting.
32 Refitting is a reversal of removal, bearing in mind the following points:
a) *When refitting the injectors to the fuel rail, note that the groove in the metal securing clip must engage with the lug on the injector body (see illustration).*
b) *Tighten the fuel rail mounting and fuel line union bolts securely.*
c) *Ensure that all wiring connectors are securely reconnected, and that the wiring is secured in the relevant clips and brackets.*
d) *Finally, it may be necessary to have a dealer program all volatile memories.*

Crankshaft speed/position sensor

Note: *A new O-ring seal must be used on refitting.*

33 The crankshaft speed/position sensor is located at the front left-hand end of the cylinder block, below the oil filter. Access is most easily obtained from beneath the vehicle.

34 Apply the handbrake, then jack up the front of the vehicle and support it on axle stands (see *Jacking and vehicle support*). Where necessary, remove the engine undertray.

35 Disconnect the sensor wiring connector, then unscrew the retaining bolt and withdraw the sensor from the block.

Refitting

36 Refitting is a reversal of removal, but ensure that the mating surfaces of the sensor and block are clean and fit a new O-ring seal to the sensor before refitting. Tighten the bolt to the specified torque.

Camshaft position sensor

Removal

37 The camshaft position sensor is located next to the right-hand side of the throttle body.

38 Disconnect the wiring, then unscrew the mounting bolt and withdraw the sensor.

Refitting

39 Refitting is a reversal of removal.

Coolant temperature sensor

40 The coolant temperature sensor is located on the right-hand front end of the cylinder head.

41 Partially drain the cooling system as described in Chapter 1A. Alternatively, release any pressure in the cooling system by removing the expansion filler cap then refitting it, and have ready a means of plugging the sensor hole.

42 Disconnect the sensor wiring plug.

43 Unscrew the sensor, and withdraw it from the engine. Recover the sealing ring.

Refitting

44 Refitting is a reversal of removal, but use a new sealing ring, and tighten the sensor to the specified torque. On completion, top-up the cooling system as described in *Weekly checks*.

Exhaust gas oxygen sensor (mixture regulation)

Caution: The sensor will be very hot if the engine has been running within 10 or 15 minutes.

Removal

45 The mixture regulation oxygen sensor is located on the exhaust manifold/catalytic converter. With the engine top cover removed, trace the wiring back from the sensor to the connector located on the left-hand side of the cylinder head, and disconnect it.

46 Unscrew the sensor from the exhaust manifold/catalytic converter. Ideally, a special 'split' socket should be used, as this will locate over the sensor wiring.

Refitting

47 Clean the threads of the sensor then coat them with Vauxhall special grease for oxygen sensors. If a new sensor is being fitted, it will be supplied with the threads already coated with the special grease to prevent it seizing in the manifold.

48 Screw the sensor into the exhaust manifold/catalytic converter and tighten to the specified torque.

49 Reconnect the wiring and clip it in place.

Exhaust gas oxygen sensor (catalytic converter control)

Caution: The sensor will be very hot if the engine has been running within 10 or 15 minutes.

Removal

50 The catalytic converter control oxygen sensor is located in the exhaust front pipe, just behind the flexible section. First, apply the handbrake, then jack up the front of the vehicle and support it on axle stands (see *Jacking and vehicle support*).

51 Trace the wiring back from the sensor to the connector located on the bracket, and disconnect it. Unclip the wiring from the bracket.

52 Unscrew the sensor from the exhaust front pipe. Ideally, a special 'split' socket should be used, as this will locate over the sensor wiring.

Refitting

53 Clean the threads of the sensor then coat them with Vauxhall special grease for oxygen sensors. If a new sensor is being fitted, it will be supplied with the threads already coated with the special grease to prevent it seizing in the pipe.

54 Screw the sensor into the exhaust front pipe and tighten to the specified torque.

55 Reconnect the wiring and clip it in place.

Knock sensor

Removal

56 The knock sensor is located on the rear, left-hand side of the cylinder block, just above the starter motor.

57 Apply the handbrake, then jack up the front of the vehicle and support it on axle stands (see *Jacking and vehicle support*).

58 Unscrew the oil filler cap, then unscrew the engine top cover securing bolts and lift off the cover. Screw the cap back into the camshaft cover.

59 Disconnect the wiring from the air temperature sensor located on the rear of the air cleaner-to-throttle body duct.

60 Loosen the clip and disconnect the airbox crankcase ventilation hose from the camshaft cover.

61 Loosen the clip and remove the airbox from the throttle body, then loosen the clip and separate the airbox and duct from the air cleaner cover.

62 Disconnect the knock sensor wiring at the connector on the top of the engine, then feed the wire between the fuel rail and wiring trough.

63 Note its position, then unscrew the mounting bolt and withdraw the sensor from the block.

Refitting

64 Clean the contact surfaces of the sensor and block. Also clean the threads of the sensor mounting bolt.

65 Locate the sensor on the block and insert the mounting bolt. Position the sensor as previously noted, then tighten the bolt to the specified torque. Note that the torque setting is critical for the sensor to function correctly.

66 Reconnect the wiring, making sure that it is routed as previously noted.

67 Refit the airbox and duct and tighten the clips.

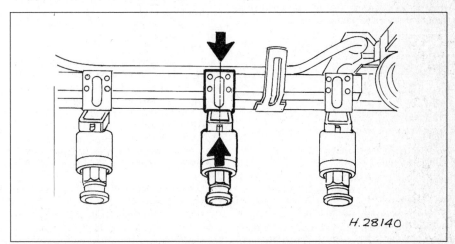

H.28140

10.32 The metal securing clip must engage with the lug on the injector body

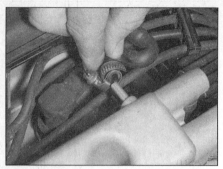

11.13 Disconnecting the breather hose from the camshaft cover

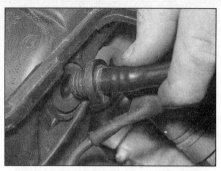

11.18 Disconnecting the brake servo vacuum hose from the upper section of the inlet manifold

68 Reconnect the airbox crankcase ventilation hose, and reconnect the wiring to the air temperature sensor.

69 Refit the engine top cover and tighten the bolts.

70 Lower the vehicle to the ground.

Electronic control unit

Removal

71 The electronic control unit is located on the rear, left-hand side of the engine.

72 Disconnect the battery negative lead (refer to *Disconnecting the battery* in the Reference Chapter).

73 Unscrew the oil filler cap, then unscrew the engine top cover securing bolts and lift off the cover. Screw the cap back into the camshaft cover.

74 Disconnect the wiring from the following components:

 a) *Mixture regulating oxygen sensor.*
 b) *Ignition module.*
 c) *Combination plug.*
 d) *Control unit.*

75 Unscrew the bolt securing the earth wire to the control unit, then unbolt and remove the engine control unit.

Refitting

76 Refitting is a reversal of removal. Finally, it may be necessary to have a Vauxhall dealer program all volatile memories.

11 Inlet manifold – removal and refitting

Upper section

Note: *A new manifold gasket must be used on refitting.*

Removal

1 Disconnect the battery negative lead (refer to *Disconnecting the battery* in the Reference Chapter).

2 Apply the handbrake, then jack up the front of the vehicle and support it on axle stands (see *Jacking and vehicle support*). Remove the right-hand front roadwheel and the wheel arch liner for access to the crankshaft pulley.

3 Partially drain the cooling system as described in Chapter 1A so that the coolant level is below the throttle body.

4 Remove the auxiliary drivebelt as described in Chapter 1A. Mark the drivebelt to indicate its running direction and ensure it is refitted correctly.

5 Unscrew and remove the inlet manifold support bracket upper bolt, then loosen only the lower bolt. Move the bracket to one side.

6 Disconnect the wiring from the oil pressure switch and release the wiring from the cable tie.

7 Unscrew the oil filler cap, then unscrew the engine top cover securing bolts and lift off the cover. Screw the cap back into the camshaft cover.

8 Remove the air cleaner assembly as described in Section 2.

9 Depressurise the fuel system as described in Section 4.

10 Unscrew the union bolt and disconnect the fuel feed line from the fuel rail. Tape over or plug the rail aperture and the end of the line.

11 Disconnect the wiring from the following components, and release the wiring from the cable ties:

 a) *Coolant temperature sensor.*
 b) *Camshaft position sensor.*
 c) *Throttle body.*
 d) *Knock sensor.*
 e) *Manifold absolute pressure (MAP) sensor.*
 f) *Catalytic converter oxygen sensor.*
 g) *EGR valve.*

12 Release the retaining clips and disconnect the two coolant hoses from the rear of the throttle body.

13 Disconnect the crankcase ventilation hose from the throttle body and camshaft cover **(see illustration)**.

14 Unscrew the two mounting bolts and remove the fuel rail, together with the injectors and wiring conduit, from the lower section of the inlet manifold.

15 Unbolt the wiring harness bracket from the alternator.

16 Unscrew the three bolts and remove the upper mounting bracket from the alternator. Loosen the lower mounting bolt. Swivel the alternator to the rear.

17 Unbolt the bracket and unclip the wiring

harness from the rear right-hand side of the inlet manifold.

18 Disconnect the brake vacuum hose from the upper section of the inlet manifold **(see illustration)**.

19 Disconnect the carbon canister purge hose from the throttle body, then unbolt and remove the throttle body from the manifold. Recover the gasket.

20 Unscrew the securing bolts, and withdraw the upper section of the inlet manifold. Recover the gasket.

Refitting

21 Commence refitting by checking the condition of the rubber gasket which fits between the upper and lower sections of the inlet manifold. Renew the gasket if necessary. Thoroughly clean the mating surfaces of the manifolds.

22 Refit the upper section of the inlet manifold, ensuring that the gasket between the upper and lower manifold sections locates correctly. Insert and tighten the securing bolts progressively to the specified torque.

23 Refit the throttle body with reference to Section 10, and reconnect the purge hose.

24 Reconnect the brake vacuum hose.

25 Refit the wiring harness and bracket and tighten the bolts.

26 Refit the alternator bracket and tighten the bolts. Also refit the wiring harness bracket.

27 Refit the fuel rail and injectors with reference to Section 10.

28 Reconnect the crankcase ventilation hose and the two coolant hoses.

29 Reconnect the wiring to the components listed in paragraph 11.

30 Refit the fuel feed line to the fuel rail and tighten the union bolt securely.

31 Refit the air cleaner assembly and engine top cover.

32 Reconnect the wiring to the oil pressure switch and secure with a new cable tie.

33 Refit the inlet manifold support bracket and tighten the bolts.

34 Refit the auxiliary drivebelt with reference to Chapter 1A.

35 Top-up the cooling system with reference to *Weekly checks*.

36 Refit the wheel arch liner and front wheel and lower the vehicle to the ground.

37 Reconnect the battery negative lead (refer to *Disconnecting the battery* in the Reference Chapter). Finally, it may be necessary to have a Vauxhall dealer program all volatile memories.

Lower section

Note: *A new manifold gasket must be used on refitting.*

Removal

38 Remove the upper section of the inlet manifold as described previously in this Section. It should be noted however, that the cooling system should be drained completely.

39 Unbolt and remove the engine lifting eye.

40 Unbolt and remove the coolant flange.

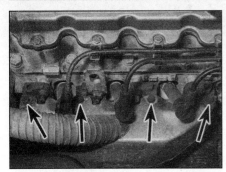

12.7a Exhaust manifold hot-air shroud upper . . .

12.7b . . . and lower securing bolts

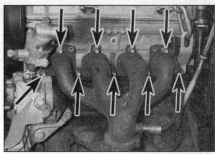

12.8 Exhaust manifold securing nuts (arrowed) – viewed with engine removed for clarity

41 Remove the coolant hose, then unscrew the 9 nuts and remove the lower section of the inlet manifold. The manufacturers recommend that the nuts are renewed.

42 Unbolt the EGR valve from the inlet manifold. Discard the gasket and obtain a new one.

Refitting

43 Thoroughly clean the mating surfaces of the manifolds, cylinder head, coolant flange and EGR valve.

44 Refit the EGR valve together with a new gasket, and tighten the bolts to the specified torque.

45 Refit the lower section of the inlet manifold together with a new gasket, and progressively tighten the nuts to the specified torque.

46 Reconnect the coolant hose and tighten the clip.

47 Refit the coolant flange and tighten the bolts to the specified torque.

48 Refit the engine lifting eye and tighten the bolt.

49 Refit the upper section of the inlet manifold as described earlier in this Section.

---

12 Exhaust manifold – removal and refitting

Note: *A new gasket must be used on refitting.*

Removal

1 Disconnect the battery negative lead (refer to *Disconnecting the battery* in the Reference Chapter).

2 Unscrew the oil filler cap, then unscrew the engine top cover securing bolts and lift off the cover. Screw the cap back into the camshaft cover.

3 Apply the handbrake, then jack up the front of the vehicle and support it on axle stands (see *Jacking and vehicle support*).

4 Refer to Section 10 and disconnect the wiring from the oxygen sensor (mixture regulation) on the exhaust manifold/catalytic converter, then unbolt the exhaust front pipe from the exhaust manifold, taking care to support the flexible section. **Note:** *Angular movement in excess of 10° can cause*

permanent damage to the flexible section. Recover the gasket.

5 Release the mounting rubbers and support the front of the exhaust pipe to one side.

6 Remove the oxygen sensor (mixture regulation) from the exhaust manifold as described in Section 10.

7 Unbolt the hot air shroud from the exhaust manifold **(see illustrations)**. Also remove the engine oil dipstick.

8 Unscrew the retaining nuts and carefully withdraw the exhaust manifold upwards from the engine **(see illustration)**. Recover the manifold gasket. The manufacturers recommend that the nuts are renewed.

Refitting

9 Thoroughly clean the mating surfaces of the exhaust manifold and cylinder head.

10 Refit the exhaust manifold to the cylinder head together with a new gasket. Tighten the (new) nuts progressively to the specified torque.

11 Refit the oil dipstick, then refit the heat shield to the manifold and tighten the bolts.

12 Refit the oxygen sensor (mixture regulation) to the exhaust manifold as described in Section 10.

13 Refit the front pipe to the manifold together with a new gasket and tighten the nuts to the specified torque. Reconnect the mounting rubbers.

14 Reconnect the wiring for the oxygen sensor (catalytic converter).

15 Lower the vehicle to the ground.

16 Refit the engine top cover, and reconnect the battery negative lead (refer to

Disconnecting the battery in the Reference Chapter). Finally, it may be necessary to have a Vauxhall dealer program all volatile memories.

---

13 Exhaust system – general information and component renewal

General information

1 The exhaust system is in two sections. The front section includes the oxygen sensor (catalytic converter control), silencer and intermediate pipe. The rear section consists of the tailpipe and silencer.

2 Periodically, the exhaust system should be checked for signs of leaks or damage. Also inspect the system rubber mountings, and renew if necessary.

3 Small holes or cracks can be repaired using proprietary exhaust repair products.

4 Before renewing an individual section of the exhaust system, it is wise to inspect the remaining section. If corrosion or damage is evident, it may prove more economical to renew the entire system.

Component renewal

5 If either part of the system is to be renewed, it is important to ensure that the correct component is obtained **(see illustration)**.

6 To remove the rear tailpipe and silencer, chock the front wheels then jack up the rear of the vehicle and support on axle stands (see *Jacking and vehicle support*). Loosen the

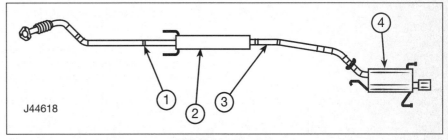

J44618

13.5 Exhaust system

1 Front exhaust pipe with flexible section   3 Intermediate exhaust pipe
2 Catalytic converter   4 Tail pipe and silencer

13.7a Exhaust system rubber mounting spring clip (arrowed)

13.7b Removing the exhaust front pipe gasket

clamp securing the intermediate pipe to the tailpipe, then release the rubber mountings and slide the tailpipe from the intermediate pipe. If the tailpipe is rusted onto the intermediate pipe, tap around the joint with a hammer to free it. Twist the tailpipe in both directions while holding the intermediate pipe.

7 To remove the front section of the exhaust, jack up the front and rear of the vehicle and support it on axle stands (see *Jacking and vehicle support*). Remove the tailpipe and silencer as described in paragraph 6, then remove the oxygen sensor (catalytic converter control) from the front pipe as described in Section 10. Unbolt the exhaust front pipe from the exhaust manifold/catalytic converter, taking care to support the flexible section. **Note:** *Angular movement in excess of 10° can cause permanent damage to the flexible section.* Recover the gasket. Release the rubber mountings and withdraw the exhaust from under the vehicle **(see illustrations)**.

8 Refitting is a reversal of removal, but renew all gaskets and tighten the clamp and front pipe flange nuts to the specified torque.

Chapter 4 Part C:
Fuel and exhaust systems – diesel engine

Contents

Degrees of difficulty

Easy, suitable for novice with little experience	Fairly easy, suitable for beginner with some experience	Fairly difficult, suitable for competent DIY mechanic	Difficult, suitable for experienced DIY mechanic	Very difficult, suitable for expert DIY or professional

Specifications

General

System type	ECD V5 direct injection system incorporating an electronically-controlled Nippon Denso V5 distributor fuel injection pump with integral transfer pump. Two stage injectors with pilot and post injection. Turbocharger fitted to all models and intercooler on Y17DT engined models

Adjustment data

Idle speed	825 to 875 rpm – controlled by ECU
Maximum speed	5060 to 5180 rpm – controlled by ECU

Injection pump

Direction of rotation	Clockwise, viewed from sprocket end
Pump timing (static):	
Checking	0.28 to 0.33 mm pump plunger travel @ TDC
Setting	0.33 mm pump plunger travel @ TDC
Transfer fuel pump pressure	8.0 ± 0.1 bars at 2200 rpm

Injectors

Opening pressure	175 bar (1st stage) to 335 bar (2nd stage)

Torque wrench settings

	Nm	lbf ft
Accelerator pedal/position sensor	9	7
Air conditioning compressor bracket	43	32
Air conditioning compressor	22	16
Charge pressure sensor	10	7
Coolant temperature sensor	22	16
Crankshaft sensor	10	7
Electronic control unit	6	4

Torque wrench settings (contnued)

	Nm	lbf ft
Exhaust front pipe-to-turbocharger nuts	67	49
Exhaust manifold:		
Retaining nuts and bolts	24	18
Support bracket bolts	51	38
Fuel injector return pipe unions	15	11
Fuel injectors	22	16
Fuel pipe union nuts	23	17
Fuel tank	20	15
Injection pump:		
Central bleed screw	25	18
Pump bracket to cylinder block	54	40
Pump to pump bracket	18	13
Pump to timing cover	20	15
Timing belt sprocket nut	69	51
Inlet manifold nuts and bolts*	25	18
Oil pressure switch	21	15
Oil return line banjo	15	11
Turbocharger:		
Exhaust flange nuts	27	20
Oil feed line adaptor to block	21	15
Oil feed line to turbocharger/block adaptor	10	7
Turbocharger-to-manifold nuts	27	20

Use new fasteners

---

1 General information and precautions

General information

1 The fuel supply system consists of a fuel tank (which is mounted under the rear of the car), a fuel filter with integral water separator (in the engine compartment), an electronically-controlled distributor fuel injection pump with integral transfer pump, injectors and associated components.

2 Fuel is drawn from the fuel tank by the fuel injection pump. Before reaching the pump, the fuel passes through a fuel filter, where foreign matter and water are removed. Excess fuel lubricates the moving components of the pump, and is then returned to the tank.

3 The fuel injection pump is driven at half-crankshaft speed by the timing belt. The high pressure required to inject the fuel into the compressed air in the cylinder is achieved by radial plungers.

4 The injection pump is electronically-controlled to meet the latest emission standards. The system consists of the engine electronic control unit, the injection electronic control unit, and the following sensors:

a) *Accelerator pedal position sensor – informs the ECUs of the accelerator pedal position.*

b) *Coolant temperature sensor – informs the ECUs of engine temperature.*

c) *Intake air temperature sensor – informs the ECUs of the temperature of the air passing through the intake duct.*

d) *Hot film mass airflow meter – informs the ECUs of the amount of air passing through the intake duct.*

e) *Crankshaft sensor – informs the ECUs of engine speed and crankshaft position.*

f) *Charge pressure sensor – informs ECUs of the pressure in the inlet manifold.*

g) *ABS control unit – informs the ECUs of the vehicle speed.*

h) *Atmospheric pressure sensor – informs the ECUs of the atmospheric pressure.*

i) *Fuel temperature sensor – informs the ECUs of the fuel temperature.*

j) *Injection pump shaft sensor – used by the ECUs to determine the exact injection timing.*

k) *Oil pressure switch – used by the engine ECU to control the instrument cluster oil warning lamp.*

l) *Clutch switch – used by the ECUs for cruise control functions.*

m) *Air conditioning system compressor switch (where fitted) – informs the ECUs when the air conditioning system is switched on.*

5 All the above information is analysed by the ECUs and, based on this, the ECUs determine the appropriate injection requirements for the engine. The engine ECU controls the injection pump timing, via the pump control unit, to provide the best setting for cranking, starting (with either a hot or cold engine), warm-up, idle, cruising, and acceleration.

6 Basic injection timing is determined when the pump is fitted. When the engine is running, it is varied automatically to suit the prevailing engine speed by a mechanism which turns the cam plate or ring – controlled by the ECU.

7 The engine ECU also controls the exhaust gas recirculation (EGR) system (see Chapter 4D) and the pre-heating system (see Chapter 5C).

8 The four fuel injectors produce a spray of fuel directly into the cylinders. The injectors are calibrated to open and close at critical pressures to provide efficient and even combustion. Each injector needle is lubricated by fuel which accumulates in the spring chamber and is channelled to the injection pump return hose by leak-off pipes.

9 The inlet manifold is a two-part assembly sealed by a metal gasket. The EGR (exhaust gas recirculation) valve and charge pressure sensor are mounted to the upper part of the manifold.

10 A turbocharger is fitted to increase engine efficiency by raising the pressure in the inlet manifold above atmospheric pressure. Instead of the air simply being sucked into the cylinders, it is forced in. Additional fuel is supplied by the injection pump in proportion to the increased air intake.

11 Energy for the operation of the turbocharger comes from the exhaust gas. The gas flows through a specially-shaped housing (the turbine housing) and in so doing, spins the turbine wheel. The turbine wheel is attached to a shaft, at the end of which is another vaned wheel known as the compressor wheel. The compressor wheel spins in its own housing, and compresses the inlet air on the way to the inlet manifold.

12 Between the turbocharger and the inlet manifold, the compressed air passes through an intercooler (except Y20DTL engine). This is an air-to-air heat exchanger mounted next to the radiator, and supplied with cooling air from the front of the vehicle. The purpose of the intercooler is to remove some of the heat gained in being compressed from the inlet air. Because cooler air is denser, removal of this heat further increases engine efficiency.

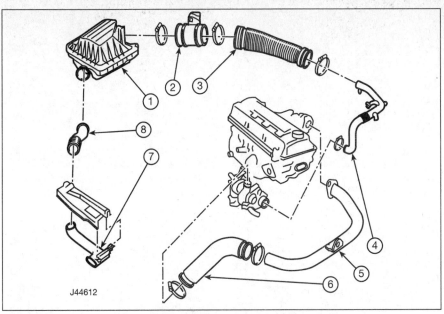

2.1a Air cleaner and ducting – 17DTL engine

1 Air cleaner housing	3 Air intake hose	6 Charge air hose
2 Hot film mass airflow	4 Air intake manifold	7 Resonator/air intake pipe
meter	5 Charge air pipe	8 Connecting hose

13 Charge pressure (the pressure in the inlet manifold) is limited by a wastegate, which diverts the exhaust gas away from the turbine wheel in response to a pressure-sensitive actuator. A pressure-operated switch operates a warning light on the instrument panel in the event of excessive charge pressure developing.

14 The turbo shaft is pressure-lubricated by an oil feed pipe from the engine main oil so that the shaft 'floats' on a cushion of oil. A drain pipe returns the oil to the sump.

15 The charge pressure wastegate is controlled by the ECU via a solenoid valve.

16 If there is an abnormality in any of the readings obtained from any sensor, the ECU enters its back-up mode. In this event, the ECU ignores the abnormal sensor signal, and assumes a preprogrammed value which will allow the engine to continue running (albeit at reduced efficiency). If the ECU enters this back-up mode, the warning light on the instrument panel will come on, and the relevant fault code will be stored in the ECU memory.

17 If the warning light comes on, the vehicle should be taken to a Vauxhall dealer at the earliest opportunity. A complete test of the injection system can then be carried out, using a special electronic diagnostic test unit which is simply plugged into the system's diagnostic connector. The connector is located behind the centre of the facia.

Precautions

⚠️ **Warning: It is necessary to take certain precautions when working on the fuel system components, particularly the fuel injectors. Before**
carrying out any operations on the fuel system, refer to the precautions given in 'Safety first!' at the beginning of this manual, and to any additional warning notes at the start of the relevant Sections.

Caution: Do not operate the engine if any of air intake ducts are disconnected or the filter element is removed. Any debris entering the engine will cause severe damage to the turbocharger.

Caution: To prevent damage to the turbocharger, do not race the engine immediately after start-up, especially if it is cold. Allow it to idle smoothly to give the oil a few seconds to circulate around the turbocharger bearings. Always allow the engine to return to idle speed before switching it off – do not blip the throttle and switch off, as this will leave the turbo spinning without lubrication.

Caution: Observe the recommended intervals for oil and filter changing, and use oil of the specified quality. Neglect of oil changing, or use of inferior oil, can cause carbon formation on the turbo shaft, leading to subsequent failure.

2 Air cleaner assembly and intake ducts – removal and refitting

Note: The intercooler is only fitted to the Y17DT engine.

Removal

1 Disconnect the wiring from the hot film mass airflow meter by releasing it towards the air cleaner cover **(see illustrations)**.

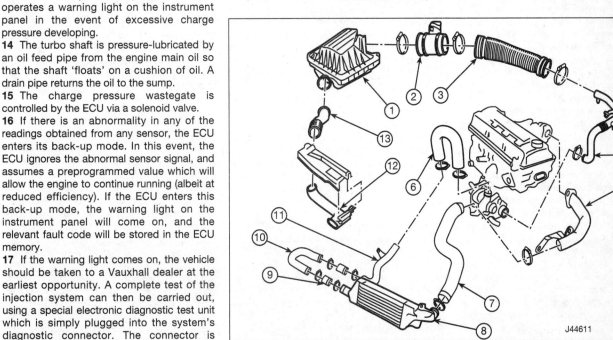

2.1b Air cleaner and ducting – 17DT engine

1 Air cleaner housing	5 Upper charge air pipe	10 Lower charge air pipe
2 Hot film mass airflow	6 Charge air hose	11 Centre charge air pipe
meter	7 Charge air hose	12 Resonator/air intake
3 Air intake hose	8 Intercooler	pipe
4 Air intake manifold	9 Charge air hose	13 Connecting hose

2.2a Loosen the clip . . .

2.2b . . . and disconnect the mass airflow meter from the air cleaner cover

2.2c Disconnecting the air duct from the pipe at the rear of the engine

2.3a Undo the screws . . .

2.3b . . . and lift the cover from the air cleaner

2.4 Removing the element

2 Loosen the clip and disconnect the hot film mass airflow meter from the air cleaner cover. Similarly, disconnect the duct from the intermediate pipe at the rear of the engine **(see illustrations)**.

3 Undo the screws and lift the cover from the air cleaner **(see illustrations)**.

4 Lift out the element **(see illustration)**.

5 Disconnect the air inlet duct from the front of the air cleaner **(see illustration)**.

6 Unscrew the crossbar mounting bolt from the rear of the air cleaner, and release the crossbar from the rear rubber mountings **(see illustration)**.

7 Pull the air cleaner body rearwards from the front mounting rubber, and withdraw from the engine compartment **(see illustration)**.

8 The remaining ducts linking the turbocharger, intercooler and inlet manifold can be removed once their retaining clips and (where necessary) bolts have been slackened.

Refitting

9 Refitting is the reverse of removal, ensuring that all intake ducts are properly reconnected and their retaining clips securely tightened.

3 Accelerator pedal and position sensor – removal and refitting

Removal

1 Disconnect the battery negative lead (refer to *Disconnecting the battery* at the end of this manual).

2 Working in the driver's footwell under the facia, disconnect the wiring from the top of the accelerator pedal/position sensor. Where necessary, pull back the footwell carpet first.

3 Unscrew the three mounting nuts, and withdraw the sensor from the bulkhead.

Refitting

4 Refitting is a reversal of removal. After reconnecting the battery, have a Vauxhall dealer reprogram the volatile memories.

4 Fuel system – priming and bleeding

1 It is not necessary to manually prime and bleed the fuel system after any operation on the system components. Start the engine, noting that this may take longer than usual, especially if the fuel system has been allowed to run dry. Operate the starter in ten second bursts with 5 seconds rest in between each operation, for a maximum of 40 seconds. When the engine starts, run it at a fast idle speed for a minute or so to purge any trapped

2.5 Removing the air inlet duct from the front of the air cleaner

2.6 Removing the mounting crossbar from the rear of the air cleaner

2.7 Removing the air cleaner assembly

5.4 Prise the plastic cover from the floor for access to the fuel gauge sender cover

5.5 Using the special tool to release the fuel line connectors

5.6 Disconnecting the main wiring plug

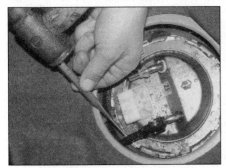

5.7 Tapping the locking ring anti-clockwise to release it

5.8 Removing the locking ring

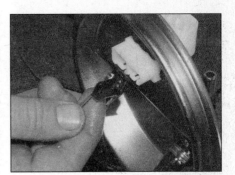

5.9 Disconnect the fuel gauge sender wiring plug

air from the fuel lines. After this time the engine should idle smoothly at a constant speed.

2 If the engine idles roughly, then there is still some air trapped in the fuel system. Increase the engine speed again for another minute or so then recheck the idle speed. Repeat this procedure as necessary until the engine is idling smoothly.

5 Fuel gauge sender unit – removal and refitting

Note: *Refer to the precautions given in Section 1 before proceeding.*
Note: *The fuel tank should be as empty as possible when carrying out this procedure.*

Removal

1 Disconnect the battery negative lead (refer to *Disconnecting the battery* at the end of this manual).

2 Syphon out any remaining fuel in the tank through the filler pipe into a clean metal container which can be sealed.

3 On Hatchback models, remove the rear seat as described in Chapter 11. On standard Van models, fold up the rear seat. On Combo Van models, unbolt the tank cover flap from the rear floor.

4 Fold up the acoustic insulation, then, using a screwdriver, carefully lever out the plastic cover to expose the fuel gauge sender cover **(see illustration)**.

5 Identify the position of the fuel feed and return lines, then disconnect the quick-release fittings. Be prepared for some loss of fuel. A Vauxhall special tool is available to release the fuel line connectors **(see illustration)**, but provided care is taken, the connectors can be released using a pair of long-nosed pliers, or a

similar tool, to depress the retaining tangs. Clamp or plug the open ends of the hoses, to prevent dirt ingress and further fuel spillage.

6 Disconnect the main wiring plug from the cover **(see illustration)**.

7 Release the fuel gauge sender cover locking ring. A special tool (Vauxhall tool No KM-797) is available for this, but the ring can be removed by tapping anti-clockwise until the locking clips release **(see illustration)**.

8 Remove the locking ring, then carefully lift off the cover, noting the location of the wiring and hose connections **(see illustration)**.

9 Disconnect the sender unit wiring from the bottom of the cover **(see illustration)**.

10 Release the clip and disconnect the fuel supply hose from the cover **(see illustration)**.

11 Disconnect the fuel return hose, and withdraw the cover.

12 Remove the cover sealing ring **(see illustration)**.

5.10 Disconnecting the fuel supply hose from the cover

5.12 Removing the cover sealing ring

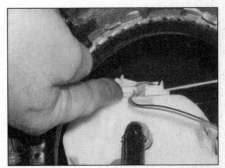

5.13a Depress the hook . . .

5.13b ... pull the sender unit from the housing

13 Depress the hook and pull the sender unit from the clips on the side of the housing **(see illustrations)**.

Refitting

14 Refitting is a reversal of removal, bearing in mind the following points:
a) *Check the condition of the sealing ring on the underside of the fuel pump cover, and renew if necessary.*
b) *Refit the fuel pump cover locking ring by tapping it clockwise until the locking clips 'click' into position.*

---

6 Fuel tank – removal and refitting

Note: *Refer to the precautions given in Section 1 before proceeding.*
Note: *The fuel tank should be as empty as possible when carrying out this procedure.*

Removal

1 Disconnect the battery negative lead (refer to *Disconnecting the battery* at the end of this manual).
2 Syphon out any remaining fuel in the tank through the filler pipe into a clean metal container which can be sealed.
3 Chock the front wheels then jack up the rear of the vehicle and support on axle stands (see *Jacking and vehicle support*). Remove both rear wheels.

8.1 Slide the lock to disconnect the wiring from the mass airflow meter

4 Refer to Chapter 9 and disconnect the front ends of the rear (secondary) handbrake cables from the underbody clips after backing off the primary cable adjustment. Unclip the cables from the underbody and the right-hand side of the fuel tank, then tie them to one side, away from the fuel tank.
5 Disconnect the rear of the exhaust system from its rubber mountings, and lower the system, then move it to one side sufficiently to enable removal of the fuel tank. Alternatively, remove the exhaust system completely to provide greater clearance (refer to Section 16).
6 Disconnect the wiring from the fuel gauge sensor, at the connector on the underbody.
7 Disconnect the fuel feed and return lines at the quick-release connectors on the underbody (if necessary, detach the line retaining bracket from the underbody). Be prepared for some loss of fuel. A Vauxhall special tool is available to release the fuel line connectors, but provided care is taken, the connectors can be released using a pair of long-nosed pliers, or a similar tool, to depress the retaining tangs.
8 Unscrew the lower filler hose mounting bolt, then unclip the ventilation hose from the bottom of the fuel tank.
9 Loosen the clip and disconnect the fuel filler hose from the fuel tank.
10 Support the weight of the fuel tank on a jack with interposed block of wood.
11 Unbolt and remove the two securing straps from the fuel tank.
12 Lower the tank sufficiently to enable access to the fuel hoses on the tank, then disconnect them. Be prepared for some loss of fuel.
13 Continue to lower the tank until it can be removed from under the vehicle.
14 Plug or clamp the fuel and vent hoses to prevent entry of dust and dirt.
15 If necessary, remove the fuel lines and hoses, heat shield and wiring from the tank for transfer to the new tank. If a new tank is being fitted, it is recommended that the filter is renewed at the same time.

Refitting

16 If the tank contains sediment or water, it may cleaned out with two or three rinses of clean fuel. Remove the fuel gauge sender unit as described in Section 5. Shake the tank vigorously, and change the fuel as necessary to remove all contamination from the tank. *This procedure should be carried out in a well-ventilated area, and it is vital to take adequate fire precautions.*
17 Any repairs to the fuel tank should be carried out by a professional. Do not under any circumstances attempt any form of DIY repair to a fuel tank.
18 Refitting is a reversal of removal, bearing in mind the following points:
a) *Ensure that all hoses are securely reconnected to their correct locations.*
b) *Check the handbrake cable adjustment, as described in Chapter 9.*

c) *On completion, fill the fuel tank, then run the engine and check for leaks. If leakage is evident, stop the engine immediately and rectify the problem without delay.*

---

7 Maximum speed – checking and adjustment

Caution: The maximum speed is controlled by the ECU and cannot be adjusted by the home mechanic. The speed can be checked using a tachometer as described below, but if adjustment is needed it will be necessary to take the vehicle to a Vauxhall dealer. They will have access to the necessary diagnostic equipment required to test and adjust the settings.
1 Run the engine to normal operating temperature.
2 Have an assistant fully depress the accelerator pedal, and check that the maximum engine speed is as given in the Specifications. Do not keep the engine at maximum speed for more than two or three seconds.

---

8 Injection system electrical components – removal and refitting

Hot film mass airflow meter

Note: *The intake air temperature sensor is built into the airflow meter.*

Removal

1 Ensure the ignition is switched off and disconnect the wiring plug from the hot film mass airflow meter. To do this, slide the lock towards the air cleaner **(see illustration)**.
2 Release the retaining clips then free the airflow meter from the air cleaner cover and intake duct. Remove it from the engine compartment.

Refitting

3 Refitting is the reverse of removal, ensuring the airflow meter is correctly seated in the air cleaner and duct and the retaining clips are securely tightened.

Crankshaft sensor

Removal

4 Apply the handbrake, then jack up the front of the vehicle and support it on axle stands (see *Jacking and vehicle support*). Remove the engine undertray.
5 The sensor is located on the rear of the cylinder block, beneath the starter motor. Working from under the vehicle, disconnect the wiring plug from the sensor.
6 Undo the retaining bolt and remove the sensor. Recover the sealing ring **(see illustration)**.

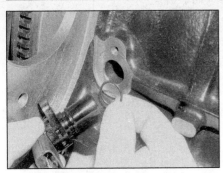

8.6 Crankshaft position sensor

8.9 Engine coolant temperature sensor

8.18 Undo the bolts and remove the charge pressure sensor

Refitting

7 Refitting is a reversal of removal. If necessary renew the sealing ring and tighten the sensor retaining bolt to the specified torque.

Coolant temperature sensor

Removal

8 With reference to Chapter 3, drain the coolant system, or be prepared for coolant spillage.

9 The coolant temperature sensor is located in the thermostat housing at the left-hand end of the cylinder head. Disconnect the wiring plug from the sensor **(see illustration)**.

10 Unscrew the sensor from the thermostat housing. Mop up any spilled coolant.

Refitting

11 Apply a little locking compound to the threads of the sensor, and refit the sensor to the housing. Tighten the sensor to the specified torque.

12 Reconnect the wiring plug to the sensor.

13 Top-up the coolant system (see *Weekly checks* or Chapter 3).

Charge pressure sensor

Removal

14 The charge pressure sensor is located on the right-hand rear end of the inlet manifold.

15 Loosen the clips and remove the air intake hose from above the inlet manifold.

16 Remove the exhaust gas recirculation (EGR) solenoid valve from the inlet manifold as described in Part D of this Chapter.

17 Disconnect the wiring plug from the sensor.

18 Unscrew the mounting bolt and remove the sensor **(see illustration)**.

Refitting

19 Refitting is a reversal of removal. Tighten the sensor retaining bolt to the specified torque.

Oil pressure switch

Removal

20 The signal from the oil pressure switch is used by the injection control unit to determine whether or not to illuminate the oil pressure warning light.

21 The oil pressure switch is located at the left-hand, rear end of the cylinder block. For improved access, remove the battery and battery tray as described in Chapter 5A.

22 Unclip the coolant expansion tank hose and position to one side.

23 Disconnect the wiring plug from the switch.

24 Unscrew the switch from the cylinder block. Be prepared for some oil spillage **(see illustration)**.

Refitting

25 Apply some suitable silicone sealant (available from Vauxhall dealers) to the threads, and screw the switch into place. Tighten the switch to the specified torque.

26 Reconnect the wiring plug, locate the expansion tank hose in the clip, and refit the battery tray and battery where removed.

27 Start the vehicle and check for oil leaks.

8.24 Oil pressure switch

Engine electronic control unit (ECU)

Removal

28 The engine control unit is located on top of the engine above the exhaust gas recirculation valve.

29 Disconnect the battery negative lead (refer to *Disconnecting the battery* in the Reference Chapter).

30 Disconnect the wiring plugs from the ECU. The two main plugs are unlocked by lifting up the metal levers, and this is best achieved using two screwdrivers **(see illustrations)**.

31 Unbolt and remove the wiring harness bracket from the top of the ECU.

32 Unscrew the mounting bolts and nuts, and remove the ECU from the mounting bracket.

33 Release the glow plug wiring, then unscrew the two mounting bolts and single nut, and remove the ECU mounting bracket.

8.30a Using two screwdrivers to lift the metal lock levers . . .

8.30b . . . in order to disconnect the main plugs from the engine ECU

8.30c Disconnecting the central wiring

8.38 Wiring plug on the injection electronic control unit

8.39 Unscrew the injection ECU retaining bolts

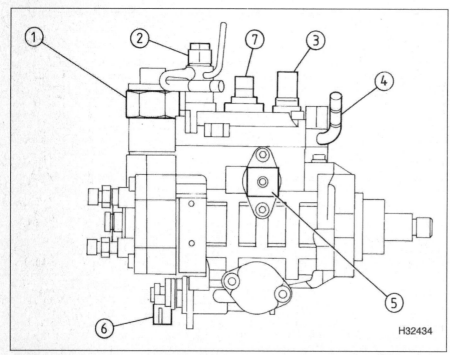

8.41 Fuel injection pump

1 Spill valve
2 Fuel return line
3 Fuel temperature sensor
4 Fuel supply line
5 Programmable read-only memory
6 Timing control solenoid
7 Injection pump shaft position sensor

Refitting

34 Refitting is a reversal of removal. Tighten the ECU retaining bolts/nuts to the specified

8.43 Screw the fuel temperature sensor into the injection pump

torque. The ECU wiring plugs are shaped such that each plug will only fit its correct socket. The plug from the left-hand side of the engine compartment connects to the rearmost socket. Take great care when refitting the plugs, as the terminals are very delicate and easily damaged. Finally, it may be necessary to have a Vauxhall dealer program all volatile memories.

Injection electronic control unit (ECU)

Removal

35 The injection ECU is located on the rear of the engine, beneath the injection pump. Access is best from beneath the vehicle.
36 Disconnect the battery negative lead (refer to *Disconnecting the battery* in the Reference Chapter).

37 Apply the handbrake, then jack up the front of the vehicle and support it on axle stands (see *Jacking and vehicle support*). Remove the engine undertray.
38 Working under the vehicle, disconnect the ECU wiring plug **(see illustration)**.
39 Undo the retaining bolts, and remove the ECU **(see illustration)**.

Refitting

40 Refitting is a reversal of removal, but tighten the bolts to the specified torque. Finally, it may be necessary to have a Vauxhall dealer program all volatile memories.

Fuel temperature sensor

Removal

41 The fuel temperature sensor is fitted to the right-hand top of the injection pump **(see illustration)**.
42 To remove the sensor, disconnect the wiring plug and unscrew the sensor from the top of the injection pump.

Refitting

43 With a new seal fitted, screw the sensor into the injection pump and tighten the nut securely **(see illustration)**.
44 Reconnect the wiring plug.

Injection pump shaft position sensor

45 The sensor is located on the side of the fuel injection pump.
46 The sensor may not be available as a separate item. Check with a Vauxhall dealer prior to any attempt to remove the sensor.

Injection commencement sensor

47 The sensor is located on the underside of the fuel injection pump at the flywheel end.
48 The sensor may not be available as a separate item. Check with a Vauxhall dealer prior to any attempt to remove the sensor.

Fuel cut-off solenoid

49 The fuel cut-off solenoid is located on top of the fuel injection pump, at the flywheel end.
50 The solenoid may not be available as a separate item. Check with a Vauxhall dealer prior to any attempt to remove the sensor.

---

9 Fuel injection pump – removal and refitting

Caution: Be careful not to allow dirt into the injection pump or injector pipes during this procedure.

Removal

1 Disconnect the battery negative lead (refer to *Disconnecting the battery* in the Reference Chapter).
2 Apply the handbrake, then jack up the front of the vehicle and support it on axle stands (see *Jacking and vehicle support*). Remove the right-hand front roadwheel and the inner

wheel arch liner for access to the crankshaft pulley. Remove the engine compartment undertray.

3 Remove the timing belt and injection pump sprocket as described in Chapter 2C.

4 Disconnect the wiring plugs from the engine electronic control unit (ECU) located on the top of the engine. The two main plugs are unlocked by lifting up the metal levers.

5 Disconnect the crankcase ventilation hose from the camshaft cover then unscrew the mounting bolts and disconnect the air intake pipe from the turbocharger. Also disconnect the clips and remove the centre charge air hose.

6 Remove the engine electronic control unit (ECU) and mounting bracket as described in Section 8.

7 Unscrew the nuts and remove the starter/ alternator wiring harness bracket from the EGR valve.

8 Unscrew the studs and bolts and remove the centre charge air metal pipe.

9 Disconnect the wiring from the glow plugs.

10 Remove the EGR valve and EGR solenoid valve as described in Part D of this Chapter.

11 Unbolt and remove the right-hand engine lifting eye.

12 Remove the charge pressure sensor as described in Section 8.

13 Place a suitable container beneath the oil filter housing, then unscrew the cover and remove the filter element.

14 Release the clip and disconnect the oil return line from the oil filter housing.

15 Remove the protective insulator (where fitted), then unscrew the bolts and remove the three clamps from the injector lines (see illustrations). Also, unscrew the union nuts and remove the lines from the injection pump and injectors.

16 Unscrew the union bolt and the mounting bolt securing the oil return line to the cylinder head, then release the clip and disconnect the oil return hose.

17 Disconnect the three wiring plugs from the injection pump (see illustration).

18 Progressively unscrew the mounting bolts and nuts, and remove the inlet manifolds from the cylinder head. Recover the gaskets.

19 Disconnect the fuel supply and return hoses from the injection pump.

20 Note its location, then carefully unscrew the fuel return check valve from the injection pump (see illustration). Do not unscrew the check valve from the banjo bolt. Tape over or plug the fuel return aperture to prevent entry of dust and dirt.

21 Unscrew the bolt and remove the injection pump outer insulation, then disconnect and unclip the engine management wiring, and carefully lever off the inner insulation. Note the routing of the various wiring looms.

22 Unbolt the mounting bracket from the left-hand end of the pump (see illustration).

23 Disconnect the PROM (Programmable Read-Only Memory) wiring harness plug, then unscrew the two retaining nuts, and manoeuvre the injection pump from the timing

9.15a Fuel injection pump protective insulator   **9.15b Injector line clamp**

9.17 Injection pump wiring plugs   **9.20 Fuel return check valve**

case. Recover the foam insulator from between the pump and cylinder block.

Caution: Never attempt to dismantle the pump assembly. If there is a problem, take the pump to a Vauxhall dealer/diesel injection specialist for testing/repair.

Refitting

24 To refit the pump, hold the correct piece of foam insulator against the cylinder block, engage the pump shaft with the corresponding hole in the timing case, and fit the two retaining nuts. Hand-tighten the nuts at this stage.

25 Refit the pump mounting bracket to the cylinder block, and tighten the bolts to the specified torque. Fit the bolts securing the bracket to the pump, then fully tighten the pump mounting nuts and bolts to the specified torque. Refit the foam insulation pieces around the pump (see illustration). Note: *Reconnect*

the wiring plug to the PROM on the side of the pump before fitting the rearmost foam insulation piece.

26 Reconnect the wiring and insulation, and tighten the bolt.

27 Refit the fuel return check valve and tighten the banjo bolt securely.

28 Reconnect the fuel supply and return hoses.

29 Refit the inlet manifolds together with new gaskets, and tighten the nuts and bolts to the specified torque.

30 Reconnect the pump wiring, then refit the oil return line and hose.

31 Reconnect the oil return line to the oil filter housing.

32 Insert a new oil filter element, then refit the cover and tighten.

33 Refit the charge pressure sensor with reference to Section 8.

34 Refit the engine lifting eye.

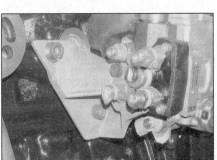

9.22 Fuel injection pump mounting bracket and bolts   **9.25 Refit the foam insulation pieces**

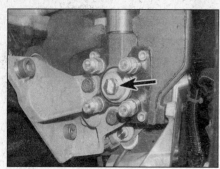

10.4 Remove the central bleed screw

35 Refer to Part D and refit the EGR solenoid valve and EGR valve.

36 Reconnect the wiring to the glow plugs.

37 Refit the timing belt and injection pump sprocket as described in Chapter 2C.

38 Carry out the injection timing checking and adjustment procedure described in Section 10.

39 Refit the injector lines and clamps.

40 Refit the centre charge air metal pipe, and starter/alternator wiring harness bracket.

41 Refit the engine electronic control unit (ECU) and mounting bracket with reference to Section 8.

42 Reconnect the centre charge air hose, turbocharger air intake pipe and crankcase ventilation hose.

43 Reconnect the wiring plugs to the ECU.

44 Refit the wheel arch liner and roadwheel, and lower the vehicle to the ground.

45 Reconnect the battery negative lead (refer to *Disconnecting the battery* in the Reference Chapter).

46 Finally, it may be necessary to have a Vauxhall dealer program all volatile memories.

10 Injection timing – checking and adjustment

Note: *Although on these models the injection timing is determined by the engine ECU, the basic injection timing has to be set when the pump is fitted. Actual checking of the injection system can only be carried out using specialist diagnostic equipment.*

10.5 Screw the adapter into the pump and mount the dial gauge

Caution: Be careful not to allow dirt into the injection pump or injector pipes during this procedure.

Caution: Some of the injection pump settings and access plugs may be sealed by the manufacturers at the factory, using paint or locking wire and lead seals. Do not disturb the seals if the vehicle is still within the warranty period, otherwise the warranty will be invalidated. Also do not attempt the timing procedure unless accurate instrumentation is available.

1 Remove the air cleaner housing and ducting (Section 2)

2 Undo the unions and remove the fuel injection delivery pipes. We found it necessary to remove the oil cooler housing retaining bolt (see Chapter 2C) and push the housing to the rear, to allow sufficient access to the rear of the pump. Be prepared for fluid spillage.

3 With reference to Chapter 2C, position the crankshaft at approximately 45° before TDC for No 1 piston.

4 Remove the central bleed screw from the centre of the four fuel delivery unions at the left-hand end of the injection pump **(see illustration)**. Recover the seal.

5 Screw the adapter into the rear of the pump and mount the dial gauge in the adapter **(see illustration)**. The special adapter and dial gauge (Vauxhall tool No KM-798) can be purchased from most good motor factors. Position the dial gauge so that its plunger is at the mid-point of its travel and securely tighten the adapter locknut.

6 Slowly rotate the crankshaft back-and-forth whilst observing the dial gauge, to determine when the injection pump plunger is at the bottom of its travel (BDC). When the pump plunger is correctly positioned, zero the dial gauge.

7 Rotate the crankshaft slowly in the correct direction until the crankshaft pulley TDC mark is correctly aligned with the pointer (No 1 cylinder at TDC on its compression stroke).

8 The reading obtained on the dial gauge should be equal to the specified pump timing measurement given in the Specifications at the start of this Chapter. If adjustment is necessary, slacken the pump front mounting nuts and rear mounting bolts and slowly rotate the pump body until the point is found where the specified reading is obtained. **Note:** *If necessary remove the upper timing belt cover for access to the nuts and bolts.* If the reading is too large turn the pump towards the engine, and if the reading is too small turn the pump away from the engine. When the pump is correctly positioned, tighten both its front and rear mounting nuts and bolts to the specified torque.

9 Rotate the crankshaft through one and three quarter rotations in the normal direction of rotation. Find the injection pump plunger BDC as described in paragraph 6 and zero the dial gauge.

10 Rotate the crankshaft slowly in the correct direction of rotation until the crankshaft pulley

mark is realigned with the pointer (bringing the No 1 cylinder piston back to TDC). Recheck the timing measurement.

11 If adjustment is necessary, slacken the pump mounting nuts and bolts and repeat the operations in paragraphs 8 to 10.

12 When the pump timing is correctly set unscrew the adapter and remove the dial gauge.

13 Inspect the seal and renew if necessary, then refit the central bleed screw and tighten it to the specified torque.

14 Refit the fuel injection pipes, tightening the unions to the specified torque, and refit the oil cooler housing and retaining bolt (if removed).

15 Where removed, refit the upper timing belt cover, then refit the air filter housing and ducting.

16 The fuel system should 'self-bleed' as the engine is cranked, although it may take longer than normal to restart. Check for fuel leaks from the disturbed pipes and unions.

11 Fuel injectors – removal and refitting

⚠️ *Warning: Exercise extreme caution when working on the fuel injectors. Never expose the hands or any part of the body to injector spray, as the high working pressure can cause the fuel to penetrate the skin, with possibly fatal results. You are strongly advised to have any work which involves testing the injectors under pressure carried out by a dealer or fuel injection specialist.*

Caution: Be careful not to allow dirt into the injection pump, injectors or pipes during this procedure.

Caution: Take care not to drop the injectors, or allow the needles at their tips to become damaged. The injectors are precision-made to fine limits, and must not be handled roughly. In particular, never mount them in a bench vice.

Removal

1 Remove the camshaft cover as described in Chapter 2C.

2 Drain the cooling system as described in Chapter 1B. **Note:** *This is recommended by the manufacturers as a precaution against coolant entering the combustion chambers when the fuel injectors are removed, as a result of the injector heat sleeves becoming displaced.*

3 Undo the five bolts and remove the inner fuel leak-back pipe. Recover the copper washers **(see illustrations)**.

4 Slacken and remove the retaining nuts, and remove the injector clamps **(see illustration)**.

5 Lift the injectors out of the cylinder head. Discard the rubber seals and copper washers; new seals/washers must be fitted prior to reassembly. Do not attempt to dismantle the injectors any further.

6 Testing of the injectors requires the use of special equipment. If any injector is thought to be faulty have it tested and, if necessary, reconditioned by a diesel engine specialist or Vauxhall dealer.

Refitting

7 Commence reassembly by ensuring that the injector and cylinder head mating faces are clean, and fitting new copper sealing washers and rubber seals to each injector. Note the correct orientation of the copper washers **(see illustration)**.
8 Carefully fit each injector into the cylinder head, and secure them in place by fitting the injector clamps. Tighten the clamp retaining nuts to the specified torque.
9 Refit the inner fuel leak-back pipe to the injectors and the camshaft housing. The larger diameter bolt secures the leak-back pipe to the camshaft housing. Note that new copper washers should be fitted to the top of each injector, and the underside of each bolt. Reconnect the pipe to the camshaft housing using new copper washers. Tighten the bolts to the specified torque.
10 Refit the camshaft cover as described in Chapter 2C.
11 Refill the cooling system as described in Chapter 1B.
12 Restart the engine and check for leaks.

12 Turbocharger – removal and refitting

Removal

1 Remove the exhaust manifold, together with the turbocharger assembly, as described in Section 15.
2 With the assembly on the bench, unbolt the turbocharger heat shield **(see illustration)**.
3 Undo the retaining nuts and remove the exhaust connection flange and gasket from the turbocharger **(see illustration)**.
4 Undo the union and remove the oil feed pipe along with the sealing washers which are fitted on each side of the pipe union **(see illustration)**.
5 Unscrew the retaining bolts and remove the

oil return pipe union and gasket **(see illustration)**.
6 Slacken and remove the four mounting nuts then remove the turbocharger and gasket from the manifold **(see illustration)**.

7 Unscrew the bolts securing the wastegate unit to the turbocharger. Release the clip and disconnect the control rod.
8 Do not attempt to dismantle the turbocharger any further. If the unit is thought

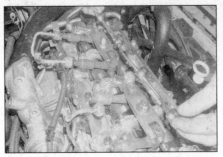
11.3a Copper washers fit either side of the fuel leak-back pipe unions on the injectors . . .

11.3b . . . and the union on the camshaft housing

11.4 The injector clamp washer fits dished with the side facing down

11.7 Note the rubber seal and copper washer

12.2 Turbocharger heat shield

12.3 Exhaust flange connection nuts

12.4 Turbocharger oil feed pipe union

12.5 Turbocharger oil return union

12.6 Undo the nuts and separate the turbocharger from the exhaust manifold

14.17a Remove the rear section of the manifold . . .

14.17b . . . and the front section

to be faulty take it to a turbo specialist or Vauxhall dealer for testing and examination. They will be able to inform you if the unit can be overhauled or will need renewing.

Refitting

9 Refitting is the reverse of removal, using new gaskets and sealing washers, and tightening the fasteners to their specified torque settings (where given). Refit the manifold and turbocharger assembly as described in Section 15.

13 Intercooler – removal and refitting

Note: The intercooler is only fitted to the Y17DT engine.

Removal

1 The intercooler is located in front of the lower part of the radiator.
2 Remove the front bumper with reference to Chapter 11.
3 Carefully unclip the air duct from the front of the radiator, and lift upwards from behind the front crossmember.
4 Loosen the clips and disconnect the two air hoses from the intercooler.
5 Release the retaining clamps and withdraw the intercooler from the front of the radiator.

Refitting

6 Refitting is a reversal of removal.

14 Inlet manifold – removal and refitting

Note: New manifold retaining nuts will be required on refitting
Note: The intercooler is only fitted to the Y17DT engine.

Removal

1 Disconnect the battery negative lead (refer to *Disconnecting the battery* in the Reference Chapter).
2 Remove the air cleaner assembly as described in Section 2.
3 Remove the engine electronic control unit (ECU) as described in Section 8.
4 Loosen the clip and disconnect the crankcase ventilation hose from the left-hand end of the camshaft cover. Unscrew the intercooler-to-turbocharger air pipe mounting bolts, then disconnect the pipe from the turbocharger and withdraw from the engine.
5 Unscrew the nuts and remove the starter/alternator wiring harness bracket from the EGR valve.
6 Loosen the clips and disconnect the charge air hose from the centre air pipe, then unbolt the centre air pipe from the inlet manifold.
7 Disconnect the wiring from the glow plugs.
8 Remove the EGR valve and gaskets with reference to Chapter 4D. To do this, unbolt the pipe then unscrew the studs and bolts, disconnect the vacuum hose and remove the valve. Recover the gaskets.

9 Disconnect the vacuum hose from the EGR solenoid valve, then disconnect the wiring and unbolt the solenoid valve.
10 Unbolt the rear engine lifting eye.
11 Disconnect the wiring then unbolt the clamp and remove the charge pressure sensor.
12 Place a suitable container beneath the oil filter housing, then unscrew the cover and remove the filter element.
13 Release the clip and disconnect the oil return line from the oil filter housing.
14 Unscrew the bolts and remove the three clamps from the injector lines, then unscrew the union nuts and remove the lines from the injection pump and injectors.
15 Unscrew the union bolt and the mounting bolt securing the oil return line to the cylinder head, then release the clip and disconnect the oil return hose.
16 Disconnect the three wiring plugs from the injection pump.
17 Progressively unscrew the mounting bolts and nuts, and remove the inlet manifold rear and front sections from the cylinder head **(see illustrations)**. Recover the gaskets.

Refitting

18 Clean the cylinder head and manifold(s) gasket faces, and fit a new gasket(s) in place.
19 The remainder of the refitting procedure is a reversal of removal, but tighten all nuts and bolts to the correct torque setting where specified. After reconnecting the battery, have a dealer reprogram the volatile memories.

15 Exhaust manifold – removal and refitting

Note: The intercooler is only fitted to the Y17DT engine.

Removal

1 The exhaust manifold is removed together with the turbocharger, then separated on the bench. First, apply the handbrake, then jack up the front of the vehicle and support it on axle stands (see *Jacking and vehicle support*). Remove the right-hand front roadwheel and the inner wheel arch liner for access to the crankshaft pulley. Remove the engine compartment undertray.
2 Disconnect the battery negative lead (refer to *Disconnecting the battery* in the Reference Chapter). Remove the air cleaner and ducting as described in Section 2.
3 Unscrew the upper and lower mounting bolts and remove the oil level dipstick tube from the sump. Note the wiring and hose supports on the tube **(see illustrations)**.
4 Remove the auxiliary drivebelt as described in Chapter 1B. Prior to removal, mark the direction of rotation on the belt to ensure the belt is refitted the same way around.
5 At the rear of the alternator, loosen the clips and remove the brake vacuum pump oil return hose from the pump and block.

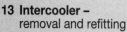
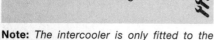

15.3a Engine oil level dipstick tube upper mounting bolt . . .

15.3b . . . and lower mounting bolts

15.6 Exhaust front pipe-to-turbocharger joint

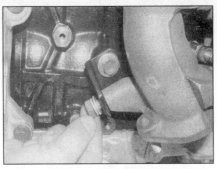

15.7 Unbolt the turbocharger from the cylinder block mounting bracket

15.8 Disconnect the oil return hose

6 Unbolt the exhaust front pipe from the turbocharger, taking care to support the flexible section **(see illustration)**. **Note:** *Angular movement in excess of 10° can cause permanent damage to the flexible section.* Release the mounting rubbers and support the front of the exhaust pipe to one side.

7 Unscrew and remove the turbocharger mounting bracket bolt **(see illustration)**.

8 Loosen the clips and remove the turbocharger oil return hose **(see illustration)**.

9 While counterholding the block adapter with one spanner, unscrew the domed nut from the oil feed line union on the block **(see illustration)**.

10 Disconnect the vacuum hose from the wastegate actuator on the turbocharger **(see illustration)**.

11 Loosen the clips securing the air intake pipe to the turbocharger and intercooler **(see illustration)**, then unscrew the mounting bolt and remove the air intake pipe.

12 On models equipped with air conditioning, disconnect the compressor wiring plug, undo the compressor mounting bolts, and move the compressor to one side. Secure the compressor with cable ties. Do not open the refrigerant hoses.

13 Undo the three bolts and remove the air conditioning compressor mounting bracket.

14 Unscrew the nuts securing the oil dipstick guide tube bracket to the camshaft cover, then unbolt the guide tube from the block, release the vacuum hoses and remove the bracket and guide tube **(see illustration)**.

15 Unscrew the bolt, loosen the clip and remove the centre charge air pipe.

16 Unbolt the heat shield from the exhaust manifold **(see illustration)**.

17 Disconnect the wiring from the engine electronic control unit.

18 Disconnect the crankcase ventilation hose from the camshaft cover then unscrew the

mounting bolts and disconnect the air intake pipe from the turbocharger. Also disconnect the clips and remove the centre charge air hose.

19 Unscrew the oil feed banjo bolt on the turbocharger and recover the seals.

20 The EGR (exhaust gas recirculation) pipe is mounted at the left-hand end of the manifold. Undo the two retaining bolts, and recover the gasket **(see illustration)**.

21 Undo the exhaust manifold retaining nuts/bolts, unscrew and remove the two manifold studs, and remove the exhaust manifold.

22 The manifold can now be separated from the turbocharger as described in Section 12.

Refitting

23 Refitting is the reverse of removal, but clean the mating surfaces and renew all gaskets/sealing washers. Tighten all nuts and bolts to their specified torques, where given.

15.9 Remove the oil feed pipe from the cylinder block

15.10 Wastegate actuator vacuum pipe

15.11 Turbocharger air intake pipe

15.14 Remove the oil dipstick guide tube mounting bolt from the block

15.16 Exhaust manifold heat shield

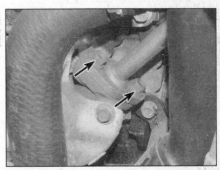

15.20 EGR pipe flange on the exhaust manifold

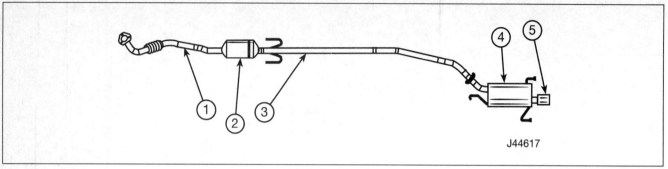

J44617

16.5 Exhaust system

1	Front exhaust pipe with flexible section	2	Catalytic converter	4	Rear silencer
		3	Intermediate exhaust pipe	5	Tail pipe

16 Exhaust system –
general information, removal and refitting

General information

1 The exhaust system is in two sections. The front section includes the catalytic converter, oxygen sensor and intermediate pipe. The rear section consists of the tailpipe and silencer.

2 Periodically, the exhaust system should be checked for signs of leaks or damage. Also inspect the system rubber mountings, and renew if necessary.

3 Small holes or cracks can be repaired using proprietary exhaust repair products.

4 Before renewing an individual section of the exhaust system, it is wise to inspect the remaining section. If corrosion or damage is evident, it may prove more economical to renew the entire system.

Component renewal

5 If either part of the system is to be renewed, it is important to ensure that the correct component is obtained **(see illustration)**.

6 To remove the rear tailpipe and silencer, chock the front wheels then jack up the rear of the vehicle and support on axle stands (see *Jacking and vehicle support*). Loosen the clamp securing the intermediate pipe to the tailpipe, then release the rubber mountings and slide the tailpipe from the intermediate pipe **(see illustrations)**. If the tailpipe is rusted onto the intermediate pipe, tap around the joint with a hammer to free it. Twist the tailpipe in both directions while holding the intermediate pipe.

7 To remove the front section of the exhaust, jack up the front and rear of the vehicle and support it on axle stands (see *Jacking and vehicle support*). Remove the tailpipe and silencer as described in paragraph 6, then unbolt the exhaust front pipe from the turbocharger, taking care to support the flexible section. **Note:** *Angular movement in excess of 10° can cause permanent damage to the flexible section.* Recover the gasket. Release the rubber mountings and withdraw the exhaust from under the vehicle **(see illustration)**.

8 Refitting is a reversal of removal, but renew all gaskets and tighten the clamp and front pipe flange nuts to the specified torque, where given.

16.6a Tailpipe-to-intermediate pipe exhaust clamp

16.6b One of the tailpipe rubber mountings

16.7 Exhaust front section rubber mountings

Chapter 4 Part D:
Emissions control systems

Contents

Degrees of difficulty

Easy, suitable for novice with little experience	Fairly easy, suitable for beginner with some experience	Fairly difficult, suitable for competent DIY mechanic	Difficult, suitable for experienced DIY mechanic	Very difficult, suitable for expert DIY or professional

Specifications

Torque wrench settings	Nm	lbf ft
EGR pipe-to-exhaust manifold (1.7 litre diesel)	28	21
EGR pipe-to-valve union nut (1.7 litre diesel)	44	33
EGR valve-to-inlet manifold:		
1.4 litre petrol	20	15
1.7 litre diesel	25	18

1 General information and precautions

1 All petrol engine models use unleaded petrol and also have various other features built into the fuel/exhaust system to help minimise harmful emissions. All models are equipped with a crankcase emission control system, a catalytic converter, an exhaust gas recirculation (EGR) system and an evaporative emission control system to keep fuel vapour/exhaust gas emissions down to a minimum.

2 All diesel engine models are also designed to meet strict emission requirements. All models are fitted with a crankcase emission control system and a catalytic converter to keep exhaust emissions down to a minimum. All models are also fitted with an exhaust gas recirculation (EGR) system to further decrease exhaust emissions.

3 The emission control systems function as follows.

Petrol models

Crankcase emissions control

4 To reduce the emission of unburned hydrocarbons from the crankcase into the atmosphere, the engine is sealed and the blow-by gases and oil vapour are drawn from the camshaft cover into the inlet manifold to be burned by the engine during normal combustion.

5 The gases are forced out of the crankcase by the relatively higher crankcase pressure; if the engine is worn, the raised crankcase pressure (due to increased blow-by) will cause some of the flow to return under all manifold conditions.

Exhaust emission control

6 To minimise the amount of pollutants which escape into the atmosphere, all models are fitted with a catalytic converter which is integral with the exhaust manifold. The system is of the closed-loop type, in which oxygen sensors in the exhaust system provide the fuel injection/ignition system ECU with constant feedback, enabling the ECU to adjust the mixture to provide the best possible conditions for the converter to operate.

7 On all engines covered by this manual, there are two heated oxygen sensors fitted to the exhaust system. The sensor on the top of the exhaust manifold/catalytic converter determines the residual oxygen content of the exhaust gases for mixture correction. The sensor in the exhaust front pipe (after the catalytic converter) monitors the function of the catalytic converter to give the driver a warning signal if there is a fault.

8 The oxygen sensor's tip is sensitive to oxygen and sends the ECU a varying voltage depending on the amount of oxygen in the exhaust gases; if the intake air/fuel mixture is too rich, the exhaust gases are low in oxygen so the sensor sends a low-voltage signal, the voltage rising as the mixture weakens and the amount of oxygen rises in the exhaust gases. Peak conversion efficiency of all major pollutants occurs if the intake air/fuel mixture is maintained at the chemically-correct ratio for the complete combustion of petrol of 14.7 parts (by weight) of air to 1 part of fuel (the 'stoichiometric' ratio). The sensor output voltage alters in a large step at this point, the ECU using the signal change as a reference point and correcting the intake air/fuel mixture accordingly by altering the fuel injector pulse width.

Fuel evaporation emission control

9 To minimise the escape into the atmosphere of unburned hydrocarbons, a fuel evaporation emission control system is fitted. The fuel tank filler cap is sealed and a charcoal canister is mounted behind the right-hand front wing. The canister collects the petrol vapours generated in the tank when the car is parked and stores them until they can be cleared from the canister (under the control of the fuel injection/ignition system ECU) via the purge valve into the inlet manifold to be burned by the engine during normal combustion.

10 To ensure that the engine runs correctly when it is cold and/or idling and to protect the catalytic converter from the effects of an over-rich mixture, the purge control valve is not opened by the ECU until the engine has warmed-up, and the engine is under load; the valve solenoid is then modulated on and off to allow the stored vapour to pass into the inlet manifold.

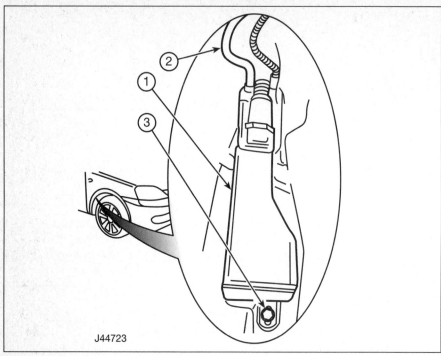

J44723

2.5 Charcoal canister location

1   *Charcoal canister*   2   *Purge hose*   3   *Mounting bolt*

Exhaust gas recirculation system

11 This system is designed to recirculate small quantities of exhaust gas into the inlet manifold, and therefore into the combustion process. This reduces the level of unburnt hydrocarbons present in the exhaust gas before it reaches the catalytic converter. On 1.0, 1.4 and early 1.2 litre engines, the system is controlled by the fuel injection/ignition ECU, using the information from its various sensors, via the electrically-operated EGR solenoid valve mounted on a housing bolted to the left-hand end of the cylinder head. Later 1.2 litre engines are not fitted with the EGR valve, although the EGR housing *is* fitted. On all engines, a metal pipe from the EGR housing links the exhaust ports in the cylinder head to the inlet manifold on the rear of the head.

Diesel models

Crankcase emission control

12 Refer to paragraphs 4 and 5.

Exhaust emission control

13 To minimise the level of exhaust pollutants released into the atmosphere, a catalytic converter is fitted in the exhaust system.
14 The catalytic converter consists of a canister containing a fine mesh impregnated with a catalyst material, over which the hot exhaust gases pass. The catalyst speeds up the oxidation of harmful carbon monoxide, unburned hydrocarbons and soot, effectively reducing the quantity of harmful products released into the atmosphere via the exhaust gases.

Exhaust gas recirculation system

15 This system is designed to recirculate small quantities of exhaust gas into the inlet manifold, and therefore into the combustion process. This reduces the level of unburnt hydrocarbons present in the exhaust gas before it reaches the catalytic converter. The system is controlled by the injection system ECU, using the information from its various sensors, via the electrically-operated EGR solenoid valve on the upper section of the inlet manifold. The EGR valve is vacuum-operated and is switched on and off by an electrical solenoid valve.

---

2   Petrol engine emission control systems – testing and component renewal

Crankcase emission control

1 The components of this system require no attention other than to check that the hose(s) are clear and undamaged at regular intervals.

Evaporative emission control

Testing

2 If the system is thought to be faulty, disconnect the hoses from the charcoal canister and purge control valve and check that they are clear by blowing through them. Full testing of the system can only be carried out using specialist electronic equipment which is connected to the engine management system diagnostic wiring connector (see

2.10 Purge valve for the evaporative emission system

Chapter 4A or 4B). If the purge control valve or charcoal canister are thought to be faulty, they must be renewed.

Charcoal canister renewal

3 At the right-hand rear corner of the engine compartment, disconnect the quick-release connector connecting the charcoal canister to the inlet manifold. A Vauxhall special tool is available to release the connectors, but provided care is taken, the connectors can be released using a pair of long-nosed pliers, or a similar tool, to depress the retaining tangs.
4 Apply the handbrake, then jack up the front of the vehicle and support it on axle stands (see *Jacking and vehicle support*). Remove the right-hand front roadwheel.
5 Remove the wheel arch liner for access to the charcoal canister which is located on the inner wing **(see illustration)**.
6 Unbolt the charcoal canister from the mounting bracket, then disconnect the purge valve hose from the top outlet.
7 Withdraw the canister, together with the ventilation inlet hose from the inner wing.
8 Where necessary, transfer the ventilation hose to the new charcoal canister. Refitting is a reversal of the removal procedure. Make sure the hoses are correctly and securely reconnected.

Purge valve renewal

9 The purge valve is mounted on the rear of the air cleaner cover.
10 Disconnect the wiring from the purge valve **(see illustration)**.
11 Release the purge valve from the air cleaner cover **(see illustration)**.

2.11 Release the purge valve from the air cleaner cover

12 Disconnect the inlet manifold vacuum hose from the purge valve.
13 Disconnect the canister hose and withdraw the purge valve.
14 Note that, if a new valve is being fitted, it is supplied complete with purge and vacuum hoses, therefore it will be necessary to disconnect these from the canister and throttle body.
15 Refitting is a reversal of the removal procedure, ensuring the valve is fitted the correct way around and the hoses are securely connected. Check the hoses carefully for cracking and damage, and where evident, renew them. **Note:** *A cracked ventilation hose is potentially a fire hazard.*

Exhaust emission control

Testing

16 The performance of the catalytic converter can be checked only by measuring the exhaust gases using a good-quality, carefully-calibrated exhaust gas analyser.
17 If the CO level at the tailpipe is too high, the vehicle should be taken to a Vauxhall dealer so that the complete fuel injection and ignition systems, including the oxygen sensor, can be thoroughly checked using the special diagnostic equipment. Once these have been checked and are known to be free from faults, the fault must be in the catalytic converter, which must be renewed.

Catalytic converter renewal

18 The catalytic converter is welded to the exhaust manifold, and the removal and refitting procedure is described in Chapter 4A or 4B.

Oxygen sensor renewal

19 Removal and refitting of both oxygen sensors is described in Chapter 4A or 4B.

Exhaust gas recirculation system

Testing

20 Comprehensive testing of the system can only be carried out using specialist electronic equipment which is connected to the engine management system diagnostic wiring connector (see Chapter 4A or 4B). If the EGR valve is thought to be faulty, it must be renewed.

EGR valve renewal (1.0 and 1.2 litre)

21 The exhaust gas recirculation valve is bolted to the left-hand end of the cylinder head **(see illustration)**. First drain the cooling system as described in Chapter 1A.
22 Where an electrically-operated EGR valve is fitted (not later 1.2 litre models), disconnect the wiring **(see illustration)**.
23 Disconnect the wiring from the ignition module, then unclip the wiring harness and position it to one side.
24 Release the clip and disconnect the coolant hose from the EGR valve **(see illustration)**.
25 Unscrew the bolts securing the EGR pipe

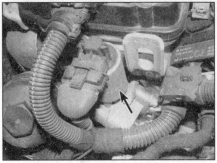

2.21 Exhaust gas recirculation (EGR) valve

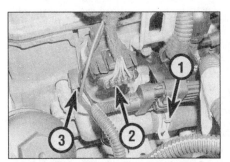

2.24 EGR valve coolant hose (1), wiring plug (2) and coolant temperature sensor wiring connector (3) – 1.0 and 1.2 litre petrol models

to the EGR valve **(see illustration)**. Recover the gasket and seal.
26 Unbolt the EGR valve/housing from the cylinder block and recover the gasket **(see illustrations)**.
27 Refitting is a reversal of removal, but clean the mating surfaces, fit new gaskets, and tighten all bolts securely. Refill the cooling system with reference to Chapter 1A.

EGR valve renewal (1.4 litre)

28 The exhaust gas recirculation valve is located on top of the inlet manifold. First, remove the engine top cover.
29 Disconnect the wiring from the EGR valve. Unclip the wiring harness and position it to one side.
30 Unscrew the mounting bolts and remove the EGR valve from the inlet manifold. Recover the gasket.

2.26a EGR valve housing securing bolts (arrowed) – 1.0 and 1.2 litre petrol models

2.22 Disconnecting the wiring from the EGR valve

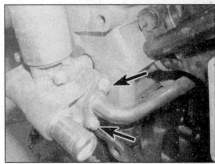

2.25 EGR pipe-to-EGR valve housing securing bolts (arrowed) – 1.0 and 1.2 litre petrol models

31 Refitting is a reversal of removal, but clean the mating surfaces, fit a new gasket, and tighten the bolts to the specified torque.

3 Diesel engine emission control systems – testing and component renewal

Crankcase emission control

1 The components of this system require no attention other than to check that the hose(s) are clear and undamaged at regular intervals.

Exhaust emission control

Testing

2 The performance of the catalytic converter

2.26b EGR housing – later 1.2 litre petrol models

3.16 Undo the large EGR valve union nut – 1.7 litre diesel models

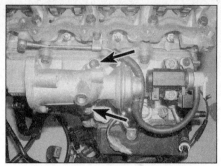

3.21 EGR valve retaining bolts (arrowed) – 1.7 litre diesel models

can be checked only by measuring the exhaust gases using a good-quality, carefully-calibrated exhaust gas analyser.

3 If the catalytic converter is thought to be faulty, first check the problem is not due to faulty injectors.

Catalytic converter renewal

4 The catalytic converter is an integral part of the exhaust system front pipe. Refer to Chapter 4C for removal and refitting details.

Exhaust gas recirculation system

Testing

5 Comprehensive testing of the system can only be carried out using specialist electronic equipment which is connected to the injection system diagnostic wiring connector (see Chapter 4C). If the EGR valve or solenoid valve are thought to be faulty, they must be renewed.

EGR valve renewal

6 The exhaust gas recirculation valve is bolted to the top of the inlet manifold, at the rear of the engine.

7 At the rear of the cylinder head, disconnect the middle and rear wiring connectors from the engine control unit (ECU).

8 Release the wiring harnesses from the air intake pipe at the left-hand rear of the engine, then unscrew the intake pipe mounting bolts.

9 Release the clamps and disconnect the crankcase ventilation hose from the intake pipe and camshaft cover.

10 Release the clamps and disconnect the

intake pipe from the mass airflow meter and turbocharger, then withdraw the intake pipe complete from the engine.

11 Unscrew the nuts, and position the alternator wiring bracket to one side.

12 Unbolt the support clamp and unscrew the mounting nut and bolt, then remove the charge air pipe.

13 Depressurise the cooling system by carefully removing then retightening the expansion tank filler cap.

14 Loosen the clip securing the coolant hose to the thermostat housing, then carefully push the hose back by approximately 1.0 cm. **Do not** disconnect the hose, or coolant will be lost.

15 Remove the EGR pipe support bracket from the camshaft housing.

16 Unscrew the bolts securing the EGR pipe to the exhaust manifold, then unscrew the union nut and remove the EGR pipe from the EGR valve **(see illustration)**. Recover the gasket.

17 Disconnect the three wiring plugs from the engine control unit (ECU) located over the inlet manifold at the rear of the engine. The two main plugs are unlocked by lifting up the metal levers.

18 Unbolt and remove the wiring harness bracket from the top of the ECU.

19 Unscrew the mounting bolts and nuts, and remove the ECU from the mounting bracket.

20 Release the glow plug wiring, then unscrew the two mounting bolts and single nut, and remove the ECU mounting bracket.

21 Disconnect the vacuum hose, then unbolt the EGR valve from the inlet manifold **(see illustration)**. Recover the gasket.

22 If the EGR valve is faulty, it must be renewed.

23 Refitting is a reversal of removal, but clean the mating surfaces, use new gaskets and tighten all nuts and bolts to the specified torque, where given.

EGR solenoid valve renewal

24 At the rear of the engine, loosen the clips and remove the convoluted hose leading from the mass airflow meter to the metal air pipe.

25 Disconnect the wiring, then note the locations of the vacuum hoses and disconnect them from the EGR solenoid valve **(see illustration)**.

26 Unscrew the mounting bolts and remove the EGR solenoid valve from the inlet manifold **(see illustration)**.

27 Refitting is a reversal of removal.

---

4   Catalytic converter – general information and precautions

The catalytic converter is a reliable and simple device which needs no maintenance in itself, but there are some facts of which an owner should be aware if the converter is to function properly for its full service life.

Petrol models

a) DO NOT use leaded petrol or LRP – the lead will coat the precious metals and reduce their efficiency, and will eventually destroy the converter.

b) Always keep the ignition and fuel systems well-maintained in accordance with the manufacturer's schedule.

c) If the engine develops a misfire, do not drive the car at all (or at least as little as possible) until the fault is cured.

d) DO NOT push- or tow-start the car.

e) Remember that the catalytic converter is FRAGILE – do not strike it with tools during servicing work.

f) The catalytic converter, used on a well-maintained and well-driven car, should last for between 50 000 and 100 000 miles – if the converter is no longer effective it must be renewed.

Diesel models

a) Always keep the fuel system well-maintained in accordance with the manufacturer's schedule.

b) If the engine develops a misfire, do not drive the car at all (or at least as little as possible) until the fault is cured.

c) DO NOT push- or tow-start the car.

d) Remember that the catalytic converter is FRAGILE – do not strike it with tools during servicing work.

e) The catalytic converter, used on a well-maintained car, should last for between 50 000 and 100 000 miles – if the converter is no longer effective it must be renewed.

3.25 Vacuum hoses on the EGR solenoid valve

3.26 EGR solenoid valve retaining bolts (arrowed) – 1.7 litre diesel models

Chapter 5 Part A:
Starting and charging systems

Contents

Degrees of difficulty

Easy, suitable for novice with little experience	**Fairly easy,** suitable for beginner with some experience	**Fairly difficult,** suitable for competent DIY mechanic	**Difficult,** suitable for experienced DIY mechanic	**Very difficult,** suitable for expert DIY or professional

Specifications

General

Electrical system type	12 volt negative earth

Battery

Type	Lead-acid, 'maintenance-free' (sealed for life)
Battery capacity	36, 44, 55, 60, 66 or 70 Ah (depending on model)

Alternator

Type	Bosch or Delco-Remy
Maximum output:	
Bosch	55 or 70 amps (depending on model)
Delco-Remy	67 or 100 amps (depending on model)
Regulated voltage	13.7 to 14.7 volts (approximately)
Brush minimum length:	
Bosch	5.0 mm
Delco-Remy:	
67 amp	12.0 mm
100 amp	20.0 mm

Starter motor

Type	Pre-engaged, Delco-Remy or Valeo
Brush minimum length:	
Delco-Remy:	
Except code number 09 000 756	4.0 mm
Code number 09 000 756	8.5 mm
Valeo	13.0 mm

Torque wrench settings

	Nm	lbf ft
Alternator:		
1.0 and 1.2 litre petrol engines	35	26
1.4 litre petrol engine:		
Top shackle	20	15
Mounting bolt	35	26
1.7 litre diesel engine:		
M10 bolt	46	34
M8 bolt	19	14
Brake vacuum servo pump line	19	14
Brake vacuum servo pump banjo bolt	22	16

Torque wrench settings (continued)

	Nm	lbf ft
Auxiliary drivebelt tensioner:		
1.0 and 1.2 litre petrol engines:		
M8 bolt	20	15
M10 bolt	55	41
1.4 litre petrol engine	35	26
1.7 litre diesel engine	50	37
Oil pressure warning light switch	26	19
Starter motor:		
Petrol engines	25	18
Diesel engines	38	28

1 General information and precautions

General information

1 The engine electrical system consists mainly of the charging and starting systems. Because of their engine-related functions, these components are covered separately from the body electrical devices such as the lights, instruments, etc (which are covered in Chapter 12). On petrol engine models refer to Part B for information on the ignition system, and on diesel models refer to Part C for information on the pre-heating system.

2 The electrical system is of 12 volt negative earth type.

3 The battery is of 'maintenance-free' (sealed for life) type, and is charged by the alternator, which is belt-driven from the crankshaft.

4 The starter motor is of the pre-engaged type, incorporating an integral solenoid. On starting, the solenoid moves the drive pinion into engagement with the flywheel ring gear before the starter motor is energised. Once the engine has started, a one-way clutch prevents the motor armature being driven by the engine.

Precautions

5 Further details of the various systems are given in the relevant Sections of this Chapter. While some repair procedures are given, the usual course of action is to renew the component concerned. The owner whose interest extends beyond mere component renewal should obtain a copy of the *Automotive Electrical & Electronic Systems Manual*, available from the publishers of this manual.

6 It is necessary to take extra care when working on the electrical system, to avoid damage to semi-conductor devices (diodes and transistors), and to avoid the risk of personal injury. In addition to the precautions given in *Safety first!* at the beginning of this manual, observe the following when working on the system:

7 *Always remove rings, watches, etc, before working on the electrical system.* Even with the battery disconnected, capacitive discharge could occur if a component's live terminal is earthed through a metal object. This could cause a shock or nasty burn.

8 *Do not reverse the battery connections.* Components such as the alternator, electronic control units, or any other components having semi-conductor circuitry, could be irreparably damaged.

9 If the engine is being started using jump leads and a slave battery, connect the batteries *positive-to-positive* and *negative-to-negative* (see *Jump starting*). This also applies when connecting a battery charger.

10 Never disconnect the battery terminals, the alternator, any electrical wiring or any test instruments when the engine is running.

11 Do not allow the engine to turn the alternator when the alternator is not connected.

12 Never 'test' for alternator output by 'flashing' the output lead to earth.

13 Never use an ohmmeter of the type incorporating a hand-cranked generator for circuit or continuity testing.

14 Always ensure that the battery negative lead is disconnected when working on the electrical system.

15 Before using electric-arc welding equipment on the car, disconnect the battery, alternator and components such as the fuel injection/ignition electronic control units to protect them from the risk of damage.

16 The radio/cassette unit fitted as standard equipment by Vauxhall is equipped with a built-in security code to deter thieves. If the power source to the unit is cut, the anti-theft system will activate. Even if the power source is immediately reconnected, the radio/cassette unit will not function until the correct security code has been entered. Therefore, if you do not know the correct security code for the radio/cassette unit **do not** disconnect the battery negative terminal of the battery or remove the radio/cassette unit from the vehicle.

2 Electrical fault finding – general information

Refer to Chapter 12.

3 Battery – testing and charging

Testing

Traditional and low maintenance battery

1 If the vehicle covers a small annual mileage, it is worthwhile checking the specific gravity of the electrolyte every three months to determine the state of charge of the battery. Use a hydrometer to make the check and compare the results with the following table. Note that the specific gravity readings assume an electrolyte temperature of 15°C (60°F); for every 10°C (18°F) below 15°C (60°F) subtract 0.007. For every 10°C (18°F) above 15°C (60°F) add 0.007.

	Ambient temperature:	
	above 25°C (77°F)	below 25°C (77°F)
Fully-charged	1.210 to 1.230	1.270 to 1.290
70% charged	1.170 to 1.190	1.230 to 1.250
Discharged	1.050 to 1.070	1.110 to 1.130

2 If the battery condition is suspect, first check the specific gravity of electrolyte in each cell. A variation of 0.040 or more between any cells indicates loss of electrolyte or deterioration of the internal plates.

3 If the specific gravity variation is 0.040 or more, the battery should be renewed. If the cell variation is satisfactory but the battery is discharged, it should be charged as described later in this Section.

Maintenance-free battery

4 Where a 'sealed for life' maintenance-free battery is fitted, topping-up and testing of the electrolyte in each cell is not possible. The condition of the battery can therefore only be tested using a battery condition indicator or a voltmeter.

5 Later models are fitted with a maintenance-free battery with a built-in 'magic-eye' charge condition indicator. The indicator is located in the top of the battery casing, and indicates the condition of the battery from its colour **(see illustration)**. If the indicator shows green, then the battery is in a good state of charge. If the indicator turns darker, eventually to black, then the battery requires charging, as described later in this Section. If the indicator shows clear/yellow, then the electrolyte level in the battery is too low to allow further use, and the battery should be renewed. Do not attempt to charge, load or jump start a battery when the indicator shows clear/yellow.

All battery types

6 If testing the battery using a voltmeter, connect the voltmeter across the battery and compare the result with those given in the Specifications under 'charge condition'. The test is only accurate if the battery has not been subjected to any kind of charge for the previous six hours. If this is not the case, switch on the headlights for 30 seconds, then wait four to five minutes before testing the battery after switching off the headlights. All other electrical circuits must be switched off, so check that the doors and tailgate are fully shut when making the test.

7 If the voltage reading is less than 12.2 volts, then the battery is discharged, whilst a reading of 12.2 to 12.4 volts indicates a partially-discharged condition.

8 If the battery is to be charged, remove it from the vehicle (Section 4) and charge it as described later in this Section.

Charging

Note: *The following is intended as a guide only. Always refer to the manufacturer's recommendations (often printed on a label attached to the battery) before charging a battery.*

Traditional and low maintenance battery

9 Charge the battery at a rate of 3.5 to 4 amps and continue to charge the battery at this rate until no further rise in specific gravity is noted over a four hour period.

10 Alternatively, a trickle charger charging at the rate of 1.5 amps can safely be used overnight.

11 Specially rapid 'boost' charges which are claimed to restore the power of the battery in 1 to 2 hours are not recommended, as they can cause serious damage to the battery plates through overheating.

12 While charging the battery, note that the temperature of the electrolyte should never exceed 37.8°C (100°F).

Maintenance-free battery

13 This battery type takes considerably longer to fully recharge than the standard type, the time taken being dependent on the extent of discharge, but it will take anything up to three days.

14 A constant voltage type charger is required, to be set, when connected, to 13.9 to 14.9 volts with a charger current below 25 amps. Using this method, the battery should be usable within three hours, giving a voltage reading of 12.5 volts, but this is for a partially-

3.5 Battery condition indicator (arrowed)

discharged battery and, as mentioned, full charging can take considerably longer.

15 If the battery is to be charged from a fully-discharged state (condition reading less than 12.2 volts), have it recharged by your Vauxhall dealer or local automotive electrician, as the charge rate is higher and constant supervision during charging is necessary.

4 Battery – removal and refitting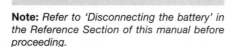

Note: *Refer to 'Disconnecting the battery' in the Reference Section of this manual before proceeding.*

Removal

1 On right-hand drive models, the battery is located on the left-hand side of the engine compartment bulkhead, beneath the windscreen cowl panel **(see illustration)**. On left-hand drive models, the battery is located on the right-hand side of the bulkhead.

2 Pull off the rubber seal from the firewall at the rear of the engine compartment.

3 Remove the water deflector from in front of the windscreen by first removing the windscreen wiper arms then undoing the retaining screws. Also disconnect the hose from the windscreen washer nozzle.

4 Disconnect the lead(s) at the negative (–) terminal by unscrewing the retaining nut and removing the terminal clamp. If necessary, the auxiliary lead may also be unbolted from the terminal **(see illustration)**.

4.1 Battery position on RHD models

5 Disconnect the lead(s) at the positive (+) terminal by unscrewing the retaining nut and removing the terminal clamp. If necessary, the auxiliary lead may also be unbolted from the terminal.

6 On the inner side of the battery, unscrew the bolt and remove the retaining clamp.

7 Carefully lift the battery from its location and remove from the car. Make sure the battery is kept upright at all times.

Refitting

Note: *As a precaution, before refitting the battery check that all doors are unlocked.*

8 Refitting is a reversal of removal, but smear petroleum jelly on the terminals after reconnecting the leads to reduce corrosion, and always reconnect the positive lead first, followed by the negative lead.

5 Charging system – testing

Note: *Refer to the precautions given in 'Safety first!' and in Section 1 of this Chapter before starting work.*

1 If the ignition no-charge warning light fails to illuminate when the ignition is switched on, first check the alternator wiring connections for security. If satisfactory, check that the warning light bulb has not blown, and that the bulbholder is secure in its location in the instrument panel. If the light still fails to illuminate, check the continuity of the warning light feed wire from the alternator to the bulbholder. If all is satisfactory, the alternator is at fault, and should be renewed, or taken to an auto-electrician for testing and repair.

2 If the ignition warning light illuminates when the engine is running, stop the engine and check that the drivebelt is correctly tensioned (see Chapter 1A or 1B) and that the alternator connections are secure. If all is so far satisfactory, have the alternator checked by an auto-electrician for testing and repair.

3 If the alternator output is suspect even though the warning light functions correctly, the regulated voltage may be checked as follows.

4 Connect a voltmeter across the battery terminals, and start the engine.

4.4 Auxiliary lead on the main positive battery lead

7.2 Auxiliary drivebelt upper and lower mounting bolts on 1.0 and 1.2 litre petrol engines

5 Increase the engine speed until the voltmeter reading remains steady; the reading should be approximately 12 to 13 volts, and no more than 14 volts.

6 Switch on as many electrical accessories (eg, the headlights, heated rear window and heater blower) as possible, and check that the alternator maintains the regulated voltage at around 13.5 to 14.5 volts.

7 If the regulated voltage is not as stated, the fault may be due to worn brushes, weak brush springs, a faulty voltage regulator, a faulty diode, a severed phase winding, or worn or damaged slip rings. The alternator should be renewed or taken to an auto-electrician for testing and repair.

6 Auxiliary drivebelt – removal and refitting

Refer to Chapter 1A or 1B.

7 Auxiliary drivebelt tensioner – removal and refitting

Removal

1 Remove the auxiliary drivebelt as described in Chapter 1A or 1B. On 1.0 litre petrol engines with air conditioning, it will be necessary to remove the locking bolt before removal of the tensioner.

2 On 1.0 and 1.2 litre petrol engine models, unscrew the upper and lower mounting bolts and withdraw the tensioner pulley and spring assembly **(see illustration)**. Note that the tensioner spring plunger has an internal hydraulic valve and must be stored with the arrow pointing upwards.

3 On 1.4 litre petrol and 1.7 litre diesel engine models, unscrew the pivot bolt and withdraw the tensioner pulley and spring housing **(see illustration)**.

Refitting

4 Before refitting the tensioner on 1.0 and 1.2 litre petrol engines, check that it has been stored upright. If a new unit is being fitted, or

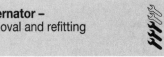

7.3 Auxiliary drivebelt tensioner on the 1.4 litre petrol engine

| 1 | Pivot bolt | 2 | Locking bolt |

if there is any doubt, it must be bled by mounting in a vice and operating it over five full strokes. Each stroke must be at constant load and speed to avoid damage to the unit.

5 Refitting is a reversal of removal, but tighten the mounting bolt(s) to the specified torque.

8 Alternator – removal and refitting

1.0 and 1.2 litre engines

Removal

1 The alternator is located on the rear of the cylinder block **(see illustration)**. First, apply the handbrake, then jack up the front of the vehicle and support it on axle stands (see *Jacking and vehicle support*). Remove the right-hand front roadwheel and the wheel arch liner cover for access to the right-hand side of the engine. Where necessary, remove the engine undertray.

2 Disconnect the battery negative lead (refer to *Disconnecting the battery* in the Reference Chapter).

8.1 Alternator on 1.0 and 1.2 litre petrol engines

3 With reference to Chapter 4A, remove the air cleaner housing.

4 Remove the auxiliary drivebelt tensioner as described in Section 7. Store it with the arrow pointing upwards.

5 Unscrew the nuts and disconnect the two wires from the rear of the alternator.

6 On 1.0 litre models, unscrew the nuts and remove the oxygen sensor wiring harness bracket. On 1.2 litre models, disconnect the plug and release the harness from the cable ties.

7 Unscrew the upper and lower mounting bolts/nuts and withdraw the alternator downwards from the block **(see illustration)**.

Refitting

8 Refitting is a reversal of removal, but tighten the mounting bolts to the specified torque. After reconnecting the battery leads, it may be necessary to have any volatile memories reprogrammed by a Vauxhall dealer.

1.4 litre engine

Removal

9 The alternator is located on the rear of the cylinder block. First, apply the handbrake, then jack up the front of the vehicle and support it on axle stands (see *Jacking and vehicle support*). Remove the right-hand front roadwheel and the wheel arch liner cover for access to the right-hand side of the engine.

10 Disconnect the battery negative lead (refer to *Disconnecting the battery* in the Reference Chapter).

11 With reference to Chapter 4B, remove the air cleaner housing.

12 Remove the auxiliary drivebelt as described in Chapter 1A.

13 Unbolt the inlet manifold support bracket, noting the location of the earth cable.

14 Disconnect the wiring from the oil pressure switch and unclip the harness.

15 Depressurise the fuel system with reference to Chapter 4B, then disconnect the fuel hose from the fuel rail. Tape over or plug the hose.

16 Disconnect the following engine management wiring, and release the support cable ties:

a) *Coolant temperature sensor.*
b) *Camshaft position sensor.*
c) *Throttle body module.*

8.7 Alternator upper and lower mounting bolts/nuts on 1.0 and 1.2 litre petrol engines

d) *Knock sensor.*
e) *Intake pipe pressure sensor.*
f) *Oxygen sensor.*
g) *EGR valve.*

17 Disconnect the hoses from the throttle body and the crankcase ventilation hose from the camshaft cover.
18 Remove the fuel rail, together with the injectors and wiring harness.
19 Unbolt the wiring harness bracket from the alternator.
20 Unscrew the three bolts and remove the alternator top mounting shackle **(see illustration)**. Swivel the alternator rearwards.
21 Unbolt the engine management wiring harness from above the alternator. Also unclip the brake vacuum hose.
22 Disconnect the evaporative carbon canister hose from the throttle body.
23 Unbolt and remove the inlet manifold from the cylinder head and recover the gasket.
24 Unscrew the nuts and disconnect the wiring from the rear of the alternator.
25 Unscrew the lower mounting bolt then lift the alternator from the rear of the engine **(see illustration)**.

Refitting

26 Refitting is a reversal of removal, but fit a new inlet manifold gasket and tighten all nuts and bolts to the specified torque, where given. After reconnecting the battery leads, it may be necessary to have any volatile memories reprogrammed by a Vauxhall dealer.

1.7 litre engine

Removal

27 The alternator is located on the front right-hand side of the cylinder block. First, apply

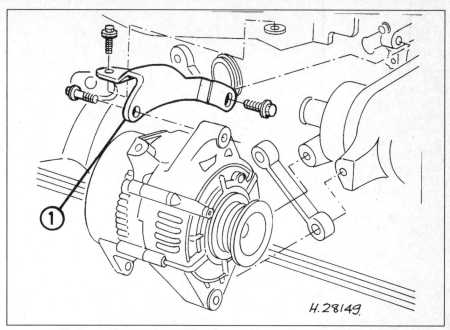

8.20 Upper alternator mounting shackle (1) on the 1.4 litre petrol engine

the handbrake, then jack up the front of the vehicle and support it on axle stands (see *Jacking and vehicle support*). Remove the right-hand front roadwheel and the wheel arch liner cover for access to the right-hand side of the engine.
28 Disconnect the battery negative lead (refer to *Disconnecting the battery* in the Reference Chapter).
29 With reference to Chapter 4C, remove the air cleaner housing.

30 On models with air conditioning, carry out the following procedures:
a) *Unclip the brake servo vacuum line from the 5 brackets and position to one side.*
b) *Loosen the clips and remove the charge air hose from the turbocharger and centre charge air pipe.*
c) *Unbolt and remove the centre charge air pipe.*
d) *Remove the front bumper as described in Chapter 11.*

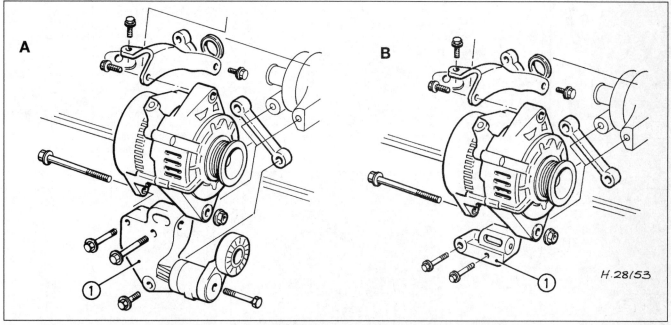

8.25 Alternator lower mounting bracket on the 1.4 litre petrol engine

A Models without air conditioning   *B Models with air conditioning*   *1 Alternator lower mounting bracket*

8.31 Vacuum hose connection on the brake vacuum pump

8.32a Disconnecting the battery cable . . .

8.32b . . . and wiring plug from the alternator

e) *Remove the auxiliary drivebelt with reference to Chapter 1B.*

f) *Loosen the clip then unbolt and remove the lower charge air pipe.*

g) *The condenser refrigerant pipe obstructs removal of the alternator. As an alternative to evacuating the air conditioning system, the engine may be lowered after removing the right-hand engine mounting, or alternatively, the condenser may be moved to one side (refer to Chapter 3).*

31 Detach the vacuum hoses from the brake vacuum pump located on the rear of the alternator **(see illustration)**.

32 Unscrew the nut and disconnect the battery cable from the alternator. Also disconnect the wiring plug **(see illustrations)**.

33 Position a container beneath the alternator, then unscrew the banjo bolt and detach the oil feed line from the vacuum pump. If necessary, the feed line may be unbolted from the cylinder block **(see illustrations)**.

34 Disconnect the vacuum pump oil return hose.

35 Unscrew the upper and lower mounting bolts **(see illustrations)**, then withdraw the alternator. Unscrew the nut and remove the brake vacuum servo vacuum line.

36 With the alternator on the bench, unbolt the vacuum pump and recover the seal **(see illustration)**.

Refitting

37 Refitting is a reversal of removal, but fit a new vacuum pump seal, and tighten all nuts and bolts to the specified torque, where given. After reconnecting the battery leads, it may be necessary to have any volatile memories reprogrammed by a Vauxhall dealer.

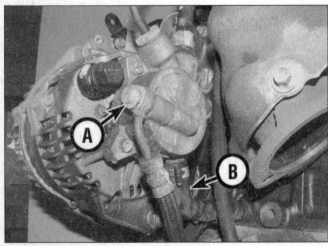

8.33a Vacuum pump oil feed pipe bolt (A) and return pipe (B) on diesel engines

8.33b Oil feed line on the cylinder block

8.35a Alternator upper mounting bolt . . .

8.35b . . . and lower mounting bolt on diesel engines

8.36 Inner view of the vacuum pump on diesel engines

9 Alternator brush holder/regulator – removal and refitting

Note: *The following procedure applies to alternators fitted to petrol engine models. Check with your Vauxhall dealer for availability on diesel models.*

Removal

1 The brush holder and voltage regulator are combined in a single assembly, which is bolted to the rear of the alternator. If the voltage regulator is faulty, the complete assembly must be renewed.

2 Remove the alternator as described in Section 8.

3 Undo the two nuts and single bolt, and remove the plastic cover from the rear of the alternator **(see illustration)**.

4 Unscrew the three bolts and remove the brush holder/voltage regulator assembly **(see illustration)**.

Refitting

5 Refitting is a reversal of removal.

10 Starting system – testing

Note: *Refer to the precautions given in 'Safety first!' and in Section 1 of this Chapter before starting work.*

1 If the starter motor fails to operate when the ignition key is turned to the appropriate position, the possible causes are as follows:

  a) *The battery is faulty.*
  b) *The electrical connections between the switch, solenoid, battery and starter motor are somewhere failing to pass the necessary current from the battery through the starter to earth.*
  c) *The solenoid is faulty.*
  d) *The starter motor is mechanically or electrically defective.*

2 To check the battery, switch on the headlights. If they dim after a few seconds, this indicates that the battery is discharged – recharge (see Section 3) or renew the battery. If the headlights glow brightly, operate the starter switch while watching the headlights. If they dim, then this indicates that current is reaching the starter motor, therefore the fault must lie in the starter motor. If the lights continue to glow brightly (and no clicking sound can be heard from the starter motor solenoid), this indicates that there is a fault in the circuit or solenoid – see the following paragraphs. If the starter motor turns slowly when operated, but the battery is in good condition, then this indicates either that the starter motor is faulty, or there is considerable resistance somewhere in the circuit.

3 If a fault in the circuit is suspected, disconnect the battery leads (including the earth connection to the body), the starter/solenoid wiring and the engine/transmission earth strap. Thoroughly clean the connections, and reconnect the leads and wiring. Use a voltmeter or test light to check that full battery voltage is available at the battery positive lead connection to the solenoid. Smear petroleum jelly around the battery terminals to prevent corrosion – corroded connections are among the most frequent causes of electrical system faults.

4 If the battery and all connections are in good condition, check the circuit by disconnecting the switched feed wire from the solenoid (the thinner wire). Connect a voltmeter or test light between the wire end and a good earth (such as the battery negative terminal), and check that the wire is live when the ignition switch is turned to the 'start' position. If it is, then the circuit is sound – if not, there is a fault in the ignition/starter switch or wiring.

5 The solenoid contacts can be checked by connecting a voltmeter or test light between the battery positive feed connection on the starter side of the solenoid and earth. When the ignition switch is turned to the 'start' position, there should be a reading or lighted bulb, as applicable. If there is no reading or lighted bulb, the solenoid is faulty and should be renewed.

6 If the circuit and solenoid are proved sound, the fault must lie in the starter motor. Begin checking the starter motor by removing it (see Section 11), and checking the brushes (see Section 12). If the fault does not lie in the brushes, the motor windings must be faulty. In this event, the starter motor must be renewed, unless an auto-electrical specialist can be found who will overhaul the unit at a cost significantly less than that of a new or exchange starter motor.

11 Starter motor – removal and refitting

1.0 and 1.2 litre engines

Removal

1 Apply the handbrake, then jack up the front of the vehicle and support it on axle stands (see *Jacking and vehicle support*).

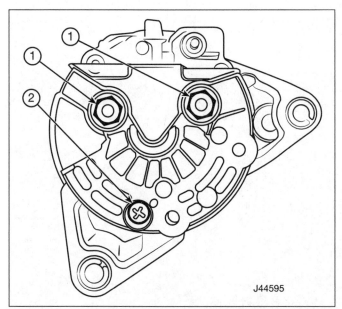

9.3 Two nuts (1) and single bolt (2) securing the plastic cover to the rear of the alternator

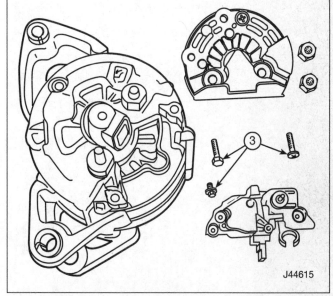

9.4 Mounting bolts (3) for the brush holder/voltage regulator assembly

11.3 Battery positive cable connection on the starter motor

11.14 Earth cable on the starter motor upper mounting bolt

2 Remove the alternator as described in Section 8.

3 Unscrew the two nuts and disconnect the battery positive cable and the starter trigger wire from the starter **(see illustration)**.

4 Unscrew the two mounting bolts and withdraw the starter motor from the rear of the engine.

Refitting

5 Refitting is a reversal of removal, but tighten the mounting bolts to the specified torque. After reconnecting the battery leads, it may be necessary to have any volatile memories reprogrammed by a Vauxhall dealer.

1.4 litre engine

Removal

6 Disconnect the battery negative lead (refer to *Disconnecting the battery* in the Reference Chapter).

7 Apply the handbrake, then jack up the front of the vehicle and support it on axle stands (see *Jacking and vehicle support*).

8 Unbolt the inlet manifold support bracket, noting the location of the earth cable.

9 Unscrew the two nuts and disconnect the battery positive cable and the starter trigger wire from the starter.

10 Unscrew the two mounting bolts and with-

draw the starter motor from the rear of the engine.

Refitting

11 Refitting is a reversal of removal, but tighten the mounting bolts to the specified torque. After reconnecting the battery leads, it may be necessary to have any volatile memories reprogrammed by a Vauxhall dealer.

1.7 litre engine

Removal

12 Disconnect the battery negative lead (refer to *Disconnecting the battery* in the Reference Chapter).

13 Apply the handbrake, then jack up the front of the vehicle and support it on axle stands (see *Jacking and vehicle support*).

14 At the rear left-hand end of the engine, unscrew the starter motor upper mounting bolt, noting that the engine earth cable is located beneath the head of the bolt **(see illustration)**.

15 Remove the gearchange bracket from the rear of the engine subframe. To do this, extract the circlip and release the gearchange link, then unbolt the bracket and remove from the splines.

16 Disconnect the wiring from the crankshaft pulse pick-up.

17 Disconnect the vacuum hose from the charge pressure control solenoid valve.

18 Place a container beneath the cylinder block, then release the clip and disconnect the oil return hose from the block.

19 Unscrew the two bolts and remove the atmospheric pressure sensor bracket.

20 Undo the screw and nut and disconnect the wiring from the starter motor **(see illustration)**.

21 Unscrew the lower mounting bolt and withdraw the starter motor from the engine **(see illustration)**.

Refitting

22 Refitting is a reversal of removal, but tighten the mounting bolts to the specified torque. After reconnecting the battery leads, it may be necessary to have any volatile memories reprogrammed by a Vauxhall dealer.

---

12 Starter motor – testing and overhaul

If the starter motor is thought to be suspect, it should be removed from the vehicle and taken to an auto-electrician for testing. Most auto-electricians will be able to supply and fit brushes at a reasonable cost. However, check on the cost of repairs before proceeding as it may prove more economical to obtain a new or exchange motor.

---

13 Ignition switch – removal and refitting

The switch is integral with the steering column lock, and removal and refitting is described in Chapter 10.

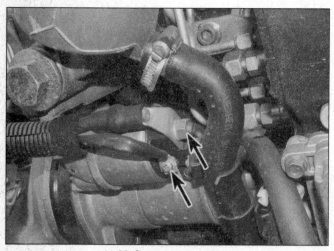

11.20 Starter motor wiring

11.21 Starter motor lower mounting bolt

14 Oil pressure warning light switch – removal and refitting

Removal

1 On 1.0 and 1.2 litre petrol engines, the oil pressure warning light switch is screwed into the front right-hand side of the cylinder head **(see illustration)**. On the 1.4 litre petrol engine, it is screwed in the end of the oil pump, on the inlet manifold side of the engine **(see illustration)**. On diesel engines it is screwed into the left-hand end of the cylinder block, just above the transmission bellhousing, below and slightly to the rear of the thermostat housing **(see illustration)**.

2 Pull back the cover and disconnect the wiring from the switch **(see illustration)**.

3 Place some cloth rags beneath the switch, then unscrew the switch from the block.

Refitting

4 Refitting is a reversal of removal, but tighten the switch to the specified torque.

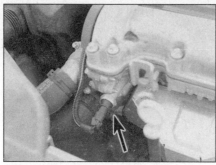

14.1a Oil pressure warning light switch location on 1.0 and 1.2 litre petrol engines

14.1b Oil pressure warning light switch location on the 1.4 litre petrol engine

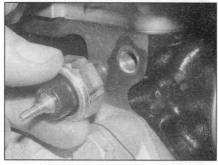

14.1c Oil pressure warning light switch location on the 1.7 litre diesel engine

14.2 Wiring to the oil pressure switch on the 1.7 litre diesel engine

Notes

Chapter 5 Part B:
Ignition system – petrol engines

Contents

Degrees of difficulty

Easy, suitable for novice with little experience	Fairly easy, suitable for beginner with some experience	Fairly difficult, suitable for competent DIY mechanic	Difficult, suitable for experienced DIY mechanic	Very difficult, suitable for expert DIY or professional

Specifications

General

System type	Distributorless ignition system (DIS)
System application:	
1.0 and 1.2 litre engines	Bosch Motronic M 1.5.5
1.4 litre engine	GM Multec-S(F)
Location of No 1 cylinder	Timing chain/timing belt end of engine
Firing order:	
All except 1.0 litre engines	1-3-4-2
1.0 litre engines	1-2-3

Torque wrench settings

	Nm	lbf ft
DIS module	8	6
Spark plugs	25	18

---

1 General information and precautions

Warning: Voltages produced by the electronic ignition system are very high, and extreme care must be taken when working on the system with the ignition switched on. Persons with surgically-implanted cardiac pacemaker devices should keep well clear of the ignition circuits, components and test equipment.

Ignition system function

1 The ignition system is integrated with the fuel injection system to form a combined engine management system under the control of one ECU (See Chapter 4A or 4B for further information). The ignition side of the system is of the distributorless type, and consists of the ignition module (mounted on top of the cylinder head) and the knock sensor (mounted on the rear of the cylinder block).

2 The ignition module consists of four ignition coils, one per cylinder, in one casing mounted directly above the spark plugs. This module eliminates the need for any HT leads as the coils locate directly onto the relevant spark plug. The ECU uses its inputs from the various sensors to calculate the required ignition advance setting.

3 The knock sensor is mounted onto the cylinder block and informs the ECU when the engine is 'pinking' under load. The sensor is sensitive to vibration and detects the knocking which occurs when the engine starts to 'pink' (pre-ignite). The knock sensor sends an electrical signal to the ECU which in turn retards the ignition advance setting until the 'pinking' ceases.

Motronic M 1.5.5 DIS

4 This system is fitted to models with 1.0 and 1.2 litre engines (see *Vehicle identification* for details of engine code locations).

5 The system is under the overall control of the Motronic electronic control unit, which controls both the ignition and fuel injection systems. The system comprises various sensors (whose inputs also provide data to control the fuel injection system), and the Motronic electronic control unit, in addition to the DIS module and spark plugs. Details of the system sensors and the electronic control unit are given in Chapter 4A.

6 The DIS module is located centrally on the camshaft cover directly over the spark plugs.

7 Information on crankshaft position, cylinder identification, and engine speed and load is supplied to the Motronic electronic control unit via inputs from the various system sensors (see Chapter 4A).

8 The electronic control unit selects the optimum ignition advance setting based on the information received from the various sensors, and fires the relevant ignition coil accordingly. The degree of advance can thus be constantly varied to suit the prevailing engine operating conditions.

Multec-S(F) DIS

9 This system is fitted to models with the 1.4 litre engine.

10 The system is under the overall control of the Multec electronic control unit, which controls both the ignition and fuel injection systems. The system comprises various sensors (whose inputs also provide data to control the fuel injection system), and the Multec electronic control unit, in addition to the DIS module and spark plugs. Details of the system sensors and the electronic control unit are given in Chapter 4B.

11 The DIS module is located centrally on the camshaft cover directly over the spark plugs.

12 Information on crankshaft position, and engine speed and load is supplied to the Multec electronic control unit via inputs from the various system sensors (see Chapter 4B).

3.2a Release the DIS module cover by sliding it towards the transmission . . .

3.2b . . . then remove it – 1.0 and 1.2 litre engines

3.3 Disconnecting the DIS module wiring plug – 1.0 and 1.2 litre engines

13 The electronic control unit selects the optimum ignition advance setting based on the information received from the various sensors, and fires the relevant ignition coil accordingly. The degree of advance can thus be constantly varied to suit the prevailing engine operating conditions.

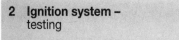

2 Ignition system – testing

1 If a fault appears in the engine management (fuel injection/ignition) system first ensure that the fault is not due to a poor electrical connection or poor maintenance; ie, check that the air cleaner filter element is clean, the spark plugs are in good condition and correctly gapped, that the engine breather hoses are clear and undamaged, referring to Chapter 1A for further information. If the engine is running very roughly, check the compression pressures as described in the relevant part of Chapter 2.
2 If these checks fail to reveal the cause of the problem, the vehicle should be taken to a suitably-equipped Vauxhall dealer for testing. A wiring block connector is incorporated in the engine management circuit into which a special electronic diagnostic tester can be plugged. The tester will locate the fault quickly and simply, alleviating the need to test all the system components individually, which is a time-consuming operation that carries a high risk of damaging the ECU.
3 The only ignition system checks which can

be carried out by the home mechanic are those described in Chapter 1A, relating to the spark plugs. If necessary, the system wiring and wiring connectors can be checked as described in Chapter 12, ensuring that the ECU wiring connector(s) have first been disconnected.

3 Ignition (DIS) module – testing, removal and refitting

Testing

1 Testing of the ignition module can only be carried out safely, and without the risk of damage to the module, using special test equipment. It should therefore be entrusted to a Vauxhall dealer or auto-electrician.

Removal

1.0 and 1.2 litre engines

2 The DIS module is mounted in the centre of the camshaft cover, directly above the spark plugs. First, remove the cover from the ignition module by sliding it towards the transmission **(see illustrations)**.
3 Disconnect the wiring plug from the end of the module **(see illustration)**.
4 Unscrew the two mounting bolts **(see illustration)**.
5 Vauxhall technicians use two special tools to lift the module from the spark plugs, however, as an alternative, two threaded rods may be screwed into the special holes. Pull on

the rods to release the module from the tops of the spark plugs **(see illustration)**. The module may also be removed by carefully easing it upwards using a screwdriver. Take care to keep the module level as it is released from the spark plugs to avoid damage to the module connectors and the upper ceramic part of the spark plugs.

1.4 litre engine

6 The DIS module is mounted in the centre of the camshaft cover, directly above the spark plugs. First, remove the engine top cover by unscrewing the oil filler cap and two mounting bolts. Refit the filler cap.
7 Disconnect the wiring plug from the end of the module.
8 Unscrew the four mounting bolts.
9 Vauxhall technicians use two special tools to lift the module from the spark plugs, however, as an alternative, two threaded rods may be screwed into the special holes. Pull on the rods to release the module from the tops of the spark plugs. The module may also be removed by carefully easing it upwards using a screwdriver. Take care to keep the module level as it is released from the spark plugs to avoid damage to the module connectors and the upper ceramic part of the spark plugs.

Refitting

10 Refitting is a reversal of removal, but tighten the mounting bolts to the specified torque.

4 Knock control system – general information

The knock control system forms part of the ignition system, and allows the ignition timing to be advanced to the point at which 'knocking' or pre-ignition is about to occur. This contributes to improved engine efficiency and reduced exhaust emission levels, as it allows the engine to run as close as possible to the 'knock limit' (the point at which pre-ignition or 'pinking' occurs) without the risk of engine damage. The ignition timing is set to a predetermined value (stored in the memory of the engine management electronic control unit), which is very close to the knock limit for the engine. Due

3.4 Undo the two retaining bolts . . .

3.5 . . . then screw two threaded rods into the DIS module and lift it upwards off the spark plugs – 1.0 and 1.2 litre engines

to slight changes in the combustion process during varying engine operating conditions, and possible slight fuel irregularities, engine knock may occur, and this is detected and controlled by the knock control system.

The system comprises a knock sensor and the Multec or Motronic engine management electronic control unit (see Chapter 4A or 4B). On all engines the knock module is an integral part of the engine management electronic control unit (ECU).

The knock sensor is located on the cylinder block, and contains a piezo-electric crystal, which has a resonance frequency which corresponds to the engine knock frequency. Mechanical vibrations in the cylinder block are converted by the sensor into an electrical signal. The output signal provided by the sensor increases with an increase in the vibrations in the cylinder block. If the signal increases beyond a preset limit, the sensor indicates the onset of 'knock' to the knock module.

The knock module acts as a signal processor, and modifies the signal produced by the sensor before providing an output to the ECU.

The ECU processes the signals received from the knock module, and retards the ignition timing to prevent knock. From the signals provided by other engine management sensors (see Chapter 4A or 4B), the ECU can determine the cylinder which fired most recently before the knocking occurred, and hence can trace the knocking to that particular cylinder. The ignition timing for the particular cylinder concerned is thus retarded ('selective knock control'), giving independent ignition timing control over all cylinders. Once knocking has been detected and prevented, the ignition timing is progressively advanced to the predetermined value, or until knocking recurs. The system processes signals many times per second, and is able to react to changes sufficiently quickly to prevent engine damage, with no perceptible effect on engine performance.

If the system develops a fault, the ignition timing is automatically retarded by a predetermined amount as a safety precaution, and this may be detected as a slight reduction in engine performance.

5 Knock sensor – removal and refitting

Refer to Chapter 4A or 4B as applicable.

6 Ignition timing – checking and adjustment

1 There are no timing marks on the flywheel or crankshaft pulley. The timing is constantly being monitored and adjusted by the engine management ECU, and nominal values cannot be given. Therefore, it is not possible for the home mechanic to check the ignition timing.

2 The only way in which the ignition timing can be checked and (where possible) adjusted is by using special electronic test equipment, connected to the engine management system diagnostic connector. Refer to your Vauxhall dealer for further information.

Chapter 5 Part C:
Pre/post-heating system

Contents

Degrees of difficulty

Easy, suitable for novice with little experience	**Fairly easy,** suitable for beginner with some experience	**Fairly difficult,** suitable for competent DIY mechanic	**Difficult,** suitable for experienced DIY mechanic	**Very difficult,** suitable for expert DIY or professional

Specifications

Glow plug

Type . . . . Vauxhall part number 97210818

Torque wrench setting	**Nm**	**lbf ft**
Glow plugs	20	15

---

1 Pre/post-heating system – description and testing

Description

1 Each cylinder of the engine is fitted with a heater plug (commonly called a glow plug) screwed into it. The plugs are electrically-operated before and during start-up when the engine is cold. Electrical feed to the glow plugs is controlled via the pre/post-heating system control unit.

2 A warning light in the instrument panel tells the driver that pre/post-heating is taking place. When the light goes out, the engine is ready to be started. The voltage supply to the glow plugs continues for several seconds after the light goes out. If no attempt is made to start, the timer then cuts off the supply, in order to avoid draining the battery and overheating the glow plugs.

3 The glow plugs also provide a 'post-heating' function, whereby the glow plugs remain switched on for a period after the engine has started. The length of time 'post-heating' takes place for is also determined by the control unit, and is anything up to 6 minutes, depending on engine temperature.

4 The fuel filter is fitted with a heating element to prevent the fuel 'waxing' in extreme cold temperature conditions and to improve combustion. The heating element is fitted between the filter and its housing and is controlled by the pre/post-heating system control unit via the temperature switch on the

filter housing. The heating element is switched on if the temperature of the fuel passing through the filter is less than 5°C (41°F) and switches off when the fuel temperature reaches 16°C (61°F).

Testing

5 If the system malfunctions, testing is ultimately by substitution of known good units, but some preliminary checks may be made as follows.

6 Connect a voltmeter or 12 volt test lamp between the glow plug supply cable and earth (engine or vehicle metal). Make sure that the live connection is kept clear of the engine and bodywork.

7 Have an assistant switch on the ignition, and check that voltage is applied to the glow plugs. Note the time for which the warning light is lit, and the total time for which voltage is applied before the system cuts out. Switch off the ignition.

8 At an underbonnet temperature of 20°C (68°F), typical times noted should be approximately 3 seconds for warning light operation. Warning light time will increase with lower temperatures and decrease with higher temperatures.

9 If there is no supply at all, the control unit or associated wiring is at fault.

10 To locate a defective glow plug, disconnect the wiring connector from each plug.

11 Use a continuity tester, or a 12 volt test lamp connected to the battery positive terminal, to check for continuity between each glow plug terminal and earth. The resistance

of a glow plug in good condition is very low (less than 1 ohm), so if the test lamp does not light or the continuity tester shows a high resistance, the glow plug is certainly defective.

12 If an ammeter is available, the current draw of each glow plug can be checked. After an initial surge of 15 to 20 amps, each plug should draw 12 amps. Any plug which draws much more or less than this is probably defective.

13 As a final check, the glow plugs can be removed and inspected as described in the following Section.

---

2 Glow plugs – removal, inspection and refitting

Caution: If the pre/post-heating system has just been energised, or if the engine has been running, the glow plugs will be very hot.

Removal

1 Disconnect the battery negative lead (refer to *Disconnecting the battery* in the Reference Chapter).

2 Remove the air cleaner assembly as described in Chapter 4C.

3 Remove the engine electronic control unit and mounting bracket as described in Chapter 4C, Section 8.

4 Disconnect the wiring from the glow plugs by squeezing the connectors with thumb and forefinger, and pulling them from the plugs.

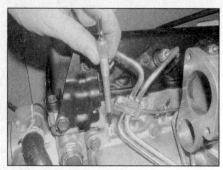

2.5 Removing the glow plugs from the cylinder head

5 Unscrew the glow plugs and remove them from the cylinder head **(see illustration)**.

Inspection

6 Inspect each glow plug for physical damage. Burnt or eroded glow plug tips can be caused by a bad injector spray pattern. Have the injectors checked if this type of damage is found.

7 If the glow plugs are in good physical condition, check them electrically using a 12 volt test lamp or continuity tester as described in the previous Section.

8 The glow plugs can be energised by applying 12 volts to them to verify that they heat up evenly and in the required time. Observe the following precautions.

  a) *Support the glow plug by clamping it carefully in a vice or self-locking pliers. Remember it will become red-hot.*

  b) *Make sure that the power supply or test lead incorporates a fuse or overload trip to protect against damage from a short-circuit.*

  c) *After testing, allow the glow plug to cool for several minutes before attempting to handle it.*

9 A glow plug in good condition will start to glow red at the tip after drawing current for 5 seconds or so. Any plug which takes much longer to start glowing, or which starts glowing in the middle instead of at the tip, is defective.

Refitting

10 Carefully refit the plugs and tighten to the specified torque. Do not overtighten, as this can damage the glow plug element.

11 Push the electrical connectors firmly onto the glow plugs.

12 Refit the electronic control unit and bracket with reference to Chapter 4C.

13 Refit the air cleaner assembly with reference to Chapter 4C.

14 Reconnect the battery negative lead (refer to *Disconnecting the battery* in the Reference Chapter). It may be necessary to have the engine management memory reprogrammed by a Vauxhall dealer after reconnecting the battery.

15 Check the operation of the glow plugs.

3 Pre/post-heating system components – removal and refitting

System control unit

Removal

1 The pre/post-heating system control unit is located on the left-hand side of the engine compartment where it is mounted beneath the fusebox on the inner wing panel.

2 Disconnect the battery negative lead (refer to *Disconnecting the battery* in the Reference Chapter).

3 Move the coolant expansion tank to one side, by releasing the retaining clip and unclipping the coolant hoses from their supports.

4 Disconnect the wiring harness from the bottom of the brake ABS control unit.

5 Unscrew the two outer mounting nuts securing the fusebox to the inner wing panel.

6 Unbolt the brake hydraulic modulator bracket from the inner wing. Also unclip the clutch pressure line.

7 Remove the cover from the fusebox, then release the tabs and unclip the relay/fuse carrier from the fusebox lower body.

8 Unclip the pre/post-heating system control unit wiring harness.

9 Detach the fusebox from the inner wing panel, then carefully push the fusebox/hydraulic modulator to one side.

10 Unclip the pre/post-heating control unit and disconnect the wiring harness plug. Withdraw the unit from the vehicle.

Refitting

11 Refitting is a reversal of removal. It may be necessary to have the engine management memory reprogrammed by a Vauxhall dealer after reconnecting the battery.

Coolant temperature switch

12 The coolant temperature switch is screwed into the thermostat housing. Refer to Chapter 3 for more details.

Fuel filter heater element

13 Prior to attempting any repair procedure, check spares availability with your Vauxhall dealer. Remove the fuel filter as described in Chapter 1B. If the filter is damaged on removal, a new one should be used on refitting.

14 Disconnect the wiring connector from the heating element.

15 Unscrew the centre bolt and remove the heating element from the filter housing. Recover the sealing ring and discard; a new one should be used on refitting.

16 Fit a new sealing ring in the heating element recess then refit the element to the filter housing and securely tighten the centre bolt.

17 Refit the fuel filter with reference to Chapter 1B.

Heater temperature switch

18 Prior to attempting any repair procedure, check spares availability with your Vauxhall dealer. Disconnect the wiring connector from the temperature switch which is screwed into the fuel filter housing.

19 Position a wad of rag beneath the filter housing to catch any spilt fuel then unscrew the switch and remove it from the housing. Plug the housing aperture to prevent the entry of dirt and minimise fuel loss. Remove the sealing ring from the switch and renew them.

20 Fit new sealing rings to the switch recesses then refit the switch to the filter housing and tighten securely. Reconnect the wiring connector to the switch.

Relays and fuses

21 The fuel heating element relays and fuses are located in the box in the engine compartment. Refer to Chapter 12 for further details.

Chapter 6
Clutch

Contents

Degrees of difficulty

Easy, suitable for novice with little experience	**Fairly easy,** suitable for beginner with some experience	**Fairly difficult,** suitable for competent DIY mechanic	**Difficult,** suitable for experienced DIY mechanic	**Very difficult,** suitable for expert DIY or professional

Specifications

Type . . . . Single dry plate with diaphragm spring, hydraulically-operated

Friction disc

Diameter:
  1.0 litre petrol engines . . . . 190 mm
  1.2 litre petrol engine:
    Standard transmission . . . . 190 mm
    Easytronic transmission . . . . 200 mm
  1.4 litre petrol engine . . . . 200 mm
  1.7 litre diesel engines . . . . 205 mm
New lining thickness . . . . 7.65 mm

Torque wrench settings

	Nm	lbf ft
Clutch master cylinder retaining nuts*	20	15
Pedal mounting bracket nuts*	20	15
Pressure plate retaining bolts*:		
M7 bolts	15	11
M8 bolts	28	21

*Use new self-locking bolts/nuts

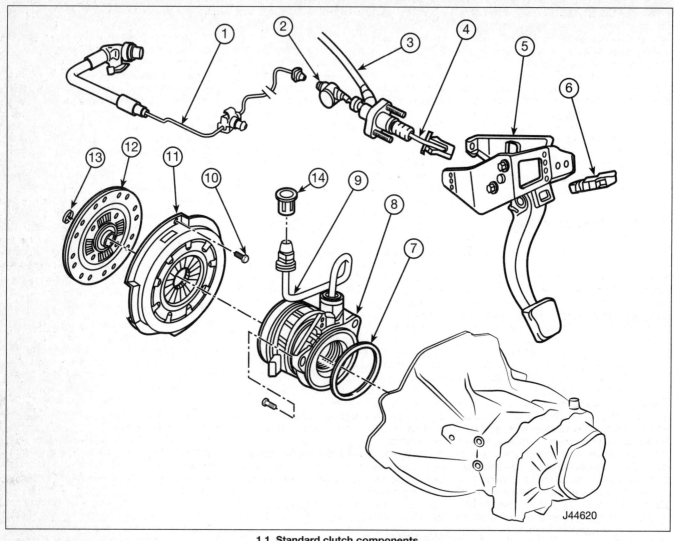

1.1 Standard clutch components

1 Pressure line	5 Clutch pedal assembly	8 Release cylinder	11 Pressure plate
2 Damper	6 Clutch pedal switch (where	9 Release cylinder pressure	12 Friction disc
3 Supply hose	fitted)	line	13 Assembly guide
4 Master cylinder	7 O-ring	10 Pressure plate bolt	14 Fastening sleeve

1 General information

Standard clutch

1 The clutch consists of a friction disc, a pressure plate assembly, and the hydraulic release cylinder (which incorporates the release bearing); all of these components are contained in the large cast-aluminium alloy bellhousing, sandwiched between the engine and the transmission **(see illustration)**.

2 The friction disc is fitted between the engine flywheel and the clutch pressure plate, and is allowed to slide on the transmission input shaft splines.

3 The pressure plate assembly is bolted to the engine flywheel. When the engine is

running, drive is transmitted from the crankshaft, via the flywheel, to the friction disc (these components being clamped securely together by the pressure plate assembly) and

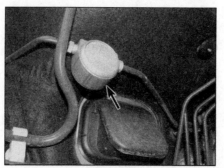

1.4 Clutch release hydraulic pipe and accumulator

from the friction disc to the transmission input shaft.

4 To interrupt the drive, the spring pressure must be relaxed. This is achieved using a hydraulic release mechanism which consists of the master cylinder, the release cylinder and the pipe/hose linking the two components **(see illustration)**. Depressing the pedal pushes on the master cylinder pushrod which hydraulically forces the release cylinder piston against the pressure plate spring fingers. This causes the springs to deform and releases the clamping force on the friction disc.

5 The clutch is self-adjusting and requires no manual adjustment.

Semi-automatic clutch (SAC)

6 Models equipped with the Easytronic MTA (Manual Transmission with Automatic shift), are fitted with a Semi Automatic Clutch (SAC). The clutch may be operated either fully automatically or semi-automatically by means of the gear selector lever. There is no conventional clutch pedal fitted.

7 The Easytronic system essentially consists of a conventional manual gearbox and clutch fitted with electrical and hydraulic controls, the clutch being operated by a clutch module attached to the side of the transmission casing. Refer to Chapter 7C for more information. The clutch component removal and refitting procedures are included in this Chapter as they are very similar to those for the standard manual transmission.

2 Clutch hydraulic system – bleeding

Note: *On models with the Easytronic semi-automatic clutch (SAC), the following manual method of bleeding the clutch is not possible since the hydraulic control unit is integral with the transmission. On these models, bleeding is carried out using the Vauxhall TECH2 diagnostic instrument, therefore this work should be entrusted to a Vauxhall dealer.*

⚠️ *Warning: Hydraulic fluid is poisonous; wash off immediately and thoroughly in the case of skin contact, and seek immediate medical advice if any fluid is swallowed or gets into the eyes. Certain types of hydraulic fluid are flammable, and may ignite when allowed into contact with hot components; when servicing any hydraulic system, it is safest to assume that the fluid is flammable, and to take precautions against the risk of fire as though it is petrol that is being handled. Hydraulic fluid is also an effective paint stripper, and will attack plastics; if any is spilt, it should be washed off immediately, using copious quantities of fresh water. Finally, it is hygroscopic (it absorbs moisture from the air) – old fluid may be contaminated and unfit for further use. When topping-up or renewing the fluid, always use the recommended type, and ensure that it comes from a freshly-opened sealed container.*

1 The correct operation of any hydraulic system is only possible after removing all air from the components and circuit; this is achieved by bleeding the system.

2 During the bleeding procedure, add only clean, unused hydraulic fluid of the recommended type; never re-use fluid that has already been bled from the system. Ensure that sufficient fluid is available before starting work.

3 If there is any possibility of incorrect fluid being already in the system, the hydraulic circuit must be flushed completely with uncontaminated, correct fluid.

4 If hydraulic fluid has been lost from the

system, or air has entered because of a leak, ensure that the fault is cured before continuing further.

5 The bleed screw is located in the hose end fitting which is situated on the top of the transmission housing **(see illustration)**. On some models access to the bleed screw is limited and it may be necessary to jack up the front of the vehicle and support it on axle stands so that the screw can be reached from below, or remove the inlet air trunking (see Chapter 4A, 4B or 4C) so that the screw can be reached from above.

6 Check that all pipes and hoses are secure, unions tight and the bleed screw is closed. Clean any dirt from around the bleed screw.

7 Unscrew the master cylinder fluid reservoir cap (the clutch shares the same fluid reservoir as the braking system), and top the master cylinder reservoir up to the upper (MAX) level line. Refit the cap loosely, and remember to maintain the fluid level at least above the lower (MIN) level line throughout the procedure, or there is a risk of further air entering the system.

8 There are a number of one-man, do-it-yourself bleeding kits currently available from motor accessory shops. It is recommended that one of these kits is used whenever possible, as they greatly simplify the bleeding operation, and reduce the risk of expelled air and fluid being drawn back into the system. If such a kit is not available, the basic (two-man) method must be used, which is described in detail below.

9 If a kit is to be used, prepare the vehicle as described previously, and follow the kit manufacturer's instructions, as the procedure may vary slightly according to the type being used; generally, they are as outlined below in the relevant sub-section.

Bleeding

Basic (two-man) method

10 Collect a clean glass jar, a suitable length of plastic or rubber tubing which is a tight fit over the bleed screw, and a ring spanner to fit the screw. The help of an assistant will also be required.

11 Remove the dust cap from the bleed screw. Fit the spanner and tube to the screw, place the other end of the tube in the jar, and

2.5 Clutch bleed screw

pour in sufficient fluid to cover the end of the tube.

12 Ensure that the fluid level is maintained at least above the lower level line in the reservoir throughout the procedure.

13 Have the assistant fully depress the clutch pedal several times to build-up pressure, then maintain it on the final down stroke.

14 While pedal pressure is maintained, unscrew the bleed screw (approximately one turn) and allow the compressed fluid and air to flow into the jar. The assistant should maintain pedal pressure and should not release it until instructed to do so. When the flow stops, tighten the bleed screw again, have the assistant release the pedal slowly, and recheck the reservoir fluid level.

15 Repeat the steps given in paragraphs 13 and 14 until the fluid emerging from the bleed screw is free from air bubbles. If the master cylinder has been drained and refilled allow approximately five seconds between cycles for the master cylinder passages to refill.

Using a one-way valve kit

16 As their name implies, these kits consist of a length of tubing with a one-way valve fitted, to prevent expelled air and fluid being drawn back into the system; some kits include a translucent container, which can be positioned so that the air bubbles can be more easily seen flowing from the end of the tube.

17 The kit is connected to the bleed screw, which is then opened.

18 The user returns to the driver's seat, depresses the clutch pedal with a smooth, steady stroke, and slowly releases it; this is repeated until the expelled fluid is clear of air bubbles.

19 Note that these kits simplify work so much that it is easy to forget the clutch fluid reservoir level; ensure that this is maintained at least above the lower level line at all times.

Using a pressure-bleeding kit

20 These kits are usually operated by the reservoir of pressurised air contained in the spare tyre. However, note that it will probably be necessary to reduce the pressure to a lower level than normal; refer to the instructions supplied with the kit.

21 By connecting a pressurised, fluid-filled container to the clutch fluid reservoir, bleeding can be carried out simply by opening the bleed screw and allowing the fluid to flow out until no more air bubbles can be seen in the expelled fluid.

22 This method has the advantage that the large reservoir of fluid provides an additional safeguard against air being drawn into the system during bleeding.

All methods

23 When bleeding is complete, no more bubbles appear and correct pedal feel is restored, tighten the bleed screw securely (do not overtighten). Remove the tube and spanner, and wash off any spilt fluid. Refit the dust cap to the bleed screw.

3.4 Slide out the retaining clip and free the hydraulic pipe from the connector

24 Check the hydraulic fluid level in the master cylinder reservoir, and top-up if necessary (see *Weekly Checks*).

25 Discard any hydraulic fluid that has been bled from the system; it will not be fit for re-use.

26 Check the operation of the clutch pedal. If the clutch is still not operating correctly, air must still be present in the system, and further bleeding is required. Failure to bleed satisfactorily after a reasonable repetition of the bleeding procedure may be due to worn master cylinder/release cylinder seals.

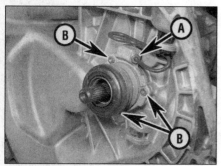

4.2a Clutch release cylinder hydraulic pipe union nut (A) and retaining bolts (B)

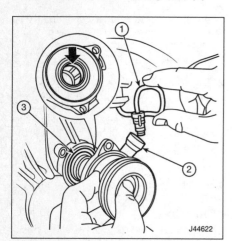

4.2b Clutch release cylinder hydraulic pipe quick-release connector (1), adaptor (2) and outer sealing ring (3)

Also note the inner sealing ring (arrowed)

3 Clutch master cylinder – removal and refitting

Note: *This procedure does not apply to models fitted with the Easytronic semi-automatic transmission.*

Removal

1 Remove the clutch pedal and bracket as described in Section 5. Note that the clutch master cylinder retaining nuts are removed during the bracket removal.

2 Remove the brake/clutch hydraulic fluid reservoir filler cap, and tighten it down onto a piece of polythene. This will reduce the loss of fluid when the master cylinder is removed. Alternatively, detach the clutch master cylinder fluid supply hose from the brake fluid reservoir, and plug the apertures.

3 Working in the engine compartment, remove all traces of dirt from the outside of the master cylinder and position some cloth beneath the cylinder to catch any spilt fluid.

4 Slide out the retaining clip, and free the hydraulic pipe from the connector in the end of the master cylinder at the engine compartment bulkhead. Plug the pipe end and master cylinder port to minimise fluid loss and prevent the entry of dirt. Recover the sealing ring from the union and discard it; a new one must be used on refitting **(see illustration)**. Gently squeeze the two legs of the retaining clip together, and re-insert the clip into the pipe end fitting.

5 Working in the engine compartment, withdraw the clutch master cylinder from the bulkhead.

Refitting

6 Ensure the mating surfaces are clean and dry, then locate the master cylinder on the bulkhead.

7 Using a new sealing ring, push the hydraulic pipe into the connector until the retaining clip engages.

8 Where applicable, reconnect the fluid supply hose to the brake fluid reservoir.

9 Refit the clutch pedal and bracket with reference to Section 5.

10 Bleed the clutch hydraulic system as described in Section 2.

4 Release cylinder – removal and refitting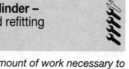

Note: *Due to the amount of work necessary to remove and refit clutch components, it is usually considered good practice to renew the clutch friction disc, pressure plate assembly and release bearing as a matched set, even if only one of these is actually worn enough to require renewal. It is also worth considering the renewal of the clutch components on a preventative basis if the engine and/or*

transmission have been removed for some other reason.

Note: *Refer to the warning concerning the dangers of asbestos dust at the beginning of Section 6.*

Removal

1 Unless the complete engine/transmission unit is to be removed from the car and separated for major overhaul (see Chapter 2D), the clutch release cylinder can be reached by removing the transmission only, as described in Chapter 7A or 7C.

2 Wipe clean the outside of the release cylinder then either unscrew the union nut or release the quick-release connector and disconnect the hydraulic pipe **(see illustrations)**. Wipe up any spilt fluid with a clean cloth.

3 Unscrew the three retaining bolts and slide the release cylinder from the transmission input shaft. Remove the sealing ring which is fitted between the cylinder and transmission housing and discard it; a new one must be used on refitting.

4 The release cylinder is a sealed unit and cannot be overhauled. If the cylinder seals leak or the release bearing is noisy or rough in operation, then the complete unit must be renewed.

Refitting

5 Ensure the release cylinder and transmission mating surfaces are clean and dry and fit the new sealing ring to the transmission recess.

6 Lubricate the release cylinder seal with a smear of transmission oil then carefully ease the cylinder along the input shaft and into position. **Note:** *Vauxhall technicians use a special tapered sleeve on the input shaft to prevent damage to the seal. If necessary, wrap suitable tape around the end of the shaft.* Ensure the sealing ring is still correctly seated in its groove then refit the release cylinder retaining bolts and tighten them securely.

7 Reconnect the hydraulic pipe to the release cylinder, making sure that the quick-release connector engages correctly. It should make an audible 'click'.

8 Refit the transmission unit as described in Chapter 7A or 7C.

9 Bleed the clutch hydraulic system as described in Section 2.

10 On Easytronic (semi-automatic transmission) models, a Vauxhall dealer must carry out a Contact Point Determination program, using the TECH2 diagnostic instrument.

5 Clutch pedal and bracket – removal and refitting

Removal

1 Remove the lower facia panel from the driver's footwell, then remove the air duct.

2 On right-hand drive models, remove the steering column as described in Chapter 10. On left-hand drive models, it is not necessary to remove the column, however, the electric power steering wiring must be disconnected from it.

3 Where fitted (according to model), remove the EGR clutch switch from the pedal bracket, and unclip the wiring harness bracket.

4 Disconnect the return spring from the clutch pedal, then remove the clip securing the pedal to the master cylinder piston rod. Vauxhall technicians use a special tool to do this, however, the clip may be released using screwdrivers. **Note:** *Do not remove the ball head clip at the master cylinder end.*

5 Remove the windscreen wiper motor from the bulkhead as described in Chapter 12.

6 In the engine compartment, unscrew the pedal support strut bolt from the bulkhead (behind the wiring harness), then unscrew the nuts in the driver's footwell and remove the support strut.

7 Unscrew the two self-locking nuts securing the clutch master cylinder to the bulkhead. Discard the nuts and obtain new ones.

8 Unscrew the three remaining self-locking nuts, and withdraw the clutch pedal and bracket from inside the vehicle **(see illustration)**. Discard the nuts and obtain new ones. To prevent any damage, make sure that all wiring is moved to one side.

9 Check the pedal and bracket for excessive wear and damage. It is not possible to renew the pedal pivot bushes separately, so if they are worn, the complete assembly must be renewed.

Refitting

10 Manoeuvre the pedal and bracket assembly into position, making sure that the surrounding wiring is not trapped. Screw on the new retaining nuts, including the master cylinder ones, and tighten to the specified torque. The pedal bracket nuts should be tightened before the master cylinder nuts.

11 Refit the pedal support strut and tighten the bolts/nuts.

12 Refit the windscreen wiper motor with reference to Chapter 12.

13 Reconnect the clutch pedal to the master cylinder piston rod, making sure that an audible 'click' is heard as the clip engages.

14 Reconnect the clutch return spring.

15 Where applicable, refit the EGR clutch switch and clip the wiring harness in place.

16 On right-hand drive models, refit the steering column with reference to Chapter 10. On left-hand drive models, reconnect the electric power steering wiring.

17 Refit the air duct and lower facia panel to the driver's footwell.

6 Clutch assembly (Standard) – removal, inspection and refitting

⚠ **Warning: Dust created by clutch wear and deposited on the clutch components may contain asbestos, which is a health hazard. DO NOT blow it out with compressed air, or** inhale any of it. DO NOT use petrol or petroleum-based solvents to clean off the dust. Brake system cleaner or methylated spirit should be used to flush the dust into a suitable receptacle. After the clutch components are wiped clean with rags, dispose of the contaminated rags and cleaner in a sealed, marked container.

Note: *To prevent possible damage to the ends of the pressure plate diaphragm spring fingers, Vauxhall recommend the use of a special jig (KM-6263) to remove the clutch assembly, however, with care it is possible to carry out the work without the jig.*

Removal

1 Unless the complete engine/transmission unit is to be removed from the car and separated for major overhaul (see Chapter 2D), the clutch can be reached by removing the transmission as described in Chapter 7A.

2 Before disturbing the clutch, use chalk or a marker pen to mark the relationship of the pressure plate assembly to the flywheel.

3 At this stage, Vauxhall technicians fit the special jig KM-6263 to the rear of the engine and compress the diaphragm spring fingers until the friction disc is released **(see illustrations overleaf)**. The pressure plate mounting bolts are then unscrewed, and the jig spindle backed off.

4 If the jig is not available, progressively unscrew the pressure plate retaining bolts in diagonal sequence by half a turn at a time, until spring pressure is released and the bolts can be unscrewed by hand.

5 Remove the pressure plate assembly and collect the friction disc, noting which way round the disc is fitted. It is recommended that new pressure plate retaining bolts are obtained.

Inspection

Note: *Due to the amount of work necessary to remove and refit clutch components, it is usually considered good practice to renew the clutch friction disc and pressure plate assembly as a matched set, even if only one of these is actually worn enough to require renewal. It is also worth checking the release cylinder and thrust bearing for wear.*

6 Wipe clean the clutch components, however, read the warning at the beginning of this Section. Remove dust using a clean, dry cloth, and working in a well-ventilated area.

7 Check the friction disc linings for signs of wear, damage or oil contamination. If the friction material is cracked, burnt, scored or damaged, or if it is contaminated with oil or grease (shown by shiny black patches), the friction disc must be renewed.

8 If the friction material is still serviceable, check that the centre boss splines are unworn, that the torsion springs are in good condition and securely fastened, and that all the rivets are tight. If any wear or damage is found, the friction disc must be renewed.

9 If the friction material is fouled with oil, this

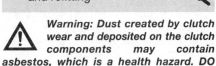

5.8 Clutch pedal and master cylinder

J44616

1 *Clutch master cylinder*	3 *Seal*	5 *Foot pad*
2 *Clutch pedal and bracket*	4 *Support strut*	6 *Pedal stop/bumper*

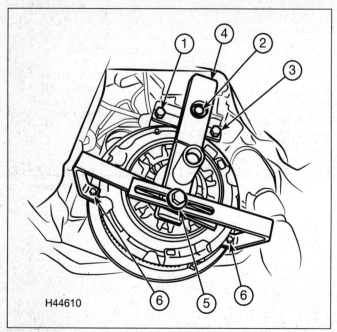

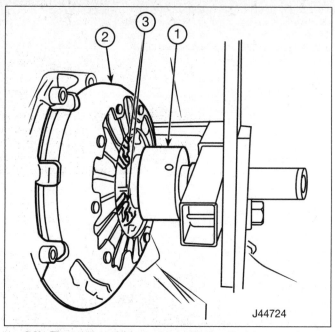

6.3a Vauxhall special jig KM-6263 for removing the clutch pressure plate and friction disc

6.3b Thrust piece (1) in contact with the diaphragm spring fingers (3) of the pressure plate (2)

1, 3 and 6 Bolts securing the jig   2 and 5   Bolts for adjusting the jig
*   to the engine   to the centre of the crankshaft*

must be due to an oil leak from the crankshaft oil seal, from the sump-to-cylinder block joint, or from the release cylinder assembly (either the main seal or the sealing ring). Renew the crankshaft oil seal or repair the sump joint as described in the relevant part of Chapter 2, before installing the new friction disc. The clutch release cylinder work is covered in Section 4.

10 Check the pressure plate assembly for obvious signs of wear or damage by shaking it to check for loose internal components. If the diaphragm spring is worn or damaged, or if its pressure is in any way suspect, the pressure plate assembly should be renewed.

11 Check that the machined surfaces of the pressure plate and flywheel are clean, completely flat, and free from scratches or scoring. If either is discoloured from excessive heat, or shows signs of cracks, it should be renewed.

12 Check that the release cylinder bearing rotates smoothly and easily, with no sign of noise or roughness. Also check that the surface itself is smooth and unworn, with no signs of cracks, pitting or scoring. If there is any doubt about its condition, the clutch release cylinder should be renewed (it is not possible to renew the bearing separately).

Refitting

13 On reassembly, ensure that the friction surfaces of the flywheel and pressure plate are completely clean, smooth, and free from oil or grease. Use solvent to remove any protective grease from new components.

14 Lightly grease the teeth of the friction disc

hub with high melting-point grease. Do not apply too much, otherwise it may eventually contaminate the friction disc linings.

Using the Vauxhall jig

15 Fit the special Vauxhall guide bush to the centre of the crankshaft, and locate the friction disc on it, making sure that the lettering 'transmission side' points towards the transmission.

16 Locate the pressure plate on the special centring pins on the flywheel, then compress the diaphragm spring fingers with the jig, until the friction disc is in full contact with the flywheel.

17 Insert new pressure plate retaining bolts, and progressively tighten them to the specified torque. If necessary, hold the flywheel stationary while tightening the bolts, using a screwdriver engaged with the teeth of the starter ring gear.

6.23 Centralise the friction disc using a clutch aligning tool or similar

18 Back off the jig spindle so that the diaphragm spring forces the pressure plate against the friction disc and flywheel, then remove the jig and guide bush from the engine.

19 Refit the transmission as described in Chapter 7A.

Without using the Vauxhall jig

20 Locate the friction disc on the flywheel, making sure that the lettering 'transmission side' points towards the transmission.

21 Refit the pressure plate assembly, aligning the marks made on dismantling (if the original pressure plate is re-used). Fit new pressure plate bolts, but tighten them only finger-tight so that the friction disc can still be moved.

22 The friction disc must now be centralised so that, when the transmission is refitted, its input shaft will pass through the splines at the centre of the friction disc.

23 Centralisation can be achieved by passing a screwdriver or other long bar through the friction disc and into the hole in the crankshaft. The friction disc can then be moved around until it is centred on the crankshaft hole. Alternatively, a clutch-aligning tool can be used to eliminate the guesswork; these can be obtained from most accessory shops. A home-made aligning tool can be fabricated from a length of metal rod or wooden dowel which fits closely inside the crankshaft hole, and has insulating tape wound around it to match the diameter of the friction disc splined hole **(see illustration)**.

24 When the friction disc is centralised,

tighten the pressure plate bolts evenly and in a diagonal sequence to the specified torque setting.

25 Refit the transmission as described in Chapter 7A.

7 Clutch assembly (Easytronic) – removal, inspection and refitting

Note: *After fitting the clutch assembly, a Vauxhall dealer must carry out a Contact Point Determination program, using the TECH2 diagnostic instrument.*

Note: *To prevent possible damage to the pressure plate diaphragm spring fingers, Vauxhall recommend the use of a special jig KM-6263 to remove the clutch assembly. Additionally, Vauxhall tool KM-6289 will be required when removing the pressure plate. The following procedure assumes these tools are available.*

Removal

1 Unless the complete engine/transmission unit is to be removed from the car and separated for major overhaul (see Chapter 2D), the clutch can be reached by removing the transmission as described in Chapter 7C.

2 Prepare Vauxhall tool KM-6289 in accordance with the clutch diameter, then fit the tool onto the outside of the pressure plate, making sure that the two inner pins are in contact with the pressure plate adjusting ring. Insert the two spring hooks in the pressure plate **(see illustrations)**.

3 Fit the Vauxhall jig KM-6263 to the rear of the engine, and compress the diaphragm spring fingers until the friction disc is released. Check that as the fingers are compressed, tool KM-6289 rotates the pressure plate anti-clockwise.

4 Progressively unscrew and remove the pressure plate retaining bolts, then back off the jig spindle and remove the pressure plate, together with the friction disc.

5 Remove tool KM-6289 if the pressure plate is to be renewed and fit it to the new pressure plate, otherwise leave it in position on the original pressure plate.

Inspection

6 Refer to Section 6, paragraphs 6 to 12.

Refitting

7 On reassembly, ensure that the friction surfaces of the flywheel and pressure plate are completely clean, smooth, and free from oil or grease. Use solvent to remove any protective grease from new components.

8 Lightly grease the teeth of the friction disc hub with high melting-point grease. Do not apply too much, otherwise it may eventually contaminate the friction disc linings.

9 Fit the special Vauxhall guide bush to the centre of the crankshaft, and locate the friction disc on it, making sure that the

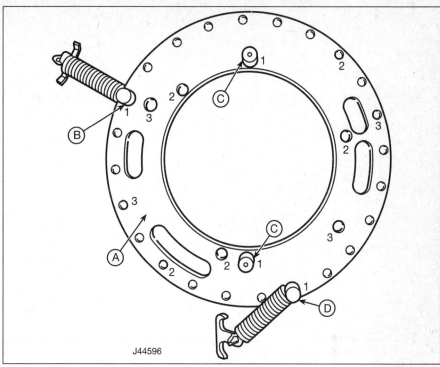

7.2a Vauxhall tool KM-6289 required to hold the adjusting ring when removing the pressure plate

A   Tool
B   Attach pin for pre-tensioning spring
C   Pins adjusted for clutch diameter
D   Attach pin for pretensioning spring
1, 2 and 3 Connection points for different diameter clutches

lettering 'transmission side' points towards the transmission.

10 Locate the pressure plate on the special centring pins on the flywheel, then compress the diaphragm spring fingers with the jig, until the friction disc is in full contact with the flywheel.

11 Insert new pressure plate retaining bolts, and progressively tighten them to the specified torque. If necessary, hold the flywheel stationary while tightening the bolts,

using a screwdriver engaged with the teeth of the starter ring gear.

12 Back off the jig spindle so that the diaphragm spring forces the pressure plate against the friction disc and flywheel, then remove the jig and guide bush from the engine.

13 Remove Vauxhall tool KM-6289 from the pressure plate.

14 Refit the transmission as described in Chapter 7C.

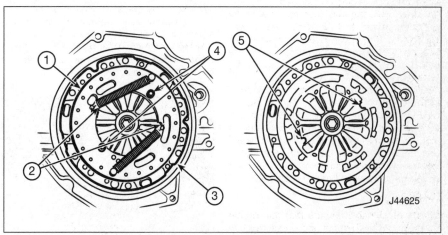

7.2b Vauxhall tool KM-6289 fitted to the pressure plate

1   Tool
2   Hooks
3   Pressure plate
4   Pins
5   Adjusting ring contact

Chapter 7 Part A:
Manual transmission

Contents

Degrees of difficulty

Easy, suitable for novice with little experience	**Fairly easy,** suitable for beginner with some experience	**Fairly difficult,** suitable for competent DIY mechanic	**Difficult,** suitable for experienced DIY mechanic	**Very difficult,** suitable for expert DIY or professional

Specifications

General

Type . . . . Five forward speeds and one reverse, synchromesh on all forward gears. Integral differential

Manufacturer's designation:
Petrol engines . . . . F 13/5 CR
Diesel engine:
   Without intercooler . . . . F 13/5 WR
   With intercooler . . . . F 17/5 WR

Gear ratios

F 13/5 CR transmission:
1st 3.73:1
2nd 2.14:1
3rd 1.41:1
4th 1.12:1
5th 0.89:1
Reverse 3.31:1
F 13/5 WR and F 17/5 WR transmissions:
1st 3.73:1
2nd 1.96:1
3rd 1.31:1
4th 0.95:1
5th 0.76:1
Reverse 3.31:1

Final drive ratios

F 13/5 CR transmission:
1.0 and 1.2 litre petrol engines . . . . 3.74:1 or 3.94:1
1.4 litre petrol engine 3.94:1
F 13/5 WR and F 17/5 WR transmissions:
Except Combo models 3.55:1
Combo models 3.74:1

Torque wrench settings

	Nm	lbf ft
Differential housing cover plate bolts:		
Alloy plate	18	13
Steel plate	30	22
Gearchange mechanism selector rod clamp bolt:		
Stage 1	12	9
Stage 2	Angle-tighten a further 225°	
Left-hand engine mounting	See Chapter 2A, 2B or 2C	
Reversing light switch	20	15
Transmission-to-engine/sump bolts	See Chapter 2A, 2B or 2C	
Vehicle speed sensor retaining plate bolt	4	3

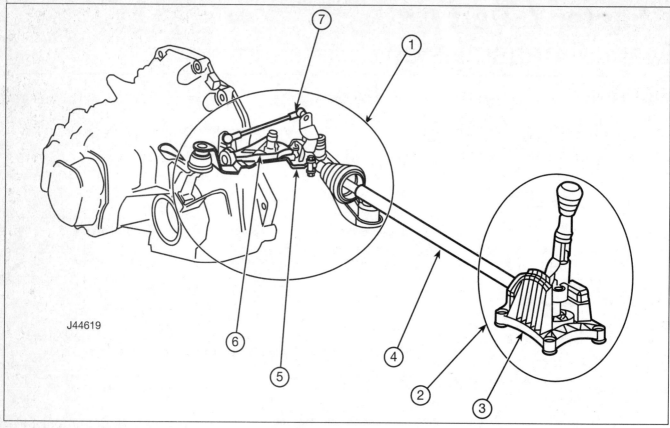

J44619

1.1 Transmission and gearchange

1 Linkage guide components
2 Gear lever/housing
  assembly

3 Housing
4 Control rod
5 Shift guide bearing support

6 Gear shift guide lever
7 Shift guide rod

1 General information

1 One of three different CR (close ratio) or WR (wide ratio) manual transmissions may be fitted, depending on model and engine fitted (see Specifications); there are only minor internal differences between the transmission types **(see illustration)**.

2 Drive from the clutch is transmitted to the input shaft, which runs in parallel with the mainshaft. The input shaft and mainshaft gears are in constant mesh, and selection of gears is by sliding synchromesh hubs, which lock the appropriate mainshaft gear to the mainshaft.

3 The 5th speed gear components are located in an extension housing at the end of the transmission.

4 Reverse gear is obtained by sliding an idler gear into mesh with two straight-cut gears on the input shaft and mainshaft.

5 The differential is mounted in the main transmission casing, and drive is transmitted to the differential by a pinion gear on the end of the mainshaft. The inboard ends of the

driveshafts locate directly into the differential. The transmission and differential unit share the same lubricating oil.

6 Gear selection is by a floor-mounted gearchange lever, via a remote control linkage.

2 Transmission oil – draining and refilling

Note: Changing the transmission oil is not a

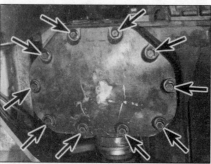

2.3 Differential cover plate securing bolts

routine job, however, it may be considered necessary if the vehicle has completed a high mileage or if a second-hand transmission is being fitted. No drain plug is fitted.

Draining

1 Apply the handbrake, then jack up the front of the vehicle and support it on axle stands (see Jacking and vehicle support). Remove the engine undertray where fitted.

2 Unbolt the rear engine torque link from the transmission and pivot it to one side.

3 Place a suitable container under the differential cover plate. Unscrew the securing bolts and withdraw the cover plate, allowing the transmission oil to drain into the container **(see illustration)**. Recover the gasket and, if necessary, renew it.

4 Refit the differential cover plate together with the gasket, and tighten the securing bolts, then refit the rear engine torque link and tighten the bolts.

Refilling

5 Wipe clean the area around the level plug. The level plug is located behind the driveshaft inner joint on the left-hand side of the transmission **(see illustration)**. Unscrew the plug and clean it.

2.5 Transmission oil level hole

2.6 Fill the transmission through the reversing light switch aperture

3.3 Gear selector rod-to-clamp sleeve clamp nut

6 The transmission is refilled via the reversing light switch aperture **(see illustration)**. Wipe clean the area around the reversing light switch, and remove the switch as described in Section 7. Refill the transmission with the specified grade of oil given in *Lubricants and fluids*, until it reaches the bottom of the level plug aperture. Allow any excess oil to drain, then refit and tighten the level plug. **Note:** *When new, the transmission is originally filled by weight, and the level may be 20 mm below the level hole.*

7 Refit the reversing light switch with reference to Section 7, then refit the engine undertray (where fitted) and lower the vehicle to the ground.

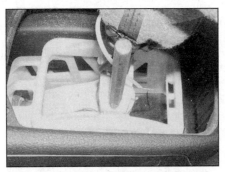

3.5 Insert a 5 mm drill or punch through the clamp and into the locating hole

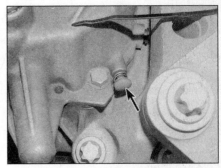

3.6 Lock the selector mechanism by pressing in the spring-loaded locking pin

3 Gearchange linkage/mechanism – adjustment

Note: *A 5 mm drill or metal rod will be required to carry out this procedure.*

1 Adjustment of the gearchange linkage/mechanism is not a routine operation and should only be needed if the mechanism has been disconnected or removed. The mechanism is adjusted on the clamp bolt which secures the selector rod to the transmission linkage at the rear of the engine compartment. Access is best from under the vehicle.

2 Apply the handbrake, then jack up the front of the vehicle and support it on axle stands (see *Jacking and vehicle support*). Remove the engine undertray where fitted.

3 Slacken the gearchange selector rod clamp bolt which is situated at the front of the rod **(see illustration)**. Do not remove the bolt completely.

4 From inside the vehicle, unclip the gear lever gaiter from the console and fold it back.

5 Push the gear lever to the left in neutral, then insert a 5 mm drill or metal rod through the special hole in the lever base to lock it in the adjusting position **(see illustration)**.

6 Working in the engine compartment, with the selector mechanism in neutral, turn the selector shaft anti-clockwise against the spring pressure towards the third gear position, and lock the selector mechanism by

pressing in the spring-loaded locking pin which is located on the top of the transmission unit **(see illustration)**.

7 With both the lever and transmission locked in position, tighten the selector rod clamp bolt to the specified torque Stage 1, then through the Stage 2 angle.

8 Remove the locking rod from the gear lever and check the operation of the gearchange mechanism; the transmission locking pin will automatically release when the lever is moved into the reverse position.

9 Ensure the transmission locking pin has released, then refit the engine undertray (where necessary) and lower the vehicle to the ground.

10 Finally check that all gears can be engaged easily, first with the engine off, then with the engine running and the clutch disengaged.

4 Gearchange linkage/mechanism – removal and refitting

1 The gearchange mechanism consists of the gear lever, the selector rod and the linkage assembly on the transmission. The lever and selector rod and the linkage assembly can be removed separately.

Gear lever

Note: *To remove the gear lever, it is necessary to destroy the ball socket. Obtain a new socket before carrying out the work.*

Removal

2 Ensure that the lever is in neutral, then carefully unclip the edge of the gearchange lever gaiter from the centre console. There are two retaining lugs at the front and two at the rear of the centre console aperture. Pull the gaiter upwards over the gear lever knob, then release the cable tie and remove it completely.

3 Using a screwdriver, depress the tabs at the bottom of the gear lever housing to release the ball socket from the housing **(see illustration)**. Pull up the gear lever together with the ball socket.

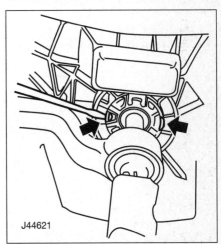

J44621

4.3 Depress the tabs at the bottom of the gear lever housing to release the ball socket from the housing

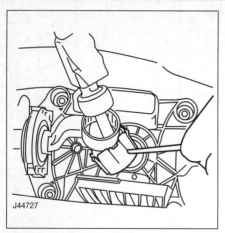

4.4 Lever the ball socket from the bottom of the gear lever

4 Using a screwdriver, lever the ball socket from the bottom of the gear lever (see illustration). Note that this will destroy the socket.

5 Withdraw the gear lever from the gearchange rod guide.

Refitting

6 Wipe clean all lubricant from the bearing surfaces of the gear lever and guide, then apply new silicone grease to the surfaces.

7 Insert the gear lever through the gearchange rod guide, then press the new ball socket firmly onto the end of the gear lever until it engages. Note that the lugs on the ball

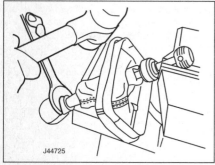

4.21 Driving the knob from the gear lever

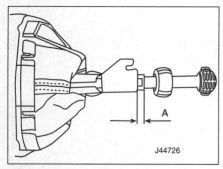

4.22 Correct position of the gear lever knob

A = 8.0 to 10.0 mm

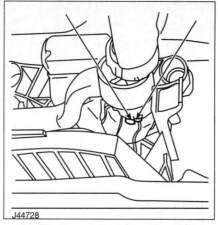

4.7 The lugs on the ball end must be aligned with the grooves of the ball socket

end must be aligned with the grooves of the ball socket (see illustration).

8 Align the gearchange lever with the gearchange rod guide, then press the ball socket firmly into the housing. Note that the retaining clips must be heard to engage.

9 Refit the gaiter to the gear lever, using a new cable tie, then clip the edge of the gaiter firmly into the centre console. To prevent any subsequent noise, the loose end of the cable tie should be cut off.

Lever housing and control rod

Removal

10 Apply the handbrake, then jack up the front of the vehicle and support it on axle stands (see *Jacking and vehicle support*). Where fitted, remove the engine undertray.

11 Reach up behind the transmission and loosen the clamp bolt of the shift guide clamp (do not remove it). Push the control rod rearwards and separate it from the shift guide.

12 Prise the gaiter from the bulkhead and withdraw from the control rod.

13 Remove the centre console as described in Chapter 11.

14 Unscrew the nut and release the wiring trough from the left-hand side of the gear lever housing.

15 Unscrew the four bolts, then withdraw the gear lever housing and control rod assembly from the vehicle.

4.26 Shift guide viewed from the top of the transmission

16 If necessary, the control rod may be removed from the housing.

Refitting

17 Clean the bush guide in the housing, and apply some silicone grease. Insert the control rod through the guide.

18 The remaining refitting procedure is a reversal of removal, tightening the housing mounting bolts securely, and adjusting the linkage as described in Section 3.

Gear lever knob

Renewal

19 Using a small screwdriver, carefully prise the position indicator plate from the top of the gear lever knob.

20 Remove the gear lever as described earlier in this Section.

21 Make sure you note the fitted position of the knob, and also check that the pressure spring fitted below the knob stays in place. Mount the gear lever in a soft-jawed vice, then drive the knob from the lever using a suitable spanner and mallet (see illustration).

22 Locate the new knob on the lever and drive into position with the mallet. The distance from the lower edge of the lever guide to the lower edge of the stop lever with reverse gear button lock applied, must be between 8.0 and 10.0 mm (see illustration).

23 Refit the gear lever as described earlier in this Section.

24 Place the position indicator plate on the gear lever knob with the tab and knob groove aligned with each other, then press firmly into position.

Gearchange shift guide

Removal

25 Apply the handbrake, then jack up the front of the vehicle and support it on axle stands (see *Jacking and vehicle support*). Where fitted, remove the engine undertray.

26 Reach up behind the transmission and loosen the clamp bolt of the shift guide clamp (do not remove it). Push the control rod rearwards and separate it from the shift guide (see illustration).

27 Remove the two clips and disconnect the linkage from the shift guide bracket (see illustration).

4.27 Shift guide bracket

28 Depress the retaining spring and lever out the pin. Detach the universal joint from the shift rod **(see illustration)**.

29 Withdraw the shift pivot together with the shift guide.

Refitting

30 Refitting is a reversal of removal, but adjust the linkage as described in Section 3.

---

5 Vehicle speed sensor – removal and refitting

Note: *On later models (with or without ABS), a wheel speed sensor provides the engine ECU(s) with vehicle speed data. On these vehicles no speed sensor is fitted to the transmission.*

Removal

1 The sensor is located on the rear of the transmission casing, above the left-hand driveshaft. Working in the engine compartment, reach down and disconnect the wiring plug from the top of the sensor.

2 Unscrew the retaining bolt and remove the sensor from the casing **(see illustration)**.

Refitting

3 With a new sealing ring fitted, insert the sensor into the transmission casing aperture.

4 Tighten the retaining bolt to the specified torque and reconnect the wiring plug.

---

6 Oil seals – renewal

Driveshaft oil seals

1 Apply the handbrake, then jack up the front of the vehicle and support it on axle stands (see *Jacking and vehicle support*). Remove the relevant front roadwheel.

2 Drain the transmission oil as described in Section 2 or be prepared for oil loss as the seal is changed.

3 Disconnect the inner end of the relevant driveshaft from the differential as described in Chapter 8. There is no need to disconnect the driveshaft from the swivel hub. Support the driveshaft by suspending it with wire or string – do not allow the driveshaft to hang down under its own weight, or the joints may be damaged.

4 Prise the now-exposed oil seal from the differential housing, using a screwdriver or similar instrument **(see illustration)**.

5 Smear the sealing lip of the new oil seal with a little transmission oil, then using a metal tube or socket of suitable diameter, drive the new seal into the differential casing until the outer surface of the seal is flush with the outer surface of the differential casing **(see illustration)**.

6 Reconnect the driveshaft to the differential as described in Chapter 8.

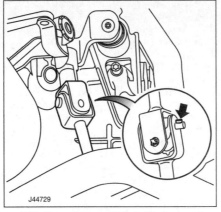

4.28 Gearchange shift guide removal

Arrow shows position of hollow pin retaining spring

7 Refill or top up the transmission oil level with reference to Section 2.

8 Refit the roadwheel, then lower the vehicle to the ground.

Input shaft oil seal

9 The input shaft oil seal is an integral part of the clutch release cylinder; if the seal is leaking the complete release cylinder assembly must be renewed. Before condemning the release cylinder, check that the leak is not coming from the sealing ring which is fitted between the cylinder and the transmission housing; the sealing ring can be renewed once the release cylinder assembly

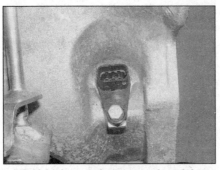

5.2 Vehicle speed sensor and retaining bolt

6.5 Fitting a new driveshaft oil seal using a socket as a tubular drift

has been removed. Refer to Chapter 6 for removal and refitting details.

Selector rod oil seal

10 Renewal of the selector rod oil seal requires the selector mechanism cover to be unbolted from the transmission and dismantled. This task is considered to be beyond the scope of the DIY mechanic, and should therefore be entrusted to a Vauxhall dealer or specialist.

---

7 Reversing light switch – testing, removal and refitting

Testing

1 The reversing light circuit is operated by a plunger-type switch, mounted on the upper/front of the transmission casing.

2 To test the switch, disconnect the wiring **(see illustration)**, and use a suitable meter or a battery-and-bulb test circuit to check for continuity between the switch terminals. Continuity should only exist when reverse gear is selected. If this is not the case, and there are no obvious breaks or other damage to the wires, the switch is faulty and must be renewed.

Removal

3 The reversing light switch is located on the front of the transmission casing, and is accessible from the left-hand side of the engine compartment or from beneath the vehicle.

6.4 Prising out a driveshaft oil seal

7.2 Disconnecting the wiring from the reversing light switch

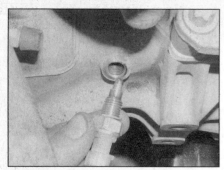

7.5 Removing the reversing light switch and sealing washer

4 On Y17DT diesel engine models, remove the air duct leading to the intercooler for access to the top of the transmission. If necessary, also remove the engine undertray.
5 Disconnect the wiring from the switch, then unscrew the switch from the transmission **(see illustration)**. Recover the O-ring seal.

Refitting

6 Refitting is a reversal of removal, but tighten the switch to the specified torque.

8 Manual transmission – removal and refitting

Note: *This is an involved procedure, and it may well prove easier to remove the transmission complete with the engine as an assembly (see Chapter 2D), then separate the transmission. However, this Section describes removing the transmission leaving the engine in position. Suitable equipment will be required to support the engine and transmission, and the help of an assistant will be required.*

Removal

1 Apply the handbrake, then jack up the front of the vehicle and support it on axle stands (see *Jacking and vehicle support*). Allow sufficient working room to remove the transmission from under the left-hand side of the engine compartment. Remove both front roadwheels then, where necessary, undo the retaining clips/screws and remove the engine

undertray. Also remove the engine top cover where fitted.
2 Remove the air cleaner housing and intake trunking (see Chapter 4A, 4B or 4C).
3 Drain the transmission oil as described in Section 2 or be prepared for oil loss as the transmission is removed.
4 On diesel engines, remove the crash box from the rear of the engine compartment **(see illustration)**. To do this, first remove the fuel filter as described in Chapter 1B, then unscrew the nut and remove the add-on heater from the crash box. Release the coolant hose from the bracket on the front of the crash box. Next to the crash box, release the coolant expansion tank and position to one side. Unscrew the mounting nuts and withdraw the crash box from the bulkhead. Note that it is only necessary to loosen the outer mounting nut.
5 Remove the filler cap from the brake/clutch fluid reservoir on the bulkhead, then tighten it onto a piece of polythene. This will reduce the loss of fluid when the clutch hydraulic hose is disconnected. Alternatively, fit a hose clamp to the flexible hose next to the clutch hydraulic connection on the transmission housing.
6 Place some cloth rags beneath the hose, then prise out the retaining clip securing the clutch hydraulic pipe/hose end fitting to the top of the transmission bellhousing and detach the end fitting from the transmission **(see illustration)**. Gently squeeze the two legs of the retaining clip together and re-insert the retaining clip back into position in the end fitting. Discard the sealing ring from the pipe end; a new sealing ring must be used on refitting. Plug/cover both the union and pipe ends to minimise fluid loss and prevent the entry of dirt into the hydraulic system. **Note:** *Whilst the hose/pipe is disconnected, do not depress the clutch pedal.*
7 Disconnect the wiring from the reversing lamp switch on the front of the transmission.
8 Unscrew and remove the three upper bolts securing the transmission to the rear of the engine. Where necessary, pull up the coolant hoses and secure them away from the transmission using plastic cable ties.
9 Tie the radiator to the engine compartment front crossmember in preparation for lowering the front subframe.

10 Remove the hub caps, then extract the split pins and unscrew the driveshaft outer hub nuts while holding the hubs stationary. To do this, temporarily insert the wheel bolts and have an assistant depress the brake pedal while the nuts are loosened.
11 Remove the front brake discs with reference to Chapter 9.
12 Refer to Chapter 10 and disconnect the track rods from the hub carrier steering arms. Also detach the anti-roll bar links from the front suspension struts, and detach the front suspension lower arms from the hub carriers.
13 Disconnect the driveshafts from the hub carriers by carefully tapping them through the hubs while pulling out the carriers. Do not allow the driveshafts to hang down under their own weight, or the joints may be damaged – support the driveshafts with wire or string.
14 On models with air conditioning, remove the auxiliary drivebelt (Chapter 1A or 1B), then unbolt the compressor from the engine **without disconnecting the refrigerant lines** and support the compressor to one side.
15 Remove the exhaust system as described in Chapter 4A, 4B or 4C.
16 Refer to Section 4 and disconnect the gearchange/selector rod from the transmission.
17 Support the front suspension subframe on trolley jacks, then mark the position of the subframe on the front underbody **(see Haynes Hint)**, and unscrew the four mounting bolts. Discard the bolts as new ones must be used for refitting. Unscrew and remove the bolt securing the engine rear torque link to the subframe. With the help of an assistant, carefully lower the subframe to the ground and withdraw from under the vehicle.
18 Attach a suitable hoist and lifting tackle to the lifting bracket located on the left-hand side of the cylinder head, and support the weight of the engine/transmission. Alternatively, the engine can be supported using a jack and interposed block of wood under the sump, however, great care must be taken when removing the transmission not to move the engine off the jack.

8.4 Crash box and fuel filter on the bulkhead

To ensure correct repositioning, we bolted two lengths of metal bar to the subframe, and marked their position on the underbody.

8.6 Prise out the clip to disconnect the clutch hydraulic hose from the release cylinder pipe

19 Unbolt and remove the left-hand mounting bracket from the transmission and body with reference to Chapter 2A, 2B or 2C.

20 Lower the engine and transmission by approximately 5 cm making sure that the coolant hoses and wiring harnesses are not stretched.

21 Disconnect the gearchange linkage from the transmission with reference to Section 4.

22 Refer to Chapter 8 and remove the driveshafts from the transmission. To do this, disconnect the front suspension lower arm balljoints from the hub carriers, and also disconnect the steering track rod ends from the steering arms. It is not necessary to remove the driveshafts from the hub carriers. Tie the driveshafts to one side.

23 On diesel engine models, unbolt and remove the front left-hand engine mounting with reference to Chapter 2C.

24 Unbolt and remove the rear engine mounting torque link with reference to Chapter 2A, 2B or 2C.

25 Unscrew the four lower bolts securing the transmission to the engine sump.

26 Support the weight of the transmission on a trolley jack, then unscrew the remaining transmission-to-engine bolts, noting the location of the earth cable **(see illustration)**.

27 Make a final check that all components have been disconnected, and are positioned clear of the transmission so that they will not hinder the removal procedure.

28 With the help of an assistant, carefully withdraw the transmission from the engine, taking care not to allow the weight of the transmission to hang on the input shaft otherwise the clutch friction disc hub may be damaged. Note that there are two locating dowels which may be tight, and it may be necessary to rock the transmission from side-to-side to release it from them. Once the transmission is free, lower the jack and manoeuvre the unit out from under the car.

Refitting

29 Commence refitting by positioning the transmission on the trolley jack beneath the engine compartment. With the help of an assistant, raise the transmission and locate it on the engine, making sure that the input shaft engages accurately with the splines of the friction disc hub. With the transmission located on the dowels, insert all of the retaining bolts and tighten to the specified torque.

30 The remaining refitting procedure is a reversal of removal, noting the following points:

a) *Tighten all nuts and bolts to the specified torque (where given). Note that the torque for the transmission-to-sump bolts is different than the bolts to the rest of the engine.*

b) *Renew the driveshaft oil seals (see Section 6) before refitting the driveshafts.*

c) *Refit the front subframe assembly with reference to Chapter 10.*

d) *Fit a new sealing ring to the transmission clutch hydraulic pipe before clipping the hose/pipe end fitting into position. Ensure the end fitting is securely retained by its clip then bleed the hydraulic system as described in Chapter 6.*

e) *Refill the transmission with the specified type and quantity of oil, as described in Section 2.*

f) *On completion, adjust the gearchange linkage/mechanism as described in Section 3.*

9 Manual transmission overhaul – general information

1 Overhauling a manual transmission unit is a difficult and involved job for the DIY home mechanic. In addition to dismantling and reassembling many small parts, clearances must be precisely measured and, if necessary, changed by selecting shims and spacers. Internal transmission components

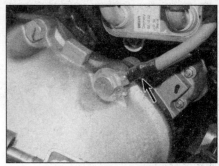

8.26 Earth cable on a transmission mounting bolt

are also often difficult to obtain, and in many instances, extremely expensive. Because of this, if the transmission develops a fault or becomes noisy, the best course of action is to have the unit overhauled by a specialist repairer, or to obtain an exchange reconditioned unit.

2 Nevertheless, it is not impossible for the more experienced mechanic to overhaul the transmission, provided the special tools are available, and the job is done in a deliberate step-by-step manner, so that nothing is overlooked.

3 The tools necessary for an overhaul include internal and external circlip pliers, bearing pullers, a slide hammer, a set of pin punches, a dial test indicator, and possibly a hydraulic press. In addition, a large, sturdy workbench and a vice will be required.

4 During dismantling of the transmission, make careful notes of how each component is fitted, to make reassembly easier and more accurate **(see illustration overleaf)**.

5 Before dismantling the transmission, it will help if you have some idea what area is malfunctioning. Certain problems can be closely related to specific areas in the transmission, which can make component examination and replacement easier. Refer to the *Fault finding* Section of this manual for more information.

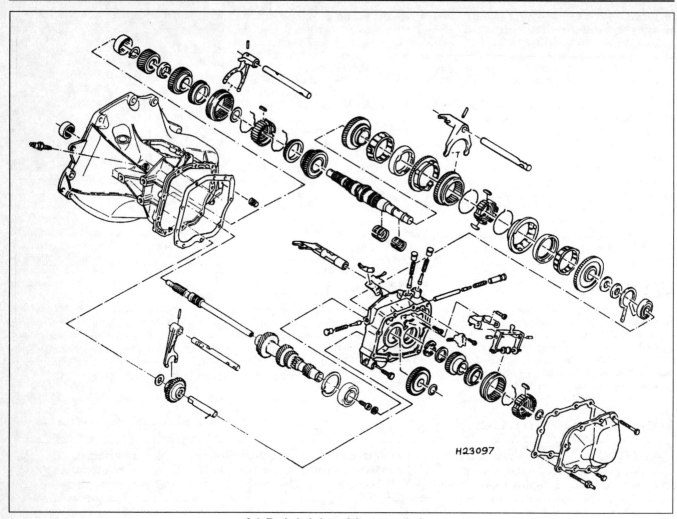

H23097

9.4 Exploded view of the transmission

Chapter 7 Part B:
Automatic transmission

Contents

Degrees of difficulty

Easy, suitable for novice with little experience		Fairly easy, suitable for beginner with some experience		Fairly difficult, suitable for competent DIY mechanic		Difficult, suitable for experienced DIY mechanic		Very difficult, suitable for expert DIY or professional	

Specifications

General

Type	Hydrodynamic torque converter with electronically-controlled mechanical lock-up system, two epicyclic gearsets giving four forward speeds and reverse, integral final drive. Gearchanging under full electronic control, with three 'driving' modes selectable
Manufacturer's designation	AF 13

Gear ratios

1st	2.81:1
2nd	1.48:1
3rd	1.00:1
4th	0.74:1
Reverse	2.77:1
Final drive	4.12:1

Torque wrench settings

	Nm	lbf ft
Fluid cooler pipe union bolts	25	18
Fluid filler tube support	60	44
Position switch hub-to-shaft nut	8	6
Selector lever position switch to transmission	25	18
Selector lever to selector lever shaft	16	12
Torque converter-to-driveplate bolts*	50	37
Transmission-to-engine block bolts	60	44
Transmission to engine sump	40	30

*Use new bolts

1 General information

1 A 4-speed fully-automatic transmission is available as an option on certain Corsa models. The transmission consists of a torque converter, an epicyclic geartrain and hydraulically-operated clutches and brakes. The differential is integral with the transmission, and is similar to that used in manual gearbox models **(see illustration)**.

2 The torque converter provides a fluid coupling between the engine and transmission which acts as an automatic 'clutch', and also provides a degree of torque multiplication when accelerating.

3 The epicyclic geartrain provides either one of the four forward gear ratios, or reverse gear, according to which of its component parts are held stationary or allowed to turn. The components of the geartrain are held or released by brakes and clutches, which are activated by a hydraulic control unit. A fluid pump within the transmission provides the necessary hydraulic pressure to operate the brakes and clutches.

4 The transmission is electronically-controlled, and three driving modes – Economy, Sport and Winter – are provided. The transmission electronic control unit (ECU) operates in conjunction with the engine management ECU to control the gear-changes. The transmission ECU receives information on transmission fluid temperature, throttle position, engine coolant temperature, and input-versus-output speed. The ECU controls the hydraulically-operated clutches and brakes via four solenoids. The control system can also retard the engine ignition timing, via the engine management ECU, to permit smoother gearchanges.

5 Due to the complexity of the automatic transmission, any repair or overhaul work must be entrusted to a Vauxhall dealer, who will have the necessary specialist equipment and knowledge for fault diagnosis and repair. Refer to the *Fault finding* section at the end of this manual for further information.

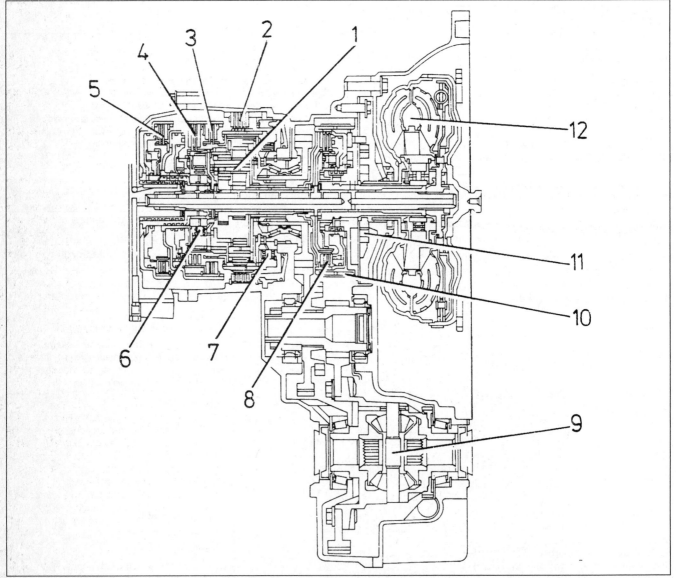

1.1 Cutaway view of the AF 13 automatic transmission

1 *Gear assembly*	4 *Multi-plate clutch*
2 *Multi-disc brake*	5 *Multi-plate clutch*
3 *Multi-plate clutch*	6 *Freewheel assembly*
7 *Freewheel assembly*	10 *Brake band*
8 *Multi-plate clutch*	11 *Fluid pump*
9 *Differential*	12 *Torque converter*

2 Automatic transmission fluid renewal

Refer to Chapter 1A.

3 Selector cable – removal, refitting and adjustment

Removal

1 Apply the handbrake, then jack up the front of the vehicle and support it on axle stands (see *Jacking and vehicle support*). Where applicable, remove the engine undertray.
2 Remove the centre console as described in Chapter 11.
3 Release the wiring trough from the front of the selector housing.
4 Using a screwdriver, prise off the retaining clip and release the outer selector cable from the mounting bracket.
5 Working in the engine compartment, press the cable end fitting from the lever on the position switch.
6 Using a screwdriver, prise off the retaining clip and release the outer selector cable from the mounting bracket on the transmission.
7 Working beneath the vehicle, pull the selector cable through the rubber grommet in the bulkhead and withdraw. Do not remove the grommet.

Refitting and adjustment

8 Apply soapy water solution to the outer cable, then insert it through the rubber grommet into the passenger compartment.
9 The remaining refitting procedure is a reversal of removal, but adjust the cable as follows before lowering the vehicle to the ground.
10 In the engine compartment, use a screwdriver to prise up the locking clamp at the support mounting on the transmission **(see illustration)**.
11 Move the selector lever inside the vehicle to position P. Check that the lever has engaged properly by moving it back-and-forth without depressing the lock knob.
12 Working at the transmission, move the lever to the stop (position 2), then rotate the front wheels until the parking lock pawl engages.
13 Press down the locking clamp to lock the cable in position.
14 Check the adjustment by selecting P, R, N, D, 3, 2, 1 and checking that the relative positions on the transmission are engaged.

4 Selector lever housing – removal and refitting

Removal

1 Remove the centre console as described in Chapter 11.
2 Release the wiring trough from the front of the selector housing.
3 On the left-hand side of the housing, use a screwdriver to lever off the cable end fitting from the selector lever.
4 Release the clip and remove the outer selector cable from the mounting bracket.
5 Disconnect the wiring from the right-hand front of the housing.
6 Unscrew the mounting bolts and withdraw the selector lever housing from the floor.

Refitting

7 Refitting is a reversal of removal, but tighten the mounting bolts securely, and adjust the cable as described in Section 3.

5 Selector lever lock components – removal and refitting

General

1 The transmission selector lever assembly incorporates an electrically-operated selector lever lock mechanism that prevents the lever being moved out of the P position unless the ignition is switched on and the brake pedal or handbrake operated. The components associated with the system are as follows:
 a) *Selector lever lock contact switch.*
 b) *Selector lever lock solenoid switch.*
 c) *Ignition key contact switch.*
 d) *Footbrake stop-light switch.*
 e) *Handbrake 'on' switch.*
2 Apart from the footbrake and handbrake switches, all the components are located on the selector lever housing, and removal and refitting is described in the following sub-Sections. Stop-light and handbrake 'on' switch removal and refitting procedures are given in Chapters 9 and 12.
3 If the selector lever is in the P position and there is an interruption of the power supply to the ignition switch (ie, if the battery is disconnected, or if the battery is flat) it will not be possible to move the selector lever out of position P by the normal means. To overcome this problem, it is possible, in an emergency, to manually release the selector lever lock solenoid switch as described in *Lever lock manual override* later in this Section.

Lever lock contact switch

Note: *New contact switch retaining clip washers will be required for refitting.*

Removal

4 Remove the selector lever housing as described in Section 4.
5 Remove the cable tie then disconnect the earth lead from the earth terminal on the base of the selector lever housing **(see illustration)**.
6 Disconnect the wiring connector from the solenoid switch for the lock lever.
7 Release the two securing clip washers and press the selector lever contact switch out of the housing. Note that new clip washers will be required for refitting.

Refitting

8 Locate the switch on the housing ensuring that it is positioned correctly and secure with two new clip washers.
9 Reconnect the wiring connector and the earth lead. Secure the earth lead with a new cable tie.

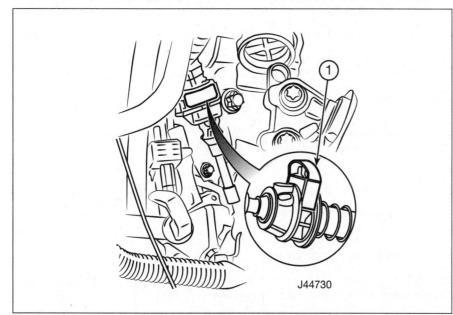

3.10 Selector cable locking clamp (1)

J44730

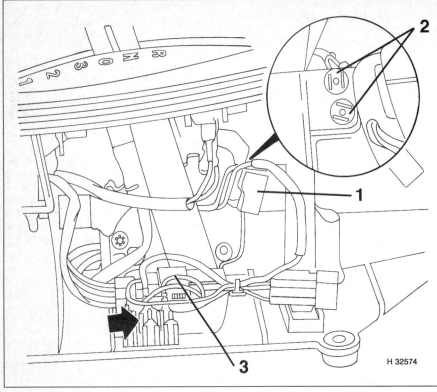

5.5 Selector lever lock contact switch details

1 Selector lever lock contact switch
2 Securing clip washers

3 Wiring connector
Arrow indicates earth lead connection

10 Refit the selector lever housing as described in Section 4.

Lever lock solenoid switch

Removal

11 Remove the selector lever housing as described in Section 4.
12 Unbolt the lever lock solenoid switch from the housing and disconnect the wiring, noting its location.

Refitting

13 Refitting is a reversal of removal.

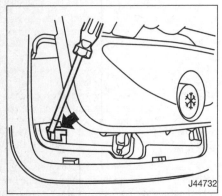

5.22 To release the selector lever lock, depress the plunger on the selector lever lock solenoid switch

Ignition lock release switch

Removal

14 Remove the selector lever housing as described in Section 4.
15 Release the two securing clip washers and press the ignition lock release contact switch out of the housing. Note that new clip washers will be required for refitting.
16 Remove the cable ties from the wiring harness.
17 Release the switch wiring contact pin from the wiring connector (pin 1 in the connector). Vauxhall special tool MKM-923-22 is available for releasing the contact pin, but it should be possible to carefully release the pin using conventional tools.
18 Disconnect the relevant earth cable, then remove the contact switch.

Refitting

19 Refitting is a reversal of removal.

Lever lock manual override

20 If it is not possible to move the selector lever out of the P position due to a disconnected or flat battery, proceed as follows.
21 Carefully prise up the indicator cover from the base of the selector lever.
22 Using a ballpoint pen or small screwdriver, push the release lever on the solenoid switch forwards and hold in this

position **(see illustration)**. Now depress the knob and move the selector lever out of the P position.
23 Refit the indicator cover.

6 Transmission input/ output speed sensors – removal and refitting

Note: *On later models (with or without ABS), a wheel speed sensor provides the engine ECU(s) with vehicle speed data. On these vehicles no speed sensor is fitted to the transmission.*

Removal

1 The input and output speed sensors are located on the rear of the transmission casing, above the left-hand driveshaft **(see illustration)**. Working in the engine compartment, reach down and disconnect the wiring plug from the top of the sensor.
2 Unscrew the retaining bolt and remove the sensor from the casing.

Refitting

3 With a new sealing ring fitted, insert the sensor into the transmission casing aperture.
4 Tighten the retaining bolt securely and reconnect the wiring plug.

7 Driveshaft oil seals – renewal

1 Apply the handbrake, then jack up the front of the vehicle and support it on axle stands (see *Jacking and vehicle support*). Remove the relevant front roadwheel.
2 Drain the transmission fluid as described in Chapter 1A or be prepared for fluid loss as the seal is changed.
3 Disconnect the inner end of the relevant driveshaft from the differential as described in Chapter 8. There is no need to disconnect the driveshaft from the swivel hub. Support the driveshaft by suspending it with wire or string

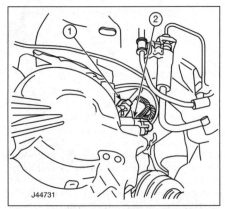

6.1 Transmission output (1) and input (2) speed sensors

– do not allow the driveshaft to hang down under its own weight, or the joints may be damaged.

4 Prise the now-exposed oil seal from the differential housing, using a screwdriver or similar instrument.

5 Smear the sealing lip of the new oil seal with a little transmission oil, then using a metal tube or socket of suitable diameter, drive the new seal into the differential casing until the outer surface of the seal is flush with the outer surface of the differential casing.

6 Reconnect the driveshaft to the differential as described in Chapter 8.

7 Refill or top-up the transmission fluid level with reference to Chapter 1A.

8 Refit the roadwheel, then lower the vehicle to the ground.

8 Fluid cooler – general information

1 The transmission fluid cooler is an integral part of the radiator assembly; radiator removal and refitting is described in Chapter 3.

2 The hoses running from the transmission to the cooler should be checked at regular intervals, and renewed if there is any doubt about their condition.

3 Always take note of the pipe and hose connections before disturbing them, and take note of the hose routing.

4 To minimise the loss of fluid, and to prevent the entry of dirt into the system, clamp the hoses before disconnecting them, and plug the unions once the hoses have been disconnected.

5 When reconnecting the hoses, ensure that they are connected to their original locations, and route them so that they are not kinked or twisted.

6 Always renew the sealing washers if the banjo union bolts (where fitted) are disturbed, and tighten the bolts to their specified torque wrench setting. Be particularly careful when tightening the cooler unions.

9 Selector lever position switch – adjustment, removal and refitting

Adjustment

1 Adjustment of the switch entails the use of Vauxhall special tool KM-962, which is then connected to the selector lever position switch wiring connector on the transmission. The tool contains a series of LEDs (light emitting diodes), that illuminate in sequence, with the ignition switched on, as each selector position is engaged. If the LEDs do not illuminate correctly in each selector lever position, the position switch securing screws must be slackened and the switch repositioned accordingly. As accurate

adjustment of the position switch can only be carried out using this tool, the work should be entrusted to a Vauxhall dealer.

Removal

Note: *It will be necessary to have the adjustment of the switch carried out by a Vauxhall dealer on completion (see adjustment above). Bearing this in mind, it may be beneficial to have the complete operation (removal, refitting and adjustment) carried out by the dealer at the same time.*

2 Remove the transmission electronic control unit as described in Section 11. Also remove the control unit mounting bracket.

3 Working in the engine compartment, press the cable end fitting from the lever on the position switch.

4 Using a screwdriver, prise off the retaining clip and release the outer selector cable from the mounting bracket on the transmission.

5 Remove the wiring harness plug bracket, and disconnect the wiring from the lever position switch.

6 Unscrew the nut and remove the lever from the transmission selector shaft.

7 Bend up the lockplate, then unscrew the switch hub retaining nut and withdraw from the shaft. It is recommended that the lockplate is renewed.

8 Mark the position of the selector lever position switch, then unscrew the adjustment lockbolts and withdraw the switch from the transmission **(see illustration)**.

Refitting

9 Locate the position switch over the shaft and onto the transmission in the previously-noted position. Insert the adjustment lock-bolts and tighten them to the specified torque.

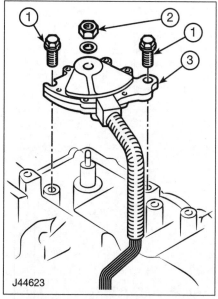

9.8 Selector lever position switch (3)

1 Adjustment lock bolts
2 Switch hub retaining nut

10 Refit the switch hub nut together with a new lockplate and tighten to the specified torque. Bend the lockplate onto the nut to lock it.

11 Locate the lever on selector shaft and tighten the nut to the specified torque.

12 Reconnect the wiring and refit the bracket.

13 Refit the outer cable to the bracket and secure with the clip.

14 Press the cable end fitting onto the lever on the position switch.

15 Refit the electronic control unit and bracket with reference to Section 11.

16 Have a Vauxhall dealer adjust the switch.

10 Transmission 'mode' switches – removal and refitting

Economy/Sport switch

1 Removal of the Economy/Sport mode switch entails complete dismantling of the selector lever housing so that the switch can be pushed out of the selector lever using a length of welding rod, or similar. The switch wires must then be unsoldered from the switch. It is recommended that this operation is entrusted to a Vauxhall dealer.

Winter switch

Removal

2 Remove the centre console as described in Chapter 11.

3 Remove the selector lever housing as described in Section 4.

4 Unclip the indicator cover, then press out the winter mode switch upwards.

5 Cut free the cable ties and remove the harness from the bracket.

6 Release the relevant switch wiring contact pins from the wiring connector, noting their location. Vauxhall special tool MKM-923-22 is available for releasing the contact pins, but it should be possible to carefully release the pin using conventional tools.

7 Remove the winter mode switch through the hole in the indicator cover.

Refitting

8 Refitting is a reversal of removal.

11 Electronic control unit – removal and refitting

Note: *The electronic control units vary according to model, and it is important that the correct unit if fitted.*

Removal

1 The automatic transmission electronic control unit is located on the left-hand side of the engine compartment, on the side of the ABS unit.

2 Disconnect the battery negative lead (refer to *Disconnecting the battery* in the Reference Chapter).

3 Disconnect the wiring plugs from the front and rear of the electronic control unit **(see illustration)**.

4 At the front of the unit, press out the retaining tab, then withdraw the control unit forwards from the mounting bracket.

Refitting

5 Refitting is a reversal of removal.

12 Automatic transmission – removal and refitting

Note: *This is an involved procedure, and it may prove easier in many cases to remove the transmission complete with the engine as an assembly, as described in Chapter 2D. If removing the transmission on its own, it is suggested that this Section is read through thoroughly before commencing work. Suitable equipment will be required to support the engine and transmission, and the help of an assistant will be required. New torque converter-to-driveplate bolts must be used on refitting, and if the original torque converter is being used, an M10 x 1.25 mm tap will be required.*

Removal

1 Apply the handbrake, then jack up the front of the vehicle and support it on axle stands (see *Jacking and vehicle support*). Allow sufficient working room to remove the transmission from under the left-hand side of the engine compartment. Remove both front roadwheels then, where necessary, undo the retaining clips/screws and remove the engine undertray. Also remove the engine top cover where fitted.

2 Drain the transmission fluid as described in Chapter 1A.

3 Remove the engine control unit from the top of the engine as described in Chapter 4A or 4B.

4 On the top of the transmission, unclip the selector lever cable, then unbolt the cable bracket.

5 Release the wiring plug and selector lever position switch from the bracket, then disconnect and separate them.

6 Pull the bleeder hose from the top of the transmission.

7 Unscrew and remove the two uppermost bolts securing the transmission to the rear of the engine. Note that the front one secures the fluid filler tube. Withdraw the filler tube and dipstick upwards from the engine.

8 Working beneath the engine compartment, remove the rear torque link as described in Chapter 2A or 2B.

9 Tie the radiator to the engine compartment front crossmember in preparation for lowering the front subframe.

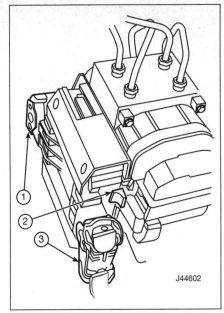

11.3 Automatic transmission electronic control unit

1 *Rear wiring plug*
2 *ECU retaining tab*
3 *Front wiring plug*

10 Remove the hub caps, then extract the split pins and unscrew the driveshaft outer hub nuts while holding the hubs stationary. To do this, temporarily insert the wheel bolts and have an assistant depress the brake pedal while the nuts are loosened.

11 Remove the front brake discs with reference to Chapter 9.

12 Refer to Chapter 10 and disconnect the track rods from the hub carrier steering arms. Also detach the anti-roll bar links from the front suspension struts, and detach the front suspension lower arms from the hub carriers.

13 Disconnect the driveshafts from the hub carriers by carefully tapping them through the hubs while pulling out the carriers. Do not allow the driveshafts to hang down under their own weight, or the joints may be damaged – support the driveshafts with wire or string.

To ensure correct repositioning, we bolted two lengths of metal bar to the subframe, and marked their position on the underbody.

14 On models with air conditioning, remove the auxiliary drivebelt (Chapter 1A), then unbolt the compressor from the engine without disconnecting the refrigerant lines and support the compressor to one side.

15 Remove the exhaust system as described in Chapter 4A or 4B.

16 Support the front suspension subframe on trolley jacks, then mark the position of the subframe on the front underbody **(see Haynes Hint)**, and unscrew the four mounting bolts. Discard the bolts as new ones must be used for refitting. With the help of an assistant, carefully lower the subframe to the ground and withdraw from under the vehicle.

17 Place a suitable container beneath the transmission quick-release fluid cooler hose connections at the transmission. Clamp the transmission fluid cooler hoses, then lever off the retaining clamps and disconnect them from the transmission, noting their locations. Be prepared for fluid spillage, and plug the open ends of the hoses and transmission, to minimise fluid loss and prevent dirt ingress. Tie the lines to one side.

18 Prise out the two access covers from the transmission housing.

19 Working through the bellhousing access holes, unscrew the three torque converter-to-driveplate bolts. It will be necessary to turn the engine, using a suitable spanner or socket on the crankshaft pulley or sprocket bolt (as applicable), to gain access to each bolt in turn through the aperture. Use a screwdriver or a similar tool to jam the driveplate ring gear, preventing the driveplate from rotating as the bolts are loosened. Discard the bolts.

20 Disconnect the inner ends of the driveshafts from the transmission as described in Chapter 8. There is no need to disconnect the driveshafts from the swivel hubs. Be prepared for transmission fluid spillage, and plug the openings in the transmission, to prevent dirt ingress and further fluid loss. Do not allow the driveshafts to hang down under their own weight, or the joints may be damaged – support the driveshafts with wire or string.

21 Attach a suitable hoist and lifting tackle to the lifting bracket located on the left-hand side of the cylinder head, and support the weight of the engine/transmission. Alternatively, the engine can be supported using a jack and interposed block of wood under the sump, however, great care must be taken when removing the transmission, not to move the engine off the jack.

22 Mark the position of the left-hand engine mounting and bracket, then unbolt and remove it from the transmission and body with reference to Chapter 2A or 2B.

23 Lower the engine and transmission by approximately 5 cm making sure that the coolant hoses and wiring harnesses are not stretched.

24 Disconnect the wiring from the TDC pick-up sensor at the left-hand front of the engine.

25 Support the weight of the transmission on

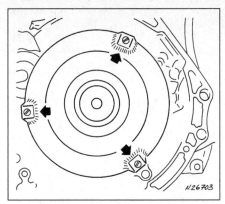

12.30 Torque converter-to-driveplate bolt threads must be recut on refitting

a trolley jack. Ensure that the engine is adequately supported as previously described.

26 Unscrew and remove the transmission-to-engine bolts.

27 Make a final check that all components have been disconnected, and are positioned clear of the transmission so that they will not hinder the removal procedure.

28 With the help of an assistant, carefully withdraw the transmission from the rear of the engine, taking care to ensure that the torque converter remains firmly in place in the transmission. Note that there are two locating dowels in the rear of the engine which may be tight, and it may be necessary to rock the transmission from side-to-side to release it from them. If this precaution is not taken, the torque converter could fall out, resulting in fluid spillage and possible damage.

29 Lower the transmission to the ground and withdraw it from under the vehicle. Retain the torque converter while the transmission is removed by bolting a strip of metal across the transmission bellhousing end face.

Refitting

30 If the original torque converter is being refitted, commence refitting by recutting the torque converter-to-driveplate bolt threads in the torque converter using an M10 x 1.25 mm tap **(see illustration)**. Clean any rust from the centre stub of the torque converter and the hole in the centre of the driveplate. Apply a little grease to the contact surfaces.

31 Check that the torque converter is fully entered inside the transmission bellhousing by measuring the distance from the flange to

the bolt holes in the torque converter, using a straight-edge and vernier calipers **(see illustration)**. The distance must measure approximately 12.0 mm.

32 If a new transmission is being fitted, the manufacturers recommend that the radiator's fluid cooler passages are flushed clean before the new transmission is installed. Ideally, compressed air should be used (in which case, ensure that adequate safety precautions are taken; in particular, eye protection should be worn). Alternatively, the cooler can be flushed with clean automatic transmission fluid until all the old fluid has been removed, and fresh fluid runs clear from the cooler outlet.

33 Position the transmission under the front of the vehicle, and support with the trolley jack. Remove the strip of metal retaining the torque converter in the transmission, and hold the torque converter in position as the transmission is located on the engine.

34 With the help of an assistant, raise the transmission and locate it on the rear of the engine. Refit all of the engine-to-transmission bolts hand-tight with the exception of the one which secures the fluid filler tube support bracket, then tighten them to their specified torque.

35 Raise the engine and transmission, then refit the left-hand mounting and bracket with reference to Chapter 2A or 2B. Make sure it is aligned with the previously-made marks. Remove the hoist and lifting tackle.

36 Align the holes of the torque converter with the holes in the driveplate. Apply locking fluid to the threads of the new bolts, then insert them separately and tighten to the specified torque while holding the driveplate ring gear stationary with the screwdriver. Refit the two access covers to the transmission housing.

37 Reconnect the wiring to the TDC pick-up sensor.

38 Reconnect the driveshafts to the transmission with reference to Chapter 8.

39 Reconnect the quick-release fluid cooler hoses together with new O-ring seals to the transmission.

40 Refit the front subframe assembly with reference to Chapter 10, making sure that it is aligned with the previously-made marks.

41 Refit the rear torque link as described in Chapter 2A or 2B.

42 Refit the fluid filler tube together with a new O-ring seal to the cylinder block. Insert

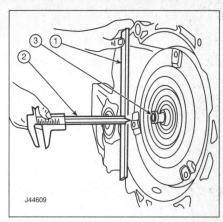

12.31 Check that the torque converter is fully entered

1 Straight-edge
2 Vernier calipers on bolt hole
3 Torque converter centre stub

the dipstick, then fit the final transmission-to-engine bolt (which also secures the filler tube support) and tighten to the specified torque.

43 Refit the bleeder hose, selector lever position switch and selector lever cable with bracket.

44 Refit the engine control unit with reference to Chapter 4A or 4B.

45 Refill the transmission with the specified fluid with reference to Chapter 1A.

46 Where fitted, refit the engine undertray, then refit the roadwheels and lower the vehicle to the ground. Refit the engine top cover where applicable.

13 Automatic transmission overhaul – general information

1 In the event of a fault occurring on the transmission, it is first necessary to determine whether it is of an electrical, mechanical or hydraulic nature, and to achieve this, special test equipment is required. It is therefore essential to have the work carried out by a Vauxhall dealer if a transmission fault is suspected.

2 Do not remove the transmission from the car for possible repair before professional fault diagnosis has been carried out, since most tests require the transmission to be in the vehicle.

Chapter 7 Part C:
Easytronic transmission

Contents

Degrees of difficulty

Easy, suitable for novice with little experience		Fairly easy, suitable for beginner with some experience		Fairly difficult, suitable for competent DIY mechanic		Difficult, suitable for experienced DIY mechanic		Very difficult, suitable for expert DIY or professional	

Specifications

General

Type	Five forward speeds and one reverse, automatic or manual selection. Integral differential
Manufacturer's designation	MTA

Gear ratios

1st	3.73:1
2nd	2.14:1
3rd	1.41:1
4th	1.12:1
5th	0.89:1
Reverse	3.31:1

Torque wrench settings

	Nm	lbf ft
Clutch module with MTA control unit	11	8
Left-hand engine mounting	See Chapter 2A or 2B	
Oil level plug:		
Stage 1	4	3
Stage 2	Angle-tighten a further 45° to 135°	
Transmission shift module	11	8
Transmission-to-engine/sump bolts	See Chapter 2A or 2B	
Transmission vent plug:		
Stage 1	4	3
Stage 2	Angle-tighten a further 45° to 135°	

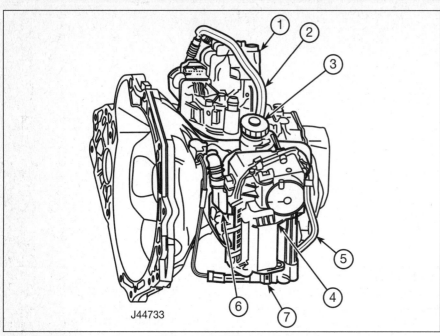

J44733

1.1 Easytronic (MTA) transmission

1 Transmission shift module
2 Wiring harness
3 Hydraulic fluid reservoir

4 Clutch control module
5 Hydraulic supply line to clutch control module

6 Wiring harness for clutch control module
7 Hydraulic pressure line to clutch release cylinder

1 General information

1 The Easytronic MTA transmission (Manual Transmission Automatic-shift) is essentially a conventional manual transmission with the addition of a clutch module and shift module, used in conjunction with a self-adjusting clutch plate **(see illustration)**.
2 The description of the MTA transmission is basically as for the manual transmission given in Chapter 7A, but with an electronically-operated hydraulic clutch control module and gear selection module. The transmission can be switched between fully automatic and manual mode, even while driving.
3 The clutch control module incorporates its own master cylinder and push rod, which is operated electrically by a worm gear.
4 The gear selection module is fitted with a shifting motor and a selector motor, which together position the selector lever to move the selector forks in the transmission. It is located in exactly the same position as the gear selection cover fitted to the conventional manual transmission.
5 Since the transmission is electronically-controlled, in the event of a problem, in the first instance the vehicle should be taken to a Vauxhall dealer who will have the TECH2 diagnostic equipment necessary to pin-point the faulty area. Note also that if the transmission assembly, shift module or clutch module are renewed, the vehicle must be taken to a Vauxhall dealer in order to have the fault memory erased and new parameters programmed into the ECU.

2 Transmission oil – draining and refilling

Note: Changing the transmission oil is not a routine job, however, it may be considered necessary if the vehicle has completed a high mileage or if a second-hand transmission is being fitted. No drain plug is fitted.

Draining

1 Apply the handbrake, then jack up the front of the vehicle and support it on axle stands (see Jacking and vehicle support). Remove the engine undertray where fitted.
2 Unbolt the rear engine torque link from the transmission and pivot it to one side.
3 Place a suitable container under the differential cover plate. Unscrew the securing bolts and withdraw the cover plate, allowing the transmission oil to drain into the container **(see illustration)**. Recover the gasket, and if necessary, renew it.
4 Refit the differential cover plate together with the gasket, and tighten the securing bolts, then refit the rear engine torque link and tighten the bolts.

Refilling

5 Wipe clean the area around the level plug. The level plug is located behind the driveshaft inner joint on the left-hand side of the transmission **(see illustration)**. Unscrew the plug and clean it.
6 The transmission is refilled through the vent on top of the transmission. Wipe clean the area around the vent, then unscrew and remove it. Refill the transmission with the specified grade of oil given in Lubricants and fluids, until it reaches the bottom of the level plug aperture. Allow any excess oil to drain, then refit and tighten the level plug. **Note:** When new, the transmission is originally filled by weight, and the level may be 20 mm below the level hole.
7 Refit and tighten the vent, then refit the engine undertray (where fitted) and lower the vehicle to the ground.

3 Selector lever assembly – removal and refitting

Removal

1 Remove the centre console as described in Chapter 11.
2 Disconnect the wiring from the selector lever.
3 Unscrew the mounting bolts and withdraw the selector lever assembly from the floor.
4 If required, the panel may be removed from the top of the gear lever using a small screwdriver.

Refitting

5 Refitting is a reversal of removal.

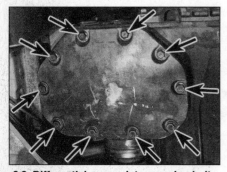

2.3 Differential cover plate securing bolts

2.5 Transmission oil level plug

4 Transmission shift module – removal and refitting

Removal

1 Switch on the ignition, then depress the footbrake pedal and move the selector lever to position N. Switch off the ignition.

2 Working in the engine compartment, disconnect the two wiring plugs and release the harness from the support cable ties on the top of the transmission.

3 Unbolt and remove the transmission shift module from the top of the transmission. To do this, lift it and tilt it slightly forwards before removing. Recover the gasket.

4 If the module cannot be removed because of internal jamming, unbolt the selector motor followed by the shifting motor **(see illustration)**, and use a screwdriver to move the selector lever to its neutral position first. The selector motor is the uppermost unit. **Note:** *The manufacturers recommend that the shift module assembly is never re-used if dismantled.*

Refitting

5 Clean the gasket faces of the module and transmission, and obtain a new gasket.

6 Make sure that the selector lever is in neutral, by checking that the mark on the segment is aligned with the pinion tooth. Check also that the lever is fully extended so that the annular groove is visible. The shift forks in the transmission must also be in neutral – use a screwdriver to move them if necessary **(see illustrations)**.

7 Refit the shift module together with a new gasket, then insert the bolts and tighten to the specified torque.

8 Reconnect the wiring and secure with new cable ties.

9 Finally, it may be necessary to have a Vauxhall dealer program all volatile memories. If a new control unit has been fitted, a Vauxhall dealer must program the unit specifically for the model to which it is fitted.

5 Clutch module with MTA control unit – removal and refitting

Note: *Bleeding the module is carried out using the Vauxhall TECH2 diagnostic instrument, therefore this work should be entrusted to a Vauxhall dealer.*

Removal

1 Apply the handbrake, then jack up the front of the vehicle and support it on axle stands (see *Jacking and vehicle support*). Where necessary, remove the engine undertray.

2 Remove the cover from the clutch hydraulic fluid reservoir.

3 Disconnect the wiring from the Easytronic

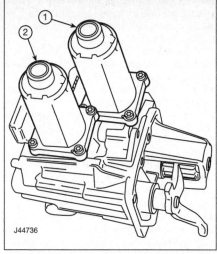

4.4 Shift motor (1) and selector motor (2) on the transmission shift module

transmission and release it from the cable tie supports.

4 Place a suitable container beneath the front of the transmission to catch spilt hydraulic fluid.

5 Fit a hose clamp to the hydraulic hose leading from the brake fluid reservoir to the clutch control unit, then disconnect the hose.

6 Disconnect the hydraulic quick-release pressure hose from the clutch control unit.

7 Unscrew the mounting bolts and remove the clutch module with MTA control unit from the transmission.

Refitting

8 Refitting is a reversal of removal, but tighten the mounting bolts to the specified torque. Make sure that the quick-release pressure hose is fully engaged – it must make an audible sound. Bleed the hydraulic circuit. Finally, it may be necessary to program all volatile memories. If a new control unit has been fitted, a Vauxhall dealer must program the unit specifically for the model to which it is fitted.

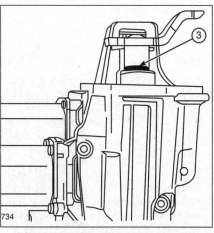

4.6b Groove (3) visible when the shift module is in neutral

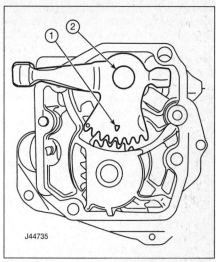

4.6a Neutral mark (1) and shift lever shaft (2) on the transmission shift module

6 Driveshaft oil seals – renewal

1 Apply the handbrake, then jack up the front of the vehicle and support it on axle stands (see *Jacking and vehicle support*). Remove the relevant front roadwheel.

2 Drain the transmission oil as described in Section 2 or be prepared for oil loss as the seal is changed.

3 Disconnect the inner end of the relevant driveshaft from the differential as described in Chapter 8. There is no need to disconnect the driveshaft from the swivel hub. Support the driveshaft by suspending it with wire or string – do not allow the driveshaft to hang down under its own weight, or the joints may be damaged.

4 Prise the now-exposed oil seal from the differential housing, using a screwdriver or similar instrument.

5 Smear the sealing lip of the new oil seal

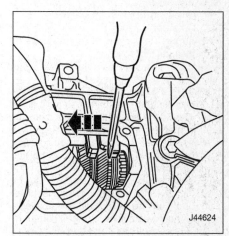

4.6c Using a screwdriver to move the transmission shift forks into neutral

with a little transmission oil, then using a metal tube or socket of suitable diameter, drive the new seal into the differential casing until the outer surface of the seal is flush with the outer surface of the differential casing.

6 Reconnect the driveshaft to the differential as described in Chapter 8.

7 Refill or top-up the transmission oil level with reference to Section 2.

8 Refit the roadwheel, then lower the vehicle to the ground.

7 Easytronic transmission – removal and refitting

Note: *This is an involved procedure, and it may well prove easier to remove the transmission complete with the engine as an assembly (see Chapter 2D), then separate the transmission. However, this Section describes removing the transmission leaving the engine in position. Suitable equipment will be required to support the engine and transmission, and the help of an assistant will be required.*

Removal

1 Apply the handbrake, then jack up the front of the vehicle and support it on axle stands (see *Jacking and vehicle support*). Allow sufficient working room to remove the transmission from under the left-hand side of the engine compartment. Remove both front roadwheels then, where necessary, undo the retaining clips/screws and remove the engine undertray. Also remove the engine top cover where fitted.

2 Remove the air cleaner housing and intake trunking (see Chapter 4A or 4B).

3 Drain the transmission oil as described in Section 2 or be prepared for oil loss as the transmission is removed.

4 Tie the radiator to the engine compartment front crossmember in preparation for lowering the front subframe.

5 Remove the hub caps, then extract the split pins and unscrew the driveshaft outer hub nuts while holding the hubs stationary. To do this, temporarily insert the wheel bolts and have an assistant depress the brake pedal while the nuts are loosened.

6 Remove the front brake discs with reference to Chapter 9.

7 Refer to Chapter 10 and disconnect the track rods from the hub carrier steering arms. Also detach the anti-roll bar links from the front suspension struts, and detach the front suspension lower arms from the hub carriers.

8 Disconnect the driveshafts from the hub carriers by carefully tapping them through the hubs while pulling out the carriers. Do not allow the driveshafts to hang down under their own weight, or the joints may be damaged – support the driveshafts with wire or string.

9 On models with air conditioning, remove the auxiliary drivebelt (Chapter 1A), then unbolt the compressor from the engine **without disconnecting the refrigerant lines** and support the compressor to one side.

10 Remove the exhaust system as described in Chapter 4A or 4B.

11 Disconnect the wiring from the transmission clutch and shift modules, and release the wiring from the support cables.

12 Support the front suspension subframe on trolley jacks, then mark the position of the subframe on the front underbody **(see Haynes Hint)**, and unscrew the four mounting bolts. Discard the bolts as new ones must be used for refitting. Unscrew and remove the bolt securing the engine rear torque link to the subframe. With the help of an assistant, carefully lower the subframe to the ground and withdraw from under the vehicle.

13 Unscrew and remove the three upper bolts securing the transmission to the rear of the engine. Where necessary, pull up the coolant hoses and secure them away from the transmission using plastic cable ties.

14 Attach a suitable hoist and lifting tackle to the lifting bracket located on the left-hand side of the cylinder head, and support the weight of the engine/transmission. Alternatively, the engine can be supported using a jack and interposed block of wood under the sump, however, great care must be taken when removing the transmission not to move the engine off the jack.

15 Unbolt and remove the left-hand mounting bracket from the transmission and body with reference to Chapter 2A or 2B.

16 Lower the engine and transmission by approximately 5 cm making sure that the coolant hoses and wiring harnesses are not stretched.

17 Refer to Chapter 8 and remove the driveshafts from the transmission. To do this, disconnect the front suspension lower arm balljoints from the hub carriers, and also disconnect the steering track rod ends from the steering arms. It is not necessary to remove the driveshafts from the hub carriers. Tie the driveshafts to one side.

18 Unbolt and remove the rear engine mounting torque link with reference to Chapter 2A or 2B.

To ensure correct repositioning, we bolted two lengths of metal bar to the subframe, and marked their position on the underbody.

19 Unscrew the four lower bolts securing the transmission to the engine sump.

20 Support the weight of the transmission on a trolley jack, then unscrew the remaining transmission-to-engine bolts.

21 Make a final check that all components have been disconnected, and are positioned clear of the transmission so that they will not hinder the removal procedure.

22 With the help of an assistant, carefully withdraw the transmission from he engine, taking care not to allow the weight of the transmission to hang on the input shaft otherwise the clutch friction disc hub may be damaged. Note that there are two locating dowels which may be tight, and it may be necessary to rock the transmission from side-to-side to release it from them. Once the transmission is free, lower the jack and manoeuvre the unit out from under the car.

Refitting

23 Commence refitting by positioning the transmission on the trolley jack beneath the engine compartment. With the help of an assistant, raise the transmission and locate it on the engine, making sure that the input shaft engages accurately with the splines of the friction disc hub. With the transmission located on the dowels, insert all of the retaining bolts and tighten to the specified torque.

24 The remaining refitting procedure is a reversal of removal, noting the following points:

a) Tighten all nuts and bolts to the specified torque (where given). Note that the torque for the transmission to sump bolts is different than the bolts to the rest of the engine.

b) Renew the driveshaft oil seals (see Section 6) before refitting the driveshafts.

c) Refit the front subframe assembly with reference to Chapter 10.

d) Refill the transmission with the specified type and quantity of oil, as described in Section 2.

e) If disturbed, bleed the clutch hydraulic circuit as described in Chapter 6.

f) Finally, it may be necessary to have a dealer program all volatile memories.

8 Easytronic transmission overhaul – general information

In the event of a fault occurring on the transmission, it is first necessary to determine whether it is of an electrical, mechanical or hydraulic nature, and to achieve this, special test equipment is required. It is therefore essential to have the work carried out by a Vauxhall dealer if a transmission fault is suspected.

Do not remove the transmission from the car for possible repair before professional fault diagnosis has been carried out, since most tests require the transmission to be in the vehicle.

Chapter 8
Driveshafts

Contents

Degrees of difficulty

Easy, suitable for novice with little experience	Fairly easy, suitable for beginner with some experience	Fairly difficult, suitable for competent DIY mechanic	Difficult, suitable for experienced DIY mechanic	Very difficult, suitable for expert DIY or professional

Specifications

Type

1.0 litre models	Unequal length shafts with outer ball-and-cage type and inner tripod type constant velocity joints
All except 1.0 litre models	Unequal length shafts with ball-and-cage type constant velocity joint at each end

Lubrication (overhaul only – see text)

Lubricant type/specification	Use only special grease supplied in sachets with gaiter kits – joints are otherwise pre-packed with grease and sealed

Torque wrench settings

	Nm	lbf ft
Driveshaft retaining nut*:		
Stage 1	120	89
Stage 2	Slacken the nut completely	
Stage 3	20	15
Stage 4	Angle-tighten through a further 90°	
Drop link retaining nut*	65	48
Lower arm balljoint clamp bolt nut*	60	44
Roadwheel bolts	110	81

*Use new nuts/bolts.

1 General information

Drive is transmitted from the differential to the front wheels by means of two solid steel driveshafts of unequal length. The right-hand driveshaft is longer than the left-hand one, due to the position of the transmission unit.

Both driveshafts are splined at their outer ends to accept the wheel hubs, and are threaded so that each hub can be fastened by a large nut. The inner end of each driveshaft is splined to accept the differential sun gear. On some models, a vibration damper is attached to the right-hand driveshaft.

Constant velocity (CV) joints are fitted to each end of the driveshafts, to ensure the smooth and efficient transmission of drive at all the angles possible as the roadwheels move up-and-down with the suspension, and as they turn from side-to-side under steering. Both inner and outer constant velocity joints are of the ball-and-cage type on all except 1.0 litre models; on these vehicles, the inner constant velocity joints are of the tripod type.

2.2 Extract the split pin from the driveshaft retaining nut

2.3 Using a fabricated tool to hold the front hub stationary whilst the driveshaft retaining nut is slackened

2.5 Holding the joint stub with an open-ended spanner

2 Driveshafts – removal and refitting

Note: *A new driveshaft retaining nut, split pin and balljoint clamp bolt nut will be needed on refitting.*

Removal

> **HAYNES HiNT** *If work is being carried out without the aid of an assistant, remove the wheel trim/hub cap (as applicable) then withdraw the split pin and slacken the driveshaft retaining nut with the vehicle resting on its wheels.*

1 Firmly apply the handbrake, then jack up the front of the car and support it securely on axle stands (see *Jacking and vehicle support*). Remove the relevant front roadwheel.

2 Extract the split pin from the driveshaft retaining nut and discard it; a new one must be used on refitting **(see illustration)**.

3 Refit at least two roadwheel bolts to the front hub, and tighten them securely. Have an assistant firmly depress the brake pedal to prevent the front hub from rotating, then using a socket and extension bar, slacken and remove the driveshaft retaining nut. Alternatively, a tool can be fabricated from two lengths of steel strip (one long, one short) and a nut an bolt; the nut and bolt forming the pivot of a forked tool. Bolt the tool to the hub using two wheel bolts, and hold the tool to prevent the hub from rotating as the driveshaft retaining nut is undone **(see illustration)**.

4 Unscrew the driveshaft retaining nut, and remove the washer. Discard the nut; a new one must be used on refitting.

5 Unscrew and remove the nut securing the anti-roll bar drop link to the strut, while holding the joint stub on the flats provided with a further spanner **(see illustration)**. Release the link from the strut and move it to one side.

6 Slacken and remove the lower arm balljoint clamp nut and bolt, and free the lower arm from the swivel hub **(see illustration)**. Discard the clamp bolt nut; a new one must be used on refitting.

7 Use a chisel or screwdriver as a wedge to expand the balljoint clamp at the bottom of the swivel hub **(see illustration)**.

8 Using a lever, push down on the lower arm to free the balljoint from the swivel hub **(see illustration)**, then move the swivel hub to one side and release the balljoint, taking care not to damage the balljoint rubber boot.

9 The swivel hub must now be freed from the end of the driveshaft. It should be possible to pull the hub off the driveshaft, but if the end of the driveshaft is tight in the hub, then tap the end of the driveshaft with a soft-faced hammer while pulling outwards on the swivel hub **(see illustrations)**. Support the driveshaft by suspending it with wire or string; **Do not** *allow the driveshaft to hang down under its own weight, or the joints may be damaged.*

10 Where fitted, remove the splash shield from under the engine compartment. Position a container beneath the transmission to catch any oil that may be spilt.

11 A suitable lever will now be required to release the inner end of the driveshaft from the differential. To release the right-hand driveshaft, a flat steel bar with a good chamfer

2.6 Withdraw the clamp bolt from the lower arm balljoint

2.7 Using a chisel to expand the balljoint clamp at the bottom of the hub carrier

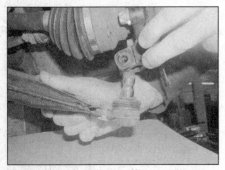

2.8 Push down the lower suspension arm to free the balljoint from the hub carrier

2.9a Use a soft-faced hammer to drive the driveshaft from the hub splines . . .

2.9b . . . then pull the hub carrier outwards

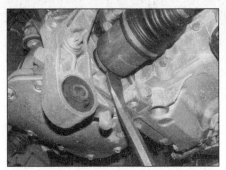

2.12 Lever the driveshaft CV joint out from the transmission to release its circlip from the differential

2.15 Prior to refitting, ensure that the circlip (arrowed) is correctly located in the inner CV joint groove

2.18 Using a punch on the CV joint weld bead to drive the joint into the differential until the circlip engages positively

on one end can be used. The left-hand driveshaft may prove more difficult to release, and a suitable square- or rectangular-section bar may be required.

12 Lever between the driveshaft and the differential housing to release the driveshaft circlip from the differential. Carefully withdraw the driveshaft from the transmission unit, taking great care not to damage the driveshaft oil seal, and remove the driveshaft from underneath the vehicle **(see illustration)**.

13 Plug the opening in the differential, to prevent further oil loss and dirt ingress.

Caution: Do not allow the vehicle to rest on its wheels with one or both driveshaft(s) removed, as damage to the wheel bearing(s) may result. If the vehicle must be moved on its wheels, clamp the wheel bearings using a long threaded rod and spacers to take the place of the outer driveshaft joint through the hub.

Refitting

14 Before installing the driveshaft, examine the driveshaft oil seal in the transmission for signs of damage or deterioration. Renew if necessary, referring to the relevant part of Chapter 7 for further information.

15 Remove the circlip from the end of the inner constant velocity joint splines and discard it. Fit a new circlip, making sure it is correctly seated in its groove **(see illustration)**.

16 Thoroughly clean the driveshaft splines, and the apertures in the transmission unit and hub assembly. Apply a thin film of grease to the oil seal lips, and to the driveshaft splines

and shoulders. Check that all gaiter clips are securely fastened.

17 Remove the plug from the transmission (see paragraph 13) and offer up the driveshaft. Locate the joint splines with those of the differential sun gear, taking great care not to damage the oil seal.

18 Place a screwdriver or similar tool on the slot/weld bead on the inner driveshaft joint, not the rubber cover, and drive the shaft into the differential until the retaining circlip engages positively **(see illustration)**. Pull on the joint, not the shaft, to make sure that the joint is securely retained by the circlip.

19 Locate the outer constant velocity joint splines with those of the swivel hub, and slide the joint back into position in the hub.

20 Using the lever, push down on the lower suspension arm, then relocate the balljoint and release the arm. Make sure that the balljoint stub is fully entered in the swivel hub.

21 Insert the balljoint clamp bolt to the swivel hub, so that its threads are facing to the rear of the vehicle. Fit a new nut to the clamp bolt, and tighten it to the specified torque setting.

22 Refit the anti-roll bar drop link to the strut, and tighten the nut to the specified torque while holding the joint on its flats using a spanner.

23 Refit the washer to the end of the drive-shaft, then screw on a new nut. Using the method employed on removal to prevent rotation, tighten the new driveshaft retaining nut through the stages given in the Specifications at the start of this Chapter **(see illustration)**.

24 With the nut correctly tightened, secure it in position with a new split pin **(see**

illustrations). If the holes in the driveshaft are not aligned with any of the slots in the nut, loosen **(do not tighten)** the nut by the *smallest possible amount* until the split pin can be inserted.

25 Refit the splash shield under the engine (where fitted), then refit the roadwheel, then lower the vehicle to the ground and tighten the roadwheel bolts to the specified torque.

26 Check and if necessary top-up the transmission oil level, using the information given in the relevant part of Chapter 7.

---

3 Driveshaft rubber gaiters – renewal

Ball-and-cage type joint

All joints except 1.0 litre inner

Note: *If both driveshaft gaiters are to renewed at the same time, it is only necessary to remove one of the constant velocity joints. The second gaiter can then be slid along and removed from the exposed end of the driveshaft. The inner and outer CV joints are identical (except 1.0 litre model inner joints) and the following procedure can be used for either joint.*

1 Remove the driveshaft from the car as described in Section 2.

2 Secure the driveshaft in a vice equipped with soft jaws, and release the two retaining clips on the gaiter which is to be renewed. If necessary, the retaining clips can be cut to release them.

2.23 Refit the washer and a new retaining nut

2.24a Insert a new split pin . . .

2.24b . . . and secure in position by bending over the split pin ends

3.4a The CV joint circlip (arrowed) . . .

3.4b . . . can be expanded using circlip pliers to release the joint from the shaft

3.9 Examine the constant velocity joint balls and cage for signs of wear or damage

3.11 Components required for driveshaft gaiter renewal

3.14 Slide the gaiter onto the end of the driveshaft

3.15a Fit a new circlip . . .

3 Slide the rubber gaiter down the shaft to expose the constant velocity joint. Scoop out any excess grease.

4 Using circlip pliers, expand the circlip which secures the joint to the driveshaft **(see illustrations)**.

5 Using a soft-faced mallet, tap the joint off the end of the driveshaft.

6 Slide the rubber gaiter off the driveshaft, and discard it.

7 If both gaiters are to be renewed, release the retaining clips, then slide the second gaiter along the driveshaft and remove it. If the driveshaft is fitted with a vibration damper, mark the damper fitted position, then remove it from the driveshaft (see Section 5).

8 Thoroughly clean the constant velocity joint(s) using paraffin, or a suitable solvent, and dry thoroughly. Carry out a visual inspection as follows.

9 Move the inner splined driving member

from side-to-side, to expose each ball in turn at the top of its track. Examine the balls for cracks, flat spots, or signs of surface pitting **(see illustration)**.

10 Inspect the ball tracks on the inner and outer members. If the tracks have widened, the balls will no longer be a tight fit. At the same time, check the ball cage windows for wear or cracking between the windows.

11 If on inspection any of the constant velocity joint components are found to be worn or damaged, it will be necessary to renew the complete joint assembly. If the joint is in satisfactory condition, obtain a repair kit consisting of a new gaiter and retaining clips, a constant velocity joint circlip, and the correct type and quantity of grease **(see illustration)**. Note: *If vibration, consistent with road speed, is felt through the car when accelerating, there is a possibility of wear in the inner constant velocity joints.*

12 Wind tape around the splines on the end of the driveshaft, to protect the gaiter as it is slid into place.

13 Where both gaiters have been removed, slide on the first gaiter and proceed as described in paragraphs 15 to 18.

14 Slide the (second) gaiter onto the end of the driveshaft **(see illustration)**, then remove the tape from the driveshaft splines.

15 Fit a new circlip to the constant velocity joint, then tap the joint onto the driveshaft until the circlip engages in its groove **(see illustrations)**. Make sure that the joint is securely retained by the circlip, by pulling on the joint, not the shaft.

16 Pack the joint with the specified type of grease **(see illustration)**. Work the grease well into the bearing tracks whilst twisting the joint, and fill the rubber gaiter with any excess.

17 Ease the gaiter over the joint, and ensure

3.15b . . . ensuring it is correctly located in the joint inner member

3.15c Slide the joint onto the driveshaft until the circlip is correctly located in the driveshaft groove

3.16 Pack the CV joint and gaiter with the grease supplied

3.18a Hook the large outer retaining clip ends together . . .

3.18b . . . then secure the clip in position by compressing the raised section of the clip

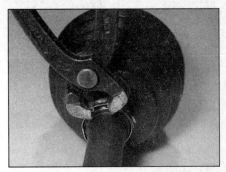

3.18c Small inner retaining clip is secured in position in the same way

that the gaiter lips are correctly located in the grooves on both the driveshaft and constant velocity joint. Lift the outer sealing lip of the gaiter, to equalise air pressure within the gaiter.

18 Fit the large metal retaining clip to the gaiter. Pull the clip as tight as possible, and locate the hooks on the clip in their slots. Remove any slack in the gaiter retaining clip by carefully compressing the raised section of the clip. In the absence of the special tool, a pair of side-cutters may be used. Secure the small retaining clip using the same procedure **(see illustrations)**.

19 Check that both constant velocity joints move freely in all directions then, where applicable, refit the vibration damper to its original position on the driveshaft (see Section 5). On completion, refit the driveshaft to the car as described in Section 2.

Tripod joints

1.0 litre models inner

20 Remove the driveshaft from the car as described in Section 2.

21 The outer CV joint on 1.0 litre models is of the same ball-and-cage type as used on all other models. Both rubber gaiters can therefore be renewed after removing the outer CV joint as described previously in paragraphs 1 to 19.

22 If the inner rubber gaiter is being renewed, and an initial inspection indicates possible wear in the inner joint, remove the joint for a detailed inspection as follows.

23 With the rubber gaiter released from the joint, mark the joint outer member in relation to the driveshaft, to ensure correct refitting. Withdraw the joint outer member from the tripod and driveshaft. As the outer member is withdrawn, take precautions to prevent the bearing rollers falling off the tripod. Wipe away all excess grease and, if necessary, wrap tape around the tripod joint to secure the rollers in position.

24 Prise the circlip from the end of the driveshaft, then using a punch, paint or a suitable marker pen, make alignment marks between the tripod joint and driveshaft, and also identify which way round the tripod is fitted **(see illustrations)**. Remove the tripod joint assembly from the end of the shaft, if the

joint is a tight fit, it maybe necessary to use a puller to draw it off the shaft – if a puller is used, take great care not to damage the rollers.

25 Slide the gaiter off the end of the driveshaft.

26 Where applicable, remove the tape from the joint, and thoroughly clean the constant velocity joint components using paraffin, or a suitable solvent, and dry the components thoroughly.

27 Check the spider, rollers and outer member for signs of wear, pitting or scuffing on their bearing surfaces. Also check that the spider rollers rotate smoothly and easily, with no traces of roughness.

28 If any of the constant velocity joint components are found to be worn or damaged, it will be necessary to renew the complete joint assembly. If the joint is in satisfactory condition, obtain a repair kit consisting of a new gaiter and retaining clips, circlips, and the correct type and quantity of grease.

29 Clean the driveshaft, and tape over the splines on its inner end to protect the new gaiter as it is fitted.

30 Slide the new gaiter onto the driveshaft then remove the tape from the driveshaft end.

31 If necessary, again wind tape around the tripod to retain the rollers then, with the previously-made marks on the tripod and driveshaft aligned, push the tripod onto the driveshaft splines. If necessary use a soft-faced mallet to drive the tripod fully onto the splines. Secure the tripod in position using the new circlip, making sure that the circlip locates correctly in the driveshaft groove.

32 Where applicable, remove the tape from around the tripod, then work the grease supplied with the repair kit fully into the roller bearings. Fill the joint outer member with any excess grease.

33 Locate the outer member over the tripod, making sure that the previously-made marks are aligned.

34 Slide the gaiter along the driveshaft, and locate it in the recesses on the driveshaft and joint outer member.

35 Ensure that the gaiter is not twisted or distorted, then carefully lift the lip of the gaiter at the outer member end to equalise air pressure in the gaiter.

36 Fit the large metal retaining clip to the gaiter. Remove any slack in the gaiter retaining clip by carefully compressing the raised section of the clip. In the absence of the special tool, a pair of side-cutters may be used. Secure the small retaining clip using the same procedure.

37 The driveshaft can now be refitted to the car as described in Section 2.

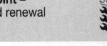

4 Driveshaft joint –
checking and renewal

Checking

1 First carry out the checks described in Chapter 1A or 1B, to reveal if there is any wear in one of the driveshaft joints.

2 Check the split pin is in position and the driveshaft nut is tight. If in doubt, the only

3.24a Prise the circlip from the end of the driveshaft. . .

3.24b . . . then make alignment marks between the tripod joint and the driveshaft

5.0 Vibration damper fitted to the right-hand driveshaft on certain models

alternative is to obtain a new nut and split pin, then fit and tighten the nut using the procedures described in Section 2. Once tightened, secure the nut in position with the new split pin, and refit the centre cap or trim. Repeat this check on the other driveshaft nut.

3 Road test the vehicle, and listen for a metallic clicking noise from the front as the vehicle is driven slowly in a circle on full-lock. If evident, this indicates wear in the outer constant velocity joint which must be renewed.

4 To check for wear on the inner joint, apply the handbrake then jack up the front of the vehicle and support it on axle stands (see *Jacking and vehicle support*). Attempt to move the inner end of the driveshaft up-and-down, then hold the joint with one hand and attempt to rotate the driveshaft with the other. If excessive wear is evident, the joint must be renewed. **Note:** *If vibration, consistent with*

road speed, is felt through the car when accelerating, there is a possibility of wear in the inner constant velocity joints.

Renewal

Note: *It may not be possible to renew the tripod type inner joint individually (as fitted to the 1.0 litre model), check with your local Vauxhall dealer for the availability of parts.*

5 To renew the ball-and-cage type constant velocity joint, follow the procedures in Section 3. If the old gaiter is going to be re-used it can be left on the driveshaft, take care not to damage the gaiter when removing the retaining clips.

---

5 Vibration damper (right-hand driveshaft) – removal and refitting

Note: *On some models a vibration damper is fitted to the right-hand driveshaft (see illustration). The vibration damper can only be separated from the driveshafts that are made by GKN. On any other make of driveshaft the complete driveshaft will have to be renewed, if there is a fault with the vibration damper.*

Removal

1 Remove the driveshaft from the car as described in Section 2.

2 Remove the transmission side constant velocity joint and gaiter as described in Section 3.

3 Clean around the vibration damper, then

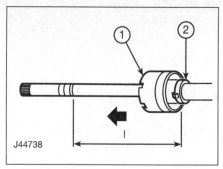

5.6 The vibration damper (1) must be secured in position with a new retaining clip (2)

Dimension I = 22.5 cm ± 5 mm

mark the dampers fitted position on the driveshaft.

4 Cut the retaining clip from around the collar of the vibration damper, discard it, a new one will be required on refitting.

5 Spray the shaft with penetrating oil, and pull the vibration damper from the driveshaft.

Refitting

6 Refitting is a reversal of removal, bearing in mind the following points:

a) Fit the vibration damper to the driveshaft using the measurement shown *(see illustration).*

b) Use the relevant Section when refitting the constant velocity joint to the driveshaft.

c) Use the relevant Section when refitting the driveshaft to the vehicle.

Chapter 9
Braking system

Contents

Degrees of difficulty

Easy, suitable for novice with little experience		Fairly easy, suitable for beginner with some experience		Fairly difficult, suitable for competent DIY mechanic		Difficult, suitable for experienced DIY mechanic	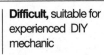	Very difficult, suitable for expert DIY or professional	

Specifications

Front brakes

	New	Minimum
Type . . . . Disc, with single-piston sliding caliper		
Disc diameter:		
1.0 and 1.2 litre petrol models . . . . 240 mm		
1.4 litre petrol models . . . . 260 mm		
1.7 litre diesel models:		
Y17DTL . . . . 240 mm		
Y17DT . . . . 260 mm		
Disc thickness:	**New**	**Minimum**
1.0 and 1.2 litre petrol models :		
With ABS	20.0 mm	17.0 mm
Without ABS	11.0 mm	8.0 mm
1.4 litre petrol models	24.0 mm	21.0 mm
1.7 litre diesel models:		
Y17DTL	20.0 mm	17.0 mm
Y17DT	24.0 mm	21.0 mm
Maximum disc run-out	0.03 mm	
Brake pad thickness:		
New (including backing plate):		
1.0 and 1.2 litre petrol models	15.0 mm	
1.4 litre petrol models	16.0 mm	
1.7 litre diesel models	16.0 mm	
Minimum thickness (including backing plate)	7.0 mm	
Brake caliper piston diameter:		
1.0 and 1.2 litre petrol models	48.0 mm	
1.4 litre petrol models	54.0 mm	
1.7 litre diesel models	54.0 mm	

Rear brakes

Type	Single leading shoe drum	
Drum diameter (inner):	**New**	**Maximum**
Corsa and Corsavan models:		
All models except Y17DTL diesel engines	200 mm	201 mm
Y17DTL diesel engines (also some Y17DT engines)	230 mm	231 mm
Combo Van models	230 mm	231 mm
Drum width:		
Corsa and Corsavan models:		
All models except Y17DTL diesel engines		
With ABS	45.0 mm	
Without ABS	28.0 mm	
Y17DTL diesel engines (also some Y17DT engines)	40.0 mm	
Combo Van models	40.0 mm	
Maximum drum out-of-round	0.8 mm	
Brake shoes thickness:		
New (without backing plate)	5.0 mm	
Minimum thickness	2.5 mm	
Wheel cylinder nominal diameter	19.05 mm	

Torque wrench settings

	Nm	lbf ft
ABS components:		
ECU-to-modulator retaining screws*	3	2
Front wheel sensor bolt	8	6
Modulator block retaining nuts	10	7
Brake hose union bolt:		
Front caliper	40	30
Rear caliper	16	12
Brake pedal bracket bolt and nuts*	20	15
Brake pipe union nut	16	12
Front brake caliper:		
Guide bolts*	27	20
Mounting bracket-to-swivel hub bolts	100	74
Front brake disc retaining screw	7	5
Master cylinder mounting nuts*	25	18
Pressure-regulating valve:		
Mounting bolts	20	15
Tension spring clamping screw	11	8
Rear drum hub nut*	175	129
Rear wheel cylinder bolts	9	7
Roadwheel bolts	110	81
Vacuum hose to vacuum pump	18	13
Vacuum servo unit mounting nuts*	20	15

Use new nuts/bolts

1 General information

The braking system is of the servo-assisted, dual-circuit hydraulic type. The arrangement of the hydraulic system is such that each circuit operates one front and one rear brake from a tandem master cylinder. Under normal circumstances, both circuits operate in unison. However, in the event of hydraulic failure in one circuit, full braking force will still be available at two wheels.

All models covered in this manual have front disc brakes and rear drum brakes (rear discs are fitted to the 1.8 litre petrol engines – not covered in this manual). An Anti-lock Braking System (ABS) is fitted as an optional extra to all vehicles covered in this manual (it

is fitted as standard to the 1.8 litre petrol model. Refer to Section 19 for further information on ABS operation.

The front disc brakes are actuated by single-piston sliding type calipers, which ensure that equal pressure is applied to each disc pad.

The rear drum brakes incorporate leading and trailing shoes, which are actuated by twin-piston wheel cylinders. A self-adjust mechanism is incorporated to automatically compensate for brake shoe wear. As the brake shoe linings wear, the footbrake operation automatically operates the adjuster mechanism, which effectively lengthens the shoe strut, and repositions the brake shoes to maintain the lining-to-drum clearance.

On models without ABS fitted, there are pressure-regulating valves which are situated in the hydraulic lines to control the pressure applied to the rear brakes. The regulating

valves help to prevent rear wheel lock-up during emergency braking. On 1.0 and 1.2 litre models, the valves are of the pressure-dependent type; on all other models, they are of the load-dependent type, which alter the pressure to suit the load being carried by the vehicle.

The cable-operated handbrake provides an independent mechanical means of rear brake application.

Note: *When servicing any part of the system, work carefully and methodically; also observe scrupulous cleanliness when overhauling any part of the hydraulic system. Always renew components (in axle sets, where applicable) if in doubt about their condition, and use only genuine Vauxhall replacement parts, or at least those of known good quality. Note the warnings given in 'Safety first!' and at relevant points in this Chapter concerning the dangers of asbestos dust and hydraulic fluid.*

2 Hydraulic system – bleeding

⚠️ **Warning: Hydraulic fluid is poisonous; wash off immediately and thoroughly in the case of skin contact, and seek immediate medical advice if any fluid is swallowed or gets into the eyes. Certain types of hydraulic fluid are inflammable, and may ignite when allowed into contact with hot components. When servicing any hydraulic system, it is safest to assume that the fluid IS inflammable, and to take precautions against the risk of fire as though it is petrol that is being handled. Hydraulic fluid is also an effective paint stripper, and will attack plastics; if any is spilt, it should be washed off immediately using copious quantities of water. Finally, it is hygroscopic (it absorbs moisture from the air) – old fluid may be contaminated, and unfit for further use. When topping-up or renewing the fluid, always use the recommended type, and ensure that it comes from a freshly-opened sealed container.**

General

1 Any hydraulic system will only function correctly once all the air has been removed from the components and circuit; this is achieved by bleeding the system.

2 During the bleeding procedure, add only clean, fresh hydraulic fluid of the recommended type; never use old fluid, nor re-use any which has already been bled from the system. Ensure that sufficient fresh fluid is available before starting work.

3 If there is any possibility of the wrong fluid being in the system, the brake components and circuit must be flushed completely with uncontaminated, correct fluid, and new seals should be fitted to the various components.

4 If hydraulic fluid has been lost from the system (or if air has entered) because of a leak, ensure that the fault is cured before proceeding further.

5 Park the vehicle on level ground, switch off the engine and select first or reverse gear, then chock the wheels and release the handbrake.

6 Check that all pipes and hoses are secure, that the pipe unions are tight, and that the bleed screws are closed. Clean any dirt from around the bleed screws.

7 Unscrew the master cylinder reservoir cap, and top the master cylinder reservoir up to the MAX level line; refit the cap loosely, and remember to maintain the fluid level at least above the MIN level line throughout the procedure, to avoid the risk of further air entering the system.

8 There are a number of one-man, do-it-yourself brake bleeding kits currently available from motor accessory shops. It is recommended that one of these kits is used whenever possible, as they greatly simplify the bleeding operation, and also reduce the risk of expelled air and fluid being drawn back into the system. If such a kit is not available, the basic (two-man) method must be used, which is described in detail below.

Caution: Vauxhall recommend using a pressure bleeding kit for this operation (see paragraphs 24 to 27).

9 If a kit is to be used, prepare the vehicle as described previously, and follow the kit manufacturer's instructions, as the procedures may vary slightly according to the type being used; generally, they will be as outlined below in the relevant sub-section.

10 Whichever method is used, the same sequence must be followed (paragraphs 11 and 12) to ensure the removal of all air from the system.

Bleeding sequence

11 If the system has been only partially disconnected, and suitable precautions were taken to minimise fluid loss, it should only be necessary to bleed that part of the system (ie, the primary or secondary circuit).

12 If the complete system is to be bled, then it should be done working in the following sequence:

a) Left-hand front brake.
b) Right-hand front brake.
c) Left-hand rear brake.
d) Right-hand rear brake.

Bleeding

Basic (two-man) method

13 Collect a clean glass jar, a suitable length of plastic or rubber tubing which is a tight fit over the bleed screw, and a ring spanner to fit the bleed screw. The help of an assistant will also be required.

14 Remove the dust cap from the first screw in the sequence. Fit the spanner and tube to the screw, place the other end of the tube in the jar, and pour in sufficient fluid to cover the end of the tube.

15 Ensure that the master cylinder reservoir fluid level is maintained at least above the MIN level line throughout the procedure.

16 Have the assistant fully depress the brake pedal several times to build-up pressure, then maintain it on the final stroke.

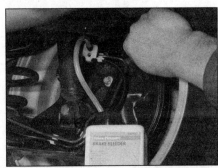

2.22 Using a one-way valve kit to bleed the rear brake

17 While pedal pressure is maintained, unscrew the bleed screw (approximately one turn) and allow the compressed fluid and air to flow into the jar. The assistant should maintain pedal pressure, following it down to the floor if necessary, and should not release it until instructed to do so. When the flow stops, tighten the bleed screw again; the pedal should then be released slowly, and the reservoir fluid level checked and topped-up.

18 Repeat the steps given in paragraphs 16 and 17 until the fluid emerging from the bleed screw is free from air bubbles. If the master cylinder has been drained and refilled, and air is being bled from the first screw in the sequence, allow approximately five seconds between cycles for the master cylinder passages to refill.

19 When no more air bubbles appear, tighten the bleed screw securely, remove the tube and spanner, and refit the dust cap. Do not over-tighten the bleed screw.

20 Repeat the procedure on the remaining screws in the sequence, until all air is removed from the system and the brake pedal feels firm again.

Using a one-way valve kit

21 As their name implies, these kits consist of a length of tubing with a one-way valve fitted, to prevent expelled air and fluid being drawn back into the system; some kits include a translucent container, which can be positioned so that the air bubbles can be more easily seen flowing from the end of the tube.

22 The kit is connected to the bleed screw, which is then opened **(see illustration)**. The user returns to the driver's seat, depresses the brake pedal with a smooth, steady stroke, then slowly releases it; this is repeated until the expelled fluid is clear of air bubbles.

23 These kits simplify work so much that it is easy to forget the master cylinder reservoir fluid level; ensure that this is maintained at least above the MIN level line at all times, or air will be drawn into the system.

Using a pressure bleeding kit

24 These kits are usually operated by the reservoir of pressurised air contained in the spare tyre, noting that it will probably be necessary to reduce the pressure to less than normal; refer to the instructions supplied with the kit.

25 By connecting a pressurised, fluid-filled container to the master cylinder reservoir, bleeding can be carried out simply by opening each screw in turn (in the specified sequence) and allowing the fluid to flow out until no more air bubbles can be seen in the expelled fluid.

26 This method has the advantage that the large reservoir of fluid provides an additional safeguard against air being drawn into the system during bleeding.

27 Pressure bleeding is particularly effective when bleeding 'difficult' systems, or when bleeding the complete system at the time of routine fluid renewal.

4.2 Unscrew the lower retaining bolt and lift the caliper up

4.3 Remove the anti-rattle springs from the caliper mounting bracket

All methods

28 When bleeding is complete and firm pedal feel is restored, wash off any spilt fluid, tighten the bleed screws securely, and refit their dust caps.

29 Check the hydraulic fluid level, and top-up if necessary (see *Weekly checks*).

30 Discard any hydraulic fluid that has been bled from the system; it will not be fit for re-use. Bear in mind that this fluid may be inflammable.

31 Check the feel of the brake pedal. If it feels at all spongy, air must still be present in the system, and further bleeding is required. Failure to bleed satisfactorily after a reasonable repetition of the bleeding procedure may be due to worn master cylinder seals.

3 Hydraulic pipes and hoses – renewal

Note: *Before starting work, refer to the warning note at the beginning of Section 2 concerning the dangers of hydraulic fluid.*

1 If any pipe or hose is to be renewed, minimise fluid loss by first removing the master cylinder reservoir cap and screwing it down onto a piece of polythene. Alternatively, flexible hoses can be sealed, if required, using a proprietary brake hose clamp. Metal brake pipe unions can be plugged (if care is taken not to allow dirt into the system) or capped immediately they are disconnected. Place a wad of rag under any union that is to be disconnected, to catch any spilt fluid.

2 If a flexible hose is to be disconnected, unscrew the brake pipe union nut before removing the spring clip which secures the hose to its mounting bracket. Where applicable, unscrew the banjo union bolt securing the hose to the caliper and recover the copper washers.

3 To unscrew the union nuts, it is preferable to obtain a brake pipe spanner of the correct size; these are available from most large motor accessory shops. Failing this, a close-fitting open-ended spanner will be required, though if the nuts are tight or corroded, their flats may be rounded-off if the spanner slips.

In such a case, a self-locking wrench is often the only way to unscrew a stubborn union, but it follows that the pipe and the damaged nuts must be renewed on reassembly. Always clean a union and surrounding area before disconnecting it. If disconnecting a component with more than one union, make a careful note of the connections before disturbing any of them.

4 If a brake pipe is to be renewed it can be obtained, cut to length and with the union nuts and end flares in place, from Vauxhall dealers. All that is then necessary is to bend it to shape, following the line of the original, before fitting it to the car. Alternatively, most motor accessory shops can make up brake pipes from kits, but this requires very careful measurement of the original to ensure that the replacement is of the correct length. The safest answer is usually to take the original to the shop as a pattern.

5 On refitting, securely tighten the union nuts but do not over-tighten (it is not necessary to exercise brute force to obtain a sound joint).

6 When refitting hoses to the calipers, always use new copper washers and tighten the banjo union bolts to the specified torque. Make sure that the hoses are positioned so that they will not touch surrounding bodywork or the roadwheels.

7 Ensure that the pipes and hoses are correctly routed, with no kinks, and that they are secured in the clips or brackets provided. After fitting, remove the polythene from the reservoir, and bleed the hydraulic system as described in Section 2. Wash off any spilt fluid, and check carefully for fluid leaks.

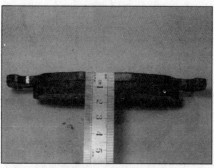

4.5 Measuring brake pad thickness

4 Front brake pads – renewal

⚠ **Warning: Renew BOTH sets of front brake pads at the same time – NEVER renew the pads on only one wheel, as uneven braking may result. Note that the dust created by wear of the pads may contain asbestos, which is a health hazard. Never blow it out with compressed air, and don't inhale any of it. An approved filtering mask should be worn when working on the brakes. DO NOT use petroleum-based solvents to clean brake parts – use brake cleaner or methylated spirit only.**

1 Firmly apply the handbrake, then jack up the front of the car and support it securely on axle stands (see *Jacking and vehicle support*). Remove the front roadwheels.

2 With the steering in the straight-ahead position, unscrew the lower guide bolt from the caliper, and lift the caliper upwards to gain access to the brake pads **(see illustration)**.

3 Remove the brake pads and anti-rattle springs from the caliper mounting bracket, noting there fitted position **(see illustration)**.

4 Brush the dirt and dust from the caliper mounting bracket, but take care not to inhale it. Carefully remove any rust from the edge of the brake disc.

5 First measure the thickness of each brake pad (friction material and backing plate) **(see illustration)**. If either pad is worn at any point to the specified minimum thickness or less, all four pads must be renewed. The pads should also be renewed if any are fouled with oil or grease; there is no satisfactory way of degreasing friction material, once contaminated. If any of the brake pads are worn unevenly, or fouled with oil or grease, trace and rectify the cause before reassembly. Check the pad anti-rattle springs, renew if required. New brake pads and springs are available from Vauxhall dealers.

6 If the brake pads are still serviceable, carefully clean them using a clean, fine wire brush or similar, paying particular attention to the sides and back of the metal backing. Clean out the grooves in the friction material, and pick out any large embedded particles of dirt or debris. Carefully clean the pad locations in the caliper body/mounting bracket.

7 Prior to fitting the pads, check that the guide pins are a snug fit in the caliper mounting bracket **(see illustration)**. Brush the dust and dirt from the caliper and piston, but do not inhale it, as it is injurious to health. Inspect the dust seal around the piston for damage, and the piston for evidence of fluid leaks, corrosion or damage. If attention to any of these components is necessary, refer to Section 8.

8 If new brake pads are to be fitted, the caliper piston must be pushed back into the cylinder to make room for them. *It is imperative that the caliper piston is pushed back as slowly as possible, using minimal force.* Either use a G-clamp or similar tool, or use suitable pieces of wood as levers. Provided that the master cylinder reservoir has not been overfilled with hydraulic fluid, there should be no spillage, but keep a careful watch on the fluid level while retracting the piston. If the fluid level rises above the MAX level line at any time, the surplus should be syphoned off or ejected via a plastic tube connected to the bleed screw (see Section 2). *Note: Do not syphon the fluid by mouth, as it is poisonous; use a syringe or an old battery hydrometer.*

 There have been some instances of damage being caused to the master cylinder seals when pushing the piston back into the caliper, and we therefore recommend that a hose clamp is fitted to the brake hose leading to the caliper and hydraulic fluid drained through the bleed nipple. Using this method will also remove any deteriorated hydraulic fluid which may have accumulated near the caliper.

9 Fit the brake pads and anti-rattle springs to the caliper mounting bracket, ensuring that its friction material is facing the brake disc **(see illustrations)**.
10 Move the caliper downwards into position over the brake pads, then install a new caliper guide bolt. Tighten the bolt to the specified torque setting **(see illustration)**.
11 Depress the brake pedal repeatedly, until normal (non-assisted) pedal pressure is restored, and the pads are pressed into firm contact with the brake disc.
12 Repeat the above procedure on the remaining front brake caliper.
13 Refit the roadwheels, aligning the marks made on removal, then lower the vehicle to the ground and tighten the roadwheel bolts to the specified torque setting.
14 Check the hydraulic fluid level as described in *Weekly checks*.

5 Rear brake shoes – renewal

⚠️ *Warning: Brake shoes must be renewed on BOTH rear wheels at the same time – NEVER renew the shoes on only one wheel, as uneven braking may result. The dust created as the shoes wear may contain asbestos, which is a health hazard. Never blow it out with compressed air, and don't inhale any of it. An approved filtering mask should be worn when working on the brakes. DO NOT use petroleum-based solvents to clean brake parts – use brake cleaner or methylated spirit only.*

4.7 Check the guide pins move freely in the caliper mounting bracket

4.9b . . . and to the caliper mounting bracket (arrowed)

1 Remove the brake drum as described in Section 7.
2 Working carefully and taking the necessary precautions, remove all traces of brake dust from the brake drum, backplate and shoes.
3 Measure the thickness of the friction material of each brake shoe, at several points. If the friction material thickness is equal to or less than the specified minimum, all four shoes must be renewed as a set **(see illustration)**. Also, the shoes should be renewed if any are fouled with oil or grease; there is no satisfactory way of degreasing friction material, once contaminated.
4 If any of the brake shoes are worn unevenly, or fouled with oil or grease, trace and rectify the cause before reassembly. If the shoes are to be renewed proceed as described below. If all is well refit the drums as described in Section 7.

5.3 Brake shoe wear can be assessed by measuring the thickness of the friction material

4.9a Fit new anti-rattle springs to the brake pads . . .

4.10 Tighten the guide bolts (arrowed) to the specified torque setting

5 Note the location and orientation of all components before dismantling, as an aid to reassembly **(see illustration)**.
6 Using a pair of pliers, carefully unhook the upper shoe return spring, and remove it from the brake shoes **(see illustration)**.
7 Prise the adjusting lever retaining spring out of the front shoe, and remove the retaining spring, lever and return spring from the brake shoe, noting each component's correct fitted position **(see illustrations)**.
8 Prise the upper ends of the brake shoes apart, and withdraw the adjuster strut from between the shoes **(see illustration)**.
9 Using a pair of pliers, remove the front shoe retainer spring cup by depressing and turning it through 90°. With the cup removed, lift off the spring and withdraw the retainer pin **(see illustration)**.
10 Detach the front shoe from the lower

5.5 Prior to disturbing the shoes, note the correct fitted locations of all components, paying particular attention to the adjuster strut components

5.6 Unhook the upper return spring, and remove it from the brake shoes

5.7a Remove the return spring . . .

5.7b . . . followed by the retaining spring . . .

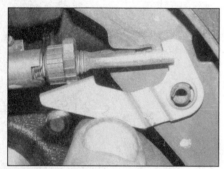

5.7c . . . and the operating lever

5.8 Withdraw the adjuster strut from the brake shoes

5.9 Using pliers, remove the spring cup then lift off the spring and retainer pin

return spring, and remove both the shoe and return spring **(see illustration)**.

11 Remove the rear shoe retainer spring cup, spring and retainer pin as described in

paragraph 9, then remove the shoe, detaching it from the handbrake cable **(see illustrations)**.

12 Do not depress the brake pedal until the

brakes are reassembled. As a precaution, wrap a cable tie or a strong elastic band around the wheel cylinder pistons to retain them **(see illustration)**.

13 If both brake assemblies are dismantled at the same time, take care not to mix up the components. Note that the left-hand and right-hand adjuster components are marked as such; the threaded rod is marked L or R, and the other 'handed' components are colour-coded black for the left-hand side, and silver for the right-hand side **(see illustration)**.

14 Dismantle and clean the adjuster strut. Apply a smear of silicone-based grease to the adjuster threads **(see illustration)**.

15 Examine the return springs. If they are distorted, or if they have seen extensive service, renewal is advisable. Weak springs may cause the brakes to bind.

16 If a new handbrake operating lever was

5.10 Remove the shoe from the backplate and unhook the return spring

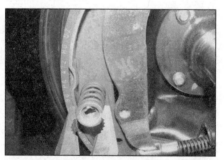

5.11a Using pliers, remove the other spring cup then lift off the spring and retainer pin

5.11b Remove the other shoe from the backplate and unhook the handbrake cable

5.12 Plastic cable tie retaining the wheel cylinder pistons

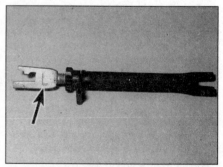

5.13 The left-hand adjuster strut assembly is marked L (arrowed)

5.14 Dismantling the adjuster strut for cleaning

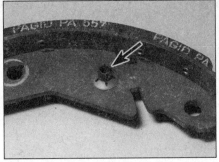

5.16 It may be necessary to transfer the adjusting lever pivot pin and clip (arrowed) from the original shoes to the new ones

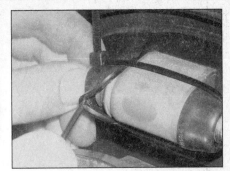

5.17 Checking the wheel cylinder for hydraulic fluid leaks

5.18 Apply a smear of anti-seize compound to the contact surfaces of the backplate (arrowed). Note the elastic band wrapped around the wheel cylinder

5.19 Make sure the handbrake cable is located behind the clip (arrowed)

5.21 Install the brake shoes and lower return spring

not supplied with the new shoes (where applicable), transfer the lever from the old shoes. The lever may be secured with a pin and circlip, or by a rivet, which will have to be drilled out. It may also be necessary to transfer the adjusting lever pivot pin and clip from the original front shoe to the new shoe **(see illustration)**.

17 Peel back the rubber protective caps, and check the wheel cylinder for fluid leaks or other damage **(see illustration)**. Ensure that both cylinder pistons are free to move easily. Refer to Section 9, if necessary, for information on wheel cylinder overhaul.

18 Prior to installation, clean the backplate thoroughly. Apply a thin smear of high-temperature copper-based brake grease or anti-seize compound to all those surfaces of

the backplate which bear on the shoes, particularly the wheel cylinder pistons and lower pivot point **(see illustration)**. Do not allow the lubricant to foul the friction material.

19 Ensure that the handbrake cable is correctly retained by the clip on the lower brake shoe pivot point, then engage the rear shoe with the cable. Locate the shoe on the backplate **(see illustration)**.

20 Install the rear shoe retainer pin and spring, and secure it in position with the spring cup.

21 Hook the lower return spring onto the rear shoe, then engage the front shoe with the return spring. Locate the front shoe on the backplate, and secure it in position with its retainer pin, spring and spring cup **(see illustration)**.

22 Screw the adjuster strut wheel fully onto

the forked end of the adjuster, so that the adjuster strut is set to its shortest possible length. Back the wheel off a half a turn, and check that it is free to rotate easily.

23 Manoeuvre the adjuster strut assembly into position between the brake shoes. Make sure that both ends of the strut are correctly engaged with the shoes, noting that the forked end of the strut must be positioned so that its longer, straight fork is to the back of the shoe **(see illustration)**.

24 Engage the adjusting lever return spring with the front shoe and adjusting lever, and locate the lever on its pivot pin **(see illustration)**. Check that the lever and spring are correctly located, and secure the lever in position with the retaining spring, making sure the spring ends are securely located **(see illustration)**.

5.23 Refit the adjuster strut, noting that the shorter part of the fork (arrowed) must be to the front of the shoe

5.24a Refit the adjusting lever and retaining spring . . .

5.24b . . . then refit the return spring, making sure that the spring is correctly engaged in the correct hole (arrowed)

5.25 Cut the plastic cable tie from the wheel cylinder

25 Remove the cable tie or rubber band from the wheel cylinder **(see illustration)**. Make sure that both shoes are correctly positioned on the wheel cylinder pistons, then fit the upper return spring **(see illustration)**.

26 Ensure that the handbrake operating lever stop peg is correctly positioned against the edge of the shoe web, then refit the brake drum as described in Section 7.

27 Repeat the operation on the remaining brake.

28 Once both sets of rear shoes have been renewed, with the handbrake fully released, adjust the lining-to-drum clearance by repeatedly depressing the brake pedal 20 to 25 times. Whilst depressing the pedal, have an assistant listen to the rear drums, to check that the adjuster strut is functioning correctly; if so, a clicking sound will be emitted by the strut as the pedal is depressed.

29 Check and, if necessary, adjust the handbrake as described in Section 14.

30 On completion, check the hydraulic fluid level as described in *Weekly checks*.

6 Front brake disc – inspection, removal and refitting

Note: *Before starting work, refer to the warning at the beginning of Section 4 concerning the dangers of asbestos dust.*

Inspection

Note: *If either disc requires renewal, BOTH*

should be renewed at the same time, to ensure even and consistent braking.

1 Chock the rear wheels, firmly apply the handbrake, then jack up the front of the car and support it on axle stands. Remove the appropriate front roadwheel.

2 Slowly rotate the brake disc so that the full area of both sides can be checked; remove the brake pads if better access is required to the inner surface. Light scoring is normal in the area swept by the brake pads, but if heavy scoring is found, the disc must be renewed.

3 It is normal to find a lip of rust and brake dust around the disc's perimeter; this can be scraped off if required. If, however, a lip has formed due to excessive wear of the brake pad swept area, then the disc's thickness must be measured using a micrometer. Take measurements at several places around the disc, at the inside and outside of the pad swept area; if the disc has worn at any point to the specified minimum thickness or less, the disc must be renewed.

4 If the disc is thought to be warped, it can be checked for run-out either using a dial gauge mounted on any convenient fixed point, while the disc is slowly rotated, or by using feeler gauges to measure (at several points all around the disc) the clearance between the disc and a fixed point such as the caliper mounting bracket. To ensure that the disc is squarely seated on the hub, fit two wheel bolts, complete with spacers approximately 10 mm thick, and tighten them securely. If the measurements obtained are at the specified maximum or beyond, the disc is excessively warped and must be renewed; however, it is worth checking first that the hub bearing is in good condition (Chapter 1A or 1B).

5 Check the disc for cracks, especially around the wheel bolt holes, and for any other wear or damage, and renew if necessary.

Removal

6 Unscrew the two bolts securing the brake caliper assembly to the swivel hub, and slide the caliper assembly off the disc **(see illustrations)**. Using a piece of wire or string, tie the caliper to the front suspension coil spring, to avoid placing any strain on the hydraulic brake hose.

7 Remove the screw securing the brake disc to the hub, and remove the disc. If it is tight, lightly tap its rear face with a hide or plastic mallet **(see illustration)**.

Refitting

8 Refitting is the reverse of the removal procedure, noting the following points:

a) *Ensure that the mating surfaces of the disc and hub are clean and flat.*

b) *Tighten the disc retaining screw to the specified torque setting.*

c) *If a new disc has been fitted, use a suitable solvent to wipe any preservative coating from the disc before refitting the caliper.*

d) *Remove all traces of old thread-locking compound from the brake caliper bolts and holes in the swivel hub, ideally by running a tap of the correct size and pitch through them. Apply a suitable thread-locking compound to the threads of the caliper mounting bracket bolts. Slide the caliper assembly into position over the disc, then fit the mounting bolts and tighten them to the specified torque setting.*

e) *Refit the roadwheel, aligning the marks made on removal, then lower the vehicle to the ground and tighten the roadwheel bolts to the specified torque. On completion, repeatedly depress the brake pedal until normal (non-assisted) pedal pressure returns.*

7 Rear brake drum – removal, inspection and refitting

Note: *Before starting work, refer to the warning at the beginning of Section 5 concerning the dangers of asbestos dust. A new hub nut and dust cap will be required on refitting.*

Removal

1 Chock the front wheels, then jack up the rear of the vehicle and support it on axle stands. Remove the appropriate rear wheel and release the handbrake. Proceed as described under the relevant sub-heading.

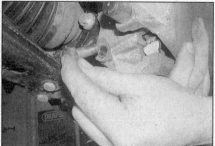

6.6a Slacken and remove the two bolts securing the brake caliper mounting bracket to the hub . . .

6.6b . . . then slide the caliper assembly off the brake disc

6.7 Undo the retaining screw and remove the brake disc from the hub

Corsa and Corsavan

2 Use a chisel to prise out the cap from the centre of the drum **(see illustration)**.

3 Slacken and remove the rear hub nut, then withdraw the brake drum assembly from the stub axle by hand. It may be difficult to remove the drum, due to the brake shoes binding on the inner circumference of the drum. If the brake shoes are binding, first check that the handbrake is fully released, then proceed as follows.

4 Referring to Section 14 for further information, fully slacken the handbrake cable adjuster nut to obtain maximum free play in the cable.

5 Remove the plug from the inspection hole in the brake backplate, and push the handbrake operating lever outwards away from the brake shoe. This will release the handbrake lever stop-peg from the edge of the brake shoe, and further collapse the shoes **(see illustrations)**. The brake drum can then be withdrawn from the stub axle.

Combo Van

6 Slacken and remove the drum retaining screw, and remove the drum from the vehicle **(see illustrations)**. It may be difficult to remove the drum due to the brake shoes binding on the inner circumference of the drum. If the brake shoes are binding, first check that the handbrake is fully released, then proceed as described above in paragraphs 4 and 5.

Inspection

Note: *If either drum requires renewal, BOTH should be renewed at the same time, to ensure even and consistent braking.*

7 Working carefully, remove all traces of brake dust from the drum, but *avoid inhaling the dust, as it is a health-hazard.*

8 Scrub clean the outside of the drum, and check it for obvious signs of wear or damage (such as cracks around the roadwheel bolt holes); renew the drum if necessary.

9 Examine the inside of the drum carefully. Light scoring of the friction surface is normal, but if heavy scoring is found, the drum must be renewed. It is usual to find a lip on the drum's inboard edge which consists of a mixture of rust and brake dust;

7.2 Remove the cap from the centre of the drum to gain access to the hub nut

7.5b ... release the handbrake lever stop-peg by inserting a screwdriver in through the hole in the rear of the backplate ...

this should be scraped away, to leave a smooth surface which can be polished with fine (120- to 150-grade) emery paper. If, however, the lip is due to the friction surface being recessed by excessive wear, then the drum must be renewed.

10 If the drum is thought to be excessively worn, or oval, its internal diameter must be measured at several points using an internal micrometer. Take measurements in pairs, the second at right-angles to the first, and compare the two to check for signs of ovality. Provided that it does not enlarge the drum to beyond the specified maximum diameter, it may be possible to have the drum refinished by skimming or grinding; if this is not possible, the drums on both sides must be renewed. Note that if the drum is to be skimmed, both drums must be refinished, to maintain a consistent internal diameter on both sides.

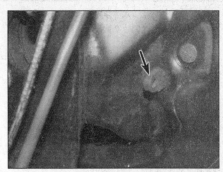

7.5a Remove the rubber plug (arrowed) from the brake backplate ...

7.5c ... and use screwdriver (A) to push the handbrake lever away from the brake shoe in the direction of arrow (B) – shown with drum removed

Refitting

11 If a new brake drum is to be installed, use a suitable solvent to remove any preservative coating that may have been applied to its interior. Note that it may also be necessary to shorten the adjuster strut length by rotating the strut wheel, to allow the new drum to pass over the brake shoes.

Corsa and Corsavan

12 Ensure that the handbrake lever stop-peg is correctly repositioned against the edge of the brake shoe web **(see illustration)**.

13 Slide the drum into position, then fit a new hub nut, and tighten it to the specified torque setting.

14 Fit the new dust cap to the centre of the brake drum.

15 With the handbrake fully released, adjust the lining-to-drum clearance by repeatedly

7.6a Remove the securing screw ...

7.6b ... and withdraw the brake drum

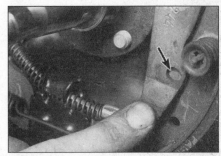

7.12 Prior to refitting the drum, check that the handbrake lever is correctly positioned on the shoe

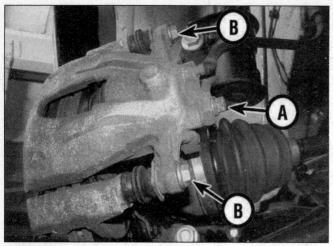
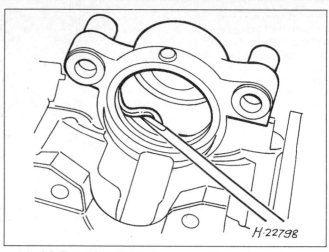

8.3 Slacken the brake hose union (A), then undo the caliper retaining bolts (B)

8.7 Removing the piston seal from the caliper body

depressing the brake pedal 20 to 25 times. Whilst depressing the pedal, have an assistant listen to the rear drums, to check that the adjuster strut is functioning correctly; if so, a clicking sound will be emitted by the strut as the pedal is depressed.

16 With the lining-to-drum clearance set, check and, if necessary, adjust the handbrake as described in Section 14.

17 Refit the roadwheel, aligning the marks made on removal, then lower the vehicle to the ground and tighten the roadwheel bolts to the specified torque setting.

Combo Van

18 Ensure that the drum and hub flange mating surfaces are clean and dry, and remove all traces of corrosion.

19 Ensure that the handbrake lever stop-peg is correctly repositioned against the edge of the brake shoe web, and locate the drum on the hub. Refit the drum retaining screw, and tighten it securely.

20 Carry out the operations described in paragraphs 15 to 17.

8 Front brake caliper – removal, overhaul and refitting

Note: New caliper guide bolts and brake hose sealing washers will be required when refitting. Before starting work, refer to the warning at the beginning of Section 2 concerning the dangers of hydraulic fluid, and to the warning at the beginning of Section 4 concerning the dangers of asbestos dust.

Removal

1 Chock the rear wheels, apply the handbrake, then jack up the front of the vehicle and support it on axle stands. Remove the appropriate roadwheel.

2 Minimise fluid loss by first removing the master cylinder reservoir cap, then tightening

it down onto a piece of polythene to obtain an airtight seal. Alternatively, use a brake hose clamp, a G-clamp or a similar tool to clamp the flexible hose.

3 Clean the area around the caliper brake hose union **(see illustration)**. Slacken and remove the union bolt, and recover the sealing washer from either side of the hose union. Discard the washers; new ones must be used on refitting. Plug the hose end and caliper hole, to minimise fluid loss and prevent the ingress of dirt into the hydraulic system.

4 Slacken and remove the lower and upper caliper guide bolts and remove the brake caliper from the vehicle **(see illustration 8.3)**.

Overhaul

Note: Before starting work, check with your local dealer for the availability of parts to overhaul the caliper.

5 With the caliper on the bench, wipe away all traces of dust and dirt, but avoid inhaling the dust, as it is a health hazard.

6 Withdraw the partially-ejected piston from the caliper body, and remove the dust seal. The piston can be withdrawn by hand, or if necessary pushed out by applying compressed air to the brake hose union hole. Only low pressure should be required, such as is generated by a foot pump, and as a precaution a block of wood should be positioned to prevent any damage to the piston.

7 Using a small screwdriver, carefully remove the piston seal from the caliper, taking great care not mark the bore **(see illustration)**.

8 Carefully press the guide bushes out of the caliper body.

9 Thoroughly clean all components, using only methylated spirit, isopropyl alcohol or clean hydraulic fluid as a cleaning medium. Never use mineral-based solvents such as petrol or paraffin, which will attack the hydraulic system's rubber components. Dry the components immediately, using compressed air or a clean, lint-free cloth. If

compressed air is available, use it to blow through the fluid passages to make sure they are clear

⚠ **Warning: Always wear eye protection when using compressed air.**

10 Check all components, and renew any that are worn or damaged. Check particularly the cylinder bore and piston; these should be renewed (note that this means the renewal of the complete body assembly) if they are scratched, worn or corroded in any way. Similarly check the condition of the guide bushes and bolts; both bushes and bolts should be undamaged and (when cleaned) a reasonably tight sliding fit in each other. If there is any doubt about the condition of any component, renew it.

11 If the assembly is fit for further use, obtain the necessary components (from your Vauxhall dealer). Renew the caliper seals as a matter of course; these should never be re-used.

12 On reassembly, ensure that all components are absolutely clean and dry.

13 Soak the piston and the new piston (fluid) seal in clean hydraulic fluid. Smear clean fluid on the cylinder bore surface.

14 Fit the new piston (fluid) seal, using only the fingers to manipulate it into the cylinder bore groove.

15 Fit the new dust seal to the piston, refit it to the cylinder bore using a twisting motion, and ensure that the piston enters squarely into the bore. Press the dust seal fully into the caliper body, and push the piston fully into the caliper bore.

16 Ease the guide bushes into position in the caliper body.

Refitting

17 Using new guide bolts, refit the caliper and brake pads (where removed) as described in paragraphs 9 and 10 of Section 4.

18 Position a new sealing washer on each side of the hose union, and connect the brake hose to the caliper. Ensure that the hose is correctly positioned against the caliper body lug, then install the union bolt and tighten it to the specified torque setting.

19 Remove the brake hose clamp or the polythene, where fitted, and bleed the hydraulic system as described in Section 2. Note that, providing the precautions described were taken to minimise brake fluid loss, it should only be necessary to bleed the relevant front brake.

20 Refit the roadwheel, aligning the marks made on removal, then lower the vehicle to the ground and tighten the roadwheel bolts to the specified torque.

9.2 Using a pair of pliers to unhook the upper return spring from the brake shoes

9.4 Brake pipe union nut (A) and wheel cylinder retaining bolt (B)

---

9 Rear wheel cylinder –
removal, overhaul and refitting

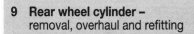

Note: *Before starting work, refer to the warning at the beginning of Section 2 concerning the dangers of hydraulic fluid, and to the warning at the beginning of Section 5 concerning the dangers of asbestos dust.*

Removal

1 Remove the brake drum as described in Section 7.

2 Using pliers, carefully unhook the upper brake shoe return spring, and remove it from both brake shoes **(see illustration)**. Pull the upper ends of the shoes away from the wheel cylinder to disengage them from the pistons.

3 Minimise fluid loss by first removing the master cylinder reservoir cap, then tightening it down onto a piece of polythene to obtain an airtight seal. Alternatively, use a brake hose clamp, a G-clamp or a similar tool to clamp the flexible hose at the nearest convenient point to the wheel cylinder.

4 Wipe away all traces of dirt around the brake pipe union at the rear of the wheel cylinder, and unscrew the union nut. Carefully ease the pipe out of the wheel cylinder, and plug or tape over its end to prevent dirt entry. Wipe off any spilt fluid immediately **(see illustration)**.

5 Unscrew the wheel cylinder retaining bolt from the rear of the backplate **(see illustration 9.4)**, and remove the cylinder, taking great care not to allow surplus hydraulic fluid to contaminate the brake shoe linings.

Overhaul

Note: *Before starting work, check with your local dealer for the availability of parts to overhaul the wheel cylinder.*

6 Brush the dirt and dust from the wheel cylinder, but take care not to inhale it.

7 Pull the rubber dust seals from the ends of the cylinder body **(see illustration)**.

8 The pistons will normally be ejected by the pressure of the coil spring, but if they are not, tap the end of the cylinder body on a piece of wood, or apply low air pressure (eg, from a foot pump) to the hydraulic fluid union hole to eject the pistons from their bores.

9 Inspect the surfaces of the pistons and their bores in the cylinder body for scoring, or evidence of metal-to-metal contact. If evident, renew the complete wheel cylinder assembly.

10 If the pistons and bores are in good condition, discard the seals and obtain a repair kit, which will contain all the necessary renewable items.

11 Lubricate the piston seals with clean brake fluid, and insert them into the cylinder bores, with the spring between them, using finger pressure only.

12 Dip the pistons in clean brake fluid, and insert them into the cylinder bores.

13 Fit the dust seals, and check that the pistons can move freely in their bores.

Refitting

14 Ensure that the backplate and wheel cylinder mating surfaces are clean, then spread the brake shoes and manoeuvre the wheel cylinder into position.

15 Engage the brake pipe, and screw in the union nut two or three turns to ensure that the thread has started.

16 Insert the wheel cylinder retaining bolt, and tighten it to the specified torque setting. Now tighten the brake pipe union nut to the specified torque.

17 Remove the clamp from the flexible brake hose, or the polythene from the master cylinder reservoir (as applicable).

18 Ensure that the brake shoes are correctly located against the cylinder pistons, then carefully refit the brake shoe upper return spring, using a screwdriver to stretch the spring into position.

19 Refit the brake drum as described in Section 7.

20 Bleed the brake hydraulic system as described in Section 2. Providing suitable precautions were taken to minimise loss of fluid, it should only be necessary to bleed the relevant rear brake.

---

10 Master cylinder –
removal, overhaul and refitting

Note: *New master cylinder retaining nuts will be required when refitting. Before starting work, refer to the warning at the beginning of Section 2 concerning the dangers of hydraulic fluid.*

Removal

1 Remove the master cylinder reservoir cap,

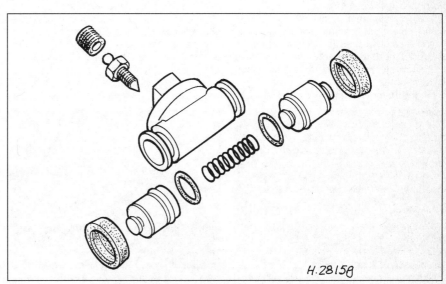

H.28158

9.7 Exploded view of a rear brake wheel cylinder

10.4a Peel the bonnet seal off the engine compartment bulkhead . . .

10.4b . . . then unclip the cover from the battery cables

10.5 Release the battery cables from the water deflector

10.6a Undo the retaining screw (arrowed) from the right-hand side of the water deflector . . .

10.6b . . . the retaining screw (arrowed) from the left-hand side of the water deflector . . .

10.6c . . . and the retaining screw from the middle of the water deflector

and syphon the hydraulic fluid from the reservoir. **Note:** *Do not syphon the fluid by mouth, as it is poisonous; use a syringe or an old hydrometer.* Alternatively, open any convenient bleed screw in the system, and gently pump the brake pedal to expel the fluid through a plastic tube connected to the screw (see Section 2).

2 Disconnect the battery negative terminal (refer to *Disconnecting the battery* in the Reference Chapter).

3 Remove both windscreen wiper arms as described in Chapter 12.

4 Peel the bonnet seal off the engine compartment bulkhead, then unclip the cover from the battery cables **(see illustrations)**.

5 Unclip the battery cables from the wind deflector, and move them to one side **(see illustration)**.

6 Undo the three retaining screws – one at

each end and one in the middle **(see illustrations)**. Remove both halves of the wind deflector trim, release the trim from the engine compartment bulkhead and wiper spindles. Disconnect the washer pipe for the washer jets as the trim is removed from the vehicle.

7 Unclip the rubber guide/grommet from the bulkhead for the brake pipes.

8 Disconnect the wiring connector from the brake fluid level sender unit **(see illustration)**.

9 Detach the fluid supply hose for the clutch master cylinder from the reservoir.

10 Wipe clean the area around the brake pipe unions on the side of the master cylinder, and place absorbent rags beneath the pipe unions to catch any surplus fluid. Make a note of the correct fitted positions of the unions, then unscrew the union nuts and carefully withdraw the pipes **(see illustration)**. Plug or

tape over the pipe ends and master cylinder orifices, to minimise the loss of brake fluid and to prevent the entry of dirt into the system. Wash off any spilt fluid immediately with cold water.

11 Slacken and remove the two nuts securing the master cylinder to the vacuum servo unit and discard them; new ones must be used on refitting **(see illustration)**. Withdraw the master cylinder assembly from the engine compartment.

12 Where applicable, recover the seal which is fitted between the master cylinder and servo.

Overhaul

13 At the time of writing, master cylinder overhaul is not possible as no spares are available.

14 The only parts available individually are

10.8 Disconnecting the master cylinder brake fluid level sender wiring connector

10.10 Slacken and remove the brake pipes (arrowed) from the brake master cylinder

10.11 Undo the two retaining nuts (arrowed) and remove the master cylinder from the servo unit

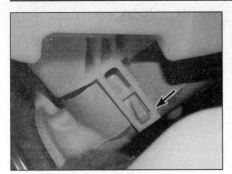

10.14 Where necessary, unclip the reservoir (arrowed) from the master cylinder

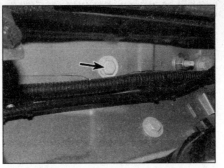

11.2 Slacken and remove the brake pedal upper retaining bolt (arrowed)

11.4 Unhook the pedal return spring (A), then withdraw the locking clip (B) and remove the clevis pin from the pedal/pushrod

the fluid reservoir, its mounting seals, the filler cap and the master cylinder mounting seals. The reservoir can be unclipped **(see illustration)**, then the seals can be removed from the master cylinder.

15 If the master cylinder is worn excessively, it must be renewed.

Refitting

16 Remove all traces of dirt from the master cylinder and servo unit mating surfaces. Inspect the master cylinder seal for signs of wear or damage, and renew if necessary.

17 Where applicable, fit a new seal to the servo and refit the master cylinder, ensuring that the pushrod enters the master cylinder bore centrally. Fit the new master cylinder mounting nuts, and tighten them to the specified torque.

18 Wipe clean the brake pipe unions, refit them to the master cylinder ports, and tighten them to the specified torque.

19 Ensure that the brake pipes are correctly clipped back into position in the bulkhead rubber guide/grommet.

20 Reconnect the wiring connector to the brake fluid level sender unit.

21 Fill the master cylinder reservoir with new fluid, and bleed the complete hydraulic system as described in Section 2.

22 Install the components removed for access by reversing the removal procedure.

11 Brake pedal –
removal and refitting

Removal

1 Remove the clutch pedal as described in Chapter 6.

2 Working in the engine compartment, unscrew the brake pedal mounting bracket upper retaining bolt **(see illustration)**.

3 From inside the vehicle, remove the stop-light switch as described in Section 18.

4 Unhook the return spring from the brake pedal, then slide off the spring clip, and withdraw the clevis pin securing the pedal to the servo unit pushrod **(see illustration)**.

5 Undo the mounting bracket retaining nuts

and remove the pedal and support bracket assembly from the vehicle **(see illustration)**.

6 Inspect the pedal pivot bush and shaft for signs of wear, and renew if necessary.

Refitting

7 Apply a smear of multi-purpose grease to the pedal pivot bush, then manoeuvre the pedal and support bracket assembly into place, fitting new retaining nuts.

8 Make sure the brake servo pushrod fits correctly in the brake pedal bracket.

9 Align the pedal hole with the pushrod end, and insert the clevis pin. Secure the pin in position with the spring clip **(see illustration)**.

10 Refit the return spring to the brake pedal.

11 Refit the stop-light switch as described in Section 18.

12 Working in the engine compartment, refit the brake pedal mounting bracket upper retaining bolt.

13 Refit the clutch pedal as described in Chapter 6.

12 Vacuum servo unit –
testing, removal and refitting

Testing

1 To test the operation of the servo unit, with the engine off, depress the footbrake several times to exhaust the vacuum. Now start the engine, keeping the pedal firmly depressed. As the engine starts, there should be a noticeable 'give' in the brake pedal as the

vacuum builds-up. Allow the engine to run for at least two minutes, then switch it off. The brake pedal should now feel normal, but further applications should result in the pedal feeling firmer, the pedal stroke decreasing with each application.

2 If the servo does not operate as described, first inspect the servo unit check valve as described in Section 13.

3 If the servo unit still fails to operate satisfactorily, the fault lies within the unit itself. Repairs to the unit are not possible; if faulty, the servo unit must be renewed.

Removal

4 Remove the master cylinder as described in Section 10. On some models, it may prove sufficient to unbolt the master cylinder and position it clear of the servo, taking great care not to strain the brake pipes. This removes the need to disconnect the brake pipes and open the hydraulic system.

5 Carefully ease the vacuum hose out of the servo unit, taking care not to displace the sealing grommet **(see illustration)**.

6 Working from inside the vehicle, unhook the return spring, slide off the spring clip and withdraw the clevis pin securing the brake pedal to the servo unit pushrod **(see illustration)**.

7 Slacken and remove the nuts securing the servo unit to the pedal mounting bracket **(see illustration)**.

8 Return to the engine compartment, and lift the servo unit out of position. Where fitted,

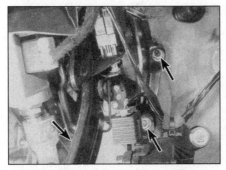

11.5 Remove the pedal mounting assembly retaining nuts (arrowed)

11.9 Ensure that the servo pushrod clevis pin is securely retained by its spring clip

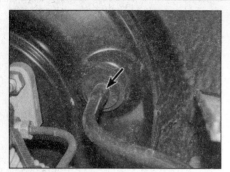

12.5 Carefully ease the vacuum hose (arrowed) out of the servo unit

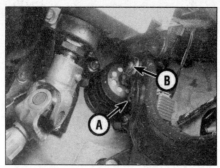

12.6 Unhook the pedal return spring (A), then withdraw the locking clip (B) and remove the clevis pin

12.7 Servo unit retaining nuts (arrowed)

recover the gasket from the rear of the servo unit. Discard the gasket and retaining nuts; new ones should be used on refitting.

Refitting

9 Inspect the servo unit check valve sealing grommet for signs of damage or deterioration, and renew if necessary.
10 Ensure that the servo and bulkhead mating surfaces are clean and dry.
11 Fit a new gasket to the rear of the servo, and reposition the unit in the engine compartment.
12 From inside the vehicle, ensure that the servo unit pushrod is correctly engaged with the brake pedal, then fit the new servo unit mounting nuts. Tighten the nuts to the specified torque setting.

13.1 Vacuum servo unit check valve is integral with the hose, and cannot be renewed separately

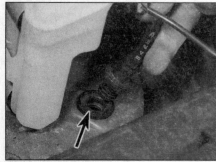

13.2 Ease the vacuum hose out from the servo unit, taking care not to displace the grommet (arrowed)

13 Refit the servo unit pushrod-to-brake pedal clevis pin, and secure it in position with the spring clip.
14 Refit the return spring to the brake pedal.
15 Ease the vacuum hose end piece into place in the servo unit, taking great care not to displace or damage the grommet.
16 Refit the master cylinder as described in Section 10.
17 On completion, start the engine and check for air leaks at the vacuum hose-to-servo unit connection. Check the operation of the braking system.

13 Vacuum servo unit check valve – removal, testing and refitting

1 The check valve is located in the vacuum hose running from the inlet manifold to the brake servo. If the valve is faulty, it will need to be renewed with the hose as a complete assembly (see illustration).

Removal

2 Carefully ease the vacuum hose out of the servo unit, taking care not to displace the grommet (see illustration).
3 Note the correct routing of the hose, then undo the union nut securing the hose to the inlet manifold and remove the hose assembly from the vehicle.

Testing

4 Examine the check valve and vacuum hose for signs of damage, and renew if necessary.
5 The valve may be tested by blowing through it in both directions. Air should flow through the valve in one direction only: when blown through from the servo unit end of the valve. Renew the valve if this is not the case.
6 Examine the servo unit rubber sealing grommet for signs of damage or deterioration, and renew as necessary.

Refitting

7 Ensure that the sealing grommet is correctly fitted to the servo unit.
8 Ease the hose union into position in the servo, taking great care not to displace or damage the grommet.

9 Ensure that the hose is correctly routed, and connect it to the inlet manifold, tightening its union nut securely.
10 On completion, start the engine and check for air leaks at the check valve-to-servo unit connection.

14 Handbrake – adjustment

1 To check the handbrake adjustment, fully release the handbrake lever, and apply the footbrake firmly several times. This will establish correct shoe-to-drum clearance, and ensure that the self-adjust mechanism is fully adjusted. Applying normal, moderate pressure, pull the handbrake lever to the fully-applied position, counting the number of clicks emitted from the handbrake ratchet mechanism. If adjustment is correct, there should be 7 clicks before the handbrake is fully applied; if this is not the case, adjust as follows.
2 Chock the front wheels, then jack up the rear of the vehicle, and support securely on axle stands.
3 The handbrake cable adjuster nut is situated is situated by the handbrake lever inside the vehicle, unclip the cover from around the handbrake lever (see illustration).
4 With the handbrake set on the third notch of the ratchet mechanism, rotate the adjusting nut until a reasonable amount of force is required to turn each wheel/hub (see

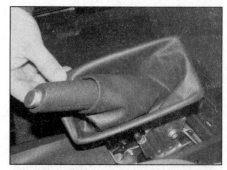

14.3 Unclipping the cover from around the handbrake lever

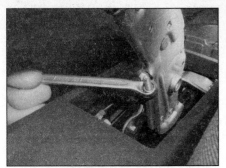

14.4 Adjusting the handbrake cable

15.4 Unclip the storage tray from the rear of the centre console

15.5 Disconnect the wiring connector from the handbrake warning light switch

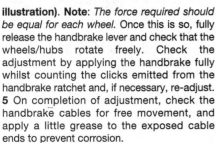

15.6 Slacken and remove the handbrake cable adjuster nut

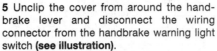
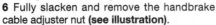

15.7 Unscrew the four retaining bolts (arrowed), then lift the handbrake lever out of position

15.9 To remove the warning light switch from the handbrake lever, undo the retaining bolt (arrowed)

illustration). **Note:** *The force required should be equal for each wheel.* Once this is so, fully release the handbrake lever and check that the wheels/hubs rotate freely. Check the adjustment by applying the handbrake fully whilst counting the clicks emitted from the handbrake ratchet and, if necessary, re-adjust.
5 On completion of adjustment, check the handbrake cables for free movement, and apply a little grease to the exposed cable ends to prevent corrosion.
6 Refit the handbrake lever cover and lower the vehicle to the ground. If the roadwheels have been removed, tighten the roadwheel bolts to the specified torque setting.

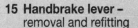

15 Handbrake lever – removal and refitting

Removal

1 Chock the front wheels, then jack up the rear of the vehicle, and support securely on axle stands.
2 Disengage the exhaust system from the rubber mountings and lower it until it comes to rest on the rear axle. Disconnect the wiring block connectors to the oxygen sensor(s).
3 Undo the retaining nuts, and remove the exhaust heat shield from underneath the vehicle to gain access to the underside of the handbrake lever.
4 From inside the vehicle, unclip the storage tray from the rear of the centre console **(see illustration)**.

5 Unclip the cover from around the hand-brake lever and disconnect the wiring connector from the handbrake warning light switch **(see illustration)**.
6 Fully slacken and remove the handbrake cable adjuster nut **(see illustration)**.
7 Unscrew the four handbrake lever mounting bolts **(see illustration)**.
8 From under the vehicle, disconnect the front handbrake cable from the handbrake lever connecting bracket.
9 The handbrake lever can now be withdrawn from inside the vehicle. The warning light switch can be removed from the lever assembly after unscrewing its retaining bolt **(see illustration)**.

Refitting

10 Refitting is a reversal of the removal procedure, adjusting the cable as described in Section 14.

16 Handbrake cables – removal and refitting

Corsa and Corsavan

1 The handbrake cable consists of two main sections, a long cable linking the handbrake lever to the left-hand drum brake, and a short cable linking the right-hand drum brake to the equaliser. The equaliser links both cables together, and is situated above the rear axle crossmember. Each cable can be renewed individually as follows. **Note:** *There are also*

two short rear sections of cable which attach the main cables to the brake shoes **(see illustration)**.

Long cable

2 Undo the retaining nuts, and remove the exhaust heat shield from underneath the vehicle to gain access to the underside of the handbrake lever.
3 Unscrew the handbrake cable adjuster nut, from inside the vehicle (see Section 14).
4 Remove the left-hand rear brake drum as described in Section 7.
5 Referring to Section 5, remove the upper and lower return springs, then remove the spring cup, spring and retainer pin, and remove the rear brake shoe. Note that the front shoe and adjuster strut mechanism can be left in position on the backplate.
6 Free the handbrake cable from the retaining clip on the shoe lower pivot, then remove the

16.1 Handbrake cable connector (arrowed) in front of the rear brake drum assembly on each side

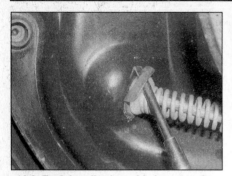

16.6 Each handbrake cable is secured to the backplate on the inside by a retaining clip

16.7 Free the cable from any relevant clips or guides (arrowed) securing it to the vehicle underbody

16.8 Remove the rubber grommet (arrowed) and withdraw the cable

retaining clip and withdraw the cable from the rear of the backplate **(see illustration)**.

7 Work back along the cable, releasing it from any relevant retaining clips and guides, whilst noting its correct routing **(see illustration)**.

8 Detach the front end of the cable from the handbrake lever assembly, then remove the rubber grommet from around the equaliser link and withdraw the cable from underneath the vehicle **(see illustration)**.

9 On refitting, attach the front end of the cable to the handbrake lever, then hook the cable through the equaliser link. Secure the cable in position with the rubber grommet.

10 Work back along the cable, securing it in position with all the relevant clips and guides, and routing it as noted on removal.

11 Insert the cable through the backplate, and secure it in position with the clip.

12 Ensure that the cable is securely retained by the clip on the shoe lower pivot point **(see illustration)**, and refit the rear brake shoe as described in Section 5.

13 Ensure that the brake shoes and adjuster strut components are correctly fitted, then refit the brake drum as described in Section 7.

14 Adjust the handbrake cable as described in Section 14.

Short cable

15 Remove the cable as described above in paragraphs 3 to 7, removing the right-hand brake drum instead of the left-hand drum. Remove the rubber grommet from around the equaliser link and withdraw the cable.

16 Attach the front end of the cable to the

equaliser link, securing the cable in position with the rubber grommet. Refit the cable as described in paragraphs 10 to 14.

Combo Van

17 The handbrake cable consists of two sections of equal length, which run from each rear brake to the equaliser plate. The equaliser plate is secured to the handbrake lever by a short cable which is secured to the handbrake lever by the adjuster nut. The two cables from the rear brake assemblies can only be bought as a complete item and cannot be separated from the equaliser plate, therefore the cable arrangement can only be removed and refitted as an assembly **(see illustration)**.

Removal

18 Where applicable, undo the retaining nuts, and remove the exhaust heat shield from underneath the vehicle to gain access to the underside of the handbrake lever.

19 Unscrew the handbrake cable adjuster nut from inside the vehicle (see Section 14).

20 Remove the left-hand rear brake drum as described in Section 7.

21 Referring to Section 5, remove the upper and lower return springs, then remove the spring cup, spring and retainer pin, and remove the rear brake shoe. Note that the front shoe and adjuster strut mechanism can be left in position on the backplate.

22 Free the handbrake cable from the retaining clip on the shoe lower pivot, then remove the retaining clip and withdraw the cable from the rear of the backplate.

23 Repeat the operations in paragraphs 20 to 22 on the right-hand rear brake.

24 Work back along both cables, releasing them from any relevant retaining clips and ties, whilst noting the correct routing. Remove the cable/equaliser plate assembly from the underneath the vehicle, releasing it from the short cable to the handbrake lever **(see illustration)**.

Refitting

25 Connect the equaliser plate to the short front handbrake cable, and screw on the adjuster nut.

26 Work back along both cables, securing them in position with all the relevant clips and ties, and routing them as noted on removal.

27 Insert the cable through the left-hand backplate, and secure it in position with the clip.

28 Ensure that the cable is securely retained by the clip on the shoe lower pivot point, and refit the rear brake shoe as described in Section 5.

29 Ensure that the brake shoes and adjuster strut components are correctly fitted, then refit the left-hand brake drum as described in Section 7. **Note:** *Do not apply the brake pedal until the right-hand drum has also been installed.*

30 Repeat the operations in paragraphs 27 to 29 on the right-hand brake.

31 Once both drums are in position, with the handbrake fully released, adjust the lining-to-drum clearance by repeatedly depressing the brake pedal 20 to 25 times. Whilst depressing

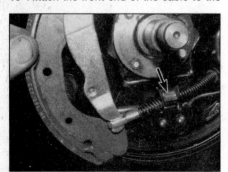

16.12 Make sure the handbrake cable is located behind the clip (arrowed) correctly

16.17 Handbrake linkage/equaliser plate on the Combo Van model

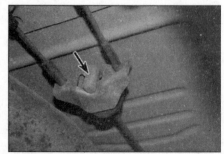

16.24 Twist the handbrake short cable (arrowed), to release it from the equaliser plate

17.1 Rear brake pressure-regulating valves (arrowed) – 1.0 and 1.2 litre models

17.7 Rear brake pressure-regulating valve assembly – Corsa and Corsavan models

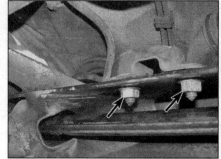

17.9 Undo the two retaining nuts (arrowed) and remove the spring securing bracket

the pedal, have an assistant listen to the rear drums, to check that the adjuster strut is functioning correctly; if so, a clicking sound will be emitted by the strut as the pedal is depressed

32 Adjust the handbrake cable as described in Section 14.

17 Rear brake pressure-regulating valve(s) – removal and refitting

Note: *Before starting work, refer to the warning at the beginning of Section 2 concerning the dangers of hydraulic fluid.*

Removal

1.0 and 1.2 litre models

1 The rear brake pressure-regulating valves are of the pressure-dependent type, and are located underneath the bonnet of the vehicle, directly above the transmission on the left-hand side of the vehicle **(see illustration)**. There are two valves, one for each rear brake. The purpose of the valves is to prevent the rear wheels locking up under heavy braking.

2 Minimise fluid loss by first removing the master cylinder reservoir cap and screwing it down onto a piece of polythene.

3 Wipe clean the area around the brake pipe unions on the relevant valve, and place absorbent rags beneath the pipe unions to catch any surplus fluid.

4 Retain the relevant pressure-regulating valve with a suitable open-ended spanner, slacken the union nuts and disconnect both brake pipes, and remove the valve from the vehicle. Plug or tape over the pipe ends and valve orifices, to minimise the loss of brake fluid and to prevent the entry of dirt into the system. Wash off any spilt fluid immediately with cold water.

5 Where necessary, remove the other valve in the same way.

6 If renewal is necessary, both valves should be renewed as a matched pair.

All other models

7 The pressure-regulating valve is of the load-dependent type, and is mounted underneath

the rear of the vehicle. The valve is mounted onto the vehicle underbody, and is connected to the rear axle by a spring **(see illustration)**. As the load being carried by the vehicle is altered, the suspension moves in relation to the vehicle body, altering the tension in the spring. The spring then adjusts the pressure-regulating valve lever so that the correct pressure is applied to the rear brakes to suit the load being carried. The purpose of the valve is to prevent the rear wheels locking up under heavy braking.

8 Minimise fluid loss by first removing the master cylinder reservoir cap and screwing it down onto a piece of polythene.

9 Undo the two retaining nuts from the spring securing bracket **(see illustration)**, then carefully unhook the spring and detach it from the valve.

10 Wipe clean the area around the brake pipe unions on the brake pressure-regulating valve, and place absorbent rags beneath the pipe unions to catch any surplus fluid. Make identification marks on the brake pipes; these marks can then be used on refitting to ensure that each pipe is correctly reconnected **(see illustration)**.

11 Slacken the union nuts, and disconnect the brake pipes from the valve. Plug or tape over the pipe ends and valve orifices, to minimise the loss of brake fluid and to prevent the entry of dirt into the system. Wash off any spilt fluid immediately with cold water.

12 Undo the two bolts, and remove the pressure-regulating valve from underneath the vehicle **(see illustration)**.

Refitting

1.0 and 1.2 litre models

13 Refitting is the reverse of the removal procedure, tightening the pipe union nuts to the specified torque setting. On completion, bleed the complete hydraulic system as described in Section 2.

All other models

14 Refitting is the reverse of the removal procedure, noting the following points:

 a) Tighten the valve mounting bolts to the specified torque.
 b) Ensure that the brake pipes are correctly connected to the valve, and tighten the union nuts to the specified torque settings.
 c) Coat the ends of the spring with grease prior to installation.
 d) Bleed the complete hydraulic system as described in Section 2.

15 On completion, adjust the valve as follows.

16 With the vehicle completely unladen and approximately 5 litres of fuel in the fuel tank, position the car over an inspection pit, or drive it onto ramps so that it is resting on all four wheels.

17 Make sure the spring on the pressure-regulating valve is not under any tension.

18 Remove the clamping screw from the pressure-regulating valve spring **(see illustration)**.

19 Move the spring forwards or backwards until it lies against the regulator lever without

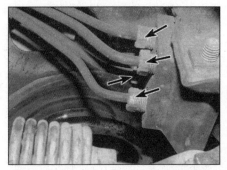

17.10 Brake pipe unions (arrowed) on the valve

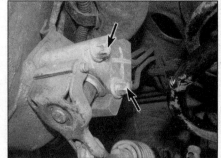

7.12 Undo the two retaining bolts (arrowed) to remove the valve

17.18 Slacken the clamping screw (arrowed) to adjust the spring

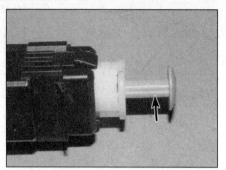

18.4a Pull out the centre actuating pin arrowed (switch removed for clarity) . . .

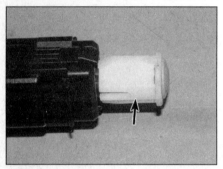

18.4b . . . and unclip the locking sleeve (arrowed) . . .

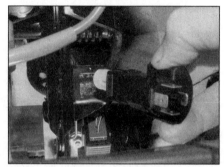

18.5 . . . then withdraw the switch from the pedal bracket

tension. Refit the clamping screw (using thread locking compound) and tighten to specified torque. Repeat procedure if required.

18 Stop-light switch – removal and refitting

Removal

1 The stop-light switch is located on the pedal bracket in the driver's footwell, behind the facia.
2 To remove the switch, the lower facia trim

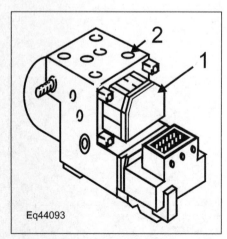

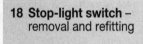

19.4 ABS ECU (1) and integral hydraulic modulator (2)

will have to be removed for better access, then remove the securing clip and withdraw the heating duct.
3 Disconnect the wiring plug from the stop-light switch.
4 Push the brake pedal down, pull out the brake switch actuating pin, then unclip the locking sleeve from around the actuating pin **(see illustrations)**.
5 Release the securing clips and pull the switch to disengage it from the pedal mounting bracket **(see illustration)**.

Refitting

6 Refitting is a reversal of removal, making sure the locking sleeve is located correctly.

19 Anti-lock braking system (ABS) – description and system operation

General description

1 The anti-lock braking system fitted to Corsa models covered by this manual is the Bosch 5.3 type, comprising a hydraulic modulator assembly, electronic control unit and four wheel speed sensors, in addition to the normal braking system components.
2 The purpose of the system is to apply the vehicle brakes at maximum efficiency without wheel lock or loss of directional stability. Inductive-type wheel speed sensors monitor the speed of the roadwheels by generating an electrical signal as the wheel is rotated. This information is passed to the ABS electronic

control unit (ECU) which compares the signals received from each wheel and uses the speed of the fastest wheel as a reference value. The ECU continually monitors the speed of each wheel and if the onset of lock at any wheel is detected (a received speed signal being less than the reference value) a signal is sent to the hydraulic modulator which regulates the brake pressure for the relevant wheel(s).

Electronic control unit

3 The ECU continually monitors wheel speed from the signals provided by the wheel speed sensors, and brake application from the brake light switch signal. If the ECU detects the incidence of wheel lock on one or more wheels, a signal is sent to the hydraulic modulator to regulate the hydraulic pressure to the brake of the locking wheel(s). The ECU contains two microprocessors and uses digital technology to complete this and other functions such as fault code memory and power modules for valve and relay activity.
4 To reduce external electrical connections to a minimum and improve reliability, the ECU is integral with the hydraulic modulator **(see illustration)**.
5 The ECU is equipped with a self-test capability that initially examines the ABS system when the ignition is switched on, and then examines the wheel speed sensor signals after a wheel speed of approximately 4 mph is reached from all wheels. The ABS self-test program continues to examine the signals from the various components as long as the ignition is switched on. If self-test determines that faults are not present, the ABS is ready for operation once a specified vehicle speed has been achieved.
6 If the ECU detects that a fault is present, all ABS functions are switched off and the warning lamp is turned on. The conventional braking system continues to operate as normal without ABS assistance.
7 If the ECU detects a fault during the self-test routine, an internal fault code is stored in the ECU memory. Stored fault codes can be retrieved from the vehicle diagnostic connector with the aid of a suitable fault code reader. If the fault clears, the code will remain stored until cleared with the fault code reader.

Hydraulic modulator

8 Bosch 5.3 is a four-channel system with a separate hydraulic circuit for each brake. The hydraulic modulator consists of an electric motor and radial piston return pump, inlet and outlet solenoid valves, pressure accumulators and pulsation dampers **(see illustration)**. The unit controls the hydraulic pressure applied to the brake for each individual front and rear wheel. The return pump is switched on when the ABS is activated and returns hydraulic fluid, drained off during the pressure reduction phase, back into the brake circuit.
9 The 'select-low' principle is employed for control of the rear brakes during ABS operation. With the 'select-low' principle, the wheel with the lowest adhesion determines

the amount of hydraulic pressure to be supplied to both rear brakes during a controlled ABS cycle.

Wheel speed sensors

10 The rotational speed of the roadwheels and any changes in the rotational speed are recorded by inductive wheel speed sensors, one located at each roadwheel.

11 Each wheel speed sensor assembly comprises a toothed sensor ring which rotates at roadwheel speed, and an adjacent sensor mounted a set distance from the sensor ring **(see illustration)**.

12 The sensors are permanent magnet pulse generator types producing an AC voltage sine wave as the sensor ring teeth pass through the magnetic field of the sensor.

13 The frequency of the waveform produced by the wheel speed sensor is proportional to the road speed. This AC voltage signal is continually being delivered to the ECU for processing.

14 The peak-to-peak voltage of the speed signal can vary considerably according to wheel speed and an analogue-to-digital converter in the ECU transforms the AC pulse into a digital signal.

Wiring, switches and warning lamps

15 An integrated main wiring harness is used for ECU power supply and earth connections, and enables sensor signals to reach the ECU and the ECU, in turn, to send output signals to the ABS warning lamp and diagnostic connector. The main relay and return pump relay are an integral part of the ECU and cannot be separately removed. Internal connections between the ECU and hydraulic modulator are used to activate the return pump motor.

16 The stop-light switch comprises a switch body and contact pin and is located above the brake pedal. When the brake pedal is depressed, closing the stop-light switch, a signal is sent to the ECU indicating that the brakes are being applied. Once this signal is received, the ECU will begin monitoring the wheel speed via the wheel speed sensors and activate the ABS if necessary.

17 After the ignition is switched on, the ABS warning lamp on the instrument panel is illuminated for approximately 2 to 4 seconds during the system initial self-test cycle, then extinguished. During vehicle operation above a predetermined wheel speed, the ECU continues the self-test cycle whereby the system status is continually monitored. If a fault is detected, the ECU illuminates the warning lamp on the instrument panel and the ECU switches off the ABS, although the conventional braking system continues to operate as normal. The warning lamp will remain illuminated until the fault is no longer present.

18 When the ECU detects a fault, the fault code is stored and the ABS warning lamp activated. If the fault no longer exists after the next system start (ignition on/off) the ABS

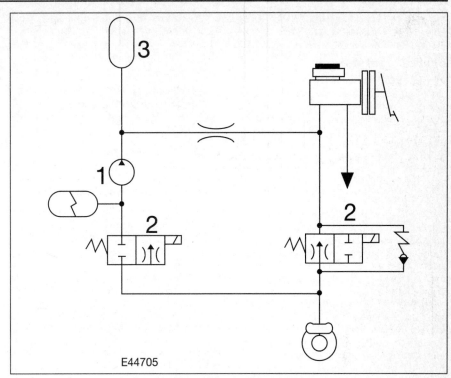

E44705

19.8 ABS hydraulic circuit schematic

1 Pump motor	2 Inlet and outlet solenoid valves	3 Pulsation damper

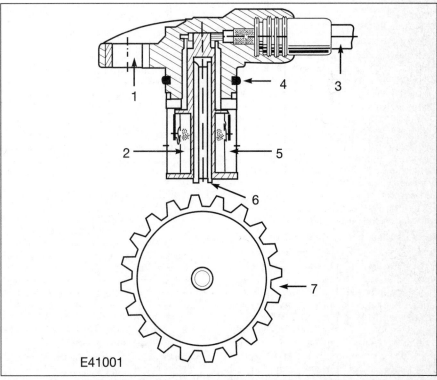

E41001

19.11 Sectional view of a wheel speed sensor

1 Mounting bolt location	3 Wiring harness	6 Sensor tip
2 Permanent magnet	4 O-ring	7 Toothed sensor ring
	5 Coil	

warning lamp is extinguished after the self-test cycle, however the fault code remains stored in the ECU memory.

System operation

19 The ECU continually monitors wheel speed from the signals provided by the wheel speed sensors. If the ECU detects the incidence of wheel lock on one or more wheels, ABS is automatically initiated in three phases. As the system operates individually on each wheel, all or any of the wheels could be in any one of the following phases at any particular moment.

First phase, pressure holding

20 To prevent any further build-up of hydraulic pressure in the circuit being controlled, the ECU closes the inlet solenoid valve and allows the outlet solenoid valve to remain closed. The hydraulic fluid line from the master cylinder to the brake caliper or wheel cylinder is closed, and the hydraulic fluid in the controlled circuit is maintained at a constant pressure. This effectively removes the braking force from the controlled circuit. The pressure cannot now be increased in that circuit by any further application of the brake pedal.

21 If the wheel speed sensor signals indicate that wheel rotation has now stabilised, the ECU will instigate the pressure build-up phase, allowing braking to continue. If wheel lock is still detected after the pressure holding phase, the ECU instigates the pressure reduction phase.

Second phase, pressure reduction

22 If the ECU detects wheel instability, a pressure reduction phase is initiated. The inlet solenoid valve remains closed and the outlet solenoid valve is opened by means of a series of short activation pulses. The pressure in the controlled circuit decreases rapidly as the fluid flows from the brake caliper or wheel cylinder into the pressure accumulator. At the same time, the ECU actuates the electric motor to operate the return pump. The hydraulic fluid is then pumped back into the pressure side of the master cylinder. This process creates a pulsation which can be felt in the brake pedal action, but which is softened by the pulsation damper.

Third phase, pressure build-up

23 The pressure build-up phase is instigated after the wheel rotation has stabilised. The inlet and outlet solenoid valves are returned to the at rest position (inlet solenoid valve open and outlet solenoid valve closed) which re-opens the hydraulic fluid line from the master cylinder to the brake caliper or wheel cylinder. Hydraulic pressure is reinstated, thus re-introducing operation of the brake. After a brief period, a short pressure holding phase is re-introduced and the ECU continually shifts between pressure build-up and pressure holding until the wheel has decelerated to a sufficient degree where pressure reduction is once more required.

24 The whole ABS control cycle takes place 4 to 10 times per second for each affected wheel and this ensures maximum braking effect and control during ABS operation.

20 Anti-lock Braking system (ABS) components – removal and refitting

Modulator assembly

Note: *Before starting work, refer to the note at the beginning of Section 2 concerning the dangers of hydraulic fluid.*

Removal

1 Disconnect the battery negative terminal (refer to *Disconnecting the battery* in the Reference Chapter).

2 Pull out the locking bar and disconnect the wiring harness multi-plug connector from the electronic control unit located on the hydraulic modulator.

3 Unscrew the master cylinder reservoir filler cap, and top-up the reservoir to the MAX mark (see *Weekly checks*). Place a piece of polythene over the filler neck, and secure the polythene with the filler cap. This will minimise brake fluid loss during subsequent operations. As a precaution, place absorbent rags beneath the modulator brake pipe unions when unscrewing them.

4 Wipe clean the area around the modulator brake pipe unions, then make a note of how the pipes are arranged, to use as a reference on refitting. Unscrew the union nuts, and carefully withdraw the pipes.

5 Plug or tape over the pipe ends and modulator orifices, to minimise the loss of brake fluid and to prevent the entry of dirt into the system. Wash off any spilt fluid immediately with cold water.

6 Slacken and remove the mounting nuts, and release the modulator assembly from its mounting bracket. Remove the assembly from the engine compartment.

Refitting

7 Refitting is the reverse of the removal procedure, noting the following points:
a) *Tighten the modulator block mounting nuts to the specified torque setting.*
b) *Refit the brake pipes to their respective unions, and tighten the union nuts to the specified torque.*
c) *Ensure that the wiring is correctly routed, and that the multi-plug connector is firmly pressed into position and secured with the locking bar.*
d) *On completion, and prior to refitting the battery, bleed the complete hydraulic system as described in Section 2. Ensure that the system is bled in the correct order, to prevent air entering the modulator return pump.*

Electronic control unit (ECU)

Caution: Separation of the ECU from the

hydraulic modulator is not recommended by the manufacturers of the ABS system (Bosch). Information on this operation is, however, given by Vauxhall. If difficulties are experienced when refitting the ECU to the modulator, it may be necessary to renew the complete assembly.
Note: *New ECU retaining screws and a new gasket will be required for refitting.*

Removal

8 Remove the hydraulic modulator from the car as described previously in this Section.

9 Disconnect the return pump motor wiring plug from the ECU.

10 Undo the six retaining screws and carefully withdraw the ECU upwards and off the hydraulic modulator. Recover the gasket.

Refitting

11 Prior to refitting, clean and then carefully inspect, the condition of the gasket sealing surfaces on the ECU and hydraulic modulator. If the surfaces are in any way deformed, damaged, or rough to the extent that a perfect gasket seal cannot be maintained, the complete modulator and ECU assembly must be renewed.

12 Check to see if there is a spring plate located over the solenoid valves on the hydraulic modulator. If a spring plate is present, it should be removed and discarded.

13 With a new gasket in position, and holding the ECU centrally, carefully lower it over the solenoid valves on the modulator, keeping it square and level.

14 Fit the six new retaining screws, and tighten the four screws around the solenoid area of the modulator, evenly and progressively until they all just make contact with the ECU body. Continue tightening these four screws alternately and progressively until the ECU body just makes contact with the hydraulic modulator. Now tighten the remaining two screws until they also just make contact with the ECU body.

15 Progressively, and working in a diagonal sequence, tighten the four screws in the vicinity of the solenoid area to the specified torque. Now tighten the remaining two screws to the specified torque. The ECU must make complete contact with the hydraulic modulator, with no visible gap around any of the sealing area. If this cannot be achieved, release all the screws and tighten them progressively again. If it is still not possible to obtain correct seating of the unit, the complete assembly must be renewed.

16 Reconnect the return pump motor wiring plug, then refit the hydraulic modulator as described previously in this Section.

Front wheel speed sensor

Removal

17 Disconnect the battery negative terminal (refer to *Disconnecting the battery* in the Reference Chapter).

18 Firmly apply the handbrake, then jack up

20.19 Disconnect the wiring connector . . .

20.20a . . . then undo the retaining bolt (arrowed) . . .

20.20b . . . and remove the front wheel speed sensor from the vehicle

the front of the car and support it securely on axle stands (see *Jacking and vehicle support*). Remove the appropriate front roadwheel.

19 Trace the wheel speed sensor wiring back to its wiring connector, and release it from its retaining clip. Disconnect the connector **(see illustration)**, and work back along the sensor wiring, freeing it from all the relevant retaining clips and ties.

20 Slacken and remove the bolt securing the sensor to the mounting bracket, and remove the sensor and lead assembly from the vehicle **(see illustrations)**.

Refitting

21 Prior to refitting, apply a thin coat of multi-purpose grease to the sensor mounting bracket.

22 Ensure that the sensor and mounting bracket sealing faces are clean, then fit the sensor to the hub. Refit the retaining bolt, and tighten it to the specified torque.

23 Ensure that the sensor wiring is correctly routed, and retained by all the necessary clips. Reconnect it to its wiring connector, and fit the connector into the retaining clip.

24 Refit the roadwheel, aligning the marks

made on removal, then lower the vehicle to the ground and tighten the roadwheel bolts to the specified torque.

Rear wheel speed sensor

25 The rear wheel sensors is part of the rear hub/stub axle assembly. At the time of writing, the sensor could not be bought separately; see your local Vauxhall dealer.

26 To remove the hub/stub axle units, refer to the relevant section in Chapter 10.

Front speed sensor toothed rings

27 The front toothed rings are an integral part of the driveshaft outer constant velocity (CV) joints, and cannot be renewed separately. Examine the rings for such damage as chipped or missing teeth. If renewal is necessary, the complete outer constant velocity joint must be renewed, as described in Chapter 8.

Rear speed sensor toothed rings

Removal

28 The rear sensor pick-up rings are on the inside of the rear brake drums, remove the

20.30 Rear wheel speed sensor toothed ring is an integral part of the brake drum

rear brake drum as described in Section 7.

29 Examine the rings for signs of damage such as chipped or missing teeth, use a puller to withdraw the ring from the inside of the brake drum.

Refitting

30 Refit the sensor pick-up ring to the inside of the brake drum, taking care not to damage it as it is being pressed onto the hub assembly **(see illustration)**. Refitting is the reverse of the removal procedure.

Chapter 10
Suspension and steering

Contents

Degrees of difficulty

Easy, suitable for novice with little experience	Fairly easy, suitable for beginner with some experience	Fairly difficult, suitable for competent DIY mechanic	Difficult, suitable for experienced DIY mechanic	Very difficult, suitable for expert DIY or professional
				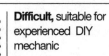

Specifications

Front suspension
Type .... Independent, with MacPherson struts and anti-roll bar

Rear suspension
Type .... Semi-independent torsion beam, with trailing arms, coil springs and telescopic shock absorbers. Anti-roll bar on some models

Steering
Type .... Rack-and-pinion. Electric motor in EPS steering column

Roadwheels
Type .... Pressed-steel or aluminium alloy (depending on model)
Size .... 5J x 13, 5.5J x 14 and 6J x 15

Front wheel alignment and steering angles
Camber angle:
  All models except Sport:
    Corsa and Corsavan .... -1°10' ± 45'
    Corsa ECO .... -1°25' ± 45'
    Combo Van .... -1°05' ± 45'
  Sport models .... -1°20' ± 45'
  Maximum difference between sides .... 1°
Castor angle:
  All models except Sport:
    Corsa and Corsavan .... 1°35' ± 1°
    Corsa ECO .... 1°40' ± 1°
    Combo Van .... 1°25' ± 1°
    Combo Van with increased pay load .... 1°15' ± 1°
  Sport models .... 1°30' ± 1°
  Maximum difference between sides .... 1°
Toe setting:
  Corsa and Corsavan .... +0°10' ± 10'
  Combo Van .... -0°10' ± 10'

Rear wheel alignment

Camber angle (not adjustable):
Corsa and Corsavan .... -1°30' ± 30'
Combo Van .... -1°40' ± 30'
Maximum difference between sides .... 35'
Toe setting (not adjustable):
Corsa and Corsavan .... +0°10' +30' / -15'
Combo Van .٫... +0°00' +30' / -15'
Maximum difference between sides .... 15'

Tyres

Corsa and Corsavan:
1.0 litre petrol models .... 155/80 R 13-79 T, 175/65 R 14-82 T
1.2 litre petrol models .... 155/80 R 13-79 T, 175/65 R 14-82 T, 185/55 R 15-82 H
1.4 litre petrol models .... 175/65 R 14-82 T, 185/55 R 15-82 H
1.7 litre diesel models:
Y17DT .... 175/65 R 14-82 T, 185/55 R 15-82 H
Y17DTL .... 175/65 R 14-82 T
Combo:
Van .... 175/65 R 14-90 T
Tour .... 175/65 R 14-86 T

Torque wrench settings

	Nm	lbf ft
Steering		
Airbag unit to steering wheel	8	6
Intermediate shaft-to-steering pinion clamp bolt	24	18
Steering column mounting bolts	22	16
Steering column-to-intermediate shaft clamp bolt	22	16
Steering gear-to-front axle body bolts*:		
Stage 1	45	33
Stage 2	Angle tighten a further 45°	
Stage 3	Angle tighten a further 15°	
Steering wheel bolt	25	18
Track rod axial joint to steering rack	70	52
Track rod balljoint locknut	50	37
Track rod balljoint-to-swivel hub nut*	35	26
Front suspension		
Anti-roll bar clamp bolts	20	15
Balljoint-to-lower arm bolts/nuts*	55	41
Brake caliper mounting bracket-to-swivel hub bolts	100	74
Driveshaft retaining nut*:		
Stage 1	120	89
Stage 2	Slacken the nut completely	
Stage 3	20	15
Stage 4	Angle-tighten a further 90°	
Front subframe mounting bolts*:		
Stage 1	90	66
Stage 2	Angle-tighten a further 45°	
Stage 3	Angle-tighten a further 15°	
Link rod-to-strut nut*	65	48
Link rod-to-anti-roll bar nut*	65	48
Lower arm balljoint clamp bolt nut*	60	44
Lower arm pivot bolts/nut to engine subframe*:		
Stage 1	90	66
Stage 2	Angle-tighten a further 75°	
Stage 3	Angle-tighten a further 15°	
Lower arm-to-inner front bush bolts/nuts*	55	41
Suspension strut piston rod upper mounting nut*	50	37
Suspension strut-to-swivel hub bolts*:		
Stage 1	80	59
Stage 2	Angle-tighten a further 60°	
Stage 3	Angle-tighten a further 15°	
Suspension strut upper mounting nut	55	41
Wheel sensor retaining bracket bolt	8	6

Torque wrench settings (continued)

	Nm	lbf ft
Rear suspension – Corsa and Corsavan models		
Anti-roll bar bolts*:		
Stage 1	60	44
Stage 2	Angle-tighten a further 15°	
Drum/hub nut*	175	129
Shock absorber:		
Lower bolt:		
M10 x 1.25 bolt	65	48
M14 x 1.50 bolt	110	81
Upper nut	20	15
Stub axle bolts*:		
Stage 1	50	37
Stage 2	Angle-tighten a further 30°	
Stage 3	Angle-tighten a further 15°	
Trailing arm pivot bolts*:		
Stage 1	50	37
Stage 2	Angle-tighten a further 45°	
Stage 3	Angle-tighten a further 15°	
Rear suspension – Combo Van models		
Shock absorber:		
Lower bolt	110	81
Upper bolt	90	66
Stub axle/bearing unit bolts*:		
Stage 1	50	37
Stage 2	Angle-tighten a further 30°	
Stage 3	Angle-tighten a further 15°	
Trailing arm mounting bolts*:		
Stage 1	90	66
Stage 2	Angle-tighten a further 30°	
Stage 3	Angle-tighten a further 15°	
Trailing arm pivot centre bolt*:		
Stage 1	90	66
Stage 2	Angle-tighten a further 60°	
Stage 3	Angle-tighten a further 15°	
Roadwheels		
Roadwheel bolts	110	81

*Use new nuts/bolts.

1 General information

1 The independent front suspension is of the MacPherson strut type, incorporating coil springs and integral telescopic shock absorbers. The MacPherson struts are located by transverse lower suspension arms, which utilise rubber inner mounting bushes, and incorporate a balljoint at the outer ends. The front swivel hubs, which carry the wheel bearings, brake calipers and the hub/disc assemblies, are bolted to the MacPherson struts, and connected to the lower arms via the balljoints. A front anti-roll bar is fitted, which has link rods with balljoints at each end to connect it to the strut.

2 The rear suspension is of semi-independent type, consisting of a torsion beam axle and trailing arms, with double-conical coil springs and telescopic shock absorbers. The front ends of the trailing arms are attached to the vehicle underbody by horizontal bushes; the rear ends are located by the shock absorbers,

which are bolted to the underbody at their upper ends. The coil springs are mounted independently of the shock absorbers, and act directly between the trailing arms and the underbody. Certain models are fitted with an anti-roll bar, which is bolted onto the underside of each trailing arm.

3 The steering column is linked to the steering gear by an intermediate shaft. The intermediate shaft has a universal joint fitted to its upper end, and is secured to the column by a clamp bolt. The lower end of the intermediate shaft is attached to the steering gear pinion by means of a clamp bolt.

4 The rack-and-pinion type steering gear is rubber-mounted onto the engine compartment bulkhead, and is connected by two track rods, with balljoints at their outer ends, to the steering arms projecting rearwards from the swivel hubs. The track rod ends are threaded, to facilitate adjustment.

5 Electric power-assisted steering is fitted as standard, whereby an electric motor, drive gear assembly and torque sensor incorporated in the upper steering column provide a variable degree of power assistance

according to roadspeed. The system is controlled by an electronic control unit with self-diagnostic capability, located on the steering column.

2 Front swivel hub assembly – removal and refitting

Note: *New retaining nuts and/or bolts will be required for most attachments when refitting (see text).*

Removal

If work is being carried out without the aid of an assistant, remove the wheel trim/hub cap (as applicable), then withdraw the split pin and slacken the driveshaft retaining nut prior to jacking up the vehicle.

1 Firmly apply the handbrake, then jack up the front of the car and support it securely on

2.2 Extract the split pin from the driveshaft retaining nut

2.3 Using a fabricated tool to hold the front hub stationary whilst the driveshaft retaining nut is slackened

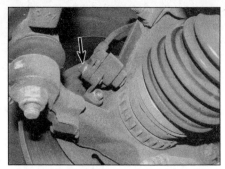

2.6 Undo the bolt (arrowed) and remove the wheel sensor – where applicable

axle stands (see *Jacking and vehicle support*). Remove the appropriate front roadwheel.

2 Where fitted, remove the dust cap from the centre of the hub assembly, then extract the split pin from the driveshaft retaining nut and discard it; a new one must be used on refitting **(see illustration)**.

3 Refit at least two roadwheel bolts to the front hub, and tighten them securely. Have an assistant firmly depress the brake pedal to prevent the front hub from rotating, then using a socket and extension bar, slacken and remove the driveshaft retaining nut. Alternatively, a tool can be fabricated from two lengths of steel strip (one long, one short) and a nut and bolt; the nut and bolt forming the pivot of a forked tool. Bolt the tool to the hub using two wheel bolts, and hold the tool to prevent the hub from rotating as the driveshaft retaining nut is undone **(see illustration)**.

4 Unscrew the driveshaft retaining nut, and remove the washer. Discard the nut and washer; new ones must be used on refitting.

5 Remove the brake disc as described in Chapter 9. The procedure involves removing the brake caliper, using a piece of wire or string, tie the caliper to the front suspension coil spring to avoid placing any strain on the hydraulic brake hose.

6 On models with ABS, undo the bolt securing the wheel speed sensor mounting bracket to the swivel hub, and position the sensor assembly clear of the hub **(see illustration)**.

7 On all models, slacken and remove the nut securing the steering gear track rod balljoint to the swivel hub, and release the balljoint tapered shank using a universal balljoint separator. Discard the nut; it should be renewed whenever it is disturbed.

8 Slacken and remove the lower arm balljoint clamp nut and bolt, and free the lower arm

from the swivel hub **(see illustration)**. Discard the clamp bolt nut; a new one must be used on refitting.

9 Slacken and remove the two nuts and bolts securing the suspension strut to the swivel hub, noting which way around the bolts are inserted **(see illustration)**. Discard the nuts and bolts; they should be renewed whenever they are disturbed.

10 Carefully pull the swivel hub assembly outwards, and withdraw the driveshaft outer constant velocity joint from the hub assembly. If necessary, the shaft can be tapped out of the hub using a soft-faced mallet. Support the driveshaft by suspending it with wire or string, and do not allow it to hang under its own weight. Remove the hub assembly from the vehicle **(see illustration)**.

Refitting

11 Ensure that the driveshaft outer constant velocity joint and hub splines are clean, then slide the hub onto the driveshaft splines. Fit the washer and new driveshaft retaining nut, tightening it by hand only at this stage **(see illustration)**.

12 Engage the swivel hub with the suspension strut, and insert the new bolts from the front of the strut so that their threads are facing to the rear. Fit the new nuts, tightening them by hand only at this stage.

13 Locate the lower arm balljoint in the swivel hub. Insert the clamp bolt from the front of the swivel hub, so that its threads are facing to the rear. Fit the new nut to the clamp bolt, and tighten it to the specified torque setting.

14 With the hub correctly located, tighten the strut-to-swivel hub bolts through the various stages given in the Specifications at the start of this Chapter.

15 Engage the track rod balljoint in the swivel hub, then fit the new retaining nut and tighten it to the specified torque setting.

16 Refit the brake disc and caliper to the swivel hub, referring to Chapter 9 for further information.

17 Where necessary, refit the ABS wheel speed sensor to the hub, making sure it is located correctly, and tighten the retaining bolt to the specified torque.

18 Using the method employed on removal to prevent rotation, tighten the driveshaft

2.8 Withdraw the clamp bolt, and free the lower arm balljoint from the swivel hub

2.9 Unscrew the nuts and withdraw the bolts securing the suspension strut to the swivel hub

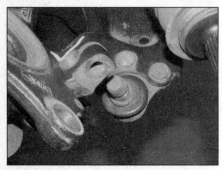

2.10 Free the swivel hub and withdraw it from the vehicle

2.11 Engage the swivel hub with the driveshaft constant velocity joint

retaining nut through the stages given in the Specifications.

19 With the nut correctly tightened, secure it in position with a new split pin. If the holes in the driveshaft are not aligned with any of the slots in the nut, loosen (do not tighten) the nut by the *smallest possible amount* until the split pin can be inserted.

20 Refit the roadwheel, then lower the vehicle to the ground and tighten the roadwheel bolts to the specified torque. Refit the wheel trim/hub cap, where applicable.

3 Front hub bearings – renewal

Note: *The bearing is sealed, pre-adjusted and prelubricated. Never overtighten the driveshaft nut beyond the specified torque wrench setting in an attempt to 'adjust' the bearing.*

Note: *A press will be required to dismantle and rebuild the assembly; if such a tool is not available, a large bench vice and spacers (such as large sockets) will serve as an adequate substitute. The bearing's inner races are an interference fit on the hub; if the inner race remains on the hub when it is pressed out of the hub carrier, a knife-edged bearing puller will be required to remove it.*

1 Remove the swivel hub assembly as described in Section 2.

2 Align the holes in the hub and undo the screws, to remove the brake disc shield from the hub **(see illustration)**.

3 Support the swivel hub securely on blocks or in a vice. Using a tubular spacer/socket which bears only on the inner end of the hub flange, press the hub flange out of the bearing. If the bearing's outboard inner race remains on the hub, remove it using a bearing puller – see note above **(see illustrations)**.

4 Extract the bearing retaining circlip from the swivel hub assembly **(see illustration)**.

5 Using a drift or tubular spacer which bears only on the inner race, press the complete bearing assembly out of the swivel hub **(see illustration)**.

6 Thoroughly clean the hub and swivel hub, removing all traces of dirt and grease. Polish away any burrs or raised edges which might hinder reassembly. Check both assemblies for cracks or any other signs of wear or damage, and renew as necessary. Renew the circlip regardless of its apparent condition.

7 On reassembly, apply a light film of oil to the bearing outer race and hub flange shaft, to aid installation of the bearing. Remove all traces of old thread-locking compound from the disc shield retaining screw holes, ideally by running a tap of the correct size and pitch through them.

8 Securely support the swivel hub, and locate the bearing in the hub. Press the bearing fully into position, ensuring that it enters the hub squarely, using the old wheel bearing or a tubular spacer which bears only on the bearing outer race **(see illustration)**.

3.2 Disc shield retaining screws are accessed through holes in the hub flange

3.3b Use a chisel to remove the inner bearing race from the hub flange

9 Once the bearing is correctly seated, secure the bearing in position with the new inner circlip. Make sure that the circlip is correctly located in its groove **(see illustration)**.

10 Securely support the swivel hub in a vice,

3.5 Using a drift to remove the bearing from the swivel hub

3.9 . . . then refit the circlip securely into the groove (arrowed)

3.3a Using a socket to drift out the hub flange out from the bearing

3.4 Use circlip pliers to remove the circlip

then locate the hub flange into the bearing inner race. Press the flange into the swivel hub bearing, using a tubular spacer/sockets and threaded rod, until it seats against the hub shoulder **(see illustration)**. Check that

3.8 Use a threaded rod and spacers to press the bearing squarely into position . . .

3.10 Using a threaded rod and spacers/sockets to press the hub flange into the bearing

3.11 Refit the disc shield to the hub assembly

4.2 Hold the joint stub with an open-ended spanner and undo the retaining nut (arrowed)

4.4 Unscrew the nuts and withdraw the bolts (arrowed) securing the suspension strut to the swivel hub

the hub flange rotates freely, and wipe off any excess oil or grease.

11 Fit the disc shield to the hub assembly **(see illustration)**, and apply a few drops of thread-locking compound to the new screws. Fit the screws, and tighten them securely.

12 Refit the swivel hub assembly as described in Section 2.

4 Front strut – removal, overhaul and refitting

Note: *When refitting, new strut-to-swivel hub bolts and nuts, and strut link rod nut, will be required.*

Removal

1 Firmly apply the handbrake, then jack up the front of the car and support it securely on axle stands (see *Jacking and vehicle support*). Remove the appropriate roadwheel.

2 Unscrew the retaining nut and disconnect the anti-roll bar link rod from the strut, discard it; a new one should be used on refitting. Use a spanner on the flats to hold the link while the nut is being loosened **(see illustration)**.

3 On models with ABS, release the front wheel speed sensor wiring from its clip on the suspension strut.

4 Slacken and remove the two nuts and bolts securing the suspension strut to the swivel hub. Discard both nuts and bolts; these must be renewed whenever they are disturbed **(see illustration)**.

5 Support the front strut assembly then, from within the engine compartment, remove the plastic cap from the upper strut mounting. Unscrew the suspension strut upper mounting nut and remove the retaining plate **(see illustrations)**.

6 Release the strut from the swivel hub, and withdraw it from under the wheel arch **(see illustration)**.

Overhaul

Note: *A spring compressor tool will be required for this operation. Before overhaul, mark the position of each component in relationship with each other for reassembly.*

7 With the suspension strut resting on a bench, or clamped in a vice, fit a spring compressor tool, and compress the coil spring to relieve the pressure on the spring seats. Ensure that the compressor tool is securely located on the spring, in accordance with the tool manufacturer's instructions **(see illustration)**.

8 Mark the position of the spring relevant to the top and bottom mountings, then counter-hold the strut piston rod with a spanner, and unscrew the piston rod nut **(see illustration)**.

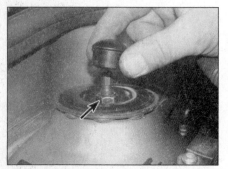

4.5a Remove the plastic cap, unscrew the mounting nut (arrowed) . . .

4.5b . . . and withdraw the upper retaining plate

4.6 Release the lower end of the strut from the swivel hub . . .

4.7 Ensure that the compressor tool is securely located on the spring

4.8 Counterhold the strut piston rod with a spanner, and unscrew the piston rod nut

4.9 Withdraw the upper damping ring . . .

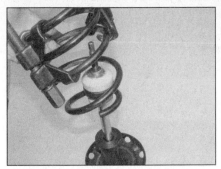

4.10a . . . and the coil spring . . .

4.10b . . . then the buffer

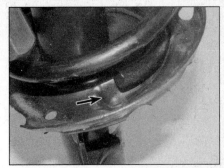

4.15 Locate the spring against the raised stop (arrowed) in the strut

9 Remove the upper damping ring with support bearing and upper spring seat **(see illustration)**.
10 Remove the spring and buffer from the strut **(see illustrations)**.
11 With the strut assembly now completely dismantled, examine all the components for wear, damage or deformation, and check the support bearing for smoothness of operation. Renew any of the components as necessary.
12 Examine the strut for signs of fluid leakage. Check the strut piston for signs of pitting along its entire length, and check the strut body for signs of damage. While holding it in an upright position, test the operation of the strut by moving the piston through a full stroke, and then through short strokes of 50 to 100 mm. In both cases, the resistance felt should be smooth and continuous. If the resistance is jerky or uneven or if there is any visible sign of wear or damage to the strut, renewal is necessary.
13 If any doubt exists as to the condition of the coil spring, carefully remove the spring compressors and check the spring for distortion and signs of cracking. Renew the spring if it is damaged or distorted, or if there is any doubt as to its condition.
14 Inspect all other components for damage or deterioration, and renew any that are suspect.
15 With the spring compressed with the compressor tool, locate the spring on the strut making sure that it is correctly seated with its lower end against the raised stop **(see illustration)**.

16 Refit the buffer, upper spring seat, and upper damping ring.
17 Refit the piston rod nut and tighten it to the specified torque while counterholding the piston rod with a spanner.
18 Slowly slacken the spring compressor tool to relieve the tension in the spring. Check that the ends of the spring locate correctly against the stops on the spring seats. If necessary, turn the spring and the upper seat so that the components locate correctly before the compressor tool is removed. Remove the compressor tool when the spring is fully seated.

Refitting

19 Manoeuvre the strut assembly into position, ensuring that the top mounting is correctly located in the inner wing panel. Fit the upper mounting plate and retaining nut, and tighten it to the specified torque setting.
20 Engage the lower end of the strut with the swivel hub. Insert the new bolts from the front of the strut so that their threads are facing to the rear. Fit the new nuts to the bolts, and tighten them through the various stages given in the Specifications at the start of this Chapter.
21 Refit the anti-roll bar link rod to the strut, using a new retaining nut. Use a spanner on the flats to hold the link, while the nut is being tightened to the specified torque setting.
22 On models with ABS, clip the sensor wiring back into its retaining clip.
23 Refit the roadwheel, then lower the vehicle to the ground and tighten the roadwheel bolts to the specified torque.

5 Front lower arm –
removal, overhaul and refitting

Note: *When refitting, new pivot bolt/nuts, and new lower arm-to-balljoint nut/bolt, will be required.*

Removal

1 Firmly apply the handbrake, then jack up the front of the car and support it securely on axle stands (see *Jacking and vehicle support*). Remove the appropriate front roadwheel.
2 Slacken and remove the lower arm balljoint clamp nut and bolt, and free the lower arm from the swivel hub **(see illustration)**. Discard the clamp bolt nut; a new one must be used on refitting.
3 Unscrew the nut and withdraw the pivot bolt securing the front of the lower arm to the engine subframe **(see illustration)**. Discard the bolt/nut; new ones should be used on refitting.
4 Undo the securing bolt and withdraw it from the lower arm rear mounting to the engine subframe **(see illustration)**. Discard the bolt; a new one should be used on refitting. Remove the lower arm from the vehicle.

Overhaul

5 Thoroughly clean the lower arm and the area around the arm mountings, removing all traces of dirt and underseal if necessary. Check carefully for cracks, distortion, or any other signs of wear or damage, paying

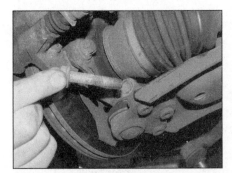

5.2 Slacken and remove the nut and clamp bolt . . .

5.3 . . . the front lower arm pivot bolt (arrowed) . . .

5.4 . . . and the rear lower arm retaining bolt

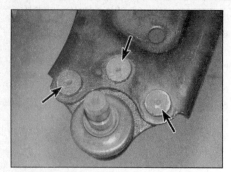

6.2 Drill out the balljoint securing rivets (arrowed) using a 10mm drill bit

6.6 Drill out the front bush securing rivets (arrowed) using a 10mm drill bit

particular attention to the pivot bushes. If rear bush renewal is necessary, the lower arm should be taken to a Vauxhall dealer or suitably-equipped garage. A hydraulic press and spacers are required to press the bushes out of the arm, and to install the new ones. To renew the lower arm balljoint or front inner bush see Section 6.

Refitting

6 Offer up the lower arm, aligning the inner end of the arm with its mountings, insert new pivot bolt and nut to the front and rear mounting points. **Note:** *Only tighten the mounting bolts/nut hand tight at this stage.*
7 Locate the lower balljoint stub fully in the bottom of the swivel hub, then refit the clamp bolt and tighten to the specified torque. Make sure the bolt head is facing the front of the vehicle.
8 The lower arm inner mounting bolts/nut can now be tightened through the various stages given in the Specifications at the start of this Chapter.
9 Refit the roadwheel, aligning any marks made on removal, lower the vehicle to the ground, and tighten the roadwheel bolts to the specified torque setting.
10 Have the front wheel alignment settings checked by a suitably-equipped garage.

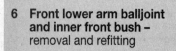

6 Front lower arm balljoint and inner front bush – removal and refitting

Note: *When refitting, a new clamp bolt/nut*

and new balljoint-to-lower arm nuts and bolts will be required.

Balljoint

Removal

1 Remove the front lower arm assembly as described in Section 5.
2 Using a 10mm drill bit, drill out the three rivets which hold the balljoint to the lower arm **(see illustration)**, and remove the balljoint. Coat the holes in the lower arm where the rivets had been with anti-corrosion paint.

Refitting

3 Align the new balljoint with the lower arm, then insert the new special bolts (supplied by the dealer) from the top downwards through the lower arm. Fit the new nuts to the bolts, tightening them to the specified torque setting at the beginning of this Chapter.
4 Refit the front lower arm assembly as described in Section 5.

Inner front bush (Hydro-bush)

Removal

5 Remove the front lower arm assembly as described in Section 5.
6 Using a 10mm drill bit, drill out the three rivets which hold the bush to the lower arm **(see illustration)**, and remove the bush. Coat the holes in the lower arm where the rivets had been with anti-corrosion paint.

Refitting

7 Align the new bush with the lower arm, then insert the new special bolts (supplied by the

dealer) from the top downwards through the lower arm. Fit the new nuts to the bolts, tightening them to the specified torque setting at the beginning of this Chapter.
8 Refit the front lower arm assembly as described in Section 5.

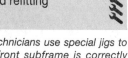

7 Front subframe – removal and refitting

Note: *Vauxhall technicians use special jigs to ensure that the front subframe is correctly aligned. Without the use of these tools it is important to note the position of the subframe accurately before removal.*

Removal

1 Set the front wheels in the straight-ahead position, then remove the ignition key and lock the column by turning the steering wheel as required.
2 In the driver's footwell, unscrew the bolt securing the bottom of the steering column intermediate shaft to the steering gear pinion **(see illustration)**. Pull the shaft from the pinion and position to one side.
3 Working under the bonnet, connect a hoist to the engine/transmission assembly and support its weight. If available, the type of support bar which locates in the engine compartment side channels is to be preferred, as this will ensure correct repositioning during refitting. Where applicable, remove the engine upper cover.
4 Use cable-ties to secure the top mountings on each side of the radiator to prevent the radiator dropping when the subframe is removed **(see illustration)**.
5 Apply the handbrake, then jack up the front of the vehicle and support it on axle stands (see *Jacking and vehicle support*). Remove both front wheels.
6 Remove the front bumper as described in Chapter 11.
7 Disconnect the steering track rod ends from the hub carriers by unscrewing the nuts and using a balljoint separator tool **(see illustration)**.
8 Unscrew the nuts and disconnect the anti-roll bar link rods from the struts on both sides.

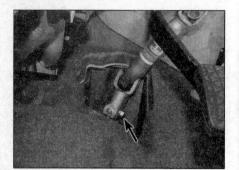

7.2 Unscrew the bolt (arrowed) securing the bottom of the steering column

7.4 Use cable-ties to prevent the radiator dropping

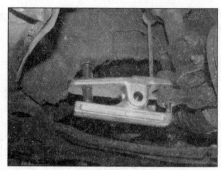

7.7 Using a balljoint separator tool to free the balljoint

7.8 Holding the joint stub with an open-ended spanner, while removing the retaining nut

7.9 Withdraw the clamp bolt, and free the lower arm balljoint from the swivel hub

7.13a Undo the centre bolt (arrowed) from the rear torque link mounting

7.13b On diesel models, remove the mounting bolt (arrowed) from the front torque link

7.14 Release the retaining clip from the gearchange guide bracket

Use a further spanner to hold the studs while the nuts are being loosened **(see illustration)**.

9 Unscrew and remove the clamp bolts securing the front suspension lower arm balljoints in the hub carriers **(see illustration)**, noting which way round they are fitted.

10 Using a suitable lever, push down the lower arms and separate them from the hub carriers. When releasing the lower arms, take care not to damage the balljoint rubber boots on the bottom of the hub carriers; if necessary protect them with a piece of card or plastic. **Note:** *If the balljoint stub is tight in the hub carrier, use a screwdriver or cold chisel as a wedge to force the clamp apart.*

11 On petrol models, disconnect the oxygen sensor wiring and position to one side.

12 Remove the front section of the exhaust as described in the relevant part of Chapter 4.

13 Undo the centre bolt from the torque link mounting at the rear of the engine/transmission **(see illustration)**. **Note:** *On diesel models, there is a torque link mounting bolt on the front of the engine/transmission that will need to be removed* **(see illustration)**.

14 Remove the retaining clip and release the gearchange guide bracket **(see illustration)**.

15 Support the subframe with a cradle across a trolley jack. Alternatively, two trolley jacks and the help of an assistant will be required.

16 Accurately mark the position of the subframe in relation with the mounting points to ensure correct refitting. Note that Vauxhall technicians use a special jig with guide pins located through the alignment holes in the subframe and underbody.

17 Unscrew the four subframe mounting bolts and carefully lower the subframe to the ground **(see illustrations)**. As the subframe is lowered, make sure there are no cables or wiring still attached.

18 Remove the lower suspension arms from the subframe with reference to Section 5, the anti-roll bar with reference to Section 8, the rear engine mounting with reference to the relevant part of Chapter 2, and the steering gear with reference to Section 20.

Refitting

19 Refitting is a reversal of removal, but tighten all nuts and bolts to the specified

7.17a Unscrew the rear mounting bolts (one side arrowed) . . .

torque where necessary in the stages given. Make sure that the alignment holes in the subframe and underbody are correctly aligned before fully tightening the mounting bolts.

8.4 Undo the link rod retaining nut (arrowed) from the end of the anti-roll bar

7.17b . . . and the front mounting bolts (one side shown)

8 Front anti-roll bar – removal and refitting

Removal

1 Firmly apply the handbrake, then jack up the front of the car and support it securely on axle stands (see *Jacking and vehicle support*).

2 Remove the front engine subframe assembly as described in Section 7.

3 Prior to removal of the anti-roll bar, mark the position of each anti-roll bar mounting clamp rubber.

4 Unscrew the retaining nut and disconnect the link rod from the ends of the anti-roll bar, discard the retaining nut; a new one should be used on refitting **(see illustration)**. Use a spanner on the flats to hold the link while the nut is being loosened.

8.5 Unscrew the anti-roll bar clamp retaining nuts . . .

5 Unscrew the two bolts from each mounting clamp, and remove the clamp **(see illustration)**. As the last clamp is removed, support the anti-roll bar and remove it from the subframe.
6 Inspect the mounting clamp rubbers for signs of damage and deterioration, and renew if necessary **(see illustration)**.

Refitting

7 Align the mounting rubbers with the marks made on the anti-roll bar prior to removal.
8 Refit the anti-roll bar to the subframe, and fit the mounting clamps. Ensure that the clamp half is correctly engaged with the anti-roll bar rubbers, then tighten each clamp retaining bolt, by hand only at this stage.
9 With the two clamps loosely installed, check the position of the anti-roll bar to the marks made on removal, then tighten the clamp bolts to the specified torque setting.

9.1 The drum and hub assembly on the Corsa and Corsavan models

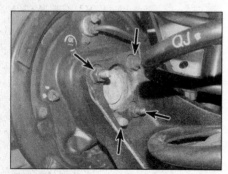

9.6 Undo the four retaining nuts (arrowed) from the rear of the trailing arm

8.6 . . . and remove the mounting rubber from the tie-bar

10 Refit the link rods to the ends of the anti-roll bar using new retaining nuts, tighten to the specified torque setting.
11 Refit the front engine subframe assembly as described in Section 7.
12 Refit the roadwheels if not already done, then lower the vehicle to the ground and tighten the roadwheel bolts to the specified torque setting.

| 9 | **Rear hub assembly –** removal and refitting | |

Removal

Corsa and Corsavan models

1 On these models, the rear hub is an integral part of the brake drum **(see illustration)**.

9.3 Examine the stub axle shaft (arrowed) for signs of wear or damage

10.2 Use circlip pliers to remove the circlip

Refer to Chapter 9 for drum removal and refitting details.
2 Check the hub bearing for signs of roughness or damage, and renew if necessary as described in Section 10.
3 With the hub removed, examine the stub axle shaft for signs of wear or damage **(see illustration)**, if necessary, renew it as described in Section 11.

Combo Van models

4 Remove the rear brake drum as described in Chapter 9.
5 On models with ABS, disconnect the wiring for the wheel speed sensor, located on the rear of the brake backplate.
6 Support the hub assembly then undo the four retaining nuts from the rear of the trailing arm. Withdraw the hub assembly from the vehicle **(see illustration)**.

Refitting

Corsa and Corsavan models

7 Refit the brake drum as described in Chapter 9.

Combo Van models

8 Ensure that the backplate is clean, then locate the hub assembly onto the trailing arm and fit new retaining nuts to secure.
9 Tighten the new retaining nuts to the specified torque and angles in the stages given at the beginning of this Chapter.
10 Where applicable, reconnect the wiring for the wheel speed sensor.
11 Refit the brake drum as described in Chapter 9.

| 10 | **Rear hub bearings –** renewal | |

Note: *On Combo Van models, the bearing and hub assembly can only be bought as a complete unit (see your local dealer for availability of parts). To remove the hub/bearing assembly on the Combo Van see Section 9.*

1 Remove the rear brake drum as described in Chapter 9, Section 7.
2 Extract the bearing retaining circlip from the inside of the brake drum assembly **(see illustration)**.
3 Turn the drum/hub over, then supporting it on two blocks of wood, use a drift to tap the complete bearing out of the hub.
4 Thoroughly clean the hub, removing all traces of dirt and grease. Polish away any burrs or raised edges which might hinder reassembly. Check the drum/hub surface for cracks or any other signs of wear or damage, and renew it if necessary. The bearings must be renewed whenever they are disturbed, as removal will almost certainly damage the outer races. Obtain new bearings from your Vauxhall dealer.
5 On reassembly, apply a light film of clean

10.6a Press the bearing squarely into position . . .

10.6b . . . then use a threaded rod and spacers to press the bearing into the hub

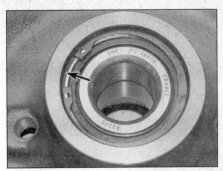

10.7 Refit the circlip securely into the groove (arrowed)

engine oil to each bearing outer race, to aid installation.

6 Securely support the drum/hub, and locate the bearing in the hub. Press the bearing fully into position, ensuring that it enters the hub squarely. Use a tubular spacer/sockets which bears only on the bearing outer race and threaded rod to press the bearing into position **(see illustrations)**.

 The old wheel bearing can be used to press the new bearing into the hub.

7 Once the bearing is correctly seated, secure the bearing in position with the new inner circlip. Make sure that the circlip is correctly located in its groove **(see illustration)**.

8 Refit the brake drum as described in Chapter 9, Section 7.

11 Rear stub axle – removal and refitting

Corsa and Corsavan models

Note: *When refitting, new stub axle retaining bolts/nuts must be used.*

Removal

1 Remove the brake drum as described in Chapter 9.

2 Position a jack underneath the relevant trailing arm, and raise the jack until it is just supporting the weight of the arm.

3 Undo the lower shock absorber mounting bolt **(see illustration)**, and swing the shock absorber away from the trailing arm to gain access to the stub axle retaining bolts.

4 Slacken and remove the retaining bolts, and remove the stub axle from the trailing arm **(see illustration)**. Discard the retaining bolts; new ones must be used on refitting.

5 Inspect the stub axle surface for signs of damage such as scoring, and renew if necessary.

Refitting

6 Ensure that the mating surfaces of the stub axle and backplate are clean and dry. Check the backplate for signs of damage, and remove any burrs with a fine file or emery cloth.

7 Offer up the stub axle, and fit the new retaining bolts. Tighten the retaining bolts through the various stages given in the Specifications at the start of this Chapter.

8 Align the shock absorber with the trailing arm, then fit its lower mounting bolt, tightening it to the specified torque.

9 Remove the jack from underneath the trailing arm, and refit the brake drum as described in Chapter 9.

Combo Van models

10 On Combo Van models, the stub axle/bearing hub assembly is one unit. Refer to Section 9 to remove the hub bearing assembly.

12 Rear shock absorber – removal, testing and refitting

Note: *Always renew shock absorbers in pairs and the correct version for model, to maintain good handling.*

Removal

Corsa and Corsavan models

1 Chock the front wheels then jack up the rear of the car and support it on axle stands (see *Jacking and vehicle support*).

2 Position a jack underneath the relevant trailing arm, and raise the jack until it is just supporting the weight of the arm.

3 Working in the luggage compartment, unclip the trim cover cap to gain access to the shock absorber upper mounting nut **(see illustration)**.

4 Slacken and remove the nut, and lift off the plate and rubber mounting damper, noting their fitted position. If necessary, to prevent the shock absorber piston rotating as the nut is slackened, retain it using an open-ended spanner on the flats on the upper end of the piston **(see illustration)**.

5 Slacken and remove the lower shock absorber mounting bolt, then lower the shock absorber out of position and remove it from underneath the vehicle **(see illustration)**.

Combo Van

6 Chock the front wheels then jack up the

11.3 Remove the lower mounting bolt then free the shock absorber from the trailing arm

11.4 Undo the four retaining bolts (arrowed) from the rear of the trailing arm

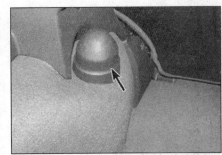

12.3 Remove the cap (arrowed) to gain access to the shock absorber upper mounting nut

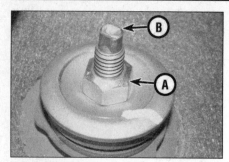

12.4 Slacken the mounting nut (A) whilst retaining the piston (B) with an open-ended spanner

12.5 Remove the lower mounting bolt (arrowed) then manoeuvre the shock absorber out from under the vehicle

13 From inside the luggage compartment, refit the rubber mounting damper and plate to the piston. Fit the upper mounting nut, and tighten it to the specified torque setting. If necessary, prevent the piston rotating as described in paragraph 4. Refit the trim cover cap.

14 Lower the vehicle to the ground and withdraw the jack from underneath the trailing arm.

Combo Van

15 Operate the shock absorber fully through several strokes to prime it, then manoeuvre it into position underneath the vehicle.

16 Ensure that the shock absorber is positioned the correct way up, and insert both the upper and lower mounting bolts. Tighten both mounting bolts to their specified torque settings.

17 Lower the vehicle to the ground and withdraw the jack from underneath the trailing arm.

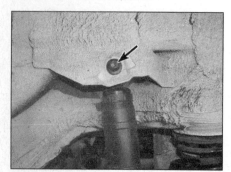

12.8a On Combo Van models, slacken and remove the upper (arrowed) . . .

12.8b . . . and lower mounting bolts (arrowed)

rear of the car and support it on axle stands (see *Jacking and vehicle support*).

7 Position a jack underneath the axle, and raise the jack until it is just supporting the weight of the axle.

8 Note the orientation of the shock absorber, then slacken and remove the upper and lower shock absorber mounting bolts, and remove the shock absorber from underneath the vehicle **(see illustrations)**.

Testing

9 Examine the shock absorber for signs of fluid leakage or damage. Test the operation of the strut, while holding it in an upright position, by moving the piston through a full stroke, and then through short strokes of 50 to 100 mm. In both cases, the resistance felt should be smooth and continuous. If the resistance is jerky, or uneven, or if there is any visible sign of wear or damage to the strut, renewal is necessary. Also check

the rubber mounting bush(es) for damage and deterioration. If the bushes are damaged or worn, the complete shock absorber will have to be renewed, as the mounting bushes are not available separately. Inspect the shanks of the mounting bolts for signs of wear or damage, and renew as necessary.

10 On Corsa and Corsavan models, examine the upper mounting rubber dampers for signs of damage or deterioration, and renew if necessary.

Refitting

Corsa and Corsavan

11 Manoeuvre the shock absorber into position, ensuring that the piston is correctly located in the hole in the vehicle body.

12 Insert the shock absorber lower mounting bolt, and tighten it to the specified torque setting.

13 Rear coil spring – removal and refitting

Note: *Always renew coil springs in pairs and the correct version for model, to maintain good handling.*

Removal

1 Chock the front wheels then jack up the rear of the car and support it on axle stands (see *Jacking and vehicle support*). Remove both rear roadwheels.

Corsa and Corsavan

2 Position a jack underneath the relevant trailing arm, and raise the jack until it is just supporting the weight of the arm.

3 Undo the shock absorber lower mounting bolt, and disengage the shock absorber from the trailing arm.

4 Slowly lower the jack, keeping watch on the brake pipes to ensure no excess strain is placed on them, until it is possible to withdraw the coil spring. Note which way around the spring is installed, and recover the upper damping ring and lower spring seat **(see illustrations)**.

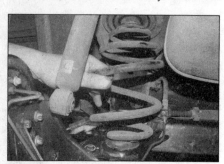

13.4a Lower the rear axle, then remove the coil spring (noting which way around it is installed) . . .

13.4b . . . then recover the lower . . .

13.4c . . . and upper damping rings/spring seats

5 If the vehicle is to be left for some time with the spring removed, lift up the trailing arms and refit the shock absorber lower mounting bolts. **Note:** *Do not allow the rear axle assembly to hang unsupported.*

6 Inspect the springs closely for signs of damage, such as cracking, and check the spring seats and damping ring for signs of wear or damage. Renew worn components as necessary.

Combo Van

Note: *A spring compressor tool will be required for this operation.*

7 Fit the spring compressor tool, and compress the coil spring to relieve the pressure on the spring seats. Ensure that the compressor tool is securely located on the spring, in accordance with the tool manufacturer's instructions.

8 Withdraw the coil spring, noting which way around the spring is installed, and recover the upper damping ring and lower spring seat.

9 Inspect the springs closely for signs of damage, such as cracking, and check the spring seats and damping ring for signs of wear or damage. Renew worn components as necessary.

Refitting

All models

10 Refitting is a reversal of removal, but note the following points.

   a) *Ensure that the spring locates correctly on the upper and lower seats, as well as on the trailing arm and underbody.*

   b) *On Corsa and Corsavan models, tighten the shock absorber lower mounting bolt to the specified torque.*

   c) *If the spring is being renewed, repeat the procedure on the remaining side of the vehicle.*

   d) *Refit the roadwheels, then lower the vehicle to the ground, and tighten the roadwheel bolts to the specified torque.*

---

14 Rear axle –
removal and refitting

Note: *Vauxhall technicians use special jigs to*

14.7a Slacken the union nut (arrowed) . . .

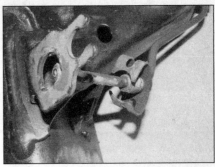

14.7b . . . and disconnect the brake pipe

ensure that the rear axle is correctly aligned. Without the use of these tools it is important to note the position of the axle mounting points accurately before removal. New trailing arm pivot bolts and nuts will be required when refitting.

Removal

1 Chock the front wheels then jack up the rear of the car and support it on axle stands (see *Jacking and vehicle support*). Remove both rear roadwheels, marking the position in relation with the hub for refitting.

2 Unscrew the brake master cylinder fluid reservoir cap and screw it down onto a piece of polythene to minimise fluid loss during the following procedure. Proceed as described under the relevant sub-heading.

Corsa and Corsavan models

3 On models with ABS, disconnect the rear wheel speed sensors at the wiring connectors. Free the sensor wiring from all its retaining clips, so that it is free to be removed with the axle.

4 Follow the brake pipes and ABS wiring and disconnect from any retaining clips along the axle.

5 With the handbrake lever in the off position, unscrew the handbrake cable adjuster nut (referring to Chapter 9), then detach the handbrake cable at the centre of the rear axle, unclipping it from the guide on the axle.

6 On ECO models, undo the retaining screws and remove the cover from under the rear of the vehicle.

7 Trace the brake pipes back from the

backplates to their unions situated directly above the axle. A brake hose clamp or similar can be used to clamp the nearest flexible hose. Slacken the union nuts, and disconnect the pipes. Plug the pipe ends, to minimise fluid loss and prevent the entry of dirt into the hydraulic system. Remove the retaining clips, and release the pipes from the axle/vehicle body **(see illustrations)**.

8 Undo the two retaining nuts and disconnect the brake pressure-regulating valve spring bracket from the axle **(see illustration)**.

9 Remove the rear coil springs as described in Section 13, then place the jack underneath the centre of the axle.

10 Accurately mark the position of the axle mounting points in relation with the vehicle underbody to ensure correct refitting. Note that Vauxhall technicians use a special jig with guide pins located through alignment holes in the underbody.

11 Slacken and remove the nut and pivot bolt securing each trailing arm to the vehicle underbody **(see illustration)**. Discard the nuts and bolts; new ones should be used on refitting.

12 Make a final check that all necessary components have been disconnected and positioned so that they will not hinder the removal procedure. Carefully lower the axle assembly out of position, and remove it from underneath the vehicle.

13 Inspect the trailing arm bushes for signs of damage or deterioration, and renew if necessary. The bushes can be pressed out of the axle and new ones fitted **(see illustrations)**. Always mark the position of the

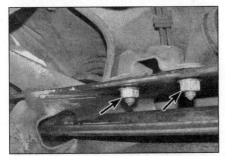

14.8 Undo the two retaining nuts (arrowed) to release the bracket from the axle

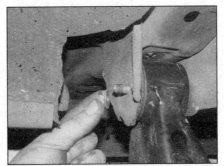

14.11 Slacken and remove the front pivot bolt

14.13a Using a drift to remove the trailing arm bush (note the fitted position)

14.13b Using a threaded rod and spacers to press the bush into the trailing arm

14.14 Detach the handbrake cable from the connector (arrowed)

14.17 Slacken and remove the brake pipe (arrowed) from the brake cylinders

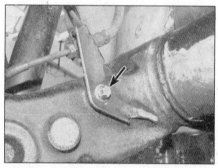

14.18 Undo the retaining bolt (arrowed) to disconnect the bracket from the axle

bush before removal, so that the new bushes can be refitted in the same position.

Combo Van

14 With the handbrake lever in the off position, unscrew the handbrake cable adjuster nut (referring to Chapter 9), then detach the handbrake cables at each side from the connections at the rear hub units **(see illustration)**.

15 Remove the rear coil springs as described in Section 13.

16 On vehicles with ABS fitted, disconnect the wiring connectors from each of the sensors on the rear hub units.

17 Disconnect the brake pipes from the brake cylinders at their unions on the back-plates **(see illustration)**. Slacken the union nuts, and disconnect the pipes. Plug the pipe ends, to minimise fluid loss and prevent the entry of dirt into the hydraulic system.

18 Follow the brake pipes and ABS wiring and disconnect any brackets or unclip from any retaining clips along the axle **(see illustration)**.

19 Position a jack beneath the centre of the axle, and raise the jack until it is supporting the weight of the axle.

20 Unscrew both the rear shock absorber lower mounting bolts, and free both shock absorbers from the axle.

21 Accurately mark the position of the axle mounting points in relation with the vehicle underbody to ensure correct refitting. Note that Vauxhall technicians use a special jig with guide pins located through alignment holes in the underbody.

22 Unscrew the three retaining bolts (at each side) for the axle front mounting brackets to vehicle underbody **(see illustration)**.

23 Make a final check that all necessary components have been disconnected and

positioned so that they will not hinder the removal procedure. Carefully lower the axle assembly out of position, and remove it from underneath the vehicle.

Refitting

Corsa and Corsavan models

24 Refitting is a reverse of the removal procedure, bearing in mind the following points:

a) Ensure that the trailing arm and mounting bracket surfaces are clean and dry. Lubricate the bushes with 'red grease' see Vauxhall dealer for specification of grease. Raise the axle assembly into position, and insert the new trailing arm pivot bolts, tightening them by hand only at this stage.

b) Raise the axle until the distance between the lower coil spring mounting on the axle and the upper coil spring mounting on the vehicle underbody is 100 ± 5mm **(see illustration)**.

c) The axle front mounting retaining bolts can now be tightened to their specified torque setting.

d) Refit the rear coil springs as described in Section 13.

e) Ensure that the brake pipes, handbrake cables and wiring (as applicable) are correctly routed, and retained by all the necessary retaining clips.

f) Tighten all the brake pipe union nuts to the specified torque, and bleed the braking system, with reference to Chapter 9.

g) Adjust the handbrake cable as described in Chapter 9. Where applicable, also adjust the rear brake pressure-regulating valve once the vehicle is on the ground.

h) Tighten the shock absorber lower mounting bolts to the specified torque.

i) On completion, lower the vehicle to the ground, and tighten the roadwheel bolts to the specified torque.

Combo Van models

25 Refitting is a reverse of the removal procedure, bearing in mind the following points:

a) Ensure that the trailing arm and mounting bracket surfaces are clean and dry. Raise the axle assembly into position, and insert the new trailing arm retaining bolts, tightening them by hand only at this stage. Make sure that the alignment holes in the mounting bracket and underbody are correctly aligned

b) Raise the axle until the distance between the lower coil spring mounting on the axle and the upper coil spring mounting on the vehicle underbody is 172 ± 10mm **(see illustration 14.24)**.

c) The axle front mounting retaining bolts can now be tightened to their specified torque setting.

d) Refit the rear coil springs as described in Section 13.

e) Ensure that the brake pipes, handbrake cables and wiring (as applicable) are

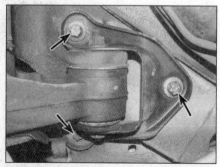

14.22 The axle front mounting bracket retaining bolts (arrowed) – one side shown

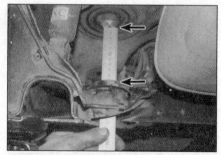

14.24 The height (arrowed) should be set at 100 mm ± 5 mm (172 mm ± 10 mm for Combo Van)

correctly routed and retained by all the necessary retaining clips.

f) Tighten all the brake pipe union nuts to the specified torque, and bleed the braking system, with reference to Chapter 9.

g) Adjust the handbrake cable and rear brake pressure-regulating valve (where applicable) as described in Chapter 9.

h) Tighten the shock absorber lower mounting bolts to the specified torque.

i) On completion, lower the vehicle to the ground, and tighten the roadwheel bolts to the specified torque.

15 Rear anti-roll bar – removal and refitting

Note: New retaining bolts will be required on refitting.

Removal

1 Chock the front wheels then jack up the rear of the car and support it on axle stands (see *Jacking and vehicle support*). Remove both rear roadwheels, marking the position in relation with the hub for refitting.

2 Prior to removal, mark the position of the rubber dampers on the axle crossmember **(see illustration)**.

3 Slacken and remove the bolts securing the ends of the anti-roll bar to the trailing arms, noting the fitted position **(see illustration)**. Discard the bolts; new ones must be used on refitting.

4 Withdraw the anti-roll bar from one side of the rear axle, if the bar is tight, drift the bar out using a hammer and soft metal drift from the opposite side. Recover the dampers from the bar as they are released **(see illustrations)**.

5 Inspect the rubber dampers for signs of damage or deterioration, and renew as necessary.

Refitting

6 Insert the anti-roll bar in through the trailing arm, and locate the rubber dampers on the bar. Align the rubber dampers with the marks made prior to removal, and seat them in the axle crossmember.

7 Slide the anti-roll bar fully into position, so

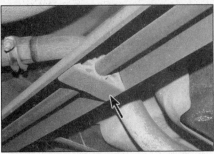

15.2 Prior to removal, mark the position of the rubber damper (arrowed) on the axle crossmember

15.4a . . . then withdraw the anti-roll bar . . .

that it is correctly engaged in the opposite trailing arm.

8 Install the new retaining bolts in the same position as noted on removal. Tighten both bolts first to the specified torque, and then through the specified angle given in the Specifications at the start of this Chapter.

9 Refit the roadwheel(s), aligning the marks made on removal. Lower the vehicle to the ground, and tighten the roadwheel bolts to the specified torque.

16 Steering wheel – removal and refitting

⚠️ **Warning: Make sure that the airbag safety recommendations given in Chapter 12 are followed, to prevent personal injury.**

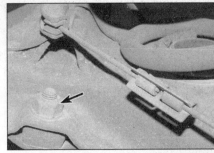

15.3 Slacken and remove the nut and bolt (arrowed) securing the anti-roll bar to each trailing arm . . .

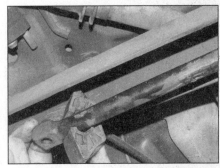

15.4b . . . and recover the rubber damper

Removal

1 Remove the airbag as described in Chapter 12.

2 Set the front wheels in the straight-ahead position, then lock the column in position after removing the ignition key.

3 Release the horn wiring connector and, where fitted, the radio remote control wiring from the steering wheel, and disconnect the connectors **(see illustration)**.

4 Unscrew the Torx retaining bolt securing the steering wheel to the column **(see illustration)**.

5 Make alignment marks between the steering wheel and the steering column shaft **(see illustration)**. Refit the steering wheel retaining bolt back into the steering column approximately two full turns.

6 Grip the steering wheel with both hands and carefully rock it from side-to-side to

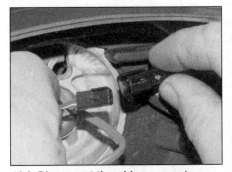

16.3 Disconnect the wiring connectors . . .

16.4 . . . then remove the steering wheel retaining bolt

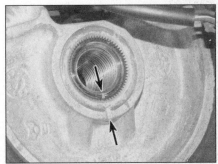

16.5 If not already marked, make alignment marks (arrowed)

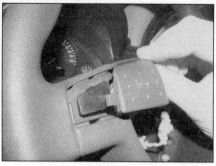

16.7 Carefully guide the wiring (arrowed) for the contact unit through the hole in the steering wheel

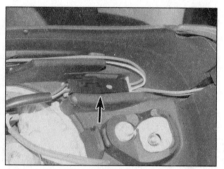

16.8a Unclip the horn button cover . . .

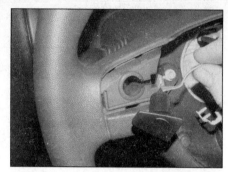

16.8b . . . then remove the switch and wiring from the steering wheel

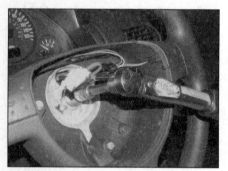

16.10 Tighten the retaining bolt to the specified torque setting

16.11 Clip the wiring connector (arrowed) into the recess in the steering wheel

withdraw the switch and wiring from the steering wheel **(see illustrations)**.

Refitting

9 Refit the steering wheel, aligning the marks made prior to removal. Route the wiring connectors through the steering wheel aperture. **Note:** *Make sure the steering wheel centre hub locates correctly with the contact unit on the steering column.*

10 Clean the threads on the retaining bolt and the threads in the steering column. Coat the retaining bolt with locking compound, then fit the retaining bolt and tighten to the specified torque setting **(see illustration)**.

11 Reconnect the horn wiring connector and, where fitted, the radio remote control wiring, then clip the connectors into the steering wheel recess **(see illustration)**.

12 Release the steering lock, and refit the airbag as described in Chapter 12.

release it from the splines on the steering column.

7 With the steering wheel loose on the splines, the retaining bolt can now be completely removed. As the steering wheel is being

removed, guide the wiring for the contact unit through the hole, taking care not to damage the wiring contact unit **(see illustration)**.

8 To remove the horn switch from the steering wheel, unclip the cover, then

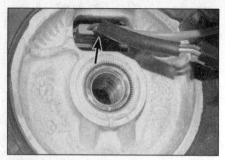

17.3 Unclipping the upper steering column shroud

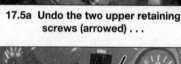
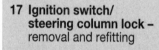

17.5a Undo the two upper retaining screws (arrowed) . . .

17 Ignition switch/ steering column lock – removal and refitting

Removal

1 Disconnect the battery negative terminal (refer to *Disconnecting the battery* in the Reference Chapter).

2 Remove the steering wheel as described in Section 16.

3 Unclip the upper steering column shroud from the lower shroud **(see illustration)**.

4 Where necessary, undo the retaining screw and release the steering column adjustment handle from under the steering column.

5 Undo the two upper retaining screws and the lower retaining screw and remove the lower steering column shroud from the vehicle **(see illustrations)**.

6 Remove the windscreen wiper switch by releasing the upper and lower lugs and sliding the switch out of its mounting bracket **(see illustration)**.

Lock cylinder

7 Remove the rubber trim from around the lock cylinder. Insert the ignition key into the ignition switch/lock, and turn it to position I.

8 Insert a thin rod into the hole in the lock

17.5b . . . then the lower shroud retaining screw

17.6 Depress the retaining clips (arrowed) and slide the combination switch out from the column

17.8 Insert a thin rod (arrowed) into the hole in the lock housing to release the detent spring

17.9 Release the locking clip (arrowed) and disconnect the wiring connector

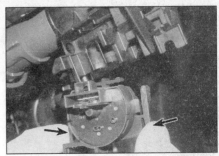

17.10 Depress the retaining clips (arrowed) and slide downwards out from the column

housing, press the rod to release the detent spring, and pull out the lock cylinder using the key **(see illustration)**.

Ignition switch wiring block

9 Release the securing clip and disconnect the wiring connector from the ignition switch wiring block **(see illustration)**.
10 Press the two lugs in (one at each side) and slide the switch wiring block down out of its mounting bracket **(see illustration)**.

Refitting

Lock cylinder

11 With the wiring block in position, insert the ignition switch/lock into the lock housing, while the key is in position I.
12 Ensure that the centre of the ignition switch wiring block is correctly aligned with the lock cylinder rod flats. If necessary, rotate the switch centre using a suitable screwdriver **(see illustration)**. If the steering column lock has been actuated, release the lock by depressing the locking mechanism recess in the column housing.
13 Press the lock cylinder into the housing until the detent spring clicks into position, then check the operation of the lock cylinder and steering lock.
14 Refit the rubber trim around the lock cylinder **(see illustration)**. Refit the lower steering column shroud, tightening its retaining screws securely, then clip the upper shroud back in position.
15 Where necessary, refit the steering column adjustment handle under the steering column.

17.12 Align the lock cylinder recess (arrowed) in the switch housing

16 Refit the steering wheel as described in Section 16, and check the operation of the switch.

Ignition switch wiring block

17 Slide the switch wiring block back up into its mounting bracket on the steering column, making sure it is located correctly.
18 Reconnect the wiring connector to switch wiring block.
19 Refit the ignition/lock cylinder as described in paragraphs 11 to 16.

---

18 Steering column –
 removal and refitting

Removal

1 Disconnect the battery negative terminal

17.14 Refit the rubber trim to the lock cylinder

(refer to *Disconnecting the battery* in the Reference Chapter).
2 Remove the airbag wiring contact unit as described in Chapter 12, Section 23.
3 Release the securing clips and disconnect the wiring connectors from the ignition switch wiring block, the immobiliser control unit and the horn contact, then release the wiring cables from the steering column **(see illustrations)**.
4 Unclip the driver's side lower storage tray, then undo the retaining screws and remove the driver's side lower trim panels **(see illustrations)**.
5 Release the retaining clip and withdraw the air duct from the driver's side footwell **(see illustrations)**.
6 Undo the four retaining bolts and remove the crossmember from the footwell on the driver's side, then cut the facia panel padding web from the footwell on the driver's side **(see illustrations)**.

18.3a Release the locking clip (arrowed) and disconnect the wiring connector from the switch . . .

18.3b . . . and the immobiliser control unit

18.4a Release the locking clips (arrowed) and withdraw the storage tray

18.4b Undo the two retaining screws (arrowed) . . .

18.4c . . . then release the lower facia panel . . .

18.4d . . . and the lower trim above the pedal assembly

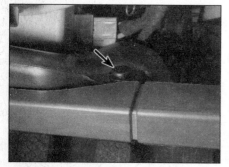

18.5a Remove the retaining clip (arrowed) . . .

18.5b . . . and withdraw the heater duct from the driver's footwell

10 Unscrew the lower mounting nuts securing the steering column to the bulkhead (see illustration).

11 Two fasteners must now be extracted from the column upper mounting bracket, and the bolts at the middle of the steering column must be removed too (see illustration).

12 Release the column assembly from its mountings, then detach it from the intermediate shaft and remove it from the vehicle. DO NOT release the steering lock while the steering column is off the vehicle, as it will alter the position of the angular adjustment setting for refitting.

Refitting

13 Manoeuvre the steering column into position, and engage it with the intermediate shaft universal joint, aligning the marks made on removal.

7 Disconnect the wiring connectors from the EPS control unit on the steering column (see illustration).

8 Using paint or similar, make alignment marks between the steering column and

intermediate shaft, then slacken and remove the clamp bolt securing the intermediate shaft to the steering column (see illustration).

9 If applicable, make sure the steering column adjustment handle is in the locked position.

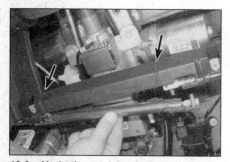

18.6a Undo the retaining bolts and remove the crossmember, then cut the trim in the places arrowed

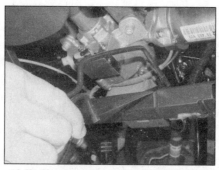

18.6b Using a junior hacksaw to remove the trim section

18.7 Disconnect the wiring connectors (arrowed) from the EPS control unit

18.8 Remove the clamp bolt (arrowed) securing the intermediate shaft to the steering column

18.10 Steering column lower mounting bolts (arrowed) . . .

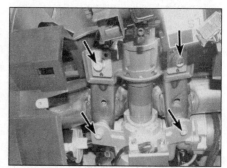

18.11 . . . and upper mounting bolts (arrowed)

19.3a Remove the upper clamp bolt (arrowed) . . .

19.3b . . . and the lower clamp bolt (arrowed)

19.9 Locate hole in the length compensator, then insert the locating pin

14 Refit the column upper, lower and middle mounting nut/bolts. Tighten all bolts by hand only at this stage.

15 Align the intermediate shaft bolt hole with the steering column shaft cut-out so that the clamp bolt can be slid into position (use thread locking compound). Tighten the bolt by hand only.

16 With the steering column in position, tighten the column mounting bolts to the specified torque setting. Start at the lower bolts first, then the middle, and finally the upper bolts.

17 Tighten the intermediate shaft upper clamp bolt to the specified torque setting.

18 The remainder of refitting is reverse of the removal procedure, noting the following points:

 a) *Ensure that the wiring is correctly routed, and reconnect to the ignition switch, horn, EPS control unit and, where applicable, the immobiliser.*

 b) *Clip the left-and right-hand switches back into position, and reconnect their wiring connectors.*

 c) *Refit the contact unit to the top of the steering column, making sure it is located correctly (see Chapter 12).*

 d) *Refit the trim panels to the driver's side lower footwell and the upper and lower steering column shrouds.*

 e) *Refit the steering column adjustment handle under the steering column.*

 f) *Refit the steering wheel and airbag as described in Section 16.*

 g) *Reconnect the battery negative terminal (refer to 'Disconnecting the battery' in the Reference Chapter).*

20.3a Undo the right-hand mounting bolt (arrowed) . . .

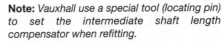

19 Steering column intermediate shaft – removal, inspection and refitting

Note: *Vauxhall use a special tool (locating pin) to set the intermediate shaft length compensator when refitting.*

Removal

1 Set the front wheels in the straight-ahead position. Undo the retaining screws and remove the driver's side lower storage tray panel and instrument panel lower padding as described in Section 18, paragraph 4.

2 If there are no alignment marks on the joints, use paint or a suitable marker pen to make alignment marks between the intermediate shaft joints and the steering column and steering gearshafts.

3 Slacken and remove the upper clamp bolt and the lower clamp bolt and nut **(see illustrations)**. Discard the nut from the lower joint, as a new one will be required when refitting.

4 Disengage the shaft universal joint from the steering column, then slide the shaft from the steering gear pinion and remove it from the vehicle.

Inspection

5 The steering column intermediate shaft incorporates a telescopic safety section, in the event of a front-end crash, the shaft shortens on the splines and prevents the steering wheel injuring the driver. Inspect the intermediate shaft universal joint for excessive wear or damage. If either joint is worn or damaged in any way, the complete shaft assembly must be renewed.

Refitting

6 Check that the front wheels are still in the straight-ahead position, and that the steering wheel is correctly positioned.

7 Aligning the marks made on removal, locate the upper universal joint onto the steering column.

8 Install the steering column upper clamp bolt (use thread locking compound) and tighten to the specified torque setting.

9 Aligning the marks made on removal, locate the lower universal joint onto the with the

steering gear pinion. Push the joint down onto the steering gear pinion until the hole in the length compensator is in line, then insert the locating pin (Vauxhall tool No KM-6181) can be inserted **(see illustration)**.

10 Install the lower clamp bolt and new retaining nut, then tighten to the specified torque setting.

11 Remove the Vauxhall tool (locating pin) from the intermediate shaft, after the lower retaining bolt has been tightened in the correct position.

12 The remainder of refitting is reverse of the removal procedure

20 Steering gear assembly – removal, inspection and refitting

Note: *New track rod balljoint-to-swivel hub nuts and steering gear to subframe nuts, bolts and washers will be required when refitting.*

Removal

1 Firmly apply the handbrake, then jack up the front of the car and support it securely on axle stands (see *Jacking and vehicle support*). Remove both front roadwheels.

2 Remove the engine front subframe as described in Section 7.

3 Slacken and remove the two bolts, nuts and washers securing the steering gear to the subframe **(see illustrations)**, then remove the steering gear from the subframe. Discard the bolts, nuts and washers as new ones will be required when refitting.

20.3b . . . and left-hand mounting bolt (arrowed)

4 If a new steering gear is to be fitted, then the track rod end balljoints will need to be removed from each end of the steering track rod arms (see Section 23).

Inspection

5 Examine the steering gear assembly for signs of wear or damage, and check that the rack moves freely throughout the full length of its travel, with no signs of roughness or excessive free play between the steering gear pinion and rack. Check with your Vauxhall dealer to see if it is possible to overhaul the steering gear assembly. The only components which can be renewed easily by the home mechanic are the steering gear gaiters, the track rod balljoints and the track rods. Steering gear gaiter, track rod balljoint and track rod renewal procedures are covered in Sections 22, 23 and 24 respectively.

Refitting

6 Refitting is a reverse of the removal procedure, bearing in mind the following points:
 a) *Refit the front subframe as described in Section 7.*
 b) *Locate the track rod balljoints in position using new nuts, and tighten them to the specified torque.*
 c) *On completion, check and, if necessary, adjust the front wheel alignment – see Section 25 for general information.*

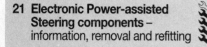

21 Electronic Power-assisted Steering components –
information, removal and refitting

EPS motor

1 The electronic power-assisted steering motor is part of the steering column assembly, at the time of writing the motor was not available separately and could only be bought as a complete unit with the steering column.
2 To remove the steering column, follow the procedures as described in Section 18.

EPS control unit

3 Disconnect the battery negative terminal (refer to *Disconnecting the battery* in the Reference Chapter).

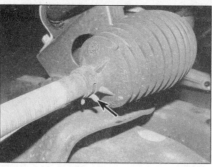

22.2a Release the gaiter outer retaining clip (arrowed) . . .

4 Unclip the drivers side lower storage tray, then undo the retaining screws and remove the driver's side lower trim panels.
5 Disconnect the wiring connectors from the EPS control unit on the steering column **(see illustration 18.7)**.
6 Undo the retaining bolts and remove the control unit from the steering column.
7 Refitting is a reversal of removal.

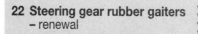

22 Steering gear rubber gaiters – renewal

1 Remove the track rod balljoint as described in Section 23.
2 Mark the correct fitted position of the gaiter on the track rod, then release the retaining clips **(see illustrations)**, and slide the gaiter off the steering gear housing and track rod end.
3 Thoroughly clean the track rod and the steering gear housing, clean off any corrosion, burrs or sharp edges which might damage the new gaiter's sealing lips on installation. Scrape off all the old grease, and apply new grease to the track rod inner balljoint.
4 Carefully slide the new gaiter onto the track rod end, and locate it on the steering gear housing. Align the outer edge of the gaiter with the mark made on the track rod prior to removal, then secure it in position with new retaining clips.
5 Refit the track rod balljoint as described in Section 23.

23.3 Use an open-ended spanner to hold the track rod arm, then slacken the locknut

23.4a Using a universal balljoint separator . . .

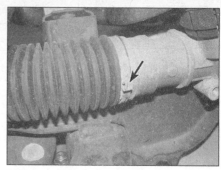

22.2b . . . and inner retaining clip (arrowed)

23 Track rod balljoint – removal and refitting

Note: *A new track rod balljoint-to-swivel hub nut will be required when refitting.*

Removal

1 Firmly apply the handbrake, then jack up the front of the car and support it securely on axle stands (see *Jacking and vehicle support*). Remove the appropriate front roadwheel.
2 If the balljoint is to be re-used, use a scriber, or similar, to mark its relationship to the track rod.
3 Hold the track rod arm, and unscrew the balljoint locknut by a quarter of a turn **(see illustration)**.
4 Slacken and remove the nut securing the track rod balljoint to the swivel hub, and release the balljoint tapered shank using a universal balljoint separator **(see illustrations)**. Discard the nut; a new one must be used of refitting.
5 Counting the exact number of turns necessary to do so, unscrew the balljoint from the track rod arm.
6 Count the number of exposed threads between the end of the track rod and the locknut, and record this figure. If a new gaiter is to be fitted, unscrew the locknut from the track rod.
7 Carefully clean the balljoint and the track rod threads. Renew the balljoint if there is excessive free play of the balljoint shank, or if the shank is excessively stiff. If the balljoint

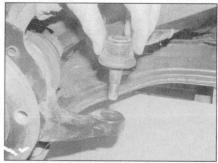

23.4b . . . release the track rod balljoint from the swivel hub

gaiter is damaged, the complete balljoint assembly must be renewed; it is not possible to obtain the gaiter separately.

Refitting

8 If it was removed, screw the locknut onto the track rod threads, and position it so that the same number of exposed threads are visible as was noted prior to removal.

9 Screw the balljoint on to the track rod by the number of turns noted on removal. This should bring the balljoint locknut to within approximately quarter of a turn from the locknut, with the alignment marks that were noted on removal.

10 Refit the balljoint shank to the swivel hub, then fit a new retaining nut and tighten it to the specified torque setting. If the balljoint stud turns as the nut is being tightened, press down on the track rod balljoint to force the tapered part of the stud into the arm on the swivel hub.

11 Tighten the track rod balljoint securing locknut on the track rod arm while holding the track rod arm stationary with a second spanner on the flats provided **(see illustration 23.3)**. **Note:** *If possible tighten the nut to the specified torque using a special crow's-foot adapter for the torque wrench.*

12 Refit the roadwheel, then lower the vehicle to the ground and tighten the roadwheel bolts to the specified torque setting.

13 Have the front wheel alignment checked and if necessary, adjusted at the earliest opportunity. See Section 25 for general information on wheel alignment

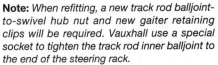

24 Track rod –
renewal

Note: *When refitting, a new track rod balljoint-to-swivel hub nut and new gaiter retaining clips will be required. Vauxhall use a special socket to tighten the track rod inner balljoint to the end of the steering rack.*

1 Remove the track rod balljoint as described in Section 23.

2 Release the retaining clips, and slide the steering gear gaiter off the end of the track rod as described in Section 22.

3 Turn the steering on full lock, so that the rack protrudes from the steering gear housing on the relevant side, slide the cover (where fitted) off the inner balljoint.

4 Prevent the rack from rotating using an open-ended spanner located on the rack flats, then unscrew and remove the track rod inner balljoint from the end of the steering rack. Where fitted remove any spacers/washers noting the correct position for refitting.

5 Remove the track rod assembly, and examine the track rod inner balljoint for signs of slackness or tight spots. Check that the track rod itself is straight and free from damage. If necessary, renew the track rod; it

is also recommended that the steering gear gaiter/dust cover is renewed.

6 Where applicable, locate the spacer on the end of the steering rack, and screw the balljoint into the end of the steering rack. Tighten the track rod inner balljoint to the specified torque, whilst retaining the steering rack with an open-ended spanner.

7 Install the steering gaiter and track rod balljoint as described in Sections 22 and 23.

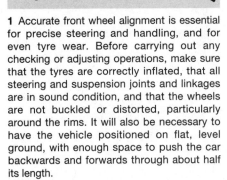

25 Wheel alignment
and steering angles –
general information

1 Accurate front wheel alignment is essential for precise steering and handling, and for even tyre wear. Before carrying out any checking or adjusting operations, make sure that the tyres are correctly inflated, that all steering and suspension joints and linkages are in sound condition, and that the wheels are not buckled or distorted, particularly around the rims. It will also be necessary to have the vehicle positioned on flat, level ground, with enough space to push the car backwards and forwards through about half its length.

2 Front wheel alignment consists of four factors **(see illustration)**:

Camber is the angle at which the roadwheels are set from the vertical, when viewed from the front or rear of the vehicle. Positive camber is the angle (in degrees) that the wheels are tilted outwards at the top from the vertical.

Castor is the angle between the steering axis and a vertical line when viewed from each side of the vehicle. Positive castor is indicated when the steering axis is inclined towards the rear of the vehicle at its upper end.

Steering axis inclination is the angle, when viewed from the front or rear of the vehicle, between the vertical and an imaginary line drawn between the upper and lower front suspension strut mountings.

Toe setting is the amount by which the distance between the front inside edges of the roadwheels differs from that between the rear inside edges, when measured at hub height. If the distance between the front edges is less than at the rear, the wheels are said to 'toe-in'. If it is greater than at the rear, the wheels are said to 'toe-out'.

3 Camber, castor and steering axis inclination are set during manufacture, and are not adjustable. Unless the vehicle has suffered accident damage, or there is gross wear in the suspension mountings or joints, it can be assumed that these settings are correct. If for any reason it is believed that they are not correct, the task of checking them should be left to a Vauxhall dealer, who will have the necessary special equipment needed to measure the small angles involved.

4 It is, however, within the scope of the home mechanic to check and adjust the front wheel

toe setting. To do this, a tracking gauge must first be obtained. Two types of gauge are available, and can be obtained from motor accessory shops. The first type measures the distance between the front and rear inside edges of the roadwheels, as previously described, with the vehicle stationary. The second type, known as a 'scuff plate', measures the actual position of the contact surface of the tyre, in relation to the road surface, with the vehicle in motion. This is

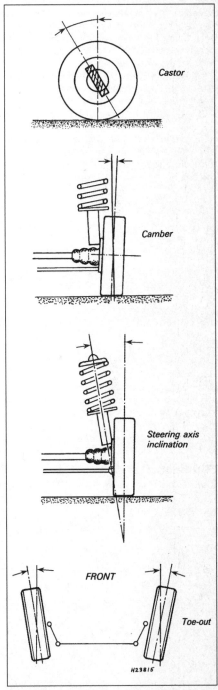

25.2 Wheel alignment and steering angles

achieved by pushing or driving the front tyre over a plate, which then moves slightly according to the scuff of the tyre, and shows this movement on a scale. Both types have their advantages and disadvantages, but either can give satisfactory results if used correctly and carefully.

5 Many tyre specialists will also check toe settings free, or for a nominal charge. Considering the initial cost of obtaining a tracking gauge, and then becoming experienced with its use, it may actually be beneficial to have the whole job done by a tyre specialist or similar company. The actual procedure for using a tracking gauge is, however, outlined in the following paragraphs to show the work involved.

6 Make sure that the steering is in the straight-ahead position when making measurements.

7 If adjustment is necessary, chock the rear wheels, apply the handbrake, then jack up the front of the vehicle and support it securely on axle stands. Turn the steering wheel onto full-left lock, and record the number of exposed threads on the right-hand track rod end. Now turn the steering onto full-right lock, and record the number of threads on the left-hand side. If there are the same number of threads visible on both sides, then subsequent adjustment should be made equally on both sides. If there are more threads visible on one side than the other, it will be necessary to compensate for this during adjustment. It is most important that, after adjustment, the same number of threads are visible on each track rod end.

8 First clean the track rod threads; if they are corroded, apply penetrating fluid before starting adjustment. Release the rubber gaiter outer clips, then peel back the gaiters and apply a smear of grease, so that the gaiters will not be twisted or strained as their respective track rods are rotated.

9 Use a straight-edge and a scriber, or similar, to mark the relationship of each track rod to its balljoint then, holding each track rod in turn, unscrew its locknut fully.

10 Alter the length of the track rods, bearing in mind the note made in paragraph 7, screwing them into or out of the balljoints by rotating the track rod using an open-ended spanner fitted to the track rod flats provided. Shortening the track rods (screwing them into their balljoints) will reduce toe-in/increase toe-out.

11 When the setting is correct, hold the track rods and securely tighten the balljoint locknuts. Check that the balljoints are seated correctly in their sockets, and count the exposed threads to check the length of both track rods. If they are not the same, then the adjustment has not been made equally, and problems will be encountered with tyre scrubbing in turns; also, the steering wheel spokes will no longer be horizontal when the wheels are in the straight-ahead position.

12 If the track rod lengths are the same, check that the toe setting has been correctly adjusted by lowering the vehicle to the ground and rechecking the toe setting; re-adjust if necessary. If the setting is correct, tighten the track rod balljoint locknuts to the specified torque setting. Ensure that the rubber gaiters are seated correctly and are not twisted or strained, and secure them in position with the retaining clips.

Chapter 11
Bodywork and fittings

Contents

Degrees of difficulty

Easy, suitable for novice with little experience	Fairly easy, suitable for beginner with some experience	Fairly difficult, suitable for competent DIY mechanic	Difficult, suitable for experienced DIY mechanic	Very difficult, suitable for expert DIY or professional

Specifications

Torque wrench settings	Nm	lbf ft
Facia-to-bulkhead nuts	22	16
Front seat bolts	20	15
Rear seat:		
Corsa and Corsavan (split rear seat):		
Seat back-to-bracket bolts	30	22
Seat back-to-centre bearing bolts	20	15
Seat back-to-hinge bolts	20	15
Combo Van:		
Seat back bolts	20	15
Seat belt anchorage bolts	35	26
Seat belt height adjuster ratchet bolts	20	15
Seat belt inertia reel bolt	35	26

1 General information

The bodyshell is made of pressed-steel sections, and is available in three- and five-door Hatchback versions, as well as two different forms of Van. Most components are welded together, but some use is made of structural adhesives; the front wings are bolted on.

The bonnet, doors, and some other vulnerable panels, are made of zinc-coated metal, and are further protected by being coated with an anti-chip primer, prior to being sprayed.

Extensive use is made of plastic materials, mainly on the interior, but also in exterior components. The front and rear bumpers are injection-moulded from a synthetic material which is very strong and yet light. Plastic components such as wheel arch liners are fitted to the underside of the vehicle, to improve the body's resistance to corrosion.

2 Maintenance – bodywork and underframe

The general condition of a vehicle's bodywork is the one thing that significantly affects its value. Maintenance is easy, but needs to be regular. Neglect, particularly after minor damage, can lead quickly to further deterioration and costly repair bills. It is important also to keep watch on those parts of the vehicle not immediately visible, for instance the underside, inside all the wheel arches, and the lower part of the engine compartment.

The basic maintenance routine for the bodywork is washing – preferably with a lot of water, from a hose. This will remove all the loose solids which may have stuck to the vehicle. It is important to flush these off in such a way as to prevent grit from scratching the finish. The wheel arches and underframe need washing in the same way, to remove any accumulated mud, which will retain moisture and tend to encourage rust. Paradoxically enough, the best time to clean the underframe and wheel arches is in wet weather, when the mud is thoroughly wet and soft. In very wet weather, the underframe is usually cleaned of large accumulations automatically, and this is a good time for inspection.

Periodically, except on vehicles with a wax-based underbody protective coating, it is a good idea to have the whole of the underframe of the vehicle steam-cleaned, engine compartment included, so that a thorough inspection can be carried out to see what minor repairs and renovations are necessary. Steam-cleaning is available at many garages, and is necessary for the removal of the accumulation of oily grime, which sometimes is allowed to become thick in certain areas. If steam-cleaning facilities are not available, there are some excellent grease solvents available which can be brush-applied; the dirt can then be simply hosed off. Note that these methods should not be used on vehicles with wax-based underbody protective coating, or the coating will be removed. Such vehicles should be inspected annually, preferably just prior to Winter, when the underbody should be washed down, and any damage to the wax coating repaired. Ideally, a completely fresh coat should be applied. It would also be worth considering the use of such wax-based protection for injection into door panels, sills, box sections, etc, as an additional safeguard against rust damage, where such protection is not provided by the vehicle manufacturer.

After washing paintwork, wipe off with a chamois leather to give an unspotted clear finish. A coat of clear protective wax polish will give added protection against chemical pollutants in the air. If the paintwork sheen has dulled or oxidised, use a cleaner/polisher combination to restore the brilliance of the shine. This requires a little effort, but such dulling is usually caused because regular washing has been neglected. Care needs to be taken with metallic paintwork, as special non-abrasive cleaner/polisher is required to avoid damage to the finish. Always check that the door and ventilator opening drain holes and pipes are completely clear, so that water can be drained out. Brightwork should be treated in the same way as paintwork. Windscreens and windows can be kept clear of the smeary film which often appears, by the use of proprietary glass cleaner. Never use any form of wax or other body or chromium polish on glass.

3 Maintenance of upholstery and carpets – general

Mats and carpets should be brushed or vacuum-cleaned regularly, to keep them free of grit. If they are badly stained, remove them from the vehicle for scrubbing or sponging, and make quite sure they are dry before refitting. Seats and interior trim panels can be kept clean by wiping with a damp cloth. If they do become stained (which can be more apparent on light-coloured upholstery), use a little liquid detergent and a soft nail brush to scour the grime out of the grain of the material. Do not forget to keep the headlining clean in the same way as the upholstery. When using liquid cleaners inside the vehicle, do not over-wet the surfaces being cleaned. Excessive damp could get into the seams and padded interior, causing stains, offensive odours or even rot.

If the inside of the vehicle gets wet accidentally, it is worthwhile taking some trouble to dry it out properly, particularly where carpets are involved. Do not leave oil or electric heaters inside the vehicle for this purpose.

4 Minor body damage – repair

Minor scratches

If the scratch is very superficial, and does not penetrate to the metal of the bodywork, repair is very simple. Lightly rub the area of the scratch with a paintwork renovator, or a very fine cutting paste, to remove loose paint from the scratch, and to clear the surrounding bodywork of wax polish. Rinse the area with clean water.

Apply touch-up paint to the scratch using a fine paint brush; continue to apply fine layers of paint until the surface of the paint in the scratch is level with the surrounding paintwork. Allow the new paint at least two weeks to harden, then blend it into the surrounding paintwork by rubbing the scratch area with a paintwork renovator or a very fine cutting paste. Finally, apply wax polish.

Where the scratch has penetrated right through to the metal of the bodywork, causing the metal to rust, a different repair technique is required. Remove any loose rust from the bottom of the scratch with a penknife, then apply rust-inhibiting paint to prevent the formation of rust in the future. Using a rubber or nylon applicator, fill the scratch with bodystopper paste. If required, this paste can be mixed with cellulose thinners to provide a very thin paste which is ideal for filling narrow scratches. Before the stopper-paste in the scratch hardens, wrap a piece of smooth cotton rag around the top of a finger. Dip the finger in cellulose thinners, and quickly sweep it across the surface of the stopper-paste in the scratch; this will ensure that the surface of the stopper-paste is slightly hollowed. The scratch can now be painted over as described earlier in this Section.

Dents

When deep denting of the vehicle's bodywork has taken place, the first task is to pull the dent out, until the affected bodywork almost attains its original shape. There is little point in trying to restore the original shape completely, as the metal in the damaged area will have stretched on impact, and cannot be reshaped fully to its original contour. It is better to bring the level of the dent up to a point which is about 3 mm below the level of the surrounding bodywork. In cases where the dent is very shallow anyway, it is not worth trying to pull it out at all. If the underside of the dent is accessible, it can be hammered out gently from behind, using a mallet with a wooden or plastic head. Whilst doing this, hold a suitable block of wood firmly against the outside of the panel, to absorb the impact from the hammer blows and thus prevent a large area of the bodywork from being 'belled-out'.

Should the dent be in a section of the

bodywork which has a double skin, or some other factor making it inaccessible from behind, a different technique is called for. Drill several small holes through the metal inside the area – particularly in the deeper section. Then screw long self-tapping screws into the holes, just sufficiently for them to gain a good purchase in the metal. Now the dent can be pulled out by pulling on the protruding heads of the screws with a pair of pliers.

The next stage of the repair is the removal of the paint from the damaged area, and from an inch or so of the surrounding 'sound' bodywork. This is accomplished most easily by using a wire brush or abrasive pad on a power drill, although it can be done just as effectively by hand, using sheets of abrasive paper. To complete the preparation for filling, score the surface of the bare metal with a screwdriver or the tang of a file, or alternatively, drill small holes in the affected area. This will provide a really good 'key' for the filler paste.

To complete the repair, see the Section on filling and respraying.

Rust holes or gashes

Remove all paint from the affected area, and from an inch or so of the surrounding 'sound' bodywork, using an abrasive pad or a wire brush on a power drill. If these are not available, a few sheets of abrasive paper will do the job most effectively. With the paint removed, you will be able to judge the severity of the corrosion, and therefore decide whether to renew the whole panel (if this is possible) or to repair the affected area. New body panels are not as expensive as most people think, and it is often quicker and more satisfactory to fit a new panel than to attempt to repair large areas of corrosion.

Remove all fittings from the affected area, except those which will act as a guide to the original shape of the damaged bodywork (eg headlight shells etc). Then, using tin snips or a hacksaw blade, remove all loose metal and any other metal badly affected by corrosion. Hammer the edges of the hole inwards, in order to create a slight depression for the filler paste.

Wire-brush the affected area to remove the powdery rust from the surface of the remaining metal. Paint the affected area with rust-inhibiting paint, if the back of the rusted area is accessible, treat this also.

Before filling can take place, it will be necessary to block the hole in some way. This can be achieved by the use of aluminium or plastic mesh, or aluminium tape.

Aluminium or plastic mesh, or glass-fibre matting, is probably the best material to use for a large hole. Cut a piece to the approximate size and shape of the hole to be filled, then position it in the hole so that its edges are below the level of the surrounding bodywork. It can be retained in position by several blobs of filler paste around its periphery.

Aluminium tape should be used for small or very narrow holes. Pull a piece off the roll, trim it to the approximate size and shape required, then pull off the backing paper (if used) and stick the tape over the hole; it can be overlapped if the thickness of one piece is insufficient. Burnish down the edges of the tape with the handle of a screwdriver or similar, to ensure that the tape is securely attached to the metal underneath.

Filling and respraying

Before using this Section, see the Sections on dent, deep scratch, rust holes and gash repairs.

Many types of bodyfiller are available, but generally speaking, those proprietary kits which contain a tin of filler paste and a tube of resin hardener are best for this type of repair. A wide, flexible plastic or nylon applicator will be found invaluable for imparting a smooth and well-contoured finish to the surface of the filler.

Mix up a little filler on a clean piece of card or board – measure the hardener carefully (follow the maker's instructions on the pack), otherwise the filler will set too rapidly or too slowly. Using the applicator, apply the filler paste to the prepared area; draw the applicator across the surface of the filler to achieve the correct contour and to level the surface. As soon as a contour that approximates to the correct one is achieved, stop working the paste – if you carry on too long, the paste will become sticky and begin to 'pick-up' on the applicator. Continue to add thin layers of filler paste at 20-minute intervals, until the level of the filler is just proud of the surrounding bodywork.

Once the filler has hardened, the excess can be removed using a metal plane or file. From then on, progressively-finer grades of abrasive paper should be used, starting with a 40-grade production paper, and finishing with a 400-grade wet-and-dry paper. Always wrap the abrasive paper around a flat rubber, cork, or wooden block – otherwise the surface of the filler will not be completely flat. During the smoothing of the filler surface, the wet-and-dry paper should be periodically rinsed in water. This will ensure that a very smooth finish is imparted to the filler at the final stage.

At this stage, the 'dent' should be surrounded by a ring of bare metal, which in turn should be encircled by the finely 'feathered' edge of the good paintwork. Rinse the repair area with clean water, until all of the dust produced by the rubbing-down operation has gone.

Spray the whole area with a light coat of primer – this will show up any imperfections in the surface of the filler. Repair these imperfections with fresh filler paste or bodystopper, and once more smooth the surface with abrasive paper. Repeat this spray-and-repair procedure until you are satisfied that the surface of the filler, and the feathered edge of the paintwork, are perfect.

Clean the repair area with clean water, and allow to dry fully.

The repair area is now ready for final spraying. Paint spraying must be carried out in a warm, dry, windless and dust-free atmosphere. This condition can be created artificially if you have access to a large indoor working area, but if you are forced to work in the open, you will have to pick your day very carefully. If you are working indoors, dousing the floor in the work area with water will help to settle the dust which would otherwise be in the atmosphere. If the repair area is confined to one body panel, mask off the surrounding panels; this will help to minimise the effects of a slight mis-match in paint colours. Bodywork fittings (eg chrome strips, door handles etc) will also need to be masked off. Use genuine masking tape, and several thicknesses of newspaper, for the masking operations.

Before commencing to spray, agitate the aerosol can thoroughly, then spray a test area (an old tin, or similar) until the technique is mastered. Cover the repair area with a thick coat of primer; the thickness should be built up using several thin layers of paint, rather than one thick one. Using 400-grade wet-and-dry paper, rub down the surface of the primer until it is really smooth. While doing this, the work area should be thoroughly doused with water, and the wet-and-dry paper periodically rinsed in water. Allow to dry before spraying on more paint.

Spray on the top coat, again building up the thickness by using several thin layers of paint. Start spraying at one edge of the repair area, and then, using a side-to-side motion, work until the whole repair area and about 2 inches of the surrounding original paintwork is covered. Remove all masking material 10 to 15 minutes after spraying on the final coat of paint.

Allow the new paint at least two weeks to harden, then, using a paintwork renovator, or a very fine cutting paste, blend the edges of the paint into the existing paintwork. Finally, apply wax polish.

Plastic components

With the use of more and more plastic body components by the vehicle manufacturers (eg bumpers. spoilers, and in some cases major body panels), rectification of more serious damage to such items has become a matter of either entrusting repair work to a specialist in this field, or renewing complete components. Repair of such damage by the DIY owner is not really feasible, owing to the cost of the equipment and materials required for effecting such repairs. The basic technique involves making a groove along the line of the crack in the plastic, using a rotary burr in a power drill. The damaged part is then welded back together, using a hot-air gun to heat up and fuse a plastic filler rod in the groove. Any excess plastic is then removed, and the area rubbed down to a smooth finish. It is important that a filler rod of the correct plastic is used, as body components can be made of

6.2a undo the retaining nut . . .

6.2b . . . and release the wheel arch trim panel from the end of the bumper

a variety of different types (eg polycarbonate, ABS, polypropylene).

Damage of a less serious nature (abrasions, minor cracks etc) can be repaired by the DIY owner using a two-part epoxy filler repair material. Once mixed in equal proportions, this is used in similar fashion to the bodywork filler used on metal panels. The filler is usually cured in twenty to thirty minutes, ready for sanding and painting.

If the owner is renewing a complete component himself, or if he has repaired it with epoxy filler, he will be left with the problem of finding a suitable paint for finishing which is compatible with the type of plastic used. At one time, the use of a universal paint was not possible, owing to the complex range of plastics encountered in body component applications. Standard paints, generally speaking, will not bond to plastic or rubber satisfactorily. However, it is now possible to

obtain a plastic body parts finishing kit which consists of a pre-primer treatment, a primer and coloured top coat. Full instructions are normally supplied with a kit, but basically, the method of use is to first apply the pre-primer to the component concerned, and allow it to dry for up to 30 minutes. Then the primer is applied, and left to dry for about an hour before finally applying the special-coloured top coat. The result is a correctly-coloured component, where the paint will flex with the plastic or rubber, a property that standard paint does not normally possess.

5 Major body damage repair – general

Where serious damage has occurred, or large areas need renewal due to neglect, it

means that complete new panels will need welding-in, and this is best left to professionals. If the damage is due to impact, it will also be necessary to check completely the alignment of the bodyshell, and this can only be carried out accurately by a Vauxhall dealer, using special jigs. If the body is left misaligned, it is primarily dangerous as the car will not handle properly, and secondly, uneven stresses will be imposed on the steering, suspension and possibly transmission, causing abnormal wear, or complete failure, particularly to such items as the tyres.

6 Front bumper – removal and refitting

Removal

1 Firmly apply the handbrake, then jack up the front of the car and support it securely on axle stands (see *Jacking and vehicle support*).
2 Remove the two retaining nuts (one on each side) securing either end of the bumper to the vehicle **(see illustrations)**.
3 Undo the four screws (two on either side) securing the ends of the bumper to the wheel arch liner **(see illustration)**.
4 Unscrew the three bolts securing the top of the radiator grille to the crossmember **(see illustration)**. Note the radiator grille is part of the bumper assembly.
5 Withdraw the centre pins, then release the three clips securing the bottom of the bumper to the vehicle body **(see illustrations)**.
6 Where applicable, disconnect any wiring block connector(s) from the rear of the bumper **(see illustration)**.
7 With the aid of an assistant, release the bumper ends from the wheel arch outer trim covers, and remove the bumper from the front of the vehicle. On models with headlight washers, note that it will be necessary to disconnect the supply hose from the T-piece as it becomes accessible.

Refitting

8 Refitting is a reversal of the removal procedure, ensuring that all bumper fasteners are securely tightened.

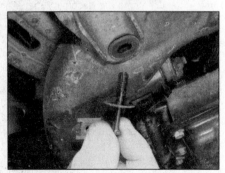

6.3 Undo the screws (arrowed) securing the inner wheel arch trim to the bumper (two on each side)

6.4 Front grille to crossmember securing bolts (arrowed)

6.5a Release the centre pins . . .

6.5b . . . then withdraw the lower bumper retaining clips (arrowed)

6.6 Disconnect the wiring block connector as the bumper is removed

7.1 Undo the rear bumper upper retaining screws (arrowed)

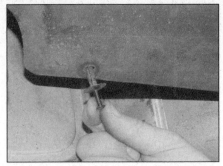

7.2 Release the centre pins, then withdraw the lower bumper retaining clips

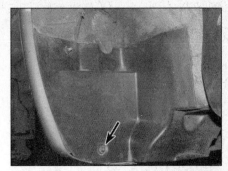

7.3 Undo the retaining screws (one side arrowed) from the bumper inner wing panel

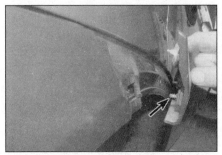

7.4 Carefully ease the wheel arch trim covers away from the vehicle to release the bumper

7.5 Disconnect the wiring block connector as the bumper is removed

7.7 Release the centre pins, then withdraw the upper bumper retaining clips

7 Rear bumper –
removal and refitting

Removal

Corsa and Corsavan

1 Open the tailgate, and undo the four screws securing the top of the bumper to the vehicle **(see illustration)**.
2 Withdraw the centre pins, then remove the two plastic securing clips from the bottom of the bumper to the vehicle body **(see illustration)**.
3 Undo the two retaining screws (one on either side) securing the ends of the bumper to the wheel arch liner **(see illustration)**.
4 Remove the two retaining nuts (one on

each side) securing either end of the bumper to the vehicle **(see illustration)**.
5 With the aid of an assistant, unclip the bumper ends from the wheel arch outer trim covers, and remove the bumper from the rear of the vehicle. Disconnect the wiring connector as the bumper is being removed **(see illustration)**.

Combo Van

6 Remove both rear number plate light units as described in Chapter 12, Section 7.
7 Prise out the centre pins, then release the two clips (one each side) securing the top of the bumper to the vehicle body **(see illustration)**.
8 Remove the two retaining nuts (one on each side) securing either end of the bumper to the vehicle **(see illustration)**.
9 Undo the six fasteners securing the bottom

of the bumper to the vehicle, and the four screws (two each side) securing the bumper to the inner wing panels.
10 Lift the bumper away from the rear of the vehicle. If necessary, slide the foam wedges out from between the bumper mountings, and unbolt the mountings from the vehicle body.

Refitting

11 Refitting is a reverse of the relevant removal procedure, ensuring that all disturbed fasteners are securely tightened. Before finally bolting the bumper in position, ensure that any wiring is securely connected.

8 Bonnet –
removal, refitting and adjustment

Removal

1 Open the bonnet, and have an assistant support it. It may be useful, to mark the outline position of each bonnet hinge relative to the bonnet (using a pencil or felt-tip pen), to use as a guide on refitting.
2 Undo the bonnet retaining bolts **(see illustration)**, two each side, then with the help of an assistant, carefully lift the bonnet clear. Store the bonnet out of the way, in a safe place.
3 Inspect the hinge for signs of wear or damage. If hinge renewal is necessary, the lower hinge bolts (three each side) will need to be removed from the inner wing panel.

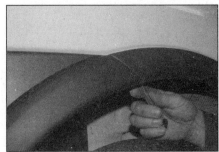

7.8 Undo the retaining nut and release the wheel arch trim panel from the end of the bumper

8.2 Undo the bonnet retaining bolts (arrowed) and lift the bonnet away from the vehicle

Refitting and adjustment

4 With the aid of an assistant, offer up the bonnet, and loosely fit the retaining bolts. Align the hinges with the marks made on removal, then tighten the retaining bolts securely.

5 Close the bonnet, and check for alignment with the adjacent panels. If necessary, slacken the bonnet support bolts, and realign the bonnet to suit. Once the bonnet is correctly aligned, securely tighten the bolts.

6 Once the bonnet is correctly aligned, check that the bonnet fastens and releases in a satisfactory manner, and if necessary adjust the lock striker as described in Section 10.

9	Bonnet release cable – removal and refitting

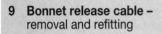

Removal

1 Open the bonnet, and unscrew the three bolts securing the top of the radiator grille to the crossmember **(see illustration 6.4)**.

2 Carefully pull back the top of the grille, to access the crossmember securing bolts (three on each side). Slacken and remove the bolts **(see illustrations)**, then lift the crossmember to one side. **Note:** *Bonnet release cable will still be attached.*

3 Undo the two retaining bolts and remove the cover from the lock assembly **(see illustrations)**.

9.2a Undo the retaining bolts (one side arrowed) . . .

4 Unscrew the clamp bolt from the crossmember and release the outer cable, then detach the inner cable from the lock spring **(see illustrations)**.

5 Work back along the cable, releasing it from all the relevant retaining clips and ties, whilst noting its correct routing. Release the rubber sealing grommet from the engine compartment bulkhead, and tie a piece of string to the cable end, this can then be used to draw the cable back into position.

6 From inside the vehicle, release the retaining clip, then withdraw the bonnet release lever from the side of the driver's footwell **(see illustrations)**.

7 Withdraw the lever and cable assembly from inside the vehicle. Once the cable end appears, untie the string and leave it in position in the vehicle.

9.2b . . . and remove the crossmember

Refitting

8 Refitting is a reverse of the relevant removal procedure, noting the following points:

a) *Tie the string to the end of the cable, and use the string to draw the bonnet release cable through from inside the vehicle into the engine compartment. Once the cable is through, untie the string.*

b) *Ensure that the cable is correctly routed and retained by all the relevant clips and ties, then seat the outer cable grommet in the engine compartment bulkhead.*

c) *Connect the inner cable to the lock spring, and seat the outer cable in its retaining clamp. Position the outer cable so that all free play is removed from the inner cable, then securely tighten its clamp screw.*

d) *Refit the crossmember, then check the operation of the bonnet release lever before shutting the bonnet.*

9.3a Undo the two retaining bolts (arrowed) . . .

9.3b . . . and remove the cover from the lock assembly

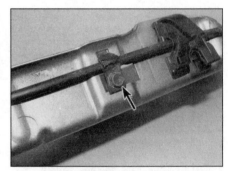

9.4a Slacken the bonnet release cable clamp screw . . .

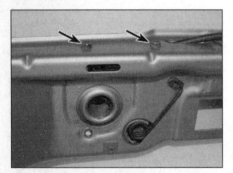

9.4b . . . then unhook the inner cable from the spring

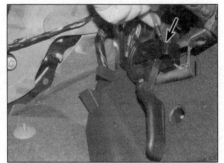

9.6a Release the retaining clip (arrowed), slide the mounting bracket forwards . . .

9.6b . . . and withdraw the bonnet release lever

10.1 Bonnet lock hook is removed by drilling out its pivot pin (arrowed)

10.5 When refitting, adjust the position of the bonnet lock striker as described in text

10.7 Free the spring from the crossmember

10 Bonnet lock components – removal and refitting

Bonnet lock hook

1 Drill out the pivot pin, and remove the lock hook and return spring from the bonnet **(see illustration)**.
2 On refitting, locate the hook and spring in the bonnet bracket, and insert a new pivot pin. Secure the pin in position by flattening its end with a suitable pair of pliers.

Lock striker

3 Slacken the striker locknut, then unscrew the striker from the bonnet and recover the washer. If necessary, unscrew the locknut from the end of the striker, and remove the spring and spring seats.
4 Where necessary, fit the spring and spring seats to the striker, and screw on the locknut. Fit the washer to the striker, and screw the striker into position in the bonnet, tightening it only lightly at this stage.
5 Hold the locknut, and adjust the position of the striker so that the distance from the lower spring seat to the inside of the bonnet is 40 to 45 mm **(see illustration)**.
6 When the striker is correctly positioned, securely tighten the locknut.

Lock spring

7 Unhook the bonnet release cable from the

spring (see Section 9), then free the spring from the body crossmember and remove it from the vehicle **(see illustration)**.
8 On refitting, ensure that the spring is correctly engaged with the cable and crossmember. Check the operation of the bonnet release lever before shutting the bonnet.

11 Door – removal, refitting and adjustment

Removal

All front and Corsa rear doors

1 Open the door to gain access to the wiring connector which is fitted to the front edge of the door.

11.2a On front doors, release the locking clip in the direction of the arrow

2 On the front doors, slide the locking clip out, then rotate the wiring connector to disconnect it from the front edge of the door **(see illustration)**. On the rear doors, slide the locking collar in, then carefully withdraw the wiring connector to disconnect it from the front edge of the door **(see illustration)**.
3 Undo the retaining bolt securing the door check link to the door pillar **(see illustration)**.
4 Remove the plastic covers (where fitted) from the door hinge pins. Have an assistant support the door, then drive both hinge pins out of position using a hammer and suitable punch **(see illustrations)**. Remove the door from the vehicle.
5 Inspect the hinge pins for signs of wear or damage, and renew if necessary.

Combo Van rear door

6 Open the rear door, and release the check link spring from the door pin **(see illustration)**.

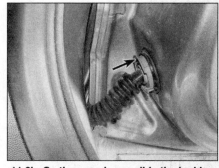

11.2b On the rear doors, slide the locking collar (arrowed) inwards

11.3 Undo the retaining bolt (arrowed) securing the door check link to the door pillar

11.4a Remove the lower plastic cover . . .

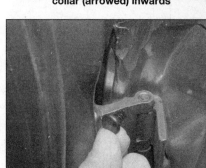

11.4b . . . and upper plastic cover . . .

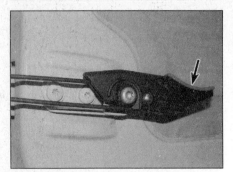

11.6 Release the check link spring (arrowed) from the door pin

11.7 Release the wiring grommet from the door pillar

11.8a Remove the upper hinge bolts (arrowed) . . .

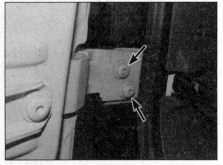

11.8b . . . and lower hinge bolts (arrowed)

11.13 Door lock striker retaining bolts (arrowed)

7 Where necessary, trace the wiring back into the door to its wiring connectors. Disconnect the wiring connectors, then free the grommet from the door **(see illustration)**, and withdraw the wiring loom so that it is free from the door.
8 Have an assistant support the door, then slacken and remove the four hinge retaining bolts and remove the door from the vehicle **(see illustrations)**. It may be useful to mark the outline position of each hinge relative to the body (using a pencil or felt-tip pen), to use as a guide on refitting.
9 If necessary, the hinge(s) can then be unbolted and removed from the door.

Refitting

All front and Corsa rear doors

10 Refitting is the reversal of removal procedure, tightening the check link bolts

securely, and ensuring that the wiring is securely reconnected.

Combo Van rear door

11 Refitting is a reversal of the removal procedure, tightening the hinge bolts securely, and ensuring that the wiring is securely reconnected.

Adjustment

All front and Corsa rear doors

12 Adjustment of the door position is not possible; the hinges are welded to the vehicle body and door, and cannot be repositioned. Misalignment of the door can only be caused by accident damage or wear of the hinge pins.
13 Door closure may be adjusted by altering the position of the door lock striker on the body. Slacken the striker retaining bolts,

reposition the striker as required, then securely retighten the bolts **(see illustration)**.

Combo Van rear door

14 Slight adjustment of the doors can be achieved by slackening the hinge retaining bolts and repositioning the hinge/door.
15 Door closure may be adjusted by altering the position of the upper and lower door lock strikers on the door/body (as applicable). Slacken the striker retaining bolts, reposition the striker as required, then securely retighten the bolts **(see illustrations)**.

---

12 Door inner trim panel – removal and refitting

Removal

Front door

1 Carefully unclip the exterior mirror inner trim panel from the door. On models with manually-operated mirrors, it will be necessary to pull the knob off the adjusting lever in order to remove the panel **(see illustrations)**. Depending on vehicle model, disconnect any wiring connectors as they become accessible.
2 Lift the inner door lock handle, and carefully prise the handle trim cover out from the door trim panel **(see illustration)**.
3 Unclip the electric window switch assembly from the door trim panel, then disconnect the wiring connector **(see illustration)**.

11.15a Rear upper door lock catch retaining bolts (arrowed) – Combo Van

11.15b Slacken the retaining bolt (arrowed) to adjust the door striker – Combo Van

12.1a Unclip the exterior mirror inner trim panel from the door . . .

12.1b . . . and disconnect the wiring connector

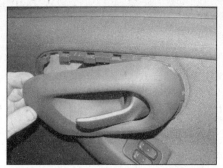

12.2 Unclip the trim cover from the door inner handle

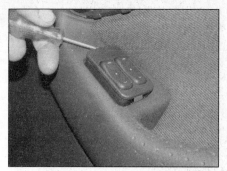

12.3 Carefully unclip the electric window switch from the door trim panel

12.4 Prise out the window sealing strip from the top of the door

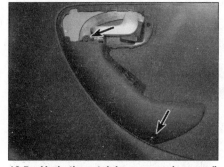

12.5a Undo the retaining screws (arrowed) from the door handle . . .

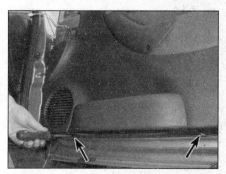

12.5b . . . the trim panel lower retaining screws (arrowed) . . .

4 Carefully prise the window inner sealing strip from the top edge of the door trim panel **(see illustration)**.

5 Unscrew the door grab handle retaining screws, the two lower trim panel screws and the upper trim panel securing screw **(see illustrations)**.

6 Working your way around the door, carefully unclip the door trim panel, and remove it from the door **(see illustration)**.

Rear door

7 Undo the retaining screws, and remove the handle from the rear door **(see illustration)**.

8 Lift the inner door lock handle, and carefully prise the handle trim cover out from the door trim panel, then undo the retaining screw from the trim panel **(see illustrations)**.

9 On models with manually-operated windows, release the securing clip, and remove the window regulator handle. To

release the securing clip, either use a special forked tool, or insert a length of wire with a hooked end between the handle and the trim bezel on the door trim panel, and manipulate it to free the securing clip from the handle.

12.5c . . . and the trim panel front retaining screw

Take care not to damage the door trim panel. Recover the trim bezel **(see illustrations)**.

10 Carefully prise the triangle trim panel away from the top of the door inner trim panel **(see illustration)**.

12.6 Remove the trim panel from the door

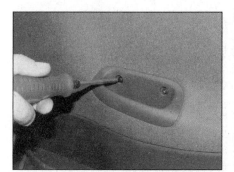

12.7 Undo the two screws, and remove the handle from the rear door

12.8a Unclip the trim cover from the door inner handle . . .

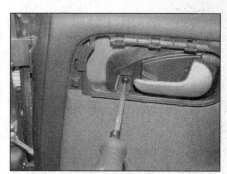

12.8b . . . and undo the retaining screw

12.9a Using a special forked tool to release the securing clip

12.9b Recover the bezel from the door trim panel

12.10 Unclip the inner trim panel from the rear door . . .

12.11 . . . then prise out the window sealing strip from the top of the door

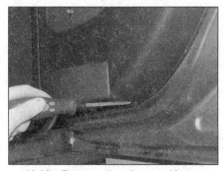

12.12a Remove the trim panel lower retaining screws . . .

12.12b . . . and remove the trim panel from the door

11 Carefully prise the window inner sealing strip from the top edge of the door trim panel **(see illustration)**.
12 Undo the lower trim panel securing screw, then working your way around the door,

12.13 Fit the clip (arrowed) to the regulator handle before fitting the handle to the door

carefully unclip the door trim panel, and remove it from the door **(see illustrations)**.

Refitting

13 Refitting is the reverse of the relevant removal procedure. On models with manual windows, fit the retaining clip to the regulator handle before fitting the handle onto the regulator **(see illustration)**.

---

13 Door handle and lock components –
removal and refitting

Removal

Interior handle

1 Remove the door inner trim panel as described in Section 12.

2 Peel the polythene weathershield away from the door to gain access to the inner handle components **(see illustration)**.
3 Slide the inner handle towards the rear of the door to release it from the door panel **(see illustration)**.
4 Pull the operating cable to release it from the inner handle assembly, and remove the inner handle from the door **(see illustration)**.

Front exterior handle

5 Remove the door inner trim panel as described in Section 12, then peel back the weathershield (see paragraph 2).
6 With the window fully raised, disconnect the wiring connector from the central locking unit, then undo the retaining bolts and remove the shield from around the door locking mechanism **(see illustrations)**.

13.2 Carefully peel the weathershield away from the door to gain access to the lock components

13.3 Slide the interior handle forwards to release it from door

13.4 Release the outer cable (arrowed) from the inner handle assembly

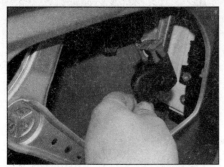

13.6a Release the securing clip and disconnect the wiring block connector . . .

13.6b . . . then remove the shield from the door locking mechanism

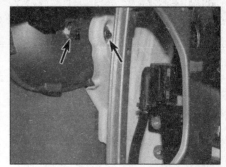

13.7a Undo the two nuts . . .

7 Undo the two retaining nuts from the inside of the door handle, and remove the handle from the outside of the door (see illustration).

Front lock cylinder

8 Remove the exterior door handle as described above, then unhook the inner door handle shell from the link rod (see illustration).

9 Unclip the locking washer from the rear of the lock cylinder, and remove the lever and springs, note the fitted position of the lever and springs for refitting (see illustrations).

10 Insert the key into the lock cylinder, then remove the roll-pin from the lock housing (see illustration).

11 Turn the lock housing anti-clockwise and carefully remove the lock cylinder upwards out of the housing (see illustration).

12 Remove the key, then withdraw the lock

13.7b . . . then withdraw the door handle from the vehicle

13.8 Unhook the link rod (arrowed) from the door lock lever

barrel from the housing, taking care the tumblers do not fall out of the barrel (see illustrations).

13 If the collar is removed from the lock shell,

note the position for refitting. Make sure the two ball-bearings and locating ring are located correctly when refitting (see illustrations).

13.9a Remove the C-clip (arrowed) . . .

13.9b . . . then lift off the lever. . .

13.9c . . . and spring, noting the correct fitted position

13.10 Use long-nose pliers to remove the roll-pin

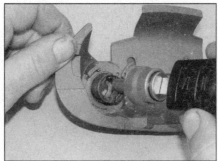

13.11 Remove the lock cylinder out of the housing

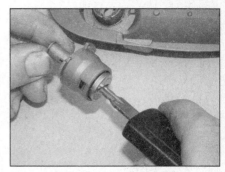

13.12a Remove the key . . .

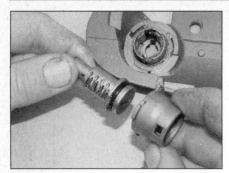

13.12b . . . then withdraw the lock barrel from the housing

13.13a Remove the collar from the lock shell . . .

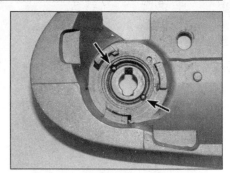

13.13b . . . then the ball-bearings (arrowed) . . .

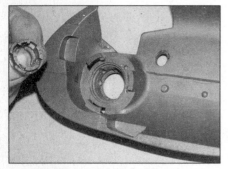

13.13c . . . and the locating ring

Front lock assembly

14 Remove the exterior door handle as described in paragraphs 5 to 7, then unhook the inner door handle shell from the link rod to the lock assembly.

13.15 Undo the three retaining screws (arrowed)

15 Undo the three retaining screws, and manoeuvre the lock assembly to gain access to the operating cables (see illustration).
16 Release the retaining clips, and free the

operating cables from the lock assembly (see illustrations).
17 Withdraw the lock assembly from the door frame (see illustration).

Corsa rear exterior handle

18 Remove the door inner trim panel as described in Section 12, and peel back the weathershield (see paragraph 2).
19 Wind the window fully down, and release the window sealing strip from the rear of the door and window guide (see illustration).
20 Undo the window guide retaining bolts, and manoeuvre the window guide upwards and out from the door (see illustrations).
21 Wind the window fully up, then undo the two nuts, and free the mounting plate assembly from the rear of the handle (see illustration).
22 Remove the handle from the outside of

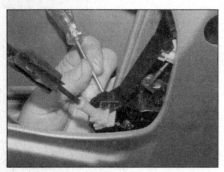

13.16a Release the outer cable . . .

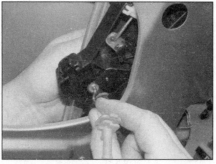

13.16b . . . then unclip the inner cable

13.16c Release the outer cable and unclip the inner cable

13.17 Withdraw the lock assembly from the door frame

13.19 Free the sealing strip from the rear of the door

13.20a Slacken and remove the retaining bolts (arrowed) . . .

13.20b ... then manoeuvre the guide upwards and out of the rear door

13.21 Undo the two nuts, and free the mounting plate assembly

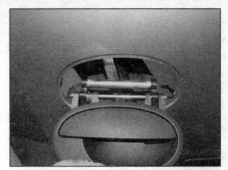

13.22a Withdraw the handle from the door ...

13.22b ... the link rod length can be adjusted by turning the plastic stop nut (arrowed)

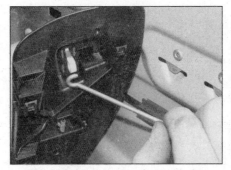

13.23 Unhook the operating cable from the door handle lever

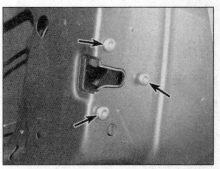

13.25 Undo the three retaining screws (arrowed)

the door, freeing its link rod from the lock assembly **(see illustrations)**.

Corsa rear lock assembly

23 Remove the interior handle as described in paragraphs 1 to 4 above **(see illustration)**.
24 Undo the window guide retaining bolts, and manoeuvre the window guide out from the door **(see illustrations 13.20a and 13.20b)**.
25 Undo the three retaining screws, and manoeuvre the lock assembly to gain access to the central locking wiring connector **(see illustration)**.
26 Slide the locking clip out and disconnect the central locking wiring connector from the lock assembly **(see illustration)**.
27 Undo the retaining screw and unclip the operating cables from the door and withdraw the lock assembly from door frame complete with operating cables **(see illustrations)**.

28 Release the cable from the lock assembly by unclipping the outer cable and disconnecting the inner cable from the operating lever on the lock assembly, the link rod can be removed by pivoting the retaining

clip away from the link rod, and free the link rod from the lock assembly **(see illustrations)**.

Combo Van rear lock assembly

29 Release the securing clip, and remove the

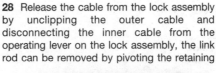

13.26 Release the securing clip (arrowed) and disconnect the wiring block connector

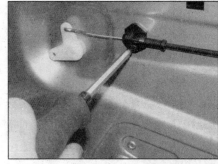

13.27a Undo the retaining screw ...

13.27b ... and unclip the operating cables (arrowed)

13.28a Release the outer cable and unclip the inner cable ...

13.28b ... then release the securing clip and disconnect the link rod

13.29a Release the securing clip using a special forked tool . . .

13.29b . . . then withdraw the handle

13.30 Remove the trim panel from the door

13.32 Release the securing clips and disconnect the linkage rods (arrowed)

31 Remove the upper and lower latches as described in paragraphs 40 to 42.
32 Release the retaining clips from the link rods, and free both link rods from the lock mechanism **(see illustration)**.
33 Undo the three retaining screws from the lock assembly **(see illustration)**.
34 Disconnect the central locking wiring connector from the lock assembly.
35 Withdraw the actuation unit complete with the operating cables. To detach the cables from the unit, first unclip the covers, then release the outer cables from the bracket and unclip the inner cables from the linkage **(see illustrations)**.

Combo Van rear handle

36 Remove the lock assembly as described in paragraphs 29 to 35.
37 Undo the two retaining nuts and remove the inner door handle shell from the door handle. Withdraw and remove the handle from the outside of the door **(see illustration)**.

Combo Van rear lock cylinder

38 Remove the rear handle as described in paragraphs 36 and 37.
39 Remove the lock cylinder as described in paragraphs 8 to 13.

Combo Van rear latches

40 Undo the two bolts securing the latch to the door, and guide the latch out of position **(see illustration)**.
41 Release the operating cable and free it from the latch assembly **(see illustration)**.
42 If necessary, remove the second latch in the same way.

door handle. To release the securing clip, either use a special forked tool, or insert a length of wire with a hooked end between the handle and the door trim panel, and manipulate it to free the securing clip from the

handle. Take care not to damage the door trim panel **(see illustrations)**.
30 Carefully unclip the inner trim panel, and remove it from the rear door **(see illustration)**.

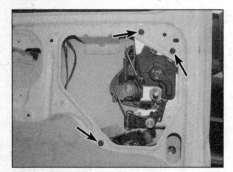

13.33 Undo the retaining screws (arrowed)

13.35a Withdraw the lock assembly from the door . . .

13.35b . . . unclip the cover . . .

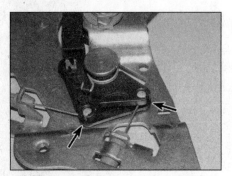

13.35c . . . and disconnect the operating cables (arrowed) from the lever

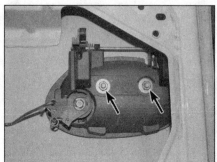

13.37 Undo the two nuts (arrowed) and free the mounting plate assembly

13.40 Undo the two bolts and remove the latch from the door . . .

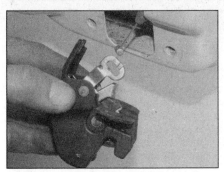

13.41 . . . then disconnect the operating cable from the lever

Refitting

43 Refitting is the reverse of the removal sequence, noting the following points:

a) If a lock cylinder has been removed, on refitting ensure that all the components are refitted in the correct position, as noted on removal and are securely held in place by the C-clip. Check the operation of the lock cylinder, making sure that the spring returns the cylinder to its central position, before refitting the plate to the door.

b) Ensure that all link rods are securely held in position by their retaining clips.

c) Apply grease to all lock and link rod pivot points.

d) Before installing the relevant trim panel, thoroughly check the operation of all the door lock handles and, where necessary, the central locking system, and ensure

that the weathershield is correctly positioned.

e) Make sure the polythene weathershield fitted behind the trim panel is undamaged and perfectly sealed to the door around its complete contact area. If a perfect seal cannot be made, renew the weathershield.

14 Door window glass and regulator – removal and refitting

Removal

1 Remove the door inner trim panel as described in Section 12.

2 Peel the polythene weathershield away from the door to gain access to the door lock components. Proceed as described under the relevant sub-heading.

Front window glass

3 Remove the regulator assembly as described below. The glass can then be lifted out from the door **(see illustration)**.

Rear window glass

4 Carefully prise the window outer sealing strip from the top edge of the door trim panel **(see illustration)**.

5 Wind the window fully down, and release the window sealing strip from the rear of the door and window guide **(see illustration 13.19)**.

6 Undo the window guide retaining bolts, and

manoeuvre the window guide upwards and out from the door **(see illustrations 13.20b)**.

7 Tilt the window glass forwards, and free the window guide from the regulator mechanism (it may be necessary to raise the window mechanism slightly to disengage the window guide). The glass can then be manoeuvred out from the door **(see illustration)**.

Front regulator

Note: *A pop-rivet gun and suitable rivets will be required when refitting. The rivet heads should be approximately 4.8 mm in diameter and 11 mm in length.*

8 With the window set in the raised position, secure the window glass in position, then undo the retaining bolts from the base of the window guide **(see illustration)**.

9 Using an 8.5 mm drill bit, drill out the rivets securing the regulator assembly and the guide rails to the door, taking great care not to damage the door panel **(see illustrations)**.

10 With all the rivets removed, free the regulator rollers from the ends of the window glass guide rail, and manoeuvre the guide rails and regulator assembly out through the door aperture **(see illustrations)**.

11 On models with electric windows, disconnect the wiring connector from the regulator as it becomes accessible.

Rear regulator

Note: *A pop-rivet gun and suitable rivets will be required when refitting. The rivet heads should be approximately 4.8 mm in diameter and 11 mm in length.*

14.3 Removing the front door window glass

14.4 Prise out the window sealing strip from the top of the door

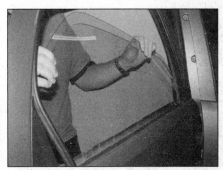

14.7 Removing the rear door window glass

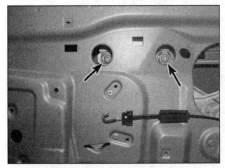

14.8 Undo the two retaining bolts (arrowed)

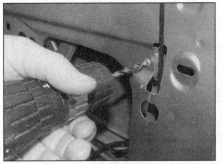

14.9a Using a suitable drill . . .

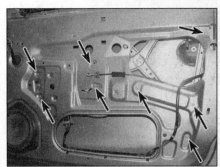

14.9b . . . carefully drill out the rivets (arrowed)

14.10a Free the regulator rollers from the window glass runner . . .

14.10b . . . and remove the regulator assembly from the door

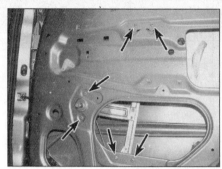

14.13 Drill out the rivets (arrowed)

14.15a Engage the regulator at the front (arrowed) . . .

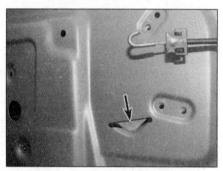

14.15b . . . and at the rear (arrowed)

12 Remove the rear window glass as described in paragraphs 4 to 7.

13 Using an 8.5 mm drill bit, drill out the rivets securing the regulator assembly to the door, taking great care not to damage the door panel **(see illustration)**.

14 With all the rivets removed, manoeuvre the regulator out through the door aperture. On models with electric windows, disconnect the wiring connector from the regulator as it becomes accessible.

Refitting

15 Refitting is the reverse of the removal procedure, noting the following points:

a) *Where the regulator has been removed, remove the remains of the old rivets before fitting the regulator to the door. Engage the regulator in position on the door* **(see illustrations)** *and with the window glass, and secure it with new pop-rivets.*

b) *Check the window moves smoothly and easily up-and-down, without any sign of tight spots. If the window movement is stiff, trace and rectify the cause. On the front window, movement is adjustable by slackening the regulator guide bolts and moving them in the slotted holes. Find the position where the window movement is the easiest, then securely tighten the bolts.*

c) *Refit the weathershield, making sure it is securely stuck to the door, then install the trim panel as described in Section 12.*

15 Tailgate and support struts – removal and refitting

Removal

Tailgate

1 Disconnect the battery negative terminal (refer to *Disconnecting the battery* in the Reference Chapter).

2 Open the tailgate, and detach the parcel shelf cords from the tailgate. Undo the four retaining screws from the tailgate trim panel.

3 Carefully prise the inner trim panel from the tailgate, taking care not to break the retaining clips on removal **(see illustration)**.

4 Disconnect the wiring block connector from the tailgate. Tie a suitable length of string to the end of the wiring loom block connector, then free the grommet from the top of the tailgate and withdraw the wiring loom **(see illustrations)**. When the end of the loom appears, untie the string and leave it in position in the tailgate; it can then be used to draw the wiring back into position when refitting.

5 Prise out the washer jet from the top of the tailgate, and disconnect it from the washer hose **(see illustration)**. Tie a suitable length of

15.3 Unclip the inner trim panel from the tailgate

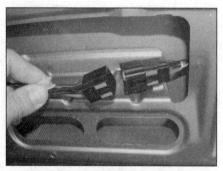

15.4a Disconnect the wiring block connector . . .

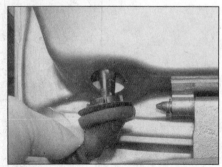

15.4b . . . then remove the grommet and withdraw the wiring from the tailgate

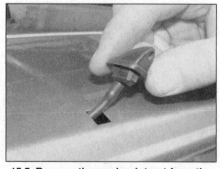

15.5 Remove the washer jet out from the tailgate

string to the hose end, then withdraw the hose, leaving the string in position in the same way as for the wiring.

6 Have an assistant support the tailgate, then raise the spring clips and pull the support struts off their balljoint mountings on the tailgate (see paragraphs 8 and 9). Prise out the hinge pin retaining clips, then tap both hinge pins out of position and remove the tailgate from the vehicle **(see illustrations)**.

7 Examine the hinge pins for signs of wear or damage, and renew if necessary.

Support struts

8 Support the tailgate in the open position using a suitable piece of wood, or with the help of an assistant.

9 Raise the spring clips, and pull the support strut off its balljoint mountings on the tailgate and vehicle body **(see illustrations)**.

Refitting

Tailgate

10 Refitting is a reversal of the removal procedure, noting the following points:

  a) *Prior to refitting, apply a smear of multi-purpose grease to the hinge pins.*

  b) *Ensure that the hinge pins are securely retained by their clips, and that the support struts are securely held in position by their spring clips.*

  c) *Use the string to draw the wiring loom and washer hose through into position, and ensure that the wiring connector is securely reconnected.*

Support struts

11 Refitting is a reverse of the removal procedure, ensuring that the strut is securely retained by its spring clips.

---

16 Tailgate lock components –
removal and refitting

Removal

1 Open the tailgate, and detach the parcel shelf cords from the tailgate. Undo the four retaining screws from the tailgate trim panel.

2 Carefully prise the inner trim panel from the tailgate, taking care not to break the retaining clips on removal **(see illustration 15.3)**.

3 Proceed as described under the relevant sub-heading.

Lock assembly

4 From inside the tailgate, release the retaining clip by pivoting it away from the link rod, and detach the rod from the lock assembly **(see illustration)**.

5 Slacken and remove the three screws, and remove the lock, complete with link rod, from the tailgate **(see illustrations)**.

Lock cylinder assembly

6 From inside the tailgate, release the

retaining clip by pivoting it away from the link rod, and detach the rod from the lock cylinder **(see illustration)**.

7 Release the retaining clip and detach the central locking wiring connector from the

15.6a Remove the retaining clips . . .

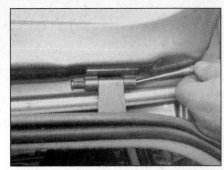
15.6b . . . then drift out the hinge pin and lift off the tailgate

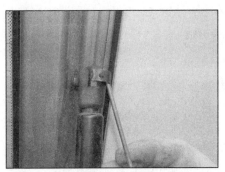
15.9a Lift the retaining clip

15.9b . . . and free the support strut from its balljoints

16.4 Release the retaining clip (arrowed) and detach the link rod from the tailgate lock

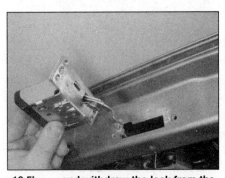
16.5b . . . and withdraw the lock from the tailgate

servo unit on the lock cylinder assembly **(see illustration)**.

8 Undo the two nuts and the lock cylinder assembly can then be manoeuvred out of the tailgate **(see illustration)**. **Note:** *The lock*

16.5a Remove the three screws (arrowed) . . .

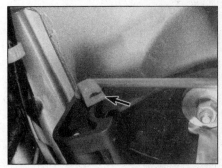
16.6 Release the retaining clip (arrowed) and detach the link rod

cylinder assembly can only be replaced as a complete unit, check with your local Vauxhall dealer for the availability of parts.

Refitting

9 Refitting is a reverse of the removal procedure.

17 Central locking components – removal and refitting

Front door servo

1 The servo motor is part of the lock assembly and can only be purchased as a complete assembly. Remove the lock assembly as described in Section 13.

17.4a Undo the two retaining screws (arrowed) . . .

17.7 Slide the wiring connector away from the lock cylinder to release it from the bracket

17.8b . . . and unclip the servo unit from the lock cylinder lever

16.7 Release the retaining clip (arrowed) and disconnect the wiring connector

Rear door servo

Corsa

2 The servo motor is part of the lock assembly and can only be purchased as a

17.4b . . . and disconnect the servo unit from the lock mechanism

17.8a Undo the two retaining screws (arrowed) . . .

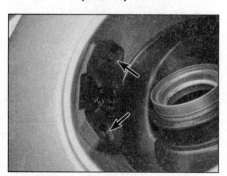

17.11a Undo the two retaining screws (arrowed) . . .

16.8 Undo the nuts (arrowed) and remove the lock assembly

complete assembly. Remove the lock assembly as described in Section 13.

Combo Van

3 Remove the lock assembly as described in Section 13.
4 Undo the two retaining screws and remove the servo unit from the lock assembly, detaching its actuating arm from the lock mechanism **(see illustrations)**.
5 Refitting is the reverse of removal. Prior to installing the trim panel, check the operation of the servo unit.

Tailgate servo

6 Remove the tailgate lock cylinder assembly as described in Section 16.
7 Release the wiring harness plug from the bracket by sliding it away from the lock cylinder **(see illustration)**.
8 Undo the two retaining screws, withdraw the circlip (where fitted) from the actuating rod and unclip the servo unit from the lock cylinder assembly **(see illustrations)**.
9 Refitting is the reverse of removal, ensuring that the actuating rod is correctly engaged with the lock mechanism. Prior to installing the trim panel, check the operation of the servo unit.

Fuel filler cap servo

Corsa

10 Open the fuel filler flap and remove the fuel tank cap.
11 Undo the two retaining screws from the fuel filler flap catch and withdraw the servo unit assembly, disconnect the wiring

17.11b . . . and withdraw the servo unit assembly

17.12 Unclip the servo unit and withdraw it from the housing

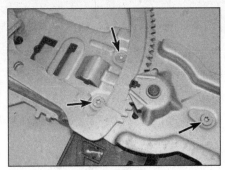

18.3a Undo the retaining screws (arrowed) . . .

18.3b . . . and remove the electric window motor

connector as it becomes accessible **(see illustrations)**.

12 The servo motor can then be unclipped and withdrawn from the catch assembly **(see illustration)**.

13 Refitting is the reverse of removal, ensuring that the servo unit assembly is correctly engaged in the filler neck aperture.

Combo Van

14 Remove the right-hand rear quarter inner trim panel.

15 Release the servo retaining clips then manoeuvre the servo out from the rear quarter panel, disconnect the servo unit wiring connector.

16 Refitting is the reverse of removal, ensuring that the servo unit is correctly engaged. Check the operation of the servo unit before refitting the inner trim panel.

---

18 Electric window components – removal and refitting

Note: *Every time the battery is disconnected, or the electric window motors are disconnected, it will be necessary to reprogramme the motors to restore the one-touch function of the buttons. To do this, fully close both front windows. With the windows closed, depress the up button of the driver's side window for approximately 5 seconds, then release it and depress the passenger side window up button for approximately 5 seconds.*

18.4a Check the drive gear is located correctly on the motor . . .

Window switches

1 Refer to Chapter 12.

Window winder motors

2 Remove the regulator mechanism as described in Section 14.

3 With the regulator removed, slacken and remove the three retaining screws, and separate the motor and regulator **(see illustrations)**. Do not attempt to dismantle the motor assembly, as it is a sealed unit.

4 Before refitting the motor, check the drive gear is located correctly on the motor, and the washer is clipped into place on the regulator assembly **(see illustrations)**.

5 Fit the motor assembly to the regulator, and securely tighten its retaining screws.

6 Install the regulator mechanism as described in Section 14.

18.4b . . . and the washer is clipped into place on the regulator assembly

---

19 Exterior mirror and associated components – removal and refitting

Mirror assembly

1 Unclip the exterior mirror inner trim panel from the door, on manually-adjusted mirrors detach the knob from the adjustment lever **(see illustration)**.

2 Disconnect the wiring connector from the speaker in the trim panel **(see illustration)**.

3 On electrically-operated mirrors, disconnect the wiring connector to the mirror assembly.

4 Undo the three retaining bolts, and remove the mirror assembly from the outside of the door **(see illustrations)**.

5 Refitting is a reverse of the removal procedure.

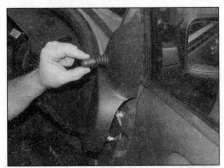

19.1 Unclip the exterior mirror inner trim panel from the door . . .

19.2 . . . and disconnect the wiring connector

19.4a Undo the retaining screws (arrowed) . . .

19.4b . . . and remove the exterior mirror

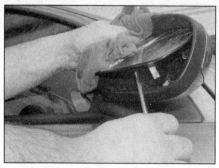

19.6a Press against the top face of the mirror . . .

19.6b . . . and carefully prise the glass from its balljoints

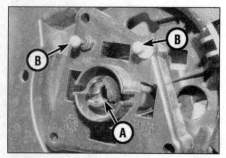

19.8 Ensure that the mirror is correctly located on the balljoint socket (A) and on each of its cable balljoints (B)

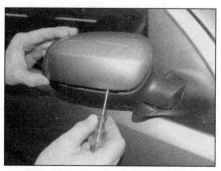

19.12a Carefully unclip the cover . . .

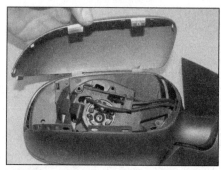

19.12b . . . and remove it from the mirror housing

Mirror glass

6 While pressing against the top face of the mirror, insert a wide plastic or wooden wedge between the lower edge of the mirror glass and mirror housing, and carefully prise the glass from its balljoints (see illustrations). Take great care when removing the glass; do not use excessive force, as the glass is easily broken (use a rag or wear thick gloves, particularly if removing an already-broken mirror).

7 Remove the glass from the mirror. Where applicable, disconnect the wiring connector from the mirror heating element as it become accessible.

8 When refitting, carefully clip the glass back into position, ensuring that it is correctly located on each of its balljoints (see illustration).

Mirror motor

9 Remove the mirror glass as described above.

10 Undo the three screws and remove the motor assembly, disconnecting its wiring connectors as they become accessible.

11 Refitting is the reverse of removal.

Mirror cover

12 Fold the mirror in partially, then carefully unclip the cover from the mirror housing (see illustrations).

13 Refitting is the reverse of removal.

Mirror switch

14 Refer to Chapter 12.

20 Windscreen, tailgate and fixed window glass – general information

These areas of glass are secured by the tight fit of the weatherstrip in the body aperture, and are bonded in position with a special adhesive. The removal and refitting of these areas of fixed glass is a difficult, messy and time-consuming task, which is considered beyond the scope of the home mechanic. It is difficult, unless one has plenty of practice, to obtain a secure, waterproof fit. Furthermore, the task carries a high risk of breakage; this applies especially to the laminated glass windscreen. In view of this, owners are strongly advised to have this sort of work carried out by one of the many specialist windscreen fitters, or a Vauxhall dealer.

21 Sunroof – general information

1 A manual or electric sunroof was offered as an optional extra on most models, and is fitted as standard equipment on some models.

2 Due to the complexity of the sunroof mechanism, considerable expertise is needed to repair, renew or adjust the sunroof components successfully. Removal of the roof first requires the headlining to be removed, which is a complex and tedious operation in itself, and not a task to be undertaken lightly (See Section 26). Therefore, any problems with the sunroof should be referred to a Vauxhall dealer.

3 On models with an electric sunroof, if the sunroof motor fails to operate, first check the relevant fuse. If the fault cannot be traced and rectified, the sunroof can be opened and closed manually using a suitable Allen wrench to turn the motor spindle. To gain access to the motor spindle, carefully prise out the trim cover situated at the rear of the sunroof. Insert the Allen key in the motor spindle, and turn to move the sunroof to the required position. A suitable Allen key is supplied with the vehicle, and should be found in the glovebox.

22 Body exterior fittings – removal and refitting

Radiator grille

1 The radiator grille is part of the front bumper assembly, remove the bumper as described in Section 6.

Wheel arch liners and body under-panels

2 The various plastic covers fitted to the underside of the vehicle are secured in position by a mixture of screws, nuts and retaining clips, and removal will be fairly obvious on inspection. Work methodically around the liner/panel, removing its retaining

screws and releasing its retaining clips until it is free to be removed from the underside of the vehicle. Most clips used on the vehicle, with the exception of the fasteners which are used to secure the wheel arch liners, are simply prised out of position. The wheel arch liner clips are released by tapping their centre pins through the clip, and then removing the outer section of the clip; new clips will be required on refitting if the centre pins are not recovered.

3 When refitting, renew any retaining clips that may have been broken on removal, and ensure that the panel is securely retained by all the relevant clips, nuts and screws. Vauxhall also recommend that plastic nuts (where used) are renewed, regardless of their apparent condition, whenever they are disturbed.

Body trim strips and badges

4 The various body trim strips and badges are held in position with a special adhesive tape. Removal requires the trim/badge to be heated, to soften the adhesive, and then cut away from the surface. Due to the high risk of damage to the vehicle's paintwork during this operation, it is recommended that this task should be entrusted to a Vauxhall dealer.

23 Seats –
removal and refitting

> **Warning: The front seats are equipped with seat belt tensioners, and side airbags may be built into the outer sides of the seats. The seat belt tensioners and side airbags may cause injury if triggered accidentally. If the tensioner has been triggered due to a sudden impact or accident, the unit must be renewed, as it cannot be reset. If a seat is to be disposed of, the tensioner must be triggered before the seat is removed from the vehicle. Due to safety considerations, tensioner renewal or seat disposal must be entrusted to a Vauxhall dealer. Where side airbags are fitted, refer to Chapter 12 for the precautions which should be observed when dealing with an airbag system.**

1 Disconnect the battery negative terminal (refer to *Disconnecting the battery* in the Reference Chapter). Wait 2 minutes for capacitors to discharge, before working on the seat electrics.

Front seat removal

Note: *On Combo models, the front passenger seat needs a special Vauxhall tool (KM-6290) to slide the seat forwards, to access the rear mounting bolts. It is a bar which fits under the front of the seat and locates into the locking levers on the two seat guide rails. When the locking levers are released, the seat can slide forward to access the rear mounting bolts.*

2 Slide the seat adjustment fully to the rear.

23.2a Unclip the cover . . .

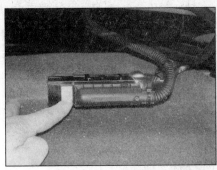

23.2b . . . then release the locking clip . . .

23.2c . . . and disconnect the wiring connector from the seat wiring harness

Where applicable, unclip the cover then disconnect the wiring connector from the seat wiring harness **(see illustrations)**.

3 Slacken and remove the seat retaining bolts from the front of the seat guide rails **(see illustration)**.

4 Slide the seat fully forwards, then slacken and remove the seat retaining bolts from rear of the guide rails **(see illustration)**. See note above for passenger seat in Combo models.

5 The seat can now be lifted out of the vehicle. On Combo models, note the position of any spacers under the seat guide rails on the floor panel.

Rear seat removal

Cushion – Corsa and Corsavan

6 Pull the rear seat cushion forwards and fold it upwards.

7 Press the two hinge retaining rods towards

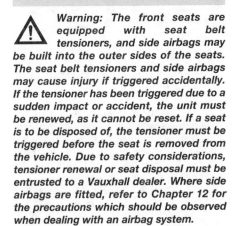

23.4 Undo the seat retaining bolts (one side arrowed) from the rear of the seat rails

23.3 Undo the seat retaining bolts (one side arrowed) from the front of the seat rails

the centre, to release them from the seat hinge brackets on the base of the seat cushion.

One-piece backrest – Corsa and Corsavan

8 Open up the tailgate, and remove the rear parcel shelf.

9 Fold the rear seat backrest forwards, and release the pivot pin from the left- and right-hand seat backrest pivot catch **(see illustration)**.

10 The seat backrest can then be manoeuvred out of the vehicle.

Two-piece backrest – Corsa and Corsavan

11 Open up the tailgate, and remove the rear parcel shelf.

12 Fold the left-hand backrest forward, unclip the trim cover from the right-hand seat backrest hinge and remove the retaining

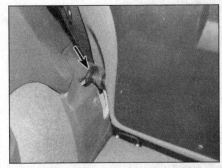

23.9 Release the pivot pin (arrowed) from the seat backrest pivot catch

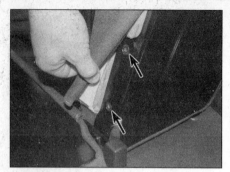

23.12a Unclip the trim cover and remove the retaining bolts (arrowed)

23.12b Release the pivot pin (arrowed) from the seat backrest pivot catch

23.13 Unscrew the seat belt/stalk mounting bolt

23.14a Unclip the trim cover and remove the retaining bolts (arrowed)

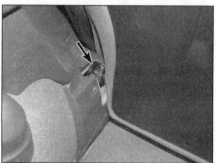

23.14b Release the pivot pin (arrowed) from the seat backrest pivot catch

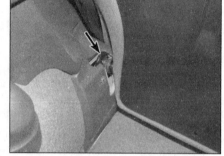

23.22 Press the end of the wiring block connector to secure

bolts. Push the right-hand backrest to the right and detach it from the pivot bracket to withdraw the backrest **(see illustrations)**.

13 Prise off the trim cover from the seat belt stalk/lap belt mounting bolt. Unscrew the mounting bolt, and recover the washer and spacer from behind the belt anchorage **(see illustration)**.

14 Fold the left-hand backrest upwards, unclip the trim cover from the seat backrest hinge and remove the retaining bolts. Push the backrest to the left and detach it from the pivot bracket to withdraw the left-hand backrest **(see illustrations)**.

Cushion – Combo Van

15 Fold back the carpet from front of the seat to gain access to the seat pivot pins.

16 Prise off the covers from each pin, then release the pins and remove the seat cushion from the vehicle.

Backrest – Combo Van

17 Where necessary, undo the retaining bolts and remove the luggage compartment grille from the vehicle.

18 Fold the seat backrest forwards slightly, then unclip the cover at the centre seat to access the seat hinge bolts.

19 Prise off the trim cover from the seat belt stalk/lap belt mounting bolts. Unscrew the mounting bolts, and recover the washer and spacer from behind the belt anchorage.

20 Fold the left-hand backrest forward, push the right-hand backrest to the right and detach it from the pivot bracket to withdraw the backrest.

21 Fold the left-hand backrest upwards, push the backrest to the left and detach it from the pivot bracket to withdraw the left-hand backrest.

Refitting front seats

22 Refitting is a reverse of the removal procedure, noting the following points:

a) *Remove all traces of old thread-locking compound from the threads of the seat retaining bolts, and clean the threaded holes in the vehicle floor, ideally by running a tap of the correct size and pitch down them.*

b) *Apply a suitable thread-locking compound to the threads of the seat bolts. Refit the bolts, and tighten them to the specified torque setting.*

c) *Reconnect the seat wiring block connector (see illustration) making sure it has locked securely, then reconnect the battery negative terminal.*

Refitting rear seats

23 Refitting is a reverse of the removal procedure, tightening the seat mounting bolts to the specified torque (where applicable).

24 Front seat belt tensioning mechanism – general information

All models covered in this manual are fitted with a front seat belt pyrotechnic tensioner system. The system is designed to instantaneously take up any slack in the seat

belt in the case of a sudden frontal impact, therefore reducing the possibility of injury to the front seat occupants. Each front seat is fitted with its own system, the components of which are mounted in the seat frame.

The seat belt tensioner is triggered by a frontal impact causing a deceleration of six times the force of gravity or greater. Lesser impacts, including impacts from behind, will not trigger the system.

When the system is triggered, a pretensioned spring draws back the seat belt via a cable which acts on the seat belt stalk. The cable can move by up to 80.0 mm, which therefore reduces the slack in the seat belt around the shoulders and waist of the occupant by a similar amount.

There is a risk of injury if the system is triggered inadvertently when working on the vehicle, and it is therefore strongly recommended that any work involving the seat belt tensioner system is entrusted to a Vauxhall dealer. Refer to the warning given at the beginning of Section 23 before contemplating any work on the front seats.

25 Seat belt components – removal and refitting

Front belt removal

Three-door models

1 Prise off the trim cover from the upper seat belt mounting. Unscrew the mounting bolt,

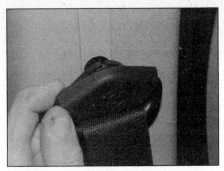

25.1a Prise off the trim cover . . .

25.1b . . . and unscrew the mounting bolt

25.2a Remove the trim cap and unscrew the retaining bolt . . .

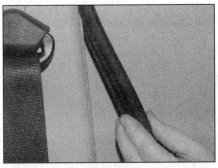

25.2b . . . then disengage the seat belt mounting rail from the floor and seat belt, and remove it from the vehicle

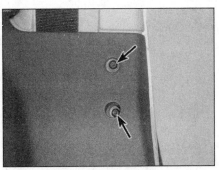

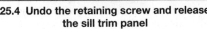

25.4 Undo the retaining screw and release the sill trim panel

4 Undo the retaining screw, and release the sill trim panel from the front edge of the rear seat side trim panel **(see illustration)**.

5 Peel the door sealing strip away from the front edge of the rear seat side panel, then undo the two retaining screws, release the two securing clips and unclip the panel from the rear side panel of the vehicle **(see illustrations)**.

6 Undo the two retaining screws, and remove the seat belt guide from the pillar **(see illustration)**.

7 Undo the inertia reel retaining bolt, and remove the seat belt assembly from the vehicle **(see illustration)**.

Five-door and Combo Van models

8 Unclip the storage tray from along the sill trim panel, then unclip the sill trim from the bottom of the door pillar **(see illustrations)**.

and recover any washer/spacers from behind the belt anchorage **(see illustrations)**.

2 Slacken and remove bolt and washer securing the seat belt mounting rail to the

floor. Disengage the rail from the floor and the seat belt, and remove it **(see illustrations)**.

3 Remove the rear seat backrest as described in Section 23.

25.5a Peel the door sealing strip away from the panel . . .

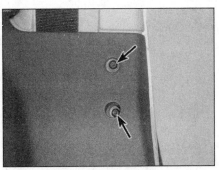

25.5b . . . undo the upper retaining screws (arrowed) . . .

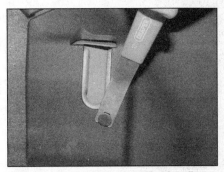

25.5c . . . unclip the lower rear trim clip . . .

25.5d . . . unclip the lower front trim clip . . .

25.5e . . . then unclip the trim panel from the vehicle

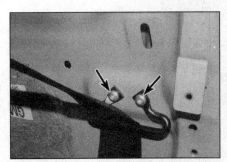

25.6 Undo the retaining screws (arrowed) and remove the seat belt guide from the pillar

25.7 Undo the inertia reel retaining bolt (arrowed) and remove the seat belt assembly

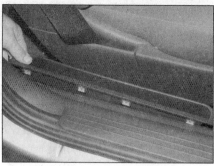

25.8a Unclip the storage tray . . .

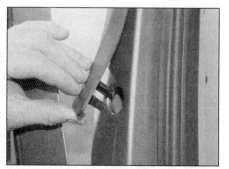

25.8b . . . then unclip the sill trim panel

25.9a Prise out the circular plug (where fitted) . . .

25.9b . . . . then undo the retaining screw

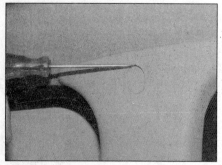

25.10a Remove the trim from the outside of the door pillar . . .

9 Prise out the trim cap from upper trim panel and undo the retaining screw (see illustrations). Peel the door sealing strip away from the door pillar.
10 Remove the trim from the outside of the

door pillar to reveal the retaining nuts, then undo both bolts and free the upper inner trim panel (see illustrations). Unclip the two panel sections, and remove them from the vehicle.
11 Prise out the trim cap from the outside of

the door pillar to reveal the seat belt inertia reel mounting nut. Using a deep socket (Vauxhall use an extra long deep socket) unscrew the mounting nut and remove the inertia reel from inside the vehicle (see illustrations).

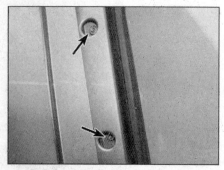

25.10b . . . undo the retaining nuts (arrowed) . . .

25.10c . . . and withdraw the inner trim panel

25.11a Remove the trim from the outside of the door pillar . . .

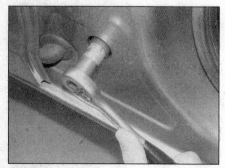

25.11b . . . undo the retaining nut, using a deep socket . . .

25.11c . . . and withdraw the inertia seat belt assembly

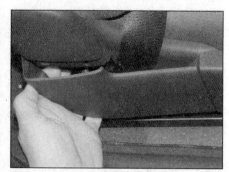

25.12a Unclip the trim panel . . .

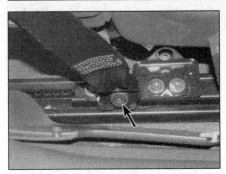

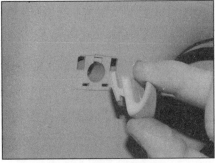
25.15a Unclip the trim/hook . . .

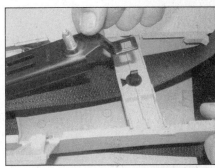
25.15b . . . undo the retaining screw . . .

25.12b . . . and remove the anchorage bolt (arrowed) from the seat frame

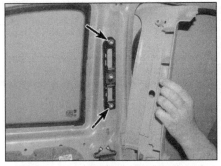
25.15c . . . and remove the trim panel

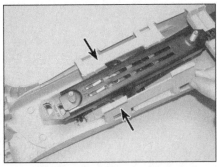
25.17a Release the securing trim clips . . .

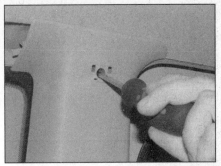
25.17b . . . unclip the height adjuster . . .

12 Unclip the trim panel from the side of the seat and remove the seat belt anchorage bolt from the seat frame **(see illustrations)**.

Height adjuster – three-door models

13 Prise off the trim cover from the upper seat belt mounting. Unscrew the mounting bolt, and recover any washer/spacers from behind the belt anchorage **(see illustrations 25.1a and 25.1b)**.

14 Peel the door sealing strip away from the front edge of the rear seat side panel, then undo the two retaining screws and unclip the panel from the rear side panel of the vehicle **(see illustrations 25.5a, 25.5b and 25.5e)**.

15 Unclip the trim cap/hook at the top of the upper door trim panel and undo the retaining screw. Remove the trim panel and undo the two retaining bolts and withdraw the adjuster from the pillar **(see illustrations)**.

Height adjuster – five-door models

16 Remove the upper B-pillar trim/height adjuster as described in paragraphs 9 and 10.

17 Unclip the height adjuster from the trim panel, then feed the seat belt through the trim panel to remove **(see illustrations)**.

18 To remove the seat belt from the height adjuster, unscrew the mounting bolt, and recover the washer and spacer from behind the belt anchorage **(see illustrations)**.

Rear belt removal

Side belts

19 Prise off the trim cover from the upper seat belt mounting. Unscrew the mounting bolt, and recover any washer/spacers from

behind the belt anchorage **(see illustrations)**.

20 Remove the rear seat backrest as described in Section 23. Unbolt the seat belt lower anchorage bolt from the floor panel **(see illustration)**

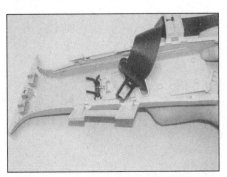
25.17c . . . then feed the seat belt through the trim panel to remove

25.18b . . . and recover the washer . . .

21 Peel the sealing strip away from the tailgate aperture and, on five-door vehicles, from the door aperture **(see illustration)**.

22 On five-door vehicles, undo the retaining screw at the rear of the upper trim panel, then

25.18a Unscrew the mounting bolt . . .

25.18c . . . and spacer from behind the belt anchorage

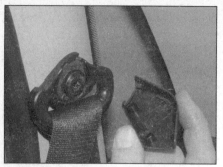

25.19a Prise off the trim cover . . .

25.19b . . . and unscrew the mounting bolt

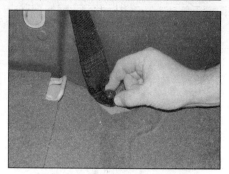

25.20 Unbolt the seat belt lower anchorage bolt

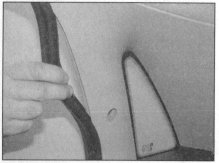

25.21 Peel the sealing strip away from the from the door aperture – 5-door models

25.22a Undo the retaining screw . . .

lower trim panel from the rear quarter panel. As the panel is removed feed the seat belt through the panel to disengage it **(see illustration)**. Disconnect wiring connectors for speakers or interior lights as they come into view.

26 Unscrew the inertia reel retaining bolt, free the belt and remove the belt reel from the vehicle **(see illustration)**.

Centre buckles

27 Fold the rear seat cushion forwards, and unscrew the relevant bolt securing the buckle to the floor **(see illustration)**.

Centre belt

28 Remove the rear seat backrest as described in Section 23.

29 Unclip the trim cover from around the rear seat locking button **(see illustrations)**.

30 With the aid of an assistant, unclip the

unclip the trim and remove it from the vehicle **(see illustrations)**.

23 On three-door models, unclip the trim panel from the upper B-pillar trim panel **(see illustration)**.

24 Undo the two retaining bolts and remove the seat locking arm from the inner panel **(see illustration)**. Make alignment marks to aid the correct fitting of the arm.

25 Undo the retaining screws and unclip the

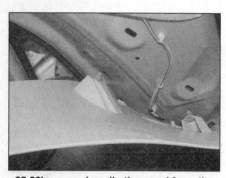

25.22b . . . and unclip the panel from the vehicle

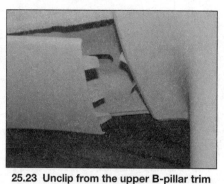

25.23 Unclip from the upper B-pillar trim panel – 3 door models

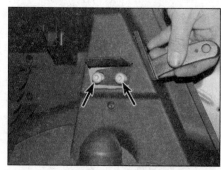

25.24 Undo the retaining bolts (arrowed) and remove the seat locking arm

25.25 Feed the seat belt through the trim panel

25.26 Unscrew the inertia reel retaining bolt

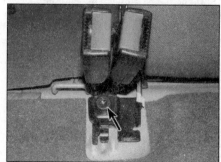

25.27 Unscrew the bolt (arrowed) to remove the seat belt buckle

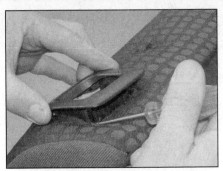

25.29a Use a screwdriver to carefully release the trim cover . . .

25.29b . . . then remove it from around the rear seat locking button

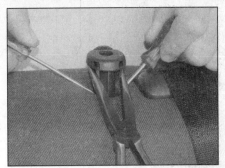

25.30a Unclip the headrest locking sleeves from the seat . . .

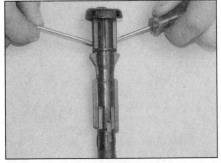

25.30b . . . press in at each side to release the locking tangs

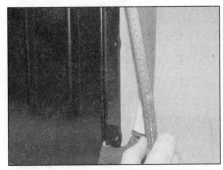

25.31a Carefully peel the seat cover from the seat frame . . .

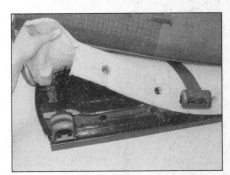

25.31b . . . then move the foam to one side to access the seat belt

headrest locking sleeves from the seat **(see illustrations)**.

31 Working your way around the seat frame, unclip the seat cover from the seat frame, then pull back the foam cushion to access the inertia reel seat belt **(see illustrations)**.

32 Undo the four retaining bolts and remove the bracket from around the inertia reel seat belt **(see illustration)**.

33 Undo the inertia reel mounting bolt, then withdraw the reel and disconnect the cable from the bottom of the inertia reel **(see illustrations). Note:** *This cable is a safety feature which is linked to the seat locking catches, if the seat is not located correctly on the seat catches then the seat belt will not operate correctly and will lock.*

Refitting

34 Refitting is a reversal of the removal procedure, ensuring that all the mounting

bolts are tightened to the specified torque, where applicable. Make sure that any trim panels disturbed during removal are securely retained by all the relevant retaining clips.

26 Interior trim – removal and refitting

Interior trim panels

1 The interior trim panels are secured using either screws or various types of trim fasteners, usually studs or clips.

2 Check that there are no other panels overlapping the one to be removed; usually there is a sequence that has to be followed that will become obvious on close inspection.

3 Remove all obvious fasteners, such as

screws. If the panel will not come free, it is held by hidden clips or fasteners. These are usually situated around the edge of the panel, and can be prised up to release them; note, however, that they can break quite easily, so new ones should be available. The best way of releasing such clips (in the absence of the correct type of tool) is to use a large flat-bladed screwdriver. Note in many cases that the adjacent sealing strip must be prised back to release a panel.

4 When removing a panel, **never** use excessive force, or the panel may be damaged; always check carefully that all fasteners have been removed or released before attempting to withdraw a panel.

5 Refitting is the reverse of the removal procedure; secure the fasteners by pressing them firmly into place, and ensure that all disturbed components are secured correctly, to prevent rattles.

25.32 Undo the four retaining bolts (arrowed)

25.33a Undo the inertia reel mounting bolt . . .

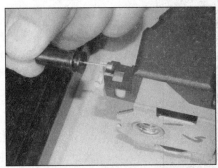

25.33b . . . then withdraw the reel and disconnect the locking cable

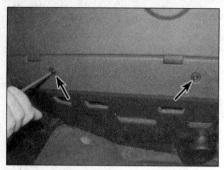

26.6 Undo the lower retaining screws (arrowed) . . .

26.7 . . . and the upper retaining screws (arrowed)

26.8a Pull out the two hinge pins . . .

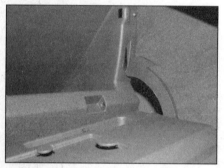

26.8b . . . then unhook the guide rails

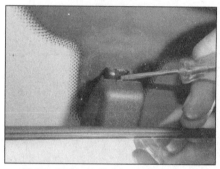

26.15a Release the retaining clip . . .

26.15b . . . and slide the mirror down out of the mounting plate

Glovebox

6 Slacken and remove the two glovebox lower retaining screws **(see illustration)**.
7 Open up the glovebox lid, and undo the two upper retaining screws situated inside the glovebox. Slide the glovebox out of position, disconnecting the wiring connector from the glovebox illumination light (where fitted) as it becomes accessible **(see illustration)**.
8 To remove the lid from the glovebox housing, press out the two hinge pins (from the inside to the outside), then press the lugs on the guide rails upwards to release the lid from the glovebox housing **(see illustrations)**.
9 Refitting is the reverse of removal.

Carpets

10 The passenger compartment floor carpet is in one piece, and is secured at its edges by screws or clips, usually the same fasteners used to secure the various adjoining trim panels.
11 Carpet removal and refitting is reasonably straightforward, but very time-consuming. All adjoining trim panels must be removed first, as must components such as the seats, the centre console and seat belt lower anchorages.

Headlining

12 The headlining is clipped to the roof, and can only be withdrawn once all fittings such as the grab handles, sunvisors, sunroof (if fitted), windscreen and rear quarter windows and related trim panels have been removed, and the door, tailgate and sunroof aperture sealing strips have been prised clear.
13 Note that headlining removal requires considerable skill and experience if it is to be carried out without damage, and is therefore best entrusted to an expert.

Interior mirror

14 On models with rain sensor fitted, unclip and remove the sensor trim panel and release the retaining clip(s) and disconnect the wiring connectors from the mirror assembly.
15 Press the retaining clip at the top of the interior mirror mounting bracket, then carefully release the interior mirror in the downwards direction to remove it from the windscreen **(see illustrations)**.
16 Refitting is the reverse of removal.

27 Centre console – removal and refitting

Removal

1 Unclip the handbrake lever gaiter from the centre console, and fold it back over the handbrake lever **(see illustration)**.
2 On models with manual transmission, unclip the gear lever gaiter from the centre console, and fold it back over the gear lever **(see illustration)**. On automatic models unclip the trim from around the gear lever.
3 Slide both front seats fully forwards and undo the two retaining screw from the rear of the centre console **(see illustration)**.
4 Slide both front seats fully backwards, undo the four retaining screws (two at each side of the front of the centre console) and withdraw the front trim panels **(see illustrations)**.
5 Unclip the switch panel from the front of the

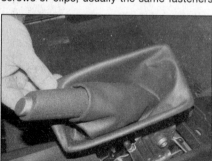

27.1 Unclip the handbrake lever gaiter . . .

27.2 . . . and the gear lever gaiter

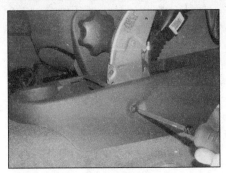

27.3 Remove the retaining screws from the rear of the centre console . . .

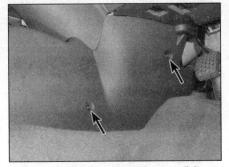

27.4a . . . and the screws (arrowed) from the front of the console . . .

27.4b . . . then release from the front trim panel

centre console and disconnect the wiring block connectors **(see illustration)**.

6 On all models, slide the console to the rear to disengage it from its retaining clip, and lift it upwards and over the gear/selector lever and handbrake **(see illustration)**.

Refitting

7 Refitting is the reverse of removal.

28 Facia panel assembly –
removal and refitting

HAYNES HiNT *Label each wiring connector as it is disconnected from its relevant component. The labels will prove useful when refitting, as a guide to routing the wiring and feeding it through the facia apertures.*

Removal

1 Disconnect the battery negative terminal (refer to *Disconnecting the battery* in the Reference Chapter).
2 Undo the retaining screws and remove the two sill inner trim panels and the lower A-pillar trim panels – see Section 26.
3 Remove the steering column as described in Section 18 of Chapter 10.
4 Remove the following components as described in Chapter 12:

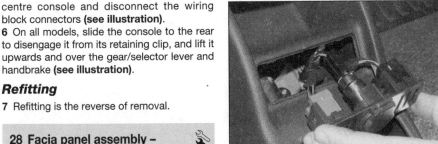

27.5 Unclip the switch panel from the centre console

a) *Instrument panel.*
b) *Windscreen wiper motor.*
c) *Radio/cassette player.*
d) *Clock/multi/function unit display.*
e) *Light switch.*
f) *Passenger side airbag.*
5 Slide the light switch wiring connector out from its clip on the right-hand side of the facia.
6 Undo the screw securing the radio/cassette mounting bracket in position, then slide out the bracket, freeing it from the aerial lead and wiring connector **(see illustrations)**.
7 Remove the glovebox as described in Section 26.
8 Remove the centre console as described in Section 27.
9 Remove the following components as described in Chapter 3:
a) *Heater/ventilation control unit.*
b) *Driver's side vent housing.*

27.6 Lift the console upwards and over the gear/selector lever and handbrake

c) *Passenger side heater duct.*
10 Release the retaining clips and, noting its correct routing, free the wiring loom from the metal frame of the facia panel. Also slide the instrument panel wiring connector out from its clip on the facia.
11 Slide the diagnostic plug wiring connector out from its clip on the lower part of the facia **(see illustration)**.
12 Undo the two retaining screws, one from the left-hand end and one from the right-hand end of the facia panel **(see illustration)**.
13 Return to the engine compartment, and undo the two retaining nuts securing the facia to the bulkhead.
14 The facia panel is now free to be removed. Pull the panel away from the bulkhead, then remove the facia assembly, noting the correct routing of the wiring harnesses, and feeding the wiring back through the facia apertures.

28.6a Undo the screw and slide the radio retaining bracket from the facia . . .

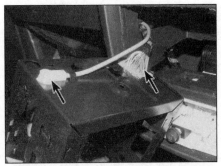

28.6b . . . then free the aerial lead and wiring connector (arrowed)

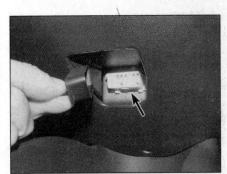

28.11 Diagnostic plug wiring connector in the lower part of the facia at the centre

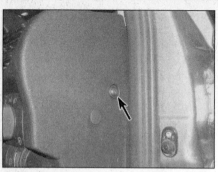

28.12 Undo the facia side retaining screws (one side arrowed)

Refitting

15 Refitting is a reversal of the removal procedure, noting the following points:

a) *Manoeuvre the facia into position and, using the labels stuck on during removal, ensure that the wiring is correctly routed and fed through the relevant facia apertures.*

b) *Clip the facia back into position, then refit all the facia fasteners and tighten them to their specified torque settings.*

c) *On completion, reconnect the battery and check that all the electrical components and switches function correctly.*

Chapter 12
Body electrical systems

Contents

Degrees of difficulty

Easy, suitable for novice with little experience	**Fairly easy,** suitable for beginner with some experience	**Fairly difficult,** suitable for competent DIY mechanic	**Difficult,** suitable for experienced DIY mechanic	**Very difficult,** suitable for expert DIY or professional

Specifications

System type	12 volt negative earth

Bulbs	Wattage
Direction indicator side repeater	5
Direction indicator	21
Front foglight	55
Headlight	60/55
Instrument panel illumination lights	2
Instrument panel warning lights	1.2
Interior lights	10
Number plate light	10
Rear foglight	21
Reversing light	21
Sidelight	5
Stop/tail-light	21/5

Torque wrench settings	Nm	lbf ft
Airbag unit retaining screws	8	6
Windscreen wiper motor	14	10

1 General information and precautions

Warning: Before carrying out any work on the electrical system, read through the precautions given in 'Safety first!' at the beginning of this manual, and in Chapter 5A.

1 The electrical system is of the 12 volt negative earth type. Power for the lights and all electrical accessories is supplied by a lead-acid type battery, which is charged by the engine-driven alternator.

2 This Chapter covers repair and service procedures for the various electrical components not associated with the engine. Information on the battery, alternator and starter motor can be found in Chapter 5A.

3 It should be noted that, prior to working on any component in the electrical system, the battery negative terminal should first be disconnected, to prevent the possibility of electrical short-circuits and/or fires.

Caution: Before proceeding, refer to 'Disconnecting the battery' in the Reference Chapter for further information.

2 Electrical fault finding – general information

Note: *Refer to the precautions given in 'Safety first!' and in Section 1 before starting work. The following tests relate to testing of the main electrical circuits, and should not be used to test delicate electronic circuits (such as the anti-lock braking system or fuel injection system), particularly where an electronic control module is used.*

General

1 A typical electrical circuit consists of an electrical component, any switches, relays, motors, fuses, fusible links or circuit breakers related to that component, and the wiring and connectors which link the component to both the battery and the vehicle body. To help to pinpoint a problem in an electrical circuit, wiring diagrams are shown at the end of this Chapter.

2 Before attempting to diagnose an electrical fault, first study the appropriate wiring diagram to obtain a complete understanding of the components included in the particular circuit concerned. The possible sources of a fault can be narrowed down by noting if other components related to the circuit are operating properly. If several components or circuits fail at one time, the problem is likely to be related to a shared fuse or earth connection.

3 Electrical problems usually stem from simple causes, such as loose or corroded connections, a faulty earth connection, a blown fuse, a melted fusible link, or a faulty relay (refer to Section 3 for details of testing relays). Inspect the condition of all fuses, wires and connections in a problem circuit before testing the components. Use the wiring diagrams to determine which terminal connections will need to be checked in order to pinpoint the trouble-spot.

4 The basic tools required for electrical fault finding include a circuit tester or voltmeter (a 12 volt bulb with a set of test leads can also be used for certain tests); a self-powered test light (sometimes known as a continuity tester); an ohmmeter (to measure resistance); a battery and set of test leads; and a jumper wire, preferably with a circuit breaker or fuse incorporated, which can be used to bypass suspect wires or electrical components. Before attempting to locate a problem with test instruments, use the wiring diagram to determine where to make the connections.

5 To find the source of an intermittent wiring fault (usually due to a poor or dirty connection, or damaged wiring insulation), a 'wiggle' test can be performed on the wiring. This involves wiggling the wiring by hand to see if the fault occurs as the wiring is moved. It should be possible to narrow down the source of the fault to a particular section of wiring. This method of testing can be used in conjunction with any of the tests described in the following sub-Sections.

6 Apart from problems due to poor connections, two basic types of fault can occur in an electrical circuit – open-circuit, or short-circuit.

7 Open-circuit faults are caused by a break somewhere in the circuit, which prevents current from flowing. An open-circuit fault will prevent a component from working, but will not cause the relevant circuit fuse to blow.

8 Short-circuit faults are caused by a 'short' somewhere in the circuit, which allows the current flowing in the circuit to 'escape' along an alternative route, usually to earth. Short-circuit faults are normally caused by a breakdown in wiring insulation, which allows a feed wire to touch either another wire, or an earthed component such as the bodyshell. A short-circuit fault will normally cause the relevant circuit fuse to blow.

Finding an open-circuit

9 To check for an open-circuit, connect one lead of a circuit tester or voltmeter to either the negative battery terminal or a known good earth.

10 Connect the other lead to a connector in the circuit being tested, preferably nearest to the battery or fuse.

11 Switch on the circuit, bearing in mind that some circuits are live only when the ignition switch is turned to a particular position.

12 If voltage is present (indicated either by the tester bulb lighting or a voltmeter reading, as applicable), this means that the section of the circuit between the relevant connector and the battery is problem-free.

13 Continue to check the remainder of the circuit in the same fashion.

14 When a point is reached at which no voltage is present, the problem must lie between that point and the previous test point with voltage. Most problems can be traced to a broken, corroded or loose connection.

Finding a short-circuit

15 To check for a short-circuit, first disconnect the load(s) from the circuit (loads are the components which draw current from a circuit, such as bulbs, motors, heating elements, etc).

16 Remove the relevant fuse from the circuit, and connect a circuit tester or voltmeter to the fuse connections.

17 Switch on the circuit, bearing in mind that some circuits are live only when the ignition switch is turned to a particular position.

18 If voltage is present (indicated either by the tester bulb lighting or a voltmeter reading, as applicable), this means that there is a short-circuit.

19 If no voltage is present, but the fuse still blows with the load(s) connected, this indicates an internal fault in the load(s).

Finding an earth fault

20 The battery negative terminal is connected to 'earth' – the metal of the engine/ transmission unit and the car body – and most systems are wired so that they only receive a positive feed, the current returning via the metal of the car body. This means that the component mounting and the body form part of that circuit. Loose or corroded mountings can therefore cause a range of electrical faults, ranging from total failure of a circuit, to a puzzling partial fault. In particular, lights may shine dimly (especially when another circuit sharing the same earth point is in operation), motors (eg, wiper motors or the radiator cooling fan motor) may run slowly, and the operation of one circuit may have an apparently-unrelated effect on another. Note that on many vehicles, earth straps are used between certain components, such as the engine/transmission and the body, usually where there is no metal-to-metal contact between components, due to flexible rubber mountings, etc.

21 To check whether a component is properly earthed, disconnect the battery, and connect one lead of an ohmmeter to a known good earth point. Connect the other lead to the wire or earth connection being tested. The resistance reading should be zero; if not, check the connection as follows.

22 If an earth connection is thought to be faulty, dismantle the connection, and clean back to bare metal both the bodyshell and the wire terminal or the component earth connection mating surface. Be careful to remove all traces of dirt and corrosion, then use a knife to trim away any paint, so that a clean metal-to-metal joint is made. On reassembly, tighten the joint fasteners securely; if a wire terminal is being refitted, use serrated washers between the terminal and the bodyshell, to ensure a clean and secure connection. When the connection is remade, prevent the onset of corrosion in the future by applying a coat of petroleum jelly or silicone-based grease. Alternatively, at regular intervals, spray on a proprietary ignition sealer or a water-dispersant lubricant.•

3 Fuses and relays – general information

Fuses

1 Most of the fuses are located in the junction box in the engine compartment **(see illustration)**. The junction box is located next

3.1 Fuses and relays are located in the engine compartment on the left-hand side

to the coolant expansion bottle on the left-hand side inner wing panel.

2 To gain access to the fusebox, unclip the junction box lid **(see illustration)**.

3 To remove a fuse, first switch off the circuit concerned (or the ignition), then pull the fuse out of its terminals **(see illustration)**. The wire within the fuse is clearly visible; if the fuse is blown, it will be broken or melted.

4 Always renew a fuse with one of an identical rating; never use a fuse with a different rating from the original, nor substitute anything else. Never renew a fuse more than once without tracing the source of the trouble. The fuse rating is stamped on top of the fuse; note that the fuses are also colour-coded for easy recognition.

5 If a new fuse blows immediately, find the cause before renewing it again; a short to earth as a result of faulty insulation is most likely. Where a fuse protects more than one circuit, try to isolate the defect by switching on each circuit in turn (if possible) until the fuse blows again. Always carry a supply of spare fuses of each relevant rating on the vehicle, a spare of each rating should be clipped into the base of the fusebox.

Relays

6 Most of the relays are located in the junction box in the engine compartment **(see illustration 3.1)**. The junction box is located next to the coolant expansion bottle on the left-hand side inner wing panel.

7 If a circuit or system controlled by a relay develops a fault and the relay is suspect, operate the system; if the relay is functioning, it should be possible to hear it click as it is energised. If this is the case, the fault lies with the components or wiring of the system. If the relay is not being energised, then either the relay is not receiving a main supply or a switching voltage, or the relay itself is faulty. Testing is by the substitution of a known good unit, but be careful; while some relays are identical in appearance and in operation, others look similar but perform different functions.

8 To renew a relay, first ensure that the ignition switch is off. The relay can then simply be pulled out from the socket and the new relay pressed in.

3.2 Unclip the cover to gain access to the fuses and relays

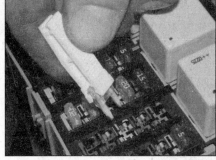

3.3 Removing a fuse from the fusebox

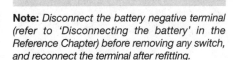

4 Switches – removal and refitting

Note: *Disconnect the battery negative terminal (refer to 'Disconnecting the battery' in the Reference Chapter) before removing any switch, and reconnect the terminal after refitting.*

Ignition switch/ steering column lock

1 Refer to Chapter 10.

Steering column switch

2 With the steering wheel in the straight-ahead position, turn the wheel 90° to the left, then prise the clip to release one side of the upper shroud. Turn the wheel 180° to the right, then release the clip to release the other side of the upper shroud **(see illustrations)**. Withdraw the upper shroud from the steering column.

3 Undo the lower retaining screw and the upper retaining screws, then remove the lower steering column shroud **(see illustrations)**. On models with steering adjustment handle, undo the retaining bolt and remove the handle from the steering column.

4 Depress the retaining clips, and release the relevant switch assembly from the column bracket. Disconnect the wiring connector, and remove the switch assembly from the vehicle **(see illustrations)**. If necessary, remove the opposite switch assembly in the same way.

5 Refitting is a reversal of the removal procedure, making sure the wiring connector is fitted correctly **(see illustration)**.

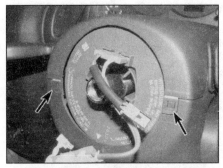

4.2a Release the two retaining clips (arrowed) . . .

4.2b . . . and unclip the upper shroud – steering wheel removed for clarity

4.3a Unscrew the lower shroud retaining screw . . .

4.3b . . . and upper screws (arrowed) and remove shroud from the column

4.4a Depress the retaining clips (arrowed) and slide out the switch . . .

4.4b . . . then release the securing clip (arrowed) and disconnect its wiring connector

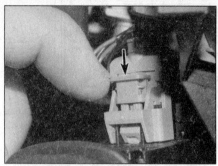

4.5 Make sure the securing clip is locked (arrowed)

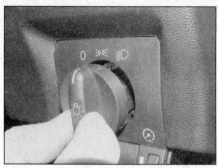

4.6 Pull off the lighting switch knob

4.7a Release the retaining clips . . .

4.7b . . . and withdraw the lighting switch from the facia

4.10 Removing the hazard warning light switch cover

Lighting switch assembly

6 Turn the knob to the headlight 'on' position, and pull the knob out **(see illustration)**.

7 Insert two small screwdrivers through the holes in each side of the turn knob recess to release the retaining clips, then slide the switch assembly out from the facia **(see illustrations)**.

8 Note that the switch assembly cannot be dismantled; if any of its functions are faulty, the complete assembly must be renewed.

9 Refitting is a reversal of the removal procedure.

Hazard warning switch

10 Unclip the front cover from the hazard switch **(see illustration)**.

11 Release the upper and lower retaining clips and withdraw the hazard switch out of facia **(see illustration)**.

12 On refitting, refit the front cover to the switch first **(see illustration)**, then push the complete switch back into position until it clicks into the facia.

Heated rear window/ blower motor switch

13 Remove the heater control panel as described in Chapter 3. Carefully unclip the heated rear window and blower motor switch assembly from the heater control housing **(see illustrations)**

Handbrake warning light switch

14 Unclip the cover from around the handbrake lever **(see illustration)**.

15 Disconnect the wiring connector, then undo the retaining bolt and remove the switch from the handbrake lever mounting bracket **(see illustration)**.

16 Install the new switch, securely tightening its retaining bolt and refit the wiring connector. Refit the cover around the handbrake lever.

4.11 Release the retaining clips (arrowed) and withdraw the switch

4.12 Refit the switch as a complete assembly

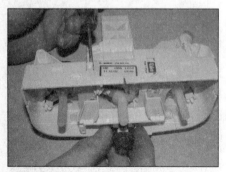

4.13a Release the retaining clips . . .

4.13b . . . and withdraw the switch assembly

14.14 Unclip the cover from around the handbrake lever

4.15 Undo the retaining bolt (arrowed) and remove the handbrake warning light switch from the lever

4.18a Undo the retaining screw (arrowed) . . .

Stop-light switch

17 Refer to Chapter 9.

Courtesy light switch

18 Open the door, then undo the switch retaining screw. Withdraw the switch from the pillar, disconnecting its wiring connector as it becomes accessible **(see illustrations)**. Tie a piece of string to the wiring, to prevent it falling back into the door pillar.
19 Refitting is a reverse of the removal procedure.

Luggage area light switch

20 On Corsa and Corsavan models, the switch is fitted to the bottom of the tailgate. On Combo Van models, the switch is fitted to the right-hand side of the vehicle body, on the outside edge of the rear door.
21 Undo the retaining screw, then withdraw the switch and disconnect it from its wiring connector **(see illustration)**. Tie a piece of string to the wiring, to prevent it falling back into the tailgate/vehicle body (as applicable).
22 Refitting is a reverse of the removal procedure.

Electric window switches

Driver's door

23 Release the retaining clips, taking care not to damage the door trim panel and remove the switch assembly. Disconnect the wiring block connector **(see illustrations)**.
24 Refitting is the reverse of removal,

4.18b . . . and withdraw the switch from the door pillar, then disconnect its wiring connector

ensuring that the wiring is correctly routed inside the door pocket.

Passenger door

25 Carefully release the retaining clips and remove the switch from the panel, then disconnect the switch wiring connector and remove the switch from the vehicle.
26 Refitting is the reverse of removal.

Electric mirror switch

27 Carefully unclip the switch from the door trim panel, then disconnect the switch wiring connector, and remove the switch from the vehicle.
28 Refitting is the reverse of removal.

Electric sunroof switch

29 Carefully prise the sunroof switch out of

4.21 Undo the retaining screw (arrowed) and withdraw the switch

position, and disconnect it from its wiring connector.
30 When refitting, connect the wiring connector, and clip the switch back into position.

Air conditioning system switch

31 The air conditioning system control switch is an integral part of the heating/ventilation control unit, and cannot be removed. Should the switch become faulty, the complete control unit assembly must be renewed (see Chapter 3).

Horn switch

32 Remove the driver's airbag as described in Section 23.
33 Using a small screwdriver, carefully release the relevant switch cover from the switch in the steering wheel **(see illustration)**.

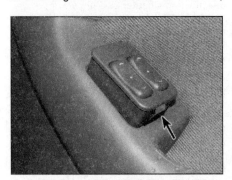

4.23a Release the retaining clips . . .

4.23b . . . and remove the switch assembly, then disconnect its wiring connector

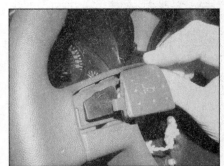

4.33 Unclip the horn switch cover from the steering wheel

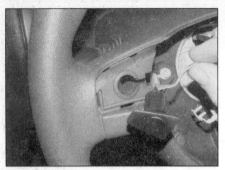

4.34a Withdraw the horn switch . . .

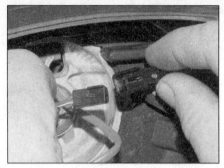

4.34b . . . then disconnect its wiring connector

34 Unclip the switch from the steering wheel, disconnect the wiring connector and remove the switch **(see illustrations)**.
35 Refit the wiring connector and switch and the switch cover, then refit the airbag as described in Section 23.

5 Bulbs (exterior lights) – renewal

General

1 Whenever a bulb is renewed, note the following points:
a) Make sure the switch is in the OFF position, for the respective bulb you are working on.
b) Remember that if the light has just been in use, the bulb may be extremely hot.

c) Always check the bulb contacts and holder, ensuring that there is clean metal-to-metal contact between the bulb and its live(s) and earth. Clean off any corrosion or dirt before fitting a new bulb.
d) Wherever bayonet-type bulbs are fitted, ensure that the live contact(s) bear firmly against the bulb contact.
e) Always ensure that the new bulb is of the correct rating, and that it is completely clean before fitting it; this applies particularly to headlight/foglight bulbs (see below).

Headlight

Dipped beam

2 Working in the engine compartment, twist the cover and remove the cover, complete with bulb, from the light unit **(see illustration)**. Note that if the right-hand bulb is being renewed, it will be necessary to unclip the

intake duct from the air cleaner housing to improve access **(see illustration)**.
3 Unclip and release the bulb from the cover **(see illustration)**. When handling the new bulb, use a tissue or clean cloth to avoid touching the glass with the fingers; moisture and grease from the skin can cause blackening and rapid failure of this type of bulb. If the glass is accidentally touched, wipe it clean using methylated spirit.
4 Install the new bulb, ensuring that it is located in the cover correctly.
5 Refit the cover to the rear of the light unit.

Main beam

6 Working in the engine compartment, twist the cover and remove from the light unit **(see illustration)**.
7 Disconnect the wiring connector from the bulb **(see illustration)**.
8 Unclip and withdraw the bulb from the rear of the light unit **(see illustration)**.
9 When handling the new bulb, use a tissue or clean cloth to avoid touching the glass with the fingers; moisture and grease from the skin can cause blackening and rapid failure of this type of bulb. If the glass is accidentally touched, wipe it clean using methylated spirit.
10 Install the new bulb, ensuring that its locating tabs are correctly located in the light cut-outs and reconnect the wiring connector.
11 Refit the dust cover to the rear of the unit.

Front sidelight

12 Working in the engine compartment, twist the cover to release it from the rear of the headlight unit **(see illustration 5.6)**. Note that

5.2a Twist the cover complete with bulb to release it from the light unit

5.2b To improve access to the right-hand headlight unit remove the air intake duct

5.3 Unclip and release the bulb from the cover

5.6 Remove the cover from the rear of the headlight . . .

5.7 . . . disconnect the wiring connector . . .

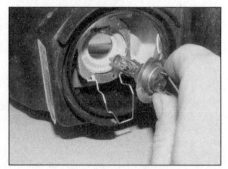

5.8 . . . release the retaining clip and withdraw the headlight bulb

5.13a Remove the sidelight bulbholder from the headlight unit . . .

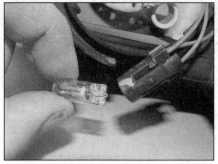

5.13b . . . and withdraw the capless bulb

5.15 Release the front indicator bulb . . .

5.16 . . . it is a bayonet fit in its holder

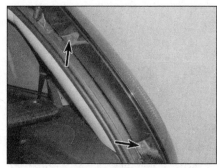

5.27 Remove the two retaining screws (arrowed) . . .

5.28 . . . disconnect the wiring block connector . . .

if the right-hand bulb is being renewed, it will be necessary to unclip the intake duct from the air cleaner housing to improve access.

13 Withdraw the sidelight holder from the rear of the light unit. The bulb is of the capless (push-fit) type, and can be removed by simply pulling it out of the bulbholder **(see illustrations)**.

14 Refitting is the reverse of the removal procedure, ensuring that the bulbholder is securely clipped into position.

Front indicator

15 Working in the engine compartment, twist the bulbholder anti-clockwise, and remove it from the rear of the headlight unit **(see illustration)**. Note that if the right-hand bulb is being renewed, it will be necessary to unclip the intake duct from the air cleaner housing to improve access.

16 The bulb is a bayonet fit in the holder, and can be removed by pressing in and twisting in an anti-clockwise direction **(see illustration)**.

17 Refitting is a reverse of the removal procedure.

Indicator side repeater

18 Carefully prise the rear edge of the indicator side repeater light out from the wing, if necessary using a suitable plastic wedge, taking great care not damage the painted finish of the wing.

19 Withdraw the light unit from the wing, and pull the bulbholder out of the light unit. The bulb is of the capless (push-fit) type, and can be removed by simply pulling it out of the bulbholder.

20 Refitting is a reverse of the removal procedure.

Front foglight

21 If necessary, to improve access to the rear of the foglight, firmly apply the handbrake, then jack up the front of the car and support it securely on axle stands (see *Jacking and vehicle support*).

22 Twist the cover and free it from the foglight, disconnect the wiring connector from the foglight bulb.

23 Release the spring clip and withdraw the foglight bulb from the light unit.

24 When handling the new bulb, use a tissue or clean cloth to avoid touching the glass with the fingers; moisture and grease from the skin can cause blackening and rapid failure of this type of bulb. If the glass is accidentally touched, wipe it clean using methylated spirit.

25 Insert the new bulb, making sure it is

correctly located, and secure it in position with the spring clip.

26 Connect the bulb wire to the terminal, then refit the cover to the rear of the unit, and lower the vehicle to the ground (where applicable).

Rear light cluster

Corsa and Corsavan models

27 Open the tailgate and remove the two retaining screws from the rear light unit **(see illustration)**.

28 Disconnect the wiring block connector from the rear of the light unit **(see illustration)**.

29 Undo the four retaining screws and remove the bulbholder from the rear of the light unit **(see illustration)**.

30 The relevant bulb can then be renewed; all bulbs have a bayonet fitting **(see illustration)**.

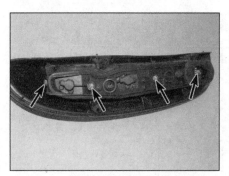

5.29 . . . undo the four retaining screws and remove the bulbholder . . .

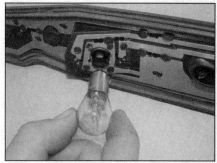

5.30 . . . then withdraw the relevant bulb

5.32 Open the trim panel flap . . .

5.33a . . . disconnect the wiring block connector . . .

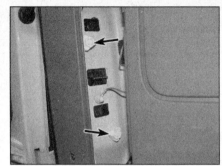

5.33b . . . undo the two retaining nuts . . .

Note that the stop/tail-light bulb has offset locating pins, to prevent it being installed incorrectly.

31 Refitting is the reverse of the removal sequence, ensuring that the light unit locates securely into position.

Combo Van models

32 From inside the vehicle luggage compartment, depress the retaining catches, and open the trim panel flap to gain access to the rear of the light unit (see illustration).

33 Undo the two rear light cluster retaining nuts, disconnect the wiring connector and free the rear light unit from the vehicle (see illustrations).

34 Release the bulbholder from the rear of the light unit, then the relevant bulb can then

be renewed; all bulbs have a bayonet fitting (see illustrations). Note that the stop/tail-light bulb has offset locating pins, to prevent it being installed incorrectly.

35 Refitting is the reverse of the removal sequence, ensuring that the bulbholder is securely clipped into position.

Number plate light

Corsa and Corsavan models

36 Using a small flat-bladed screwdriver, carefully prise the light out from the rear bumper.

37 Twist the bulbholder to remove it from the light unit, and remove the bulb.

38 Refitting is a reverse of the removal procedure.

Combo Van models

39 Undo the two retaining screws, then unclip the light unit from the rear trim panel (see illustration).

40 The bulb is a festoon type which can be removed by unclipping it from the contact springs (see illustrations).

41 Refitting is a reverse of the removal procedure.

High-level stop-light

42 The high-level stop-light bulbs are of the LED (light emitting diode) type and cannot be individually renewed. Remove the complete light unit as described in Section 7.

5.33c . . . and withdraw the light unit from the vehicle

5.34a Press the clips together to release the bulbholder from the light unit . . .

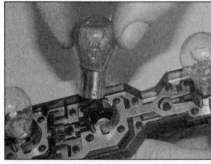

5.34b . . . then withdraw the relevant bulb

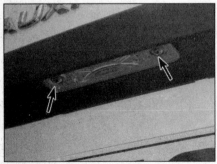

5.39 Undo the two retaining screws . . .

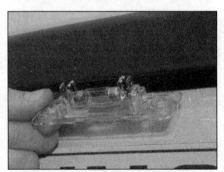

5.40a . . . withdraw the light unit . . .

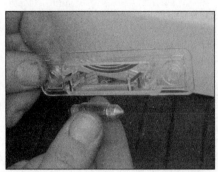

5.40b . . . and release the festoon bulb

6.2a Carefully prise the courtesy light unit out of position . . .

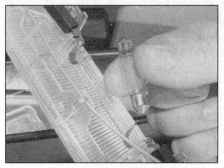

6.2b . . . and release the festoon bulb from its wiring contacts

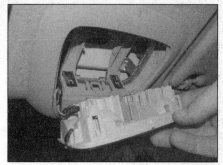

6.4 Release the interior light unit from the surround trim

6 Bulbs (interior lights) – renewal

General

1 Refer to Section 5, paragraph 1.

Front courtesy light

2 Using a suitable screwdriver, carefully prise the light unit out of position, and release the bulb from the light unit contacts **(see illustrations)**.

3 Install the new bulb, ensuring that it is securely held in position by the contacts, and clip the light unit back into position.

Courtesy light with map reading lights

4 Using a small flat-bladed screwdriver, carefully prise the light unit out from its surround. Disconnect the wiring connector, and remove the light **(see illustration)**.

5 Unclip the lens from the light unit, and release the bulb from its contacts **(see illustrations)**.

6 Install the new bulb, ensuring that it is securely held in position by the contacts, and clip the lens back into position.

7 Connect the wiring connector, and clip the light back into position in the surround.

Luggage compartment light

8 Using a suitable screwdriver, carefully prise the light unit out of position, and release the

bulb from the light unit contacts **(see illustration)**.

9 Install the new bulb, ensuring that it is securely held in position by the contacts, and clip the light unit back into position.

Instrument illumination/ warning lights

10 Remove the instrument panel as described in Section 9.

11 Twist the relevant bulbholder anti-clockwise, and withdraw it from the rear of the panel **(see illustration)**.

12 All bulbs are integral with their holders. Be very careful to ensure that the new bulbs are of the correct rating, the same as those removed; this is especially important in the case of the ignition/no-charge warning light.

13 Refit the bulbholder to the rear of the instrument panel, then refit the instrument panel as described in Section 9.

Clock/multi-function display illumination

14 Remove the clock/multi-function display unit as described in Section 10.

15 Twist the bulbholder anti-clockwise, and withdraw it from the rear of the clock **(see illustrations)**. The bulb is integral with its holder.

16 Refit the bulbholder to the rear of the unit, then refit the unit as described in Section 10.

6.5a Unclip the lens from the light unit . . .

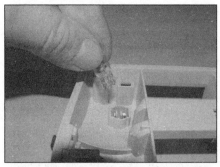

6.5b . . . and remove the capless bulb

6.8a Unclip the luggage compartment light unit . . .

6.8b . . . and remove the festoon bulb

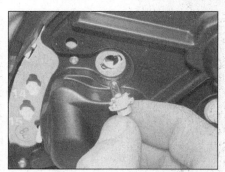

6.11 Removing an instrument panel illumination/warning light bulb

6.15a Use a screwdriver to twist the bulbholder . . .

6.15b . . . and remove the clock/multi-function display illumination bulb

6.17 Unclip the cigarette lighter/switch panel from the centre console

6.22a Unclip the cover from the switch assembly . . .

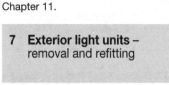

6.22b . . . and remove the illumination bulbs

Cigarette lighter/ashtray illumination

17 Unclip the cigarette lighter surround from the centre console **(see illustration)**.
18 Slide the illumination bulbholder out of the panel, and renew the bulb. The bulbs is of the capless (push-fit) type; pull the old bulb out of the holder, and press the new one into position.
19 Slide the illumination bulbholder back into position, and refit the trim by reversing the removal procedure.

Heater control panel illumination

20 Withdraw the heater control panel as described in Chapter 3, so that access to the rear of the panel can be gained. Note there is no need to remove the panel completely; the control cables can be left attached.
21 Carefully unclip the heated rear window and blower motor switch assembly from the

heater control housing as described in Section 4, paragraph 13.
22 Unclip the bulbholder cover. The bulbs are of the capless (push-fit) type; pull the relevant bulb out of the holder, and press the new one into position **(see illustrations)**.
23 Refit the bulbholder, and install the control panel as described in Chapter 3.

Glovebox light

24 Open the glovebox. Using a small flat-bladed screwdriver, carefully prise the light unit out of position, then release the bulb from its contacts. Install the new bulb, ensuring it is securely held in position by the contacts, and clip the light unit back into position.

Switch illumination

25 All the switches are fitted with illumination bulbs; some are also fitted with a bulb to show when the circuit concerned is operating.

These bulbs are an integral part of the switch assembly, and cannot be obtained separately.

Automatic transmission selector illumination

26 Remove the centre console as described in Chapter 11.
27 Unclip the selector lever cover from the selector housing and lift it upwards.
28 Withdraw the relevant bulbholder from the underside of the selector lever cover and release the bulb from the bulbholder.
29 Install the new bulb, refit the bulbholder and clip the selector lever cover back into position.
30 Refit the centre console as described in Chapter 11.

7 Exterior light units – removal and refitting

Note: *Disconnect the battery negative terminal (refer to 'Disconnecting the battery' in the Reference Chapter) before removing any light unit, and reconnect the terminal after refitting.*

Headlight

1 Remove the front bumper as described in Section 6 of Chapter 11.
2 Disconnect the wiring connectors from rear of the headlight unit, then undo the three retaining bolts and remove the headlight unit from the vehicle **(see illustrations)**.
3 On models with a headlight beam adjust-

7.2a Disconnect the wiring connector . . .

7.2b . . . then undo the upper retaining bolts (arrowed) . . .

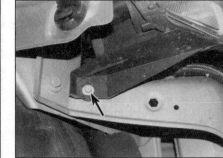

7.2c . . . and the lower retaining bolt (arrowed)

7.3a unclip the cover from the rear of the light unit . . .

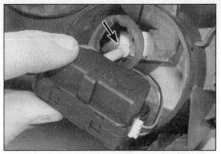

7.3b . . . then rotate the adjustment motor clockwise and unclip the balljoint (arrowed) . . .

7.3c . . . and disconnect the wiring connector

ment system, if necessary, unclip the cover then rotate the adjustment motor clockwise to free the motor from the rear of the headlight unit. Unclip the balljoint from the rear of the light reflector and disconnect the wiring connector (**see illustrations**).

4 On refitting, align the motor balljoint with the light unit socket, and clip it into position. Engage the motor assembly with the light, and twist it anti-clockwise to secure it in position.

5 Refitting is a reverse of the removal procedure. On completion, check the headlight beam alignment using the information given in Section 8.

Front indicator light

6 The front direction indicator lights are integral with the headlight units. Removal and refitting is as described above.

Indicator side repeater light

7 Carefully prise the rear edge of the indicator side repeater light out from the wing, if necessary using a suitable plastic wedge, taking great care not damage the painted finish of the wing.

8 Withdraw the light unit from the wing, and disconnect its wiring connector. Tie a piece of string to the wiring, to prevent it falling back into the wing.

9 On refitting, connect the wiring connector, and clip the light unit back into position.

Front foglight

10 Remove the front bumper as described in Section 6 of Chapter 11.

11 Disconnect the wiring connector, then undo the three foglight retaining screws and remove the light unit from the bumper.

12 Refit the light unit to the bumper, and securely tighten its retaining screws.

13 Secure the front bumper in position, then adjust the foglight aim through the hole in the bumper to the side of the foglight.

Rear light cluster

Corsa and Corsavan models

14 Open the tailgate and remove the two retaining screws from the rear light unit (**see illustration 5.27**).

15 Disconnect the wiring block connector from the rear of the light unit (**see illustration 5.28**).

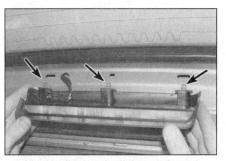

7.25a Unclipping the light unit from the rear tailgate – Corsa and Corsavan models . . .

16 Refitting is the reverse of the removal sequence, ensuring that the light unit locates securely into position.

Combo Van models

17 From inside the vehicle luggage compartment, depress the retaining catches, and open the trim panel flap to gain access to the rear of the light unit (**see illustration 5.32**).

18 Undo the two rear light cluster retaining nuts, disconnect the wiring connector and free the rear light unit from the vehicle (**see illustrations 5.33a, 5.33b and 5.33c**).

19 Refitting is the reverse of the removal sequence, ensuring that the light unit locates securely into position.

Number plate light

Corsa and Corsavan models

20 Using a small flat-bladed screwdriver, carefully prise the light out from the rear

7.26a Disconnecting the wiring connector – Corsa and Corsavan models . . .

bumper and disconnect it from the wiring connectors.

21 Refitting is a reversal of removal.

Combo Van models

22 Undo the two retaining screws, then unclip the light unit from the rear trim panel (**see illustration 5.40a**).

23 Refitting is a reversal of removal.

High-level stop-light

24 Open the tailgate or rear doors as applicable.

25 Unclip the light unit from the rear tailgate/door door panel and withdraw it from its location (**see illustrations**).

26 Release the wiring harness, disconnect the wiring connector and remove the light unit (**see illustrations**).

27 Refitting is a reversal of removal.

7.25b . . . and the rear door panel on Combo Van models

7.26b . . . and on Combo Van models

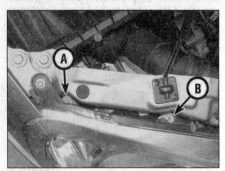

8.2 Adjust the headlight vertical beam using adjuster screw (A) and the headlight horizontal beam using adjuster screw (B)

8 Headlight beam alignment – general information

1 Accurate adjustment of the headlight beam is only possible using optical beam-setting equipment, and this work should therefore be carried out by a Vauxhall dealer or suitably-equipped workshop.
2 For reference, the headlights can be adjusted using the adjuster assemblies fitted to the top of each light unit. The inner adjuster, alters the horizontal position of the beam. The outer adjuster alters the vertical aim of the beam **(see illustration)**.
3 Some models have an electrically-operated headlight beam adjustment system, controlled via a switch in the facia. The recommended settings are as follows.

Corsa and Corsavan with rear seats

0 Front seat(s) occupied
1 All seats occupied
2 All seats occupied, and load in luggage compartment
3 Driver's seat occupied and load in the luggage compartment

Combo Van and Corsavan without rear seats

0 Seat(s) occupied
1 Seats occupied and load compartment approximately half-loaded
2 Seats occupied and luggage compartment fully-loaded
3 Driver's seat only occupied and luggage compartment fully-loaded

Note: When adjusting the headlight aim, ensure that the switch is set to position 0.

9 Instrument panel – removal and refitting

Note: The instrument panel is a complete assembly, and no dismantling of the instrument panel is possible. The only additional work possible is the renewal of a bulb (see Section 6).

Removal

1 Disconnect the battery negative terminal (refer to *Disconnecting the battery* in the Reference Chapter).
2 Unclip the driver's side lower storage tray, then undo the retaining screws and remove the driver's side lower trim panels **(see illustration)**
3 With the steering wheel in the straight-ahead position, turn the wheel 90° to the left, then prise the clip to release one side of the upper shroud. Turn the wheel 180° to the right, then release the clip to release the other side of the upper shroud **(see illustration)**. Withdraw the upper shroud from the steering column.
4 Undo the lower retaining screw and the upper retaining screws, then remove the lower steering column shroud. On models with steering adjustment handle, undo the retaining bolt and remove the handle from the steering column.
5 Undo the three retaining screws, and remove the instrument panel shroud from the facia **(see illustrations)**.
6 Unscrew the two retaining screws from the base of the instrument panel **(see illustration)**.
7 Depress the panel upper retaining clip, and withdraw the instrument panel from the facia. The wiring connector disconnects automatically as the panel is removed **(see illustration)**.

Refitting

8 Clip the instrument panel back into position, aligning it with its wiring connector, and secure it in position with the two retaining screws.
9 Refit the instrument panel shroud, and securely tighten its retaining screws.
10 Install the upper and lower steering column shrouds, and securely tighten all the

9.2 Undo the retaining screws and remove the driver's side lower trim panels

9.3 Release the two retaining clips (arrowed) and unclip the upper shroud – steering wheel removed for clarity

9.5a Unscrew the lower retaining screws (arrowed) . . .

9.5b . . . and the upper retaining screw (arrowed)

9.6 Unscrew the instrument panel lower retaining screws (arrowed)

9.7 Release the upper securing clip (arrowed) and remove the instrument panel

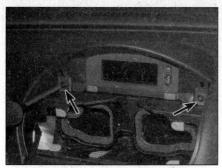

10.3a Undo the retaining screws (arrowed) . . .

10.3b . . . and remove the multi-function display unit

10.4 Release the securing clip (arrowed), then disconnect the wiring connector

retaining screws. Fit the rubber seal to the ignition switch/lock and the trim caps to the upper screws.

11 Refit the driver's side lower trim panels and storage tray.

12 Reconnect the battery, and check the operation of the panel warning lights to ensure that they are functioning correctly.

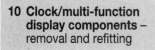

10 Clock/multi-function display components – removal and refitting

Removal

1 Disconnect the battery negative terminal (refer to *Disconnecting the battery* in the Reference Chapter).

2 Remove the central air vents as described in Section 10 of Chapter 3.

3 Undo the two retaining screws located in the vent apertures, then withdraw the clock/multi-function display from the facia **(see illustrations)**.

4 Release the securing clip and disconnect the wiring connector, then remove the unit from the vehicle **(see illustration)**.

Refitting

5 Reconnect the wiring connector, then manoeuvre the unit back into position.

6 Securely tighten the screws, and install the vents as described in Chapter 3.

7 Reconnect the battery negative terminal, then reset the clock and enter the radio security code.

11 Cigarette lighter – removal and refitting

Removal

1 Unclip the cigarette lighter surround from the centre console.

2 Disconnect the wiring connector from the rear of the cigarette lighter **(see illustration)**.

3 Release the retaining tangs and push out the metal insert, then remove the plastic outer section of the lighter.

Refitting

4 Refitting is a reversal of the removal procedure.

12 Horn – removal and refitting

Removal

1 Undo the retaining screws and remove the inner wheel arch liner from the right-hand front wing.

2 Undo the retaining nut/bolt and remove the horn, disconnecting its wiring connectors as they become accessible **(see illustration)**.

Refitting

3 Refitting is the reverse of removal.

13 Wiper arm – removal and refitting

Removal

1 Operate the wiper motor, then switch it off so that the wiper arm returns to the at-rest (parked) position.

> **HAYNES HiNT** *Stick a piece of masking tape along the edge of the wiper blade, to use as an alignment aid on refitting.*

2 Unclip the wiper arm spindle nut cover, then slacken and remove the spindle nut **(see illustration)**.

3 Lift the blade off the glass, and pull the wiper arm off its spindle. If necessary, the arm can be levered off the spindle using a suitable flat-bladed screwdriver. **Note:** *If both windscreen wiper arms are to be removed at the same time, mark them for identification. The arms are not interchangeable; the passenger-side wiper arm is longer than the driver's-side arm, and its shaft is also cranked slightly.*

Refitting

4 Ensure that the wiper arm and spindle splines are clean and dry, then refit the arm to the spindle, aligning the wiper blade with the tape fitted on removal. Refit the spindle nut, tightening it securely, and clip the nut cover back in position.

11.2 Disconnecting the wiring connector from the cigarette lighter

12.2 Undo the retaining nut (arrowed) and remove the horn

13.2 Unclip the cover and remove the spindle nut (arrowed)

14.3a Peel the seal off the engine compartment bulkhead . . .

14.3b . . . then unclip the cover from the battery cables

14.4 Unclipping the battery cables from the water deflector

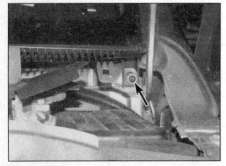

14.5a Undo the retaining screw (arrowed) from the left-hand end . . .

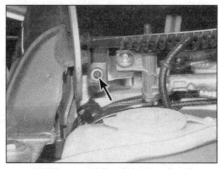

14.5b . . . and the right-hand end (arrowed) . . .

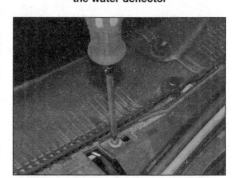

14.5c . . . then the centre of the deflector

14 Windscreen wiper motor and linkage – removal and refitting

Removal

1 Disconnect the battery negative terminal (refer to *Disconnecting the battery* in the Reference Chapter).

2 Remove the wiper arms as described in the previous Section.

3 Peel the bonnet seal off the engine compartment bulkhead, then unclip the cover from the battery cables **(see illustrations)**.

4 Unclip the battery cables from the water deflector, and move them to one side **(see illustration)**.

5 Undo the three retaining screws (one at each end and one in the middle **(see illustrations)**. Remove both halves of the water deflector trim, release the trim from the engine compartment bulkhead and wiper spindles. Disconnect the washer pipe for the washer jets as the trim is removed from the vehicle.

6 Remove the large rubber grommets from each wiper spindle **(see illustration)**.

7 Disconnect the wiring connector from the wiper motor. Undo the two retaining bolts, and remove the wiper motor and linkage assembly out from the vehicle **(see illustrations)**.

8 If necessary, mark the relative positions of the motor shaft and linkage arm, then unscrew the retaining nut from the motor spindle. Free the wiper linkage from the

spindle, then remove the three motor retaining bolts, and separate the motor and linkage **(see illustrations)**. **Note:** *It is not necessary to remove the linkage assembly from the vehicle to remove the motor.*

Refitting

9 Where necessary, assemble the motor and linkage, and securely tighten the motor retaining bolts. Locate the linkage arm on the motor spindle, aligning the marks made prior

14.6 Removing the large rubber grommet from the wiper spindle

14.7a Disconnect the wiring connector . . .

14.7b . . . undo the two retaining bolts (arrowed) and remove the wiper assembly

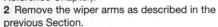
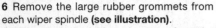
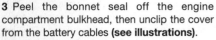

14.8a Undo the retaining nut and free the wiper linkage . . .

14.8b . . . then remove the three motor retaining bolts (arrowed)

15.1 Using a puller on the wiper arm to release it from the spindle

15.2 Undo the retaining screws and unclip the trim panel

to removal, and securely tighten its retaining nut.

10 Manoeuvre the motor assembly back into position in the vehicle. Refit the retaining bolts, and tighten them to the specified torque setting.

11 Reconnect the wiper motor wiring connector and refit the large rubber grommets to the wiper spindles.

12 Refit the water deflector, making sure it is correctly located on the bulkhead and wiper spindles, install both halves of the trim, and securely tighten the retaining screws.

13 Refit the battery cables and cover into position then refit the bonnet seal to the engine compartment bulkhead.

14 Install both the wiper arms as described in Section 13, and reconnect the battery negative terminal.

15.3 Disconnect the wiper motor wiring . . .

4 Slacken and remove the wiper motor mounting bolts and remove the wiper motor. Where applicable, recover any spacers from the motor mounting bracket, and slide the inner mounting rubber off the motor spindle **(see illustration)**.

5 Examine the motor mounting rubbers for signs of damage or deterioration, and renew as necessary.

15.4 . . . and undo the retaining bolts (arrowed)

that it is securely retained by all of its screws and clips.

10 Refit the wiper arm as described in Section 13.

15 Tailgate wiper motor – removal and refitting

Removal

1 Remove the wiper arm as described in Section 13. It may be necessary to use a puller on the wiper arm if it is tight on the wiper motor spindle **(see illustration)**.

2 Open the tailgate, undo the four retaining screws then unclip the inner trim panel from the tailgate **(see illustration)**.

3 Disconnect the wiper motor wiring connector, and release the wiring from any relevant retaining clips **(see illustration)**.

Refitting

6 Where applicable, slide the inner mounting rubber onto the motor spindle, and ensure that any rubbers are correctly fitted to the motor mountings.

7 Refit the wiper motor mounting bolts and tighten them securely.

8 Reconnect the wiper motor wiring connector.

9 Refit the trim panel to the tailgate, ensuring

16 Windscreen/tailgate washer system components – removal and refitting

Washer system reservoir

1 Slide the fluid reservoir upwards to release it from its retaining bracket **(see illustration)**.

2 Disconnect the wiring connector from the washer pump, then disconnect the hose(s) from the base of the pump and remove the reservoir from the vehicle **(see illustrations)**. Wash off any spilt fluid with cold water.

3 Refitting is the reverse of removal, ensuring that the washer hose(s) are securely connected.

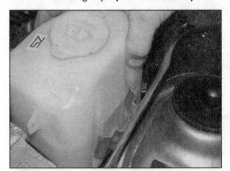

16.1 Slide upwards to release from its retaining bracket

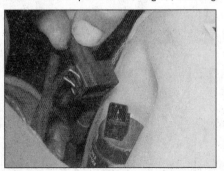

16.2a Disconnect the wiring connector . . .

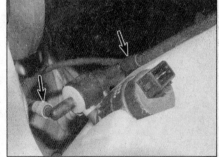

16.2b . . . and washer hoses (arrowed)

16.8a Using a screwdriver to release the retaining clip . . .

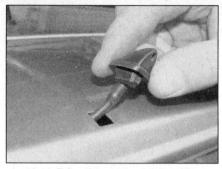

16.8b . . . then withdraw the washer jet

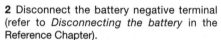

16.11 Prise the washer jet from the tailgate

Washer pump

4 Remove the washer reservoir as described above.

5 Tip out the contents of the reservoir, then carefully ease the pump out from the reservoir and recover its sealing grommet.

6 Refitting is the reverse of removal, using a new sealing grommet if the original one shows signs of damage or deterioration.

Windscreen washer jets

7 Remove the water deflector trim panels as described in paragraphs 3 to 5 of Section 14.

8 Carefully prise the nozzle from the rear of the trim panel, taking great care not to damage the trim **(see illustration)**.

9 Disconnect the nozzle from its fluid hose, and remove it from the vehicle.

10 On refitting, securely connect the nozzle to the hose, and clip it into position in the trim

17.3 Unscrew the four grub screws . . .

17.4 . . . insert the tools and withdraw the radio/cassette player out of the facia

panel. Check the operation of the jet. If necessary, adjust the nozzle using a pin, aiming the spray to a point slightly above the centre of the swept area.

Tailgate washer jet

11 Carefully prise the washer jet out of the top of the tailgate/spoiler **(see illustration)**, and disconnect it from its supply pipe. Whilst the jet is removed, tie a piece of string to the supply pipe, to ensure that it does not fall back into the tailgate.

12 When refitting, ensure that the jet is clipped securely in position. Check the operation of the jet. If necessary, adjust the nozzle using a pin, aiming the spray to a point slightly above the centre of the swept area.

17 Radio/cassette player – removal and refitting

Note: *The following removal and refitting procedure is for the range of radio/cassette units which Vauxhall fit as standard equipment. Removal and refitting procedures of non-standard units may differ slightly.*

Removal

1 All the radio/cassette players fitted by Vauxhall have DIN standard fixings. Two special tools, obtainable from most car accessory shops, are required for removal. Alternatively, suitable tools can be fabricated from 3 mm diameter wire, such as welding rod.

2 Disconnect the battery negative terminal (refer to *Disconnecting the battery* in the Reference Chapter).

3 Unscrew the four grub screws from the corners of the radio/cassette player, using a suitable Allen key **(see illustration)**.

4 Insert the tools into the holes exposed by removal of the grub screws, and push them until they snap into place. The radio/cassette player can then be slid out of the facia **(see illustration)**.

Refitting

5 To refit the radio/cassette player, simply push the unit into the facia until the retaining lugs snap into place, then refit the grub screws. On completion, reconnect the battery and enter the radio security code, where applicable.

18 Speakers – removal and refitting

Front small (treble) speaker

1 Carefully unclip the exterior mirror inner trim panel from the door. On models with manually-operated mirrors, it will be necessary to pull the knob off the adjusting lever in order to remove the panel **(see illustration)**.

2 Unclip the speaker from the handle, disconnecting its wiring connectors as they become accessible **(see illustration)**.

3 Refitting is the reverse of removal.

18.1 Unclipping the exterior mirror inner trim panel from the door

18.2 Disconnect the wiring connector(s)

18.5a Undo the retaining screws (arrowed) . . .

18.5b . . . remove the speaker and disconnect the wiring connector

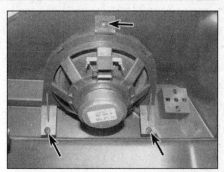

18.10 Undo the retaining screws (arrowed) and remove the speaker

Front large (bass) speaker

4 Remove the front door inner trim panel as described in Section 12 of Chapter 11.
5 Undo the retaining screws, then free the speaker from the door. Disconnect the wiring connectors and remove the speaker (**see illustrations**).
6 Refitting is the reverse of removal.

Rear speaker

7 Remove the rear parcel shelf. If the left speaker is to be removed, remove the interior light unit from the trim panel as described in Section 6.
8 Remove the rear trim panels as described in Section 26 of Chapter 11.
9 Turn the panel around to gain access to the speaker and disconnect the speaker wiring connector. Note that it is not necessary to detach the seat belt completely unless the trim panel is to be removed.

10 Undo the three retaining screws, and remove the speaker from the trim panel (**see illustration**).
11 Refitting is a reverse of the removal procedure. Make sure that the trim panel is securely retained by all the relevant clips and screws. If the left trim panel is being installed, do not forget to feed the interior light wiring through the trim panel aperture before fastening the panel in position.

---

19 Radio aerial – removal and refitting

Corsa and Corsavan

Removal

1 Open the tailgate, then prise out the trim clips and release the rear of the headlining from

the roof. Carefully peel the headlining back until access is gained to the aerial retaining nut and wiring connectors (**see illustrations**).
2 Disconnect wiring connector, then undo the retaining nut and remove the aerial from the roof (**see illustrations**).

Refitting

3 Locate the aerial in roof hole and refit its retaining nut, tightening it securely. Reconnect the wiring connectors, then clip the headlining back into position

Combo Van

Removal

4 Unclip and remove the front interior light from the headlining trim surround (**see illustration**).
5 Trace the wiring from the aerial then disconnect wiring connector. Undo the retaining nut and remove the aerial from the roof (**see illustration**).

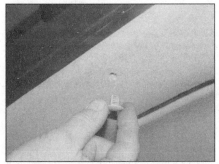

19.1a Prise out the trim clips . . .

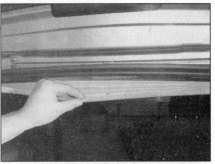

19.1b . . . and release the headlining

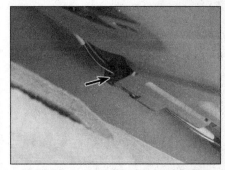

19.2a Disconnect the wiring connector (arrowed) . . .

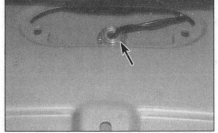

19.2b . . . and undo the retaining nut (arrowed)

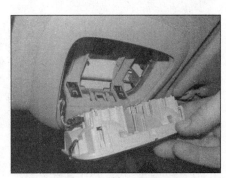

19.4 Unclip the interior light from the surround

19.5 Disconnect the wiring connector and undo the retaining nut (arrowed)

Refitting

6 Locate the aerial in roof hole and refit its retaining nut, tightening it securely. Reconnect the wiring connectors, then clip the interior light back into position.

20 Anti-theft alarm system – general information

Note: *This information is applicable only to the anti-theft alarm system fitted by Vauxhall as standard equipment.*

1 Some models in the range are fitted with an anti-theft alarm system as standard equipment. The alarm is automatically armed and disarmed when the deadlocks are operated using the driver's door lock. The alarm has switches on all the doors (including the tailgate), the bonnet, the radio/cassette player and the ignition and starter circuits. If the tailgate, bonnet or any of the doors are opened whilst the alarm is set, the alarm horn will sound and the hazard warning lights will flash. The alarm also has an immobiliser function which makes the ignition and starter circuits inoperable whilst the alarm is triggered.

2 The alarm system performs a self-test every time it is switched on; this test takes approximately 10 seconds. During the self-test, the LED (light emitting diode) in the hazard warning light switch will come on. If the LED flashes, then either the tailgate, bonnet or one of the doors is open, or there is a fault in the circuit. After the initial 10-second period, the LED will flash to indicate that the alarm is switched on. On unlocking the driver's door lock, the LED will illuminate for approximately 1 second, then go out, indicating that the alarm has been switched off.

3 With the alarm set, if the tailgate is unlocked, the tailgate switch sensing will automatically be switched off, but the door and bonnet switches will still be active. Once the tailgate is shut and locked again, the tailgate switch sensing will be switched back on after approximately 10 seconds.

4 Should the alarm system develop a fault, the vehicle should be taken to a Vauxhall dealer for examination.

21 Heated front seat components – general information

On models with heated front seats, a heater mat is fitted to the both the seat back and seat cushion. Renewal of either heater mat involves peeling back the upholstery, removing the old mat, sticking the new mat in position and then refitting the upholstery.

Note that upholstery removal and refitting requires considerable skill and experience if it is to be carried out successfully, and is therefore best entrusted to your Vauxhall dealer. In practice, it will be very difficult for the home mechanic to carry out the job without ruining the upholstery.

22 Airbag system – general information and precautions

General information

A driver's airbag is fitted as standard equipment on all models. The airbag is fitted in the steering wheel centre pad. Additionally, a passenger's airbag located in the facia, and side airbags located in the front seats are optionally available.

The system is armed only when the ignition is switched on, however, a reserve power source maintains a power supply to the system in the event of a break in the main electrical supply. The steering wheel and facia airbags are activated by a 'g' sensor (deceleration sensor), and controlled by an electronic control unit located under the centre console. The side airbags are activated by severe side impact and operate independently of the main system and of each other. A separate electrical supply, control unit and sensor is provided for each side airbag.

The airbags are inflated by a gas generator, which forces the bag out from its location in the steering wheel, facia or seat back frame.

Precautions

⚠ **Warning: The following precautions must be observed when working on vehicles equipped with an airbag system, to prevent the possibility of personal injury.**

General precautions

The following precautions **must** be observed when carrying out work on a vehicle equipped with an airbag:

a) *Do not disconnect the battery with the engine running.*
b) *Before carrying out any work in the vicinity of the airbag, removal of any of the airbag components, or any welding work on the vehicle, de-activate the system as described in the following sub-Section.*
c) *Do not attempt to test any of the airbag system circuits using test meters or any other test equipment.*
d) *If the airbag warning light comes on, or any fault in the system is suspected, consult a Vauxhall dealer without delay.* **Do not** *attempt to carry out fault diagnosis, or any dismantling of the components.*

Precautions when handling an airbag

a) *Transport the airbag by itself, bag upward.*
b) *Do not put your arms around the airbag.*
c) *Carry the airbag close to the body, bag outward.*
d) *Do not drop the airbag or expose it to impacts.*
e) *Do not attempt to dismantle the airbag unit.*
f) *Do not connect any form of electrical equipment to any part of the airbag circuit.*

Precautions when storing an airbag

a) *Store the unit in a cupboard with the airbag upward.*
b) *Do not expose the airbag to temperatures above 80ºC.*
c) *Do not expose the airbag to flames.*
d) *Do not attempt to dispose of the airbag – consult a Vauxhall dealer.*
e) *Never refit an airbag which is known to be faulty or damaged.*

De-activation of airbag system

The system must be de-activated before carrying out any work on the airbag components or surrounding area:

a) *Switch on the ignition and check the operation of the airbag warning light on the instrument panel. The light should illuminate when the ignition is switched on, then extinguish.*
b) *Switch off the ignition.*
c) *Remove the ignition key.*
d) *Switch off all electrical equipment.*
e) *Disconnect the battery negative terminal (refer to 'Disconnecting the battery' in the Reference Section of this manual).*
f) *Insulate the battery negative terminal and the end of the battery negative lead to prevent any possibility of contact.*
g) *Wait for at least two minutes before carrying out any further work. Wait at least ten minutes if the airbag warning light did not operate correctly.*

Activation of airbag system

To activate the system on completion of any work, proceed as follows:

a) *Ensure that there are no occupants in the vehicle, and that there are no loose objects around the vicinity of the steering wheel. Close the vehicle doors and windows.*
b) *Ensure that the ignition is switched off then reconnect the battery negative terminal.*
c) *Open the driver's door and switch on the ignition, without reaching in front of the steering wheel. Check that the airbag warning light illuminates briefly then extinguishes.*
d) *Switch off the ignition.*
e) *If the airbag warning light does not operate as described in paragraph c), consult a Vauxhall dealer before driving the vehicle.*

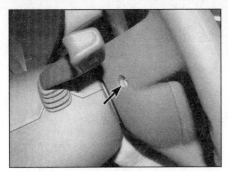

23.2 Undo the two retaining screws (one side arrowed)

23.3a Lift the airbag assembly away from the steering wheel . . .

23.3b . . . release the locking pin (arrowed) and disconnect the wiring connector

23 Airbag system components – removal and refitting

 Warning: Refer to the precautions given in Section 26 before attempting to carry out work on any of the airbag components.

1 De-activate the airbag system as described in the previous Section, then proceed as described under the relevant heading.

Driver's airbag

2 With the steering wheel in the straight-ahead position, undo the two retaining screws from the rear of the steering wheel **(see illustration)**.

3 Carefully lift the airbag assembly away from the steering wheel, release the locking pin and disconnect the wiring connector from the rear of the unit **(see illustrations)**. Note that the airbag must not be knocked or dropped, and should be stored the correct way up, with its padded surface uppermost.

4 Refitting is a reversal of the removal procedure. Make sure the locking pin is secure in the wiring block connector **(see illustration)**, then tighten the airbag retaining screws to the specified torque setting.

Passenger's airbag

5 Disconnect the battery negative terminal (refer to *Disconnecting the battery* in the Reference Chapter).

6 Remove the glovebox as described in Chapter 11, Section 26.

7 Release the locking pin and disconnect the airbag wiring plug from the side of the unit.

8 Undo the screws securing the airbag to the mounting brackets, and withdraw the airbag out through the glovebox aperture. Note that the airbag must not be knocked or dropped, and should be stored the correct way up (as mounted in the vehicle).

9 Refitting is a reversal of the removal procedure. Make sure the locking pin is secure in the wiring block connector, then tighten the airbag retaining screws to the specified torque setting.

Side airbags

10 The side airbags are located internally within the front seat back and no attempt should be made to remove them. Any suspected problems with the side airbag system should be referred to a Vauxhall dealer.

Airbag control unit

11 Remove the centre console as described in Chapter 11.

12 Disconnect the control unit wiring connector, then undo the retaining nuts and remove the control unit from the vehicle **(see illustrations)**. Note the fitted position of the control unit – the arrow on the top of the unit is facing forwards.

13 Refitting is the reverse of removal. If a new control unit is being installed, the vehicle must be taken to a Vauxhall dealer for the control unit to be reprogrammed at the earliest possible opportunity. **Note:** *The airbag system will not be operational until the new control unit is reprogrammed; this will be indicated by the warning light in the instrument panel being illuminated.*

Airbag wiring contact unit

14 Disconnect the battery negative terminal (refer to *Disconnecting the battery* in the Reference Chapter) and wait for 2 minutes.

15 Remove the steering wheel as described in Chapter 10, Section 16.

16 Where necessary, undo the retaining screw and release the steering column adjustment handle from under the steering column.

17 Unclip the upper steering column shroud from the lower shroud, then undo the retaining screws and remove the lower steering column shrouds **(see illustrations)**.

18 Depress the retaining clips, and release the left- and right-hand combination switches from the column. Release the securing clips

23.4 Make sure the locking pin (arrowed) is secure

23.12a Release the locking clip (arrowed) and disconnect the wiring connector . . .

23.12b . . . then undo the retaining nuts (arrowed)

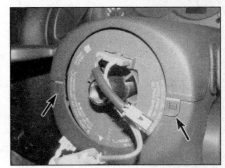

23.17a Release the two retaining clips (arrowed) and unclip the upper shroud

23.17b Undo the lower shroud upper screws (arrowed) . . .

23.17c . . . and the lower retaining screw then unclip the shroud

23.18 Depress the retaining clips (arrowed) and slide out the switch

23.19 Disconnect the wiring connector from the back of the contact unit

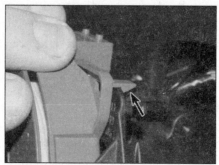

23.20a Release the securing lugs (one arrowed) . . .

23.20b . . . and withdraw the contact unit from the steering column

and disconnect the wiring connectors, then remove the switches from the vehicle **(see illustration)**.

19 Release the retaining clip and disconnect the wiring connector from the contact unit **(see illustration)**.

20 Unclip the four securing lugs and slide the contact unit from the top of the steering column. DO NOT turn the contact unit centre, as it is set in the vehicle straight ahead position for refitting **(see illustrations)**.

21 Refitting is the reverse of removal noting the following points:

  a) If a new contact unit is being installed, remove the transport lock (sticker) before refitting, this locks the contact unit in the centre position ready for refitting.

  b) Press the contact unit on squarely, taking care not to damage the securing lugs

Vauxhall Corsa 2000 to 2003 wiring diagrams

Diagram 1

Key to symbols

Bulb	
Switch	
Multiple contact switch (ganged)	
Fuse/fusible link and current rating	F5 30A
Resistor	
Variable resistor	
Connecting wires	
Plug and socket contact	
Item no.	2
Pump/motor	M
Earth point and location	E22
Gauge/meter	
Diode	
Wire splice or soldered joint	
Solenoid actuator	
Light emitting diode (LED)	
Wire colour (brown with black tracer)	Br/Sw
Screened cable	

Dashed outline denotes part of a larger item, containing in this case an electronic or solid state device.

6 - unspecified connector pin 6.

X54/9 - connector X54, pin 9.

Earth locations

E1	Engine	E7	Steering column
E2	Left bulkhead	E8	Right bulkhead
E3	Tunnel	E9	Body rear right
E4	Left engine earth	E10	Chassis
E5	Right engine earth	E11	Tailgate
E6	Body rear left	E12	Drivers 'A' pillar

Key to circuits

Diagram 1	Information for wiring diagrams
Diagram 2	Starting, charging, airbag and radio
Diagram 3	Engine management system Motronic Z10XE
Diagram 4	ABS, cigarette lighter and Motronic Z10XE continued
Diagram 5	Engine management system Motronic Z12XE
Diagram 6	Heating, heater blower, horn and Motronic Z12XE continued
Diagram 7	Engine management system Multec Z14XE
Diagram 8	Power steering, speed sensor (without ABS) and Multec Z14XE continued
Diagram 9	Engine management Diesel
Diagram 10	Easytronic transmission, engine cooling Diesel and Z14XE with A/C, sunroof and seat heating
Diagram 11	Automatic transmission, engine cooling Motronic Z10XE and Z12XE with A/C, engine cooling Multec Z14XE with A/C
Diagram 12	Wash/wipe, engine cooling Motronic Z10XE and Z12XE without A/C, engine cooling Diesel with A/C
Diagram 13	Electric windows, air conditioning, heated and power mirrors
Diagram 14	Instrument module, multi-timer supply, licence plate lights triple info display, fog lights and diagnostic connector supply
Diagram 15	Side lights, tail lights, head lights, headlight leveling, clutch switch, brake, tail and reverse lights (combo)
Diagram 16	Interior lights, auto rear view mirror (combo), direction indicators, hazard lights, brake and reverse lights (not combo)
Diagram 17	Interior lights, auto rear view mirror (not combo) and central locking

Fuses

Fuse	Rating	Circuit protected	Fuse	Rating	Circuit protected
F1	7.5A	Multi-timer	F25	10A	Brake lights
F2	7.5A	Engine control modules	F26	20A	Automatic transmission, reverse lights, cigarette lighter
F3	7.5A	Terminal 15a relay, horn, light switch, wash/wipe, diagnostic connector, instruments, triple info display, licence plate lights, air conditioning, climate control hazard warning switch,	F27	15A	Heated seats
			F28	15A	Heated seats
			F29	20A	Rear wiper
			F30	15A	Engine control module
			F31	15A	Air conditioning
			F32	5A	ABS, diesel control module, speed sensor, automatic transmission, easytronic transmission, airbag
F4	5A	Licence plate lights			
F5	20A	Electric windows			
F6	10A	Automatic transmission			
F7	30A	Headlight washer	F34	30A	Diesel control module
F8	10A	Ignition switch	F35	5A	Radio, GPS, electric windows, sunroof
F9	20A	Engine control modules			
F10	10A	Horn	F45	30A	Heating, air conditioning
F11	15A	Multi-timer	F46	20A	Engine control module
F12	20A	Radio, multi info display, GPS	F47	30A	Heated rear window
F13	10A	Alarm	F49	50A	Power steering
F14	7.5A	Power mirrors	F50	40A	ABS
F15	10A	Wash/wipe	F51	60A	Easytronic transmission
F16	5A	Interior lights		80A	Diesel control module
F17	20A	Multi-timer	F52	20A	Engine cooling (Z10XE, Z12XE without A/C)
F18	20A	Sun roof		30A	Engine cooling (Z14XE with A/C)
F19	5A	Alarm		40A	Engine cooling (Z10XE, Z12XE with A/C)
F20	20A	Electric windows			(Z14XE without A/C) (Diesel)
F22	5A	Instruments			
F23	30A	Wash/wipe	F53	30A	Engine cooling (petrol)
F24	5A	Triple info display, radio, multi info display, interior lights, wash/wipe		40A	Engine cooling (diesel)

H32797

Wire colours

Bl	Blue	**Ro**	Red
Br	Brown	**Sw**	Black
Gr	Grey	**Vi**	Violet
Gn	Green	**Ws**	White
Or	Orange	**Ye**	Yellow
Pu	Purple		

★ Manual only

Key to items

1 Battery
2 Ignition switch
3 Main fuse box
4 Multi-timer
5 Starter motor
6 Starter relay
7 Alternator
8 Diagnostic connector

9 Airbag module
10 Terminal 15 relay
11 Passenger's seat sensor
12 Driver's side airbag sensor
13 Passenger's side airbag sensor
14 Driver's side airbag
15 Passenger's side airbag
16 Driver's head airbag

17 Passenger's head airbag
18 RH seatbelt pretensioner
19 LH seatbelt pretensioner
20 Driver's airbag
21 Passenger's airbag
22 Airbag contact unit
23 Radio
24 Aerial amplifier

25 LH rear speaker
26 RH rear speaker
27 LH front speaker
28 LH front tweeter
29 RH front tweeter
30 RH front speaker
31 Outside temperature sensor

Diagram 2

MTS
H32798

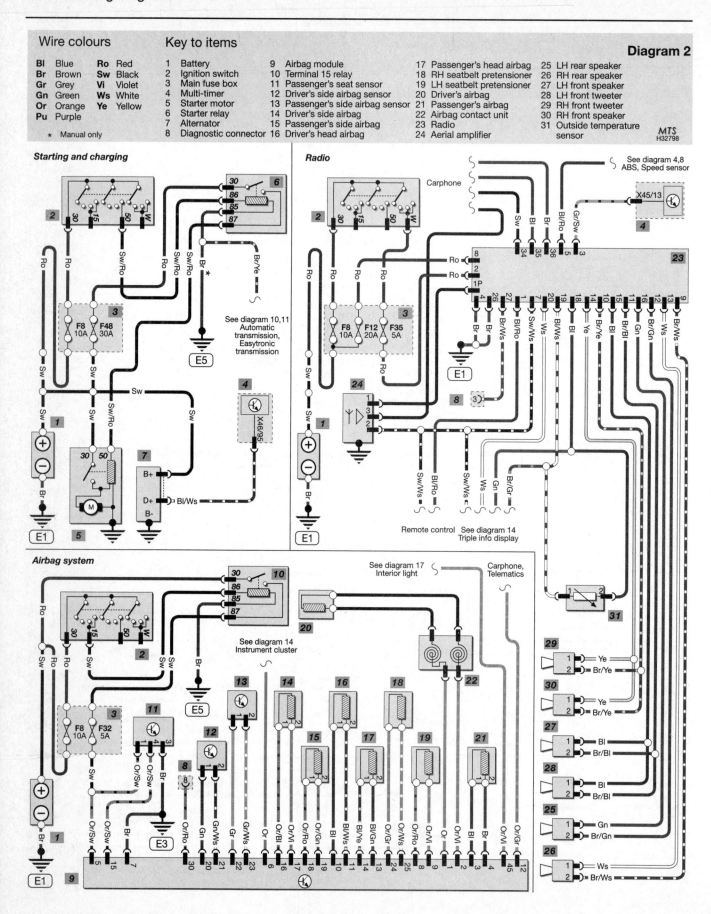

Starting and charging

Radio

Airbag system

Wire colours

Bl	Blue	Ro	Red
Br	Brown	Sw	Black
Gr	Grey	Vi	Violet
Gn	Green	Ws	White
Or	Orange	Ye	Yellow
Pu	Purple		

Key to items

1   Battery
2   Ignition switch
3   Main fuse box
4   Multi-timer
10 Terminal 15 relay
32 Motronic control module

33 Ignition coil
34 Spark plugs
35 Motronic control
    module relay
36 Fuel pump relay
37 Pedal position sensor

38 Air conditioning
    pressure sensor
39 Fuel injector cylinder 1
40 Fuel injector cylinder 2
41 Fuel injector cylinder 3
42 Fuel pump

43 Oil pressure switch
44 Throttle position sensor
45 Knock sensor

Diagram 3

* Air conditioning only

MTS
H32799

Engine management system Motronic Z10XE engines

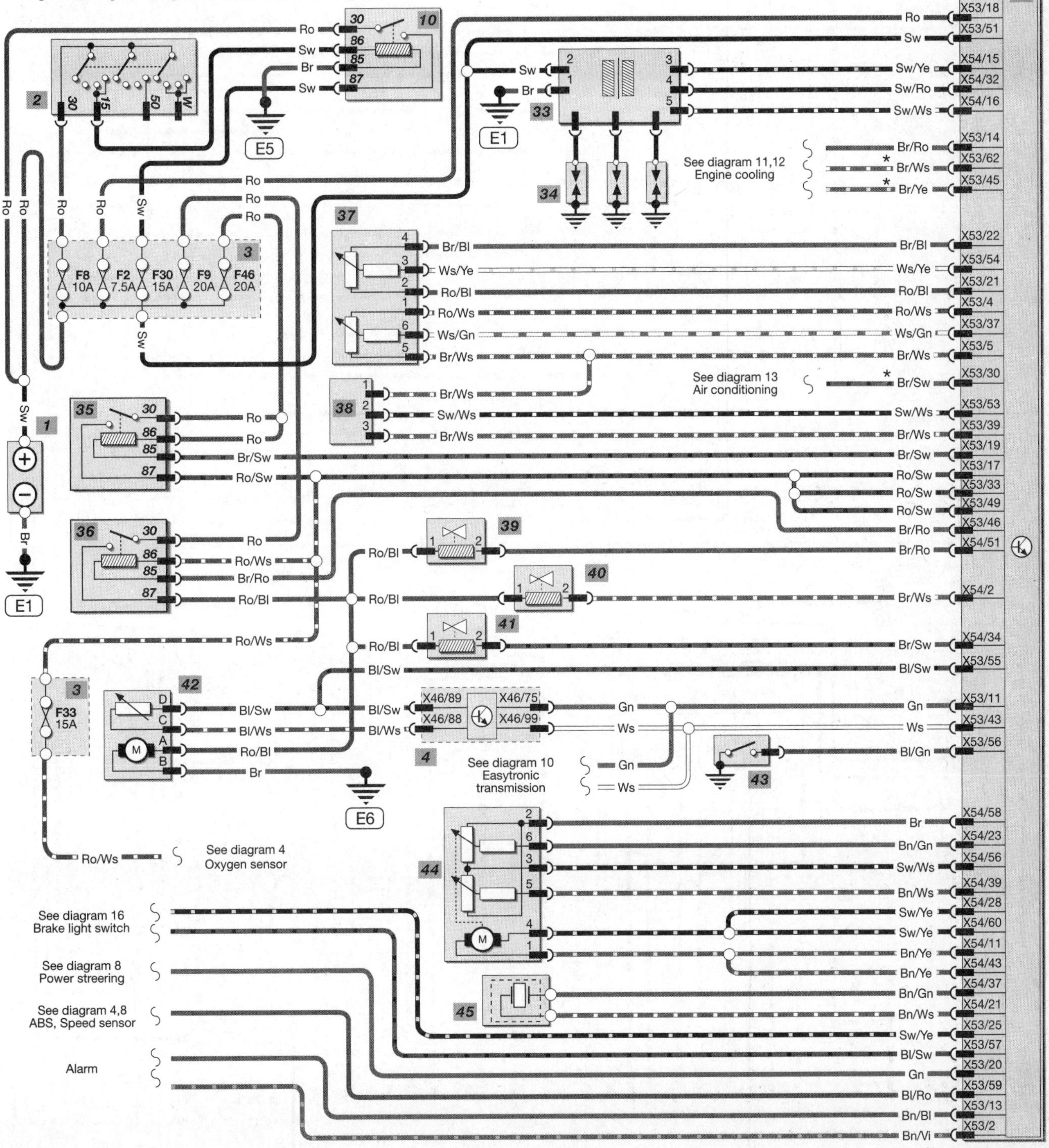

Wire colours

Bl	Blue	**Ro**	Red
Br	Brown	**Sw**	Black
Gr	Grey	**Vi**	Violet
Gn	Green	**Ws**	White
Or	Orange	**Ye**	Yellow
Pu	Purple		

Key to items

1 Battery
2 Ignition switch
3 Main fuse box
4 Multi-timer
10 Terminal 15 relay
32 Motronic control module
46 Pre-cat oxygen sensor

47 Post-cat oxygen sensor
48 Crankshaft sensor
49 Camshaft position sensor
50 Tank vent valve
51 Air mass meter
52 EGR solenoid valve

53 Coolant temperature sensor
54 ABS control module
55 LH front wheel speed sensor
56 RH front wheel speed sensor
57 LH rear wheel speed sensor
58 RH rear wheel speed sensor
59 Cigarette lighter

Diagram 4

MTS
H32800

Engine management system Motronic Z10XE engines

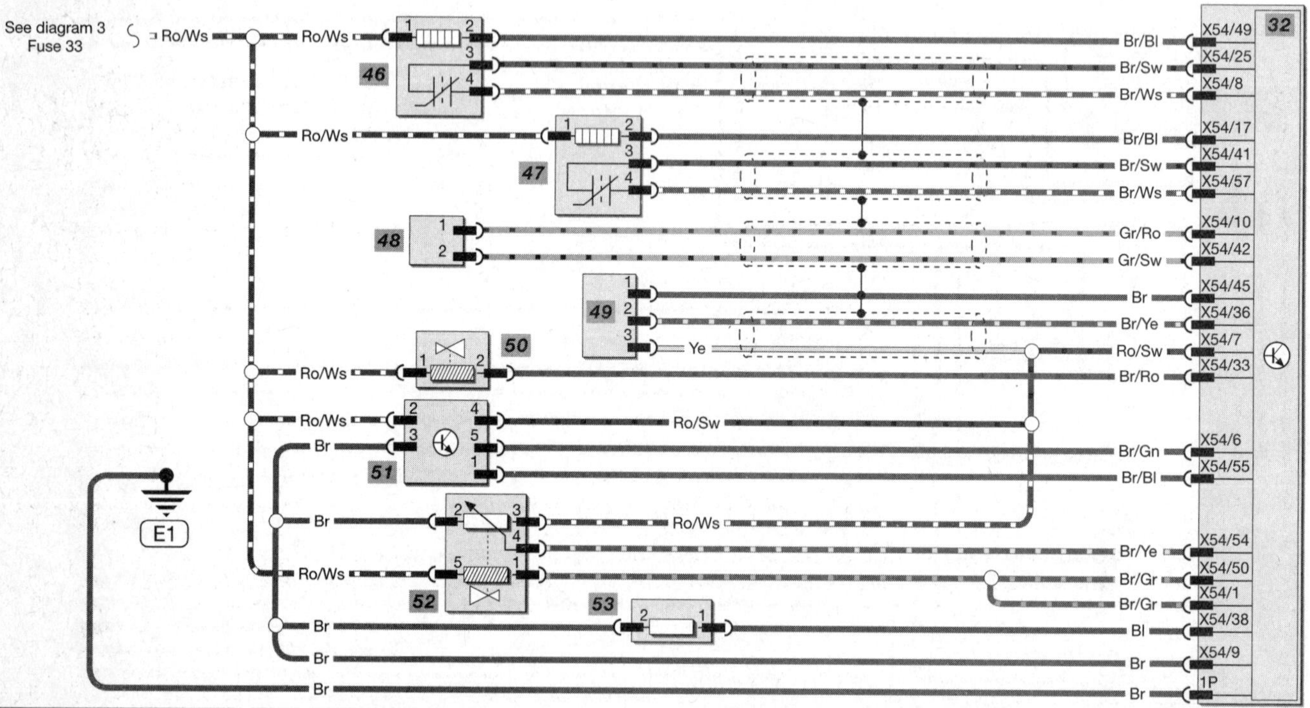

ABS

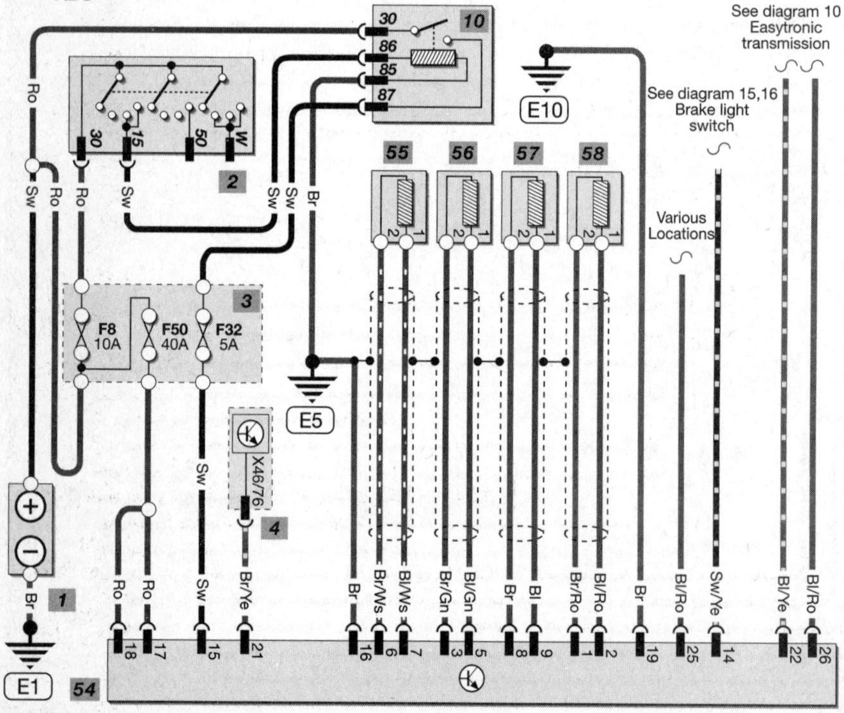

Cigarette lighter

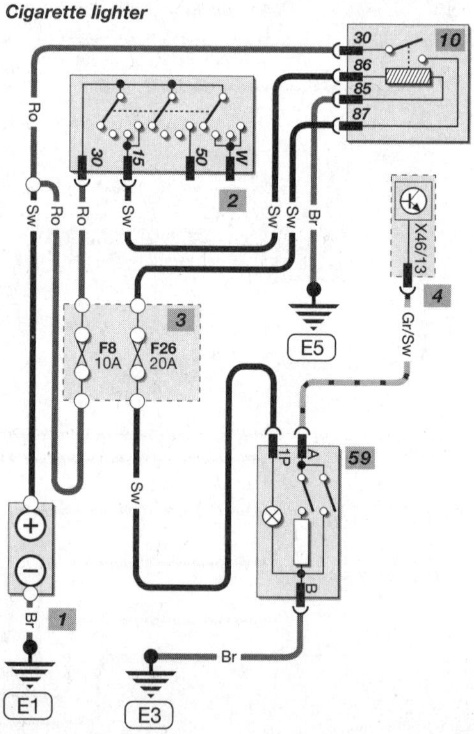

Wire colours

Bl	Blue	**Ro**	Red
Br	Brown	**Sw**	Black
Gr	Grey	**Vi**	Violet
Gn	Green	**Ws**	White
Or	Orange	**Ye**	Yellow
Pu	Purple		

Key to items

1 Battery
2 Ignition switch
3 Main fuse box
4 Multi-timer
10 Terminal 15 relay
32 Motronic control module
33 Ignition coil
34 Spark plugs
35 Motronic control module relay
36 Fuel pump relay
37 Pedal position sensor
38 Air conditioning pressure sensor
39 Fuel injector cylinder 1
40 Fuel injector cylinder 2
41 Fuel injector cylinder 3
42 Fuel pump
43 Oil pressure switch
44 Throttle position sensor
45 Knock sensor
60 Fuel injector cylinder 4

★ Air conditioning only

Diagram 5

MTS
H32801

Engine management system Motronic Z12XE engines

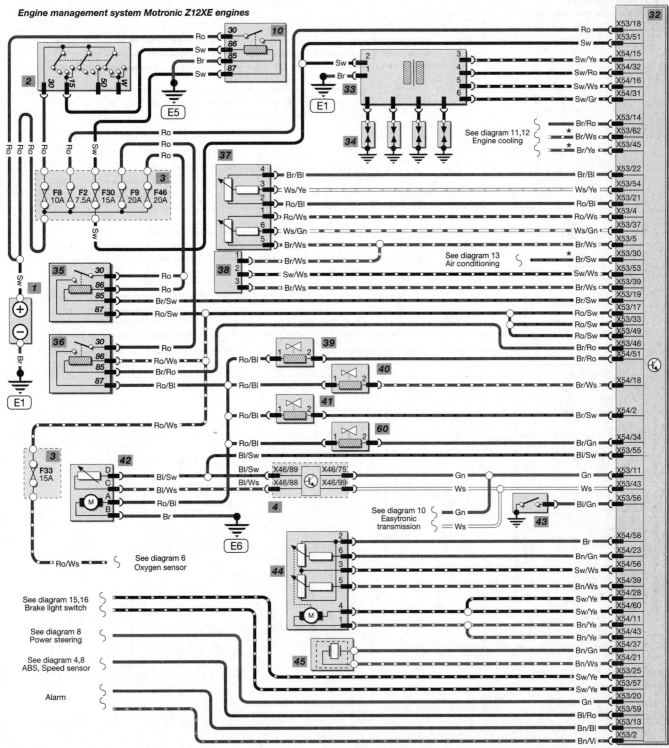

Wire colours

Bl	Blue	**Ro**	Red
Br	Brown	**Sw**	Black
Gr	Grey	**Vi**	Violet
Gn	Green	**Ws**	White
Or	Orange	**Ye**	Yellow
Pu	Purple		

Key to items

1   Battery
3   Main fuse box
4   Multi-timer
32 Motronic control module
46 Pre-cat oxygen sensor
47 Post-cat oxygen sensor
48 Crankshaft sensor
49 Camshaft position
    sensor
50 Tank vent valve
51 Air mass meter
52 EGR solenoid valve
53 Coolant temperature sensor
61 Heated rear window relay
62 Terminal 15a relay
63 Heated rear window
64 Heater blower controls
65 Resistor pack
66 Blower motor
67 Horn relay
68 Horn

★ Air conditioning only

Diagram 6

MTS
H32802

Engine management system Motronic Z12XE engines

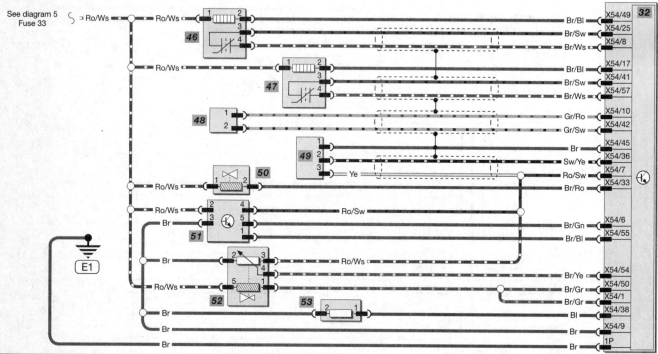

Heating and heated rear window

Horn

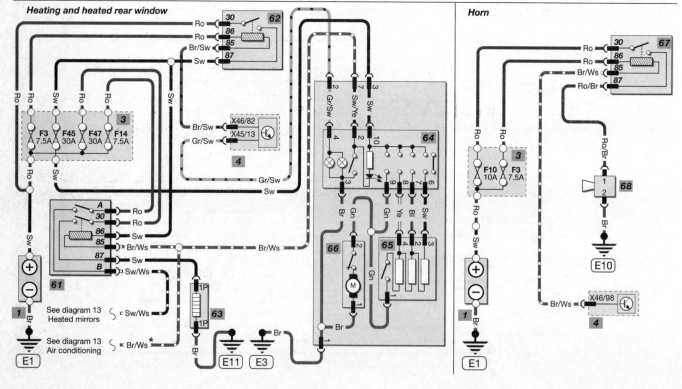

Wire colours

Bl	Blue	Ro	Red
Br	Brown	Sw	Black
Gr	Grey	Vi	Violet
Gn	Green	Ws	White
Or	Orange	Ye	Yellow
Pu	Purple		

Key to items

1　Battery
2　Ignition switch
3　Main fuse box
4　Multi-timer
10　Terminal 15 relay
33　Ignition coil
34　Spark plugs
36　Fuel pump relay
37　Pedal position sensor
39　Fuel injector cylinder 1
40　Fuel injector cylinder 2
41　Fuel injector cylinder 3
42　Fuel pump
43　Oil pressure switch
44　Throttle position sensor
60　Fuel injector cylinder 4
69　Multec control module
70　Intake absolute pressure sensor
71　Multec control module relay

Diagram 7

* Air conditioning only

MTS
H32803

Engine management system Multec Z14XE engines

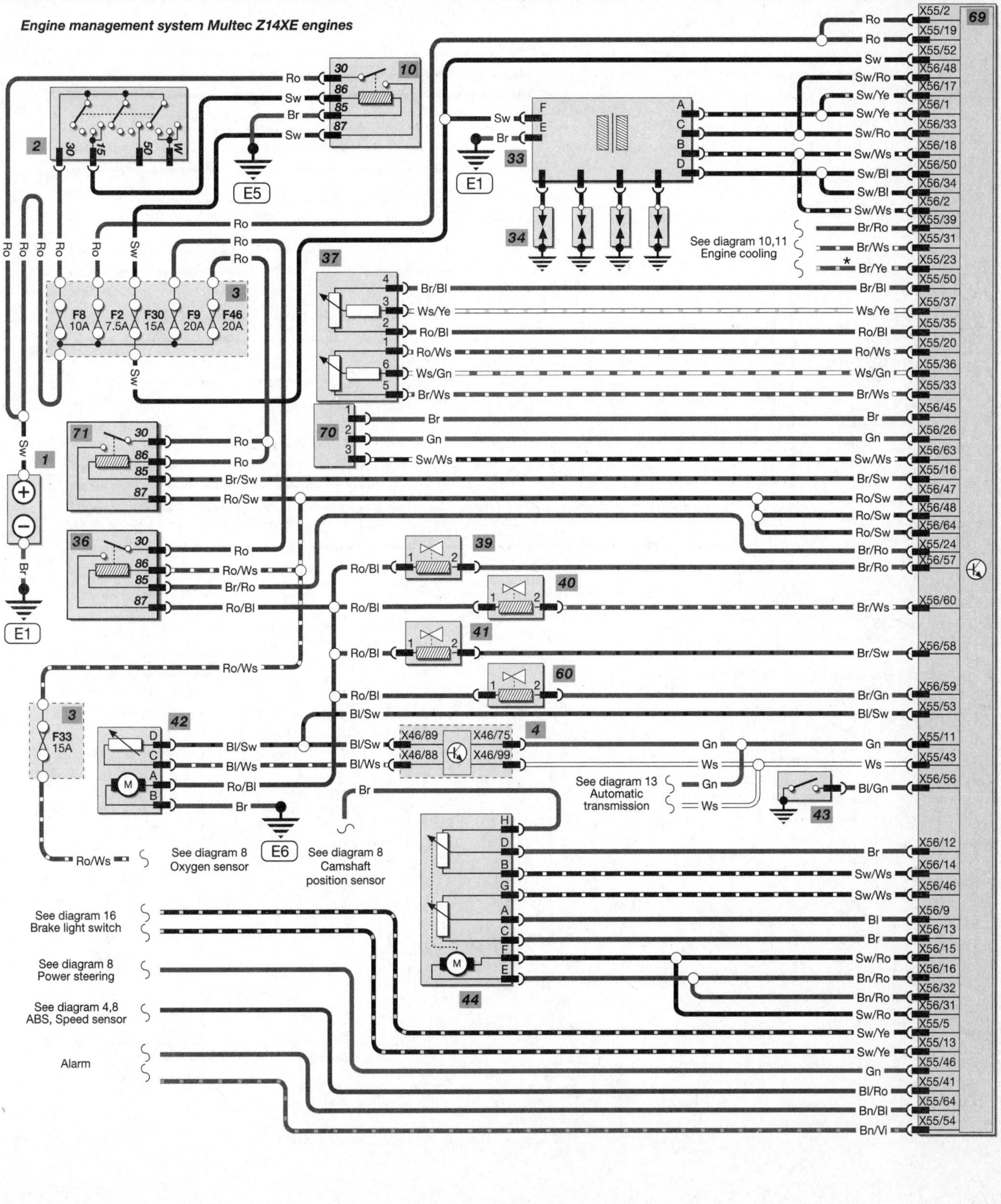

Wire colours

Bl	Blue	**Ro**	Red
Br	Brown	**Sw**	Black
Gr	Grey	**Vi**	Violet
Gn	Green	**Ws**	White
Or	Orange	**Ye**	Yellow
Pu	Purple		

Key to items

1 Battery
3 Main fuse box
4 Multi-timer
8 Diagnostic connector
10 Terminal 15 relay
38 Air conditioning pressure sensor
46 Pre-cat oxygen sensor
47 Post-cat oxygen sensor
48 Crankshaft sensor
49 Camshaft position sensor
50 Tank vent valve
52 EGR solenoid valve
53 Coolant temperature sensor
55 LH font wheel speed sensor
56 RH front wheel speed sensor
69 Multec control module
72 Air intake temperature sensor
73 Power steering unit
74 LH speed signal converter
75 RH speed signal converter

★ Air conditioning only
★★ Easytronic only

Diagram 8

MTS
H32804

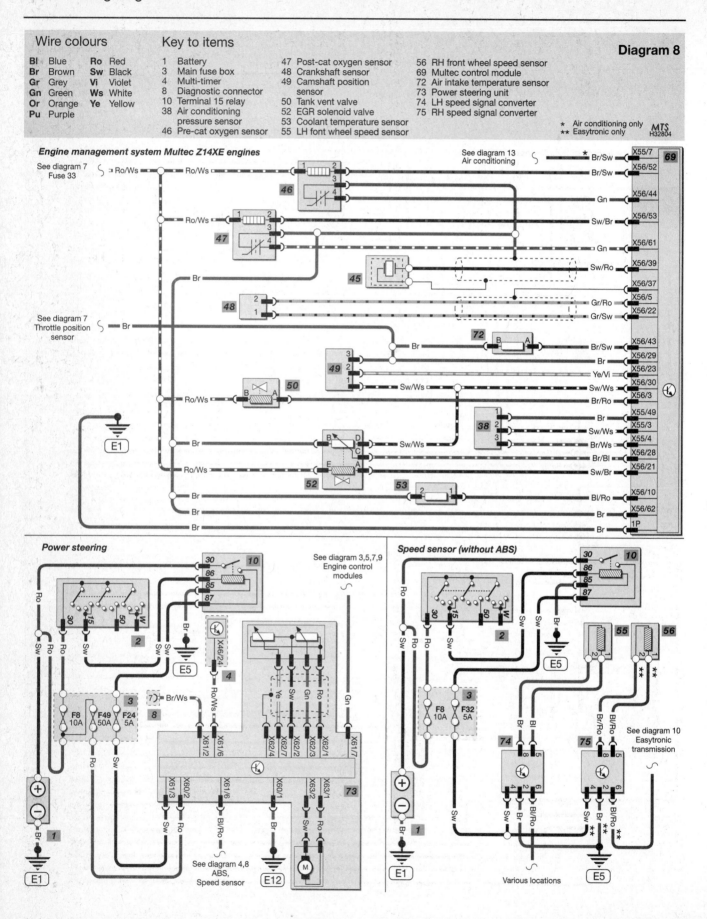

Engine management system Multec Z14XE engines

Power steering

Speed sensor (without ABS)

Wire colours

Bl Blue
Br Brown
Gr Grey
Gn Green
Or Orange
Pu Purple

Ro Red
Sw Black
Vi Violet
Ws White
Ye Yellow

★ Air conditioning only

Key to items

1 Battery
2 Ignition switch
3 Main fuse box
4 Multi-timer
10 Terminal 15 relay
37 Pedal position sensor
38 Air conditioning pressure sensor

43 Oil pressure switch
44 Throttle position sensor
48 Crankshaft sensor
51 Air mass meter
52 EGR solenoid valve
53 Coolant temperature sensor
62 Terminal 15a relay
76 Diesel control module

77 Diesel control module relay
78 Filter heater
79 Atmospheric pressure sensor
80 Boost pressure sensor
81 Boost pressure regulation valve
82 Glow time control unit

83 Injection pump shaft position sensor
84 Glow plugs
85 Fuel temperature sensor
86 Spill valve relay
87 Timing control valve
88 Spill valve
89 Injection pump

Diagram 9

MTS H32805

Engine management system diesel engines

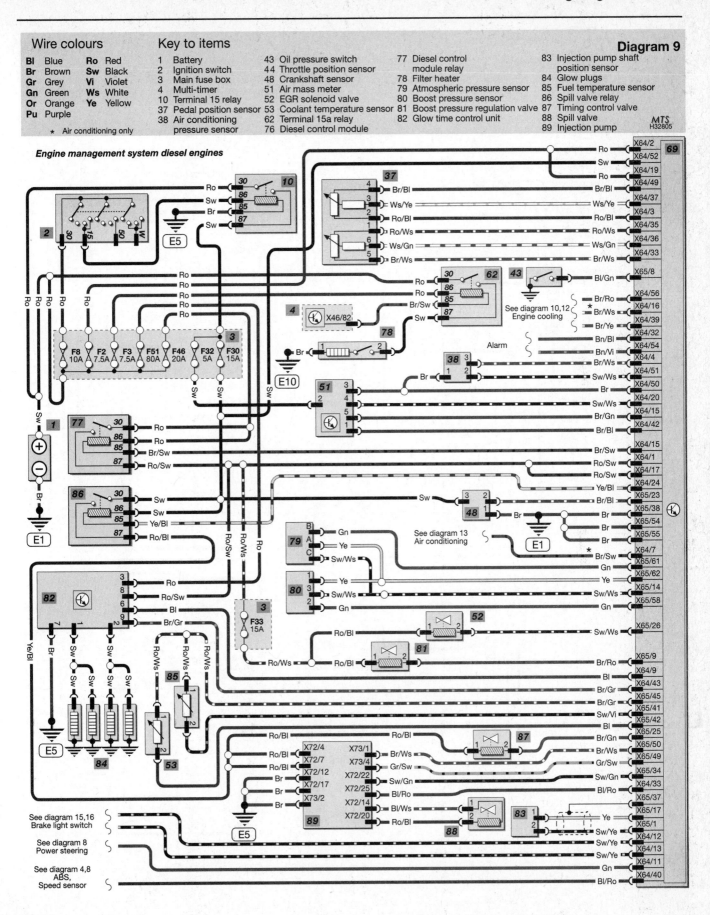

Wire colours

Bl	Blue	Ro	Red
Br	Brown	Sw	Black
Gr	Grey	Vi	Violet
Gn	Green	Ws	White
Or	Orange	Ye	Yellow
Pu	Purple		

Key to items

1 Battery
3 Main fuse box
4 Multi-timer
10 Terminal 15 relay
90 Selector lever

91 Easytronic transmission module
92 Transmission actuator unit
93 Sunroof motor
94 Sunroof switch

95 LH seat heating switch
96 RH seat heating switch
97 LH seat heater
98 RH seat heater
99 Radiator fan relay
100 Radiator fan

★ Multec Z14XE only
★★ Denso V5 only

Diagram 10

MTS H32806

Easytronic transmission

See diagram 4,8
ABS pin 26
RH speed signal converter

See diagram 4,8
ABS pin 25
LH speed signal converter

See diagram 4
ABS pin 22

See diagram 16
Reverse lights

See diagram 3,5
Motronic control module

Alarm

See diagram 2
Starter relay

Sunroof

Seat heating

Engine cooling Multec Z14XE and Diesel engines without air conditioning

See diagram 7,9
Multec control module
Diesel control module

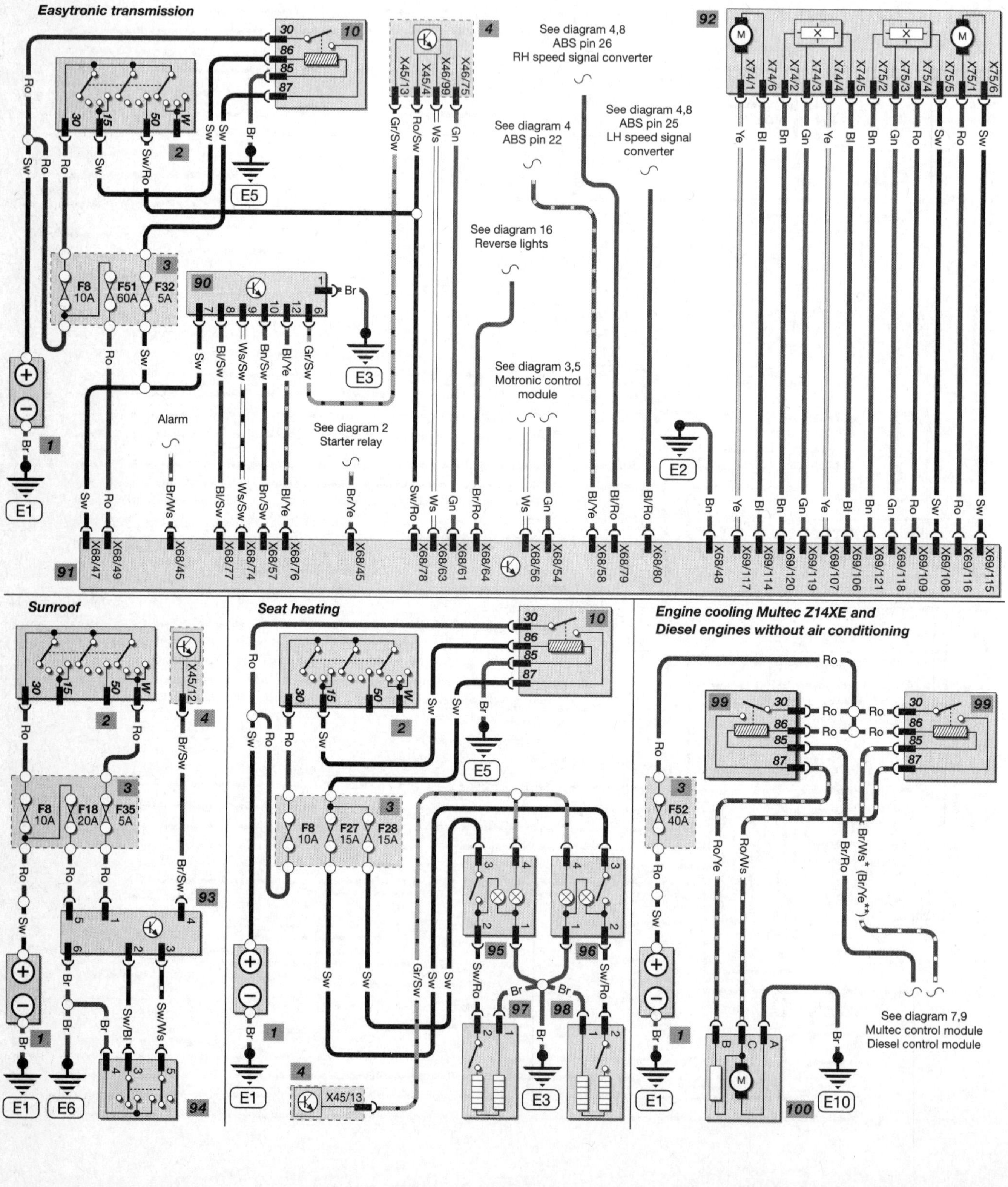

Wire colours

Bl	Blue	Ro	Red
Br	Brown	Sw	Black
Gr	Grey	Vi	Violet
Gn	Green	Ws	White
Or	Orange	Ye	Yellow
Pu	Purple		

Key to items

1 Battery
3 Main fuse box
4 Multi-timer
10 Terminal 15 relay
99 Radiator fan relay
100 Radiator fan

101 Automatic transmission
    control module
102 Switch unit
103 Gear selector lever
104 Transmission oil
    temperature sensor
105 Transmission output sensor

106 Transmission input sensor
107 Hydraulic pressure
    control solenoid valve
108 2/3 shift valve
109 1/2 - 3/4 shift valve
110 Neutral control valve
111 Converter clutch valve

Diagram 11

MTS
H32807

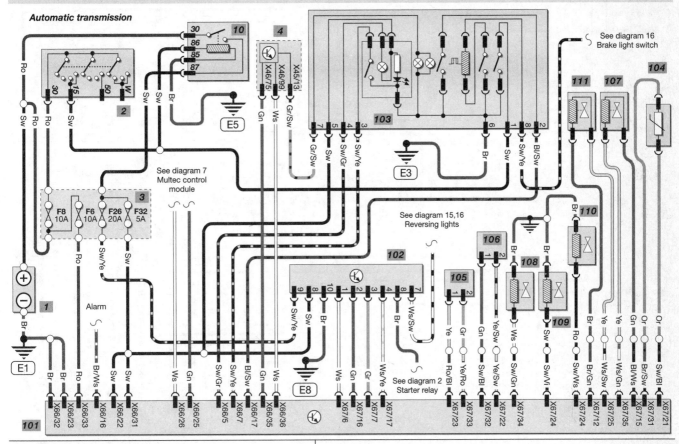

Automatic transmission

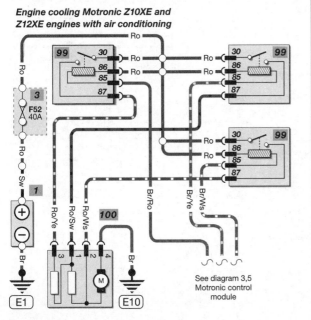

Engine cooling Motronic Z10XE and
Z12XE engines with air conditioning

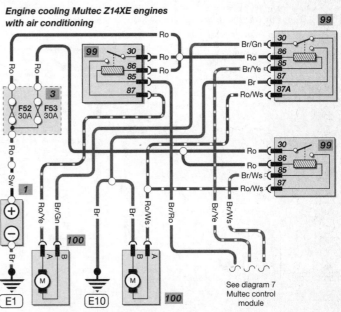

Engine cooling Multec Z14XE engines
with air conditioning

Diagram 12

Wire colours

Bl	Blue	**Ro**	Red
Br	Brown	**Sw**	Black
Gr	Grey	**Vi**	Violet
Gn	Green	**Ws**	White
Or	Orange	**Ye**	Yellow
Pu	Purple		

Key to items

1	Battery
3	Main fuse box
4	Multi-timer
10	Terminal 15 relay
99	Radiator fan relay
100	Radiator fan
112	Rear window wiper relay
113	Rear window wiper
114	LH rear window wiper
115	RH rear window wiper
116	Rear window washer pump relay
117	Windscreen window washer pump relay
118	Washer pump
119	Headlight washer pump relay
120	Headlight washer pump
121	Windscreen wiper relay stage 1/ interval
122	Windscreen wiper relay stage 2
123	Windscreen wiper motor
124	Rain sensor
201	Wiper switch unit

* Combo only
** Not Combo

MTS
H32808

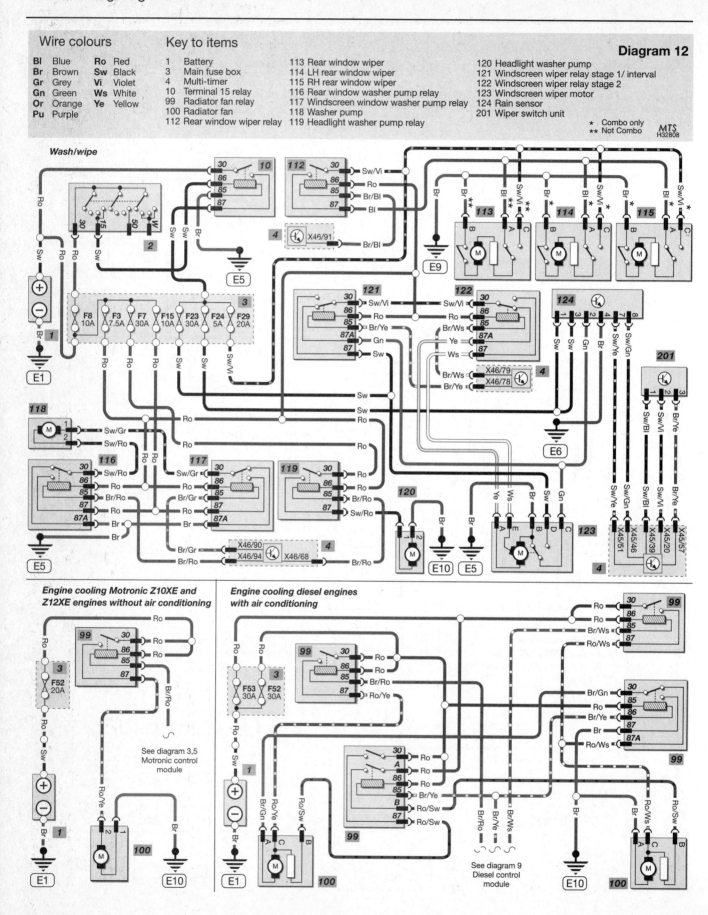

Wire colours

Bl	Blue	**Ro**	Red
Br	Brown	**Sw**	Black
Gr	Grey	**Vi**	Violet
Gn	Green	**Ws**	White
Or	Orange	**Ye**	Yellow
Pu	Purple		

Key to items

1 Battery
3 Main fuse box
4 Multi-timer
10 Terminal 15 relay
62 Terminal 15a relay
65 Resistor pack
66 Blower motor

125 Driver's door window switch
126 Passenger's door window switch
127 Driver's electric window unit

128 Passenger's electric window unit
129 Power mirror switch
130 LH power mirror
131 RH power mirror

132 A/C compressor relay
133 A/C compressor clutch
134 Air conditioning controls
135 Bosch recirculation actuator
136 Hella recirculation actuator

* Hella recirculation actuator only
** Bosch recirculation actuator only

Diagram 13

MTS
H32809

Electric windows

Heated and power mirrors

Air conditioning

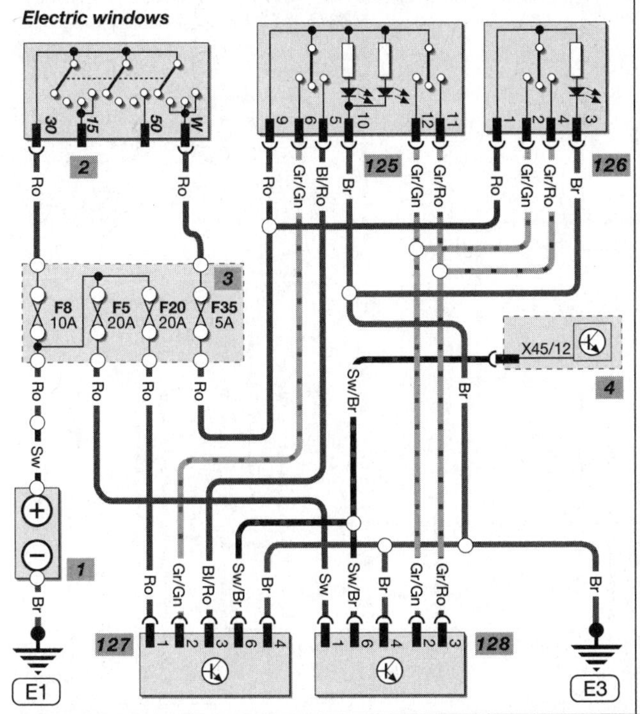

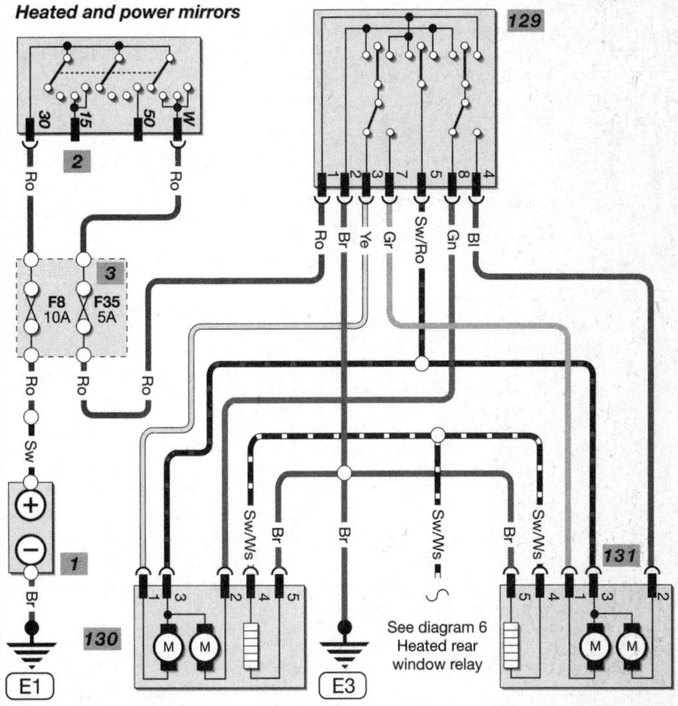

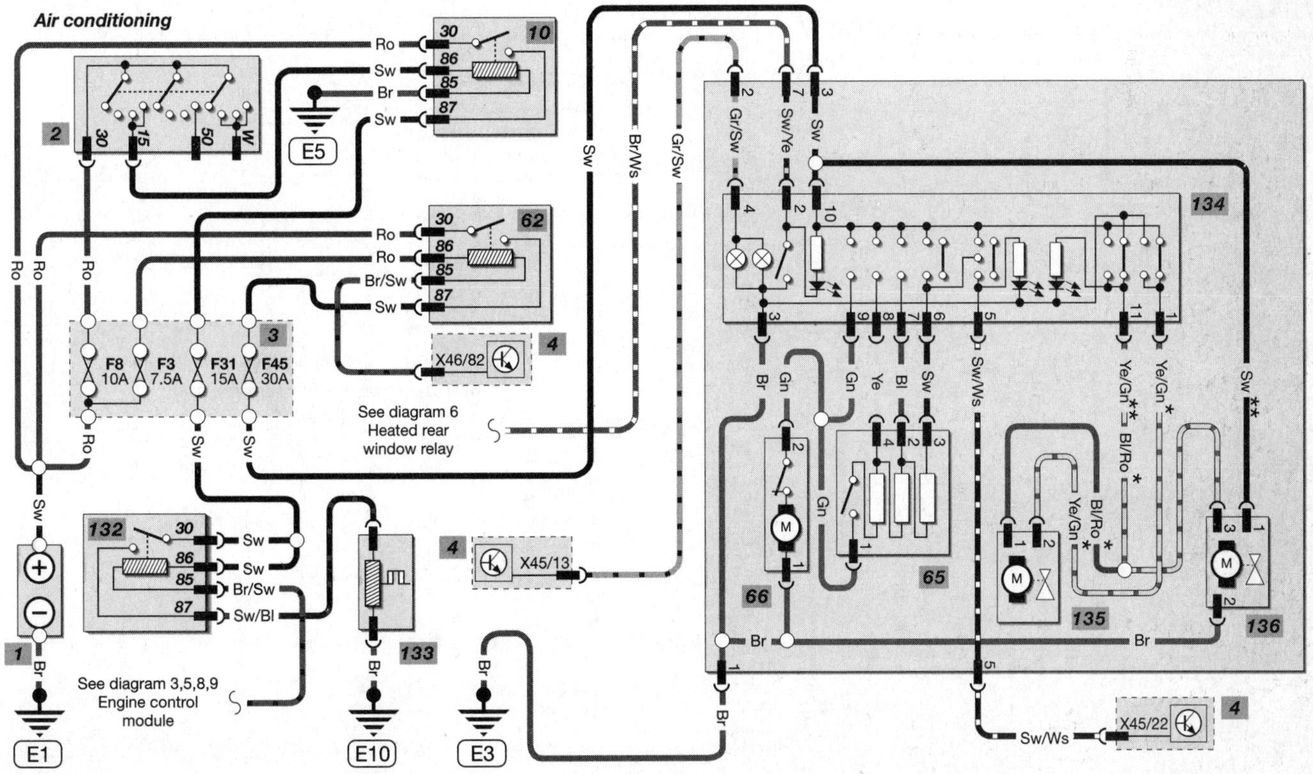

Wire colours

Bl	Blue	Ro	Red
Br	Brown	Sw	Black
Gr	Grey	Vi	Violet
Gn	Green	Ws	White
Or	Orange	Ye	Yellow
Pu	Purple		

Key to items

1 Battery
3 Main fuse box
4 Multi-timer
8 Diagnostic connector
10 Terminal 15 relay
137 Instrument module

138 Outside temperature sensor
139 Triple info display
140 LH front fog light
141 RH front fog light
142 LH rear fog light
143 RH rear fog light

144 LH combo rear light cluster
   a) fog light
145 RH combo rear light cluster (as 144)
146 Rear fog light relay

147 Front fog light relay
148 Licence plate light relay
149 LH licence plate light
150 RH licence plate light

* Combo only
** Not combo

Diagram 14

MTS
H32810

Instrument module

Multi-timer supply

Licence plate lights

See diagram 2 Airbag

Triple info display

Fog lights

Diagnostic connector supply

See diagram 4,8 ABS, Speed sensor

See diagram 2 Radio

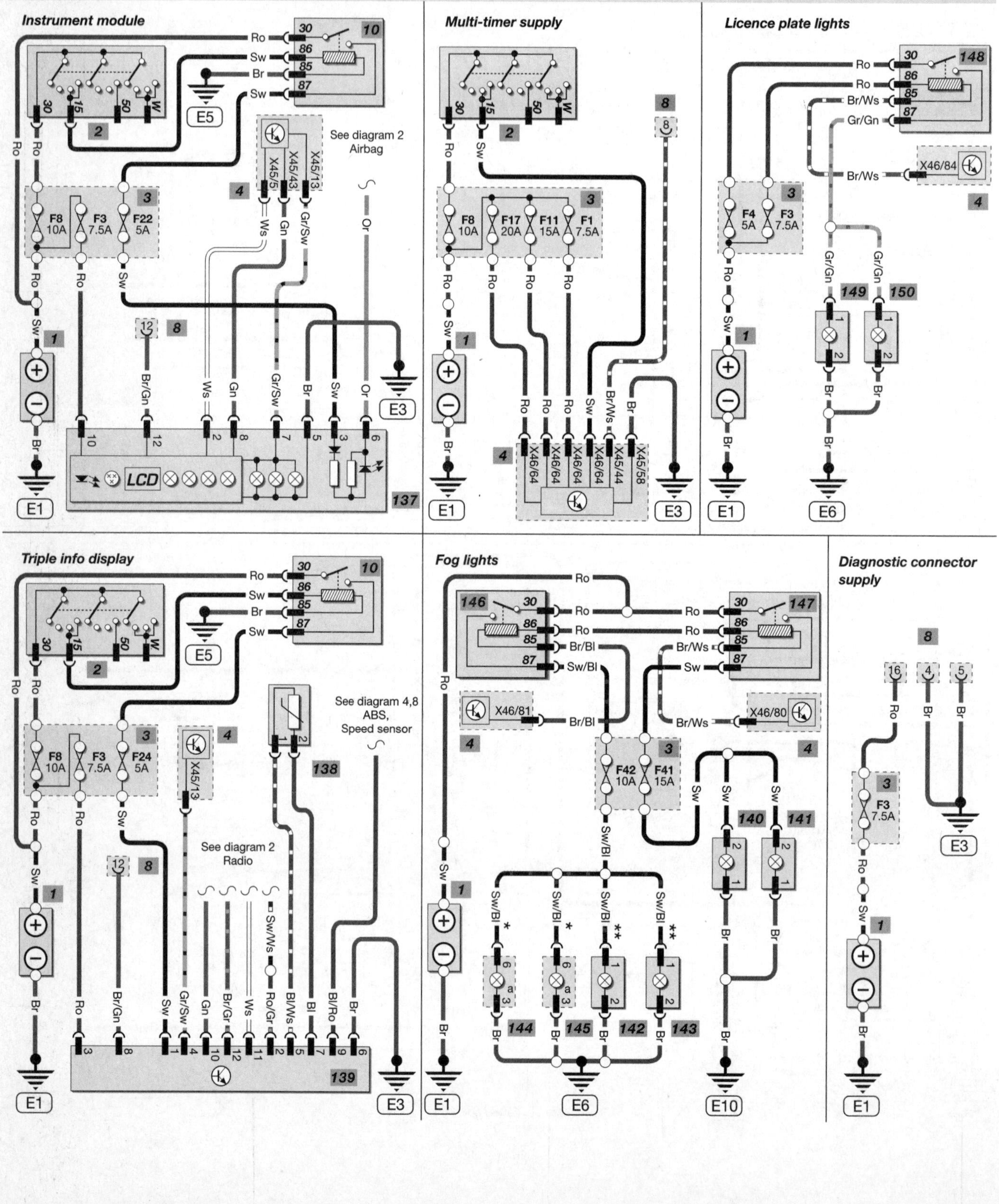

Wire colours

Bl	Blue	Ro	Red
Br	Brown	Sw	Black
Gr	Grey	Vi	Violet
Gn	Green	Ws	White
Or	Orange	Ye	Yellow
Pu	Purple		

Key to items

1 Battery
3 Main fuse box
4 Multi-timer
10 Terminal 15 relay
144 LH combo rear light cluster
   b) tail light
   c) brake light
   d) reverse light
145 RH combo rear light cluster (as 144)
151 Light switch
152 Low beam relay
153 LH side light relay
154 Hi beam relay
155 RH side light relay
156 LH headlight cluster
   a) low beam
   b) hi beam
   c) side light
   d) headlight leveling
157 RH headlight cluster (as 156)
158 LH rear light cluster
   a) tail light
159 RH rear light cluster (as 158)
160 Brake light switch
161 Reverse switch
162 LH rear door high level brake light
163 RH rear door high level brake light
164 Clutch switch
165 Steering column switches
   a) hi beam
   b) direction indicators
   c) cruise control

Diagram 15

MTS
H32811

Side lights, headlights and headlight leveling, tail lights

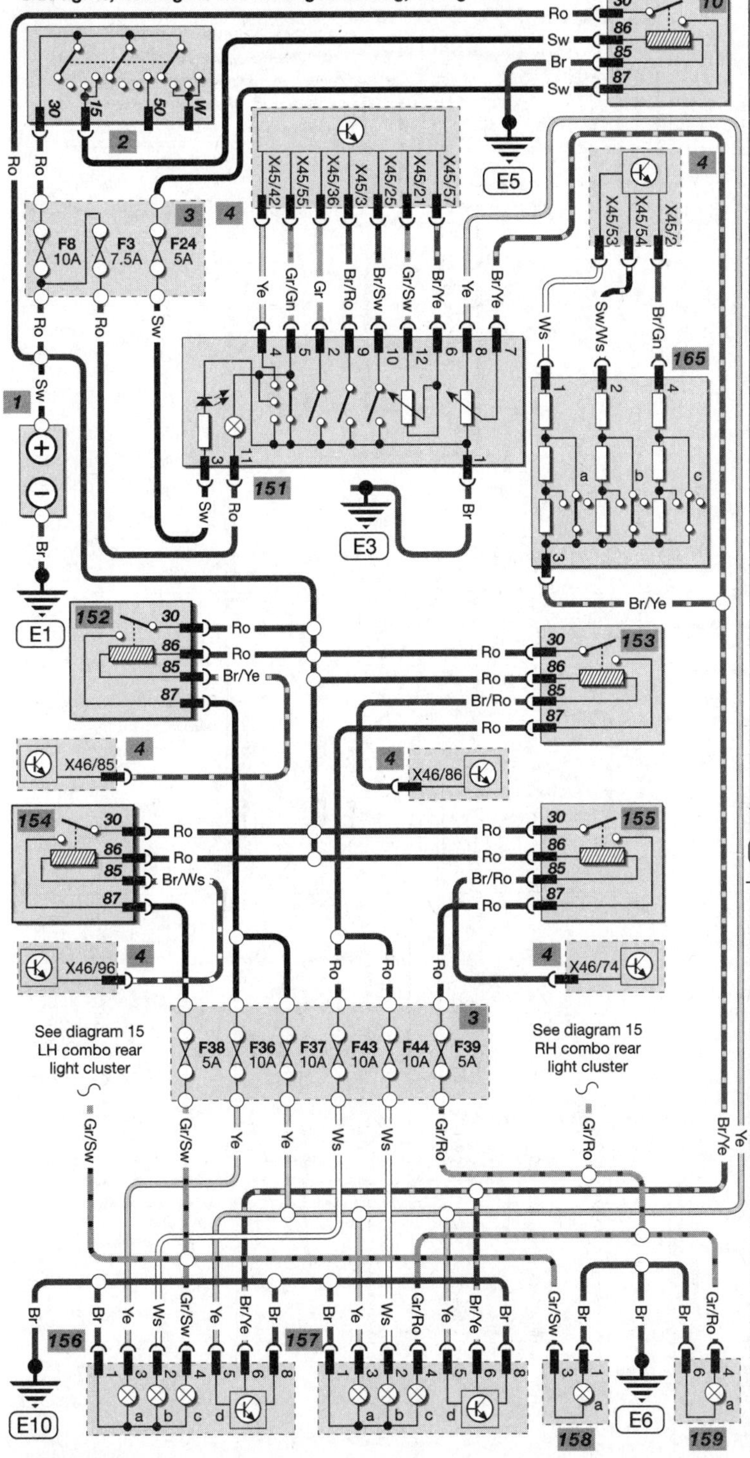

Brake lights, tail lights and reverse lights (combo)

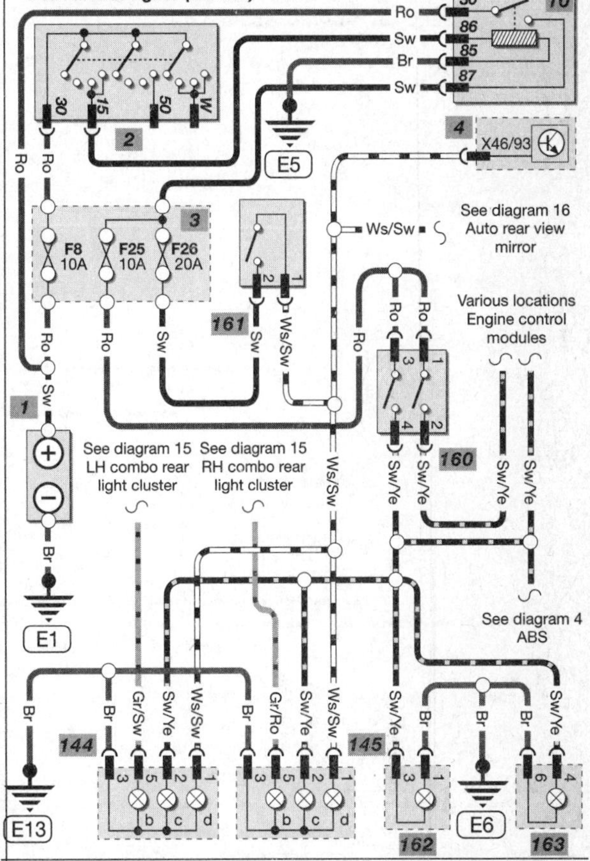

Clutch switch (cruise control only)

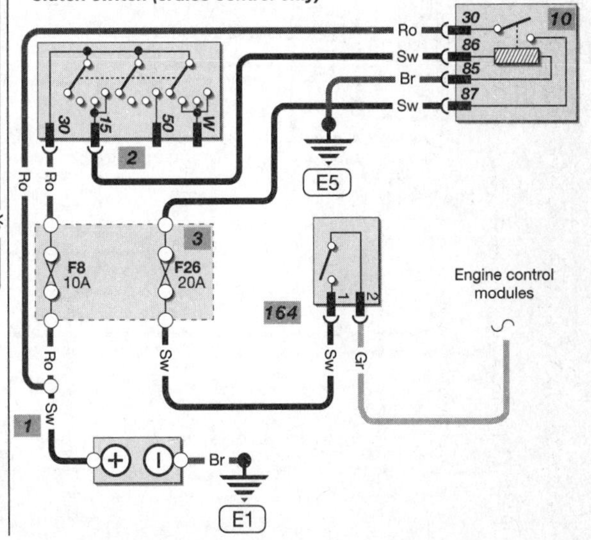

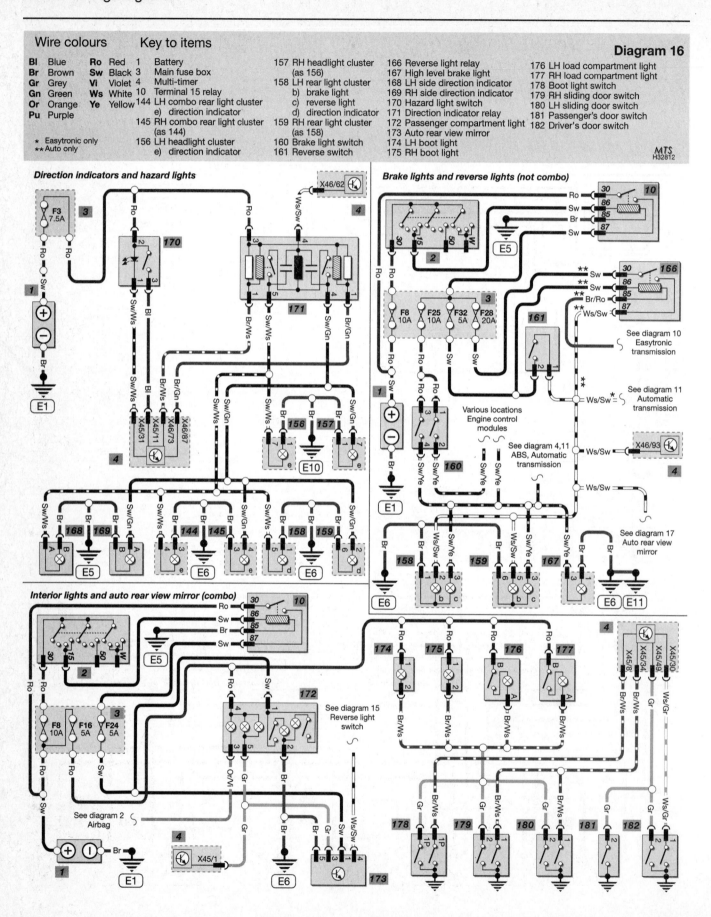

Wire colours

Bl	Blue	Ro	Red
Br	Brown	Sw	Black
Gr	Grey	Vi	Violet
Gn	Green	Ws	White
Or	Orange	Ye	Yellow
Pu	Purple		

★ Easytronic only
★★ Auto only

Key to items

1 Battery
3 Main fuse box
4 Multi-timer
10 Terminal 15 relay
144 LH combo rear light cluster
   e) direction indicator
145 RH combo rear light cluster (as 144)
156 LH headlight cluster
   e) direction indicator
157 RH headlight cluster (as 156)
158 LH rear light cluster
   b) brake light
   c) reverse light
   d) direction indicator
159 RH rear light cluster (as 158)
160 Brake light switch
161 Reverse switch
166 Reverse light relay
167 High level brake light
168 LH side direction indicator
169 RH side direction indicator
170 Hazard light switch
171 Direction indicator relay
172 Passenger compartment light
173 Auto rear view mirror
174 LH boot light
175 RH boot light
176 LH load compartment light
177 RH load compartment light
178 Boot light switch
179 RH sliding door switch
180 LH sliding door switch
181 Passenger's door switch
182 Driver's door switch

Diagram 16

MTS
H32812

Direction indicators and hazard lights

Brake lights and reverse lights (not combo)

Interior lights and auto rear view mirror (combo)

See diagram 10
Easytronic transmission

See diagram 11
Automatic transmission

Various locations
Engine control modules

See diagram 4,11
ABS, Automatic transmission

See diagram 17
Auto rear view mirror

See diagram 15
Reverse light switch

See diagram 2
Airbag

Wire colours

Bl	Blue	**Ro**	Red
Br	Brown	**Sw**	Black
Gr	Grey	**Vi**	Violet
Gn	Green	**Ws**	White
Or	Orange	**Ye**	Yellow
Pu	Purple		

Key to items

1	Battery
3	Main fuse box
4	Multi-timer
10	Terminal 15 relay
172	Passenger compartment light
173	Auto rear view mirror
178	Boot light switch
181	Passenger's door switch
182	Driver's door switch
183	Single front interior light
184	Boot light
185	Rear reading light
186	LH rear door switch
187	RH rear door switch
188	Driver's door lock relay
189	Unlock relay
190	Deadlock relay
191	Lock relay
192	Driver's door lock assembly
193	Passenger's door lock motor
194	LH door lock motor
195	RH door lock motor
196	Fuel filler flap lock
197	Tailgate/boot lock motor
198	LH sliding door lock motor
199	RH sliding door lock motor
200	Rear door lock motor
★	Without 172 only
★★	Combo only

Diagram 17

MTS
H32813

Interior lights and auto rear view mirror (not combo)

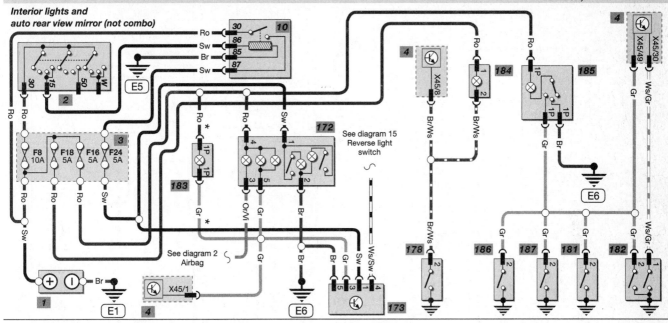

Central locking

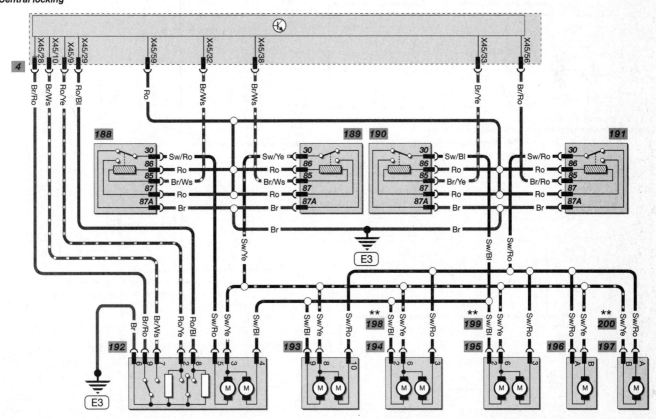

Dimensions and Weights

Note: *All figures are approximate and may vary according to model. Refer to manufacturer's data for exact figures.*

Dimensions

Overall length:
All models except Combo Van . . . . 3817 mm
Combo Van models . . . . 4322 mm
Overall width:
All models except Combo Van:
    Excluding door mirrors . . . . 1646 mm
    Including door mirrors . . . . 1955 mm
Combo Van models:
    Excluding door mirrors . . . . 1684 mm
    Including door mirrors . . . . 1892 mm
Overall height (unladen):
All models except Combo Van . . . . 1440 mm
Combo Van models . . . . 1801 mm
Wheelbase:
All models except Combo Van . . . . 2491 mm
Combo Van models . . . . 2716 mm
Turning circle diameter (wall to wall):
All models except Combo Van . . . . 10.45 metres
Combo Van models . . . . 11.25 metres
Front track . . . . 1429 mm
Rear track . . . . 1420 mm
Ground clearance . . . . 122 mm

Weights

	Kerb weight	Gross vehicle weight
3-door Hatchback:		
1.0 litre petrol models	913 kg to 980 kg	1405 kg
1.2 litre petrol models	935 kg to 1026 kg	1430 kg to 1455 kg
1.4 litre petrol models	998 kg to 1048 kg	1500 kg to 1550 kg
1.7 litre diesel models	1020 kg to 1117 kg	1505 kg to 1580 kg
5-door Hatchback:		
1.0 litre petrol models	940 kg to 1005 kg	1405 kg
1.2 litre petrol models	960 kg to 1051 kg	1430 kg to 1455 kg
1.4 litre petrol models	1023 kg to 1073 kg	1525 kg to 1570 kg
1.7 litre diesel models	1045 kg to 1142 kg	1505 kg to 1605 kg
Corsavan models:		
1.2 litre petrol models	965 kg to 1060 kg	1430 kg to 1455 kg
1.7 litre diesel models:	1050 kg to 1085 kg	1505 kg to 1580 kg
Combo Van models:		
1.7 litre diesel engines	1210 kg	1780 kg to 1995 kg
Maximum roof load (including weight of rack)	100 kg	

Conversion factors

Length (distance)

Inches (in)	x 25.4	= Millimetres (mm)	x 0.0394	= Inches (in)
Feet (ft)	x 0.305	= Metres (m)	x 3.281	= Feet (ft)
Miles	x 1.609	= Kilometres (km)	x 0.621	= Miles

Volume (capacity)

Cubic inches (cu in; in³)	x 16.387	= Cubic centimetres (cc; cm³)	x 0.061	= Cubic inches (cu in; in³)
Imperial pints (Imp pt)	x 0.568	= Litres (l)	x 1.76	= Imperial pints (Imp pt)
Imperial quarts (Imp qt)	x 1.137	= Litres (l)	x 0.88	= Imperial quarts (Imp qt)
Imperial quarts (Imp qt)	x 1.201	= US quarts (US qt)	x 0.833	= Imperial quarts (Imp qt)
US quarts (US qt)	x 0.946	= Litres (l)	x 1.057	= US quarts (US qt)
Imperial gallons (Imp gal)	x 4.546	= Litres (l)	x 0.22	= Imperial gallons (Imp gal)
Imperial gallons (Imp gal)	x 1.201	= US gallons (US gal)	x 0.833	= Imperial gallons (Imp gal)
US gallons (US gal)	x 3.785	= Litres (l)	x 0.264	= US gallons (US gal)

Mass (weight)

Ounces (oz)	x 28.35	= Grams (g)	x 0.035	= Ounces (oz)
Pounds (lb)	x 0.454	= Kilograms (kg)	x 2.205	= Pounds (lb)

Force

Ounces-force (ozf; oz)	x 0.278	= Newtons (N)	x 3.6	= Ounces-force (ozf; oz)
Pounds-force (lbf; lb)	x 4.448	= Newtons (N)	x 0.225	= Pounds-force (lbf; lb)
Newtons (N)	x 0.1	= Kilograms-force (kgf; kg)	x 9.81	= Newtons (N)

Pressure

Pounds-force per square inch (psi; lbf/in²; lb/in²)	x 0.070	= Kilograms-force per square centimetre (kgf/cm²; kg/cm²)	x 14.223	= Pounds-force per square inch (psi; lbf/in²; lb/in²)
Pounds-force per square inch (psi; lbf/in²; lb/in²)	x 0.068	= Atmospheres (atm)	x 14.696	= Pounds-force per square inch (psi; lbf/in²; lb/in²)
Pounds-force per square inch (psi; lbf/in²; lb/in²)	x 0.069	= Bars	x 14.5	= Pounds-force per square inch (psi; lbf/in²; lb/in²)
Pounds-force per square inch (psi; lbf/in²; lb/in²)	x 6.895	= Kilopascals (kPa)	x 0.145	= Pounds-force per square inch (psi; lbf/in²; lb/in²)
Kilopascals (kPa)	x 0.01	= Kilograms-force per square centimetre (kgf/cm²; kg/cm²)	x 98.1	= Kilopascals (kPa)
Millibar (mbar)	x 100	= Pascals (Pa)	x 0.01	= Millibar (mbar)
Millibar (mbar)	x 0.0145	= Pounds-force per square inch (psi; lbf/in²; lb/in²)	x 68.947	= Millibar (mbar)
Millibar (mbar)	x 0.75	= Millimetres of mercury (mmHg)	x 1.333	= Millibar (mbar)
Millibar (mbar)	x 0.401	= Inches of water (inH₂O)	x 2.491	= Millibar (mbar)
Millimetres of mercury (mmHg)	x 0.535	= Inches of water (inH₂O)	x 1.868	= Millimetres of mercury (mmHg)
Inches of water (inH₂O)	x 0.036	= Pounds-force per square inch (psi; lbf/in²; lb/in²)	x 27.68	= Inches of water (inH₂O)

Torque (moment of force)

Pounds-force inches (lbf in; lb in)	x 1.152	= Kilograms-force centimetre (kgf cm; kg cm)	x 0.868	= Pounds-force inches (lbf in; lb in)
Pounds-force inches (lbf in; lb in)	x 0.113	= Newton metres (Nm)	x 8.85	= Pounds-force inches (lbf in; lb in)
Pounds-force inches (lbf in; lb in)	x 0.083	= Pounds-force feet (lbf ft; lb ft)	x 12	= Pounds-force inches (lbf in; lb in)
Pounds-force feet (lbf ft; lb ft)	x 0.138	= Kilograms-force metres (kgf m; kg m)	x 7.233	= Pounds-force feet (lbf ft; lb ft)
Pounds-force feet (lbf ft; lb ft)	x 1.356	= Newton metres (Nm)	x 0.738	= Pounds-force feet (lbf ft; lb ft)
Newton metres (Nm)	x 0.102	= Kilograms-force metres (kgf m; kg m)	x 9.804	= Newton metres (Nm)

Power

Horsepower (hp)	x 745.7	= Watts (W)	x 0.0013	= Horsepower (hp)

Velocity (speed)

Miles per hour (miles/hr; mph)	x 1.609	= Kilometres per hour (km/hr; kph)	x 0.621	= Miles per hour (miles/hr; mph)

Fuel consumption*

Miles per gallon, Imperial (mpg)	x 0.354	= Kilometres per litre (km/l)	x 2.825	= Miles per gallon, Imperial (mpg)
Miles per gallon, US (mpg)	x 0.425	= Kilometres per litre (km/l)	x 2.352	= Miles per gallon, US (mpg)

Temperature

Degrees Fahrenheit = (°C x 1.8) + 32   Degrees Celsius (Degrees Centigrade; °C) = (°F - 32) x 0.56

It is common practice to convert from miles per gallon (mpg) to litres/100 kilometres (l/100km), where mpg x l/100 km = 282

Spare parts are available from many sources, including maker's appointed garages, accessory shops, and motor factors. To be sure of obtaining the correct parts, it will sometimes be necessary to quote the vehicle identification number. If possible, it can also be useful to take the old parts along for positive identification. Items such as starter motors and alternators may be available under a service exchange scheme – any parts returned should be clean.

Our advice regarding spare parts is as follows.

Officially appointed garages

This is the best source of parts which are peculiar to your car, and which are not otherwise generally available (eg, badges, interior trim, certain body panels, etc). It is also the only place at which you should buy parts if the vehicle is still under warranty.

Accessory shops

These are very good places to buy materials and components needed for the maintenance of your car (oil, air and fuel filters, light bulbs, drivebelts, greases, brake pads, touch-up paint, etc). Components of this nature sold by a reputable shop are of the same standard as those used by the car manufacturer.

Besides components, these shops also sell tools and general accessories, usually have convenient opening hours, charge lower prices, and can often be found close to home. Some accessory shops have parts counters where components needed for almost any repair job can be purchased or ordered.

Motor factors

Good factors will stock all the more important components which wear out comparatively quickly, and can sometimes supply individual components needed for the overhaul of a larger assembly (eg, brake seals and hydraulic parts, bearing shells, pistons, valves). They may also handle work such as cylinder block reboring, crankshaft regrinding, etc.

Tyre and exhaust specialists

These outlets may be independent, or members of a local or national chain. They frequently offer competitive prices when compared with a main dealer or local garage, but it will pay to obtain several quotes before making a decision. When researching prices, also ask what 'extras' may be added – for instance fitting a new valve and balancing the wheel are both commonly charged on top of the price of a new tyre.

Other sources

Beware of parts or materials obtained from market stalls, car boot sales or similar outlets. Such items are not invariably sub-standard, but there is little chance of compensation if they do prove unsatisfactory. In the case of safety-critical components such as brake pads, there is the risk not only of financial loss, but also of an accident causing injury or death.

Second-hand components or assemblies obtained from a car breaker can be a good buy in some circumstances, but his sort of purchase is best made by the experienced DIY mechanic.

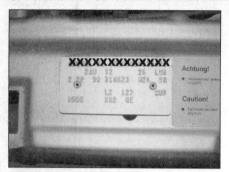

Vehicle Identification Number (VIN) plate on the front crossmember

Modifications are a continuing and unpublished process in vehicle manufacture, quite apart from major model changes. Spare parts manuals and lists are compiled upon a numerical basis, the individual vehicle numbers being essential to correct identification of the component required.

When ordering spare parts, always give as much information as possible. Quote the car model, year of manufacture and vehicle identification and/or engine numbers as appropriate.

The *vehicle identification plate* is riveted to the engine compartment front crossmember **(see illustration)** and includes the Vehicle Identification Number (VIN), vehicle weight information and paint and trim colour codes. This information also appears on the right-hand front door B-pillar or on the right-hand front suspension tower in the engine compartment **(see illustration)**.

The *Vehicle Identification Number (VIN)* is given on the vehicle identification plate and is also stamped into the body floor panel between the right-hand front seat and the door sill panel **(see illustration)**; lift the flap in the carpet to see it. The number is also fixed to the left-hand end of the instrument panel, and can be viewed through the windscreen **(see illustration)**.

The engine number is stamped on a horizontal flat located on the front of the cylinder block, at the transmission end. The first part of the engine number gives the engine code – eg Z12XE **(see illustration)**.

Engine codes are as follows:
1.0 litre DOHC petrol engine
    Z10XE and Z10XE-ECO
1.2 litre DOHC petrol engine
    Z12XE
1.4 litre DOHC petrol engine
    Z14XE
1.7 litre DOHC diesel engine
    Y17DTL and Y17DT

Vauxhall/Opel use a 'Car pass' scheme for vehicle identification. This is a card which is issued to the customer when the car is first purchased. It contains important information, eg, VIN number, key number and radio code. It also includes a special code for diagnostic equipment, therefore it must be kept in a secure place and not in the vehicle.

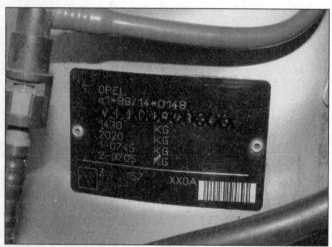

The VIN plate also appears on the right-hand front suspension tower

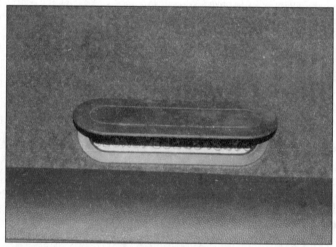

The VIN number is stamped into the body floor next to the right-hand front seat

The VIN number can also be viewed through the left-hand side of the windscreen

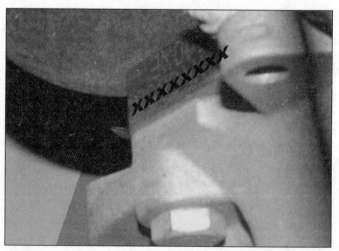

The engine number is stamped on the front of the cylinder block

Whenever servicing, repair or overhaul work is carried out on the car or its components, observe the following procedures and instructions. This will assist in carrying out the operation efficiently and to a professional standard of workmanship.

Joint mating faces and gaskets

When separating components at their mating faces, never insert screwdrivers or similar implements into the joint between the faces in order to prise them apart. This can cause severe damage which results in oil leaks, coolant leaks, etc upon reassembly. Separation is usually achieved by tapping along the joint with a soft-faced hammer in order to break the seal. However, note that this method may not be suitable where dowels are used for component location.

Where a gasket is used between the mating faces of two components, a new one must be fitted on reassembly; fit it dry unless otherwise stated in the repair procedure. Make sure that the mating faces are clean and dry, with all traces of old gasket removed. When cleaning a joint face, use a tool which is unlikely to score or damage the face, and remove any burrs or nicks with an oilstone or fine file.

Make sure that tapped holes are cleaned with a pipe cleaner, and keep them free of jointing compound, if this is being used, unless specifically instructed otherwise.

Ensure that all orifices, channels or pipes are clear, and blow through them, preferably using compressed air.

Oil seals

Oil seals can be removed by levering them out with a wide flat-bladed screwdriver or similar implement. Alternatively, a number of self-tapping screws may be screwed into the seal, and these used as a purchase for pliers or some similar device in order to pull the seal free.

Whenever an oil seal is removed from its working location, either individually or as part of an assembly, it should be renewed.

The very fine sealing lip of the seal is easily damaged, and will not seal if the surface it contacts is not completely clean and free from scratches, nicks or grooves. If the original sealing surface of the component cannot be restored, and the manufacturer has not made provision for slight relocation of the seal relative to the sealing surface, the component should be renewed.

Protect the lips of the seal from any surface which may damage them in the course of fitting. Use tape or a conical sleeve where possible. Lubricate the seal lips with oil before fitting and, on dual-lipped seals, fill the space between the lips with grease.

Unless otherwise stated, oil seals must be fitted with their sealing lips toward the lubricant to be sealed.

Use a tubular drift or block of wood of the appropriate size to install the seal and, if the seal housing is shouldered, drive the seal down to the shoulder. If the seal housing is unshouldered, the seal should be fitted with its face flush with the housing top face (unless otherwise instructed).

Screw threads and fastenings

Seized nuts, bolts and screws are quite a common occurrence where corrosion has set in, and the use of penetrating oil or releasing fluid will often overcome this problem if the offending item is soaked for a while before attempting to release it. The use of an impact driver may also provide a means of releasing such stubborn fastening devices, when used in conjunction with the appropriate screwdriver bit or socket. If none of these methods works, it may be necessary to resort to the careful application of heat, or the use of a hacksaw or nut splitter device.

Studs are usually removed by locking two nuts together on the threaded part, and then using a spanner on the lower nut to unscrew the stud. Studs or bolts which have broken off below the surface of the component in which they are mounted can sometimes be removed using a stud extractor. Always ensure that a blind tapped hole is completely free from oil, grease, water or other fluid before installing the bolt or stud. Failure to do this could cause the housing to crack due to the hydraulic action of the bolt or stud as it is screwed in.

When tightening a castellated nut to accept a split pin, tighten the nut to the specified torque, where applicable, and then tighten further to the next split pin hole. Never slacken the nut to align the split pin hole, unless stated in the repair procedure.

When checking or retightening a nut or bolt to a specified torque setting, slacken the nut or bolt by a quarter of a turn, and then retighten to the specified setting. However, this should not be attempted where angular tightening has been used.

For some screw fastenings, notably cylinder head bolts or nuts, torque wrench settings are no longer specified for the latter stages of tightening, "angle-tightening" being called up instead. Typically, a fairly low torque wrench setting will be applied to the bolts/nuts in the correct sequence, followed by one or more stages of tightening through specified angles.

Locknuts, locktabs and washers

Any fastening which will rotate against a component or housing during tightening should always have a washer between it and the relevant component or housing.

Spring or split washers should always be renewed when they are used to lock a critical component such as a big-end bearing retaining bolt or nut. Locktabs which are folded over to retain a nut or bolt should always be renewed.

Self-locking nuts can be re-used in non-critical areas, providing resistance can be felt when the locking portion passes over the bolt or stud thread. However, it should be noted that self-locking stiffnuts tend to lose their effectiveness after long periods of use, and should then be renewed as a matter of course.

Split pins must always be replaced with new ones of the correct size for the hole.

When thread-locking compound is found on the threads of a fastener which is to be re-used, it should be cleaned off with a wire brush and solvent, and fresh compound applied on reassembly.

Special tools

Some repair procedures in this manual entail the use of special tools such as a press, two or three-legged pullers, spring compressors, etc. Wherever possible, suitable readily-available alternatives to the manufacturer's special tools are described, and are shown in use. In some instances, where no alternative is possible, it has been necessary to resort to the use of a manufacturer's tool, and this has been done for reasons of safety as well as the efficient completion of the repair operation. Unless you are highly-skilled and have a thorough understanding of the procedures described, never attempt to bypass the use of any special tool when the procedure described specifies its use. Not only is there a very great risk of personal injury, but expensive damage could be caused to the components involved.

Environmental considerations

When disposing of used engine oil, brake fluid, antifreeze, etc, give due consideration to any detrimental environmental effects. Do not, for instance, pour any of the above liquids down drains into the general sewage system, or onto the ground to soak away. Many local council refuse tips provide a facility for waste oil disposal, as do some garages. If none of these facilities are available, consult your local Environmental Health Department, or the National Rivers Authority, for further advice.

With the universal tightening-up of legislation regarding the emission of environmentally-harmful substances from motor vehicles, most vehicles have tamperproof devices fitted to the main adjustment points of the fuel system. These devices are primarily designed to prevent unqualified persons from adjusting the fuel/air mixture, with the chance of a consequent increase in toxic emissions. If such devices are found during servicing or overhaul, they should, wherever possible, be renewed or refitted in accordance with the manufacturer's requirements or current legislation.

OIL CARE
FOLLOW THE CODE

OIL BANK LINE
0800 66 33 66
www.oilbankline.org.uk

Note: It is antisocial and illegal to dump oil down the drain. To find the location of your local oil recycling bank, call this number free.

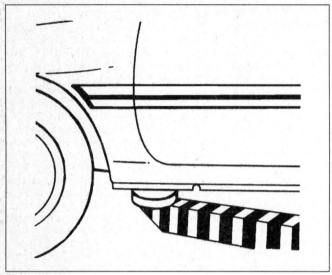

Front jacking point for hydraulic jack or axle stands

Rear jacking point for hydraulic jack or axle stands

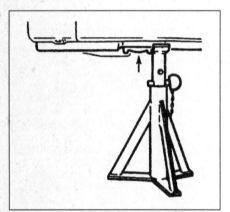

Axle stands should be placed under, or adjacent to the jacking point (arrowed)

The jack supplied with the vehicle tool kit should only be used for changing roadwheels – see Wheel changing at the front of this manual. Ensure the jack head is correctly engaged before attempting to raise the vehicle. When carrying out any other kind of work, raise the vehicle using a hydraulic jack, and always supplement the jack with axle stands positioned under the vehicle jacking points.

When jacking up the vehicle with a trolley jack, position the jack head under one of the relevant jacking points (note that the jacking points for use with a hydraulic jack are different to those for use with the vehicle jack). Use a block of wood between the jack or axle stand and the sill – the block of wood should have a groove cut into it , in which the welded flange of the sill will locate. **Do not** jack the vehicle under the sump or any of the steering or suspension components. Supplement the jack using axle stands **(see illustrations)**.

 Warning: Never work under, around, or near a raised vehicle, unless it is adequately supported in at least two places.

Numerous systems fitted to the vehicle require battery power to be available at all times, either to ensure their continued operation (such as the clock) or to maintain control unit memories which would be erased if the battery were to be disconnected. Whenever the battery is to be disconnected therefore, first note the following, to ensure that there are no unforeseen consequences of this action:

a) *First, on any vehicle with central locking, it is a wise precaution to remove the key from the ignition, and to keep it with you, so that it does not get locked in, if the central locking should engage accidentally when the battery is reconnected.*

b) *Depending on model and specification, the Vauxhall anti-theft alarm system may be of the type which is automatically activated when the vehicle battery is disconnected and/or reconnected. To prevent the alarm sounding on models so equipped, switch the ignition on, then off, and disconnect the battery within15 seconds. If the alarm is activated when the battery is reconnected, switch the ignition on then off to deactivate the alarm.*

c) *If a security-coded audio unit is fitted, and the unit and/or the battery is disconnected, the unit will not function again on reconnection until the correct security code is entered. Details of this procedure, which varies according to the unit fitted, are given in the vehicle audio system operating instructions. Ensure you have the correct code before you disconnect the battery. If you do not have the code or details of the correct procedure, but can supply proof of ownership and a legitimate reason for wanting this information, a Vauxhall dealer may be able to help.*

d) *The engine management electronic control unit is of the 'self-learning' type, meaning that as it operates, it also monitors and stores the settings which give optimum engine performance under all operating conditions. When the battery is disconnected, these settings are lost and the ECU reverts to the base settings programmed into its memory at the factory. On restarting, this may lead to the engine running/idling roughly for a short while, until the ECU has re-learned the optimum settings. This process is best accomplished by taking the vehicle on a road test (for approximately 15 minutes), covering all engine speeds and loads, concentrating mainly in the 2500 to 3500 rpm region.*

e) *On models equipped with automatic transmission, the transmission selector lever assembly incorporates an electrically-operated selector lever lock mechanism that prevents the lever being moved out of the P position unless the ignition is switched on and the brake pedal is depressed. If the selector lever is in the P position and the battery is disconnected, it will not be possible to move the selector lever out of position P by the normal means. Although it is possible to manually override the system (see Chapter 7B), it is sensible to move the selector lever to the N position before disconnecting the battery.*

f) *On all models, when reconnecting the battery after disconnection, switch on the ignition and wait 10 seconds to allow the electronic vehicle systems to stabilise and re-initialise.*

Devices known as 'memory-savers' (or 'code-savers') can be used to avoid some of the above problems. Precise details vary according to the device used. Typically, it is plugged into the cigarette lighter, and is connected by its own wires to a spare battery; the vehicle's own battery is then disconnected from the electrical system, leaving the 'memory-saver' to pass sufficient current to maintain audio unit security codes and any other memory values, and also to run permanently-live circuits such as the clock.

⚠️ *Warning: Some of these devices allow a considerable amount of current to pass, which can mean that many of the vehicle's systems are still operational when the main battery is disconnected. If a 'memory saver' is used, ensure that the circuit concerned is actually 'dead' before carrying out any work on it!*

Introduction

A selection of good tools is a fundamental requirement for anyone contemplating the maintenance and repair of a motor vehicle. For the owner who does not possess any, their purchase will prove a considerable expense, offsetting some of the savings made by doing-it-yourself. However, provided that the tools purchased meet the relevant national safety standards and are of good quality, they will last for many years and prove an extremely worthwhile investment.

To help the average owner to decide which tools are needed to carry out the various tasks detailed in this manual, we have compiled three lists of tools under the following headings: *Maintenance and minor repair, Repair and overhaul*, and *Special*. Newcomers to practical mechanics should start off with the *Maintenance and minor repair* tool kit, and confine themselves to the simpler jobs around the vehicle. Then, as confidence and experience grow, more difficult tasks can be undertaken, with extra tools being purchased as, and when, they are needed. In this way, a *Maintenance and minor repair* tool kit can be built up into a *Repair and overhaul* tool kit over a considerable period of time, without any major cash outlays. The experienced do-it-yourselfer will have a tool kit good enough for most repair and overhaul procedures, and will add tools from the *Special* category when it is felt that the expense is justified by the amount of use to which these tools will be put.

Maintenance and minor repair tool kit

The tools given in this list should be considered as a minimum requirement if routine maintenance, servicing and minor repair operations are to be undertaken. We recommend the purchase of combination spanners (ring one end, open-ended the other); although more expensive than open-ended ones, they do give the advantages of both types of spanner.

☐ *Combination spanners:*
  Metric - 8 to 19 mm inclusive
☐ *Adjustable spanner - 35 mm jaw (approx.)*
☐ *Spark plug spanner (with rubber insert) - petrol models*
☐ *Spark plug gap adjustment tool - petrol models*
☐ *Set of feeler gauges*
☐ *Brake bleed nipple spanner*
☐ *Screwdrivers:*
  Flat blade - 100 mm long x 6 mm dia
  Cross blade - 100 mm long x 6 mm dia
  Torx - various sizes (not all vehicles)
☐ *Combination pliers*
☐ *Hacksaw (junior)*
☐ *Tyre pump*
☐ *Tyre pressure gauge*
☐ *Oil can*
☐ *Oil filter removal tool*
☐ *Fine emery cloth*
☐ *Wire brush (small)*
☐ *Funnel (medium size)*
☐ *Sump drain plug key (not all vehicles)*

Repair and overhaul tool kit

These tools are virtually essential for anyone undertaking any major repairs to a motor vehicle, and are additional to those given in the *Maintenance and minor repair* list. Included in this list is a comprehensive set of sockets. Although these are expensive, they will be found invaluable as they are so versatile - particularly if various drives are included in the set. We recommend the half-inch square-drive type, as this can be used with most proprietary torque wrenches.

The tools in this list will sometimes need to be supplemented by tools from the *Special* list:

☐ *Sockets (or box spanners) to cover range in previous list (including Torx sockets)*
☐ *Reversible ratchet drive (for use with sockets)*
☐ *Extension piece, 250 mm (for use with sockets)*
☐ *Universal joint (for use with sockets)*
☐ *Flexible handle or sliding T "breaker bar" (for use with sockets)*
☐ *Torque wrench (for use with sockets)*
☐ *Self-locking grips*
☐ *Ball pein hammer*
☐ *Soft-faced mallet (plastic or rubber)*
☐ *Screwdrivers:*
  Flat blade - long & sturdy, short (chubby), and narrow (electrician's) types
  Cross blade - long & sturdy, and short (chubby) types
☐ *Pliers:*
  Long-nosed
  Side cutters (electrician's)
  Circlip (internal and external)
☐ *Cold chisel - 25 mm*
☐ *Scriber*
☐ *Scraper*
☐ *Centre-punch*
☐ *Pin punch*
☐ *Hacksaw*
☐ *Brake hose clamp*
☐ *Brake/clutch bleeding kit*
☐ *Selection of twist drills*
☐ *Steel rule/straight-edge*
☐ *Allen keys (inc. splined/Torx type)*
☐ *Selection of files*
☐ *Wire brush*
☐ *Axle stands*
☐ *Jack (strong trolley or hydraulic type)*
☐ *Light with extension lead*
☐ *Universal electrical multi-meter*

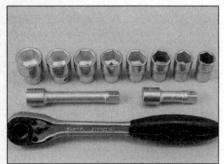

Sockets and reversible ratchet drive

Brake bleeding kit

Torx key, socket and bit

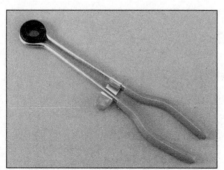

Hose clamp

Angular-tightening gauge

Special tools

The tools in this list are those which are not used regularly, are expensive to buy, or which need to be used in accordance with their manufacturers' instructions. Unless relatively difficult mechanical jobs are undertaken frequently, it will not be economic to buy many of these tools. Where this is the case, you could consider clubbing together with friends (or joining a motorists' club) to make a joint purchase, or borrowing the tools against a deposit from a local garage or tool hire specialist. It is worth noting that many of the larger DIY superstores now carry a large range of special tools for hire at modest rates.

The following list contains only those tools and instruments freely available to the public, and not those special tools produced by the vehicle manufacturer specifically for its dealer network. You will find occasional references to these manufacturers' special tools in the text of this manual. Generally, an alternative method of doing the job without the vehicle manufacturer's special tool is given. However, sometimes there is no alternative to using them. Where this is the case and the relevant tool cannot be bought or borrowed, you will have to entrust the work to a dealer.

- [ ] Angular-tightening gauge
- [ ] Valve spring compressor
- [ ] Valve grinding tool
- [ ] Piston ring compressor
- [ ] Piston ring removal/installation tool
- [ ] Cylinder bore hone
- [ ] Balljoint separator
- [ ] Coil spring compressors (where applicable)
- [ ] Two/three-legged hub and bearing puller
- [ ] Impact screwdriver
- [ ] Micrometer and/or vernier calipers
- [ ] Dial gauge
- [ ] Stroboscopic timing light
- [ ] Dwell angle meter/tachometer
- [ ] Fault code reader
- [ ] Cylinder compression gauge
- [ ] Hand-operated vacuum pump and gauge
- [ ] Clutch plate alignment set
- [ ] Brake shoe steady spring cup removal tool
- [ ] Bush and bearing removal/installation set
- [ ] Stud extractors
- [ ] Tap and die set
- [ ] Lifting tackle
- [ ] Trolley jack

Buying tools

Reputable motor accessory shops and superstores often offer excellent quality tools at discount prices, so it pays to shop around.

Remember, you don't have to buy the most expensive items on the shelf, but it is always advisable to steer clear of the very cheap tools. Beware of 'bargains' offered on market stalls or at car boot sales. There are plenty of good tools around at reasonable prices, but always aim to purchase items which meet the relevant national safety standards. If in doubt, ask the proprietor or manager of the shop for advice before making a purchase.

Care and maintenance of tools

Having purchased a reasonable tool kit, it is necessary to keep the tools in a clean and serviceable condition. After use, always wipe off any dirt, grease and metal particles using a clean, dry cloth, before putting the tools away. Never leave them lying around after they have been used. A simple tool rack on the garage or workshop wall for items such as screwdrivers and pliers is a good idea. Store all normal spanners and sockets in a metal box. Any measuring instruments, gauges, meters, etc, must be carefully stored where they cannot be damaged or become rusty.

Take a little care when tools are used. Hammer heads inevitably become marked, and screwdrivers lose the keen edge on their blades from time to time. A little timely attention with emery cloth or a file will soon restore items like this to a good finish.

Working facilities

Not to be forgotten when discussing tools is the workshop itself. If anything more than routine maintenance is to be carried out, a suitable working area becomes essential.

It is appreciated that many an owner-mechanic is forced by circumstances to remove an engine or similar item without the benefit of a garage or workshop. Having done this, any repairs should always be done under the cover of a roof.

Wherever possible, any dismantling should be done on a clean, flat workbench or table at a suitable working height.

Any workbench needs a vice; one with a jaw opening of 100 mm is suitable for most jobs. As mentioned previously, some clean dry storage space is also required for tools, as well as for any lubricants, cleaning fluids, touch-up paints etc, which become necessary.

Another item which may be required, and which has a much more general usage, is an electric drill with a chuck capacity of at least 8 mm. This, together with a good range of twist drills, is virtually essential for fitting accessories.

Last, but not least, always keep a supply of old newspapers and clean, lint-free rags available, and try to keep any working area as clean as possible.

Micrometers

Dial test indicator ("dial gauge")

Strap wrench

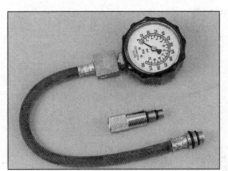

Compression tester

Fault code reader

This is a guide to getting your vehicle through the MOT test. Obviously it will not be possible to examine the vehicle to the same standard as the professional MOT tester. However, working through the following checks will enable you to identify any problem areas before submitting the vehicle for the test.

Where a testable component is in borderline condition, the tester has discretion in deciding whether to pass or fail it. The basis of such discretion is whether the tester would be happy for a close relative or friend to use the vehicle with the component in that condition. If the vehicle presented is clean and evidently well cared for, the tester may be more inclined to pass a borderline component than if the vehicle is scruffy and apparently neglected.

It has only been possible to summarise the test requirements here, based on the regulations in force at the time of printing. Test standards are becoming increasingly stringent, although there are some exemptions for older vehicles.

An assistant will be needed to help carry out some of these checks.

The checks have been sub-divided into four categories, as follows:

1 Checks carried out **FROM THE DRIVER'S SEAT**

2 Checks carried out **WITH THE VEHICLE ON THE GROUND**

3 Checks carried out **WITH THE VEHICLE RAISED AND THE WHEELS FREE TO TURN**

4 Checks carried out on **YOUR VEHICLE'S EXHAUST EMISSION SYSTEM**

---

1 Checks carried out **FROM THE DRIVER'S SEAT**

Handbrake

☐ Test the operation of the handbrake. Excessive travel (too many clicks) indicates incorrect brake or cable adjustment.
☐ Check that the handbrake cannot be released by tapping the lever sideways. Check the security of the lever mountings.

Footbrake

☐ Depress the brake pedal and check that it does not creep down to the floor, indicating a master cylinder fault. Release the pedal, wait a few seconds, then depress it again. If the pedal travels nearly to the floor before firm resistance is felt, brake adjustment or repair is necessary. If the pedal feels spongy, there is air in the hydraulic system which must be removed by bleeding.

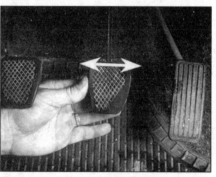

☐ Check that the brake pedal is secure and in good condition. Check also for signs of fluid leaks on the pedal, floor or carpets, which would indicate failed seals in the brake master cylinder.
☐ Check the servo unit (when applicable) by operating the brake pedal several times, then keeping the pedal depressed and starting the engine. As the engine starts, the pedal will move down slightly. If not, the vacuum hose or the servo itself may be faulty.

Steering wheel and column

☐ Examine the steering wheel for fractures or looseness of the hub, spokes or rim.
☐ Move the steering wheel from side to side and then up and down. Check that the steering wheel is not loose on the column, indicating wear or a loose retaining nut. Continue moving the steering wheel as before, but also turn it slightly from left to right.
☐ Check that the steering wheel is not loose on the column, and that there is no abnormal

movement of the steering wheel, indicating wear in the column support bearings or couplings.

Windscreen, mirrors and sunvisor

☐ The windscreen must be free of cracks or other significant damage within the driver's field of view. (Small stone chips are acceptable.) Rear view mirrors must be secure, intact, and capable of being adjusted.

290mm

☐ The driver's sunvisor must be capable of being stored in the "up" position.

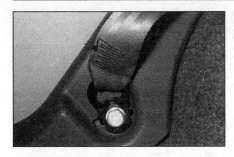

Seat belts and seats

Note: *The following checks are applicable to all seat belts, front and rear.*

☐ Examine the webbing of all the belts (including rear belts if fitted) for cuts, serious fraying or deterioration. Fasten and unfasten each belt to check the buckles. If applicable, check the retracting mechanism. Check the security of all seat belt mountings accessible from inside the vehicle.

☐ Seat belts with pre-tensioners, once activated, have a "flag" or similar showing on the seat belt stalk. This, in itself, is not a reason for test failure.

☐ The front seats themselves must be securely attached and the backrests must lock in the upright position.

Doors

☐ Both front doors must be able to be opened and closed from outside and inside, and must latch securely when closed.

2 Checks carried out **WITH THE VEHICLE ON THE GROUND**

Vehicle identification

☐ Number plates must be in good condition, secure and legible, with letters and numbers correctly spaced – spacing at (A) should be at least twice that at (B).

☐ The VIN plate and/or homologation plate must be legible.

Electrical equipment

☐ Switch on the ignition and check the operation of the horn.

☐ Check the windscreen washers and wipers, examining the wiper blades; renew damaged or perished blades. Also check the operation of the stop-lights.

☐ Check the operation of the sidelights and number plate lights. The lenses and reflectors must be secure, clean and undamaged.

☐ Check the operation and alignment of the headlights. The headlight reflectors must not be tarnished and the lenses must be undamaged.

☐ Switch on the ignition and check the operation of the direction indicators (including the instrument panel tell-tale) and the hazard warning lights. Operation of the sidelights and stop-lights must not affect the indicators - if it does, the cause is usually a bad earth at the rear light cluster.

☐ Check the operation of the rear foglight(s), including the warning light on the instrument panel or in the switch.

☐ The ABS warning light must illuminate in accordance with the manufacturers' design. For most vehicles, the ABS warning light should illuminate when the ignition is switched on, and (if the system is operating properly) extinguish after a few seconds. Refer to the owner's handbook.

Footbrake

☐ Examine the master cylinder, brake pipes and servo unit for leaks, loose mountings, corrosion or other damage.

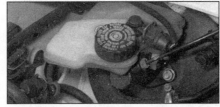

☐ The fluid reservoir must be secure and the fluid level must be between the upper (**A**) and lower (**B**) markings.

☐ Inspect both front brake flexible hoses for cracks or deterioration of the rubber. Turn the steering from lock to lock, and ensure that the hoses do not contact the wheel, tyre, or any part of the steering or suspension mechanism. With the brake pedal firmly depressed, check the hoses for bulges or leaks under pressure.

Steering and suspension

☐ Have your assistant turn the steering wheel from side to side slightly, up to the point where the steering gear just begins to transmit this movement to the roadwheels. Check for excessive free play between the steering wheel and the steering gear, indicating wear or insecurity of the steering column joints, the column-to-steering gear coupling, or the steering gear itself.

☐ Have your assistant turn the steering wheel more vigorously in each direction, so that the roadwheels just begin to turn. As this is done, examine all the steering joints, linkages, fittings and attachments. Renew any component that shows signs of wear or damage. On vehicles with power steering, check the security and condition of the steering pump, drivebelt and hoses.

☐ Check that the vehicle is standing level, and at approximately the correct ride height.

Shock absorbers

☐ Depress each corner of the vehicle in turn, then release it. The vehicle should rise and then settle in its normal position. If the vehicle continues to rise and fall, the shock absorber is defective. A shock absorber which has seized will also cause the vehicle to fail.

Exhaust system

☐ Start the engine. With your assistant holding a rag over the tailpipe, check the entire system for leaks. Repair or renew leaking sections.

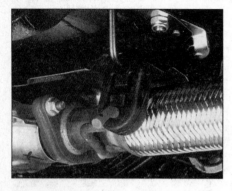

3 Checks carried out **WITH THE VEHICLE RAISED AND THE WHEELS FREE TO TURN**

Jack up the front and rear of the vehicle, and securely support it on axle stands. Position the stands clear of the suspension assemblies. Ensure that the wheels are clear of the ground and that the steering can be turned from lock to lock.

Steering mechanism

☐ Have your assistant turn the steering from lock to lock. Check that the steering turns smoothly, and that no part of the steering mechanism, including a wheel or tyre, fouls any brake hose or pipe or any part of the body structure.
☐ Examine the steering rack rubber gaiters for damage or insecurity of the retaining clips. If power steering is fitted, check for signs of damage or leakage of the fluid hoses, pipes or connections. Also check for excessive stiffness or binding of the steering, a missing split pin or locking device, or severe corrosion of the body structure within 30 cm of any steering component attachment point.

Front and rear suspension and wheel bearings

☐ Starting at the front right-hand side, grasp the roadwheel at the 3 o'clock and 9 o'clock positions and rock gently but firmly. Check for free play or insecurity at the wheel bearings, suspension balljoints, or suspension mountings, pivots and attachments.
☐ Now grasp the wheel at the 12 o'clock and 6 o'clock positions and repeat the previous inspection. Spin the wheel, and check for roughness or tightness of the front wheel bearing.

☐ If excess free play is suspected at a component pivot point, this can be confirmed by using a large screwdriver or similar tool and levering between the mounting and the component attachment. This will confirm whether the wear is in the pivot bush, its retaining bolt, or in the mounting itself (the bolt holes can often become elongated).

☐ Carry out all the above checks at the other front wheel, and then at both rear wheels.

Springs and shock absorbers

☐ Examine the suspension struts (when applicable) for serious fluid leakage, corrosion, or damage to the casing. Also check the security of the mounting points.
☐ If coil springs are fitted, check that the spring ends locate in their seats, and that the spring is not corroded, cracked or broken.
☐ If leaf springs are fitted, check that all leaves are intact, that the axle is securely attached to each spring, and that there is no deterioration of the spring eye mountings, bushes, and shackles.

☐ The same general checks apply to vehicles fitted with other suspension types, such as torsion bars, hydraulic displacer units, etc. Ensure that all mountings and attachments are secure, that there are no signs of excessive wear, corrosion or damage, and (on hydraulic types) that there are no fluid leaks or damaged pipes.
☐ Inspect the shock absorbers for signs of serious fluid leakage. Check for wear of the mounting bushes or attachments, or damage to the body of the unit.

Driveshafts (fwd vehicles only)

☐ Rotate each front wheel in turn and inspect the constant velocity joint gaiters for splits or damage. Also check that each driveshaft is straight and undamaged.

Braking system

☐ If possible without dismantling, check brake pad wear and disc condition. Ensure that the friction lining material has not worn excessively, (A) and that the discs are not fractured, pitted, scored or badly worn (B).

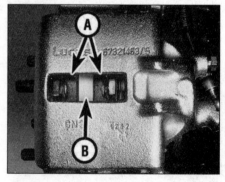

☐ Examine all the rigid brake pipes underneath the vehicle, and the flexible hose(s) at the rear. Look for corrosion, chafing or insecurity of the pipes, and for signs of bulging under pressure, chafing, splits or deterioration of the flexible hoses.
☐ Look for signs of fluid leaks at the brake calipers or on the brake backplates. Repair or renew leaking components.
☐ Slowly spin each wheel, while your assistant depresses and releases the footbrake. Ensure that each brake is operating and does not bind when the pedal is released.

□ Examine the handbrake mechanism, checking for frayed or broken cables, excessive corrosion, or wear or insecurity of the linkage. Check that the mechanism works on each relevant wheel, and releases fully, without binding.

□ It is not possible to test brake efficiency without special equipment, but a road test can be carried out later to check that the vehicle pulls up in a straight line.

Fuel and exhaust systems

□ Inspect the fuel tank (including the filler cap), fuel pipes, hoses and unions. All components must be secure and free from leaks.

□ Examine the exhaust system over its entire length, checking for any damaged, broken or missing mountings, security of the retaining clamps and rust or corrosion.

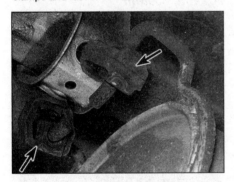

Wheels and tyres

□ Examine the sidewalls and tread area of each tyre in turn. Check for cuts, tears, lumps, bulges, separation of the tread, and exposure of the ply or cord due to wear or damage. Check that the tyre bead is correctly seated on the wheel rim, that the valve is sound and properly seated, and that the wheel is not distorted or damaged.

□ Check that the tyres are of the correct size for the vehicle, that they are of the same size and type on each axle, and that the pressures are correct.

□ Check the tyre tread depth. The legal minimum at the time of writing is 1.6 mm over at least three-quarters of the tread width. Abnormal tread wear may indicate incorrect front wheel alignment.

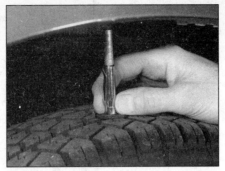

Body corrosion

□ Check the condition of the entire vehicle structure for signs of corrosion in load-bearing areas. (These include chassis box sections, side sills, cross-members, pillars, and all suspension, steering, braking system and seat belt mountings and anchorages.) Any corrosion which has seriously reduced the thickness of a load-bearing area is likely to cause the vehicle to fail. In this case professional repairs are likely to be needed.

□ Damage or corrosion which causes sharp or otherwise dangerous edges to be exposed will also cause the vehicle to fail.

4 Checks carried out on YOUR VEHICLE'S EXHAUST EMISSION SYSTEM

Petrol models

□ Have the engine at normal operating temperature, and make sure that it is in good tune (ignition system in good order, air filter element clean, etc).

□ Before any measurements are carried out, raise the engine speed to around 2500 rpm, and hold it at this speed for 20 seconds. Allow the engine speed to return to idle, and watch for smoke emissions from the exhaust tailpipe. If the idle speed is obviously much too high, or if dense blue or clearly-visible black smoke comes from the tailpipe for more than 5 seconds, the vehicle will fail. As a rule of thumb, blue smoke signifies oil being burnt (engine wear) while black smoke signifies unburnt fuel (dirty air cleaner element, or other carburettor or fuel system fault).

□ An exhaust gas analyser capable of measuring carbon monoxide (CO) and hydrocarbons (HC) is now needed. If such an instrument cannot be hired or borrowed, a local garage may agree to perform the check for a small fee.

CO emissions (mixture)

□ At the time of writing, for vehicles first used between 1st August 1975 and 31st July 1986 (P to C registration), the CO level must not exceed 4.5% by volume. For vehicles first used between 1st August 1986 and 31st July 1992 (D to J registration), the CO level must not exceed 3.5% by volume. Vehicles first

used after 1st August 1992 (K registration) must conform to the manufacturer's specification. The MOT tester has access to a DOT database or emissions handbook, which lists the CO and HC limits for each make and model of vehicle. The CO level is measured with the engine at idle speed, and at "fast idle". The following limits are given as a general guide:

At idle speed -
   CO level no more than 0.5%
At "fast idle" (2500 to 3000 rpm) -
   CO level no more than 0.3%
   (Minimum oil temperature 60ºC)

□ If the CO level cannot be reduced far enough to pass the test (and the fuel and ignition systems are otherwise in good condition) then the carburettor is badly worn, or there is some problem in the fuel injection system or catalytic converter (as applicable).

HC emissions

□ With the CO within limits, HC emissions for vehicles first used between 1st August 1975 and 31st July 1992 (P to J registration) must not exceed 1200 ppm. Vehicles first used after 1st August 1992 (K registration) must conform to the manufacturer's specification. The MOT tester has access to a DOT database or emissions handbook, which lists the CO and HC limits for each make and model of vehicle. The HC level is measured with the engine at "fast idle". The following is given as a general guide:

At "fast idle" (2500 to 3000 rpm) -
   HC level no more than 200 ppm
   (Minimum oil temperature 60ºC)

□ Excessive HC emissions are caused by incomplete combustion, the causes of which can include oil being burnt, mechanical wear and ignition/fuel system malfunction.

Diesel models

□ The only emission test applicable to Diesel engines is the measuring of exhaust smoke density. The test involves accelerating the engine several times to its maximum unloaded speed.

Note: *It is of the utmost importance that the engine timing belt is in good condition before the test is carried out.*

□ The limits for Diesel engine exhaust smoke, introduced in September 1995 are:
Vehicles first used before 1st August 1979:
   Exempt from metered smoke testing, but must not emit "dense blue or clearly visible black smoke for a period of more than 5 seconds at idle" or "dense blue or clearly visible black smoke during acceleration which would obscure the view of other road users".
Non-turbocharged vehicles first used after 1st August 1979: 2.5m⁻¹
Turbocharged vehicles first used after 1st August 1979: 3.0m⁻¹

□ Excessive smoke can be caused by a dirty air cleaner element. Otherwise, professional advice may be needed to find the cause.

Engine

☐ Engine fails to rotate when attempting to start
☐ Engine rotates, but will not start
☐ Engine difficult to start when cold
☐ Engine difficult to start when hot
☐ Starter motor noisy or excessively-rough in engagement
☐ Engine starts, but stops immediately
☐ Engine idles erratically
☐ Engine misfires at idle speed
☐ Engine misfires throughout the driving speed range
☐ Engine hesitates on acceleration
☐ Engine stalls
☐ Engine lacks power
☐ Engine backfires
☐ Oil pressure warning light illuminated with engine running
☐ Engine runs-on after switching off
☐ Engine noises

Cooling system

☐ Overheating
☐ Overcooling
☐ External coolant leakage
☐ Internal coolant leakage
☐ Corrosion

Fuel and exhaust systems

☐ Excessive fuel consumption
☐ Fuel leakage and/or fuel odour
☐ Excessive noise or fumes from exhaust system

Clutch

☐ Pedal travels to floor – no pressure or very little resistance
☐ Clutch fails to disengage (unable to select gears)
☐ Clutch slips (engine speed increases, with no increase in vehicle speed)
☐ Judder as clutch is engaged
☐ Noise when depressing or releasing clutch pedal

Manual transmission

☐ Noisy in neutral with engine running
☐ Noisy in one particular gear
☐ Difficulty engaging gears
☐ Jumps out of gear
☐ Vibration
☐ Lubricant leaks

Automatic transmission

☐ Fluid leakage
☐ Transmission fluid brown, or has burned smell
☐ General gear selection problems
☐ Transmission will not downshift (kickdown) with accelerator pedal fully depressed
☐ Engine will not start in any gear, or starts in gears other than Park or Neutral
☐ Transmission slips, shifts roughly, is noisy, or has no drive in forward or reverse gears

Driveshafts

☐ Vibration when accelerating or decelerating
☐ Clicking or knocking noise on turns (at slow speed on full-lock)

Braking system

☐ Vehicle pulls to one side under braking
☐ Noise (grinding or high-pitched squeal) when brakes applied
☐ Excessive brake pedal travel
☐ Brake pedal feels spongy when depressed
☐ Excessive brake pedal effort required to stop vehicle
☐ Judder felt through brake pedal or steering wheel when braking
☐ Brakes binding
☐ Rear wheels locking under normal braking

Suspension and steering

☐ Vehicle pulls to one side
☐ Wheel wobble and vibration
☐ Excessive pitching and/or rolling around corners, or during braking
☐ Wandering or general instability
☐ Excessively-stiff steering
☐ Excessive play in steering
☐ Lack of power assistance
☐ Tyre wear excessive

Electrical system

☐ Battery will not hold a charge for more than a few days
☐ Ignition/no-charge warning light remains illuminated with engine running
☐ Ignition/no-charge warning light fails to come on
☐ Lights inoperative
☐ Instrument readings inaccurate or erratic
☐ Horn inoperative, or unsatisfactory in operation
☐ Windscreen wipers inoperative, or unsatisfactory in operation
☐ Windscreen washers inoperative, or unsatisfactory in operation
☐ Electric windows inoperative, or unsatisfactory in operation
☐ Central locking system inoperative, or unsatisfactory in operation

Introduction

The vehicle owner who does his or her own maintenance according to the recommended service schedules should not have to use this section of the manual very often. Modern component reliability is such that, provided those items subject to wear or deterioration are inspected or renewed at the specified intervals, sudden failure is comparatively rare. Faults do not usually just happen as a result of sudden failure, but develop over a period of time. Major mechanical failures in particular are usually preceded by characteristic symptoms over hundreds or even thousands of miles. Those components which do occasionally fail without warning are often small and easily carried in the vehicle.

With any fault-finding, the first step is to decide where to begin investigations. Sometimes this is obvious, but on other occasions, a little detective work will be necessary. The owner who makes half a dozen haphazard adjustments or replacements may be successful in curing a fault (or its symptoms), but will be none the wiser if the fault recurs, and ultimately may have spent more time and money than was necessary. A calm and logical approach will be found to be more satisfactory in the long run. Always take into account any warning signs or abnormalities that may have been noticed in the period preceding the fault – power loss, high or low gauge readings, unusual smells, etc – and remember that failure of components such as fuses or spark plugs may only be pointers to some underlying fault.

The pages which follow provide an easy-reference guide to the more common problems which may occur during the operation of the vehicle. These problems and their possible causes are grouped under headings denoting various components or systems, such as Engine, Cooling system, etc. The general Chapter which deals with the problem is also shown in brackets; refer to the relevant part of that Chapter for system-specific information. Whatever the fault, certain basic principles apply. These are as follows:

Verify the fault. This is simply a matter of being sure that you know what the symptoms are before starting work. This is particularly important if you are investigating a fault for someone else, who may not have described it very accurately.

Don't overlook the obvious. For example, if the vehicle won't start, is there fuel in the tank? (Don't take anyone else's word on this particular point, and don't trust the fuel gauge either!) If an electrical fault is indicated, look for loose or broken wires before digging out the test gear.

Cure the disease, not the symptom. Substituting a flat battery with a fully-charged one will get you off the hard shoulder, but if the underlying cause is not attended to, the new battery will go the same way. Similarly, changing oil-fouled spark plugs for a new set will get you moving again, but remember that the reason for the fouling (if it wasn't simply an incorrect grade of plug) will have to be established and corrected.

Don't take anything for granted. Particularly, don't forget that a 'new' component may itself be defective (especially if it's been rattling around in the boot for months), and don't leave components out of a fault diagnosis sequence just because they are new or recently-fitted. When you do finally diagnose a difficult fault, you'll probably realise that all the evidence was there from the start.

Consider what work, if any, has recently been carried out. Many faults arise through careless or hurried work. For instance, if any work has been performed under the bonnet, could some of the wiring have been dislodged or incorrectly routed, or a hose trapped? Have all the fasteners been properly tightened? Were new, genuine parts and new gaskets used? There is often a certain amount of detective work to be done in this case, as an apparently-unrelated task can have far-reaching consequences.

Engine

Engine fails to rotate when attempting to start

☐ Battery terminal connections loose or corroded (see *Weekly checks*)
☐ Battery discharged or faulty (Chapter 5A)
☐ Broken, loose or disconnected wiring in the starting circuit (Chapter 5A)
☐ Defective starter solenoid or ignition switch (Chapter 5A or 12)
☐ Defective starter motor (Chapter 5A)
☐ Starter pinion or flywheel ring gear teeth loose or broken (Chapter 2 or 5A)
☐ Engine earth strap broken or disconnected (Chapter 5A)
☐ Engine suffering 'hydraulic lock' (eg from water drawn into the engine after traversing flooded roads, or from a serious internal coolant leak) – consult a main dealer for advice
☐ Automatic transmission not in position P or N (Chapter 7B)

Engine rotates, but will not start

☐ Fuel tank empty
☐ Battery discharged (engine rotates slowly) (Chapter 5A)
☐ Battery terminal connections loose or corroded (see *Weekly checks*)
☐ Ignition components damp or damaged – petrol models (Chapter 1A or 5B)
☐ Immobiliser fault, or 'uncoded' ignition key being used (Chapter 12 or Roadside repairs)
☐ Crankshaft sensor fault (Chapter 4A, 4B or 4C)
☐ Broken, loose or disconnected wiring in the ignition circuit – petrol models (Chapter 1A or 5B)
☐ Worn, faulty or incorrectly-gapped spark plugs – petrol models (Chapter 1A)
☐ Preheating system faulty – diesel models (Chapter 5C)
☐ Fuel injection system fault (Chapter 4A, 4B or 4C)
☐ Air in fuel system – diesel models (Chapter 4C)
☐ Major mechanical failure (eg timing chain snapped) (Chapter 2A, 2B, 2C or 2D)

Engine difficult to start when cold

☐ Battery discharged (Chapter 5A)
☐ Battery terminal connections loose or corroded (see *Weekly checks*)
☐ Worn, faulty or incorrectly-gapped spark plugs – petrol models (Chapter 1A)
☐ Other ignition system fault – petrol models (Chapter 1A or 5B)
☐ Preheating system faulty – diesel models (Chapter 5C)
☐ Fuel injection system fault (Chapter 4A, 4B or 4C)
☐ Wrong grade of engine oil used (*Weekly checks*, Chapter 1A or 1B)
☐ Low cylinder compression (Chapter 2A, 2B, 2C or 2D)

Engine difficult to start when hot

☐ Air filter element dirty or clogged (Chapter 1A or 1B)
☐ Fuel injection system fault (Chapter 4A, 4B or 4C)
☐ Low cylinder compression (Chapter 2A, 2B, 2C or 2D)

Starter motor noisy or excessively-rough in engagement

☐ Starter pinion or flywheel ring gear teeth loose or broken (Chapter 2 or 5A)
☐ Starter motor mounting bolts loose or missing (Chapter 5A)
☐ Starter motor internal components worn or damaged (Chapter 5A)

Engine starts, but stops immediately

☐ Loose or faulty electrical connections in the ignition circuit – petrol models (Chapter 1A or 5B)
☐ Vacuum leak at the throttle body or inlet manifold – petrol models (Chapter 4A or 4B)
☐ Blocked injectors/fuel injection system fault (Chapter 4A or 4B)
☐ Air in fuel, possibly due to loose fuel line connection – diesel models (Chapter 4C)

Engine idles erratically

☐ Air filter element clogged (Chapter 1A or 1B)
☐ Vacuum leak at the throttle body, inlet manifold or associated hoses – petrol models (Chapter 4A or 4B)
☐ Worn, faulty or incorrectly-gapped spark plugs – petrol models (Chapter 1A)
☐ Valve clearances incorrect (Chapter 2C)
☐ Uneven or low cylinder compression (Chapter 2A, 2B, 2C or 2D)
☐ Camshaft lobes worn (Chapter 2A, 2B, 2C or 2D)
☐ Blocked injectors/fuel injection system fault (Chapter 4A, 4B or 4C)
☐ Air in fuel, possibly due to loose fuel line connection – diesel models (Chapter 4C)

Engine misfires at idle speed

☐ Worn, faulty or incorrectly-gapped spark plugs – petrol models (Chapter 1A)
☐ Faulty spark plug HT leads – petrol models (Chapter 1A)
☐ Vacuum leak at the throttle body, inlet manifold or associated hoses – petrol models (Chapter 4A or 4B)
☐ Blocked injectors/fuel injection system fault (Chapter 4A, 4B or 4C)
☐ Faulty injector(s) – diesel models (Chapter 4C)
☐ Uneven or low cylinder compression (Chapter 2A, 2B, 2C or 2D)
☐ Disconnected, leaking, or perished crankcase ventilation hoses (Chapter 4D)

Engine (continued)

Engine misfires throughout the driving speed range

- ☐ Fuel filter choked (Chapter 1A or 1B)
- ☐ Fuel pump faulty, or delivery pressure low – petrol models (Chapter 4A or 4B)
- ☐ Fuel tank vent blocked, or fuel pipes restricted (Chapter 4A, 4B or 4C)
- ☐ Vacuum leak at the throttle body, inlet manifold or associated hoses – petrol models (Chapter 4A or 4B)
- ☐ Worn, faulty or incorrectly-gapped spark plugs – petrol models (Chapter 1A)
- ☐ Faulty spark plug HT leads (where fitted) – petrol models (Chapter 1A)
- ☐ Faulty injector(s) – diesel models (Chapter 4C)
- ☐ Faulty ignition coil – petrol models (Chapter 5B)
- ☐ Uneven or low cylinder compression (Chapter 2A, 2B, 2C or 2D)
- ☐ Blocked injector/fuel injection system fault (Chapter 4A, 4B or 4C)
- ☐ Blocked catalytic converter (Chapter 4A, 4B or 4C)
- ☐ Engine overheating – petrol models (Chapter 3)

Engine hesitates on acceleration

- ☐ Worn, faulty or incorrectly-gapped spark plugs – petrol models (Chapter 1A)
- ☐ Vacuum leak at the throttle body, inlet manifold or associated hoses – petrol models (Chapter 4A or 4B)
- ☐ Blocked injectors/fuel injection system fault (Chapter 4A, 4B or 4C)
- ☐ Faulty injector(s) – diesel models (Chapter 4C)

Engine stalls

- ☐ Vacuum leak at the throttle body, inlet manifold or associated hoses – petrol models (Chapter 4A or 4B)
- ☐ Fuel filter choked (Chapter 1A or 1B)
- ☐ Fuel pump faulty, or delivery pressure low – petrol models (Chapter 4A or 4B)
- ☐ Fuel tank vent blocked, or fuel pipes restricted (Chapter 4A, 4B or 4C)
- ☐ Blocked injectors/fuel injection system fault (Chapter 4A, 4B or 4C)
- ☐ Faulty injector(s) – diesel models (Chapter 4C)

Engine lacks power

- ☐ Air filter element blocked (Chapter 1A or 1B)
- ☐ Fuel filter choked (Chapter 1A or 1B)
- ☐ Fuel pipes blocked or restricted (Chapter 4A, 4B or 4C)
- ☐ Valve clearances incorrect (Chapter 2A, 2B, 2C or 2D)
- ☐ Worn, faulty or incorrectly-gapped spark plugs – petrol models (Chapter 1A)
- ☐ Engine overheating – petrol models (Chapter 4A or 4B)
- ☐ Fuel tank level low – diesel models (Chapter 4C)
- ☐ Accelerator cable problem – petrol models (Chapter 4A or 4B)
- ☐ Accelerator position sensor faulty – diesel models (Chapter 4C)
- ☐ Vacuum leak at the throttle body, inlet manifold or associated hoses – petrol models (Chapter 4A or 4B)
- ☐ Blocked injectors/fuel injection system fault (Chapter 4A, 4B or 4C)
- ☐ Faulty injector(s) – diesel models (Chapter 4C)
- ☐ Fuel pump faulty, or delivery pressure low – petrol models (Chapter 4A or 4B)
- ☐ Uneven or low cylinder compression (Chapter 2A, 2B, 2C or 2D)
- ☐ Blocked catalytic converter (Chapter 4A, 4B or 4C)
- ☐ Injection pump timing incorrect – diesel models (Chapter 4C)
- ☐ Brakes binding (Chapter 1A, 1B or 9)
- ☐ Clutch slipping (Chapter 6)

Engine backfires

- ☐ Vacuum leak at the throttle body, inlet manifold or associated hoses – petrol models (Chapter 4A or 4B)
- ☐ Blocked injectors/fuel injection system fault (Chapter 4A, 4B or 4C)
- ☐ Blocked catalytic converter (Chapter 4A, 4B or 4C)
- ☐ Spark plug HT leads incorrectly fitted – petrol models (Chapter 1A or 5B)
- ☐ Ignition DIS module faulty – petrol models (Chapter 5B)

Oil pressure warning light illuminated with engine running

- ☐ Low oil level, or incorrect oil grade (see Weekly checks)
- ☐ Faulty oil pressure sensor, or wiring damaged (Chapter 2A, 2B, 2C or 2D)
- ☐ Worn engine bearings and/or oil pump (Chapter 2A, 2B, 2C or 2D)
- ☐ High engine operating temperature (Chapter 3)
- ☐ Oil pump pressure relief valve defective (Chapter 2A, 2B, 2C or 2D)
- ☐ Oil pump pick-up strainer clogged (Chapter 2A, 2B, 2C or 2D)

Engine runs-on after switching off

- ☐ Excessive carbon build-up in engine (Chapter 2)
- ☐ High engine operating temperature (Chapter 3)
- ☐ Fuel injection system fault (Chapter 4A, 4B or 4C)

Engine noises

Pre-ignition (pinking) or knocking during acceleration or under load

- ☐ Ignition timing incorrect/ignition system fault – petrol models (Chapter 1A or 5B)
- ☐ Incorrect grade of spark plug – petrol models (Chapter 1A)
- ☐ Incorrect grade of fuel (Chapter 4A or 4B)
- ☐ Knock sensor faulty – some petrol models (Chapter 4A or 4B)
- ☐ Vacuum leak at the throttle body, inlet manifold or associated hoses – petrol models (Chapter 4A or 4B)
- ☐ Excessive carbon build-up in engine (Chapter 2A, 2B, 2C or 2D)
- ☐ Blocked injector/fuel injection system fault (Chapter 4A, 4B or 4C)
- ☐ Faulty injector(s) – diesel models (Chapter 4C)

Whistling or wheezing noises

- ☐ Leaking inlet manifold or throttle body gasket – petrol models (Chapter 4A or 4B)
- ☐ Leaking exhaust manifold gasket or pipe-to-manifold joint (Chapter 4A, 4B or 4C)
- ☐ Leaking vacuum hose (Chapter 4, 5 or 9)
- ☐ Blowing cylinder head gasket (Chapter 2A, 2B, 2C or 2D)
- ☐ Partially blocked or leaking crankcase ventilation system (Chapter 4D)

Tapping or rattling noises

- ☐ Valve clearances incorrect (Chapter 2A, 2B, 2C or 2D)
- ☐ Worn valve gear or camshaft (Chapter 2A, 2B, 2C or 2D)
- ☐ Ancillary component fault (coolant pump, alternator, etc) (Chapter 3, 5A, etc)

Knocking or thumping noises

- ☐ Worn big-end bearings (regular heavy knocking, perhaps less under load) (Chapter 2D)
- ☐ Worn main bearings (rumbling and knocking, perhaps worsening under load) (Chapter 2D)
- ☐ Piston slap – most noticeable when cold, caused by piston/bore wear (Chapter 2D)
- ☐ Ancillary component fault (coolant pump, alternator, etc) (Chapter 3, 5A, etc)
- ☐ Engine mountings worn or defective (Chapter 2A, 2B, 2C or 2D)
- ☐ Front suspension or steering components worn (Chapter 10)

Cooling system

Overheating

☐ Insufficient coolant in system (see *Weekly checks*)
☐ Thermostat faulty (Chapter 3)
☐ Radiator core blocked, or grille restricted (Chapter 3)
☐ Cooling fan faulty, or resistor pack fault on models with twin fans (Chapter 3)
☐ Inaccurate cylinder head temperature sender (Chapter 3, 4A, 4B or 4C)
☐ Airlock in cooling system (Chapter 3)
☐ Expansion tank pressure cap faulty (Chapter 3)
☐ Engine management system fault (Chapter 4A, 4B or 4C)

Overcooling

☐ Thermostat faulty (Chapter 3)
☐ Inaccurate cylinder head temperature sender (Chapter 3, 4A, 4B or 4C)
☐ Cooling fan faulty (Chapter 3)
☐ Engine management system fault (Chapter 4A, 4B or 4C)

External coolant leakage

☐ Deteriorated or damaged hoses or hose clips (Chapter 1A or 1B)
☐ Radiator core or heater matrix leaking (Chapter 3)
☐ Expansion tank pressure cap faulty (Chapter 1A or 1B)
☐ Coolant pump internal seal leaking (Chapter 3)
☐ Coolant pump gasket leaking (Chapter 3)
☐ Boiling due to overheating (Chapter 3)
☐ Cylinder block core plug leaking (Chapter 2D)

Internal coolant leakage

☐ Leaking cylinder head gasket (Chapter 2A, 2B, 2C or 2D)
☐ Cracked cylinder head or cylinder block (Chapter 2A, 2B, 2C or 2D)

Corrosion

☐ Infrequent draining and flushing (Chapter 1A or 1B)
☐ Incorrect coolant mixture or inappropriate coolant type (see *Weekly checks*)

Fuel and exhaust systems

Excessive fuel consumption

☐ Air filter element dirty or clogged (Chapter 1A or 1B)
☐ Fuel injection system fault (Chapter 4A, 4B or 4C)
☐ Engine management system fault (Chapter 4A, 4B or 4C)
☐ Crankcase ventilation system blocked (Chapter 4D)
☐ Tyres under-inflated (see *Weekly checks*)
☐ Brakes binding (Chapter 1A, 1B or 9)
☐ Fuel leak, causing apparent high consumption (Chapter 1A, 1B, 4A, 4B or 4C)

Fuel leakage and/or fuel odour

☐ Damaged or corroded fuel tank, pipes or connections (Chapter 4A, 4B or 4C)
☐ Evaporative emissions system fault – petrol models (Chapter 4D)

Excessive noise or fumes from exhaust system

☐ Leaking exhaust system or manifold joints (Chapter 1A, 1B, 4A, 4B or 4C)
☐ Leaking, corroded or damaged silencers or pipe (Chapter 1A, 1B, 4A, 4B or 4C)
☐ Broken mountings causing body or suspension contact (Chapter 1A or 1B)

Clutch

Note: *Fault finding for the Easytronic semi-automatic clutch should be entrusted to a Vauxhall dealer.*

Pedal travels to floor – no pressure or very little resistance

☐ Air in hydraulic system/faulty master or slave cylinder (Chapter 6)
☐ Faulty hydraulic release system (Chapter 6)
☐ Clutch pedal return spring detached or broken (Chapter 6)
☐ Broken clutch release bearing or fork (Chapter 6)
☐ Broken diaphragm spring in clutch pressure plate (Chapter 6)

Clutch fails to disengage (unable to select gears)

☐ Air in hydraulic system/faulty master or slave cylinder (Chapter 6)
☐ Faulty hydraulic release system (Chapter 6)
☐ Clutch disc sticking on transmission input shaft splines (Chapter 6)
☐ Clutch disc sticking to flywheel or pressure plate (Chapter 6)
☐ Faulty pressure plate assembly (Chapter 6)
☐ Clutch release mechanism worn or incorrectly assembled (Chapter 6)

Clutch slips (engine speed increases, with no increase in vehicle speed)

☐ Faulty hydraulic release system (Chapter 6)
☐ Clutch disc linings excessively worn (Chapter 6)
☐ Clutch disc linings contaminated with oil or grease (Chapter 6)
☐ Faulty pressure plate or weak diaphragm spring (Chapter 6)

Judder as clutch is engaged

☐ Clutch disc linings contaminated with oil or grease (Chapter 6)
☐ Clutch disc linings excessively worn (Chapter 6)
☐ Faulty or distorted pressure plate or diaphragm spring (Chapter 6).
☐ Worn or loose engine or transmission mountings (Chapter 2A, 2B, 2C or 2D)
☐ Clutch disc hub or transmission input shaft splines worn (Chapter 6)

Noise when depressing or releasing clutch pedal

☐ Worn clutch release bearing (Chapter 6)
☐ Worn or dry clutch pedal bushes (Chapter 6)
☐ Worn or dry clutch master cylinder piston (Chapter 6)
☐ Faulty pressure plate assembly (Chapter 6)
☐ Pressure plate diaphragm spring broken (Chapter 6)
☐ Broken clutch disc cushioning springs (Chapter 6)

Manual transmission

Note: *Fault finding for the Easytronic transmission should be entrusted to a Vauxhall dealer.*

Noisy in neutral with engine running

☐ Lack of oil (Chapter 7A or 7C)
☐ Input shaft bearings worn (noise apparent with clutch pedal released, but not when depressed) (Chapter 7A)*
☐ Clutch release bearing worn (noise apparent with clutch pedal depressed, possibly less when released) (Chapter 6)

Noisy in one particular gear

☐ Worn, damaged or chipped gear teeth (Chapter 7A)*

Difficulty engaging gears

☐ Clutch fault (Chapter 6)
☐ Worn, damaged, or poorly-adjusted gearchange (Chapter 7A)
☐ Lack of oil (Chapter 7A or 7C)
☐ Worn synchroniser units (Chapter 7A)*

Jumps out of gear

☐ Worn, damaged, or poorly-adjusted gearchange (Chapter 7A)
☐ Worn synchroniser units (Chapter 7A)*
☐ Worn selector forks (Chapter 7A)*

Vibration

☐ Lack of oil (Chapter 7A or 7C)
☐ Worn bearings (Chapter 7A)*

Lubricant leaks

☐ Leaking driveshaft or selector shaft oil seal (Chapter 7A)
☐ Leaking housing joint (Chapter 7A)*
☐ Leaking input shaft oil seal (Chapter 7A)*

Although the corrective action necessary to remedy the symptoms described is beyond the scope of the home mechanic, the above information should be helpful in isolating the cause of the condition, so that the owner can communicate clearly with a professional mechanic.

Automatic transmission

Note: *Due to the complexity of the automatic transmission, it is difficult for the home mechanic to properly diagnose and service this unit. For problems other than the following, the vehicle should be taken to a dealer service department or automatic transmission specialist. Do not be too hasty in removing the transmission if a fault is suspected, as most of the testing is carried out with the unit still fitted. Remember that, besides the sensors specific to the transmission, many of the engine management system sensors described in Chapter 4 are essential to the correct operation of the transmission.*

Fluid leakage

☐ Automatic transmission fluid is usually dark red in colour. Fluid leaks should not be confused with engine oil, which can easily be blown onto the transmission by airflow.

☐ To determine the source of a leak, first remove all built-up dirt and grime from the transmission housing and surrounding areas using a degreasing agent, or by steam-cleaning. Drive the vehicle at low speed, so airflow will not blow the leak far from its source. Raise and support the vehicle, and determine where the leak is coming from. The following are common areas of leakage:

a) *Fluid pan*
b) *Dipstick tube (Chapter 1A)*
c) *Transmission-to-fluid cooler unions (Chapter 7B)*

Transmission fluid brown, or has burned smell

☐ Transmission fluid level low (Chapter 1A)

General gear selection problems

☐ Chapter 7B deals with checking the selector cable on automatic transmissions. The following are common problems which may be caused by a faulty cable or sensor:

a) *Engine starting in gears other than Park or Neutral.*
b) *Indicator panel indicating a gear other than the one actually being used.*
c) *Vehicle moves when in Park or Neutral.*
d) *Poor gear shift quality or erratic gear changes.*

Transmission will not downshift (kickdown) with accelerator pedal fully depressed

☐ Low transmission fluid level (Chapter 1A)
☐ Engine management system fault (Chapter 4A)
☐ Faulty transmission sensor or wiring (Chapter 7B)
☐ Incorrect selector cable adjustment (Chapter 7B)

Engine will not start in any gear, or starts in gears other than Park or Neutral

☐ Faulty transmission sensor or wiring (Chapter 7B)
☐ Engine management system fault (Chapter 4)
☐ Incorrect selector cable adjustment (Chapter 7B)

Transmission slips, shifts roughly, is noisy, or has no drive in forward or reverse gears

☐ Transmission fluid level low (Chapter 1A)
☐ Faulty transmission sensor or wiring (Chapter 7B)
☐ Engine management system fault (Chapter 4)

Note: *There are many probable causes for the above problems, but diagnosing and correcting them is considered beyond the scope of this manual. Having checked the fluid level and all the wiring as far as possible, a dealer or transmission specialist should be consulted if the problem persists.*

Driveshafts

Vibration when accelerating or decelerating

☐ Worn inner constant velocity joint (Chapter 8)
☐ Bent or distorted driveshaft (Chapter 8)
☐ Worn intermediate bearing (Chapter 8)

Clicking or knocking noise on turns (at slow speed on full-lock)

☐ Worn outer constant velocity joint (Chapter 8)
☐ Lack of constant velocity joint lubricant, possibly due to damaged gaiter (Chapter 8)
☐ Worn intermediate bearing (Chapter 8)

Braking system

Note: *Before assuming that a brake problem exists, make sure that the tyres are in good condition and correctly inflated, that the front wheel alignment is correct, and that the vehicle is not loaded with weight in an unequal manner. Apart from checking the condition of all pipe and hose connections, any faults occurring on the anti-lock braking system should be referred to a Ford dealer for diagnosis.*

Vehicle pulls to one side under braking

☐ Worn, defective, damaged or contaminated brake pads/shoes on one side (Chapter 1A, 1B or 9)
☐ Seized or partially-seized brake caliper piston/wheel cylinder (Chapter 1A, 1B or 9)
☐ A mixture of brake pad/shoe lining materials fitted between sides (Chapter 1A, 1B or 9)
☐ Brake caliper/backplate mounting bolts loose (Chapter 9)
☐ Worn or damaged steering or suspension components (Chapter 1A, 1B or 10)

Noise (grinding or high-pitched squeal) when brakes applied

☐ Brake pad/shoe friction lining material worn down to metal backing (Chapter 1A, 1B or 9)
☐ Excessive corrosion of brake disc/drum (may be apparent after the vehicle has been standing for some time (Chapter 1A, 1B or 9)
☐ Foreign object (stone chipping, etc) trapped between brake disc and shield (Chapter 1A, 1B or 9)

Excessive brake pedal travel

☐ Faulty master cylinder (Chapter 9)
☐ Air in hydraulic system (Chapter 1A, 1B, 6 or 9)
☐ Faulty vacuum servo unit (Chapter 9)

Brake pedal feels spongy when depressed

☐ Air in hydraulic system (Chapter 1A, 1B, 6 or 9)
☐ Deteriorated flexible rubber brake hoses (Chapter 1A, 1B or 9)
☐ Master cylinder mounting nuts loose (Chapter 9)
☐ Faulty master cylinder (Chapter 9)

Excessive brake pedal effort required to stop vehicle

☐ Faulty vacuum servo unit (Chapter 9)
☐ Faulty vacuum pump – diesel models (Chapter 9)
☐ Disconnected, damaged or insecure brake servo vacuum hose (Chapter 9)
☐ Primary or secondary hydraulic circuit failure (Chapter 9)
☐ Seized brake caliper/wheel cylinder piston (Chapter 9)
☐ Brake pads/shoes incorrectly fitted (Chapter 9)
☐ Incorrect grade of brake pads/shoes fitted (Chapter 9)
☐ Brake pad/shoe linings contaminated (Chapter 1A, 1B or 9)

Judder felt through brake pedal or steering wheel when braking

Note: *Under heavy braking on models equipped with ABS, vibration may be felt through the brake pedal. This is a normal feature of ABS operation, and does not constitute a fault*

☐ Excessive run-out or distortion of discs/drums (Chapter 1A, 1B or 9)
☐ Brake pad/shoe linings worn (Chapter 1A, 1B or 9)
☐ Brake caliper/backplate mounting bolts loose (Chapter 9)
☐ Wear in suspension or steering components or mountings (Chapter 1A, 1B or 10)
☐ Front wheels out of balance (see *Weekly checks*)

Brakes binding

☐ Seized brake caliper/wheel cylinder piston (Chapter 9)
☐ Incorrectly-adjusted handbrake mechanism (Chapter 9)
☐ Faulty master cylinder (Chapter 9)

Rear wheels locking under normal braking

☐ Rear brake pad/shoe linings contaminated or damaged (Chapter 1 or 9)
☐ Rear brake discs/drums warped (Chapter 1 or 9)
☐ Rear brake load sensing proportioning valve faulty – Estate models (Chapter 9)

Suspension and steering

Note: *Before diagnosing suspension or steering faults, be sure that the trouble is not due to incorrect tyre pressures, mixtures of tyre types, or binding brakes.*

Vehicle pulls to one side

☐ Defective tyre (see *Weekly checks*)
☐ Excessive wear in suspension or steering components (Chapter 1A, 1B or 10)
☐ Incorrect front wheel alignment (Chapter 10)
☐ Accident damage to steering or suspension components (Chapter 1A or 1B)

Wheel wobble and vibration

☐ Front wheels out of balance (vibration felt mainly through the steering wheel) (see *Weekly checks*)
☐ Rear wheels out of balance (vibration felt throughout the vehicle) (see *Weekly checks*)
☐ Roadwheels damaged or distorted (see *Weekly checks*)
☐ Faulty or damaged tyre (see *Weekly checks*)
☐ Worn steering or suspension joints, bushes or components (Chapter 1A, 1B or 10)
☐ Wheel nuts loose (Chapter 1A or 1B)

Excessive pitching and/or rolling around corners, or during braking

☐ Defective shock absorbers (Chapter 1A, 1B or 10)
☐ Broken or weak spring and/or suspension component (Chapter 1A, 1B or 10)
☐ Worn or damaged anti-roll bar or mountings (Chapter 1A, 1B or 10)

Wandering or general instability

☐ Incorrect front wheel alignment (Chapter 10)
☐ Worn steering or suspension joints, bushes or components (Chapter 1A, 1B or 10)
☐ Roadwheels out of balance (see *Weekly checks*)
☐ Faulty or damaged tyre (see *Weekly checks*)
☐ Wheel nuts loose (Chapter 1A or 1B)
☐ Defective shock absorbers (Chapter 1A, 1B or 10)

Excessively-stiff steering

☐ Seized steering linkage balljoint or suspension balljoint (Chapter 1A, 1B or 10)
☐ Broken or incorrectly-adjusted auxiliary drivebelt (Chapter 1A or 1B)
☐ Incorrect front wheel alignment (Chapter 10)
☐ Steering rack damaged (Chapter 10)

Excessive play in steering

☐ Worn steering column/intermediate shaft joints (Chapter 10)
☐ Worn track rod balljoints (Chapter 1A, 1B or 10)
☐ Worn steering rack (Chapter 10)
☐ Worn steering or suspension joints, bushes or components (Chapter 1A, 1B or 10)

Lack of power assistance

☐ Broken or incorrectly-adjusted auxiliary drivebelt (Chapter 1A or 1B)
☐ Incorrect power steering fluid level (see *Weekly checks*)
☐ Restriction in power steering fluid hoses (Chapter 1A or 1B)
☐ Faulty power steering pump (Chapter 10)
☐ Faulty steering rack (Chapter 10)

Tyre wear excessive

Tyres worn on inside or outside edges

☐ Tyres under-inflated (wear on both edges) (see *Weekly checks*)
☐ Incorrect camber or castor angles (wear on one edge only) (Chapter 10)
☐ Worn steering or suspension joints, bushes or components (Chapter 1A, 1B or 10)
☐ Excessively-hard cornering or braking
☐ Accident damage

Tyre treads exhibit feathered edges

☐ Incorrect toe-setting (Chapter 10)

Tyres worn in centre of tread

☐ Tyres over-inflated (see *Weekly checks*)

Tyres worn on inside and outside edges

☐ Tyres under-inflated (see *Weekly checks*)

Tyres worn unevenly

☐ Tyres/wheels out of balance (see *Weekly checks*)
☐ Excessive wheel or tyre run-out
☐ Worn shock absorbers (Chapter 1A, 1B or 10)
☐ Faulty tyre (see *Weekly checks*)

Electrical system

Note: *For problems associated with the starting system, refer to the faults listed under 'Engine' earlier in this Section.*

Battery will not hold a charge for more than a few days

- ☐ Battery defective internally (Chapter 5A)
- ☐ Battery terminal connections loose or corroded (see *Weekly checks*)
- ☐ Auxiliary drivebelt worn or incorrectly adjusted (Chapter 1A or 1B)
- ☐ Alternator not charging at correct output (Chapter 5A)
- ☐ Alternator or voltage regulator faulty (Chapter 5A)
- ☐ Short-circuit causing continual battery drain (Chapter 5A or 12)

Ignition/no-charge warning light remains illuminated with engine running

- ☐ Auxiliary drivebelt broken, worn, or incorrectly adjusted (Chapter 1A or 1B)
- ☐ Internal fault in alternator or voltage regulator (Chapter 5A)
- ☐ Broken, disconnected, or loose wiring in charging circuit (Chapter 5A or 12)

Ignition/no-charge warning light fails to come on

- ☐ Warning light bulb blown (Chapter 12)
- ☐ Broken, disconnected, or loose wiring in warning light circuit (Chapter 5A or 12)
- ☐ Alternator faulty (Chapter 5A)

Lights inoperative

- ☐ Bulb blown (Chapter 12)
- ☐ Corrosion of bulb or bulbholder contacts (Chapter 12)
- ☐ Blown fuse (Chapter 12)
- ☐ Faulty relay (Chapter 12)
- ☐ Broken, loose, or disconnected wiring (Chapter 12)
- ☐ Faulty switch (Chapter 12)

Instrument readings inaccurate or erratic

Instrument readings increase with engine speed

- ☐ Faulty instrument panel voltage regulator (Chapter 12)

Fuel or temperature gauges give no reading

- ☐ Faulty gauge sender unit (Chapter 3 or 4)
- ☐ Wiring open-circuit (Chapter 12)
- ☐ Faulty gauge (Chapter 12)

Fuel or temperature gauges give continuous maximum reading

- ☐ Faulty gauge sender unit (Chapter 3 or 4)
- ☐ Wiring short-circuit (Chapter 12)
- ☐ Faulty gauge (Chapter 12)

Horn inoperative, or unsatisfactory in operation

Horn operates all the time

- ☐ Horn push either earthed or stuck down (Chapter 12)
- ☐ Horn cable-to-horn push earthed (Chapter 12)

Horn fails to operate

- ☐ Blown fuse (Chapter 12)
- ☐ Cable or connections loose, broken or disconnected (Chapter 12)
- ☐ Faulty horn (Chapter 12)

Horn emits intermittent or unsatisfactory sound

- ☐ Cable connections loose (Chapter 12)
- ☐ Horn mountings loose (Chapter 12)
- ☐ Faulty horn (Chapter 12)

Windscreen wipers inoperative, or unsatisfactory in operation

Wipers fail to operate, or operate very slowly

- ☐ Wiper blades stuck to screen, or linkage seized or binding (Chapter 12)
- ☐ Blown fuse (Chapter 12)
- ☐ Battery discharged (Chapter 5A)
- ☐ Cable or connections loose, broken or disconnected (Chapter 12)
- ☐ Faulty relay (Chapter 12)
- ☐ Faulty wiper motor (Chapter 12)

Wiper blades sweep over too large or too small an area of the glass

- ☐ Wiper blades incorrectly fitted, or wrong size used (see *Weekly checks*)
- ☐ Wiper arms incorrectly positioned on spindles (Chapter 12)
- ☐ Excessive wear of wiper linkage (Chapter 12)
- ☐ Wiper motor or linkage mountings loose or insecure (Chapter 12)

Wiper blades fail to clean the glass effectively

- ☐ Wiper blade rubbers dirty, worn or perished (see *Weekly checks*)
- ☐ Wiper blades incorrectly fitted, or wrong size used (see *Weekly checks*)
- ☐ Wiper arm tension springs broken, or arm pivots seized (Chapter 12)
- ☐ Insufficient windscreen washer additive to adequately remove road film (see *Weekly checks*)

Windscreen washers inoperative, or unsatisfactory in operation

One or more washer jets inoperative

- ☐ Blocked washer jet
- ☐ Disconnected, kinked or restricted fluid hose (Chapter 12)
- ☐ Insufficient fluid in washer reservoir (see *Weekly checks*)

Washer pump fails to operate

- ☐ Broken or disconnected wiring or connections (Chapter 12)
- ☐ Blown fuse (Chapter 12)
- ☐ Faulty washer switch (Chapter 12)
- ☐ Faulty washer pump (Chapter 12)

Washer pump runs for some time before fluid is emitted from jets

- ☐ Faulty one-way valve in fluid supply hose (Chapter 12)

Electric windows inoperative, or unsatisfactory in operation

Window glass will only move in one direction

- ☐ Faulty switch (Chapter 12)

Window glass slow to move

- ☐ Battery discharged (Chapter 5A)
- ☐ Regulator seized or damaged, or in need of lubrication (Chapter 11)
- ☐ Door internal components or trim fouling regulator (Chapter 11)
- ☐ Faulty motor (Chapter 11)

Window glass fails to move

- ☐ Blown fuse (Chapter 12)
- ☐ Faulty relay (Chapter 12)
- ☐ Broken or disconnected wiring or connections (Chapter 12)
- ☐ Faulty motor (Chapter 11)

Electrical system (continued)

Central locking system inoperative, or unsatisfactory in operation

Complete system failure

☐ Remote handset battery discharged, where applicable
☐ Blown fuse (Chapter 12)
☐ Faulty relay (Chapter 12)
☐ Broken or disconnected wiring or connections (Chapter 12)
☐ Faulty motor (Chapter 11)

Latch locks but will not unlock, or unlocks but will not lock

☐ Remote handset battery discharged, where applicable
☐ Faulty master switch (Chapter 12)
☐ Broken or disconnected latch operating rods or levers (Chapter 11)
☐ Faulty relay (Chapter 12)
☐ Faulty motor (Chapter 11)

One solenoid/motor fails to operate

☐ Broken or disconnected wiring or connections (Chapter 12)
☐ Faulty operating assembly (Chapter 11)
☐ Broken, binding or disconnected latch operating rods or levers (Chapter 11)
☐ Fault in door latch (Chapter 11)

A

ABS (Anti-lock brake system) A system, usually electronically controlled, that senses incipient wheel lockup during braking and relieves hydraulic pressure at wheels that are about to skid.

Air bag An inflatable bag hidden in the steering wheel (driver's side) or the dash or glovebox (passenger side). In a head-on collision, the bags inflate, preventing the driver and front passenger from being thrown forward into the steering wheel or windscreen.

Air cleaner A metal or plastic housing, containing a filter element, which removes dust and dirt from the air being drawn into the engine.

Air filter element The actual filter in an air cleaner system, usually manufactured from pleated paper and requiring renewal at regular intervals.

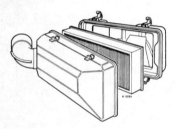

Air filter

Allen key A hexagonal wrench which fits into a recessed hexagonal hole.

Alligator clip A long-nosed spring-loaded metal clip with meshing teeth. Used to make temporary electrical connections.

Alternator A component in the electrical system which converts mechanical energy from a drivebelt into electrical energy to charge the battery and to operate the starting system, ignition system and electrical accessories.

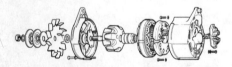

Alternator (exploded view)

Ampere (amp) A unit of measurement for the flow of electric current. One amp is the amount of current produced by one volt acting through a resistance of one ohm.

Anaerobic sealer A substance used to prevent bolts and screws from loosening. Anaerobic means that it does not require oxygen for activation. The Loctite brand is widely used.

Antifreeze A substance (usually ethylene glycol) mixed with water, and added to a vehicle's cooling system, to prevent freezing of the coolant in winter. Antifreeze also contains chemicals to inhibit corrosion and the formation of rust and other deposits that would tend to clog the radiator and coolant passages and reduce cooling efficiency.

Anti-seize compound A coating that reduces the risk of seizing on fasteners that are subjected to high temperatures, such as exhaust manifold bolts and nuts.

Anti-seize compound

Asbestos A natural fibrous mineral with great heat resistance, commonly used in the composition of brake friction materials. Asbestos is a health hazard and the dust created by brake systems should never be inhaled or ingested.

Axle A shaft on which a wheel revolves, or which revolves with a wheel. Also, a solid beam that connects the two wheels at one end of the vehicle. An axle which also transmits power to the wheels is known as a live axle.

Axle assembly

Axleshaft A single rotating shaft, on either side of the differential, which delivers power from the final drive assembly to the drive wheels. Also called a driveshaft or a halfshaft.

B

Ball bearing An anti-friction bearing consisting of a hardened inner and outer race with hardened steel balls between two races.

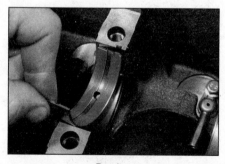

Bearing

Bearing The curved surface on a shaft or in a bore, or the part assembled into either, that permits relative motion between them with minimum wear and friction.

Big-end bearing The bearing in the end of the connecting rod that's attached to the crankshaft.

Bleed nipple A valve on a brake wheel cylinder, caliper or other hydraulic component that is opened to purge the hydraulic system of air. Also called a bleed screw.

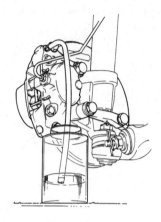

Brake bleeding

Brake bleeding Procedure for removing air from lines of a hydraulic brake system.

Brake disc The component of a disc brake that rotates with the wheels.

Brake drum The component of a drum brake that rotates with the wheels.

Brake linings The friction material which contacts the brake disc or drum to retard the vehicle's speed. The linings are bonded or riveted to the brake pads or shoes.

Brake pads The replaceable friction pads that pinch the brake disc when the brakes are applied. Brake pads consist of a friction material bonded or riveted to a rigid backing plate.

Brake shoe The crescent-shaped carrier to which the brake linings are mounted and which forces the lining against the rotating drum during braking.

Braking systems For more information on braking systems, consult the *Haynes Automotive Brake Manual*.

Breaker bar A long socket wrench handle providing greater leverage.

Bulkhead The insulated partition between the engine and the passenger compartment.

C

Caliper The non-rotating part of a disc-brake assembly that straddles the disc and carries the brake pads. The caliper also contains the hydraulic components that cause the pads to pinch the disc when the brakes are applied. A caliper is also a measuring tool that can be set to measure inside or outside dimensions of an object.

Camshaft A rotating shaft on which a series of cam lobes operate the valve mechanisms. The camshaft may be driven by gears, by sprockets and chain or by sprockets and a belt.

Canister A container in an evaporative emission control system; contains activated charcoal granules to trap vapours from the fuel system.

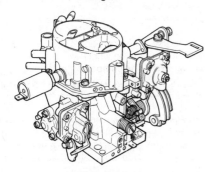

Canister

Carburettor A device which mixes fuel with air in the proper proportions to provide a desired power output from a spark ignition internal combustion engine.

Carburettor

Castellated Resembling the parapets along the top of a castle wall. For example, a castellated balljoint stud nut.

Castellated nut

Castor In wheel alignment, the backward or forward tilt of the steering axis. Castor is positive when the steering axis is inclined rearward at the top.

Catalytic converter A silencer-like device in the exhaust system which converts certain pollutants in the exhaust gases into less harmful substances.

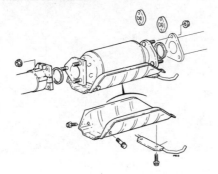

Catalytic converter

Circlip A ring-shaped clip used to prevent endwise movement of cylindrical parts and shafts. An internal circlip is installed in a groove in a housing; an external circlip fits into a groove on the outside of a cylindrical piece such as a shaft.

Clearance The amount of space between two parts. For example, between a piston and a cylinder, between a bearing and a journal, etc.

Coil spring A spiral of elastic steel found in various sizes throughout a vehicle, for example as a springing medium in the suspension and in the valve train.

Compression Reduction in volume, and increase in pressure and temperature, of a gas, caused by squeezing it into a smaller space.

Compression ratio The relationship between cylinder volume when the piston is at top dead centre and cylinder volume when the piston is at bottom dead centre.

Constant velocity (CV) joint A type of universal joint that cancels out vibrations caused by driving power being transmitted through an angle.

Core plug A disc or cup-shaped metal device inserted in a hole in a casting through which core was removed when the casting was formed. Also known as a freeze plug or expansion plug.

Crankcase The lower part of the engine block in which the crankshaft rotates.

Crankshaft The main rotating member, or shaft, running the length of the crankcase, with offset "throws" to which the connecting rods are attached.

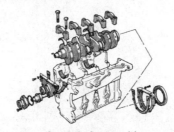

Crankshaft assembly

Crocodile clip See Alligator clip

D

Diagnostic code Code numbers obtained by accessing the diagnostic mode of an engine management computer. This code can be used to determine the area in the system where a malfunction may be located.

Disc brake A brake design incorporating a rotating disc onto which brake pads are squeezed. The resulting friction converts the energy of a moving vehicle into heat.

Double-overhead cam (DOHC) An engine that uses two overhead camshafts, usually one for the intake valves and one for the exhaust valves.

Drivebelt(s) The belt(s) used to drive accessories such as the alternator, water pump, power steering pump, air conditioning compressor, etc. off the crankshaft pulley.

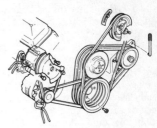

Accessory drivebelts

Driveshaft Any shaft used to transmit motion. Commonly used when referring to the axleshafts on a front wheel drive vehicle.

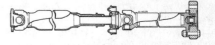

Driveshaft

Drum brake A type of brake using a drum-shaped metal cylinder attached to the inner surface of the wheel. When the brake pedal is pressed, curved brake shoes with friction linings press against the inside of the drum to slow or stop the vehicle.

Drum brake assembly

E

EGR valve A valve used to introduce exhaust gases into the intake air stream.

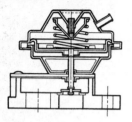

EGR valve

Electronic control unit (ECU) A computer which controls (for instance) ignition and fuel injection systems, or an anti-lock braking system. For more information refer to the *Haynes Automotive Electrical and Electronic Systems Manual.*

Electronic Fuel Injection (EFI) A computer controlled fuel system that distributes fuel through an injector located in each intake port of the engine.

Emergency brake A braking system, independent of the main hydraulic system, that can be used to slow or stop the vehicle if the primary brakes fail, or to hold the vehicle stationary even though the brake pedal isn't depressed. It usually consists of a hand lever that actuates either front or rear brakes mechanically through a series of cables and linkages. Also known as a handbrake or parking brake.

Endfloat The amount of lengthwise movement between two parts. As applied to a crankshaft, the distance that the crankshaft can move forward and back in the cylinder block.

Engine management system (EMS) A computer controlled system which manages the fuel injection and the ignition systems in an integrated fashion.

Exhaust manifold A part with several passages through which exhaust gases leave the engine combustion chambers and enter the exhaust pipe.

Exhaust manifold

F

Fan clutch A viscous (fluid) drive coupling device which permits variable engine fan speeds in relation to engine speeds.

Feeler blade A thin strip or blade of hardened steel, ground to an exact thickness, used to check or measure clearances between parts.

Feeler blade

Firing order The order in which the engine cylinders fire, or deliver their power strokes, beginning with the number one cylinder.

Flywheel A heavy spinning wheel in which energy is absorbed and stored by means of momentum. On cars, the flywheel is attached to the crankshaft to smooth out firing impulses.

Free play The amount of travel before any action takes place. The "looseness" in a linkage, or an assembly of parts, between the initial application of force and actual movement. For example, the distance the brake pedal moves before the pistons in the master cylinder are actuated.

Fuse An electrical device which protects a circuit against accidental overload. The typical fuse contains a soft piece of metal which is calibrated to melt at a predetermined current flow (expressed as amps) and break the circuit.

Fusible link A circuit protection device consisting of a conductor surrounded by heat-resistant insulation. The conductor is smaller than the wire it protects, so it acts as the weakest link in the circuit. Unlike a blown fuse, a failed fusible link must frequently be cut from the wire for replacement.

G

Gap The distance the spark must travel in jumping from the centre electrode to the side

Adjusting spark plug gap

electrode in a spark plug. Also refers to the spacing between the points in a contact breaker assembly in a conventional points-type ignition, or to the distance between the reluctor or rotor and the pickup coil in an electronic ignition.

Gasket Any thin, soft material - usually cork, cardboard, asbestos or soft metal - installed between two metal surfaces to ensure a good seal. For instance, the cylinder head gasket seals the joint between the block and the cylinder head.

Gasket

Gauge An instrument panel display used to monitor engine conditions. A gauge with a movable pointer on a dial or a fixed scale is an analogue gauge. A gauge with a numerical readout is called a digital gauge.

H

Halfshaft A rotating shaft that transmits power from the final drive unit to a drive wheel, usually when referring to a live rear axle.

Harmonic balancer A device designed to reduce torsion or twisting vibration in the crankshaft. May be incorporated in the crankshaft pulley. Also known as a vibration damper.

Hone An abrasive tool for correcting small irregularities or differences in diameter in an engine cylinder, brake cylinder, etc.

Hydraulic tappet A tappet that utilises hydraulic pressure from the engine's lubrication system to maintain zero clearance (constant contact with both camshaft and valve stem). Automatically adjusts to variation in valve stem length. Hydraulic tappets also reduce valve noise.

I

Ignition timing The moment at which the spark plug fires, usually expressed in the number of crankshaft degrees before the piston reaches the top of its stroke.

Inlet manifold A tube or housing with passages through which flows the air-fuel mixture (carburettor vehicles and vehicles with throttle body injection) or air only (port fuel-injected vehicles) to the port openings in the cylinder head.

J

Jump start Starting the engine of a vehicle with a discharged or weak battery by attaching jump leads from the weak battery to a charged or helper battery.

L

Load Sensing Proportioning Valve (LSPV) A brake hydraulic system control valve that works like a proportioning valve, but also takes into consideration the amount of weight carried by the rear axle.

Locknut A nut used to lock an adjustment nut, or other threaded component, in place. For example, a locknut is employed to keep the adjusting nut on the rocker arm in position.

Lockwasher A form of washer designed to prevent an attaching nut from working loose.

M

MacPherson strut A type of front suspension system devised by Earle MacPherson at Ford of England. In its original form, a simple lateral link with the anti-roll bar creates the lower control arm. A long strut - an integral coil spring and shock absorber - is mounted between the body and the steering knuckle. Many modern so-called MacPherson strut systems use a conventional lower A-arm and don't rely on the anti-roll bar for location.

Multimeter An electrical test instrument with the capability to measure voltage, current and resistance.

N

NOx Oxides of Nitrogen. A common toxic pollutant emitted by petrol and diesel engines at higher temperatures.

O

Ohm The unit of electrical resistance. One volt applied to a resistance of one ohm will produce a current of one amp.

Ohmmeter An instrument for measuring electrical resistance.

O-ring A type of sealing ring made of a special rubber-like material; in use, the O-ring is compressed into a groove to provide the sealing action.

O-ring

Overhead cam (ohc) engine An engine with the camshaft(s) located on top of the cylinder head(s).

Overhead valve (ohv) engine An engine with the valves located in the cylinder head, but with the camshaft located in the engine block.

Oxygen sensor A device installed in the engine exhaust manifold, which senses the oxygen content in the exhaust and converts this information into an electric current. Also called a Lambda sensor.

P

Phillips screw A type of screw head having a cross instead of a slot for a corresponding type of screwdriver.

Plastigage A thin strip of plastic thread, available in different sizes, used for measuring clearances. For example, a strip of Plastigage is laid across a bearing journal. The parts are assembled and dismantled; the width of the crushed strip indicates the clearance between journal and bearing.

Plastigage

Propeller shaft The long hollow tube with universal joints at both ends that carries power from the transmission to the differential on front-engined rear wheel drive vehicles.

Proportioning valve A hydraulic control valve which limits the amount of pressure to the rear brakes during panic stops to prevent wheel lock-up.

R

Rack-and-pinion steering A steering system with a pinion gear on the end of the steering shaft that mates with a rack (think of a geared wheel opened up and laid flat). When the steering wheel is turned, the pinion turns, moving the rack to the left or right. This movement is transmitted through the track rods to the steering arms at the wheels.

Radiator A liquid-to-air heat transfer device designed to reduce the temperature of the coolant in an internal combustion engine cooling system.

Refrigerant Any substance used as a heat transfer agent in an air-conditioning system. R-12 has been the principle refrigerant for many years; recently, however, manufacturers have begun using R-134a, a non-CFC substance that is considered less harmful to the ozone in the upper atmosphere.

Rocker arm A lever arm that rocks on a shaft or pivots on a stud. In an overhead valve engine, the rocker arm converts the upward movement of the pushrod into a downward movement to open a valve.

Rotor In a distributor, the rotating device inside the cap that connects the centre electrode and the outer terminals as it turns, distributing the high voltage from the coil secondary winding to the proper spark plug. Also, that part of an alternator which rotates inside the stator. Also, the rotating assembly of a turbocharger, including the compressor wheel, shaft and turbine wheel.

Runout The amount of wobble (in-and-out movement) of a gear or wheel as it's rotated. The amount a shaft rotates "out-of-true." The out-of-round condition of a rotating part.

S

Sealant A liquid or paste used to prevent leakage at a joint. Sometimes used in conjunction with a gasket.

Sealed beam lamp An older headlight design which integrates the reflector, lens and filaments into a hermetically-sealed one-piece unit. When a filament burns out or the lens cracks, the entire unit is simply replaced.

Serpentine drivebelt A single, long, wide accessory drivebelt that's used on some newer vehicles to drive all the accessories, instead of a series of smaller, shorter belts. Serpentine drivebelts are usually tensioned by an automatic tensioner.

Serpentine drivebelt

Shim Thin spacer, commonly used to adjust the clearance or relative positions between two parts. For example, shims inserted into or under bucket tappets control valve clearances. Clearance is adjusted by changing the thickness of the shim.

Slide hammer A special puller that screws into or hooks onto a component such as a shaft or bearing; a heavy sliding handle on the shaft bottoms against the end of the shaft to knock the component free.

Sprocket A tooth or projection on the periphery of a wheel, shaped to engage with a chain or drivebelt. Commonly used to refer to the sprocket wheel itself.

Starter inhibitor switch On vehicles with an automatic transmission, a switch that prevents starting if the vehicle is not in Neutral or Park.

Strut See MacPherson strut.

T

Tappet A cylindrical component which transmits motion from the cam to the valve stem, either directly or via a pushrod and rocker arm. Also called a cam follower.

Thermostat A heat-controlled valve that regulates the flow of coolant between the cylinder block and the radiator, so maintaining optimum engine operating temperature. A thermostat is also used in some air cleaners in which the temperature is regulated.

Thrust bearing The bearing in the clutch assembly that is moved in to the release levers by clutch pedal action to disengage the clutch. Also referred to as a release bearing.

Timing belt A toothed belt which drives the camshaft. Serious engine damage may result if it breaks in service.

Timing chain A chain which drives the camshaft.

Toe-in The amount the front wheels are closer together at the front than at the rear. On rear wheel drive vehicles, a slight amount of toe-in is usually specified to keep the front wheels running parallel on the road by offsetting other forces that tend to spread the wheels apart.

Toe-out The amount the front wheels are closer together at the rear than at the front. On front wheel drive vehicles, a slight amount of toe-out is usually specified.

Tools For full information on choosing and using tools, refer to the *Haynes Automotive Tools Manual.*

Tracer A stripe of a second colour applied to a wire insulator to distinguish that wire from another one with the same colour insulator.

Tune-up A process of accurate and careful adjustments and parts replacement to obtain the best possible engine performance.

Turbocharger A centrifugal device, driven by exhaust gases, that pressurises the intake air. Normally used to increase the power output from a given engine displacement, but can also be used primarily to reduce exhaust emissions (as on VW's "Umwelt" Diesel engine).

U

Universal joint or U-joint A double-pivoted connection for transmitting power from a driving to a driven shaft through an angle. A U-joint consists of two Y-shaped yokes and a cross-shaped member called the spider.

V

Valve A device through which the flow of liquid, gas, vacuum, or loose material in bulk may be started, stopped, or regulated by a movable part that opens, shuts, or partially obstructs one or more ports or passageways. A valve is also the movable part of such a device.

Valve clearance The clearance between the valve tip (the end of the valve stem) and the rocker arm or tappet. The valve clearance is measured when the valve is closed.

Vernier caliper A precision measuring instrument that measures inside and outside dimensions. Not quite as accurate as a micrometer, but more convenient.

Viscosity The thickness of a liquid or its resistance to flow.

Volt A unit for expressing electrical "pressure" in a circuit. One volt that will produce a current of one ampere through a resistance of one ohm.

W

Welding Various processes used to join metal items by heating the areas to be joined to a molten state and fusing them together. For more information refer to the *Haynes Automotive Welding Manual.*

Wiring diagram A drawing portraying the components and wires in a vehicle's electrical system, using standardised symbols. For more information refer to the *Haynes Automotive Electrical and Electronic Systems Manual.*

Note: *References throughout this index are in the form "Chapter Number" • "Page Number"*

Haynes Manuals – The Complete **UK Car** List

Title	Book No.
ALFA ROMEO Alfasud/Sprint (74 - 88) up to F *	0292
Alfa Romeo Alfetta (73 - 87) up to E *	0531
AUDI 80, 90 & Coupe Petrol (79 - Nov 88) up to F	0605
Audi 80, 90 & Coupe Petrol (Oct 86 - 90) D to H	1491
Audi 100 & 200 Petrol (Oct 82 - 90) up to H	0907
Audi 100 & A6 Petrol & Diesel (May 91 - May 97) H to P	3504
Audi A3 Petrol & Diesel (96 - May 03) P to 03	4253
Audi A4 Petrol & Diesel (95 - 00) M to X	3575
Audi A4 Petrol & Diesel (01 - 04) X to 54	4609
AUSTIN A35 & A40 (56 - 67) up to F *	0118
Austin/MG/Rover Maestro 1.3 & 1.6 Petrol (83 - 95) up to M	0922
Austin/MG Metro (80 - May 90) up to G	0718
Austin/Rover Montego 1.3 & 1.6 Petrol (84 - 94) A to L	1066
Austin/MG/Rover Montego 2.0 Petrol (84 - 95) A to M	1067
Mini (59 - 69) up to H *	0527
Mini (69 - 01) up to X	0646
Austin/Rover 2.0 litre Diesel Engine (86 - 93) C to L	1857
Austin Healey 100/6 & 3000 (56 - 68) up to G *	0049
BEDFORD CF Petrol (69 - 87) up to E	0163
Bedford/Vauxhall Rascal & Suzuki Supercarry (86 - Oct 94) C to M	3015
BMW 316, 320 & 320i (4-cyl) (75 - Feb 83) up to Y *	0276
BMW 320, 320i, 323i & 325i (6-cyl) (Oct 77 - Sept 87) up to E	0815
BMW 3- & 5-Series Petrol (81 - 91) up to J	1948
BMW 3-Series Petrol (Apr 91 - 99) H to V	3210
BMW 3-Series Petrol (Sept 98 - 03) S to 53	4067
BMW 520i & 525e (Oct 81 - June 88) up to E	1560
BMW 525, 528 & 528i (73 - Sept 81) up to X *	0632
BMW 5-Series 6-cyl Petrol (April 96 - Aug 03) N to 03	4151
BMW 1500, 1502, 1600, 1602, 2000 & 2002 (59 - 77) up to S *	0240
CHRYSLER PT Cruiser Petrol (00 - 03) W to 53	4058
CITROËN 2CV, Ami & Dyane (67 - 90) up to H	0196
Citroën AX Petrol & Diesel (87 - 97) D to P	3014
Citroën Berlingo & Peugeot Partner Petrol & Diesel (96 - 05) P to 55	4281
Citroën BX Petrol (83 - 94) A to L	0908
Citroën C15 Van Petrol & Diesel (89 - Oct 98) F to S	3509
Citroën C3 Petrol & Diesel (02 - 05) 51 to 05	4197
Citroen C5 Petrol & Diesel (01-08) Y to 08	4745
Citroën CX Petrol (75 - 88) up to F	0528
Citroën Saxo Petrol & Diesel (96 - 04) N to 54	3506
Citroën Visa Petrol (79 - 88) up to F	0620
Citroën Xantia Petrol & Diesel (93 - 01) K to Y	3082
Citroën XM Petrol & Diesel (89 - 00) G to X	3451
Citroën Xsara Petrol & Diesel (97 - Sept 00) R to W	3751
Citroën Xsara Picasso Petrol & Diesel (00 - 02) W to 52	3944
Citroën Xsara Picasso (03-08)	4784
Citroën ZX Diesel (91 - 98) J to S	1922
Citroën ZX Petrol (91 - 98) H to S	1881
Citroën 1.7 & 1.9 litre Diesel Engine (84 - 96) A to N	1379
FIAT 126 (73 - 87) up to E *	0305
Fiat 500 (57 - 73) up to M *	0090
Fiat Bravo & Brava Petrol (95 - 00) N to W	3572
Fiat Cinquecento (93 - 98) K to R	3501
Fiat Panda (81 - 95) up to M	0793
Fiat Punto Petrol & Diesel (94 - Oct 99) L to V	3251
Fiat Punto Petrol (Oct 99 - July 03) V to 03	4066
Fiat Punto Petrol (03-07) 03 to 07	4746
Fiat Regata Petrol (84 - 88) A to F	1167
Fiat Tipo Petrol (88 - 91) E to J	1625
Fiat Uno Petrol (83 - 95) up to M	0923
Fiat X1/9 (74 - 89) up to G *	0273
FORD Anglia (59 - 68) up to G *	0001

Title	Book No.
Ford Capri II (& III) 1.6 & 2.0 (74 - 87) up to E *	0283
Ford Capri II (& III) 2.8 & 3.0 V6 (74 - 87) up to E	1309
Ford Cortina Mk I & Corsair 1500 ('62 - '66) up to D*	0214
Ford Cortina Mk III 1300 & 1600 (70 - 76) up to P	0070
Ford Escort Mk I 1100 & 1300 (68 - 74) up to N *	0171
Ford Escort Mk I Mexico, RS 1600 & RS 2000 (70 - 74) up to N *	0139
Ford Escort Mk II Mexico, RS 1800 & RS 2000 (75 - 80) up to W *	0735
Ford Escort (75 - Aug 80) up to V *	0280
Ford Escort Petrol (Sept 80 - Sept 90) up to H	0686
Ford Escort & Orion Petrol (Sept 90 - 00) H to X	1737
Ford Escort & Orion Diesel (Sept 90 - 00) H to X	4081
Ford Fiesta (76 - Aug 83) up to Y	0334
Ford Fiesta Petrol (Aug 83 - Feb 89) A to F	1030
Ford Fiesta Petrol (Feb 89 - Oct 95) F to N	1595
Ford Fiesta Petrol & Diesel (Oct 95 - Mar 02) N to 02	3397
Ford Fiesta Petrol & Diesel (Apr 02 - 07) 02 to 57	4170
Ford Focus Petrol & Diesel (98 - 01) S to Y	3759
Ford Focus Petrol & Diesel (Oct 01 - 05) 51 to 05	4167
Ford Galaxy Petrol & Diesel (95 - Aug 00) M to W	3984
Ford Granada Petrol (Sept 77 - Feb 85) up to B *	0481
Ford Granada & Scorpio Petrol (Mar 85 - 94) B to M	1245
Ford Ka (96 - 02) P to 52	3570
Ford Mondeo Petrol (93 - Sept 00) K to X	1923
Ford Mondeo Petrol & Diesel (Oct 00 - Jul 03) X to 03	3990
Ford Mondeo Petrol & Diesel (July 03 - 07) 03 to 56	4619
Ford Mondeo Diesel (93 - 96) L to N	3465
Ford Orion Petrol (83 - Sept 90) up to H	1009
Ford Sierra 4-cyl Petrol (82 - 93) up to K	0903
Ford Sierra V6 Petrol (82 - 91) up to J	0904
Ford Transit Petrol (Mk 2) (78 - Jan 86) up to C	0719
Ford Transit Petrol (Mk 3) (Feb 86 - 89) C to G	1468
Ford Transit Diesel (Feb 86 - 99) C to T	3019
Ford Transit Diesel (00-06)	4775
Ford 1.6 & 1.8 litre Diesel Engine (84 - 96) A to N	1172
Ford 2.1, 2.3 & 2.5 litre Diesel Engine (77 - 90) up to H	1606
FREIGHT ROVER Sherpa Petrol (74 - 87) up to E	0463
HILLMAN Avenger (70 - 82) up to Y	0037
Hillman Imp (63 - 76) up to R *	0022
HONDA Civic (Feb 84 - Oct 87) A to E	1226
Honda Civic (Nov 91 - 96) J to N	3199
Honda Civic Petrol (Mar 95 - 00) M to X	4050
Honda Civic Petrol & Diesel (01 - 05) X to 55	4611
Honda CR-V Petrol & Diesel (01-06)	4747
Honda Jazz (01 - Feb 08) 51 - 57	4735
HYUNDAI Pony (85 - 94) C to M	3398
JAGUAR E Type (61 - 72) up to L *	0140
Jaguar MkI & II, 240 & 340 (55 - 69) up to H *	0098
Jaguar XJ6, XJ & Sovereign; Daimler Sovereign (68 - Oct 86) up to D	0242
Jaguar XJ6 & Sovereign (Oct 86 - Sept 94) D to M	3261
Jaguar XJ12, XJS & Sovereign; Daimler Double Six (72 - 88) up to F	0478
JEEP Cherokee Petrol (93 - 96) K to N	1943
LADA 1200, 1300, 1500 & 1600 (74 - 91) up to J	0413
Lada Samara (87 - 91) D to J	1610
LAND ROVER 90, 110 & Defender Diesel (83 - 07) up to 56	3017
Land Rover Discovery Petrol & Diesel (89 - 98) G to S	3016
Land Rover Discovery Diesel (Nov 98 - Jul 04) S to 04	4606
Land Rover Freelander Petrol & Diesel (97 - Sept 03) R to 53	3929
Land Rover Freelander Petrol & Diesel (Oct 03 - Oct 06) 53 to 56	4623

Title	Book No.
Land Rover Series IIA & III Diesel (58 - 85) up to C	0529
Land Rover Series II, IIA & III 4-cyl Petrol (58 - 85) up to C	0314
MAZDA 323 (Mar 81 - Oct 89) up to G	1608
Mazda 323 (Oct 89 - 98) G to R	3455
Mazda 626 (May 83 - Sept 87) up to E	0929
Mazda B1600, B1800 & B2000 Pick-up Petrol (72 - 88) up to F	0267
Mazda RX-7 (79 - 85) up to C *	0460
MERCEDES-BENZ 190, 190E & 190D Petrol & Diesel (83 - 93) A to L	3450
Mercedes-Benz 200D, 240D, 240TD, 300D & 300TD 123 Series Diesel (Oct 76 - 85)	1114
Mercedes-Benz 250 & 280 (68 - 72) up to L *	0346
Mercedes-Benz 250 & 280 123 Series Petrol (Oct 76 - 84) up to B *	0677
Mercedes-Benz 124 Series Petrol & Diesel (85 - Aug 93) C to K	3253
Mercedes-Benz A-Class Petrol & Diesel (98-04) S to 54	4748
Mercedes-Benz C-Class Petrol & Diesel (93 - Aug 00) L to W	3511
Mercedes-Benz C-Class (00-06)	4780
MGA (55 - 62) *	0475
MGB (62 - 80) up to W	0111
MG Midget & Austin-Healey Sprite (58 - 80) up to W *	0265
MINI Petrol (July 01 - 05) Y to 05	4273
MITSUBISHI Shogun & L200 Pick-Ups Petrol (83 - 94) up to M	1944
MORRIS Ital 1.3 (80 - 84) up to B	0705
Morris Minor 1000 (56 - 71) up to K	0024
NISSAN Almera Petrol (95 - Feb 00) N to V	4053
Nissan Almera & Tino Petrol (Feb 00 - 07) V to 56	4612
Nissan Bluebird (May 84 - Mar 86) A to C	1223
Nissan Bluebird Petrol (Mar 86 - 90) C to H	1473
Nissan Cherry (Sept 82 - 86) up to D	1031
Nissan Micra (83 - Jan 93) up to K	0931
Nissan Micra (93 - 02) K to 52	3254
Nissan Micra Petrol (03-07) 52 to 57	4734
Nissan Primera Petrol (90 - Aug 99) H to T	1851
Nissan Stanza (82 - 86) up to D	0824
Nissan Sunny Petrol (May 82 - Oct 86) up to D	0895
Nissan Sunny Petrol (Oct 86 - Mar 91) D to H	1378
Nissan Sunny Petrol (Apr 91 - 95) H to N	3219
OPEL Ascona & Manta (B Series) (Sept 75 - 88) up to F *	0316
Opel Ascona Petrol (81 - 88)	3215
Opel Astra Petrol (Oct 91 - Feb 98)	3156
Opel Corsa Petrol (83 - Mar 93)	3160
Opel Corsa Petrol (Mar 93 - 97)	3159
Opel Kadett Petrol (Nov 79 - Oct 84) up to B	0634
Opel Kadett Petrol (Oct 84 - Oct 91)	3196
Opel Omega & Senator Petrol (Nov 86 - 94)	3157
Opel Rekord Petrol (Feb 78 - Oct 86) up to D	0543
Opel Vectra Petrol (Oct 88 - Oct 95)	3158
PEUGEOT 106 Petrol & Diesel (91 - 04) J to 53	1882
Peugeot 205 Petrol (83 - 97) A to P	0932
Peugeot 206 Petrol & Diesel (98 - 01) S to X	3757
Peugeot 206 Petrol & Diesel (02 - 06) 51 to 06	4613
Peugeot 306 Petrol & Diesel (93 - 02) K to 02	3073
Peugeot 307 Petrol & Diesel (01 - 04) Y to 54	4147
Peugeot 309 Petrol (86 - 93) C to K	1266
Peugeot 405 Petrol (88 - 97) E to P	1559
Peugeot 405 Diesel (88 - 97) E to P	3198
Peugeot 406 Petrol & Diesel (96 - Mar 99) N to T	3394
Peugeot 406 Petrol & Diesel (Mar 99 - 02) T to 52	3982

* Classic reprint

Title	Book No.
Peugeot 505 Petrol (79 - 89) up to G	0762
Peugeot 1.7/1.8 & 1.9 litre Diesel Engine (82 - 96) up to N	0950
Peugeot 2.0, 2.1, 2.3 & 2.5 litre Diesel Engines (74 - 90) up to H	1607
PORSCHE 911 (65 - 85) up to C	0264
Porsche 924 & 924 Turbo (76 - 85) up to C	0397
PROTON (89 - 97) F to P	3255
RANGE ROVER V8 Petrol (70 - Oct 92) up to K	0606
RELIANT Robin & Kitten (73 - 83) up to A *	0436
RENAULT 4 (61 - 86) up to D *	0072
Renault 5 Petrol (Feb 85 - 96) B to N	1219
Renault 9 & 11 Petrol (82 - 89) up to F	0822
Renault 18 Petrol (79 - 86) up to D	0598
Renault 19 Petrol (89 - 96) F to N	1646
Renault 19 Diesel (89 - 96) F to N	1946
Renault 21 Petrol (86 - 94) C to M	1397
Renault 25 Petrol & Diesel (84 - 92) B to K	1228
Renault Clio Petrol (91 - May 98) H to R	1853
Renault Clio Diesel (91 - June 96) H to N	3031
Renault Clio Petrol & Diesel (May 98 - May 01) R to Y	3906
Renault Clio Petrol & Diesel (June '01 - '05) Y to 55	4168
Renault Espace Petrol & Diesel (85 - 96) C to N	3197
Renault Laguna Petrol & Diesel (94 - 00) L to W	3252
Renault Laguna Petrol & Diesel (Feb 01 - Feb 05) X to 54	4283
Renault Mégane & Scénic Petrol & Diesel (96 - 99) N to T	3395
Renault Mégane & Scénic Petrol & Diesel (Apr 99 - 02) T to 52	3916
Renault Megane Petrol & Diesel (Oct 02 - 05) 52 to 55	4284
Renault Scenic Petrol & Diesel (Sept 03 - 06) 53 to 06	4297
ROVER 213 & 216 (84 - 89) A to G	1116
Rover 214 & 414 Petrol (89 - 96) G to N	1689
Rover 216 & 416 Petrol (89 - 96) G to N	1830
Rover 211, 214, 216, 218 & 220 Petrol & Diesel (Dec 95 - 99) N to V	3399
Rover 25 & MG ZR Petrol & Diesel (Oct 99 - 04) V to 54	4145
Rover 414, 416 & 420 Petrol & Diesel (May 95 - 98) M to R	3453
Rover 45 / MG ZS Petrol & Diesel (99 - 05) V to 55	4384
Rover 618, 620 & 623 Petrol (93 - 97) K to P	3257
Rover 75 / MG ZT Petrol & Diesel (99 - 06) S to 06	4292
Rover 820, 825 & 827 Petrol (86 - 95) D to N	1380
Rover 3500 (76 - 87) up to E *	0365
Rover Metro, 111 & 114 Petrol (May 90 - 98) G to S	1711
SAAB 95 & 96 (66 - 76) up to R *	0198
Saab 90, 99 & 900 (79 - Oct 93) up to L	0765
Saab 900 (Oct 93 - 98) L to R	3512
Saab 9000 (4-cyl) (85 - 98) C to S	1686
Saab 9-3 Petrol & Diesel (98 - Aug 02) R to 02	4614
Saab 9-3 Petrol & Diesel (02-07) 52 to 57	4749
Saab 9-5 4-cyl Petrol (97 - 04) R to 54	4156
SEAT Ibiza & Cordoba Petrol & Diesel (Oct 93 - Oct 99) L to V	3571
Seat Ibiza & Malaga Petrol (85 - 92) B to K	1609
SKODA Estelle (77 - 89) up to G	0604
Skoda Fabia Petrol & Diesel (00 - 06) W to 06	4376
Skoda Favorit (89 - 96) F to N	1801
Skoda Felicia Petrol & Diesel (95 - 01) M to X	3505
Skoda Octavia Petrol & Diesel (98 - Apr 04) R to 04	4285
SUBARU 1600 & 1800 (Nov 79 - 90) up to H *	0995

Title	Book No.
SUNBEAM Alpine, Rapier & H120 (67 - 74) up to N *	0051
SUZUKI SJ Series, Samurai & Vitara (4-cyl) Petrol (82 - 97) up to P	1942
Suzuki Supercarry & Bedford/Vauxhall Rascal (86 - Oct 94) C to M	3015
TALBOT Alpine, Solara, Minx & Rapier (75 - 86) up to D	0337
Talbot Horizon Petrol (78 - 86) up to D	0473
Talbot Samba (82 - 86) up to D	0823
TOYOTA Avensis Petrol (98 - Jan 03) R to 52	4264
Toyota Carina E Petrol (May 92 - 97) J to P	3256
Toyota Corolla (80 - 85) up to C	0683
Toyota Corolla (Sept 83 - Sept 87) A to E	1024
Toyota Corolla (Sept 87 - Aug 92) E to K	1683
Toyota Corolla Petrol (Aug 92 - 97) K to P	3259
Toyota Corolla Petrol (July 97 - Feb 02) P to 51	4286
Toyota Hi-Ace & Hi-Lux Petrol (69 - Oct 83) up to A	0304
Toyota RAV4 Petrol & Diesel (94-06) L to 55	4750
Toyota Yaris Petrol (99 - 05) T to 05	4265
TRIUMPH GT6 & Vitesse (62 - 74) up to N *	0112
Triumph Herald (59 - 71) up to K *	0010
Triumph Spitfire (62 - 81) up to X	0113
Triumph Stag (70 - 78) up to T *	0441
Triumph TR2, TR3, TR3A, TR4 & TR4A (52 - 67) up to F *	0028
Triumph TR5 & 6 (67 - 75) up to P *	0031
Triumph TR7 (75 - 82) up to Y *	0322
VAUXHALL Astra Petrol (80 - Oct 84) up to B	0635
Vauxhall Astra & Belmont Petrol (Oct 84 - Oct 91) B to J	1136
Vauxhall Astra Petrol (Oct 91 - Feb 98) J to R	1832
Vauxhall/Opel Astra & Zafira Petrol (Feb 98 - Apr 04) R to 04	3758
Vauxhall/Opel Astra & Zafira Diesel (Feb 98 - Apr 04) R to 04	3797
Vauxhall/Opel Astra Petrol (04 - 08)	4732
Vauxhall/Opel Astra Diesel (04 - 08)	4733
Vauxhall/Opel Calibra (90 - 98) G to S	3502
Vauxhall Carlton Petrol (Oct 78 - Oct 86) up to D	0480
Vauxhall Carlton & Senator Petrol (Nov 86 - 94) D to L	1469
Vauxhall Cavalier Petrol (81 - Oct 88) up to F	0812
Vauxhall Cavalier Petrol (Oct 88 - 95) F to N	1570
Vauxhall Chevette (75 - 84) up to B	0285
Vauxhall/Opel Corsa Diesel (Mar 93 - Oct 00) K to X	4087
Vauxhall Corsa Petrol (Mar 93 - 97) K to R	1985
Vauxhall/Opel Corsa Petrol (Apr 97 - Oct 00) P to X	3921
Vauxhall/Opel Corsa Petrol & Diesel (Oct 00 - Sept 03) X to 53	4079
Vauxhall/Opel Corsa Petrol & Diesel (Oct 03 - Aug 06) 53 to 06	4617
Vauxhall/Opel Frontera Petrol & Diesel (91 - Sept 98) J to S	3454
Vauxhall Nova Petrol (83 - 93) up to K	0909
Vauxhall/Opel Omega Petrol (94 - 99) L to T	3510
Vauxhall/Opel Vectra Petrol & Diesel (95 - Feb 99) N to S	3396
Vauxhall/Opel Vectra Petrol & Diesel (Mar 99 - May 02) T to 02	3930
Vauxhall/Opel Vectra Petrol & Diesel (June 02 - Sept 05) 02 to 55	4618
Vauxhall/Opel 1.5, 1.6 & 1.7 litre Diesel Engine (82 - 96) up to N	1222
VW 411 & 412 (68 - 75) up to P *	0091
VW Beetle 1200 (54 - 77) up to S	0036
VW Beetle 1300 & 1500 (65 - 75) up to P	0039

Title	Book No.
VW 1302 & 1302S (70 - 72) up to L *	0110
VW Beetle 1303, 1303S & GT (72 - 75) up to P	0159
VW Beetle Petrol & Diesel (Apr 99 - 07) T to 57	3798
VW Golf & Jetta Mk 1 Petrol 1.1 & 1.3 (74 - 84) up to A	0716
VW Golf, Jetta & Scirocco Mk 1 Petrol 1.5, 1.6 & 1.8 (74 - 84) up to A	0726
VW Golf & Jetta Mk 1 Diesel (78 - 84) up to A	0451
VW Golf & Jetta Mk 2 Petrol (Mar 84 - Feb 92) A to J	1081
VW Golf & Vento Petrol & Diesel (Feb 92 - Mar 98) J to R	3097
VW Golf & Bora Petrol & Diesel (April 98 - 00) R to X	3727
VW Golf & Bora 4-cyl Petrol & Diesel (01 - 03) X to 53	4169
VW Golf & Jetta Petrol & Diesel (04 - 07) 53 to 07	4610
VW LT Petrol Vans & Light Trucks (76 - 87) up to E	0637
VW Passat & Santana Petrol (Sept 81 - May 88) up to E	0814
VW Passat 4-cyl Petrol & Diesel (May 88 - 96) E to P	3498
VW Passat 4-cyl Petrol & Diesel (Dec 96 - Nov 00) P to X	3917
VW Passat Petrol & Diesel (Dec 00 - May 05) X to 05	4279
VW Polo & Derby (76 - Jan 82) up to X	0335
VW Polo (82 - Oct 90) up to H	0813
VW Polo Petrol (Nov 90 - Aug 94) H to L	3245
VW Polo Hatchback Petrol & Diesel (94 - 99) M to S	3500
VW Polo Hatchback Petrol (00 - Jan 02) V to 51	4150
VW Polo Petrol & Diesel (02 - May 05) 51 to 05	4608
VW Scirocco (82 - 90) up to H *	1224
VW Transporter 1600 (68 - 79) up to V	0082
VW Transporter 1700, 1800 & 2000 (72 - 79) up to V *	0226
VW Transporter (air-cooled) Petrol (79 - 82) up to Y *	0638
VW Transporter (water-cooled) Petrol (82 - 90) up to H	3452
VW Type 3 (63 - 73) up to M *	0084
VOLVO 120 & 130 Series (& P1800) (61 - 73) up to M *	0203
Volvo 142, 144 & 145 (66 - 74) up to N *	0129
Volvo 240 Series Petrol (74 - 93) up to K	0270
Volvo 262, 264 & 260/265 (75 - 85) up to C *	0400
Volvo 340, 343, 345 & 360 (76 - 91) up to J	0715
Volvo 440, 460 & 480 Petrol (87 - 97) D to P	1691
Volvo 740 & 760 Petrol (82 - 91) up to J	1258
Volvo 850 Petrol (92 - 96) J to P	3260
Volvo 940 petrol (90 - 98) H to R	3249
Volvo S40 & V40 Petrol (96 - Mar 04) N to 04	3569
Volvo S40 & V50 Petrol & Diesel (Mar 04 - Jun 07) 04 to 07	4731
Volvo S60 Petrol & Diesel (01-08)	4793
Volvo S70, V70 & C70 Petrol (96 - 99) P to V	3573
Volvo V70 / S80 Petrol & Diesel (98 - 05) S to 55	4263

DIY MANUAL SERIES

Title	Book No.
The Haynes Air Conditioning Manual	4192
The Haynes Car Electrical Systems Manual	4251
The Haynes Manual on Bodywork	4198
The Haynes Manual on Brakes	4178
The Haynes Manual on Carburettors	4177
The Haynes Manual on Diesel Engines	4174
The Haynes Manual on Engine Management	4199
The Haynes Manual on Fault Codes	4175
The Haynes Manual on Practical Electrical Systems	4267
The Haynes Manual on Small Engines	4250
The Haynes Manual on Welding	4176

* Classic reprint

Preserving Our Motoring Heritage

< The Model J Duesenberg Derham Tourster. Only eight of these magnificent cars were ever built – this is the only example to be found outside the United States of America

Almost every car you've ever loved, loathed or desired is gathered under one roof at the Haynes Motor Museum. Over 300 immaculately presented cars and motorbikes represent every aspect of our motoring heritage, from elegant reminders of bygone days, such as the superb Model J Duesenberg to curiosities like the bug-eyed BMW Isetta. There are also many old friends and flames. Perhaps you remember the 1959 Ford Popular that you did your courting in? The magnificent 'Red Collection' is a spectacle of classic sports cars including AC, Alfa Romeo, Austin Healey, Ferrari, Lamborghini, Maserati, MG, Riley, Porsche and Triumph.

A Perfect Day Out

Each and every vehicle at the Haynes Motor Museum has played its part in the history and culture of Motoring. Today, they make a wonderful spectacle and a great day out for all the family. Bring the kids, bring Mum and Dad, but above all bring your camera to capture those golden memories for ever. You will also find an impressive array of motoring memorabilia, a comfortable 70 seat video cinema and one of the most extensive transport book shops in Britain. The Pit Stop Cafe serves everything from a cup of tea to wholesome, home-made meals or, if you prefer, you can enjoy the large picnic area nestled in the beautiful rural surroundings of Somerset.

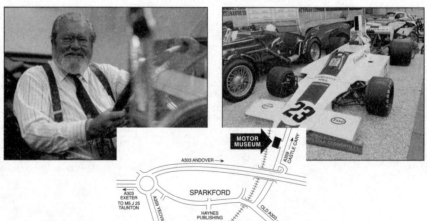

> John Haynes O.B.E., Founder and Chairman of the museum at the wheel of a Haynes Light 12.

< Graham Hill's Lola Cosworth Formula 1 car next to a 1934 Riley Sports.

The Museum is situated on the A359 Yeovil to Frome road at Sparkford, just off the A303 in Somerset. It is about 40 miles south of Bristol, and 25 minutes drive from the M5 intersection at Taunton.

Open 9.30am - 5.30pm (10.00am - 4.00pm Winter) 7 days a week, *except Christmas Day, Boxing Day and New Years Day*

Special rates available for schools, coach parties and outings Charitable Trust No. 292048